NO LIFE WITHOUT YOU

No Life Without You

Refugee Love Letters from the 1930s

Based on the Correspondence of Ernst Moritz ("Mope") Felsenstein and Vera Hirsch Felsenstein, 1936-1939

Compiled and Edited by Franklin Felsenstein with an Introduction by Rachel Pistol

https://www.openbookpublishers.com

©2024 Franklin Felsenstein (ed.)

©2024 Rachel Pistol (Introduction)

This work is licensed under an Attribution-NonCommercial 4.0 International (CC BY-NC 4.0). This license allows you to share, copy, distribute and transmit the text; to adapt the text for non-commercial purposes of the text providing attribution is made to the author (but not in any way that suggests that they endorse you or your use of the work). Attribution should include the following information:

Franklin Felsenstein (ed.), *No Life Without You: Refugee Love Letters from the 1930s. Based on the Correspondence of Ernst Moritz ("Mope") Felsenstein and Vera Hirsch Felsenstein, 1936-1939* (Cambridge, UK: Open Book Publishers, 2024), https://doi.org/10.11647/OBP.0334

Copyright and permissions for the reuse of many of the images included in this publication differ from the above. This information is provided in the captions and in the list of illustrations. Every effort has been made to identify and contact copyright holders and any omission or error will be corrected if notification is made to the publisher.

Further details about CC BY-NC licenses are available at
http://creativecommons.org/licenses/by-nc/4.0/

All external links were active at the time of publication unless otherwise stated and have been archived via the Internet Archive Wayback Machine at https://archive.org/web

Any digital material and resources associated with this volume will be available at https://doi.org/10.11647/OBP.0334#resources

ISBN Paperback: 978-1-80064-945-3
ISBN Hardback: 978-1-80064-946-0
ISBN Digital (PDF): 978-1-80064-947-7
ISBN Digital eBook (EPUB): 978-1-80064-948-4
ISBN HTML: 978-1-80064-951-4

DOI: 10.11647/OBP.0334

Front cover original images provided by Franklin Felsenstein.
Cover design by Jeevanjot Kaur Nagpal.

Contents

About the Editors — ix

Illustrations — xi

Preface and Acknowledgements — xvii

Refugees: A Contextual Introduction — 1
Rachel Pistol

PART 1: THEN — 11

One: Familien Hirsch — 13

Two: Mainly Mope — 23

Three: Victoriaschule — 33

Four: "And so What?" — 39

Five: Heising — 43

Six: Of Books and Arts (1): Max Schwimmer — 49

Seven: Of Books and Arts (2): Thomas Mann — 57

Eight: "I Will Give Up Medicine!!!!!" — 61

Nine: Under the Swastika — 73

Ten: "Did I Do the Right Thing?" — 83

Eleven: Zionism — 95

Twelve: Gretel — 103

Thirteen: Marks and Mitja — 109

PART 2: NOW	117
Fourteen: "I Stole a Kiss From You at the Train Station"	119
Fifteen: Mope in Palestine	131
Sixteen: Palestine or Vera?	139
Seventeen: Dover	149
Eighteen: "Happy and Sad at the Same Time"	159
Nineteen: Letters From a Wretched Coffee House Sitter	181
Twenty: "More of a Stranger Here Now"	197
Twenty-one: "The Letter Writing Last Guest"	205
Twenty-two: "Human Beings Are Good!"	219
Twenty-three: "Every Turn of the Wheel"	235
Twenty-four: "I Will Come to London Directly"	257
Twenty-five: "The Alpha and Omega of My Life"	285
Twenty-six: "This Ever so Long Time of Insatiable Longing"	307
Twenty-seven: "10,108 White Foxes"	349
Twenty-eight: Visas, Visas, Visas	381
Twenty-nine: "Today, for the First Time in My Life, I Wished I Were a Man!"	417
Thirty: "The Little Fruit That Fell From the Tree"	459
Thirty-one: "No Life Without You"	513
Thirty-two: Afterword	591
Glossary of Names	601
Select Bibliography	609
Index	611

For Theo Felsenstein and for another generation with perhaps different ideas to our own

About the Editors

Franklin Felsenstein (aka Frank Felsenstein) is the only son of Maurice ("Mope") and Vera Felsenstein. He is the Reed D. Voran Honors Distinguished Professor of Humanities Emeritus at Ball State University in Indiana. Before that, he was Reader in Eighteenth-Century Studies at the University of Leeds in England. He has also held appointments at the University of Geneva in Switzerland, Vanderbilt University, Yeshiva College, and Drew University. His publications include *Anti-Semitic Stereotypes: A Paradigm of Otherness in English Popular Culture* (1995), *English Trader, Indian Maid: Representing Gender, Race, and Slavery in the New World* (1999), and (with James J. Connolly) *What Middletown Read: Print Culture in an American Small City* (2015). He has edited works by Tobias Smollett (*Travels through France and Italy*), Peter Aram (*A Practical Treatise of Flowers*), and John Thelwall (*Incle and Yarico*). He and his family moved to the United States in 1998. He and his wife now live in Chicago.

Rachel Pistol, author of the Contextual Introduction to this book, is a historian, author, and leading authority on World War II refugees from Nazi oppression and internment during the Second World War. She joined the Department of Digital Humanities at King's College London in 2018 to work on the European Holocaust Research Infrastructure (EHRI), where she is part of the Project Management Board. Rachel is the National Coordinator of the UK Holocaust Research Infrastructure (EHRI-UK), for which she is based at the Parkes Institute at the University of Southampton. She is also Historical Advisor to World Jewish Relief, formerly the Central British Fund, the charity which helped German and Austrian refugees escape to the UK including the Kindertransport and Kitchener Camp rescues.

Illustrations

Unless otherwise stated, the illustrative material in this book is drawn from the private collection of its editor. VH = Vera Hirsch; VF = Vera Felsenstein EMF = Ernst Moritz ("Mope") Felsenstein.

Fig. 1   Photograph of VH (rubber stamped on verso, 6 July 1930).

Fig. 2   Photograph of the Hirsch family (hand dated 4 May 1913).

Fig. 3   Photograph of Alice Hirsch, née Ettlinger (undated but late 1890s); probably shot in Frankfurt.

Fig. 4   Cabinet photograph of Hermann Hirsch (taken by the firm of Thiele in Hanau, undated but circa late 1890s).

Fig. 5   Cabinet photograph of Alice (1875-1956) and Hermann (1870-1944) Hirsch shortly after their marriage (taken by the firm of J.B. Ciolina, Frankfurt, c. 1900).

Fig. 6   Colour photograph of Oberlindau 51, Frankfurt (taken in 2017).

Fig. 7   Photograph of EMF (hand dated May 1939).

Fig. 8   Postcard-sized photograph of Helene ("Oma Lenchen") and Isidor Felsenstein (undated but c. 1900).

Fig. 9   Group photograph of children of Helene and Isidor Felsenstein (1917); back row, Adolf, EMF (both in military uniform); middle row, Grete, Alice, Ketty, and Ruth; front row, Hanna.

Fig. 10 Present-day colour photograph of Leibnizstrasse 19, Leipzig (taken from https://www.architektur-blicklicht.de/artikel/villa-leibnizstrasse-leipzig-zentrum-nordwest-waldstrassenviertel/).

Fig. 11 EMF to VF, 23 July 1939, opening page with reference to Tischa B'Av (Jewish Fast of Av).

Fig. 12 Leipzig Schiller-Realgymnasium; undated postcard.

Fig. 13 Studio photograph of EMF as a schoolboy by Adolf Richter... Leipzig Lindenau; undated.

Fig. 14   Geschäftshaus Gebr. Felsenstein, Leipzig [Commercial Building of the Felsenstein Brothers, Leipzig] (postcard).

Fig. 15   Photograph of EMF as a young teenager.

Fig. 16   Photograph of Isidor Felsenstein (1866-1934) on entry pass to International Fur Trade Exhibition.

Fig. 17   EMF in German army uniform.

Fig. 18   Victoriaschule Frankfurt (postcard).

Fig. 19.   Victoriaschule Class in 1915, including VH, wearing a white bow, and teacher, Fraulein Albrecht.

Fig. 20   Victoriaschule Chemistry Class; VH at right hand side second row from back.

Fig. 21a   VH's Graduation Transcript from the Victoriaschule, 1928.

Fig. 21b   VH's Graduation Transcript from the Victoriaschule, 1928.

Fig. 22   Hilde Meyer with Vera on the ski slopes; Bad Homburg, winter 1930.

Fig. 23   Mope's mother, Helene Felsenstein (1874-1963), known in the family as Oma Lenchen.

Fig. 24   Hyperinflationary bank note, dated 1922.

Fig. 25   Vera with Heising on the ski slopes, hand inscribed "1930-31 Taunus" [Mountains].

Fig. 26   Mope in his study; undated but early 1930s.

Fig. 27   Anti-Nazi campaign poster by Max Schwimmer, 1924. "Wählt die VSPD – Vote for the V.S.P.D. [Independent Social Democratic Party]. Reproduced in Hellmut Radmacher, *Masters of German Poster Art* (New York: The Citadel Press, 1966, 101) and other sources.

Fig. 28   EMF on a rampart in Ragusa [Dubrovnik], June 1934.

Fig. 29   Erotic watercolour by Max Schwimmer adorning another letter from EMF to VH, Leipzig, 28 November 1936.

Fig. 30   Erotic watercolour by Max Schwimmer included with a letter from EMF to VH, Leipzig, 20 April 1937.

Fig. 31   Erotic watercolour by Max Schwimmer adorning a letter from EMF to VH, Leipzig, 10 December 1936.

Fig. 32   Later photograph of Max Schwimmer, 1950s (taken from Inge Stuhr at https://www.lehmstedt.de/schwimmer_bio.htm).

Fig. 33   Letter of Thomas Mann to VH, Munich, 29 June 1930.

Illustrations   xiii

Fig. 34   Nazi burning of "un-German" books, Berlin, 10 May 1933 (U.S. Holocaust Museum at https://www.ushmm.org/lcmedia/photo/lc/image/31/31077.jpg).

Fig. 35   Photograph of VH, rubber dated on verso as 23 July 1938 (likely a copy of an earlier shot from c. 1930).

Fig. 36   The burning of the Reichstag, Berlin, 27 February 1933; National Archives, Washington, D.C. (ARC Identifier: 535790).

Fig. 37   Cover of "Studienbuch" of VH, containing her transcript and photograph.

Fig. 38   Boycott of Jewish Businesses, Hamburg, Germany, 1 April 1933; https://www.dhm.de/archiv/ausstellungen/holocaust/r2/2.htm.

Fig. 39   Krankenhaus Sachsenhausen, Frankfurt (https://www.krankenhaus-sachsenhausen.de/geschichte/).

Fig. 40   Photograph of Dr. Franz Volhard (1872-1950), inscribed by Vera, Summer Semester 1932.

Fig. 41   Nazi Registration Card ("Anmeldekarte") obliging VH to reveal her identity as a Jew, dated 4 May 1933 (Archives of the University of Frankfurt).

Fig. 42   Boycott of Jewish businesses, 1 April 1933 (United States Holocaust Museum at https://newspapers.ushmm.org/images/nazi-boycott.jpeg).

Fig. 43   Grave of Isidor Felsenstein, Alter Israelischer Friedhof, Leipzig; photograph taken in the summer of 1947.

Fig. 44   Photograph of Adolf Felsenstein (1897-1977) outside his plumbing shop in Haifa, Palestine; undated but mid to late 1930s.

Fig. 45   Alice Homburger, née Felsenstein (1901-1993), in nurse's uniform.

Fig. 46   Post-war photograph of Fred (1906-1956) and Hanna (1910-1957) Rau entertaining at Sabbath in London.

Fig. 47   Heinz Littauer at the wheel and EMF touring in the Dolomites, 1927.

Fig. 48   Ruth (1902-1971) and Heinz (1893-1973) Littauer; undated photograph.

Fig. 49   David (1890-1944) and Ketty (1896-1944) Goldschmidt; undated photograph.

Fig. 50   Grete (1901-1975) and Norbert (1895-1974) Moschytz; undated photograph.

Fig. 51   Otto Schiff (1875-1952); photograph taken from *AJR* [Association of Jewish Refugees] *Journal*, 14, no. 6, June 2014.

Fig. 52   Dr. Paul Rothschild (1901-1965).

Fig. 53	Studio photograph of Ray Rockman Braham.
Fig. 53b	Photograph of Frank Braham.
Fig. 54a	Barmitzvah Tafellied (Table Songs) for Moritz Felsenstein, Leipzig, 29 June 1912.
Fig. 54b	Barmitzvah Tafellied (Table Songs) for Moritz Felsenstein, Leipzig, 29 June 1912.
Fig. 55	Zionistic verses dedicated to his mother, penned by EMF, on his birthday, 19 June 1923.
Fig. 56	Article by EMF that appeared in the *Leipziger Jüdische Zeitung*, 24 March 1922; accessible online at https://digital.slub-dresden.de/werkansicht/dlf/122923/2.
Fig. 57	View of the Kalmenhof, Idstein (taken from https://alt-idstein.de/wp-content/uploads/2020/07/Haupthaus_2.jpg).
Fig. 58	Telegram from the Kalmenhof at Idstein recording the death of Vera's older sister, Gretel Hirsch, 26 March 1935.
Fig. 59a	Studio photograph of Alice Hirsch with Gretel as a toddler; Atelier Blum, Frankfurt.
Fig. 59b	Grave of Margarethe ("Gretel") Hirsch at Idstein; colour photograph taken by Colin Watts, 2018.
Fig. 60	Marks & Spencer, store front of North End Road Branch, London, 1930s (https://www.pinterest.com/pin/422001427562112641/).
Fig. 61	Front of postcard from Mope to Vera, dated 15 March 1936, advertising the recent Winter Olympics in Garmisch-Partenkirchen, Germany; postage stamp removed by Hermann Hirsch, Vera's father.
Fig. 62	German film poster for *Bosambo* (1935), starring Paul Robeson with Nina Mae McKinney playing his wife, Lilongo.
Fig. 63	Photograph of steam ship Kraljica Marija.
Fig. 64	Watercolour of the shore at Lake Tiberias, 1934. Later, the picture hung on the wall of Mope's bedroom in London as a cherished memento of his earlier desire to settle in Palestine; artist's signature indecipherable.
Fig. 65	Front page of Mope's letter to Vera, Haifa, 27 March 1936.
Fig. 66a	Envelope with German Censors stamps indicating that the correspondence between Vera and Mope was frequently vetted by the Nazi authorities.
Fig. 66b	Envelope with German Censors stamps indicating that the correspondence between Vera and Mope was frequently vetted by the Nazi authorities.

Illustrations xv

Fig. 67   Postcard of Marienbad in the 1930s.

Fig. 68   Kaffeehaus Felsche, Leipzig, c. 1930 (https://www.paulinerkirche.org/tmp/augusta/fel1922.jpg).

Fig. 69   Erotic watercolour by Max Schwimmer at head of letter from Mope to Vera, 28 February 1937.

Fig. 70   Erotic watercolour by Max Schwimmer with verses included with letter from Mope to Vera, Leipzig, 5 April 1937.

Fig. 71   Erotic watercolour by Max Schwimmer accompanying letter from Mope to Vera, Leipzig, 12 May 1937.

Fig. 72a   Mope and Vera in Brussels, May 1937.

Fig. 72b   Mope and Vera in Brussels, May 1937.

Fig. 73a   Front and back of envelope to letter from Mope to Vera dated 4 June 1937 with vetting stickers added by the Nazi authorities.

Fig. 73b   Front and back of envelope to letter from Mope to Vera dated 4 June 1937 with vetting stickers added by the Nazi authorities.

Fig. 74   Hotel Metropole, Moscow.

Fig. 75   Photograph of Danäe by Rembrandt, mailed with letter from Mope to Vera, Moscow, 1 July 1937.

Fig. 76   Printed map of Yorkshire Coast included with letter from Vera to Mope, Ravenshill Farm, near Whitby, Yorkshire, 6 July 1937.

Fig. 77   Photograph of Vera (middle of second row) with vacationing Marks & Spencer shop girls.

Fig. 78a   Photographs of Vera and Mope at their wedding, London, 1 August 1937. Vera's mother, Alice Hirsch, stands behind the couple in the third of these photos.

Fig. 78b   Photographs of Vera and Mope at their wedding, London, 1 August 1937. Vera's mother, Alice Hirsch, stands behind the couple in the third of these photos.

Fig. 78c   Photographs of Vera and Mope at their wedding, London, 1 August 1937. Vera's mother, Alice Hirsch, stands behind the couple in the third of these photos.

Fig. 79   Telegram from Vera in London to Mope in Moscow, sent via Berlin, 15 March 1938.

Fig. 80   Later Certificate of Identity issued to Mope by the British Home Office in 1946. The earlier certificate has not survived.

Fig. 81   Helene Felsenstein's "Abmeldung" (Exit Accreditation), Leipzig, 15 July 1938.

Fig. 82   Georg Rosenfeld, later George Rosney, in 1937 (courtesy of Audrey Rosney, his widow).

Fig. 83   KADDISH (IN MEMORIAM): Photograph of Lies and Carl Rosenfeld typing letters to aid their escape, Karlsruhe, July 1939 (courtesy of their daughter-in-law Audrey Rosney).

Fig. 84   KADDISH (IN MEMORIAM): Card sized photograph of Ketty and David Goldschmidt.

Fig. 85   Mope's final letter from Moscow, 27 August 1939. Pepper, an enthusiastic stamp collector, tore away a corner from the sheet while removing the stamp from the envelope.

Fig. 86   Key to Her Majesty the Queen's W.C., York Race Course, entrusted to internee 80321 E. M. Felsenstein, appointed Clerk, September 1940.

Fig. 87   Mope (middle row, third from left) with his Home Guard unit, in which he served from November 1941 through to November 1944.

Fig. 88   Photograph of Mope and Vera, undated but early 1950s.

Fig. 89   Post-war photograph of Mope and Vera at a family celebration in 1960.

Online Figures

All these figures are available in the online resources to this book: https://doi.org/10.11647/OBP.0334

Online fig. 1   A photographic portrait of the artist Max Schwimmer (1895-1960).

Online fig. 2   A photograph of Dr Franz Volhard.

Online fig. 3   A photograph of a hatbox and hats designed by Eve Valère.

Online fig. 4   An image of an application form created by the Palästina Treuhand-Stelle (Palestine Trust Company).

Online fig. 5   A torn photograph of Annelie Herzberg (née Freimann), reproduced from the Holocaust Memorial Education Center website.

Online fig. 6   A photograph of Semy Felsenstein (1883-1978), head partner of Gebrüder Felsenstein.

Preface and Acknowledgements

There are near to a thousand refugee letters penned between my parents, Mope (pronounced "Mō-peh") and Vera, from January 1936 when they first met through to the latter end of August 1939, when they were reunited at the start of the Second World War. Their love letters are intimate and sensual but constantly inflected by fears brought about by the evaporation of their civil liberties under the Nazis. Even when no longer in Germany, the long arm of the fascist dictatorship continued to compromise their lives. In editing such a vast correspondence for publication, abridgment has been both inevitable and necessary. The present selection represents less than one third of the total correspondence. My aim has been to preserve the day-by-day immediacy of the letters while also omitting details that would only be of peripheral interest to the general reader.

The correspondence is partitioned by the occasions when Vera and Mope were together during which communication did not depend on the exchange of letters. When apart from one another, their letters are the life blood of their relationship. Indeed, reading into my parents' papers so many years later is not quite as good as being able to speak with them in person but it is easily the next best thing. The cadences of their voices are still remarkably fresh and captured by the moment in their letters. Their journey as refugees can be seen as an endeavor to return from turmoil and major disruption to the relative normalcy of everyday life. The integrity of their love for each other and their desire to be together are the primary forces that ultimately saved them both. As we shall discover, not everyone in their respective families was to be so fortunate.

Because Vera's letters to Mope from when he was still in Leipzig were lost to the Nazis, it is not until June 1937 that we can hear *her* voice through the correspondence. From much earlier in her life and intermittently during this period, she kept a copious private journal.

The survival of the journal is of extreme good fortune since it allows us a two-way window into the intimacies of their developing relationship. Ten months after they first met, a telling journal entry, dated 24 November 1936, reads: "I have not written anything in here for an eternity, because, whenever I have time to write, I write to my friend and lover." If we have less of her side of the story during the first eighteen months of their relationship, it is because she was devoting her energy into writing to him. In the absence of her early letters, I have been able to integrate into the correspondence extracts from her journals, allowing us to overhear her side of the story. As will be evident, there are details in these journals that were almost surely accorded a different emphasis in her lost letters. Even after we reach the point when we have both sides of the correspondence, there is still plenty that remains revealing in her journal entries, and I have incorporated portions from them as necessary.

The present book consists of thirty-two episodic chapters. It is divided into two main parts, which I have delineated as "Then" and "Now." The shorter "Then" (chs. 1-13) section concentrates on their lives before they met. By targeted burrowing into a variety of sources, I have recreated their voices even from before they knew each other. These sources include Vera's journals which long precede meeting Mope, her letters to her own mother who remained in Frankfurt for just short of a year following Vera's departure for England in May 1933, and an incomplete memoir of her childhood that she penned during the 1980s. For Mope, I have drawn from the brief *curriculum vitae* that he typed in the 1950s at the behest of German restitution authorities and on recollection of stories of his early life that he related to me at various times. These stories remain sufficiently vivid to have prompted me to expound them as closely as I can. In the chapter on his engagement with Zionism, I have been able to draw from a polemical piece that he wrote for the *Leipziger Jüdische Zeitung* in 1922 and from family papers. Throughout, I have also transferred recollections of their individual early lives that appear in their joint correspondence into the "Then" section. That is particularly the case in reconstructing Mope's awkward reminiscence of his father who died in 1934. My own visits to Leipzig during the 1970s and 1980s, when still under Communism, and, far more recently, to Frankfurt have also enhanced my knowledge of my parents' early lives. Although not included here, a personal account of the visit to Frankfurt in 2017, published by *The Times of Israel,* may be accessed at https://

blogs.timesofisrael.com/truncated-memories-berlin-and-frankfurt-in-the-afterlives-of-two-jewish-refugee-women. I have also drawn upon the privately printed *Felsenstein Family Chronicle*, created to coincide with a family reunion in Jerusalem in 2000. Some readers may feel that I have too amply interjected my own voice as the guide through the first part and in the short "Afterword" to the book. I have done so with the purpose of unraveling *their* story as best as the deficiencies and imperfections of latter-day memory will allow. My parents' story has required framing within a broader context, which positions me, as their only son, in a unique place to supply that. However, readers less interested in their background story and keen to turn directly to their letters and journals may elect to go straight to the "Now" section.

I have named the second part of this book "Now" (chs. 14-31) since my parents' letters and journals from 1936 through 1939 are written in the immediacy of the moment. The precariousness of their situation is anchored by the integrity of their relationship. Each of the chapters begins with a brief contextual overview, but I have resisted inserting my own voice beyond these preambles. Where necessary, however, I have added concise footnotes to accompany the letters. As they corresponded on a daily basis and would often pick up on the same topic, I have silently elided into individual letters details that occur in more than one. My principal criterion here has been to allow my parents to tell their own story in their own voices with minimal editorial intrusion. The brief "Afterword" (ch. 32) traces my parents' subsequent lives. A biographical who's who and glossary of terms is annexed at the end of the volume.

Looking back, it is already more years than I am prepared to count since I started thinking about editing the present volume. Both my parents saw a value in preserving family papers, and it was only after they were no longer alive that their letters to each other, unsorted but largely intact, came into my possession. At the time, I was teaching at the University of Leeds in England. Remembering that my father had spent much of the two years between 1937 and 1939 in the Soviet Union, and that the university library's Brotherton Collection contained an expanding Anglo-Russian Archive, I arranged through Richard Davies, its accomplished archivist, for the correspondence and related papers to be deposited there on a long-term loan. Shortly after the deposit, the library deputed two of its archivists, Holger Igel and Chris Butcher, to sequence the letters. They did a fine job.

When my family moved to the United States, I retrieved the letters and brought them and other related family papers with me, fearing that, if they were left in England, I would miss out on researching them more closely. In 2002, I began teaching at Ball State University. To my gratitude, the director of archives, Mr. John Straw, and the university librarian, Dr Arthur Häfner, saw a virtue in depositing the papers on a similar loan at the Bracken Library. A chance conversation with Mr. Martin Schwartz (1917-2017), a Muncie resident and long-time benefactor to the university, turned into the generous offer from the Helen and Martin Schwartz Foundation to fund translation of the letters and relevant journals into English. Among the German-speaking students capable of undertaking the translation, Hiltrud Johnting stood out for her complete fluency in the two languages. It was only as Hiltrud was completing the immense task of translating the surviving letters and journals that it became evident that they embodied a compelling story. They breathe into us the essence of what it was to be Jewish exiles in the 1930s. Unless otherwise stated, the papers and related documents, including photographs, remain in the hands of my family which retains copyright over them. Sadly, Hiltrud Johnting, a victim of the COVID-19 pandemic, is not alive to see the publication of this volume.

The everyday exigencies of teaching and research obliged me to hold off until achieving emeritus status before concentrating on the final editing of the present correspondence. Consequently, my indebtedness to those who have helped me along the way begins well before the present time. As well as those already mentioned, I should like to offer my warmest thanks to those who have both informed, encouraged or aided me at various stages in working on this volume. They include Kathryn Powell, the late James Ruebel, Warwick Gould, Raphael Homburger, Angelika Rieber, Gretchen Gerzina, Audrey Rosney, Michael Maggiotto, Michael Szajewski, George Moschytz, Lisa Herzberg, Michael and Prue Thorner, Alan Warner, Jonathan Hendrix and Adam Douglas of the Ball State University Computing Services, and Mimi-Ray and Colin Watts. I have also benefited from consultation with the Wiener Holocaust Library in London and the Leo Baeck Institute in New York. Without the valuable feedback from Stephen Ro'i, Renata Levy, Ted Wolner, and Jill Leukhardt, who read and commented on its final drafts, this book would be much less rounded. At Open Book Publishers, I have received nothing but encouragement and skillful advice from its Director, Dr. Alessandra Tosi, and from Lucy Barnes, its adroit Senior Editor. I should also like to express my special thanks to the highly resourceful and creative team at OBP that includes Anja Pritchard (proof reading), Jeevanot Kaur Nagpal (cover designer), Cameron Craig (book production), and Laura Rodríguez Pupo (dissemination, promotion and marketing). The historical introduction by Dr. Rachel Pistol is a masterly addition to the book, and I am deeply indebted to her for carving out the time to provide a valuable backdrop to my parents' story.

Very late in the day, in November 2023, a few months before this book's appearance, my only sibling, Mimi-Ray, passed away. I believe that she would have been thrilled to hold in her hands a volume that gives such an intimate picture of our parents during what will have been – with the possible exception of bringing us up – the most challenging time of their lives. Unhappily that was not to be. The strange coincidence of life cycle events is once again evidenced by the birth later in the same month of Theo, our parents' first great grandchild. In compiling this book, my most personal thanks are to my wife Carole, and to our children, Kenny and Joanna, who have witnessed its advent almost from its inception.

Refugees: A Contextual Introduction

Rachel Pistol

Discourse regarding refugees is an ever-present part of society and is multifaceted, invariably emotive, and always highly political. Sometimes the humanitarian side wins, focusing on welcoming beleaguered strangers into a country and providing hope for the future. Other times economic migrants become the focus, especially when they claim refugee status, and this is used as an excuse to whip up xenophobic hysteria against all foreigners. There is, of course, a fine line between fleeing poverty and seeking asylum because of persecution. Conflicts, natural disasters, and political, religious and ethnic persecution force people to flee from their homes and their native country into the unenviable position of attempting to find a generous nation who will take pity on their plight. Often the hardest part of this process is the stripping of identity, the loss of all that is familiar, the loss of autonomy, the ability to be self-sufficient, and the loss of dignity caused by displacement.

Terminology is important; particularly when individuals are described as economic migrants as opposed to refugees, allowing governments to pander to xenophobia. Additionally, economic migrants masquerading as refugees provide governments with the excuse to treat all refugees with suspicion. The need to consider the individual beyond the collective identity of race, gender, religion, politics, or nationality is essential if one is to respond with compassion; it is easy to become apathetic or hostile about a particular people or group when considering them *en masse*, but much harder to treat an individual with the same lack of empathy when you know their particular circumstances. The course of history demonstrates how the tide of popular opinion can ebb and

©2024 Rachel Pistol, CC BY-NC 4.0   https://doi.org/10.11647/OBP.0334.00

flow very quickly between sympathy and xenophobia. Consequently, it is imperative to keep telling refugee stories, giving a voice to those unfortunate enough to suffer persecution and the loss of all they love, whilst reminding the modern reader of the humanity of these individuals and of all the similarities they share with the reader.

There are many differences between the refugee situation of the 1930s and that of the modern day, particularly as there was no international agreement regarding the offering of asylum in the 1930s. In July 1938, in response to the growing refugee crisis due to Nazi persecution of Jews in Germany and Austria, a conference was held in Evian-les-Bains, France at which delegates from thirty-two countries and representatives from aid organizations discussed possible solutions. Sadly, the only thing the delegates agreed on was that they feared an influx of foreigners would create unacceptable economic hardship for their citizens, and therefore, although everyone present decried the treatment of Jews within Germany, only the Dominican Republic was willing to open its doors to more refugees. The conference did, however, result in the creation of the Intergovernmental Committee on Refugees (ICR), which was designed to continue considering international responses to refugees from Germany and Austria and expanded in 1943 to cover all European refugees, although it never truly achieved its goals. In 1947, the role of the ICR was taken over the by the International Refugee Organisation (IRO), who assumed responsibility for the legal protection and resettlement of refugees until 1952, when it was succeeded by the Office of the United Nations High Commissioner for Refugees. The biggest change came in the creation of the 1951 United Nations Convention relating to the Status of Refugees, which remains the central tenet of international refugee protection to this day. It has been updated since 1951, removing the geographic barriers to provide universal coverage, but the basic principles of the agreement still provide for the needs of refugees globally. According to the Refugee Convention, a refugee is a person who is unwilling or unable to return to their country of origin for fear of persecution because of their race, religion, nationality, or politics. There are also protections for refugees including that none should be forcibly returned to a country where they fear for their lives.

In the 1930s, Britain did take many more refugees than planned and proportionately more than many other countries despite its obligation being moral rather than legal. However, in recent years there has been a backlash against admitting migrants to Great Britain, and successive

Home Secretaries under the Conservative Party have created a hostile environment for immigration. It has become popular to label all asylum seekers as 'illegal immigrants', even though it is not illegal to seek asylum if it is done in a country that has signed the 1951 Convention, which includes Great Britain. While the world's population has increased around three-and-a-half-fold since 1940, the number of refugees has increased more than tenfold in the same period. This means there are many more millions of refugees globally in the twenty-first century than in the twentieth, which brings huge challenges in terms of dealing with the number of those seeking permanent residency in countries not of their birth. Only around a quarter of those emigrating to Britain are considered by the government to be refugees or asylum seekers, making it all the more important to ensure these individuals can be correctly identified and protected.

The protagonists of this story, Vera and Mope, had not expected to become refugees when they grew up in Germany. Vera was born in 1910, the second daughter of an assimilated Jewish family who lived in a large apartment in Frankfurt. By contrast, Mope was born in 1899 in Leipzig, one of seven children in an Orthodox family who lived only a short walk from the local synagogue. Vera was only a young child during the First World War, whereas by 1917 Mope was old enough to serve in the German army in France and Belgium. Almost 100,000 Jewish men served in the German military during World War I, fighting for the Fatherland despite experiencing anti-Semitism in the trenches. Around 18,000 of these men received an Iron Cross for their bravery in combat and were lauded as heroes. A special version of the Iron Cross, known as the Honour Cross, was created by President Hindenburg and bestowed on many veterans of the First World War from 1934, and these were still being awarded to Jews even after Adolf Hitler had become chancellor. Initially these medals provided some protection against persecution for those who had been awarded them, but little could anyone have imagined how worthless these medals would become in the years that followed.

Hitler's rise to power can be directly linked to the outcome of the First World War. The harsh and punitive reparations inflicted on Germany by the victors of World War I had a crippling effect on the German nation, leading to economically disastrous hyperinflation, with which the National Socialist Workers' Party (NSDAP or Nazi Party) justified their anti-Semitic policies by blaming Jewish bankers for the country's financial woes. However, before the Nazis took control, Vera and Mope lived through the 1920s in Germany, from the lows of hyperinflation to the highs of flourishing German culture under the Weimar Republic. The uncertainty and unpredictability of 1922-3, when German currency was completely devalued and thousands of Germans lost their life savings, or were bankrupted, formed the foundation for the rise of radical politics and the ultimate challenge to German democracy. Food riots and despair were a part of everyday life until a new currency, the Rentenmark, was introduced in 1924. Vera's relationship with her father was permanently affected as he all but lost the family fortune during this time, whereas Mope's father managed to successfully navigate the crisis and not suffer any major financial setbacks. No German was immune from the effects of this crisis, no matter their religious, social, or economic status, and although property and landowners were much less affected, the psychological effects of the crash were long-lasting.

Despite the economic disaster that Germany experienced in 1923, the Weimar Republic also fostered a German Renaissance where intellectual and cultural life flourished. The Bauhaus movement, in existence from 1919 to 1933, focused on crafts and the fine arts; the movement promoted artistry and function whilst emphasising the importance of mass production. These were the years of luminary scientists such as Max Plank and Albert Einstein; German philosophers such as Hannah Arendt and Martin Heidegger studied in Germany at this time; jazz and cabaret clubs were popular, the German cinema and film industry flourished, and new forms of modernist art were explored. Despite the privations that had been inflicted on Germany because of its defeat in 1918, the 1920s seemed full of possibilities. Creativity in all its forms was encouraged. This was the backdrop to Vera and Mope's formative years, when they developed their interests and education. Life was not perfect, and the association of the Weimar Republic with decadence and immorality caused concern for some, but no one could have anticipated the severity of the backlash that was to be unleashed in the 1930s.

1933 marked the turning point for not only Germany, but also Vera and Mope. As soon as Hitler was appointed chancellor of Germany by President Paul von Hindenburg, the clock was ticking down for Jews and other minority groups in Germany and beyond. By the early 1930s the German government was seen as weak, ineffectual, unable to govern or meet the needs of the nation in response to the crippling effects of the Great Depression. Dissatisfaction caused growth in political parties at both ends of the political spectrum – from the Communists on the left to the NSDAP on the right. The Nazis had come to national attention a decade before when, in November 1923, they attempted to overthrow the Bavarian government in the Beer Hall Putsch in Munich. This armed insurrection by Hitler and hundreds of stormtroopers was inspired by Mussolini's seizure of political power after the March on Rome in 1922; Hitler thought that perhaps he could achieve similar results by harnessing the discontent caused by the Weimar Republic's mishandling of the German economy. His plan backfired and led to his arrest, imprisonment, and the banning of the Nazi party. However, despite being tried for high treason, Hitler was sentenced to a mere five years in prison, and then served less than nine months in a relatively comfortable jail, which suggested that some of those in authority sympathised with his political goals. The trial was a great opportunity for spreading Nazi propaganda and gave Hitler a national platform, something previously not available to him. Hitler also made the most of his time in prison to write *Mein Kampf*, fully exploring Nazi anti-Semitic policies, racist views and aggressive foreign policy in the desire to create *Lebensraum*, extra living space for Germans through annexing parts of eastern Europe. *Mein Kampf* was not an instant bestseller, but the more recognition Hitler and the Nazis gained, the more copies were sold. The failed putsch also marked a change in Nazi policy, with an emphasis on seeking power through more legitimate methods. The years 1924 to 1929 were marked by a growth in the numbers who joined the Nazi party but a decreasing representation of the party in the Reichstag (German Parliament). It was not until the Wall Street Crash of 1929 and subsequent Great Depression that the Nazis started to see an increase in their political power. During the elections in 1930, the Nazi Party managed to attract eighteen percent of the vote, riding on a platform promising to fix the economy, create jobs, regain territory lost in the First World War, and unify the country. Hitler was campaigning on the idea of returning Germany to being a great nation. Building on the foundation of the 1930 election, the Nazi Party increased their percentage of the vote to thirty-seven percent in 1932, making it almost impossible to govern Germany without their cooperation. Hitler's appointment as chancellor did not automatically lead to dictatorship, but the position enabled him to manipulate the democratic process until, in August 1934, Hindenburg died and German democracy died with him as Hitler declared himself Führer.

It certainly cannot be said that Hitler was not clear in his manifesto as to exactly what he would do if and when he gained power. Hitler could not have been more explicit regarding his grotesque beliefs, but many people were willing to overlook the more unsavoury aspects of Nazism because they liked the sound of policies such as creating jobs, blaming others for Germany's ills, restoring Germany's economic fortunes and being led by a 'strong' leader. It is always easier to blame others for misfortune and this is a frequent rallying cry of political parties at both extremities of the political spectrum. Hitler was unashamed of lying and manipulating reality in order to orchestrate events to his benefit; one such example being the arson attack that destroyed the Reichstag and was blamed on the Communists, enabling Hitler to declare a state of emergency and suspend civil liberties. Another was using the assassination of Ernst von Rath in November 1938, a minor German diplomat posted to the German embassy in Paris, as an excuse for the outright assault on the Jewish population in the November pogrom otherwise known as *Kristallnacht*. The lenient treatment Hitler had been given at his trial and subsequent imprisonment did little to punish him for his treasonable acts, instead it inspired a culture of celebrity and intrigue around him. This should serve as a warning to all, that when an individual craving power is willing to manipulate the system, lie, and commit treason as a means of gaining power, power is the last thing they should be given. Here there are many similarities that can be drawn between the 1930s and the modern day. Once again, society is willing to accept an individual for some of their policies but willing to ignore the same individual's incitements to violence and an excessive thirst for power.

Hitler was appointed chancellor as a way of offering a concession to the far right in the expectation that his excesses could be controlled by the president and other political parties. However, once the door had been opened to the Nazis, they were not going to settle for anything less than total control. After the staged fire at the Reichstag building, the Nazi leadership passed the Law against the Founding of New Parties on 14 July 1933. All political parties and trade unions were dissolved or disbanded and their members harassed or arrested, precipitating significant emigration of these political refugees in the second half of 1933. Those who remained in Germany hoped conditions would improve and that Hitler's reign would be short-lived; however, conditions gradually deteriorated for Jews who began to be squeezed out of public life. The 1935 Nuremburg Race Laws were the first in a series of laws that sought to exclude Jews, Roma, people of colour and their descendants from an Aryan society. The Nazis wanted to create a society of white, non-Jewish people of northern European descent, typically with blonde hair and blue eyes; attributes the Nazis considered to be superior to all other races. By defining groups by racial, religious and ethnic characteristics, the Nazis created a tier of lower-class citizens, their legal and human rights stripped away, as well as actively encouraging acts of degradation, verbal abuse and violence towards those considered non-Aryan. Jews were stripped of their jobs in the civil service, medical and legal professions, which affected Vera during her medical training as she experienced the Nazification of former friends and ultimately the university system itself. Forced out of her studies, Vera had a series of tough decisions to make which ultimately led her to Britain in the hope of completing her studies there. There was opposition in Britain during the 1930s by professional bodies such as the British Medical Association (BMA) to the immigration of doctors, the British Dental Association (BDA) to dentists, and by other professions and industries in which it was felt that immigration would pose a threat to British employment, such as the retail industry. Like so many others, Vera was forced to abandon her dreams and find an alternative living in order to have the best chance of helping other family members find refuge in England.

After the Nuremburg Laws were enacted, the need for escape became apparent to many, though it was clear that leaving Germany would be challenging given the apprehension in so many countries towards the prospect of an influx of foreigners. The United States of America, for example, had strict immigration laws which they were unwilling to relax for those fleeing Germany, and other countries grew increasingly concerned about accepting refugees. Britain was not always considered to be welcoming – Germans were still aware of the way their compatriots had been treated at the end of the First World War, when they had been banished from the country because of the intensity of anti-German feeling – and immigration rules remained tight. Therefore, Britain was not usually the first choice of emigration for Jews and other refugees fleeing Nazi persecution. In the earliest waves of emigration, individuals often fled to countries bordering Germany, and sadly, those who escaped to Czechoslovakia, France, Belgium and The Netherlands were often swept up in the Nazi occupation of these countries in 1940. Vera and Mope themselves found themselves traveling away from Germany, and members of both of their families were dispersed across a wide geographic area, as was often common for those with the means and contacts to escape the deteriorating conditions at home.

There had been a growth in Zionism through the early years of the twentieth century and Mope's writings provide an important contemporary insight into the ideological attraction of the movement before the need for such a homeland became such a pressing priority. The growth of anti-Semitism in Germany after the First World War and the subsequent persecution of Jews made Zionist organisations particularly popular during the 1920s and 1930s, and Mope was no exception to the allure of such politics. The Balfour Declaration of 1917 and the 1923 Mandate of Palestine gave hope to the Zionist cause, although emigration to Palestine was not guaranteed. Many Jews tried to emigrate to British Mandated Palestine during the 1930s but it was not always possible, as the British government sought to limit the numbers arriving in Palestine to avoid aggravating political tensions with the pre-existing Arab population. Consequently, schemes were set up in Britain to train individuals with agricultural skills, which were greatly needed in Palestine. Agricultural training visas were generally available for entry to Britain provided a space was available on a suitable programme. Jewish charitable organisations such as the Central British Fund for German Jewry (CBF), under the directorship of Otto Schiff, set these schemes up from 1933 onwards with a view that the refugees, once trained, could gain entry to Palestine as experienced agricultural workers.

The letters of Vera and Mope revolve around Britain as a place of refuge; a place of hope but also of hope deferred. Upon the Nazi accession of power in Germany, leaders of the British Jewish community met with Members of Parliament to create the CBF. Like Mope, they too believed that the most effective way to provide security for German Jews was to help them to emigrate to Palestine. However, it soon became apparent it would be necessary to direct efforts at training individuals in Britain with the hope that further emigration could be organised at a later date. Refugees only arrived in Britain in relatively small numbers from 1933 to 1937. In 1938, two events changed the situation significantly: firstly the Anschluss on 12-13 March when Germany was welcomed into Austria and the two countries were declared as one, and secondly, the November pogrom, Kristallnacht, on 9 November and 10 November 1938, where Jewish shops and homes were destroyed, synagogues defiled and set on fire, and hundreds of deaths caused through injuries sustained in vicious attacks on the Jewish population. The significant deterioration of conditions within Germany and Austria hugely increased the numbers seeking to escape Nazi persecution. As part of the November pogrom, some 30,000 Jewish men were arrested and sent to concentration camps such as Dachau, Buchenwald and Sachsenhausen. Not yet extermination camps, these camps were incredibly hostile environments where harsh interrogations were undertaken and brutal punishments were meted out for the smallest of offenses, resulting in many deaths. Most of those arrested at this time were released after a few weeks or months provided they relinquished their claim on property in Germany and promised to emigrate. The CBF was an essential part of this emigration plan, creating multiple rescue schemes including the one that helped almost 4,000 of these men and some of their families to leave Germany and be accepted to Britain through the Kitchener Refugee Camp near Sandwich in Kent. Other schemes included placing individuals in domestic service, as maids or as gardeners in British households, where there was a shortage of British workers willing to carry out menial roles. The CBF was not the only charity to assist refugees from Nazi oppression during the 1930s and 1940s – the Quakers and the Church of England, for example, also helped many refugees – but the CBF was the largest and it encompassed a myriad of smaller charities who focused on assisting specific groups. Perhaps the most well-known of the refugee rescue schemes organised under their auspices was the Kindertransport. In the aftermath of Kristallnacht, when it became clear within Germany and beyond that Jews were in extreme danger, the British government agreed that an uncapped number of children from Germany, Austria and Czechoslovakia would be given visas to come temporarily to the UK, provided each child was guaranteed not to become a charge on the British taxpayer. Guarantors, foster homes and other accommodation was found for almost 10,000 minors by the outbreak of war, although more would have followed had hostilities not intervened. The anguish of parents and the desperation they must have felt to send their children into the arms of strangers can only be imagined. Mope's sister, Ketty, in Hamburg was desperate enough to use this method of escape for her four children, with no guarantee of their ever being reunited. The Kindertransport is lauded as a golden example of British charity to refugees and of humanitarianism for the thousands of lives saved, but consideration should also be given to the great emotional costs and sacrifices involved.

Vera and Mope's letters traverse this challenging and ever evolving time in Europe. Fascism and Communism in ideology and practice had taken – or were taking – hold in many countries including Spain, Russia, Germany, Austria and Italy. In response to the rise of the Nazi Party, many Jews had sought solace in Communism, and nothing could have been a bigger shock than the Molotov-Ribbentrop Pact of August 1939, which saw many Jews who had fled Germany for safety in Russia returned to Germany in a terrible betrayal. Mope's work as a furrier took him across Europe, which undoubtedly helped spare his life. His travels for business took him across country boundaries and his experiences of Russia between the years of 1937 and 1939 make for a fascinating personal insight into Russian business practices and culture. Thankfully both Vera and Mope's stories had a happy ending, but it was a particularly close call for Mope, and we now know around six million others were not so lucky. What could be more intimate than sharing the journey of two lovers through their most personal correspondence, combining matters of the heart with the complex politics and realities of the world they inhabited?

The Nazis and their Fascist regime did not spring up overnight. The road to concentration and death camps was paved with thousands of small steps of dehumanisation, as highlighted in this moving collection of letters. When Hitler came to power in 1933, Jews made up less than one percent of the German population yet were scapegoated and blamed for almost all of the ills in society. The barbaric persecution of the Holocaust did not happen in a vacuum. The Führer did not impose his will on a completely reluctant people and although not everyone supported Hitler and his thugs, many embraced the Nazi ideology and the feelings of superiority it brought with it. Blaming others serves as a convenient distraction from more serious issues that are harder to resolve in society, and it is much easier to blame someone than to take responsibility. If Mope and Vera's story teaches us anything it is the human cost of such terrifying politics. The slogan 'Never Again' is often used today in the context of preventing another genocide such as the Holocaust. Every time a politician incites hatred of a people or group and is cheered for such comments, a fundamental step against the concept of 'Never Again' has been taken. Nobody chooses to be a refugee, to uproot their lives as a result of persecution and travel to a country where they are often mistrusted and misunderstood, but those who have suffered remind us of how fragile society is, and how careful we must be to protect not only our rights, but the rights of our neighbour, no matter what his or her nationality, religion, skin colour or ethnic background might be.

PART 1: THEN

One: Familien Hirsch

Fig. 1 Photograph of VH (rubber stamped on verso, 6 July 1930).

Vera Lotte Hirsch (Felsenstein) "Lilongo"

Born Frankfurt, January 23, 1910

Died London, September 18, 1992

In her adult life, even into her final years, my mother was always more than sensitive about disclosing how old she was. Were she to find me posting her age, particularly at the very beginning of this book, she would make idle threats to do away with me, or at the very least–so she would half-jokingly declare—have me incarcerated without remission in the Tower of London. She would swear me to secrecy, insisting that I was never to reveal to the world one of life's most guarded secrets! She would consider that to be a complete and utter invasion of privacy. It at once begs the question whether publishing my mother's intimate letters and journals, alongside those of my father, is a further breach of confidentiality and an egregious step. It may come as a surprise that my mother would not have thought so.

©2024 Franklin Felsenstein, CC BY-NC 4.0   https://doi.org/10.11647/OBP.0334.01

Memorably, Leo Tolstoy began Anna Karenina *with the line that "all happy families resemble one another, each unhappy family is unhappy in its own way." I grew up in a very happy family–as well as my parents I did have a younger sister–in suburban London. In their interaction with their children, I cannot think of a single time when my mother and father opened any kind of sustained discussion of the events that had so deeply affected the early years of their relationship. Rather, it was important for them to bring us up resembling those Tolstoyan happy families, in other words as normally as possible, with almost no sense of the trauma that had beset them only a few years before. In outline, I only knew that my parents had escaped Germany and that several of their close relatives had perished. In the England in which I grew up during the late 1940s and 1950s adults constantly spoke to their children about the experience of the war but about the Holocaust they were silent.*

In everyday conversation, my parents' intonation revealed that London was not their place of birth as it was for me. Both of them spoke correct, if accented, English. That was more evident with my father who had been taught Latin as a living language, in accordance with the practice at his gymnasium or high school in Leipzig. I was quietly amused when he would pronounce "Cicero" as "Kikero" or when he would enunciate a word like "victim" as "wictim." Such occasional oddities apart, Mope spoke at least six different languages, most of them well.

The greatest linguistic compliment that my mother ever received was when a Marks & Spencer shop girl who had heard her, their personnel manager, speak with an accented English asked her without a trace of mockery whether she too hailed from the northern industrial city of Sunderland. She would often repeat that story, in jest adopting Sunderland rather than Frankfurt as her hometown! Because they wished to distance themselves from the country of their birth, at home my parents would never converse with us in German. The only time when we might hear them speaking that other language between themselves would be when they did not want us to understand what they were saying. And, in postwar England it would have marked them out as "the enemy" if they had gone around "spraching" in German.

During her nineteen years of widowhood, following Mope's death through lung cancer in 1973, Vera often found respite from her loss in re-reading the letters he had penned to her when she was in England, and he in Nazi Germany, and later, in the Soviet Union. The letters—all handwritten and occasionally typed in German—were stashed into two leather valises that she preserved on the floor of a built-in wardrobe in the main bedroom of her flat in northwest London. Every so often, when visiting her, I would find Vera perched on her bed, poring over a random selection of Mope's letters. Her bitter-sweet pleasure was in re-reading these letters, and recalling their immediacy and circumstances. She had already become inured to separation during the times when he had been abroad but by this time, so many years later, natural attrition had made that separation permanent. Reading his daily letters was her way of inviting Mope to communicate to her from beyond the grave, and for her to continue to experience the endurance of his love.

After the death of Vera, their correspondence came to me, and, given my ignorance of German, I arranged for its translation into English. Reading it, I was transfixed, appreciating that I had inherited a personal conduit through which my parents had unknowingly found a way to communicate with me after they were no longer there. Given that Vera had done everything to preserve their correspondence, I felt there was nothing preternatural or even voyeuristic about their doing that. In fact, she had more than once indicated to me a desire to have Mope's letters published, and I found her own writings no less compelling. Delving into their lives and inner thought processes was enriching to my own. Here was material that refused to remain silent. I was impelled to find out more.

Because her own letters and journals stretched back to well before she knew my father, it was easier to trace my mother's early life.

Fig. 2 Photograph of the Hirsch family (hand dated 4 May 1913).

Vera was the younger of the two girls of Hermann and Alice Hirsch. There is already tragedy in speaking about her sister. Gretel was Vera's senior by about nine years. At her delivery, an over-zealous obstetrician had clamped his forceps too tightly on to her cranium, and had irreversibly damaged her brain. Vera would describe her sister as looking perfectly normal but mentally severely impaired. Nowadays, her condition would probably be diagnosed, correctly or otherwise, as acute autism. It was only when Gretel tried to speak that you became aware of the gravity of her disability.

Fig. 3 Photograph of Alice Hirsch, née Ettlinger (undated but late 1890s); probably shot in Frankfurt.

An illustrative story is of Vera's first visit to the elegant Frankfurt Opera House, within easy walking distance of their home, when she herself will have been no more than ten years old. My grandmother was able to reserve a prime box alongside one of the balconies for the performance, and it was agreed to take Gretel too. The excitement for a young girl of Vera's age was palpable, especially so when the evening of the opera arrived. Exquisitely attired and made up for the occasion, they were ushered to their seats. Everything began accordingly, and Vera was absorbed in the beauty of the music and the novelty of the experience. However, at the height of the performance, in the middle of one of the most emotive arias, Gretel stood up and began screaming at the top of her voice, wildly gesticulating with her hands in the direction of the soprano singer. The attention of the audience was at once diverted to their box, and Gretel in company with her family had to be escorted out of the theatre. At her tender age, all that Vera could feel was complete mortification at the disturbance rather than sorrow for her sister. Given her condition, Gretel was to be institutionalized for much of her life to the extent that Vera often spoke of herself as an only child. Perhaps because my mother found it embarrassing to talk about her, I don't think I even knew that she had once had a sister until I was into my teens. It has to be said that attitudes to disability have progressed over the past hundred years.

Following her experience with Gretel, it took the advocacy, over several years, of the family doctor to persuade Alice that she should try for a second child. The real closeness of the relationship that was to develop between Alice and her younger daughter may be attributed to these circumstances. All through her journals, Vera is gushing in praise of her mother.

VERA

My life is good, and undeservedly so, and I am so lucky to have such an angel for a mother. Isn't it the happiest feeling to have that one person who loves you infinitely, admires you and worships you? If only I could pay her back somehow, even a little, but I am so self-centered.

My mother is goodness personified with an intuitive intelligence, capable, artistic–she paints very well. She is very musical and has a good and trained voice. Apart from German, she speaks a very good English, French, and a reasonably good Italian. She is immensely courageous, quick in making decisions, has a lively and keen sense of humor, is very loyal, has a natural social conscience, and literally idolizes me.

When I was about seventeen, she took me aside, and this is what she said: "Whatever may happen to you in your life, whether you will get married or not, whether you will achieve what you may set out to do, you will always be able to look back and know that you have achieved one thing to perfection. You have been the child your mother dreamt of, and you have given her all the happiness an offspring can possibly produce."

She showed me some kind of ironic aphorism that she had read in a Frankfurt newspaper: "Love is like the measles–we can only let it overwhelm us once and the later in life we find it, the worse it will be."

From the moment of her birth, Vera unwittingly displaced her sister as the focus of attention in the Hirsch household. She could easily have grown up into a very spoiled child. As a young girl, she appears to have become accustomed to getting her own way. Her habitual answer to any kind of request was a peremptory "Nein." Her mother and others tried to get her out of this awkward habit by inventing the jingle "Die Veralein sagt immer 'Nein', sagt immer 'Nein", sagt immer 'Nein'" ("Veralein always says 'No', always says 'No', always says 'No'"). It must have had some corrective effect since, in later days, my mother would often invoke it.

I never met my grandfather Hermann. He was always known as "Pepper," though I don't know where that name came from. He died three weeks to the day before I was born. I would have been his first grandchild. Hermann was five years older than Alice, having been born in Hanau, about ten miles from Frankfurt, in 1870 on the very day that the French army invaded the city during the ill-fated Franco-Prussian War. Vera's description of her father verges on the hostile.

Fig 4. Cabinet photograph of Hermann Hirsch (taken by the firm of Thiele in Hanau, undated but c. late 1890s).

VERA

Pepper grew up an only child. In appearance, he is good looking with a moustache twisted at both ends. He was a pupil at a boarding school in Friedrichsdorf near Bad Homburg because he was not up to the standard of the demands of a day school. What training he had had I do not know, probably some commercial one, and his prospective father-in-law proposed to take him into his flourishing textile business.

My mother objected strongly to the marriage. She told her father that she could not even think clearly, certainly not make such a decision as to getting married. Her father continued urging her, and pointed out that Hermann Hirsch was a kindly man, and even if he were to prove unsuccessful in making a living, it really did *not* matter, as there was more than enough wherewithal to last for their lives as well as for any children and grandchildren.

Fig. 5 Cabinet photograph of Alice (1875-1956) and Hermann Hirsch (1870-1944) shortly after their marriage (taken by the firm of J.B. Ciolina, Frankfurt, c. 1900).

My grandparents were married in April 1900 and Gretel was born in November 1901. With the dowry of a partnership in his father-in-law's wholesale cloth business and the ample wealth of the Hirsch family behind him, Hermann set up their family home in a spacious apartment on the Oberlindau in Frankfurt's fashionable West End.

When hyperinflation gripped Germany in 1923, Hermann's financial ineptitude led to the near total wipe-out of the family fortune. Vera was thirteen at the time when hyperinflation struck. It would be mistaken to ascribe her almost pathological disdain for her father as stemming from his mishandling of his business affairs. In 1923, there were countless German families who suffered a similar fate, so that the notion of placing personal blame on him alone is disproportionate. It also gives a false picture of Vera as a vindictive, spoiled child, who could never get over the loss of the family fortune. Yet, her scorn for her father remained with her throughout her life. At best, I can suggest that Vera's disdain for her father stemmed from her sense that her parents' marriage was an intellectual mismatch, that Hermann's lack of intelligence made him a hopeless and insufferable partner for his highly capable and intellectually gifted wife. She particularly objected to his obduracy.

VERA

Nothing is worse than lacking the ability to adjust. I wonder if that is a question of age. Nervousness? Lack of intelligence? Is it innate, this readiness to adjust to any given situation!!? It is completely impossible to negotiate with Papa in a kind manner: immediate screaming, stubbornness, fear of having to do something different from what he had planned. Not even the most giant strength can do anything against this kind of mountain of immovable iron, you just have to walk around it.

Fig. 6 Color photograph of Oberlindau 51, Frankfurt (taken in 2017).

In Frankfurt, we live in a large flat made up of eight rooms. Our house is situated opposite the Villa Rothschild, and five minutes from the Opera. My mother insisted on the importance of language learning, and as a young girl, we would have French or English companions lodging with us over extended periods, so as to improve our spoken knowledge of these languages. To help make ends meet following the inflation, my mother has now been taking paying guests into our household. Her fluency in English–and, more recently, my own–qualify us to give German lessons and we always give a daily lesson to our guests and of course talk only German to them all the day. We charge our lodgers a weekly rate of four guineas that includes four meals, daily German lessons, baths, etc.

Recently, I was in touch with a lady in London from a traditional English family whose seventeen-year-old daughter wants to come to Frankfurt to learn German. The charge of four guineas seemed to be no problem. The daughter wants to come over towards the end of August or the beginning of September and I expect she means to stay for six months, because she talked about Christmas and I said *all English girls are so delighted with our Christmas that they never want to go home*, and she replied how nice that would be.

I am bemused here by the irony of a Jewish family regaling gentile guests at a sumptuous dinner celebrating the birth of Jesus Christ, but the Hirsch family, like so many other German Jews of their upbringing, were very assimilated in their ways. I still possess a couple of recipe books that were compiled by my grandmother, and among the recipes is one for Christmas pudding followed by another for Passover Matzos dumplings. Both are written in Alice's almost faultless English. My grandmother was a consummate kitchen connoisseur, and what better indicator of the level of the family's pre-Nazi integration than the food that they prepared and served.

During the Second World War, Frankfurt was heavily bombed by Allied planes. Oberlindau was flattened. Miraculously, only a single house along the street was left standing, and that was the one containing my grandparents' apartment. Its survival against the odds strikes me as highly symbolic because the endurance of its bricks and mortar is the sole witness to the destruction that surrounded it. Since the war, Oberlindau has been rebuilt but, with the exception of this one building, the reality of its past history has been all but obliterated. We may wish to view the house as the sole representative of those many vanished homes, a good number of which had been inhabited by Frankfurt's former Jewish population. By extension, my parents' correspondence–and through it the story of their survival—may serve as evocative of the broader experience of so many other German-Jewish refugees from a similar social milieu.

Two: Mainly Mope

Fig. 7 Photograph of EMF (hand dated May 1939).

Ernst Moritz (Ernest Maurice) Felsenstein Mope

Born Leipzig, 19 June 1899

Died London, 27 June 1973

Ernst Moritz (or Mope as he became known) was to grow up in the socio-cultural milieu of a traditional German-Jewish family. Where the Hirsches represent Jewry at its most assimilated, the Felsenstein family may be seen as a bastion of Orthodoxy.

MOPE

I was born in Leipzig, Germany, the third one of the seven children–five girls and two boys—of Isidor and Helene Felsenstein.

Fig. 8 Postcard-sized photograph of Helene ("Oma Lenchen") and Isidor Felsenstein (undated but c. 1900).

Fig. 9 Group photograph of children of Helene and Isidor Felsenstein (1917); back row, Adolf, EMF (both in military uniform); middle row, Grete, Alice, Ketty, and Ruth; front row, Hanna.

Here we are standing together outside our home in Leipzig in 1917, a group photo of me and my six siblings. Fourteen years separated the oldest from the youngest. My oldest sister, Ketty (who is second to the right), was born in 1896, my youngest, Hanna (to the front), in 1910. Behind her are twins, Grete and Alice, who were born in 1901, and to the right of our photo is Ruth, who appeared the following year. She is the most intellectual of my sisters. The two young men in the rear are my brother, Adolf, born in 1897, and myself. Both of us appear in military uniform. The picture was taken when my brother and I were each briefly on leave from army service.

Fig. 10 Present-day color photograph of Leibnizstrasse 19, Leipzig (taken from https://www.architektur-blicklicht.de/artikel/villa-leibnizstrasse-leipzig-zentrum-nordwest-waldstrassenviertel/).

The Felsenstein family home on Leibnizstrasse in central Leipzig, in which the children grew up, was situated within walking distance of their synagogue. Both Isidor and Helene were immersed in the activities of the Jewish community. Their children passed through the Israelitische Kindergarten, of which Helene was on the steering committee. Within the family, there were plenty of joyous celebrations, such as weddings and Bar Mitzvahs, at which the children could get together with their numerous cousins. In a letter to Vera written weeks before the start of the war, the early experience of a religious education still resonated in his mind as he contemplated the Jewish Fast of Av.

MOPE

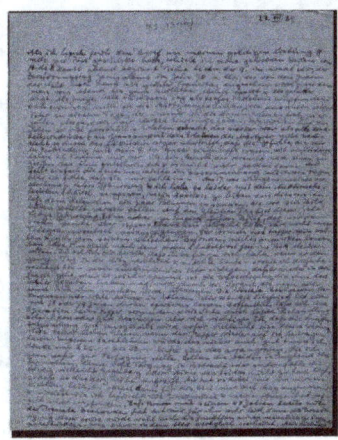

Fig. 11 EMF to VF, 23 July 1939, opening page with reference to Tischa B'Av (Jewish Fast of Av).

This evening, Tischa B'av. begins, the 9th of the month of Av., the day of Jerusalem's destruction in the year 70 A.D., which is regarded as the greatest day of mourning by Jews around the world, and it is tradition to fast from the evening of the previous day until the following evening and sing elegies. As a boy, I felt this day to be a profound religious experience and I remember the martyr stories that our blessed father would tell us on this day, and those stories made a very strong impression on me.

In the meantime, life has brought so many personal experiences that are much stronger than any childhood impressions, and the cruelty of some of them is close to the suffering of the martyrs, but maybe even exceed them because they are so acute, that the emotions related to this day, with which I was inoculated as a child, have paled. I feel like a human being who is trying to reach for something that is disappearing and cannot catch it anymore.

Though Ernst Moritz's whole childhood was in an Orthodox Jewish environment, he was to join a non-denominational school for his education.

Fig. 12 Leipzig Schiller-Real-Gymnasium; undated postcard.

MOPE

I was registered at the Schiller-Real-Gymnasium, where the curriculum included the Classics, as well as Math and Science. From early days, I dreamed of a future vocation as a scientist.

At boys' schools in Germany, as well as academic subjects, much substance was given to sport and physical fitness. My brother Adolf showed his athleticism in field sports, whereas I was less agile on my feet but a strong wrestler.

Fig. 13 Studio photograph of EMF as a schoolboy by Adolf Richter... Leipzig Lindenau; undated.

My father, Isidor, is Senior Partner of the Leipzig firm, Gebrüder Felsenstein, a three-century-old fur business. Its showroom is centrally situated on the corner of Nikolaistrasse and the Brühl, a few hundred meters from the city's main railway station.

Fig. 14 Geschäfsthaus Gebr. Felsenstein, Leipzig [Commercial Building of the Felsenstein Brothers, Leipzig] (postcard).

Through my father's astute management, the firm evaded the worst consequences of the hyperinflation of 1923. It has expanded into one of the largest fur companies in the city. Two of my father's brothers share ownership with him, and, to guarantee the future of this family partnership, it is stipulated that each in turn will be expected to place two sons in the business. As head partner, my father put the success of Gebrüder Felsenstein over almost any other consideration, and here we have the crux of the problem that has faced me from early on.

Isidor fathered seven children, but only two were boys, and, in the world of commerce at that time, girls were not in the equation.

Fig. 15 Photograph of EMF as a young teenager.

Ernst Moritz's Bar Mitzvah took place on 29 June 1912. Two years later, the so-called Great War began. Leipzig was at a distance from the fighting, and, at first, the war had little direct effect on the education of an academically gifted sixteen-year-old. However, by the spring of 1916, most of the personnel at the Gebrüder Felsenstein (including his brother Adolf) had enlisted. Isidor found a partial solution to the shortage of manpower by pulling his younger son out of school to help in the business. There was no consultation, only a paternal diktat that Ernst Moritz must leave school. It was the first of several occasions when father and son were to clash.

Fig. 16 Photograph of Isidor Felsenstein (1866-1934) on entry pass to International Fur Trade Exhibition.

MOPE

I stood in stark contrast to my father's opinions. In spite of that I tried, probably much too late, to find my way into the thought processes of my father. I learned to understand that he meant well, only wished the best for me and was convinced that, because he was an older man, he was better able to judge life with all its difficulties, than the young son whose opposition, seen from his point of view, had to be broken.

After an awkward half year working at the Gebrüder Felsenstein, a visit to his grandfather in Königsberg gave Ernst Moritz the opportunity to assert his independence. Still smarting at Isidor's intransigence, he made the decision to defy Father in favor of Fatherland. He followed his brother by enlisting.

MOPE

In the late fall of 1916, at the age of seventeen, I visited my grandfather in Königsberg and, at that time, took the opportunity to voluntarily register for military service with the Sixteenth Artillery Regiment at Rothenstein near Königsberg. In the spring of 1917, I was sent to France and participated in the war until October 1918.

Ernst Moritz left no written account of his participation in the war, and, in common with many other soldiers, found it challenging to talk about the hellish experience that he underwent. Its post-traumatic effect may account for his arbitrary shortness of temper and fits of anger, which, from early on in their courtship, Vera learned to control and to calm. In conversation with me long after he was no longer there, she would describe him as having had all the passion of a noble stallion, needing a steady rein and a long leash to bring out the best in him.

From stray comments in his later correspondence with Vera (as in one of his letters to her from Leipzig penned during a rainstorm in 1936) we can sense that the echoes of war still jangled in his head.

Fig. 17 EMF in German army uniform.

МОРЕ

There was a thunderstorm this evening. The thunder crashed like striking grenades, without rolling and without dying away. Malignant thunder, imitating the noises of war and recalling memories with their strikes that would better be forgotten. It was pouring down in streams and still did not give any release from the tension.

For all his understandable reticence to revisit the horror that he had lived through, my father did engage with me in several conversations about that period of his life. He told me that, as an observant Orthodox Jew, living conditions in the trenches were even more unbearable than for other soldiers. The food that was issued to the troops was inadequate, and, if meat was available, it was invariably pork. Some cold-hearted German soldiers who fought alongside him would taunt him with slabs of bacon and bratwurst, which they would flaunt before his eyes and, with guttural laughter, tempt him to consume. "Komm Jude, Essen." Through all this, Mope adhered to his dietary observance. The single consumable that was available in the trenches was tobacco. He became a compulsive smoker, a habit that he was unable to give up in later years. When he died in June 1973, more than a half century after the end of hostilities, it was as a result of lung cancer, a belated victim of the Great War.

The entry of the United States into the final phases of the war coincided with Mope's deployment to northern France. During the months that followed, German forces fell under increasing pressure. In an engagement in October 1918, a month prior to the signing of the Armistice, Mope was severely wounded by shrapnel from shell fire. He was carried by stretcher to an army field hospital, where, still conscious, he was informed by the surgeons that they were on the point of amputating one of his legs below the knee. As they said this, he glimpsed across from him a large basin that was brimful of amputated limbs. His reaction was to struggle, and refuse to allow the surgeons to carry out the operation. They answered that the amputation was critical to counteract gangrene. Mope fought back that he would rather die than become an amputee. Unwillingly, they agreed to have him stretchered from the front lines, where he was patched up and placed on a train to carry him back to Leipzig. For the next three days and three nights, he lay semi-comatose on the corridor floor of a moving train.

Reaching Leipzig, he was placed under the care of the best physicians, and began the slow process toward recovery. He had been proven right to refuse amputation in the field, yet he was also incredibly lucky. The surgeons at Leipzig were able to extract shrapnel, but concluded that other minor shards were too deeply embedded and would not impede his ability to walk. For the rest of his life, Mope's shins bore tiny fragments of shrapnel, though these were not visible to the naked eye and did not affect his mobility.

MOPE

During the war, my brother Adolf served as an officer in the infantry. He had what is called "a good war", being commended for his courage and leadership skills, and receiving the Iron Cross First Class. My own experience was less exalted. Although a source of some embarrassment to me in later years, since I was to receive a service decoration from the British army at the end of the Second World War, I was awarded an Iron Cross Second Class as a recompense for my combat wounds. At my discharge, I was released with the rank of *Vizewachtmeister* (lit.

"Vice–or Sub-Sergeant-Major"), and personally elected to waive my injury pension rights in favor of needier comrades.

Hitler's crude assertion, widely promulgated by the Nazis, that the cowardice of the Jews undermined the German war effort in 1914-1918, is belied by the active participation of my father and his brother no less than the sons of countless other patriotic Jewish families.

Three: Victoriaschule

Fig. 18 Victoriaschule Frankfurt (postcard).

At the same time that Ernst Moritz was serving in France, Vera was experiencing her first years at the all-girls Victoriaschule in Frankfurt. Until the advent of Hitler, a significant number of the pupils were of Jewish extraction. A story that Vera would often tell illustrates well her unfamiliarity with her own Jewishness.

Not long after she first became a pupil there–I reckon when Vera was perhaps six or seven years old–the Jewish girls were asked to withdraw from an assembly before the recitation of Christian prayers. All the Jewish girls started to file out, but my mother stayed rooted to the spot, half believing that she belonged in the assembly. Only after almost all the girls had left the room, one little classmate came running back and grabbed her, pronouncing to my mother's surprise, "Vera, you're Jewish; you're supposed to be with us!"

VERA

There are about thirty girls in our class. The class teacher, Fraulein Albrecht, will remain as our form mistress until we take the *Abitur* (graduation exam). I'm thrilled about that because I really like her, and I believe she likes me. In common with most other girls of my age, I have gone out of my way to be well-liked. My open manner soon made me one of the most popular girls in my class. In my first school year–when I was aged 6, the form was asked by Fraulein Albrecht to elect a girl as class prefect. I received 40 out of 42 votes. After one year in this position, I had become so unpopular, that I was *not* re-elected. From that time, I have learned that throwing one's weight around and being bossy is a very stupid and unworthy activity. To my good fortune, my school friends appear to have forgiven me and forgotten my electoral humiliation much more rapidly than I did.

Fig. 19. Victoriaschule Class in 1915, including VH, wearing a white bow (top righ), and teacher, Fraulein Albrecht (middle right).

When one recalls that the traumas and tragedies of the Nazi era were to scatter her surviving classmates across the world, it is testimony to the endurance of childhood friendships that Vera was able to re-establish contact with several members of her class. Like her, a few found refuge in Britain, while others affirmed their Jewishness through settling in Palestine. At least four, including Vera's best friend, Hilde Mayer, rebuilt their lives in the United States. Almost without exception, these former pupils were to choose fellow refugees as their husbands, their shared experience providing an indissoluble bond, often enhancing their identity as Jews in their post-war lives.

As with thousands of other refugees, each of these surviving school friends will have had her own personal story of fleeing from Nazism. Each would constitute a fascinating narrative. Unique as it is in its intactness, my parents' correspondence may serve as a measure of the broader experience of so many other German-Jewish refugees of an equivalent social milieu and upbringing.

Before the Abitur, which she passed with distinction, Vera, shown here in the school's science lab with more than twenty other rising Seniors, took pre-college classes in Physics and Chemistry.

Fig. 20 Victoriaschule Chemistry Class; VH at right hand side second row from back.

Her transcript shows her success.

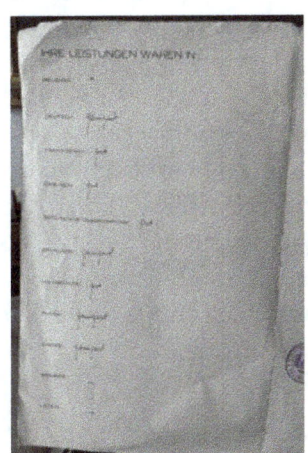

Figs. 21 (a) and (b) VH's Graduation Transcript from the Victoriaschule, 1928.

In 1929, at the age of nineteen, she matriculated with distinction, and enrolled as a student of medicine at the University of Frankfurt. In her journal, she reflects on the transition.

VERA

Today, I have to give a short overview of many things that have affected me over the last few weeks.

I used to think that, once I left high school, my time to learn would be over, but I found out that it never ends! I did not realize until just a short time ago that passing an exam does not mean reaching a *goal*, but merely a *station*, and that is the major difference between the way I used to feel and the way I feel now. The insignificance of my person and my lack of knowledge is becoming completely clear to me.

Right now, my work is very satisfying. Anatomy in the morning, after lunch an English lesson, reading and some fresh air and nice people around me. I want to go back to regarding every moment as a gift, a gift that will bring many unknown and unimagined things. I want to work, enjoy, create. I will finish my studies for sure. I want to be someone, and always have courage in my life. I want the strength to make decisions.

How wonderful it is that I am studying medicine. Because of that, I lost my silly prudishness, which used to make conversations very uncomfortable to me. I will try to analyze myself as to why. I think it is an inferiority complex: you think that you are not capable of being entertaining enough for people, not amusing enough, and then, there is that certain reticence that still haunts you from your childhood. However, these things are receding more and more into the background. In my twenty years of life, I have collected enough experiences and more are being added all the time, so it is not presumptuousness and arrogance to have self-confidence, because the self is not built on this self alone, but from the self plus experiences from outside, which together form my current self.

Fig. 22 Hilde Meyer with Vera on the ski slopes; Bad Homburg, winter 1930.

Again today: Hilde told me that she is afraid that I was going back to the small and insignificant non-person I used to be! Is that true? Actually, I am feeling quite content, that is, I know now that things are working out well for me: I have time to read, to do anything that makes me happy, and my studies fulfill me. I am not completely lazy, although my time could be put to better use. I am learning a little bit of Spanish, Chemistry, and Histology every day, read German and French books, and work on little pieces of handicraft.

Working, accomplishing things, that is the right thing for me. I am young, I am strong, I have the opportunity to learn something and that is why I will take advantage of it. I will work diligently throughout the entire semester–that is the only thing, the right thing I can do. And because of that, I am content today. The one thing one is always looking for is to give meaning to one's life!!!

Four: "And so What?"

MOPE

In Leipzig, I remain hospitalized for more than nine months. I owe it to my mother's constant attentiveness that I am receiving the finest available medical treatment in recovering from the severe injuries that I sustained in the trenches. My innermost relationship with my mother has become an enduring compass point in my life. In many ways, my closeness to her acts as a counterbalance to the often-strained relationship that I have with my father.

Fig. 23 Mope's mother, Helene Felsenstein (1874-1963), known in the family as Oma Lenchen.

Of the two, my father was certainly inferior to my dear mother intellectually as well as educationally, though he still possessed her

©2024 Franklin Felsenstein, CC BY-NC 4.0 https://doi.org/10.11647/OBP.0334.04

full love and affection. In the patriarchal world in which they lived, she was anything but the master in their marriage. However, she always understood in the most exquisite way how to balance everything and to be a wonderful and trusted friend to her husband as well as her children. Yet, I am sure that she was fully aware of her intellectual superiority after the marriage, or even before.

Mope's mother, known in the family as Oma Lenchen, grew up in a household that greatly valued intellectual pursuits. Two of her brothers, who emigrated to America, became eminent Judaic scholars. A sister was a pioneering Zionist, moving in 1910 to Palestine, where she and her husband turned mosquito-infested swamp into rich farmland. Another sister married a writer who went on to win the Nobel Prize for Literature. Oma Lenchen and her siblings exuded the charm and unassuming sophistication that came from a vibrant German-Jewish intellectual culture. Not for nothing, the great Judaic scholar Gershom Scholem extolled them as "one of the most aristocratic Orthodox Jewish families of Germany." From his mother's side, Mope inherited a natural love of learning and an almost intuitive appreciation of the importance of the life of the mind.

MOPE

During my prolonged hospital stay and recovery, I used my time to prepare myself for the baccalaureate exam, that I had been unable to take prior to my military service. I passed in May 1919. After the baccalaureate, I began to study first year Chemistry at Leipzig University, all that time remaining under supervised medical care at the military hospital until the spring of 1920. Even before my discharge, my father urged me to rejoin the Gebrüder Felsenstein, and, but for the intervention of my mother, would have succeeded in his object.

When I was near to a full recovery from my injuries, I had what was to prove for me a highly consequential one-to-one meeting with my father in the family home in Leipzig. My father held long-term grudges against me, the chief one stemming from his resentment at being excluded from the decision that I had taken at the age of seventeen to enlist. In our increasingly acrimonious exchange, he invoked his own authority, and virtually blamed my injuries on my having neglected to ask for paternal blessing prior to joining up.

Filial disobedience, my father maintained, did not make me a good Jew. Rather, in his opinion, I had shown myself a discredit to the family. Ignoring that I was in hospital and for a long period unable to attend synagogue, he invoked a malicious rumor that, as I had failed to keep Kashrut while in the trenches, it had disbarred me from being called up to read from the Torah. I was totally incensed by my father's attitude and misconstruction. I responded by recounting how, through the whole of my ordeal in the trenches, I had clung to the tenets of Orthodox Judaism that he had taught me, and, despite the privations I underwent–which I spelled out in some detail—I had adhered as far as I was capable to a kosher diet and observance.

My father's abrupt and unfeeling response was *"And So What?"* The heartlessness of the retort and the lack of understanding that went with it had a devastating effect upon me. The painful experience of war had already made me question the tenets of my belief system even as I clung to it as a matter of pride and for the sake of my family. My father's response was the proverbial straw that broke the camel's back. Though I was to remain a committed Jew and a passionate Zionist, it was the beginning of my permanent falling-out with Orthodoxy.

Mope's successful completion of his freshman year at Leipzig and his desire to continue with his academic studies caused further friction with Isidor who still insisted that his son's place was in the fur trade. Rather than allow the situation to become ever more volatile, his mother used her diplomatic skills to coax Isidor into assenting to the continuation of Mope's studies, though he made his own position clear by denying him financial support.

The Felsenstein family's prominence in the Leipzig Orthodox Community and his own estrangement from its practices persuaded Mope that he must move elsewhere. In 1921, he was to leave Leipzig and enroll at the University of Erlangen in Bavaria. From there, he was accepted at the prestigious Technische Hochschule in Karlsruhe to pursue graduate work developing new uses of plastics. Mope soon became an integral part of a highly motivated research team.

In Karlsruhe, he befriended cousins of his, Karl and Lies Rosenfeld, whom he had previously known but distantly. During the Great War, Karl, who was sixteen years older than my father, had fought in the German army, and was a decorated war veteran. Severely wounded in battle, he had been far less fortunate than Mope, and had suffered the amputation of one of his legs beneath the knee. His first wife had been a victim of the great flu epidemic in 1918, and, shortly after the war, he had taken as his second wife, Elisabeth ("Lies") Willstater, who was fourteen years his junior. By the time Mope moved to Karlsruhe, the couple were blessed with a two-year old son, Georg. Another son, Benjamin, was born to them in 1924 during my father's stay in the city. The Rosenfelds showed unstinting hospitality to him.

MOPE

My cousins, Karl and Lies, were always more than willing to give me any assistance necessary and to receive me into their home at any time. In the absence of financial support from my father, I had to earn my own money to pay for my studies and if I ran short, Carlchen always helped me out until I was able to pay the money back. At one time, I owed him over 600 Reichsmarks–and back then, that was a huge fortune to me! Of course, I paid him back.

It was a debt of gratitude that Mope never forgot, particularly so when the Rosenfelds strove to escape from Germany in the following decade. We shall return to their story.

Receiving no financial help from Isidor and with gathering hyperinflation in Germany, Mope ran short of funds. Mounting obligations forced him to approach his father in hope that he might underwrite his research. Instead, Isidor saw this as the golden opportunity to recruit his younger son into the family business. He offered to pay off his son's debts, but with an ultimatum that he must relinquish his graduate work and re-join the family business in Leipzig. An emotional appeal from Helene to her husband to allow their son to complete his doctoral work fell on deaf ears. Even the visit of two of Mope's professors, who (recognizing the potential of his research and his promise as a young physicist) traveled the considerable distance from Karlsruhe to Leipzig in order to persuade my grandfather to reconsider his decision, had no effect. Isidor had made up his mind and nothing could shift that. In the age before regular student loans, Mope was left with very little option other than to comply. In February 1925, he began once again working for the family business. For Mope, it rankled with him in later years that his academic career in the Sciences was cut short by his father's recalcitrance.

MOPE

My father was fixed in his outlook on life since his youth and, through that, in some way outdated and without understanding of modern developments and the non-patriarchal position that I had, and with his unshakeable maxims managed to undermine and destroy the development I had planned for myself.

Five: Heising

In a back drawer at home in London when I was a boy, my parents had preserved a scattering of banknotes issued at the height of the financial crisis that wrecked the German economy in 1923. They would mention the hyperinflation that struck when Vera was thirteen and Mope twenty-four. What they remembered was the immediate impact. They recounted that a loaf of bread which had cost a single Mark in 1919 was priced at one hundred billion Marks in 1923. People filled wheelbarrows with Notgelds in order to pay bills. What you earned in the morning, you spent immediately because it would have lost its value by close of day. A few years later, it was expedient for Hitler and the Nazis to put blame for the hyperinflation on the Jews.

Fig. 24 Hyperinflationary bank note, dated 1922.

My mother spelled out to me how her father, Pepper, exhausted what remained of the Hirsch family assets by honoring established agreements through selling goods at their original list price instead of renegotiating to take account of inflation. At a stroke, his honesty in business affairs–she would venture "utter naïveté"–impoverished the family.

VERA

At home the monetary situation became grim, and with it came the fear that I couldn't participate with others whose families were less affected by the hyperinflation. From our situation, there developed a constraining and insincere behavior in myself, a desire to want to be more than I was. That began when I was thirteen years old. At fifteen, I figured out that one can only enjoy life's privileges if one is willing and ready to be completely engaged in every aspect of it. In the winter of that year Fraulein Albrecht introduced a dance hour at school, and for the first time in my life I was together with the opposite sex, unbounded, shy, and excessively hurt by vanity.

Monetary pressure forced me into second guessing and self-deprecation about the choice of studies that were not so costly or time consuming, but were still practical. What followed was a zeal for work that redoubled and increased tenfold. There was no time for anything else, except to cut everything else out of my life. In between were admirers and boyfriends out of whom I didn't really form anything serious.

The incipient anti-Semitism during the era of the Weimar Republic manifested itself in less than subtle ways in the classrooms and corridors of many German universities.

VERA

As a core requirement of the university curriculum, I enrolled in a Zoology *Praktikum für Mediziner* led by a professor who had a reputation among the Jewish students for holding anti-Semitic views and being an early supporter of Adolf Hitler. I remained wary throughout the class, maintaining a low profile and expressing myself minimally. At first, this tactic seemed to work in my favor for the professor never once addressed me directly and did not appear even to know my name.

However, at the start of a class in which we were each to perform an animal dissection, he instructed us on what was expected, but ended his comments with the following: "As we all know, this is the element of the *Praktikum* for which Miss Hirsch has been awaiting so eagerly. No doubt her attention is on the rabbit fur coat that she will make for herself once you have all completed the dissection." Perhaps the remark did not go beyond the tactless, reflecting the misogyny of a male professor at a time when there were few female students of medicine. But, if it was intended to embarrass me, it surely did, though it also succeeded in provoking raucous laughter among certain of the students.

At worst, the incident, trivial as it may have been, was one more reflection of the simmering anti-Semitism which after 1933 was to become so much more barefaced and brutal. The dilemma for a Jewish student in the precarious years before the Nazis gained power was in the paranoiac uncertainty as to how to interpret such incidents.

During that period, it was not uncommon to find Jewish and non-Jewish students engaged in social pursuits that were not subject to racial segregation or prohibition in the way that they were to become from 1933. Vera was an enthusiastic sportswoman, playing tennis over the summer months, and, when her studies allowed, skiing in the nearby Taunus Mountains during the winter, the last time in 1932.

VERA

It's two days after Christmas. We spent the entire day at the meadow hut where we were surrounded by blinding snow and we went for a wonderful walk. This year, I am skiing noticeably *better*–I am sure that the reason for that are my new skis and shoes. We have decided to go there and practice every day. The sun was shining the entire time and afterwards we witnessed the Alpen-glow, absolutely indescribably beautiful. I am enjoying myself completely!!!! I am glad, aside from the fact that it is so wonderful, that I went on this trip, because one really does not get to know one's companions with all their small weaknesses and maybe great virtues until one spends an extended period of time with them.

In any case, I am feeling very well, and I feel completely *safe* and that is most precious. I am glad that I have a few reliable friends here, and they are *really* trustworthy. I think that things are really going well for me.

Photos that survive from the early 1930s show Vera amid an athletic throng of smiling young students enjoying the halcyon pleasures of winter sports. Among the medical students in the group is Heising, an Aryan-looking tall blond-haired young man, initially in thrall to his girlfriend, Edith.

Fig. 25 Vera with Heising on the ski slopes, hand inscribed "1930-31 Taunus" [Mountains].

VERA

I heard something today that made such an impression on me. From Heising, completely unknowingly. He told me how indescribably and infinitely he had loved Edith and how he had thought that he could only be happy with her. He is a young man with intense feelings. But Heising also said something that seems very true to me: He thinks—he was talking about Edith—that a man loses interest in a woman the moment he realizes that he is the only one who exists for that woman.

Six weeks later, I went walking in the *Palmen Garten* with Heising. Conscious that there had been a shift in his emotions, I told him in quick succession that I would rather not accompany him, that my presence would create a wedge between him and his girlfriend. He denied that and then said: "If both you and she were set on fire, I would rescue you first!" Something like that *is* flattering to hear! It even makes me happy, although I do *not* harbor any tender feelings toward him. As he told me (since he knows how completely out of reach I am for him), he is not interested for the moment anyway. At least that is what he said.

Now, being honest to myself, I like to see him–he is good-looking–I am glad that I have someone and I know that he is completely honest and decent. I like having someone who will carry things for me–I have lugged around tennis and swimming equipment and it is nice to have an honest and funny human being around.

In the perpetual calendar of praktika *and examinations that were required to become a medical doctor in Germany, Vera found it helpful to prepare before these exams by testing her knowledge with Heising. The result was that she came through nearly always with outstanding grades, while Heising limped behind. His devotion to her became almost dog-like to the extent that when others saw them together, they mistakenly considered them to be a couple. The truth was more complex.*

VERA

This evening, I went to the theater with Heising to see a nonsensical new play. Then on to dinner at the Ratskeller with him. He revealed to me today that he is really deeply in love with me, but (he says) he knows that I am much more mature and finished than he is, etc. (*oh, I am so vain!*), and I really like hearing things like that, of course. However, I can only feel love for someone who gives me the overwhelming feeling that he is *significantly* more intelligent than I am, at least where pure knowledge is concerned. I think Heising would have enjoyed the play, had I not been there, but after he heard me talking or rather listened to my judgment, he adjusted his to match my opinion, probably because he realized that I was right. Once I notice something like that, I tend to lean towards wistful disdain.

I did not want to tell him at first that he has been getting on my nerves quite terribly of late–I thought that he was just not worth it, but I learned something from it. No human being is so inferior that you can consider him or her as unworthy of attention and it is very stupid of me to drop such a human being without so much as an afterthought, especially one who holds me in such high esteem.

I learned that you can only ensnare a man if you always let him feel that he does not have unlimited chances with you. I should remember that for a life lesson, and if ever I should fall in love I will take that advice and use it.

I wish—not that I would like to get married right now, my studies make me much too happy for that—I would meet another human being, who will captivate me to fall in love with him! I can hardly wait to see how my life will develop. There is something delightful in not knowing your future!

Heising would frequently drop by to study alongside Vera. He was made welcome in the Hirsch household by my always hospitable grandmother. Then, from one day to the next in 1932 and with no explanation, his visits to my grandparents' home ceased. However, after a gap of several weeks, Heising unexpectedly showed up to announce to the Hirsch family that, given that they were Jewish, he was sorry that he could no longer socialize with them as he had joined the Nazi party. He considered it a patriotic duty that overrode whatever acquaintance or even friendship they may once have had.

When Vera saw him again in the medical school, he was sporting a swastika armband. His membership of the Nazi party, rather than any intellectual brilliance, would have ensured his qualification as a medical practitioner. She was never to hear from him again.

VERA

I would like to know how Heising imagines he will be able to continue his studies and for what practical purpose??? He really is reprehensible, to be so blind to everything.

In many respects, Heising's Nazification anticipates that of the medical school at Frankfurt, which was among the first to dismiss its Jewish doctors and professors in 1933, and in the following year became the home of the notorious Institut für Erbbiologie und Rassenforschung (Institute of Hereditary Biology and Racial Hygiene). The Institute's most notorious alumnus was Dr. Josef Mengele, Auschwitz's wicked "Angel of Death." Heising's wholesale disengagement from any contact with Jews was all too typical.

VERA

I was close with some cousins of mine, the Jacobsons, who lived in Fulda. There were three daughters, and a younger adopted son, Richard, with whom, when we were children, I used to play. I knew Richard as a boy. He was a few years older than I, fair, blue-eyed, tall and an unbelievably cruel and unpleasant playmate, and terribly spoilt by his parents. He was connected with a Jazz band when grown-up, and when Hitler came, he announced that he was of pure Aryan descent and only adopted by his Jewish "parents," and he abandoned them.

That abandonment placed Vera's cousins in peril. At least one of Richard's former sisters and her husband were to be murdered in the gas chambers of Auschwitz.

Six: Of Books and Arts (1): Max Schwimmer

MOPE

I resumed work at the Gebrüder Felsenstein in Leipzig toward the beginning of 1925, and, after four years during which my relationship with my father has much improved, I have been promoted to salaried partner. I think that my father has begun to appreciate whatever small talents I may possess, so long as they are directed to the fur trade. My aspiration to be a scientist means nothing to him, although my entrapment in a career I had not sought will always rankle with me.

I am sufficiently paid to have been able to move into a spacious three-room apartment on the Kaiserin Augusta Strasse. From there, I can indulge in the artistic and cultural life of the city. The most notable feature of the apartment is my library, which still reflects my former scientific pursuits, but also includes a wide-ranging collection of rare books, Judaica, and German Literature.

Fig. 26 Mope in his study; undated but early 1930s.

I have commissioned my closest friend, the artist Max Schwimmer, to design for my library a personal bookplate that will accent a Jewish theme. Schwimmer is not Jewish, and has struggled to fulfill my commission. I have other works by him, including several portraits for which I sat, though I keep these loose and unframed as they seem to me to be works in progress. To be absolutely honest, I do not find them to be particularly flattering. For all that, Schwimmer's wit, intelligence, and sheer talent make him excellent company. We often meet for a conversational smoke at the Café Merkur on the Thomasring or at his studio which attracts many fellow artists and bohemians. Both in his art and in his conversation, Schwimmer is caustic in his dismissal of the opposition Fascist mobs whom he portrays as monsters. Their stridency pushes him to the Communist left. It is a different extreme to the Nazis and not one that I could ever espouse. However, our friendship transcends politics, and I am quite certain that Schwimmer feels the same way.

Fig. 27 Anti-Nazi campaign poster by Max Schwimmer, 1924. "Wählt die VSPD–Vote for the V.S.P.D. [Independent Social Democratic Party]. Reproduced in Hellmut Radmacher, *Masters of German Poster Art* (New York: The Citadel Press, 1966, 101) and other sources.

I have often wondered–and continue to wonder–what happened to Mope's library and his other belongings. He would often talk nostalgically about the books and works of art that he had had to leave behind in Leipzig. None of these were ever recovered.

What evidence is there today? Little survives to give a sense of the composition of Mope's bachelor apartment. During the 1930s under Hitler, its contents were transferred more than once to other premises before they were impounded. Some post-war correspondence with family acquaintances in Leipzig who tried unsuccessfully on his behalf to reclaim Mope's valuables, provides a basic list of an impressive apartment. Its contents included fine furniture and fixtures, a set of white Rosenthal porcelain, an Indian tea service and a similar coffee service, a silver case, miscellaneous glassware and lamps, a painting by a Dutch old master, and a bronze Buddha. Shortly after they took power, the Aryanization laws mandated by the Nazis drove him to move more than once into smaller and less secure accommodation in areas of the town where Jews were still permitted to live. His library and papers were put into storage in one of the company warehouses. The size of his collection forced him into weeding out.

MOPE

Yesterday and today, I sorted all of my old correspondence, photographs and books. Among the photographs, there were a lot of pictures of me, most of which I had completely forgotten about. Unfortunately, I did not reduce my library nearly as much as necessary. If I took out 150 books (I did not count them), that number would not be too low, and I had counted on three or five times that many. It is so difficult to part with these friends who only talk when they are asked and never say more than is contained within them, if imagination is not involved.

Among Mope's books left in Leipzig were a number that were illustrated and inscribed to him by Max Schwimmer.[1] Mope referred to him, even in later years, as his closest male friend. Schwimmer, who was four years older than Mope, had also been drafted into the army, returning to Leipzig after the war and enrolling at the university where he studied art history and philosophy. In 1926, he was appointed as a drawing master at the Leipzig School of Fine Arts, but was dismissed in May 1933 because of his left-wing political views and his so-called "degenerate art." The following year, Mope helped fund a joint trip they made to Dalmatia, both very taken by the beauty of Ragusa (Dubrovnik). Here is a handsome photograph of Mope on the ramparts at Dubrovnik that will have been shot by Schwimmer.

---

1   A photographic portrait of the artist Max Schwimmer (1895-1960) is available in the online resources to this book, https://doi.org/10.11647/

Fig. 28 EMF on a rampart in Ragusa [Dubrovnik], June 1934.

Unlike many—or most—Germans, Schwimmer was willing to defy Nazi injunctions against socializing with Jews, and Mope was always a welcome visitor to his studio, visits he savored as a rare escape from the ostracism that he and fellow Jews encountered everywhere else. Later, in 1936 and 1937, he would use his time there to write to Vera, Schwimmer often enhancing the letters he wrote with erotic watercolors.

MOPE

Today is October 23, 1936. I am sitting at Schwimmer's writing. When I arrived, I apparently interrupted a tender *tête-à-tête* he was having with his girlfriend. Still, we soon engaged in lively conversation: art, artists, philosophy, with a few bottles of wine. The air of the studio is pregnant with smoke and the new pictures with their colors shine through the haze with great vitality. Two landscapes, in between a flower and fruit still life, decorate the walls. Max really is an exceptionally gifted artist, and it is sad that the time of patronage is over, a time in which he certainly would have had a life free from worry, at least in a material respect, and even more regrettable, given my own reduced financial circumstances, that I cannot be the patron myself.

He now says he wants to draw a sketch at the head of the letter, but I tell him I do have to hurry in order to catch the last train for mailing this letter to you.

Fig. 29 Erotic watercolor by Max Schwimmer adorning another letter from EMF to VH, Leipzig, 28 November 1936.

When it finally came time to say good-bye, I told him that the station waiting room would have to accommodate me once again, since I still wanted to complete my letter to you. While I was putting on my coat, the letterhead came into being with the help of the hands that are almost completely healed now–after he was injured in a car crash two weeks ago. I hope you like the drawing, and that you will find it as agreeable as I did and not to the shock of my dear mother–who caught sight of it just before I mailed the letter–and says to her way of thinking the sketch is obscene!

Schwimmer's erotic letterheads adorn a number of Mope's letters from Leipzig. After receiving one of Schwimmer's watercolors, Vera cautiously wondered whether they may have been intended by the artist as a friendly payback for the almost unobtainable art supplies that Mope had secured for him when traveling outside the country. Mope rushed to Schwimmer's defense.

Fig. 30 Erotic watercolor by Max Schwimmer included with a letter from EMF to VH, Leipzig, 20 April 1937.

MOPE

I definitely do not share your opinion about Max's drawing, because that was not meant to be any kind of "compensation," but was only meant as an impulsive expression of joy. He acted like a child with those colors and thanked me so ardently for them that the drawing should not be regarded as a receipt. He has often given me drawings, without equivalent, that such a thought would not even enter my mind. He is an artist and should be judged completely differently than average people. Even if I don't agree with his manner of doing things a lot of times, he is entirely clean this time.

Fig. 31 Erotic watercolor by Max Schwimmer adorning a letter from EMF to VH, Leipzig, 10 December 1936.

You owe these charming as well as lively curves to an evening spent at Max Schwimmer's–spent with a bottle of good wine. You cannot get away from here without a certain amount of alcohol. It was his birthday yesterday and since he absolutely had to see me at this opportunity, we decided on this evening, since I could not make it yesterday. When I look at those loveable parts of a charming woman while I am writing I longingly think of everything that the distance between us deprives me of and I think that it is time, finally, to come to you. Max is now lying supine on his chaise lounge and is trying out the sharpness of his saw and I am sure that he will manage to saw down a tree anytime now with his snoring!

Mope's friendship with Schwimmer reflects his immersion in the artistic and cultural life of Leipzig that became increasingly regimented after 1933. As for Schwimmer himself, he was called up during the Second World War, serving as a medical orderly. Immediately after the war, he was reinstated to his professorship as head of the graphics department in the now socialist Democratic Republic of Germany (DDR), where he was given many accolades, but because of the political divisions of the Cold War, he remained, at least until recently, almost unknown in the West. He and Mope resumed contact by mail over many years but had to wait until 1958 before they met again in London where Schwimmer was sent to represent his country at an exhibition of East German Graphic Art and Sculpture.

Fig. 32 Later photograph of Max Schwimmer, 1950s (taken from Inge Stuhr at https://www.lehmstedt.de/schwimmer_bio.htm).

Schwimmer claimed that the primary reason for coming to England was to reconnect with Mope. Their reunion was joyful. However, when it came to politics, although retaining much of his natural idealism, it was evident that he had become more and more disillusioned with Communism. He died in his native Leipzig two years later.

Seven: Of Books and Arts (2): Thomas Mann

Among the books that Vera's parents brought with them to England when they fled Germany in 1934 were leather-bound editions of Goethe, Schiller, Heine, and Shakespeare, the latter in English, and the multi-volume Meyer's Konversations Lexikon, *replete with beautifully colored chromolithographs, that had been a must-have among educated German families. These were the cultural baggage of many other educated German-Jewish escapees. It speaks to the values of these refugees that such artifacts were prized when so much else had to be abandoned.*

Over a decade younger than Mope, Vera grew up during the Weimar Republic, and was captivated by its literary and artistic freedom. In cultural terms, despite the hyperinflation, the literary and artistic flowering of the 1920s was an exciting time for an alert teenager, certainly more so than Mope's experience had been, who had gotten to that age toward the start of the war years. Beyond school, at home Vera's mother introduced her to writers in English and French whose works she expected her daughter to read and comprehend in their original languages. Reading such authors as Franz Kafka, Hermann Hesse, André Maurois, George Bernard Shaw, and Joseph Conrad, Vera absorbed much of the liberal spirit that these writers imparted.

An important manifestation of Vera's early discernment of the dangers of Nazism may be gauged from her personal reading choices. Before 1933, many Weimar-era writers and intellectuals took advantage of the relative freedom of the press to fill their pages with admonitory signals decrying the advance of totalitarianism across Europe. Soviet Bolshevism and Italian fascism were just two prime examples of an accelerating trend toward state-sponsored tyranny that these writers sought to keep at bay. In particular, Vera was enamored of the works of Thomas Mann, having read as a schoolgirl his early blockbuster novel, Buddenbrooks, *and immersing herself during her senior year at the Victoriaschule in the complexities of Der Zauberberg* (The Magic Mountain). *He was unquestionably her favorite author.*

When Mann penned his prophetic novella, Mario und der Zauberer (Mario and the Magician), *he was inspired by personal observation, during an annual family vacation to Forte dei Marmi on the Tyrrhenian coast of Italy in the mid to late 1920s, of the sinister changes wrought by Mussolini's fascism. It was published in 1929, the same year that Mann was awarded the Nobel Prize for Literature. In* Mario and the Magician, *without so much as a reference to the dictator himself, Mann delineates an Italy that has fallen under the corrupting spell that had been cast by Benito Mussolini and his militant band of flag-waving nationalists. The loosely disguised allegory at the heart of the novella presents a picture of a country that has been infected by the poison of fascism, and, although the immediate setting is in Torre di Venere (a fictive replication of Forte dei Marmi), readers quickly recognized that Mann had in mind the threat to Germany posed by Hitler no less than the state of affairs in Italy, where Mussolini had come to power in 1922. It is an extraordinary indictment of authoritarian rule and exposure of the effects of repression on individual and societal freedom.*

At the time, it was known that Thomas Mann, by then at the height of his fame, was not averse to—even encouraged–personal correspondence from his readers. Vera was deeply affected by Mario and the Magician, *at once recognizing the political topicality of Mann's latest fiction, but left wondering whether the novella was truly based on his own personal experience. If that was so, she felt, the message of the book would prove to be all the more disquieting. When she wrote to Mann in the spring of 1930 toward the end of her freshman year in medical school, she had little expectation that he would respond. In writing to such a venerated figure, she drafted her letter several times and carefully honed it before she mailed it. That Mann took it as far more than just a half-baked adulatory note from an infatuated devotee seeking his autograph is evident from his reply, dated Munich, 29 June 1930:*

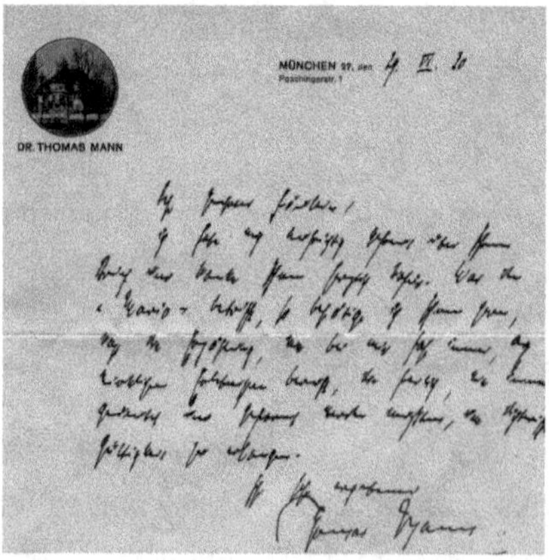

Fig. 33 Letter of Thomas Mann to VH, Munich, 29 June 1930.

Dear Miss Hirsch,

Your letter has given me real pleasure, and I thank you most warmly for it. As to the "Mario", I gladly confirm that the story–as nearly always with me–is based on real personal experiences ["*Erlebenissen*"], which of course as always only require to be formulated newly–thoughtfully— in one's mind in order to achieve poetical validity.

Yours Very Devotedly,

Thomas Mann

In his posthumously published correspondence, Mann goes into far more detail explaining the motivation for Mario and the Magician *("I should prefer to see its significance in the realm of ethics rather than politics"), yet there is little doubt that many of his contemporary readers shared with Vera a tacit understanding that the pertinence of the novella was in its implicit exposure and criticism of the threat to personal liberties posed by dictatorial regimes.*

Three years later, Mann's own acute sensitivity to the risks attached to fascism, which he had so consistently opposed, led to his self-protective exile from Germany within days of Hitler's coming to power. Writing from the safety of Switzerland in May 1933, he was to share with Albert Einstein his grave fear that out of this "terrible fall into hatred, vengeance, lust for killing, and petit bourgeois mean spiritedness... I shall never believe that any good can come... for either Germany or the world."

The ascent of Hitler as Chancellor immediately muzzled any expression of dissent against the brutal dictatorship that he imposed. The era of free thinking and plurality of political views was over.

Fig. 34 Nazi burning of "un-German" books, Berlin, 10 May 1933 (U.S. Holocaust Museum at https://www.ushmm.org/lcmedia/photo/lc/image/31/31077.jpg).

On 10 May 1933, after barely three months in power, the Nazis ordered the public burning across Germany of books by such dissident or radical writers and thinkers as Ernest Hemingway, Sigmund Freud, H.G. Wells, and Franz Werfel. On the capital's main thoroughfare, the Unter den Linden, books by Jewish and other writers deemed "un-German" were set ablaze in sight of the previously liberal University of Berlin. For Vera, the knowledge of Thomas Mann's precipitous flight from Germany in early 1933 was to have some influence upon her own decision making as she grappled with what she herself would do with her own young life and promising career under the threat of the ascendant Nazi regime.

Eight: "I Will Give Up Medicine!!!!!"

Fig. 35 Photograph of VH, rubber dated on verso as 23 July 1938 (likely a copy of an earlier shot from c. 1930).

POLITICAL TIMELINE JANUARY–MARCH 1933

- 30 January 1933: President von Hindenberg appoints Adolf Hitler Chancellor of Germany
- 27 February 1933: The Reichstag is set ablaze. The fire is blamed on the Communists.
- 28 February 1933: Presidential decree giving Chancellor Hitler emergency powers. All one hundred Communist Members of the Reichstag arrested.
- Franklin Delano Roosevelt becomes Thirty-Second President of the United States.
- 9-19 March 1933: Riots against German Jews promoted by the SA, so-called Storm Troopers of the Nazi Party.

- 22 March 1933: First concentration camp–Dachau–set up. By 1945, there were over 1,000 camps.
- 23 March 1933: Ermächtigungsgesetz (Enabling Act), passed by the Reichstag, gives Hitler's government dictatorial powers. Hitler promises that Germany's growth will be fueled by 'blood and race.'

At the end of January 1933, President Paul von Hindenburg appointed Adolf Hitler as Chancellor of Germany. Less than a month after the German Parliament–the Reichstag–was set ablaze, likely a deliberate act by the Nazis, providing the pretext to round up and arrest Communists and other dissidents whom they blamed for the fire.

Fig. 36 The burning of the Reichstag, Berlin, 27 February 1933; National Archives, Washington, D.C. (ARC Identifier: 535790).

Anti-Semitism was rife. With bewildering speed, a host of new laws were introduced and actions taken that attacked the very presence of the Jews in Germany. In Hitler's warped view, as expounded in his autobiographical manifesto Mein Kampf *(1925), the Jews' agenda was to "enslave" the Germans, and, for him, the only way to block that was to root them out. Once in power, he wasted no time pursuing his hate-filled agenda. The Jewish population in Germany in 1933 was approximately half a million out of a population of sixty-seven million, thus representing less than 0.75% of the whole.*

How did his agenda of terror affect Vera? Her surviving "Studienbuch" shows that she had enrolled at the university on 1 May 1929, proceeding over the next four years to pass all the requisite classes in such subjects as anatomy, physiology, pathology, clinical medicine, etc., but that she withdrew quite abruptly before the beginning of the summer semester of 1933, a few months after Hitler had come to power.

Fig. 37 Cover of "Studienbuch" of VH, containing her transcript and photograph.

On 1 April 1933, the new German government conducted its first nationwide boycott of Jewish businesses. "All across the country," summarizes The Holocaust Chronicle, *"Nazi Storm Troopers and SS men posted signs that advised 'Don't Buy from Jews' and 'The Jews Are Our Misfortune.' They smeared the word Jude (Jew) and painted the six-pointed Star of David in yellow and black across thousands of doors and windows. They stood menacingly in front of the homes of Jewish lawyers and doctors as well as at the entrances of Jewish-owned businesses. Germans were 'encouraged' not to enter, while Jews were arrested, beaten, harassed, and humiliated."*

Frankfurt University was a prime target for the newly empowered fascists. On the day of the boycott, its main building was taken over by eighty thugs in SA uniform, who enforced the prohibition by preventing Jewish students from entry. According to Peter Drucker, later a path-breaking management guru but then a novice teacher in the law faculty, Frankfurt had enjoyed a reputation as "the most self-confidently liberal of major German universities," and the Nazis calculated that subjugation of its faculty, which included many distinguished scientists, "would mean control of German academia altogether." Drucker had been present at a faculty meeting a few days before when, amid promises to expand funding for "racially pure science," the new Nazi commissar for Frankfurt "launched into a tirade of [anti-Semitic] abuse, filth, and four-letter words such as had rarely been heard even in the barracks and never before in academia." The fallout of this was a shameful abjuration whereby most of the Aryan professors now shunned their Jewish colleagues, keeping "a safe distance from these men who, only a few hours earlier, had been their close friends." Jewish members of faculty were henceforth forbidden from entering the university and were shortly after sacked without pay. Drucker hastily exiled himself from Germany.

In common with many others, Vera recalled 1 April as the initiation of the systematic victimization of the Jews by the Nazis. Her journal entries capture well the trauma of the moment as she wrestled with how to come to terms with an insufferable situation. Like many Jews in her situation, she began by being full of self-reproach in trying to account for the political change.

Fig. 38 Boycott of Jewish Businesses, Hamburg, Germany, 1 April 1933; https://www.dhm.de/archiv/ausstellungen/holocaust/r2/2.htm.

VERA

5 February 1933

Today, I want to put down my current views of life once again, because it is more than likely, with my good memory, that I will no longer remember anything about this time.

On Thursday, 2 February, three days after Hitler was made Chancellor, Hellmuth Winkler, a boorish medical student who prided himself on his Aryan extraction, did me a great service without knowing it. He and I were discussing the state of affairs of the Jews under the new regime. He maintained that, because of constant misgivings and hesitation and lack of self-confidence, a Jew is not able to accomplish anything.

That really hit me right in the middle. Is that not exactly the way I am? This exaggerated fear is *exclusively* a Jewish degenerative aspect. Despite our differences, I think that I have discovered a human being in Winkler. I found that even now there are young and pleasant people, well-educated, with good manners and with similar problems. This affirmed to me once again that decency of manners can protect from anti-Semitism, under certain circumstances.

It came as a profound shock to Vera that Winkler's seemingly sincere profession of friendship, to which she was initially attracted, was no more than a failed attempt to seduce her.

VERA

1 March

Something I have not mentioned so far is my *disgusting* brush with Winkler. For him to go so far and engage in that kind of thing without even feeling some kind of attachment is a stupid thing to do, and any kind of punishment I might have had to face would serve me right.

Once again–as with Heising before–Vera came face to face with the Nazi barriers between Jew and gentile. It remained still unclear whether she would be able to complete her final year as a medical student.

VERA

Uncertainty! Where should I do my clinical training? Probably in surgery, at least for part of the time, but where?? Where should I have them give me work as a doctor? What will become of me? Am I even able, with that small brain of mine, to finish this course of studies? Uncertainty is always something horrible.

Things seemed to go Vera's way when she was assigned for her clinical rotation to the public ward at the Krankenhaus Sachsenhausen, a prominent private hospital in Frankfurt. However, as a Jew, she was not permitted to practice her skills in the private ward.

Fig. 39 Krankenhaus Sachsenhausen, Frankfurt (https://www.krankenhaus-sachsenhausen.de/geschichte/).

When she approached a patient on the public ward to ask her how she was doing, the response was a vicious tirade accusing her of being "an impertinent Jewish woman" who had overstepped herself. The patient called for the Nazi doctor in charge of the ward, who, after listening to her complaint, turned to Vera and pointed her out of the hospital. Her shock at this is captured through her journal in her frightened and self-critical ruminations.

VERA

23 March

So, I was thrown out, accused of having bad manners. Entered my clinical rotation three weeks ago. Surgery in the private hospital Sachshenhausen. Because I was assigned to the 2nd class patients and actually asked a patient how she is.

Maybe I am really lacking an understanding of the discipline of medicine and all that has been taught to me, and I am actually just an impertinent Jewish woman. Can that be true???

I am sure it was right that the doctor was mad if his patient actually complained to him, but to scold me in that manner and treat me like a criminal was completely unjustified, that is, the man does not even know me and might have been thinking that he was dealing with a pert and ill-mannered person.

What can I say to justify myself? I simply did not know what to do.

I had no idea why he talked that way about the outrageousness I had committed. When I approached the patient, did I feel I was doing something I should not be doing? If I had actually done that, I would have known right away what a horrible misdeed I was committing.

Ugh, for the first time, I feel for myself what it means to be treated as an *outcast*.

3 April

Sometimes, you think that it can simply not be true. You read about the persecution of Jews in history books.

Because you are a Jew, you get thrown out of your profession, judged, scorned, and you are worthless, powerless.

I wonder what tomorrow will bring. If I could go to England–I have a decision to make, and it will not be easy for me to burn the bridges behind me. It would be best to go to a tropical country with Alicechen and Pepper–preferably not Palestine, because the pure-breed requirements of a Jewish state there are stranger to me than the one being aspired to here. Although it might actually be preferable to being scorned here!...

I wonder if I will ever finish my medical studies.

With under a year before qualification as a doctor, Vera faced a most difficult dilemma. Should she stick it out in Frankfurt with the prospect that she might still be able to graduate? Should she believe, like so many German Jews, that it would not be long before the Nazis would be ousted, and that one should therefore put up with their temporary nastiness? Or did she need to act now, leave Germany, and seek a new life elsewhere? With all these agonizing questions constantly before her, she sought some clarity by putting pen to paper. A long entry, dated 19 April 1933, addressed to herself in her private journal, lists some of the options that, as a self-declared disbelieving Jew, she saw before her:

VERA

19 April

You have to deal with this problem of being Jewish. There are three possibilities:

1. **Stay here**, that is, if you are still admitted to the university, you might be able to continue your studies, although you will always be regarded as second class, and will be treated as someone who is different. Another possibility: in the most advantageous case, you might find work at the Jewish

hospital here or start a practice that might just support you, although that is highly unlikely. As an advantage: you know the language, the books...???

2. **Go abroad**. Maybe, if the financial means allow, continue your studies and then practice there, in the best, best case possible, but that is probably not feasible, because it would not be manageable financially—if not for that, I would not hesitate at all, I would leave with joy in my heart, because I have always liked change. That is, if there is any kind of possibility for me to go abroad and find some kind of work, maybe as a domestic worker, a nanny, cook, chamber maid, etc. Something new and different, maybe even appealing in its own way!!!!!

3. Which brings me to the third possibility: **Go to Palestine**. That would mean giving up all the indulgences you have always taken for granted, like a bath, central heating, and a few other purely superficial things. No, giving up those things is not what bothers me, because no one can take away the things I really consider valuable. Wherever I will go, I will try to make a pleasant home for my family, a beautiful one, as far as my finances will allow—it will be my greatest and dearest duty, no matter where I am and what I do. The thing I do not find pleasing me about this is: I would have to adopt Jewish traditions and customs, things whose value and sense I do not accept. There is only one thing that seems valuable to me: to be a decent person, always striving!!! Even today, I still hold the unshakable belief that you can always accomplish anything with that and will do so.

Yes, I think I have made a decision, even if I will be cast out from every country again and again, driven out more forcefully the more I try to assimilate–and that is a danger that exists for anyone in this day and age. Nevertheless, my view of the world tells me that it is the right thing to move to another country in which the Jewish question is not the most burning topic and to start over again there. Maybe that is very superficial thinking, but I consider my time better used for work, instead of mulling over what cuts of meat you are allowed to eat and what you cannot. I am sure that is unforgivably arrogant and frivolous on my part. Nevertheless, that is my true attitude towards such things, exactly what

I think, without any feeling of shame. I am sure this way of thinking was created by my upbringing.

However, I think the time for us to argue about religious beliefs is over and also the question of heredity, and if those arguments rise up again anyway, I should leave the country and go to another one where these problems are not problems and where one can use one's strength for more pleasant endeavors: to be *human*!!!!!

At the medical school, she consulted an eminent teacher of hers, Dr. Franz Volhard, who was sympathetic to her situation. He advised her to petition to stay on but also undertook to write on her behalf should she seek to transfer to an equivalent program in England where he had academic contacts. Volhard was a celebrated cardiologist and nephrologist, whose anti-Nazi stance and support for his Jewish students and colleagues, led to his being stripped of his professorship in 1938, though later reinstated to his former position after the end of the war.

Fig. 40 Photograph of Dr. Franz Volhard (1872-1950), inscribed by Vera, Summer Semester 1932.[2]

On Professor Volhard's advice, she applied to the university for permission to pause her studies following the completion of her ninth semester. The documents detailing this are preserved in the university archives where they were laid open to me in 2017. They include a questionnaire, dated 4 May 1933, in which she

---

2   Another photograph of Dr Franz Volhard is available in the online resources for this book, https://doi.org/10.11647/OBP.0334#resources

was obliged to state that neither her parents nor her grandparents were of the Aryan race though the family had lived in Germany for hundreds of years, and that they had never attempted to convert from Judaism. It also asked whether her father had fought for Germany in the First World War (which she answered that he had, even including his regimental details), and if she herself was a member of a political party, to which she answered with an unambiguous "Nein."

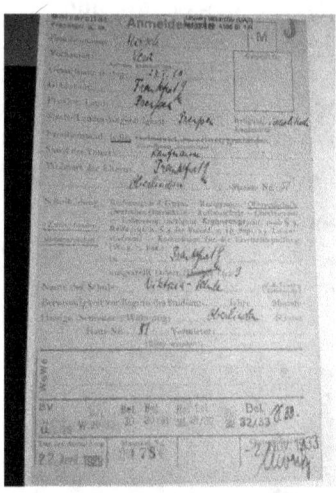

Fig. 41 Nazi Registration Card ("Anmeldekarte") obliging VH to reveal her identity as a Jew, dated 4 May 1933 (Archives of the University of Frankfurt).

This extraordinary batch of papers brought home to me the abruptness of the trauma of my mother's departure from her natal city and from the medical ambitions that, until the advent of the Nazi dictatorship less than one hundred days before, had determined the course of her young life. Ultimately, there was only one person whom Vera trusted unreservedly to help her to resolve the painful questions that confronted her. My grandmother–Alice—was adamant that her daughter must suspend her studies and leave for England. From their first conversation, she took it upon herself to spell out to her daughter how dangerous the situation was and to share her visceral sense that it could only get much worse. Alice employed an intermediary, Anna Schwab, to put her in touch with Otto Schiff, the founder of the Jewish Refugees Committee in London.

VERA

26 April

There will never be another human being like my Mutti! As soon as things started happening, on 1 April, she wrote letters explaining my situation to all the people that she knows in London. Although she does not want to be without me for so much as an hour–this self-sacrificing love, action, and flexibility is simply unmatched.

A few days later, Mutti arranged a meeting with Mrs. Schwab who was visiting [Frankfurt] from London at the Hotel Excelsior, and she had all the information Mr. Schiff thought I should have.

Following the interview, Mutti and I left the hotel just to come back again and ask her if there was a possibility of an unrestricted residence permit, because I would really hate to give up my studies. I told her that I thought and hoped that I would be able to achieve my goals *anywhere* as long as I was willing to work hard.

Otto Schiff had grown up in Frankfurt where he was an exact contemporary and erstwhile friend of my grandmother, both of them born in 1873. They may even have been distantly related and perhaps also knew each other from their school days. As soon as he learned that the daughter of Alice Hirsch, née Ettlinger, was coming to London, he reached out and invited her to be his house guest.

VERA

6 May

Tomorrow, I am leaving for London. I have been wanting to write in here for the last few days, but things happened so fast that I simply could not find the time.

Thursday at Volhard's: he advised me to stay and submit the petition to intercalate. I did that, but I will leave anyway. I will not have any chances here as a doctor to pass the German final exam, which seems so far away to me, but I still wonder if I'm doing the right thing.

Nine: Under the Swastika

POLITICAL TIMELINE 1934

- 1 January 1934: Jewish religious holidays removed from the official Nazi calendar.
- April 1934: Establishment of the Volksgericht (People's Court) to deal with enemies of the state; no trial by jury and no right of appeal.
- June 1934: Beginning of Nazi persecution of homosexuals.
- 2 August 1934: Death of German President Paul von Hindenburg; Hitler declares himself Führer of the German state and commander-in-chief of armed forces.
- 19 August 1934: Public plebiscite approves of Hitler's expanded powers by 89.9 per cent.
- 4-10 September 1934: Nazi Party Congress at Nuremberg.

In the early 1930s, the atmosphere in Leipzig was no less poisonous than in Frankfurt. Both cities contained sizeable Jewish communities, which became the targets of anti-Semitic intimidation. Even before Hitler had come to power, my grandfather Isidor had been the recipient of threats against his life. In the weeks following the Nazi takeover, similar threats led to the precipitous departure from Leipzig of most of the partners of the Gebrüder Felsenstein. Isidor stayed on until the boycott of 1 April 1933 before fleeing to Prague.

The boycott forced Jews to adopt a low profile. It was the day Mope was to attend the Bar Mitzvah of his cousin Wolfgang Felsenstein. The Bar Mitzvah had been scheduled at the orthodox Keilstrasse Synagogue, but given the dangerous situation, Wolfgang's family opted for a private ceremony at their home. Twenty-two family members had accepted the invitation to attend, but only Mope and his brother, Adolf, were willing to brave the mobs that were filling the streets with anti-Semitic signs, demonstrations, and beatings.

Fig. 42 Boycott of Jewish businesses, 1 April 1933 (United States Holocaust Museum at https://newspapers.ushmm.org/images/nazi-boycott.jpeg).

What should have been a day of joy for the young Bar Mitzvah celebrant was instead a subdued occasion with the few guests nervously voicing their anxieties and fears. The one-day boycott marked the beginning of the destruction of Jewish life in Germany. In 1938, because it had Aryan tenants in its upper stories, the Keilstrasse Synagogue, though ransacked, was the sole synagogue in Leipzig to survive the fury of Kristallnacht.

Of the members of the Gebrüder Felsenstein, until so recently a magnet of the fur trade, my father writes:

MOPE

All other members of the company had already fled to foreign countries, and Adolf and I stayed on in Leipzig as the sole family representatives in order to protect our family's interests.

My beloved father had tried to persuade his various nephews in the business to recognize the necessity of relocating the headquarters of Gebrüder Felsenstein to London or to New York while it was still possible to do so, but they showed little inclination to think strategically about the future of the company or about anybody else but themselves. In an effort to preserve the business, my father returned to Leipzig after an absence of about five or six months. Other family members followed.

Sadly, the exertions and anxiety brought on by the Nazis and other factors proved too much for my father. He was diagnosed shortly after his return with subacute bacterial endocarditis, a heart condition that was deemed untreatable and terminal. Despite our earlier differences, I felt for him very deeply. Once a father who is not as perfect as he could be becomes ill, the realization dawns on you that you are attached to him anyway. Even if he did not always think or do the right thing, my father was a completely decent man whose single concern, beyond the business, was the wellbeing of his family. He was to die on 28 May 1934, about a half year after his return to Leipzig. I am convinced that his death was exacerbated by all the agitation.

Fig. 43 Grave of Isidor Felsenstein, Alter Israelischer Friedhof, Leipzig; photograph taken in the summer of 1947.

Mope had been brought into the Gebrüder Felsenstein with the view that he and his brother would succeed to Isidor's share of the business. To help pay for the dowries of his five daughters, all of whom were married during the final years of his life, Isidor had mortgaged to his brothers and nephews part of his private stock in the business, so that, at the time of his death, his widow (Helene) was entitled to a substantially smaller percentage of the firm's assets and profits. By some dubious sleight of hand, the surviving partners manipulated this following Isidor's death so that the amount was further decreased. Both his brother Adolf and my father were mortified by this hijacking, which limited their ability to influence the future direction of the Gebrüder Felsenstein. Adolf's response was to resign his share in the partnership, and to emigrate with his wife and family to Palestine, which he did in 1935. In Haifa, where they settled, there was no demand for furriers, and, in his late thirties, Adolf showed his pioneering spirit by retraining as a plumber, a less lucrative though more essential profession.

MOPE

I receive very satisfactory reports from my brother. He is fully occupied and is as successful in his work as he could possibly wish for. My sister-in-law is also happy, despite the great adjustment there, although the idea to go to Palestine was unbelievably strange to her in the beginning. By the way, my brother writes to me about professions with which, in his opinion, I might be able to create an existence over there. These recommendations might be combined for the most part, in all likelihood. They are: chrome-plating, brass-polishing, the manufacture of aluminum signs and enameling. Whether the necessary schooling possibilities for these professions are still offered to Jews here [in Nazi Germany] appears pretty doubtful. They are occupations I could practice without much demand on my legs and a certain use of my chemical knowledge. These are practical occupations one can practice anywhere and would provide for the building of an existence–with the ability necessary in any profession.

Fig. 44 Photograph of Adolf Felsenstein (1897-1977) outside his plumbing shop in Haifa, Palestine; undated but mid to late 1930s.

A friend who recently visited Palestine met with Adolf and came back with a very satisfactory report, the one proviso being that, though he had been regarded as a "fine gentleman" in Leipzig, he had descended significantly in social rank and had to work much harder in a much less luxurious environment than when he was at the Gebrüder Felsenstein. I myself do not see any kind of downgrading in the different occupation or loss of personal worth which was only inherited anyway. Anyone who succeeds on his own to build a new existence for himself is definitely worth much more than one who is born with a silver spoon in his mouth.

Adolf is objective proof for the fact that a person's cultural standing remains untouched by his profession, and the term "downgrade" may only be considered if a lowering of the cultural disposition occurs. In Palestine, where so many academicians have taken on trade and farming professions, a guarantee is assured for the maintenance of the cultural milieu by their sheer numbers and any kind of decline won't even enter the realm of possibility until the next generation at the earliest.

Adolf's younger sister, Alice, who had married Julius Homburger, a physician, followed him by making Aliyah later the same year, also settling in Haifa. Fulfilling her own Zionist ideals, she had qualified as a nurse with the aim of going to Palestine despite objections by some family members who regarded her chosen profession as beneath her social status. They questioned how a member of the Felsenstein family could sully her hands by cleaning bed pans and wiping babies' bottoms? In Palestine, she mainly worked with typhoid cases as a private nurse, though it was becoming increasingly difficult to make ends meet. Mope felt that her husband, Julius, lacked sufficient initiative.

Fig. 45 Alice Homburger, née Felsenstein (1901-1993), in nurse's uniform.

MOPE

Alice runs around every day in order to find a chance to build an existence for her husband, herself, and her children. Sadly, they cannot seem to get ahead in Palestine. As a doctor, it should actually be her husband's job to take care of the relocation, but it is Alice who is forced to take the lead. Had Julius gone to the countryside instead of Haifa, he would probably have been more successful, but he did not pursue that option as his wife had brought out enough initial money to allow them to live in comfort, but her savings did not last.

Two of Mope's siblings—his youngest sister, Hanna, who had married an Englishman, Fred Rau, in 1932, and his second youngest sister, Ruth, with her husband Heinz, another fur man who had liquidated his business and quit Leipzig—were now living in London.

Fig. 46 Post-war photograph Fred (1906-1956) and Hanna (1910-1957) Rau entertaining at Sabbath in London.

Hanna's marriage to Fred was welcomed by all the family. He came from an Orthodox Jewish family that shared similar spiritual and ethical values. He was distinguished-looking, young and vigorous, an enthusiastic skier and mountaineer, and a knowledgeable world traveler. In London, where he and Hanna settled and started their own family, he was made partner in a lucrative metal brokerage business. In the years leading up to the war, he was to use his influence to aid the escape from Germany of an untold number of relatives and other refugees.

About Ruth, Mope admired his sister's intelligence and the breadth of her cultural interests. She had been his early confidante in many matters, but he was taken aback when, in her late twenties, she announced her engagement to Heinz Littauer, also a fur trader with a small business in Leipzig. Heinz carried with him a questionable reputation as a roué and a spendthrift. Outside his work and womanizing, his main interest was in motor cars and driving. He and Mope had spent a touring vacation together in France and Italy.

Fig. 47 Heinz Littauer at the wheel and EMF touring in the Dolomites, 1927.

Heinz did not seem to be an intellectual match for Ruth, and, although Jewish by birth, his religious knowledge was non-existent. As a condition to consenting to their marriage, Isidor insisted that Heinz, by then in his mid-thirties, should submit to a circumcision. When Mope was informed of his sister's engagement, he wept openly, and regretted that he had ever brought Heinz into their household. I suspect that he and others may have made indiscreet remarks concerning Heinz. The consequence was that the closeness that he and his sister had previously enjoyed was permanently broken. Although Heinz was unable to control his finances—it was rumored that he exhausted Ruth's dowry to pay off a former mistress—he turned out to be a loyal husband and loving father to their two children.

Fig. 48 Ruth (1902-1971) and Heinz (1893-1973) Littauer; undated photograph.

Several years before he met Vera, Mope himself had become engaged, likely through an arrangement made by his parents, to a woman who came from a similar religious background. As payback against Mope who had demurred at her own marriage to Heinz, Ruth intervened. She wrote poison-pen letters to the family of his then fiancée, imputing terrible things about him. The fiancée's family was shocked at these contemptible allegations, and called off the engagement. In later years, after my parents were happily married, Ruth claimed that what she had done was for the ultimate good of her brother, but the consequence of her action was that Mope stood wary of his sister and would never again trust her on matters of personal significance.

Three of his siblings had moved abroad. However, Ketty, his oldest sister, and her husband, David Goldschmidt, an insurance agent, with their four children, were still in Hamburg many miles to the north of Leipzig, and Grete's husband, Norbert Moschytz, a doctor, had found a situation in Freiburg im Breisgau, on the south-west tip of Germany, settling his family there.

Ketty was always very attached to Mope but living so far from Leipzig and with a young family to rear, they were only occasionally able to see one another.

Fig. 49 David (1890-1944) and Ketty (1896-1944) Goldschmidt; undated photograph.

Grete, the other twin sister, a beautiful but introverted young woman, was sensitive to the fact that she had suffered ear infections during her childhood which had caused her some hearing loss. Her impending marriage to Norbert in December 1928 came close to being called off after he demanded a twenty per cent addition to her dowry to compensate for her impairment. Isidor was afraid that Grete would stay unmarried, and reluctantly agreed to the increase, hoping that she would never find out about the brokering that had taken place. Others knew, and Norbert, who often came across as overbearing and self-important, was not well liked by his new in-laws.

Fig. 50 Grete (1901-1975) and Norbert (1895-1974) Moschytz; undated photograph.

Mope was of the opinion that the unfortunate and expensive upsets that Isidor had had to endure in his dealings with the husbands of Grete and Ruth had contributed to his death in 1934. He was now the only one of his mother's seven children not yet married and without children. He was also the only one still resident in Leipzig, and enjoyed a special closeness with her.

MOPE

There are precisely seven little children who long for her who are mommies and pappies themselves, except for me. My mother is a very special friend to all of her children and she is able to give everyone the impression that she is especially close to them so that none of us can feel jealous of the other, and to succeed in that takes a lot of sensibility and even more intelligence.

Despite increasingly vocal and urgent appeals from Hanna for her to follow her to England, Oma Lenchen was loath to leave Germany while three of her children were still living there. She also shared with Mope the belief that it was important to remain in Leipzig to protect her financial share in the Gebrüder Felsenstein and the family home.

Mope was as eager as his older brother Adolf to release himself from the clutches of the Gebrüder Felsenstein from which he felt more and more estranged following his father's death, and alienated by the mendacious jockeying of his cousins. Although he thought well of the decency of his cousin, Semy, who became senior partner following Isidor's death, the conflict with the other cousins, who were jealous of his ability, was a constant irritant.

In the face of Nazi oppression, it begs the question why the partners did not see fit to take greater collective steps to protect the assets of the company rather than acting entirely self-interestedly. By 1939, each of them had escaped from Germany but with negligible involvement in helping other family members. The criminal bent of the Nazi regime clearly brought out both the best and the worst in those they persecuted.

MOPE

I was left in Leipzig as the only representative of my direct family who could still try to protect the business interests of my mother. You cannot believe how much trouble my elbowing has caused me in the company. If I were an unimposing, inactive man, I would most likely have advanced further than I have in safeguarding my mother's share in the Gebrüder Felsenstein, because it would have been less likely to be perceived as pursuing my personal ambitions. But first of all, that is not me, and other than that, this so-called advance would have only been of a superficial nature.

A further blow to Mope was that his lease was nullified as he was living in a section of the city that was now barred to Jews. He was compelled to move at least twice more, each time to less salubrious quarters. The Nuremberg Laws of 1935 led to the rapid "Aryanization" of towns and cities across Germany.

MOPE

Because of race law threats, I was forced to give up my bachelor apartment on Empress Augusta Street and move into a sublet room on Beethoven Street; however, I also had to move on from there, since my landlady was an "Aryan." I then found lodging with Dr Jacobson, a retired Jewish attorney on Ferdinand Rhode Street, a barely comfortable situation. More worrying, I am being constantly harassed and bombarded with state-sponsored mandates to report in person again and again to the police.

Ten: "Did I Do the Right Thing?"

POLITICAL TIMELINE 1935

- 30 April 1935: Jews may no longer display the German flag.
- 31 May 1935: Jews are banned from the German armed forces.
- 15 September 1935: First Nuremberg Laws: Jews can no longer exist as German citizens or marry non-Jews. Sexual intercourse between Aryans and non-Aryans made a punishable crime.
- September 1935: The Reich Flag Law defines the official flag of Germany as a black swastika in a white circle on a red field.
- 1 November 1935: Law disqualifying Jews from German citizenship.
- 14 November 1935: National Law of Citizenship defining "Jew" as anyone with two Jewish grandparents, and quantifying "Mischlinge" (mixed race) individuals as non-German.

For most Jewish refugees arriving in London between 1933 and 1939, the brief window during which escape from Germany was viable, first impressions would have been those of confusion and bewilderment. From early on in its existence, the newly formed Jewish Refugees Committee under the guidance of Otto Schiff made it one of its principal duties to meet arriving trains from the Continent, and to provide the inflow of refugees, most of whom had no contacts or family in Britain, with a personal welcome, some basic start-up money, and short-term housing.

In contrast, because of the friendship going back to their schooldays between Alice Hirsch and Otto Schiff, Vera enjoyed the softest landing. Instead of being lodged in the most basic rooming house, she was welcomed into the opulent Schiff abode in Mayfair where she was treated as a privileged guest rather than an indigent refugee. From her arrival in England through to the emigration of her parents in early 1934, Vera wrote letters to Alice on a day-to-day basis out of which much of what follows is extracted.

VERA

8 May 1933

At the train station, they picked me up by private car and the servant took my luggage in a taxi. I arrived at the most fabulous apartment you can imagine and a dazzling room for me with roses on the table. When I came back upstairs after tea, the maid was already busy unpacking my suitcases. The bathroom is right next door to my room and I am being served like a Princess. Sometimes, I really cannot believe after all the things over there in Germany that something like this can really exist here. And I can hardly believe that I could be so lucky!!! It sounds like a wonderland, but it is real! And tomorrow, my new life will begin!

9 May 1933

First things first, I made my way this morning to London University and showed them the letter of recommendation compiled by Volhard. The man there was very nice and told me that I should turn to the three London medical schools that admit women and, because they only take a certain number, ask if they have any openings. He said that, in any case, I would need to work as a clinical resident for three years, but I would have needed to work for two and a half years back home too. Of course, if they do not agree to count the prelims, the whole process would take much longer. I called one of the medical schools and they told me that they had no more room, so I came to the unhappy conclusion this morning that I will have to give up medicine altogether, although I will make inquiries at the respective schools tomorrow anyway.

Among the circle of well-to-do women whom Vera met during her first few days in London were several who had previously been boarders at her parents' home in Frankfurt where they had gone to improve their skills in German. One of these Hirsch alumnae was an American, Betty Lawson-Johnston, a onetime salesgirl and clothes model from Albany, New York, who was married to the wealthy former husband of Barbara Guggenheim.

VERA

Also today, I was invited to join Betty Lawson-Johnston for tea. She had spent time in Frankfurt studying German with us. She told me on the telephone this morning that she would be hosting an enormous tea party at her residence after a charity event and she invited me to join and meet people.

I dressed in a brown ensemble and made myself look *smart*, which was a good thing, because just about the *smartest* ladies of London were there, simply fantastic that such things still exist (I was completely enthralled). Mrs. Lawson-Johnston was charming and took me by the hand after she had kissed me which made quite an impression!!!!!! and introduced me as *her dear friend* from Frankfurt. Among others, I met a Mrs. Brown who immediately offered to let me move in with her whenever I wanted to. The ladies decided to hold a Bridge tournament or something like that and the money gained would be for my continuing studies, and that they would help me in some way. So, tomorrow, I will ask if any of the *medical schools* still have room for me.

Looking back, it is poignant that high society women were willing to club together to support Vera's studies by organizing a bridge tournament, though the story also illustrates the lack of comprehension among such people in 1933 of the enormity of what was happening in Germany.

VERA

Even if I found people here willing to finance my education, I would not like that because it makes no sense to me to have to depend on that for years before I could even start to work.

I find it completely inconceivable that there are still so many rich people who have nothing on their minds but their parties, their clothes, and their society gossip.

As far as I can judge, I still think the following: Even if I do get the funds in such a marvelous manner, what it comes down to is that it will be futile to continue my schooling if I cannot get a position as a doctor afterwards, because there are so many already here and more continue coming over. I will make further enquiries tomorrow.

10 May 1933

This morning, I went to one of the medical schools–they said they were going to take four more girls, but I would have to register for the exam before July (the four best results of all the exams will be accepted). So, today, in order to pacify my conscience, I wrote to all three medical schools that accept girls to find out if they have any openings and I will wait for their answers. If so—and this is the best-case scenario—they will transfer my work up to the prelims and I will *only* !!! have to pass the exams in anatomy and physiology, but I will not have to attend the lectures for those exams.

First of all, I will have to take an entrance exam in English, mathematics, and one other subject (that is supposed to be quite easy). Once I have passed all of that, there will be a three-year clinical, and they will *not* budge on that despite the one and a half years' experience I had back home. I think it would make no sense, because I am sure that by the time I will be prepared to take the entrance exam and then go to the physiology and anatomy exams, another year will have passed. However, I will get the information just to quiet my conscience.

Vera realized that protracting her studies would stand in the way of her ability to help her parents and sister escape from Germany. In England, she would need to be the breadwinner for all of them, and continuing with her studies would prevent her from earning money.

VERA

11 May 1933

I went to an *examining board* again this morning–they paid me great compliments about my English, but there is nothing to be done short of four years, at best, but probably more like five, provided, of course, that an open place can even be found for a *girl-student*.

Now, I will see what new things there are for me to do and I am looking forward to it and I am satisfied with my decision. Really, about 1,000 German Marks for university studies here per year without room and board! So much charity can only be accepted if one is *absolutely* certain that something special will be achieved, but since all of it is so uncertain, it would be complete insanity.

When I think about it, if I were still at university in Frankfurt right now, I would be very unhappy. I would not be able to stand that.

12 May 1933

Fig. 51 Otto Schiff (1875-1952); photograph taken from *AJR* [Association of Jewish Refugees] *Journal*, 14, no. 6, June 2014.

I find Otto Schiff simply indescribable. He is *the* person on the refugee committee to get things done around here and he helps so many people all day long. He has not set foot in his business for three weeks now, just to help everyone and to arrange things, and that is so wonderful. He works on behalf of the refugees on Saturday and Sunday as well.

Yesterday afternoon, I went on a visit to the East End of London– that is where the building is where all the people who come over are brought to stay for a while, or rather brought through and taken care of. They have a man there for every profession, to provide information. The director and sponsor is Otto Schiff, and when the people there heard that I live in his house, all the doors opened immediately and I was the *first* one to be seen, although many people were waiting. I thought I saw two familiar faces there from Frankfurt, a boy and a girl, but since they were people I had never spoken to before and might have been people who were not too nice anyway, I did not speak to them. In confidence, Otto told me that, if he finds work for me, I cannot tell anyone, because thousands would come to him.

13 May 1933

Otto is simply charming and tells me whenever he sees me that I should act as if it were my home. The whole world and everyone in Frankfurt writes to him asking him to place their sons and daughters somewhere and he rejects many and he invites *me* into his own home!

When I talked to Otto about continuing with my medical studies, he said if I were his daughter, he would advise against it most strenuously, because the future prospects are poor. In fact, he does not even want to hear about my medical studies, since he says that it would be *completely* out of the question to open a medical practice later on.

Otto thinks that he would like to place me in a fashion shop. He asked if I can draw modern clothes–maybe I could learn! He knows the owner of Eve Valère, a high-end millinery and dress design boutique.

Schiff's paramount commitment was to the broader question of how to accommodate the influx of German refugees, a task that was beyond the capability of any single individual to accomplish. Still, as many as twelve thousand German-Jewish refugees were rescued through the efforts of Otto Schiff who is regarded by some as Britain's Oskar Schindler. There are many people alive today, the descendants of German-Jewish refugees, who unknowingly owe a debt of gratitude to the efforts of Schiff and Ernest Napier Cooper (1883-1948), the Principal of the Aliens Department and Schiff's main contact in the British Home Office.

In order to avoid any perception that she might be a burden to Schiff and also to familiarize herself with her new environment, Vera employed her leisure hours exploring London. After Germany, London in May 1933 had for her an aura of magic.

VERA

Here in England, everything is unchanged, the people look fabulous and laugh and take it easy. *I am a different girl here.* This morning, I took a walk through Hyde Park after it rained. You can simply not imagine how beautiful everything is. A rich green, and behind that red chestnut trees and green herons and rabbits, like in a fairy tale, and a few perfectly beautiful *ladies* who came riding along on horseback, just the way you see it in your dreams.

Ten: "Did I Do the Right Thing?"

17 May 1933

Around midday, I went to Hyde Park. All of a sudden, someone calls out "Miss Hirsch!" and it was that Dr. Rothschild I met at Volhard's. The world is small, isn't it? He told me that he is going to continue at the Leverhulme Institute where he has a position doing scientific research. He wants to get his *English* degree on the side, but since he has been working in physiology for many years now and knows all the professors who will test him personally, it will not be a big deal for him, or so he said.

We wrote a postcard to Volhard together in the park; Rothschild is really very pleasant and he also said that, if I was given the great chance of actually finding work, which is supposed to be horribly difficult, I should definitely do it. Getting work at a hospital here seems to be almost out of the question, but for a woman, and a German one at that, it is a thousand times more difficult.

Fig. 52 Dr. Paul Rothschild (1901-1965).

Until a few months before, Dr. Paul Rothschild had been senior research assistant to Vera's teacher, Professor Volhard, in Frankfurt. As with other Jewish physicians, his position had been axed after the Nazis came to power, and he was now in London in order to attempt to piece together his career. In this he was successful. When I was a child, Dr. Rothschild was our family physician and his family became close friends of ours.

VERA

19 May 1933

On Wednesday, I was once again at the home of Betty Lawson-Johnston who called yesterday morning to invite me for tea. There were about eighty people there and once more Betty announced to everyone that *I am her very good friend*. Mrs. Brown, who was at Betty's again, told me I should not forget that there would always be a bed for me at her place! I really think that I am taking advantage of Otto's hospitality for much too long a time. I think I will ask Betty about this Mrs. Brown.

4 June 1933

In any case, I had Mrs. Braham's address given to me (not Brown, like I thought), since Betty said that she had talked to her recently and I decided to write to her myself. She seemed extremely likable to me, has no children and told me repeatedly that the room would always be ready for me. She has a husband–both of them are quite elderly and she is in so many social service committees that her poor husband spends a lot of time by himself and she would be happy to have someone there to keep him company in the evening.

Fig. 53 (a) Studio photograph of Ray Rockman Braham.

Ten: "Did I Do the Right Thing?"

Fig. 53 (b) Photograph of Frank Braham.

"Mrs. Brown" turned out to be American-born Ray Rockman Braham, a one-time stage actress who had studied under Sarah Bernhardt, and was now a well-known London charity organizer. She subsequently persuaded Vera to become her house guest at Paultons Square in fashionable Chelsea. Diagnosing at once the predicament and financial uncertainties of a newly arrived refugee from Nazi Germany, Frank and Ray Braham made it an unqualified commitment to assist Vera in whatever manner they could. A childless couple, both she and her husband, the retired general manager of a British-owned rubber plantation in Liberia, took a quasi-parental interest in Vera during the first year of her residence in England. In gratitude many years later, she incorporated their names within those that she gave to her children.

VERA

7 June 1933

Around noon today, Mrs. Braham met with me. She said she had received my letter and that she would take me in to her home at any time with the greatest pleasure. However, she wanted to tell me in advance (and if I would not mind) that she and her husband are *busy* all day long, never at home for lunch, and did not *entertain* guests there. Would I mind regarding her house as my home and a hotel at the same time? In the evening, whenever I am home and they are gone, I could order whatever I like. Every Friday, she goes to the country until Sunday evening and I would have to run the house by myself and could invite friends over, etc. Have you ever heard anything that ideal before???

16 June 1933

My *new* abode is *fabulous*. Today, I talked to Mrs. Braham for a few minutes for the first time. Until our conversation this evening, Mrs. Braham did not know anything about me, not even what city I am from. I think Mr. Braham is very nice too (he is about 64 and she is around 62). She has snow-white hair, but quite young in her ways and the absolute master of the house and little Frank is not allowed to open his mouth or he will get doused by her. It seems that the car is hers and has *nothing* to do with him. She keeps telling me I should regard her house as my London hotel.

She is always slipping me little things when she sees me, apples, etc., etc., and she gets mad when I don't eat there. She is terribly anxious–that is her one *weak point*–she always thinks she is dying when she so much as stubs her toe. In all actuality, I have not been able to do anything for her, but, as Mr. Braham assures me, having me here is very good for Mrs. Braham's nerves because I succeed in calming her down with my medical advice.

7 August 1933

I am so completely happy here that I have to be ashamed and ask myself why I am so lucky, me of all people when I am so egotistical and unkind. This evening, I finally found the little door to Ray Braham and I found deep down such a lonely, such a horribly afraid and lonesome human being. Her haste and overwrought nerves are only used to make her forget, that hunger for a little bit of love, the kind of love she gives with full hands and she receives so little reward for it. I think that is the reason for having children, because a childless marriage leads to even more loneliness than the one all of us carry inside already.

The close friendship that developed between the Brahams and Vera lasted well into my own childhood. Frank, after whom I was named, passed away in the late 1950s, whereas Granny Ray (as she was known to me) survived until 1967 and, despite her hypochondria, had reached 102 when she died.

While happy that she had been so generously welcomed into a comfortable home, Otto Schiff continued to discourage Vera from pursuing a medical career, believing that, as a woman, it would be more than difficult for her to re-establish herself in her chosen profession. Instead, he used his connections to find work for her in the world of fashion. On Otto's recommendation, she was hired as a salesgirl in the millinery department of Eve Valère.3

VERA

15 May 1933

Otto Schiff knows Mr. Koski, the owner of Eve Valère very well, and, on his recommendation, I introduced myself to him this morning, and he said that he wanted to talk to Otto again and then, I am supposed to come in for a probational period of fourteen days starting next Monday at 10 o'clock, and now, I would like to jump to the ceiling for joy. Just think, Otto went with me personally on Saturday, his only day off. That is, at the moment, he works for the refugees on Saturday and Sunday as well and that is why it is doubly and triply sweet of him to go there with me himself.

21 May 1933

I have a free hour from one to two o'clock, and have just had lunch. So, I am in the hat department!!! Mr. Koski introduced me to a Miss Eva, said this is Miss Vera and that was that; and she showed me *all* the *work-rooms*—oh so many—and then we went into the *show room*. A really sweet little girl showed me how all the hats have to be cleaned with a brush every morning and fresh tissue paper has to be placed between them, and I will have to take care of six drawers on my own starting tomorrow. I began working on that immediately and I was laughing on the inside and felt like I was in a film. Then, they told me, that, as soon as customers came in, I was supposed to listen, etc. During the course of the morning, I sold two panama hats to a lady at thirty shillings each (*that is considered to be frightfully cheap, they are reduced!!!!*).

I am wearing my brown suit and a checkered blouse. In the store, however, everyone has to wear black and so, beginning tomorrow, I will be in black crêpe de chine. I am curious to see how this will develop. You know, the most wonderful thing about England is, no one asks where do you come from, what were you doing before, why, etc., etc. That is wonderful and would probably be completely unthinkable back home.

---

3   A photograph of a hatbox and hats designed by Eve Valère can be found in the online resources to this book, https://doi.org/10.11647/OBP.0334#resources

Even so, there was one lady who asked for a particular kind of hat. I did not know what kind–it was such an odd word–and I did not find out until later that she meant something especially *smart*. A shame that I do not remember the expression! The cheapest hat at Eve Valère costs two guineas!!! There are some fabulously *smart* people who come into the store, but also such unbelievable English shriveled up ones, that you want to burst out laughing when they turn back and forth in front of the mirror for hours, wearing the smartest hats on their impossible heads.

31 May 1933

Mr. Koski whom I saw today and who wished me *Good Yom Tov* (I did not understand until one hour later what he meant by that–it is the Jewish Pentecost) and I asked him if he was satisfied with my work and he said *you are awful, dreadful,* and laughed at me mischievously. I hope that he will not say *goodbye* after the holiday.

18 June 1933

You ask if this is something for the long run. This is the start of my fifth week and if Mr. Koski did not want to keep me, I am sure he would have said something. If I cannot take up my medical studies again in the autumn and stay here for longer, the pocket money he hands me over the counter–a pound every week–will not be sufficient in the long run, but I think, I am in no position to say anything after just four weeks.

A good number of people tell me a hundred times how extraordinarily lucky I am to have a job and that it is impossible to imagine how many highly qualified fellow German emigrés are running around only to become *lift-boys*, if they even have a chance to work in the first place.

I do now think that Otto was right–I will stay here with my hats for the time being and I will sink medicine into an anesthetics sleep which could wake from that sleep later. I do not know if that is the right thing to do! It is difficult to make a decision, but a sparrow in the hand is certainly worth more than a dove that flies over the roof.

Sometimes, when there is not so much to do, around 10 o'clock, I think, right now, Schmieden or Volhard are lecturing and I am standing in a fashion salon with lips painted red. Did I do the right thing?

Eleven: Zionism

Mope's break from the Orthodox Judaism practiced by his father did not quench his conviction that Zionism was the way forward for modern Jews or, at least, for himself. In its barest outline, I can trace Mope's fervent engagement with Zionism through to his early youth. For a fuller history, I have pieced together fragments from various sources that help to convey a consistent picture out of which his interpretation of Zionism has an appealing clarity. The geographical Palestine to which he alludes is what had become British Mandatory territory following World War I, and should not be confused with present-day aspirations for a Palestinian state.

MOPE

I believe that the function of Zionism is in the realization of the promise to create an official and legal homestead for the Jewish people in Palestine. What our generation of young Zionists is attempting is to respond to Palestine in a completely new, completely different, way from that espoused by our praying forefathers. Our concept is one that, until now, was only the stuff of stories and dreams. We try to revitalize the beauties of our religious forefathers consistent with modern demands of life today. We harmonize those dreams and make them real through plantings, irrigation and construction, a concept that was atrophied by the former "prayers only" approach.

Even as Mope entered his teens, his Zionistic leanings are unmistakable. A printed table song produced for his Bar Mitzvah on 29 June 1912 ("Tafellied zur Barmizwah-Feier von Ernst Moritz Felsenstein") balances the counterclaims of two homelands, the one natal, the other inspirational. It combines tribute to the sanctuary of the Jewish home in Germany ("the homestead fostering our childhood dreams") with the ideals of Zion ("the ancient holy land… beckons us with ties so bold"). The Zionist melodies sung at Mope's Bar Mitzvah are early indications of his growing ardor to prepare himself for the promise of a new life in Palestine.

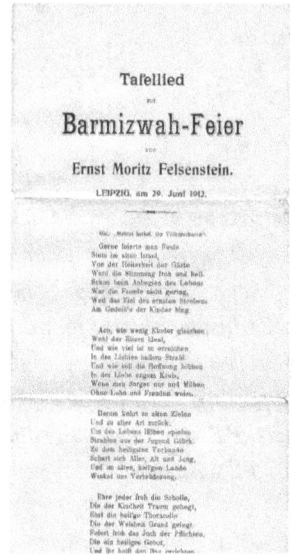 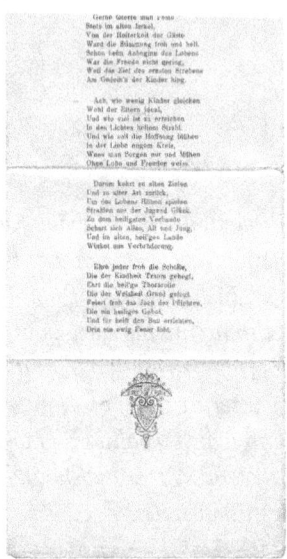

Fig. 54 (a) and (b) Bar Mitzvah Tafellied (Table Songs) for Moritz Felsenstein, Leipzig, 29 June 1912.

After 1933, hearkening to the Holy Land was transformed from aspiration into urgent necessity as German Jews sought refuge outside the clutches of the Nazi regime.

Where, following Mope's experience in the trenches, his unbending father had only succeeded in aggravating his religious disquiet, his mother appears to have been more than willing to engage with him over matters of faith. The closeness between mother and son is captured in a loosely abbreviated reconstruction of some verses that he penned to her on his own twenty fourth birthday.

Here, he nominates her as his best "critic" as he sets out his Zionist ideology. He once again distinguishes between "this cold northern land... the old Fatherland" (i.e., Germany) and the promise of a new home for the Jewish people in Palestine. Where he differs from his mother is in giving precedence to the realities of establishing a Jewish homeland over repetitive prayer in the synagogue.

Eleven: Zionism

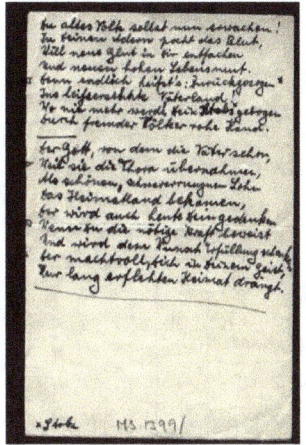 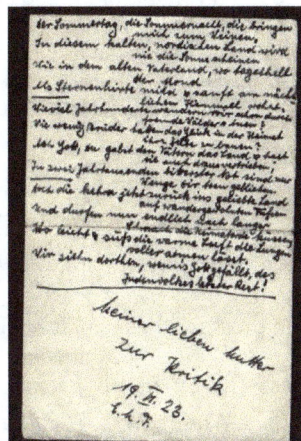

Fig. 55 Zionistic verses dedicated to his mother, penned by EMF, on his birthday, 19 June 1923.

MOPE

How many centuries have we already wandered through foreign forests?

How few of our brothers have had the good fortune to rebuild their tents in the homeland?

But now with wandering feet we are returning to our beloved land

And finally now, after centuries of humiliation, we may kiss our native earth,

And raise there, if God so wills, a permanent resting place for the Jewish people.

All good people, you should now awake

The blood should throb in your veins.

A new ardor needs to be kindled in you

And with it the courage of a new kind of higher life.

In the sad, piteous Fatherland,

Where never more will we have to bow

To the raw hand of foreign people,

They take the Torah as God's beautiful reward

When they should also be in prayer for a Jewish homeland.

If you need the proof of this

Allow it to be your desire's fulfilment

Be strong in your spirit

To press for the restoration of our long lost homeland.

Mope was steeped in the Zionist movement through membership of Blau-Weiss (Blue-White), the first Zionist youth movement in Germany which was established in the same year as his Bar Mitzvah. Blau-Weiss began as a response to the refusal of German youth movements to enlist more than a token number of non-Christian members, and it promoted social and cultural activities that helped to give its youngsters a Jewish identity and sense of togetherness. In the years after the First World War, the gathering anti-Semitism in Germany and other European countries made Zionism a very attractive ideal for many young Jews of Mope's generation.

Within his own family, Mope was aware that among the early pioneers had been his mother's sister, Rifka, and her husband Wolf Bruenn, who had successfully sought to transform mosquito-infested swamps outside Hadera in the heart of Palestine, into orange groves through the selective introduction of eucalyptus trees and other natural forms of drainage. Another of his aunts, Esther, had married the writer Shmuel Josef Agnon (later a Nobel Laureate), and they too had made Palestine their home.

During his time as a graduate student, Mope received an irregular stipend for contributing articles to Zionist newspapers and magazines. I recollect a conversation with him in which he mentioned to me that most of these pieces came to be published under a pseudonym, though (if he ever divulged the name) I cannot recollect the moniker that he used. However, the recent digitization of the Leipziger Jüdische Zeitung *has revealed a lone article, entitled "The Palestine Office in Leipzig", that he published under his own name on 24 March 1922. It was written in the context of the ongoing Kiev pogroms in which fifty thousand Jews had been massacred and half a million made homeless. I have adapted his words to give it a personal slant.*

MOPE

By the beginning of April 1920, the Balfour Declaration had received official confirmation by the Zionist Commission, and, two years later, by the League of Nations. In Leipzig as well as in other German cities, people like me considered that as a signal for the mass emigration of Jews to Palestine, but in the year 1920 just one single pioneer emigrated there from our city.

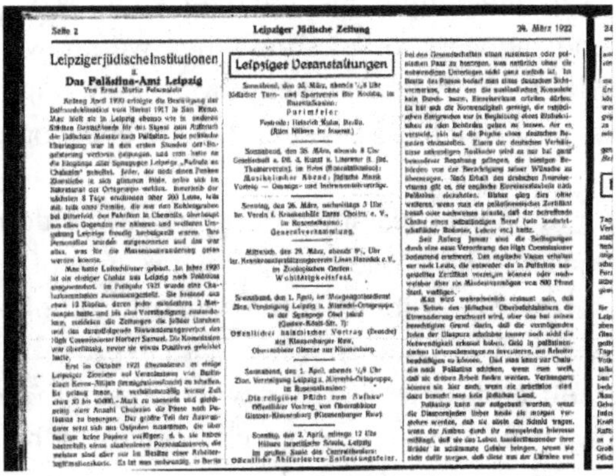

Seite 2 — Leipziger Jüdische Zeitung — 24. März 1922

Leipziger jüdische Institutionen

II.

Das Palästina-Amt Leipzig

Leipziger Veranstaltungen

Fig. 56 Article by EMF that appeared in the *Leipziger Jüdische Zeitung*, 24 March 1922; accessible online at https://digital.slub-dresden.de/werkansicht/dlf/122923/2.

In the following year, I united together with a few other committed Leipzig based Zionists. We succeeded in raising funds of around thirty to forty thousand Reichmarks and used that to furnish passports to Palestine for a number of individuals. Most of the emigrants were Eastern European Jews who rarely carried with them any personal documentation. It was essential to obtain for them Russian and Polish passports from their respective embassies in Berlin, which, without any supporting documents, was of course far from simple. No less critical was that these Eastern European emigrants should be accompanied there by one of us since we were more likely to understand the mentality of the functionaries with whom they would have to deal. A foreigner who is unfamiliar with the protocols will succeed only with extraordinary talent to convince faceless bureaucrats of their right to emigrate. In addition, an applicant would need to be furnished both with a German emigration and an English immigration visa before traveling to Palestine.

Since the start of January of the present year the conditions of entry have become immensely more difficult due to a new law from the British High Commissioner, who declared that Jewish immigration would be approved only when it could be shown that it did not do harm to the economy. For now, only people who can produce a security of at least five hundred pounds sterling will obtain an English visa.

Wealthy Jews living in the diaspora still seem not to have grasped the necessity of supporting our venture by investing in Palestinian companies that can offer employment to these emigrés once they arrive. We can only send pioneers to Palestine when we know that they will find work over there. If they are unemployed, they might just as well starve over here. In such a hopeless situation, no one would need a land for the Jews!

Better *today* rather than leaving it to tomorrow, Palestine can only be built when diaspora Jews understand the urgency of our plea. They alone will carry the responsibility if the construction of a Jewish state fails due to their lack of concern. Should that prove to be the case, hundreds and thousands of Jewish lives will be cast into terrible danger. We diaspora Jews need to take care of our brothers by helping them to emigrate from Ukraine and other such pogrom hells in order that they may enjoy a safe and secure future for themselves in Palestine.

I should end by saying that in Palestine itself, a Jew will be able to set up and run a business more successfully than anywhere else in the world because the country still has much scope to be developed economically, and, with the arrival of new immigrants, it expects an ever-increasing commerce.

We make an urgent appeal to the Leipzig Jewish community at large: **Help us with our difficult work if you can today! Likely tomorrow, it will already be too late!**

Mope's final remark is prescient. With the advent of Nazi rule in Germany, emigration to Palestine became far more complicated, particularly for those who hoped to take their material assets with them. Although his brother Adolf and his sister Alice, both still in their mid-thirties, had succeeded in bringing their families to Palestine, they had not taken into consideration the plight of their widowed mother. She would have to rely for her future on the transfer of her dwindling resources if she were to follow them. As the last of her children still living in Leipzig, Mope took it upon himself to help her in any way that he could.

When he formulated his plans for his mother and for himself to emigrate to Palestine, he realized that they would each need capital to sustain their new lives. To secure this, he turned to what he thought would be a viable scheme. Shortly after the Nazis grabbed power in 1933, an initial agreement had been reached with Zionist officials that would permit Jewish emigrants to transfer their assets to Palestine in the form of German export goods. The name of the company that was set up in Tel Aviv to administer this was Haavara, and money to be transferred had to be paid into the account of Paltreu ("Palästina Treuhandgesellschaft", the Palestine Trust Company).[4] In turn, the capital was then used to purchase German goods, which were to be sold in Palestine by Haavara. It was a way of satisfying both the Nazis who were intent of ridding Germany of its Jews, and the Jewish Agency which was no less intent in encouraging immigration to Palestine. As a committed Zionist, Mope was attracted to the scheme.

To meet British mandatory regulations, each emigrant needed to be in possession of a basic surety of £1,000. However, strict German currency restrictions prohibited the exchange or exportation of Reichmarks without formal permission. To secure the necessary amount to cover both his mother and himself, Mope turned to family members outside Germany, writing to his brother-in-law in London, Fred Rau, to ask him to act as his financial guarantor, and to a Palestine-based cousin, Dr. Julius Rosenfeld, the brother of Karl Rosenfeld of Karlsruhe, to negotiate with Haavara in Tel Aviv. Working through PalTreu, and with the participation of his brother-in-law and his cousin, he believed he had found a legal method to transfer a significant portion of his mother's and his own funds out of Nazi Germany. The goods that he decided to use for this purpose were furs. Little did he suspect that he had caught himself in what was to turn out to be a labyrinthine web that threatened to enmesh him.

MOPE

I applied for a transfer to Palestine and received permission to send merchandise valued at fifty thousand Reichmarks there under the condition that a quarter of this amount would be paid in foreign currency. My brother-in-law Frederick Rau in London provided me with the needed amount in pounds Sterling (approximately £ 1,080),

---

4 An image of an application form created by the *Palästina Treuhand-Stelle* (Palestine Trust Company) can be viewed in the online resources for this book, https://doi.org/10.11647/OBP.0334#resources

because I did not have access to any money abroad. I did not want the merchandise, a quarter of which had been paid for by my brother-in-law to remain in Germany, but on the other hand, it could not be subjected to the heat of the summer months in Palestine, so I asked for permission to warehouse the raw furs in Antwerp until the autumn.

In setting all this up, I was called a dreamer, since my brother Adolf had already tried and found it too hard a nut to crack, but it looks like my preparation was worth the effort. I had to engage in a lot of correspondence in connection with these things, but, when I discussed it with my attorney, he expressed amazement at the result of my efforts concerning *Haavara* and assured me that, in his multiple experience, he had never seen such a well-developed plan.

To my absolute frustration, I cannot undertake anything more before receiving the confirmation or permission respectively through *Haavara* in Tel-Aviv that Julius Rosenfeld, acting on my behalf, will have to present to them in writing. In my impatience to receive an answer from *Haavara*, I called and talked to Berlin yesterday and there, they put me off by telling me that such enquiries always require quite a bit of time until completion and that the waiting period was completely normal. They only promised to ask Tel-Aviv once again by airmail to expedite the matter.

Everything moves forward far too gradually. It appears that there will be more delays, most of which I probably don't even know about yet. Anyone with Zionistic aspirations, as I do, gets to suffer through this scheme. Before all of this is completed, I cannot make any firm plans for the future. The form has to be created first, before the bell is poured. In my momentary situation, it is difficult to form a clear picture of a future life in Palestine.

Twelve: Gretel

Vera was settled and in work. Although she still held out lingering hope that, come the Autumn, she would resume her medical training, her primary goal was to bring her parents and sister out of Germany. Once again, she approached Otto Schiff for advice. Between them, they developed a scheme for her parents to rent a property in London which would include temporary accommodation for arriving refugees who would pay room and board. My grandmother had already had substantial experience of a similar kind by hosting British visitors to Frankfurt. She undertook two exploratory visits to England, by the end of which she laid a deposit on a five-bedroom flat at 12A Addison Court Gardens in Kensington to which they were to move in early 1934, leaving behind the Oberlindau residence in Frankfurt. Vera left the Brahams in order to reunite with her parents under a single roof.

Two problems remained. The first concerned Pepper, my grandfather, who was reluctant to leave familiar territory and complained that he would not be understood in England. Given her low opinion of her father, Vera tried to be upbeat and not just cynical.

VERA

Pepper should be happy when he comes to England, because no one has ever achieved anything by feeling depressed and hanging their heads. Of course, he will have good prospects here. He can either help Mutti with the chores or maybe follow his hobby and buy and sell stamps. *But he has to speak English, otherwise everything will be much too difficult here!* There is no other choice. We need to give him some easy children's books to read so he can get used to the language as such and then have him translate some of it every day. I cannot repeat often enough *how* important that is. I know that it is difficult for him, but it has to be done. He needs to be a little more reasonable and not be allowed to go screaming that he cannot do something like that. For all our sakes, he must not keep walking in the same boots he wore a hundred years ago!

Far more problematic was how to accommodate Gretel in their home in London, given the severity of her mental debilities. When my grandparents were on the point of following their younger daughter out of Germany, it became apparent that, at least in the short term, they would have to leave without Gretel. If today such an outcome seems both cruel and improper, for a Jewish family living under the Nazis harsh necessity often dictated what in normal circumstances would have been unthinkable.

Initially, Vera anticipated that she would share a bedroom in London with her sister in order to open up three rooms in the new flat for the expected influx of guests. But, it did not take long for her to acknowledge how easily her sister's presence could impede her ability to support her immediate family. Gretel had been in and out of mental institutions for much of her life, and, even before the advent of the Nazi regime, her physical health had been a cause for concern. Until her parents were fully settled in England, it was expedient to return Gretel to an asylum. Their chosen locale was the Kalmenhof at Idstein in the scenic Taunus mountains not far from Frankfurt, a retreat that had been created in the late nineteenth century with support from the Jewish community.

Fig. 57 View of the Kalmenhof, Idstein (taken from https://alt-idstein.de/wp-content/uploads/2020/07/Haupthaus_2.jpg).

VERA

I think we have to find the space to accommodate *three* outside guests in our London flat. In an ideal world, Gretel and I would share a room quite well, freeing up the one originally meant for her. But, if we took Gretel along with us, it would actually be much worse for her. The situation in London would not be good for her nerves, and as we really need to make ends meet, we will need to be unhampered. Gretel's being here would restrict me and all of us terribly. Placing her at Idstein would be best by far. I hope that Gretel will settle in well there. I am certain it is the best thing for her and for all of us. Then, after a year, it might be possible to bring her here.

Alice traveled with her elder daughter to Idstein, and was met with a warm reception by the director and staff at the Kalmenhof. Satisfied that Gretel would be well looked after, she left her in their temporary care.

VERA

I am glad that the director in Idstein is so nice and that Gretel seems to have settled in well. I think it is the best for her. You will see how independent she will become there and how at home she will feel there and how good the air and the quiet will be for her. I am sure that London would have been the absolute worst for her.

Days later, in the middle of January 1934, my grandparents crossed over to London, bringing with them items from their old home to furnish their new flat. Vera had used whatever spare time she could find to prepare things for them. Her attention for Gretel was almost an afterthought.

VERA

12a Addison Court Gardens looks so delightful that my heart was in my throat. We have never had such a luxurious bathroom, simply wonderful!!! The kitchen is charming and everything is so bright and beautiful. There is a brand-new beautiful cabinet to replace the old broom closet. I measured the drapes in the dining room again and the width and length of the hall in inches and at the beginning of next week, I will find out what the carpet for the hall will cost, because Otto wants to know.

Other repair work on it was only finished yesterday morning. The porter already gave me the keys. He promised that he will look through everything with care, the windows, lighting fixtures, etc. It is absolutely beautiful! I have to repeat again and again how indescribably I am looking forward to having a real home again and how much I need that. I hope as much that Gretel will settle in well at Idstein. I am certain it is the best thing for her and for all of us.

Perhaps Vera was right that Gretel would feel more secure at the Kalmenhof than in London. That was likely wishful thinking. Sources since made available show that the "nice" director at Idstein was ejected from the institution by an SS squad and replaced by a gun-toting Nazi. The subsequent brutalization of the Kalmenhof was rapid, the new director issuing an order that "unsuitable national comrades will be reduced to an absolute minimum."

Though we do not have the details, we know that Gretel's life after her parents' departure was short. When she entered the Kalmenhof in January 1934, her health was already poor. Little over fourteen months later, on 26 March 1935, my grandfather, by then settled in London, received a telegram from the Kalmenhof with the following short notice: " = MARGARETHE HIRSCH HEUTE FRUEH LUNGENZUENDUNG UND GRIPPE VERSTORBEN = " ("Margarethe Hirsch died early today from pneumonia and influenza").

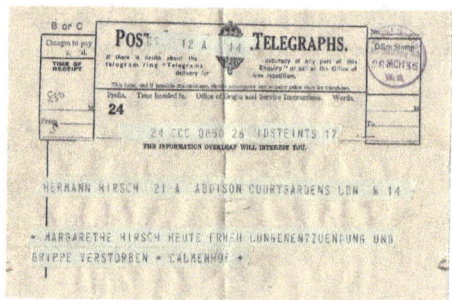

Fig. 58 Telegram from the Kalmenhof at Idstein recording the death of Vera's older sister, Gretel Hirsch, 26 March 1935.

Gretel was thirty-three years old when she died. The survival of similar telegrams from the Kalmenhof informing of the death of individual patients by natural causes such as influenza, when in fact they had been killed by lethal injection, casts a terrible shadow of suspicion over the cause of Gretel's death. Those other telegrams are of a later date.

Many years later, when I first learned that the Nazis used the Kalmenhof as an epicenter for the involuntary euthanasia of patients with chronic disabilities, I asked my mother whether she thought that Gretel may have been murdered. Vera was visibly shocked at my question, and was categorical that that was not the case. I believe that she was right since the policy of involuntary euthanasia was only instituted after Gretel's death.

It is likely, though, that Gretel was maltreated under the new regime at the Kalmenhof, which may have expedited her death. Unlike later victims who were cast into a mass grave, she was accorded individual burial in the Jewish cemetery at Idstein.

Fig. 59 (a) Studio photograph of Alice Hirsch with Gretel as a toddler; Atelier Blum, Frankfurt.

Fig. 59 (b) Grave of Margarethe ("Gretel") Hirsch at Idstein; colour photograph taken by Colin Watts, 2018.

Because she was so distant from her sister, Vera frequently identified herself as an "only child." Nevertheless, I think there remained throughout her life an undercurrent of residual guilt in her mind whenever she thought back to her unfortunate sister. For my grandmother, the loss must have been far harsher as she thought back to Gretel's childhood and mourned the passing of her first born.

Thirteen: Marks and Mitja

VERA

Selective journal entries, December 1933 through December 1934

Life–what is it?

At the moment, I am going through one of the most difficult periods in my life, no doubt.

We have never been in such a material bind, dependence, and uncertainty before. It is difficult to say how this will end. I am saying this today so that I will be more balanced and calmer this evening. I have seen that in myself before, that I waste away when I close myself off for too long.

I want to have *courage*, that is the most important thing in life. I want to take everything as valuable experience.

What a time of complete stagnancy and idle running this is for me! Why does one become such a slave to things, to stuff? How lonely every single human being is! Where are the positive things in life? Why are people so dishonest? Maybe Oscar Spengler in Germany is right when he calls social emotional impulses degenerative events: only the strong=intelligent=clever one can live. What is life? And if you feel too much pity for others and too many emotions, you will drown in them. If others are more awkward or less talented, will they have to be stepped on by your foot or at least be kicked to the side? Where is the value in life?

I worry about work. Will it be possible to find a new and more challenging position? Or must I stay forever on minimal pay at Eve Valère? How does one endure such a completely monotonous and numbingly stressful job?

A matter that is important at work is to make sure that I never look as if I have lapsed into inefficiency. Also, another observation:

I should become more tolerant, lenient, and friendly to the poor people behind the counter; these people who have no outlook in their life, with no prospect of a promotion. In this bleakest monotony, I feel a certain obligation to them, but how can they get ahead in life if they are always as undemanding as ever with their impromptu decisions, superficial friendliness, and cheerful incomprehension? Will continuing like this help with my medical studies? Maybe it's just worth it to keep my eyes open and to look for every new experience in order to learn as much as possible. It isn't altogether a bad thing that I haven't learned everything yet: with medicine, millinery, languages, etc., etc. But I have nothing, absolutely nothing that I can show for myself and declare to be my specialty.

Maybe all of this is only long-term training so that I will one day be able to give good advice to my children. What a colorful and eventful story I will be able to tell these children!

Through the recommendation of Otto Schiff and support from Ray Braham, Vera was selected as one of a cadre of a dozen individuals to be trained as staff managers in the newly established Welfare Department at Marks & Spencer, Britain's leading chain store. Schiff had received government approval to allow a hand-picked group of skilled refugees to enter the work force, though with the proviso that this did not constitute a right to permanent settlement. Vera's experience at Eve Valère, her fluency in English, and the fact that she had had a university education–at that time rare among women–all spoke in her favor. With an application in hand for working papers, she commenced what was to prove an absorbing new career as a staff manageress in the retail trade. Her enthusiasm is palpable.

Fig. 60 Marks & Spencer, store front of North End Road Branch, London, 1930s (https://www.pinterest.com/pin/422001427562112641/).

VERA

Selective journal entries, 3 June through 9 October 1935

Today I received my definite acceptance at Marks and Spencer with a salary of 3 pounds per week. How blessed I am to have such a job: I want to apply all of my strength and energy, dreading no toil, and do everything to the best of my ability and be happy in the knowledge that I could accomplish something. People who work so stressfully in a store must be able to unburden their lives. What a wonderful, encouraging endeavor.

I have been working in the Welfare department of Marks and Spencer on Oxford Street since Monday the 8th of July. I am thankful for this position. I believe that this new occupation will give me a new perspective on life. In these first six days I have learned

1. How important it is to be exact (especially with the monotonous bookwork!);
2. What a huge influence consistent friendliness, thoughtfulness, and politeness can have on the atmosphere of a business;
3. How important it is to take seriously every single person's concern, no matter how small. I want to encourage others daily and employ all my strength, without looking stressed and without pitying myself.

I am so happy at the moment that I am so much more independent. I want to find fulfillment in this work, and really take it seriously, and not as if it were just an inescapable way to make money while one cannot wait to get off work.

I have found myself falling into the practical life of the very ordinary, little average, working girl. But I am not unhappy. It has excited something in me. Maybe it's just the novelty of the adventure! This whole time of my life I am aware that I am in a transitioning period.... What next?

I strive to be a person whose existence is at least a little bit justified. I have the feeling that for the first time in my life I have found *the* occupation that speaks to my disposition and truly fits who I am.

As her professional life took a major step forward through her new career in personnel management, Vera's private life was nearly upended by an ill-starred love affair with a thirty-year old emigré from Russia whose name was Mitja

Simonoff. From the beginning, Vera recognized that Mitja was a charming lothario who enjoyed playing the field, but, from when they first met, she persuaded herself that she could alter his ways and that he was the one for her. It was love at first sight, and she was head over heels from day one.

VERA

Selective journal entries, 8 December 1934 through 27 March 1935

Is the positive in life only to be sought in the relationship between a male and a female? How long can such a relationship remain ideal? Just a short summary of the past week: eight days ago, Saturday, I was with Mitja, and he is the one that I want to marry.

The more I learn the more I like Mitja; he is the man for whom I have waited all these years. He is my final love. He is everything, *everything* that I have ever dreamed of in my ideal man. He is good, so kind, and has character. He is intelligent, energetic, and quickly resolute. He has tact, and is amusing and perceptive.

And what does he think of me?

Do I believe that he enjoys and keeps up his conversations *only* with me, since he has asked again and again for my company alone! I am sure that he can only know how much I treasure him, and there is nothing else to say. I cannot hide it from him, and yet in our last conversation he had said to me how he had these desires that only I could satisfy.

I made the suggestion that tomorrow, instead of going out, he should come over to my place. I told him by way of excuse how much I would love that he meet my angel of a mother. How shy we both are about this! Naturally, this is awfully awkward, but Mitja, I love you because I am convinced that we are both right for each other. For such a love there can and must be a wonderful and rich life's journey ahead of us!

Sunday, Mitja was at tea until 10.30, and he told me how much he liked my mother!

At the door upon leaving the house–he spoke in English because he said it was easier to say it in English!–he whispered, "Don't forget me", and then he put both arms around me, and that is as easy to say as anything else. He told me today that he is always so bashful when we are together.

Maybe Mitja only likes how I look externally. He told me today that I have good looking legs; finally a compliment, oh you child!

My dear mother always wants to remind me of the truism that after he has been with her a man will lose his interest in a woman. Well, if this happens, then it must be true! Anyone looking at this situation from the outside would say that I should prove my thankfulness for her by not taking this next step, but life is not so easy. Schooling may come easily, but life does not.

Am I aware of the consequences for me as a woman? (and, more than once, Mitja asked if it would be my first time and I didn't answer this). I told him that I am old enough to know what I am doing.

Do I really value my virginity so much? Honestly, no, I don't. And I know now for sure that I will go away with Mitja for the weekend. He asked me, and I said how much I would love to come along, but I didn't give him *any* final answer until I had a whole night to think about it. It will only be for one weekend. Yes, I know that I am definitely doing the right thing!

* * *

I almost expected this to be the first time and that I would not enjoy it; maybe that comes after many repetitions, but I am not so keen on that. I am completely calm, and not as "stirred up" as I was four weeks ago after the first unresolved time together. I feel sore, something physical hurts and I hope it will let up in the next three or four days, and that the entire matter will hopefully continue without any other side effects.

The act didn't seem so radical but there were various other things about him that were odd. I am not cold, everything on my side was really already prepared, except for the fact that the hymen was not yet broken. I hope I don't have any kind of physical defect, because my medical knowledge doesn't quite extend so far in this matter. I judged from his behavior that maybe it is abnormal, maybe it is only because my twenty-five-year-old tissue is not as flexible now. I don't know.

After our experience he didn't find it necessary to call me today to find out how I am. I don't blame him for his behavior. I am the gratified one. But a person with so little empathy cannot be my friend, much less my lover or even my husband. It's good that I've figured this out relatively early. I regret nothing. This matter has wonderfully rounded out as if it was in a cheesy novel; that is *not* my fault. I have enormously enjoyed our time together, but I intend to break up with Mitja.

I am not ashamed that I am just one of many women, many *things*, on Mitja's list. It doesn't matter because I knew what I was doing at every moment. But someone with such a shortcoming of sensitivity is unbearable to me. I am, let it be noted here, completely calm and level-headed, and I have no heartache.

For my part, everything that I gave that first time was meant to be evidence of my complete love and affection. But for him it was totally different and thus he could never understand! He said that to break up would only be better for me, but for him to never see me again would be painful and horrible.

What do I like about Mitja? It's hard to say today, he is empty! He has spent his life sleeping around with amazingly beautiful women! Why did he even befriend me? If I had the opportunity to marry a man who will even somewhat fit what I would like, I would do it and say goodbye to Mitja once and for all. It wouldn't affect him much. And despite all this, I do not regret anything, I have enjoyed our friendship and I will continue on with my life!

For three weeks now (almost to the day), I have heard *nothing* more from Mitja. Without any particular reason that I know of. It was, almost to the day, the sixth month of our friendship. And it seems that half a year is the usual amount of time he gives to a relationship. I only wish that he had stopped contact because of a mutual and honest break up, but it seems that men are this way. Externally I am opposed to him. I *cannot* give him the triumph of telling his next girlfriend how the woman he abandoned pursued him, and that he therefore had a right to completely arrest the relationship, because the abandoned girlfriend had loved him too much and had reckoned that he should marry her, and so he broke it off with her. That would indeed be about what he'd say; but by not hearing from me maybe his vanity will be a bit hurt!

It is terrifying how many men are cowards. He dared not say anything to me about breaking up, but instead decided to break contact and completely dump me. Maybe he thought he would hear from me, and through my questioning, or even better through my accusation, that I would be the one to facilitate everything. No, Mitja, that will *never* happen with me. I regret *nothing* that has happened in the course of our friendship but I will tell my next boyfriend the following: I have a tendency to be unfaithful. One day I will just dump you as if nothing happened. I'll even make this clear at the beginning of the relationship. Maybe that's the right method!!!

Is it vanity, that despite all of this my opinion of Mitja has not changed? Is it stupid that I don't want to acknowledge that I met a bad person and that I've been had? I believe that this isn't the case, and my opinion is that he is also hurting at the moment; probably completely out of vanity that this was such an unworthy departure.

I want to try and pick up the threads again. First: I believe that I am a bit better from the experience. I really am trying to give more of myself and I am working on shaking off my inhibitions.

At the beginning of last year, I was unemployed and unhappy about it, but I was mentally content and fulfilled through a friendship that grew into a romantic love, one that was cherished up to the very last moment. I have never regretted it.

Then I found myself a job, and I lost the friend and the lover without much heartbreak.

Vera's brief entanglement with Mitja made her far more circumspect in thinking about entering into a relationship with another man, though it also signaled to her that, given the right circumstances, she would most likely be emotionally ready for that. For much of the remainder of 1935, she immersed herself in her work as a staff manageress at Marks & Spencer, finding considerable satisfaction there.

PART 2: NOW

Fourteen: "I Stole a Kiss From You at the Train Station"

21 January through 16 February 1936

POLITICAL TIMELINE 1936

- 20 January 1936: Death of King George V of Great Britain (funeral 28 January).
- 6–16 February 1936: Winter Olympics staged at Garmisch-Partenkirchen, Bavaria.
- 3 March 1936: Jewish doctors officially barred from practicing in German hospitals.
- 7 March 1936: German troops occupy the Rhineland which had been demilitarized after World War I.
- March 1936: Anti-Semitic pogroms in Poland.
- April 1936: Widespread riots by Arabs in mandatory Palestine against Jewish immigration.
- 17 June 1936: Heinrich Himmler, Reichführer of the SS, made chief of all German police forces. Anti-Semitic road signs temporarily removed from Germany in anticipation of the summer games
- 17 July 1936: Beginning of the Spanish Civil War. Hitler supplies troops in support of the Spanish dictator Francisco Franco.
- 31 July 1936: Nazi decree classifying mixed-race children as Jews.
- 1-16 August 1936: Summer Olympics staged in Berlin.

- 7 September 1936: Twenty-five per cent tax on all Jewish assets in Germany.
- 23 September 1936: Sachsenhausen Concentration Camp opened.
- 15 October 1936: Decree that "Non Aryans" are prohibited from teaching in German public schools.
- 25 October 1936: Rome-Berlin Axis formed by Mussolini and Hitler.
- 14 November 1936: Statue of Felix Mendelssohn before the Gewandhaus in Leipzig destroyed.
- 27 November 1936: Film criticism banned in Germany.

In the autumn of 1935, more than a year after they left Germany, the Hirsch family hosted a visit to London by Annelie Freimann, a distant cousin whose home was in Leipzig. Vera had never met her before. From the moment she arrived, Annelie turned out to be a delight.5 She was young, energetic, full of fun, and with a most agreeable personality. Despite being Jewish, she had not been expelled from Leipzig University where she was enrolled as a dental student, and she still expected to qualify the following year. Yet, Annelie was also realistic about the situation. She told of one particular professor who had dared to speak out in the classroom against the new regime, and how she had witnessed his physical removal by Nazi thugs, adding that the poor man was never heard of or seen again. Her visit was an opportunity for Annelie to explore whether there may be options open to her in England once she graduated. On her departure, she asked Vera to visit her in Leipzig, hardly expecting that her offer would be taken up.

The open invitation that she had received from Annelie played on Vera's mind during those rare moments in which she was not engrossed in the intricacies of her new job or trying to care for the immediate wants of her parents. With her first short vacation from M&S slated for the start of 1936, she began to envision albeit wild plans. When she raised with her mother the idea of visiting Annelie in Leipzig, she inevitably received an extremely negative response. With some justification, my grandmother lectured to her on the foolishness of returning to Nazi Germany and the risks that that incurred. For whatever reason, Vera was

---

5   A torn photograph of Annelie Herzberg (née Freimann), reproduced from the Holocaust Memorial Education Center website, can be viewed in the online resources for this book, https://doi.org/10.11647/OBP.0334#resources. An extensive interview with Annelie can be found on the Holocaust Memorial Education Center website: https://www.ssbjcchec.org/survivor/anneliese-herzberg/

not prepared to listen. The more that her mother objected the more determined she was to make the journey.

In common with many other emigrants, some of whom even gave up their uncertain status as refugees in order to return to Germany at that time, Vera was perhaps lulled into a false sense of security by reports that things were really not that bad there. Indeed, during the latter part of 1935 and into 1936, with preparations well advanced for the upcoming Olympic Games, the Nazi regime temporarily relaxed its more virulent displays of anti-Semitism. Ominously, however, the first of the so-called "Nuremberg Laws," defining German citizenship by race and reducing Jews to mere "subjects," had been enunciated by Hitler as recently as mid-September 1935. The lull in the more strident propaganda against the Jews, while Germany made itself ready for the Winter Games that would take place at Garmisch-Partenkirchen in the Bavarian Alps in early February, was but a passing interlude. In retrospect, if there was a brief moment in time to revisit Germany it was then.

Fig. 61 Front of postcard from Mope to Vera, dated 15 March 1936, advertising the recent Winter Olympics in Garmisch-Partenkirchen, Germany; postage stamp removed by Hermann Hirsch, Vera's father.

Nevertheless, with her broader percipience and acumen, my grandmother was beside herself and full of fear for the safety of her daughter. When, toward the start of the fourth week of January, Vera left the relative security of London for her short holiday with Annelie in Leipzig, the parting maternal exhortation that she received was at all costs not to become romantically involved with anyone there, and, given the fluctuating political situation, above all not to become involved with a young man of the Jewish faith. There must have been intuitive angels of a higher order that guided Vera as she embarked on what was to prove the most consequential journey of her life!

VERA

Journal entry, 23 August 1935

I want to apply myself completely to my new job; avoid no effort and always keep mentally active with a goal in mind. I want to attempt to build up my position here.

Currently, every day I go to work at 7 in the morning and I return home in the evenings, and I work at home helping my mother until about 10 or 10.30, and then I am more than exhausted. I don't get out of the house at all. I don't see anyone else. I have no admirer or boyfriend. Currently the only positive thing I can find is that I can financially help my sweet mother through my work, and that I have been able to use my strengths and imagination at my job.

Recently I have discovered that it is seriously hard for me to better myself when I am at home; Mother spoils me, everything is centered around and on me; and the most essential thing —contact with other people–is difficult for me to find. Although it's my own responsibility and if I really wanted to I could figure out a way to be around others and not close myself off.

Why am I so uptight?! My heart is seemingly forced to be at a standstill: I have no friends, no lovers or suitors, and it must be my fault. I need a boyfriend! I mean a lover; but as much as I could actually fall in love I could also receive just as much pain. I don't really want to be reeling from pain like that anymore.

I want to try my best to find a new man with whom I might begin a relationship. I want to reveal little to him, if anything, of what I do. I want to be coy, and if I like someone I want to flirt, laugh, dance, and be generally light-hearted. I want to amuse a man, who I might, for example, ask if he likes it when someone wears makeup, or if he thinks it is right for a woman to go to work. I have always believed and hoped that at twenty-five years I might find myself a man whom I could marry. If I find someone I like I want to challenge him.

I am now almost 26 years old. For a woman that isn't considered young anymore. I am still too dependent. Recently I have been so horribly undisciplined, and compared with how I used to be I am weak. Have I made any steps forward in the past year?

Fourteen: "I Stole a Kiss From You at the Train Station"

Journal entry, 21 January 1936

Tomorrow I will travel to Leipzig for my vacation. Despite her opposition, my sweet mother helped to make the arrangements for me. To be completely honest, I am a bit worried today about this trip to Germany, but I wouldn't say this to anyone! I am excited about being in such a different environment–the general conditions in Germany–and I look forward to changing and leaving my everyday life for a while. I like my job now, and I do look forward to coming back to England and seeing my mother again.

It will be interesting to see how the old ways have changed in just two and a half years.

On Wednesday, 22 January, the day prior to her twenty-sixth birthday, Vera travelled to Germany for the first time since 1933, planning to return home to London at the end of the weekend in time to go to work the following morning. A hidden part of Annelie Freimann's agenda for the visit to Leipzig of her attractive cousin was at odds with the expectations of that same cousin's mother. Certainly, she wished to return her obligation to the Hirsches by welcoming Vera within her own family and to celebrate her birthday. But Annelie had other plans too. Although her circle of Jewish friends had drastically diminished since the advent of Nazi power, there were still a number of eligible bachelors to whom Annelie sought to introduce her cousin. Restrictions on Jewish life already made it hard for friends to congregate in public places, and so, on the Friday evening of 24 January, Annelie opted to invite some of them to a bridge soirée at her home. Vera had only rarely played bridge and so was a little concerned that her presence would be supernumerary.

When Annelie's friends arrived and the bridge fours sat down at their separate tables, Vera found herself placed next to a tall, debonair, well-spoken man with fine features, a light complexion and curly blond hair. One of the first things that she noticed about him was the peculiar manner with which he held his cards, denoting that he too was less than familiar with the intricacies of bridge. That turned out to be so, and, in a comparatively short time, they withdrew from the game, and engaged themselves in animated conversation. His name, she learned, was Moritz Felsenstein, and he had grown up here in Leipzig, where his family was in the fur trade, but he was planning to emigrate to Palestine.

As their individual stories began to unfold, they soon became engrossed in each other, and found themselves at the beginning of a lifelong love affair that affirms its freshness for us through their correspondence. Writing from far-away Russia three years later, Mope's recollection of their first meeting in Leipzig (on the banks of the River Pleisse) captures the intimacy of their relationship from its earliest moment.

MOPE TO VERA

Moscow, 16 January 1939

Should these lines arrive on the 24th, they have a further task to fulfill, because they are meant to express my joy concerning this day when I saw you for the very first time and my happiness and gratitude for all the infinitely many beautiful things that I have experienced in these last three years because of you. Back then, I had the feeling that I was supposed to be presented to you as a pleasing option during your visit and, prior to that, I was lacking any kind of positive sensation. Now, I know that you came to the Pleisse with the strictest prohibition against catching one from Leipzig, and you have no idea how good that little forbidden fruit tastes to me, what burning longing I feel to finally taste it again and to be allowed to lick it to taste all of its sweetness.

Writing to Mope in a more discreet recollection of their first meeting, Vera also recalls the timelessness of that moment.

VERA TO MOPE

London, 24 January 1939

Today is the 24th–three years ago, we were playing bridge although neither one of us knew how. Three years ago today, the two of us had our first rendezvous–if you could call it that. Do you know that it seems completely unimaginable to me that I am supposed to have known my beloved for only three years? And if someone asked me again today, everything I can say is that I am very grateful to a benevolent fate that gave me a 24 January 1936 with everything that goes along with it. I have the feeling that we have belonged together since time immemorial.

Shortly before Vera was to return home, a telegram arrived from her mother in London, informing that, as a mark of respect following the death of King George V, shops and businesses in England would remain closed for several days, and it would not be essential for her to go back to work until later in the week. If she was having a fine time, she could stay on with Annelie beyond the weekend. The timing of the telegram could not have been more favorable to their budding relationship.

However, as Vera was in Leipzig as a guest, most of the happenings over the additional three days of her visit involved not just Mope but Annelie and her group of friends. There was very little time for privacy. Their later correspondence is sprinkled with descriptive snapshots of those first days, including a visit to the cinema where they watched Zoltan Korda's new movie **Bosambo** (*released in the English-speaking world as* **Sanders of the River**), *starring Paul Robeson in the title role and Nina Mae McKinney as his wife, Lilongo.*

Fig. 62 German film poster for *Bosambo* (1935), starring Paul Robeson with Nina Mae McKinney playing his wife, Lilongo.

"Lilongo" became a particular and affectionate name with which Mope addressed Vera in his letters to her. For them, it was an instant link to those first days of their relationship with "the memory of the first film we watched together and the first intense holding of hands that took place then."

At the time of Vera's visit, Mope already had tickets and visas for an exploratory visit the following month to Palestine, then under British mandatory rule. After knowing Vera for fewer than four days, he found himself promising that, before his return to Leipzig, he would stop over in London. Four days earlier, he would never have imagined in his wildest dreams that he would be making such arrangements. Mope's recollection of the moment of departure and their first kiss is amusingly captured in a letter of January 1939.

MOPE TO VERA

Moscow, 22 January 1939

It has been three years now since I stole a kiss from you at the train station, a kiss I have returned to you a thousand-fold without ever giving that first one back. Its taste, which was soooo good still lies sweetly on my lips and was the beginning of my happiness. Can anyone wish for anything more beautiful? How wonderful it would be if I could spend these days with my sweetheart once again. I think I would go to a train station with you just to steal another such kiss. Do you still remember how hard Annelie was trying to be discreet and showed an enormous interest in other acquaintances who were leaving at the same time? That hussy had realized what was going on and wanted to be an unintentional matchmaker so badly and that was terribly nice of her, don't you agree?

The advancement of their relationship now depended upon correspondence. The emotional frisson brought about by their first encounter and their deepening emotions are well captured in Mope's letters. Unfortunately, all of Vera's letters to him went missing after the SS raided his Leipzig apartment in June 1937, so that their surviving correspondence remains one-sided until shortly before that date. As if to compensate, Vera continued to maintain a lively diary or journal out of which we can glean some sense of her own emergent feelings. Likely, her diary entries from this time contain inner thoughts and details that may not have been chronicled so explicitly in her missing letters. In several of their early letters to each other, when addressing one another in German, Mope and (by intimation) Vera struggle between the more intimate "Du" and the more formal "Sie". Even with only one side of the correspondence, we can sense that they are both seeking a common idiom. From the beginning, they realize too that, given Nazi censorship, discretion in what they write is essential.

MOPE TO VERA

Postcard, Leipzig, 27/28 January 1936

Dear Vera–that sounds a little less affectionate than "liebe Vera," but Annelie thinks–this will be read…. Dear reader, please stop reading. —

We are still sitting in the Café Merkur…. I hope you are sleeping well while I am writing. My heartfelt greetings to you and I will greet you in London soon, Mope

MOPE TO VERA

Leipzig, 29 January 1936

I am writing to you, Veralein, in order to thank you for your lines.[6] They include, wafted by expressions of gratitude–not deserved by me–your address–is it meant to encourage me to write?

Such a shame that your stay was too short for us to get to know each other sufficiently. I am constantly trying to form an image of you–not an external one, a photographic surrogate helps me with that, but an internal one. I am lacking impressions concerning the things you think about, and I would like to know how much of what you think you also talk about–and how strongly you regulate that. Maybe your intelligence or inner deliberations–I do not consider them repression–prevent you from thinking out loud in an easy manner. In all probability, a little more spontaneity would make the sparks fly easier from pole to pole. I am writing this–and maybe you will think it strange, at the beginning of our correspondence–in order to find a catalyst so as to make you react more easily.

In my thoughts of you, I have given you a different name–"Lilongo"–not for lack of thought or imagination, but can there be an expression of emotion that you can imbue phonetically with more feelings than this one? Even its consonants make sounds when you speak it, and it is full of tenderness that you can only feel as light that suddenly begins to shine in a lot of darkness.

Lilongo–most affectionately–Mope

VERA

Journal entry, 29 January 1936

Today, I took up my London life again!

I came back yesterday evening around 9 o'clock (Tuesday). Wednesday morning, I left London; I spent five days in Leipzig.

They admired me, and I met a human being whom I like, and I have a true and good friend in Annelie. I will continue writing another day.

---

6   Prior to leaving Leipzig, Vera must have mailed or given to Annelie Friemann a now lost first letter to Mope.

MOPE TO VERA

Leipzig, 4 February 1936

Lilongo–no, I won't be miserly with the expression of my feelings–

My beautiful, dear Lilongo! Thank you for not rejecting the name for you that maybe does not say the same thing to your ear as it does to mine, and for your letter.

"Not even a week ago, we hardly knew anything about each other," you write. Human or creature experiences cannot be measured with time pieces. They are much too rare for that, and in just a few seconds, we can experience such infinite things in happiness or pain that many years–maybe an entire life–cannot capture comparable moments with the same sense of destiny. We have known each other for one week–Lilongo–we know each other very little and still, we know each other in an immeasurably infinite place in time, as I carry you and what I feel through you inside me. And I would not write this to you if I was not sure that the feeling is mutual. We are not able to see the future and do not know what will result from our experience, but it is beautiful and full of strong emotions.

I have ordered a ticket to London and will arrive there on Friday, April 3–to visit my sister Hanna. In the long time until then, I hope to hear more about you and your well-being and wish that Lilongo will always be pleased with Mope's letters. About this one, too.

I wish you everything beautiful, Your Mope

MOPE TO VERA

Leipzig, 10 February 1936

My dear friend Lilongo, many thanks for your letter with "Du," that brought to me an advancement in the frame of your emotions, although that "little word" was paid out more by force than free will. As we sat together two weeks ago in the station restaurant in Leipzig, suddenly, I could not say "Sie" anymore. For me, it is an awakening feeling of tenderness–a desire to caress another human being–to worry about that person and to be good to her. Don't you agree that this "Du" is full of meaning?

Next Wednesday, I intend to depart from here and would like to ask you to send me a good photograph of you by then, one in which you are laughing. I can then imagine, according to my mood, that you are laughing with me or at me. If you are laughing at me, I will tell myself that you are right and that the bad mood needs to make room for a better softer one. Lilongo, if you are laughing with me, I am in a good mood and send you my heartfelt greetings, because that is what I hope.

Your friend Mope

VERA

Journal entry, London, 16 February 1936

Just a few words to say: I am feeling completely balanced in the knowledge that I have a boyfriend, a human being who is intelligent and kind. What more do you really want?

My work makes me happy; I am much more on top of the matter now and have a better overview.

My Muttilein is an angel, so full of intelligence. How she uncovered an indecisiveness resting in my subconscious during a simple conversation yesterday evening and made the right decision when we talked about the course of my life. If I should marry in the near future, I should keep working in my current profession.

Fifteen: Mope in Palestine

21 February through 3 April 1936

Mope's ambition to emigrate to Palestine filled him with excitement as he set off in mid-February on an exploratory visit during which he would advance plans with his brother Adolf, and sister Alice–both already settled there–to get their mother out of Germany. He too had every intention to relocate to Palestine. However, he was so smitten by his new relationship with Vera that he was already hoping beyond hope that he could persuade her to join him in moving to Palestine. That aspiration is semi-concealed in his letters to her in which he describes his journey, fully aware that after Palestine he will travel on to London.

MOPE TO VERA

Adria, northern Italy, 21 February 1936

Jugoslavenski Lloyd JL
   S/S Kraljica Marija

Fig. 63 Photograph of steam ship Kraljica Marija.

Off to my side, a five-man band is playing Hungarian dances. Not even two meters away from me is the cello whose constant strum is meant to provide inspiration for writing. Should I refrain from writing or should I dare to let loose a letter that will be confused by too much noise?

My dear, beautiful Lilongo, I was very pleased with your letter and the card that reached me on the morning of my departure from Leipzig. The awareness alone that a human being who stands outside my immediate circle thinks in friendship of the old bachelor makes me happy![7]

The last few days–departure–night in Munich–the drive through the Austrian Alps–sun and rain–snowy landscapes and blooming heather–eternal tunnels–psychological studies of other Palestine-bound travelers–fulfillment of 25 years of longing to come to Palestine –and so overwhelmed by an infinite number of impressions that cannot be regulated by brain functions, so that this writ is probably quite addled, even without the music right next to me. The piece that is playing now is called "A Trip to Santiago." The musicians certainly have no idea what *Erez Yisrael* [the land of Israel] means to their listeners, otherwise they would not play such kitsch. But that is neither here nor there. It is much more important that the ship, as a means of transport, seems to offer every amenity, also does not let you sense in any way that this is an emigration ship en route to Palestine. Unfortunately, travel agencies only inform you about comfort and not at all about ambience, because payment cannot be demanded for that and the agencies do not get any ambience commission–which, since Jewish, would be forbidden in Nazi Germany anyway.

I will be very happy to find mail from you on my arrival in Haifa. Will I?....

Your Mope who asks for pardon for his confusion!

VERA

Journal entry, Saturday, 8 March 1936

Just a few words to recognize, with the deepest appreciation, a fate that led us here to London; work that interests me and that makes me happy; gave me people who are good to me or led them to cross my path; let me meet Mope who seems to have many of the character traits that I had

---

7   The difference in age between Mope and Vera–almost eleven years–caused him ("the old bachelor") to be a little self-conscious at the beginning of their relationship.

hoped to find in a boyfriend. I am grateful and full of expectation in the thought of the near future, Mope's visit at the beginning of next month.

I wonder how we will get along! I will not be disappointed, but will anticipate it in the knowledge to have had these last few fulfilling weeks, filled with jubilant excitement and thankfulness. I will endeavor to let my surroundings feel my happiness!

MOPE TO VERA

Jerusalem, 9 March 1936

Yesterday was a beautiful day, the sun was shining gloriously and was blown into my face by a pleasant, fresh wind, and then, on top of it all, I received your sweet letter which is friendly and almost a little motherly–and that made the receiver feel really good.

Now you want to know a little about my travel impressions. They are still in a mess and very incomplete, because I still have to see an infinite number of things before I can give a final judgment–if that is even possible. The sea voyage was wonderful, despite partly choppy seas. As we saw the coast appear on the morning before our arrival, I was completely overwhelmed. Apart from a sentimental reaction, even when viewed from a distance, the country makes a much more grandiose impression than any other that I have come to know so far.

Mountains and valleys–Hermon and Lebanon, bright white covered with snow and shining in the sun that burnishes from a firmament that is so blue that it could never be described in a letter. The Carmel (in German "wine mountain of God"), which is green again, reaches far into the sea and behind that the hills which are becoming more fertile through Jewish labor–these hills let you understand at first sight the reason why this land was called the granary of Rome and why it was coveted by everyone who saw it.

Haifa: horrible customs control. Everything was touched, appraised, the body searched for weapons–disgusting. Outside of the customs area which they were not allowed to set foot on, my brother and my sister-in-law waited for two hours until I arrived.[8] We drove up into the city that is expanding in a hyper-American fashion. A brand–new house,

---

8   Mope's older brother, Adolf, and his wife, Gretl, who emigrated from Germany to Palestine in 1935, had settled in the port city of Haifa.

one next to the other. The roadwork cannot keep up at the same speed. And the view of the sea and the mountains, and, for the first time in many years, merry, happy, laughing human beings who don't exist in Germany any longer. Wherever I went, in the countryside and in the city, Jews who are dancing in the street after work, happy with their lives and their freedom.

They work terribly hard. The battle for survival is bitterly hard, but they laugh when work is done and that is magnificent. Besides cafes and movie theatres, I have seen no places for amusement so far. Of course there are often concerts and visiting theatre plays–even in the villages– because the people here are hungry for culture, but cabarets and variety shows are not needed here; if the joy is too much they dance on the street at night.

And the buses and cars have to get by them quietly and furtively so that they don't disrupt things. The bus drivers often sing Hebrew songs while they maneuver the difficult mountain roads in the cities up and down and are artists in their profession without any nervousness. You cannot imagine more heterogeneous elements than the ones that have come together here in the last fifteen years and still, the harmony is great and amazing–even with all the ruling political and cultural differences. The will to be free from the ghetto, to be a free human being in our own country, shines from every eye.

Here I am witness as to how quickly the people adapt to new ways of living. The ones from relatively uncivilized countries would hardly be able to exist anymore without bathtubs, shower stalls and similar comforts–even in the countryside, and they really do look like they make much use of them; and the initially over-civilized ones, especially well-to-do women who had three to six servants back there, feel happy without help, cook, fry, bake on Neft (Petroleum) and wonder why they lived differently once upon a time.

And all of these impressions are optically interwoven with the Orient in the most concentrated form. Arabs and Bedouins with donkeys and camels and in the Arabic parts of the cities the colorful, loud marketplaces where everything produced in the Orient and the Occident is traded. On the country roads large herds of goats, camel caravans and by the wells Rebekkahs with jugs, everything from clothes to forms of living and movement is like it was four thousand years ago, when our forefathers cheated their fathers-in-law out of herds of cattle because they were cheated with the women.[9]

On Saturday evening, I was asked to a surprise party. Most people wore costumes to celebrate the Purimfest[10] and spirits were high. Mope was a non-dancer, as usual, but had a wonderful time anyway. He would have danced with Lilongo: such a shame that she was not there.

I am invited tonight as well and it is already almost 9.30, so I have to go. Since I hope to receive another letter from you at my brother's address before my departure on the 27th, this report had to be written today despite the invitation.

Lilongo, I think of you all the time; I think some people call that "love." Unfortunately, I can only give you a written kiss in thanks for your letter. But I will personally retrieve it in London and am looking forward to that a lot. Your Mope

Fig. 64 Watercolor of shore at Lake Tiberias, 1934. Later, the picture hung on the wall of Mope's bedroom in London as a cherished memento of his earlier desire to settle in Palestine. Artist's signature indecipherable.

---

9   In the biblical story, Jacob was tricked by his uncle, Laban, into marrying Leah before he could marry her younger sister, Rachel. In turn, Jacob greatly increased his flocks and herds to the cost of Laban and his sons (Genesis, chs. 29-30).

10 The Feast of Purim, marking the deliverance of the Jews from genocide in Persia at the time of King Ahasuerus in the fourth century B.C.E., is celebrated with merrymaking and the wearing of masks and costumes. The event is the subject of the Book of Esther. In 1936, the first night of Purim fell on Saturday, 7 March.

MOPE TO VERA

Haifa, Hotel Villa Migdal, 27 March 1936

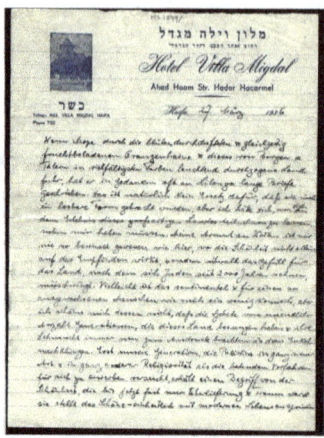

Fig. 65 Front page of Mope's letter to Vera, Haifa, 27 March 1936.

As Mope was driving through the blossoming, fragrant orange groves which were laden with fruit at the same time, and through this country crossed by mountains and valleys glowing in multihued colors, in his thoughts he often wrote long letters to Lilongo. Of course, that is no excuse for the fact that they were not put into readable form, but I would have had to have you next to me in order to let you participate in experiencing this magnificent country. I have never been so aware of my lack of words as I am here, where the beauty not only affects your own sensations, but where the overall feeling for the land that Jews have longed for these two thousand years resonates. Maybe that is sentimental and for a grown man like me a little funny, but I am not ashamed of it, that the prayers of an infinite number of generations who sang about this land and gave expression to their longing again and again, should linger in their grandchildren. Not until our generation, which is attempting to acquire Palestine for itself in a completely new way and in a completely different form of religion than our praying forefathers, have we been able to envision the true beauty that, until now, was only the stuff of stories and dreams. It reconstitutes the beautiful, consistent with modern demands of life harmonizing through plantings, irrigation and construction, what had been dried out and atrophied by "prayers only."

My dear, sweet girl, after I returned to Haifa from a trip across Palestine that lasted several days, I received your letter and I was so happy that I would have loved to have come to you via airmail in order to shorten your understandable anxiety. Now I hope that this letter reaches you before me, especially since I will be there presumably on Sunday and not, as originally intended, on Friday. Since I cannot, out of decency, arrive at my Orthodox family's home on Shabbat (Saturday), I will probably have to spend a day in Paris. I would be very grateful to you if you could let my siblings know about this because I will not write to them at this time.

The ship leaves around 6 o'clock and we home comers will take our dinner in the open Mediterranean!

Dearest Lilongo–Your Mope

VERA

Journal entry, London, Friday, 3 April 1936

Actually, I am expecting Mope today. I have not had any news for the last two and a half weeks, but such is life.

I still enjoy my work tremendously; I feel that I can achieve something and I am actually building something.

When will Mope arrive? How kind time is as a foundation. In earlier times, I would have suffered today, and how do I look at it today–as a thrilling performance. The older one gets, the more impersonal or of two minds one becomes to oneself.

Sixteen: Palestine or Vera?

4 through 24 April 1936

The essence of Mope's ten-day stopover in England, from Saturday, 4 April, through Wednesday, 15 April 1936, coinciding both with Passover and Easter, is preserved through Vera's private journal. In one of her longest journal entries, Vera captures every joyful moment as well as the comic pathos and uncertainty of their situation.

On the Monday evening following his arrival, Vera was a guest at the home of Mope's sister and brother-in-law, Hanna and Fred Rau, for the traditional Seder evening, marking the first night of Passover. Her anxieties and fear of faux-pas are well captured in her journal. Her total lack of experience of Jewish ritual observance is evident in her misspelling of "Seda" and her incorrect dowsing of a lighted match that should have been left to burn itself out.

Because of the demands of her working day at Marks & Spencer, she and Mope could spend only their evenings together, though these hours in each other's company served to strengthen their mutual feelings.

On Friday, 10 April (Good Friday), Mope proposed marriage with the goal that they should settle together in Palestine. Two days later, on Easter Sunday, they took a day trip to Canterbury. In the romantic setting of the grounds of the cathedral, Mope proposed again. Despite harboring serious reservations brought about by her hardly knowing him and doubts about Palestine, Vera tentatively consented to marry him. Three days later, Mope had to return to Leipzig. For the moment, they agreed to keep their engagement a secret.

VERA

Journal entries, London, 14 April through Saturday 18 April 1936

Actually, I meant to write in here for the last few days, but I was just too tired, too exhausted in the evening and much too absorbed and occupied with myself to put pen to paper.

I would like to recapitulate the facts, short and quick, completely objectively!

So, on Saturday, April 4, at night, Mope arrived in London.

Saturday evening, late, around 10.00 p.m., I came home from the store to find his letter in which he announced his arrival and asked me to let his siblings know; diffidently, I did so at that very late hour and found out that Fred Rau would make his way to the train station, and I declined his invitation to accompany him.

Sunday, after lunch, I met Mope at Marble Arch and found him looking better than I remembered, thinner and more tanned. He told me that he intends to emigrate to Palestine to give his mother the opportunity to pull her money from Germany and to go to the land, shall we say, of his dreams himself.

He told me about his sister Ruth and her attitude again in detail, told me that he had not seen his mother yet. To our house around 8.00 p.m., too many people at dinner.

General conversation, several unintentional, somewhat tactless remarks from one of our house guests that did not disconcert Mope at all; allusions to being a bachelor and a marriage, etc., etc., and he responded that he will be going back to Germany. Mutti's impression: a very likable man, a nice face, nothing more.

To Raus' for Seda Monday evening. I experienced a rather strange evening. To be perfectly honest, it was disappointing, but that was probably, because I had been looking forward to it way too much. I was invited to Mope's sister's for Seda, which Mope explained to me could be literally translated as "Orderliness." I dressed up as decently as was humanly possible in the greatest hurry and took a taxi to arrive on time, but when I got there no one was around. Something like that does ruin the mood just a little. It took until shortly before 7.30 p.m. when Mope and his mother arrived. Before that, Mr. Rau, whom I like very much, by the way, walked around the room praying loudly, while Hannah and I talked.

Then, as I said, Mope and his mother, who was also visiting London, joined us. The latter looks more like a distinguished officer's widow, anything, anything but a Jewish woman, especially a pious one. Another guest arrived and we sat down to dinner.

Then came the long, long rite of the Seda evening; before that, another little embarrassing scene: Mope's mother lit the candles on the table and then threw the blazing match into the flowerpot standing next to the candles and cried, "Well, burn out this instant!" and I, just to be of assistance, blew it out. Then Mope said to me in the most charming way that was an action that was forbidden, but added immediately that he would have done the same thing. However, his mother was certainly a little paralyzed by it.

I was disappointed with the evening, did not exchange a single word with Mope's mother before the rite, and only recall that she said to me, she was unfamiliar with the ritual circle in Frankfurt, but that she understood things to be very strange, especially there, and, on the other hand, much more liberal. Then good-bye.

Mope accompanied me home. Fred Rau's friend was there as well, and so, there was no opportunity to exchange even one private word. A kiss in front of the door, nothing that touched me deeply.

Wednesday: In the black coat and black dress, extremely punctual to the Regent Palace–no Mope there. To Piccadilly Circus–no Mope. Back to the Regent Palace, and there he came, twenty minutes late, since he had had a meeting with his brother-in-law and had to wait until Fred Rau's mother left.

Wandered to a small café-restaurant in Oxford Street for dinner, where we could sit without being disturbed, and I mainly told him about my work, and he asked if I was emphasizing the love for my work on purpose and that I was doing the same thing in my letters. I explained to him how this work was finally the solution to the ever so difficult choice of a profession, and that this was the reason and the explanation for that.

Then, we went on to the Ariston Café in Oxford Circus, where he told me about the corners, the hard ones, of life, on which sensitive people hurt themselves so often and so unavoidably, which makes them shy away from everything after a while.

Then he took me home with the underground, and I quickly put him on a bus here in Blythe Road. From the upper deck, he called down to ask me for another date for Thursday. Since that is the day before Good Friday, my work will continue through the afternoon, so he agreed to pick me up around 8.00 p.m. here at home.

I raced home from the store to clean up and freshen up a little, and there he was already, was led in by grinning people, and then, as fast as possible–once I was ready–I extracted him–good-bye–and off to High Street Kensington to the Majestic Restaurant for dinner.

Then a café on Earl's Court Road, where he told me about the contrariness in his company, the spite and the nitpicking of the business owners, his interrupted university studies, the suspicion of a theft from these co-partners; his obligations towards his obviously pigheaded father, who demanded he take his contractual place in the business, his need to assure that place for himself in order to avoid becoming that constantly changing, anchorless, and unstable man, and then his obligation to his mother who had lost her husband and only had him as the one single son still in Leipzig, and her expectation that he pave the way for her.

A walk home through Addison Road and back alleys, walked into a dead-end street and declined a kiss, since one does not want the other to think that one led him there for that purpose.

Nothing agreed on for the following Good Friday morning. Arranged a call between 1 and 2.

He called around 3 o'clock, and asked if I thought it would be worth it to see him for an hour. I said yes. To Marble Arch again, 12 minutes late again. First a little walk through Hyde Park, then suggested the café in the park. The main tearoom was full, but there was a small table free in the lounge. Me in the blue Trieste skirt, beige jumper, tweed coat, and a small blue cap.

He said–No, I forgot something important. Talked to Muttilein in the evening about all of my doubts, and Muttilein's good advice to tell Mope in no uncertain terms that we do not own a single penny, and wondering if he would still be so keen on me.

So back now to what Mope said: he had been plagued all that time by a very grave consideration; if he had the right to ask another human being, a girl, to come with him to a foreign country, to which he was also going with his mother's money, a girl that he supposed did not have anything herself either.

He would not demand an immediate answer, since something like that deserved some consideration. He said: to build something with two people could mean ease or burden, and I said that would of course depend on how much or little trust one had in the other.

Saturday, Easter Saturday very busy at work and no time to think. I promised to call him towards evening to make arrangements for a meeting on Sunday.

Suggested Canterbury. He would call me again at home after 10.00 p.m. to talk about an exact time, etc.

He called around 10.30 p.m. We will meet shortly before 10.00 a.m. on Easter Sunday.

He met me walking from the train station, had arranged for seats, and we found an empty compartment. We had been invited to spend the evening at Raus'.

Muttilein had impressed upon me: whatever you do, do not commit to anything, for God's sake!

On the train, after some time, I still owed him an answer and me, that really was not necessary yet and would need some more deliberation. How long until he would have to leave for Palestine? No answer.

Canterbury in the sun, after it had been hailing while we were on the train. Wandered around the city wall, then through the streets, and I told him I was glad that he had come to London. He: he hoped that I would be just as happy about it in 50 years.

Then, into the wonderful front garden of the Cathedral. Met a priest that Mope was convinced was the Archbishop–maybe it was really him–who said, "A happy Easter to you!" and I, "Thank you so much, the same to you", and both of us happy that he wished that for us of all people.[11] The Cathedral beautiful, enjoyed it together, decorated with the most precious flowers and harmoniously balanced crypt vaults. Trip back during which he talked as if I had agreed, which I had not done at all, ate in the Pullman dining car that was empty except for an old, sleepy uncle.

Then back home for tea, changed, and off to Raus'. Asked him on the train to make *no* official announcements this evening.

Him on the bus: if I would be alright that he told his mother something, and I said No, and why not, because I wanted to talk to my own mother about it first; he had assumed that I had already done so, and I said no, I had to come to my own decision first in order to be able to talk to her about it. He would not say anything. That was understood. I appreciate that very much!!!!!

A very harmonious and enjoyable evening at Raus', spent time with his mother, told him about that, made him happy, and asked that I talk to Muttilein. Made arrangements to meet the next day, Monday, at 11 o'clock in the Strand Palace Hotel.

---

11   The priest was Dr. Hewlett Johnson (1874-1966), the notorious "Red Dean", known for his left-wing ideological views. Mope was to catch sight of him again in Moscow in 1937 (28 September).

Talked to my sweet one in the evening, said that I had made my decision and only made it dependent on her final judgment. She was stunned at first, the distance, Palestine, me there, with a man without money, whom she did not know, a man she did not even believe or was sure was competent. Both of us a little anchorless and, shall we say, hysterical.

Into Muttilein's bedroom at 8 Monday morning, told Pepper that I was serious, and still a little shaky.

Then, 10 minutes late (I will have to do something about that in the future), met Mope. Asked immediately if I said anything about it, me affirmative and told him, Mutti said that she could not judge yet, she hardly knew him at all, and that he looked likable, *voilà tout*! Then home for lunch–I had never before gone home feeling so fearful.

Introduced Mope to Muttilein once again. Told him before that, how funny I felt, and him: Yes, but not yesterday at Canterbury, right? Me: That had been different circumstances from the ones at my home. I have not been that excited or have never before been excited in that way. Mutti openly off towards her goal to ask him about everything clearly and succinctly. Here until 5.

(I forgot something: on Easter Sunday, I made a decision for myself while I was in my bedroom, and the following became clear to me, "Well, what do you want? Here is a kind and nice man, and why won't you give him an answer to the question he keeps asking you, what or who are you waiting for?")

Until it was finally 5 o'clock. I felt like a slaughtered sacrificial animal, that exhausted, x times because of excitement to get to a certain place, and tried to support Mope's arguments. Changed to go to his sister Ruth in Mill Hill. Found it after hours of searching around 7.30 p.m.

Then, when we finally left, it was so late and I was so exhausted that I only wanted to go home. Mope harrying: I should come to Raus' as a favor to him. I agreed, although we were not able to announce our visit by telephone, and it was close to 9 o'clock.

Had his mother called away from dinner and only told her that Vera will go with me to Palestine. I said immediately that I do not want anyone else to hear about it, then burst in on an almost finished dinner, a matter that went completely *contre coeur for* me.

The gentlemen retired, and I had the first opportunity to talk to Mope's mother alone, and it alienated me when, after I said how difficult it was to leave my Muttilein and to have to give up my beloved job, she replied, "Well, you won't be giving up that job for the time being, will you?"

So, I went home dissatisfied, quite agitated, filled with doubts, transferring several times, all alone the entire way. And just as I was getting on, we made arrangements for me to come out to him tomorrow (Tuesday) after the store, if possible, shortly after 5.00 p.m., in order to pick him up from packing for his departure and have dinner at my house. Muttilein told me she wanted to get to know Mope and talk to him. That was quite alright with me, but I insisted on this: That I would pick up Mope out there in Golder's Green, and I did not regret it. I did not get away from the store until 5.30 and did not reach there until 6.30, and I tried to imagine what kind of a dingy digs it would be, and I was very pleasantly surprised to find a prettily furnished room.

I heard from Mope that Mutti had met his mother at lunch with the Raus and that Mutti had told her that it would be much more important for Mope to marry a rich girl, and if he insisted on going to Palestine, he should go there by himself first and try to establish an existence, before he would ask me to join him. Then Mope had come into the room, had heard that last suggestion and had refused most energetically. He would want to build something together with me and according to my wishes there.

I asked him if he was sure that we were doing the right thing, and that I did not believe that I would fit in in Palestine, and that, in my mindset, I might be thought of as an anti-Semite; and he said that I would feel at home there and that they would welcome one who was returning to Judaism with doubled joy; and I replied that I would have an easier time in America than in Palestine, and that I did know I was able to fit in anywhere in the world, but Palestine of all places!

Then he suggested to me that we should see the land together, because he could understand and appreciate that I would feel more responsibility towards Palestine compared to any other country after visiting there. I explained to him again how much I like England, my job, and everything else, and how much more I can earn here, I have relationships with people here, etc., and he responded: He would not allow me to feed him, and that his money would be worth much less here than in Palestine.

Then he said, he wanted to confess something to me that he had never told anyone else, something which he had discounted decidedly on his trip here. Should I decide to doom everything to failure because of that, he would rather do without Palestine than without me.

I thanked him, and said I was completely clear on the fact that nowadays, you could not talk Jews out of exchanging Palestine for Europe in all good conscience.

He explained to me that he was of the firm opinion that you had full responsibility for your future children and that they were put into the world for your own joy and out of your own love, and you should raise them in a country where they were not considered outsiders, and that in Palestine, children were taken care of especially well.

I told him, among other things, that I appreciate him, because I know that he is kind, but at the same time that I knew it would take him quite some time, until a thought process is executed, or better, until it had found its way down the long circuit to a full understanding between us.

I called Mutti to tell her that we would get there later and was completely blissful about how well she had liked Mrs. Felsenstein. Then I felt completely happy. Then here for dinner, and Fred Rau came around 11.00 p.m. to pick him up for his journey, and we spent a harmonious and nice evening.

MOPE TO VERA

En route from Dover to Ostend, 15 April 1936

Just now the boat was set in motion and I have to write. I am very happy that I was able to talk to you for just a bit early today and sad that we will not see each other again for quite a time. Communicating through letters is really only makeshift, and if you only knew how happy it makes me to walk arm in arm with you and to feel you with and next to me, you would understand how frozen this hand that is writing to you feels.

Dear, beautiful, tall Lilongo, I hope that our separation does not last too long and I am looking forward to a reunion, albeit when unknown to me at this time but which I hope does not keep us waiting for too long. I send my most ardent greetings and kiss your hand and your lovely beautiful mouth in my thoughts.

Now for real–Your Mope

VERA

Journal entry, Sunday, 24 April 1936

I am looking forward to a life together with Mope. Will it be here in London, when will it come to be? How will it be fashioned?

Seventeen: Dover

18 April through 1 June 1936

Mope and Vera's next rendezvous would not be until the Whitsun break at the end of May when she could take time off work. After some back and forth in their correspondence, they agreed to meet for a hurried two days in the English coastal town of Dover. None of Vera's letters from this period survive, though the journals she kept bring to light her innermost thoughts.

MOPE TO VERA

Leipzig, 23 April 1936

I am looking forward to your news and have now been sad about its absence for four evenings. Sometimes, I see Annelie and then we always talk a little of Vera, not much, because then I would have to betray what you will reveal to her before too long–that we are to be married.

Dear, dear Lilongo, do you think of me and our togetherness, of thought and feeling and everyday things that, despite the harshness of life, we want to shape into days of celebration? I think of it a lot and of you and sometimes I start brooding: Do you feel inwardly connected to me? Can you take on so many difficulties as the creation of a new existence will bring out? It is part and parcel of thinking human beings that they are racked by doubt, and they can only become closer if they write or talk about it openly, because they will come to love each other more and more through mutual understanding.

I embrace you and kiss you in my thoughts and stroke your beautiful black hair that is darker than the nights I spend dreaming about you.

MOPE TO VERA

Leipzig, 30 April 1936

My weekend was a bit soured by the embarrassing message that I would have to secure a new domicile per June 1. After three sleepless nights, my landlady has come to the heroic decision to give me notice to vacate.

I have not talked to anyone here about our plans for the future. They concern the "how." The "what" is not a problem anymore, since I know that we will do it together and I not only have the necessary will and courage, but also the urgency, because I don't want us to wait for each other for too long. Tomorrow is the first of May that reminds people of the spring and the sun one can only see as a blurred shape in this cold land.

MOPE TO VERA

Leipzig, 6 May 1936

When I arrived home late last night, I found your dear letter there. It is difficult to answer all your questions about personal strength of character, but I am glad that you ask me so openly. They show me that you have trust in me and that makes me happy (although I would have considered that understood if someone had asked me if you trusted me).

I have spent the last twenty-four hours in philosophical contemplation concerning your questions to me. There are many opportunities to prove that one is resolute and I deliberately start with the answers at a point where I show no willpower at all, that is smoking. However, you are wrong in assuming that it is contrary to my nature to have no control over my cigarette consumption. For the last few days, I have been smoking 17 cigarettes per day and I had wanted to lower that number a little more before I told you about it!

I have told you a few things about my life, and I am convinced that willpower was essential in order to emerge not only as non-debilitated, but surely as an even stronger human being. The chances to show willpower are not that numerous in a life lived in a middle-class existence, but I believe that I have fought unconditionally for everything that I believed in, even if there was strong opposition. The question whether I am resolute or not I believe I can answer with yes in all good conscience.

During my Palestine trip, I made a very far-reaching decision for the life of my dear mother as well as mine, without letting others advise me concerning the fundamental idea–the decision is known to you–and I planned to conduct the implementation of the idea regardless of all consequences. But, to complicate that, I asked Lilongo in London, if she wants to unite her life with mine. The circumstances of our situation are unusual. I am anything but a frivolous man and was fully aware of the difficulties when I asked you.

If you build a new life together with someone, the normal habits you had before undergo a big adjustment, and then both have to help each other in order to create new ways of living. The most radical change in moving to Palestine is to go into the trenches in the frame of a life led in civilization with all its comforts, in contrast to a life reclaiming land as a laborer and living in tents. The likelihood of merging that kind of life with a middle-class one is impossible. But to sink from one level of middle-class life to a lower one is hard to bear, especially if you are alone when you do it.

The unrest in Palestine has disquieted you. We old Zionists are unfortunately aware, through earlier events of the Jewish-Arabic problem, that the settlement work, like any other settlement by the way, cannot be accomplished without sacrifice. However, up to this point, it was always shown, fortunately, that such tragic events have contributed to unity and firmness in our own ranks and, in the end, aided the accomplishment of the idea. This evening, I read an editorial in *The Times* entitled "Arab and Jew," that affirmed to me that the English people will carry on with the realization of their promise to create an official and legal homestead for the Jews in Palestine. Sadly, sadly, we are not far enough to make a final decision on where we can build our tents and until it is that time, a lot of things will have to have been resolved.

If I can change and adjust, is the hardest question to answer, because it cannot be thought through to the end without given facts. Please don't be alarmed over the "where" of our future. You still have my greatest declaration of love that I could give to you, Lilongo, that I will not make our togetherness conditional on the promise that we can live in my most longed-for home country.

VERA

Journal entry, 10 May 1936

It has been quite a while now since I wrote anything in here: In the meantime, I have come to the unshakable decision to establish my marriage with Mope here in England, and judging by his last letter, he is really prepared to make that sacrifice.

This time, his words have calmed my worries and given me clarity. And I asked him openly if he has the energy, initiative, and ability to adjust. He did not misunderstand the questions, and the way in which he answered them and commented on them, made me so deeply happy. Now I hope that we will be able to spend Whitsuntide together, and I hope that many things will become clearer during those days, as far as our plans for the future are concerned. I am looking forward to seeing him, I really like him, I trust him and we understand each other.

MOPE TO VERA

Leipzig, 10 May 1936

This evening, I was in the movie theater with my mother. Marlene Dietrich movie "Desire"; very well acted and amusing. Then I accompanied her home and–with the exception of a break for a cup of coffee–went home myself. Now I am–after I finished reading a book–most definitely ready for bed. But I have two very sweet letters from you in front of me and for me not to write you back would probably not be good for the peace of my sleep, so I want to write a few lines to you and thank you, because the letters gave me a lot of joy.

The first one already told me that your doubts apparently did not become a chronic condition, and the second one told me that you want to see me over Whitsun, and I think that is so wonderful, even in my thoughts, that the reality–which I am not allowed to even imagine concretely, especially for want of housing–will surely have to be amazing.

Your reasons against Palestine that my dear mother explained to me I understand, of course. However, I intend to win you over to my way of thinking insofar as we two people are the most important people of all. Of course, that is not to say that we will forget or neglect those people to whom we are attached and spiritually connected. But the younger generation always has the right to itself and we, too, will have to understand that one day.

VERA

Journal entry, 12 May 1936

Apparently, I am much more closely connected to Mope than I wanted to admit to myself. Every time when something happens to me now that unsettles me and I just want to have a good cry about it–of course not in the literal sense–and would like to have someone to console me and talk to me, I wish for Mope and his strong embrace.

MOPE TO VERA

Leipzig, 17 May 1936

I have to and want to assume that the wish you expressed, namely that we will spend the holidays together, was meant seriously. It is very sad that you have to stay at work so late on the Saturday before the Whitsun holiday. Don't you have a few hours of overtime that you could use to set off a few hours on that day? I have to be back at the office early Tuesday morning, just like you, and if I travelled to England, we would only have Sunday in order for me to get back in time. Apart from everything else, the journey would be very exhausting, because we would hardly be able to tell each other everything and report everything in one day that two people like us have to tell each other. I am afraid that we will hardly have been able to dispel the psychological distance created by separation when we will have to say good-bye again, and that is a spiritual strain that might adversely affect our relationship, because too much will be left unsaid.

My housing situation is still in limbo, i.e. I will look at a room tomorrow at noon and will decide then which one I will take.

VERA

Journal entry, 18 May 1936

Life really does not offer too many breaks for me to take a deep breath.

So–for the moment: I do not know where or when I will be able to settle down with Mope nor what he is going to be able to do workwise. And things do not look too good where my career is concerned either. Life does ask a lot of a person and it takes a great amount of schooling in order not to become indifferent, hard, and tired of it all. However, I have now found compensation–my Mope. I wonder how our next meeting will go.

MOPE TO VERA

Leipzig, 21 May 1936

Today was Ascension Day and the rain poured down from morning till night so that many of the projected men's games were probably washed away.[12] This morning, my breakfast table had the loveliest decoration that I could possibly desire–your blue letter. The foreign exchange inspectors had opened it, but it did not suffer any delay and that made me very happy.

 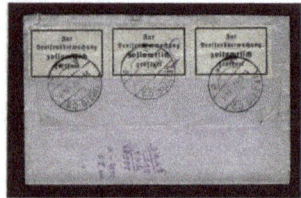

Fig. 66 (a) and (b) Envelope with German Censors stamps indicating that the correspondence between Vera and Mope was frequently vetted by the Nazi authorities.

Today too, my mother and I told my cousin Semy, the Senior Partner at the Gebrüder Felsenstein that I have a girl I want to marry. When he saw your picture, he said you were not only beautiful but extremely beautiful. He will probably be grateful to me because I procured such a cousin for him, whose excellent attributes my dear mother rightly praised very highly. The guy had tears in his eyes because my decision caught him unprepared, but he cannot object in all good conscience and only understand it. I authorized him to tell the other cousins, as far as he thinks it necessary.

---

12 Mope seems to be referring to German track and field trials prior to the Olympic Games that were to be held in Berlin in August 1936.

I was also very happy about Annelie's success with her doctoral thesis and admire her for the drive with which she asserted herself.[13] By the way, she asked me today, in a very resolute manner, if I was meeting you over Whitsun, or maybe someone else. Did you maybe tell her about us? She does not know anything from me, other than that we write back and forth.

MOPE TO VERA

Leipzig, 28 May 1936

Today is the 28th of May. A critical day for my family. The twins Grete and Alice were born thirty-five years ago and two years ago my blessed father died.

Unfortunately, I have to cause you a little trouble, because I do not know anything at all about hotels in Dover. Please make room reservations for us in a good hotel, and let me know the name of the hotel by telegraph. The address for a telegram, since Semy is the only other person here besides me, is: "Felsenstein, Leipzig." Now, here is the most important point. Please have Fred Rau give you enough money. As you know, I can only take out ten Reichsmark which won't get me very far, and I don't want to run into problems.[14] What we don't spend, you can give back to him, but the good old boy should, just for once, bleed for his brother-in-law.

By the way, don't forget your bathing suit, because I hope that the weather will be nice and the ocean warm enough for bathing.

VERA

Journal Entry, 29 May 1936

Just a few lines: tomorrow evening, I am going to meet Mope in Dover. These next few days will give me a perfectly clear picture, I hope, of whether he is the right one, if he is a man who can be a daredevil but who can also be trusted in practical things. How I want this trip to be

---

13 Annelie had just received her diploma as a dentist from the University of Leipzig.
14 A law had been passed as early as 1932, limiting the export of currency from Germany to 10 Reichmarks (equivalent to less than one Pound Sterling). The law was strictly enforced by the Nazis when they came to power with frequent censoring of letters sent abroad as an ostensible means of currency control.

a *success*! I have to tell him that I really do not want to go to Palestine and talk to him about career opportunities here, and be with the man in person. I hope this will be a satisfying, confirming, and worthwhile trip.

VERA

Journal Entry, 7 June 1936

Last Sunday, I was in Dover. I hurried there Saturday night after the store closed. Mope was waiting for me at the train station–it was after midnight when I arrived. Even that late at night, right after we arrived in our Brown House Hotel, I told him that I do not want nor was able to go to Palestine right now and he acknowledged that without argument, and he was willing to try to establish an existence here by my side and he assured me that his happiness depends on mine and not on the country.

Nevertheless, I was not completely satisfied with things that evening –and it was still resonating in my ears, even after I had been back in my room for quite some time, and then, towards morning, I dreamed about Mope behaving badly in the dining room where we were sitting at ugly tables, of bad table manners, and the surprise I was experiencing. However, that turned out to be only a dream.

Sunday morning, I got up and waited in the lobby until Mope appeared for breakfast. I told him about the ugly dream, and then, we spent the rest of the day lying on the dunes, talking and happy in the awareness of each other's closeness. We had coffee in one of the beach cafés, then a walk out to the pier, him talking about earlier friendships and experiences. I had seriously intended to tell him during this meeting that I have been with a man once before, but when he said that he did not know very much or almost nothing about me, I did not want to say anything. And when he said: In twenty-six years, you have actually never loved anyone, I only replied with a surprised question: Did he really believe that I have never really liked anyone? But I did not say anything else. At first, he misunderstood and thought I said I had never really liked anyone–how vain human beings are!

On the pier, during the course of our conversation, I mentioned that I find it dreadful when a girl offers herself to a man, but that I did not think it immoral if you did the latter in the awareness that it was the right thing to do and that every person has to decide that for him—or herself, and I think that it would be better for a future marriage if the woman went into it knowing what to expect, in most cases.

Resumé: we should always try to be just like that, so we will like each other, and with our mutually high expectations, that should be more than enough! Do I agree with that?

He probably tried to express the same thing I did, basically: energy, agility, kindness, deftness.

The last day just as agreeable and harmonious: I am looking forward to a life spent together and if I saw in him just a little ability to cope, endure, and be tough in life's battles, I will be *completely* happy.

MOPE TO VERA

Ostend and Brussels, 1 June 1936

The sea trip is already approaching its end. Until now, 7.30, I sat in the sun and, aside from turning my face to it with my eyes closed, did not do anything. She definitely used the good opportunity to give my face a new coat of paint, after the Palestine one had to give way to the city air so quickly. My eyes are still quite dazzled which you will see by the handwriting. But they are not only dazzled by the sun, but also by you. I am so happy about the two days that we were able to be together. They brought us so much closer together because they belonged only to us. They definitely belong to the most beautiful days that I have ever experienced, and I thank for the harmony and unanimity that pervaded them through your insight, intelligence and friendship.

Most passionately in love, Lilongo, Your Mope

In the meantime, I have reached Brussels where I will have a delay of about two hours. If nothing unexpected happens, I will enclose to you the last British pound note. After the exchange of my last shilling and purchase of stamps, I have almost 10.20 Belgian Francs, and I don't think the coffee will cost that much. I am telling you in such detail in order to characterize the idiotic conditions under which we live and suffer.

Eighteen: "Happy and Sad at the Same Time"

9 June through 1 October 1936

Delays in their correspondence is reflected in the frustration expressed by Mope in several of his letters and Vera in her journal. In Leipzig, the Aryanization of the city by the Nazi authorities forced Mope to change lodging yet again, while also aiding his mother who was being evicted from the Felsenstein family home. Mope was still endeavoring to sort out the complex paperwork that would allow him to leave for Palestine, where he harbored lingering hope that Vera would join him. His Zionist activities included being voted on to the Hebrew culture commission and close dealings with Haavara, the official organization concerned with the emigration of German Jews to Palestine. Vera's ultimatum that he needed to choose between his desire to settle in Palestine and his love for her took time to be fully ingested.

Vera was to spend part of her summer supervising the Marks & Spencer staff summer camp at Rhyl in North Wales. The physical distance between them and the political oppression in Germany left the two uncertain as to how and where they would next meet. The situation was aggravated in late August when a squad of Nazi police terrorized Mope by storming his Leipzig abode at five o'clock in the morning. The police left without taking him into custody but confiscated his passport. Mope alludes to the incident in coded fashion by talking about "a visitor who requested a paper that is very important to me" (24 August) and the misplacement of a "book." Eventually, with the return of the passport by the police, the couple scrambled a rendezvous during the latter part of September in Karlsbad and Marienbad in neighboring Czechoslovakia.

MOPE TO VERA

Leipzig, postcard, 9 June 1936

I was very happy about your letters here because they showed so much positive emotion as a final note of our being together.

Here, I moved my lodgings on Saturday and Sunday, and was finally able to sleep in the new bed yesterday.[15]

Additionally, I wrote a number of letters and applications, and attended consultations with the attorney on behalf of my dear mother. Of course, there are obstacles everywhere which have to be overcome.

On my blessed father's anniversary, my sisters Ketty from Hamburg and Grete from Freiburg have come to give our dear mother company.[16] Ketty will leave tomorrow while Grete will stay for a few more days. I embrace and kiss you in my thoughts, Dein Mope

MOPE TO VERA

Leipzig, 12 June 1936

I am immensely sorry that my silence agitated you and I ask you to please excuse it. Since my return, apart from the move that cost me a lot of time and strength, I have not had a moment for normal thinking. In negotiating with the authorities, everything involves a terrible amount of thought and consideration in order to avoid mistakes, and because of that, everything moves at a snail's pace with mountains of correspondence. When I went through the paperwork, I came to the realization that a larger amount loaned by my blessed father which was considered lost might be saved at least in part. This caused me quite a bit of worry, but my attorney told me that my idea was a good one. After all of that, I was, as one might say, "done for" and was unable to form clear thoughts of a personal nature.

---

15   After moving the previous year from his apartment on Kaiserin Augusta Strasse, Mope lodged on Mozartstrasse, not too far from his mother's home. His final move within Leipzig was to an address on nearby Beethovenstrasse, though he was actually sub-letting rooms around the corner from there in the apartment of Dr. Hermann Jacobson, a retired Jewish attorney.

16   Isidor Felsenstein had died two years before on 28 May 1934. The date also coincided with his daughter Grete's birthday.

Dearest Lilongo, please don't worry if I am mute once in a while, although I would experience the same thing if I didn't hear from you. Please write back soon, because I am waiting, full of longing, for detailed letters about everything that has to do with you.

VERA

Journal entry, 15 June 1936

I am so completely out of balance, so *unsettled*—I wonder what it is.

How much easier everything would be if Mope were here. Tomorrow, I will give him news about something that is not going to make him all that happy. It will let him know that I do not want to go with him right now, that I cannot. It will show him how his eight-day silence last week is completely alien and incomprehensible. I wonder if that is the right thing to do.

Is he a man who can build, who can fight and is strong enough not to fall into despair in this struggle and not to succumb to it? Did he ever have the opportunity to steel himself for that? Will I be able to instill in him those things he might not have?

MOPE TO VERA

Leipzig, 26 June 1936

I have not heard from you for a week. My matters have not made any progress since I cannot undertake anything before receiving permission through the Haavara in Tel-Aviv that I have to present in writing. My application left here on June 9 and left Berlin on June 11.

MOPE TO VERA IN RHYL, NORTH WALES

Leipzig, 28 June 1936

I would like to raise something with you that I might not have the right to write, but, as your lover, I have thought about it a lot and you, an intelligent and understanding human being, will consider if there is not something justifiable to it and not be mad at me. You only ever write about your mother and when I was with you at your house, I was left with the impression that your father is regarded as a negligible quantity.

It seems not quite right that this is so, since, in contrast to my widowed mother, your Mutti has with her the partner she chose for a life together and is not forced to a life of loneliness.

Children are like an artist's products. They are created through love and strength and soul. Aside from the fact that your father has sired an especially perfectly made child in you, there has to surely be a lot of positive in him. The world only judges people according to their material success, but the closest circle uses other rules, and it can, by recognizing the person, inspire and bring that person to material success and help him through failure as well. If a man feels very connected to his family, he needs encouragement in order to succeed. Otherwise he will resign and that seems to be the case with your father.

MOPE TO VERA IN RHYL, NORTH WALES

Leipzig, 5 July 1936

Of course, it was not all that easy for you to answer my writing and, as you yourself write, an answer like that cannot be exhaustive in treating the difficult problem, man to woman or daughter to father, like talking about it in person would make possible.

I grasp your arguments very well and your attitude as well. I tried, probably much too late and when I was older than you are now, to find my way into the thought processes of my own father. Of course, every case is different, but basically, most people of our fathers' generation are the same in that they are outdated because of their commitment to their principles, unchanged and unchangeable since their youth. My brain tries to construct your answers to my thoughts, and if you were with me, I would feel without strain that the answers are much more right and the forms much more harmonious and flawless than imagination is able to make them.

I spend quite a bit of time with Annelie and she regretted that you and I don't seem to have quite as close a friendship as she had expected and hoped for. I left her to her beliefs, because it is your business to tell her differently when you think the time is right.

VERA

Journal entry, 9 July 1936

Rhyl: I am happy and well-balanced and thankful: These are days I fancied: close to nature, and together with girls who enjoy the days simply and unspoiled, just as I do. I am completely and firmly occupied and I feel that I am actually accomplishing something. I am in the most beautiful surroundings: the sea, mountains, clean air.

Even if you do not give a minute-by-minute account in your letters of everything by writing down everything for the people you are close to, that absolutely does *not* mean that your feelings of belonging or affection are any less intense. I make a good living, I have an angel of a Mutti and a friend and lover who stand behind me. Dear God, I thank you!!!!!

MOPE TO VERA IN RHYL, NORTH WALES

Leipzig, 10 July 1936

After a constant suspense, I received your sweet and detailed letter. I am interested in everything you do and how you adjust to your new work just as much as in what is going on inside you and your thoughts, because the one is intimately connected with the other. It is very wonderful that you were able to exchange the big city for a scenically beautiful seaside place during the hottest and most uncomfortable season.

Our long-distance status is unbearable in the long run and, besides everything else, there is so much to talk about that cannot be taken care of in writing. I really feel like saying "Damn!" just once and in such a loud voice that you can hear it all the way in Rhyl and become a little respectful of my masculine anger!

In my impatience to receive an answer from the Haavara, I called and talked to Berlin yesterday and there, they put me off by telling me that such enquiries always require quite a bit of time until completion and that the waiting period was completely normal. They only promised to ask Tel-Aviv once again by airmail to expedite the matter. So I have to go on waiting and so, you have to wait for me, unfortunately.

VERA

Journal entry, 17 July 1936

Today was my day off. I do not feel well and have a cold and because of that, I spent a relatively quiet and contemplative day; I know now that, when I will be with Mope again the next time, I will go all the way with him without any misgivings; only then will I really be able to determine if I still think it right to spend the rest of my life with him. It would be small-minded and conventional or cowardly narrow-mindedness to let anything dissuade me from this.

I am completely clear on this: I am *not* passionately in love with Mope, but I consider that to be a good thing if you want to enter into a marriage and it is a much greater guarantee for long-lasting happiness in a marriage than a love that drowns out everything else with its lack of critique and judgement.

I value his refinement, his tact, his intellectual alertness and interest, and his joy in the aesthetic, aside from his decency and his sense of responsibility. I am afraid that he is not much of a daredevil and that he is not really used to really intense work. I hope, I hope that my misgivings are unfounded.

After a few days of being together completely, of sleeping together, I will be able to see how far the man loses sight of the necessity to make decisions. Should that happen in too great a measure, I am not sure if he is the most suitable life partner for me, because, as much as I love that feeling of reverie, it is completely unacceptable under the circumstances in which we want to enter this marriage. If he cannot see that or does not want to, then his incompetence will be proven to the degree that I consider unsuitable in my husband and the father of my children.

I hope that our next meeting will convince me even more than the last one that I have made the right decision.

But there is something else that scares me: his war injury to his leg; how much does that handicap him physically? I had planned on asking him that both of us should be examined, but I did not do it. However, I do not think he is so unscrupulous to get married when he is not healthy and not physically able.

Mope, despite all of these ever so doubting and weighing thoughts, I do love you and I would love to marry you. It's just that I know if you confirm any of these misgivings, I am convinced that our marriage would be a very unhappy one, and I do not want that for either of us.

MOPE TO VERA IN RHYL, NORTH WALES

Leipzig, 18 July 1936

Your letter arrived at the same time as the approval of the Haavara in Tel-Aviv, which I took to the attorney immediately. His work really only starts now in negotiations with the authorities. Please excuse the fact that I write about these things, but they do interest you as well.

Since yesterday, after a chill and rain, the weather has been beautiful. Today, it is even hot in a tropical way, a humid air that lays itself on the skin. In Palestine, the heat is much more bearable and comfortable due to its dryness.

You are perfectly right when you say that one has to construct everything in life according to one's will and that the togetherness of two people depends on the realization of one's wishes, but the realities of fate usually hamper that. It takes a lot of conviction and even more love to each other in order to let the harmony you talk about ring together even in everyday life. It is impossible to judge for oneself and determine if this great love–lasting love–is there. That can only be determined in those times when love has to prove itself, and that is where the lottery game of marriage lies with human beings who don't marry just because marriage has to be or because that is what people do, but because they wish to be together, one with the other, and firmly believe that one is the partner to the other intellectually, spiritually and physically.

In the meantime, the sky clouded up and a thunderstorm is approaching, hopefully it will clear the air and make way for the sun tomorrow morning, so that one can enjoy a day off, even if it is not in the way I would prefer–with you. Your body is probably already tanned by the air and the sun and beautiful in its form and color, and I am jealous of the other people who see you and caress you with their eyes, while I just long to do that.

MOPE TO VERA IN RHYL, NORTH WALES

Leipzig, 22 July 1936

Monday brought me a wonderful letter from you and a beautiful beginning to the week which usually lacks diversion. We have nothing to do in the store, and that is really troublesome and exhausting. We are imprisoned inwardly and life is ghetto-like, surrounded by walls whose gates are barricaded, but the culture that the ghetto used to breathe is missing. The nature of the people in our circle is strange and shy, their intellectual development is curbed and the feeling of inner atrophy is clearly worn on their faces. Maybe this atmospheric overload is not so much in the air as in us whose respiratory organs no longer dare to fill with the aroma of blooming linden trees and the evening wind pulsing with summer, because we have been detached from our connection to the environment that was familiar and our own, and have not found a new environment that can satisfy us.

There is a photograph of the Erechtheum of the Acropolis in front of me. An ocean of rocks that attained form. The Caryatides, the girls from Carya who turned to stone, with the stone gable on their heads–from ancient times–have more freedom of movement in their beautiful forms than we who represent unhappy figures paralyzed by fate. If we don't manage to create a new habitat for ourselves in the near future, we will freeze in place with a stony burden on our heads, just like the Caryatides, but the beauty that even today lets the eye glow in appreciation of the beauty in the lines, will be torpor and distortion in us and whoever looks at us will be frightened like he would be of the head of the Medusa.[17]

Many years ago, on a bridge in Stambul,[18] I saw two vagabonds, dressed in rags. Their bellies were big and content like that of Crassus[19] and their faces shone like those of happy people. Sometimes, when I think of them, I wish that I could change into one of them, to wander across the wide, beautiful bridge and over the country roads with the other for a friend, to gain new impressions day in and day out, to live on the kernels of maize and the grain that bends under its own weight and to be without my very own environment, because the ALL surrounds me then. I would rather be dressed in rags and be satisfied by that which nature provides than be banned in a circle in which you are a banned man, to vegetate and cry out in spiritual hunger.

---

17 Mope's remarks in these two paragraphs subtly allegorize the political situation and the plight of Germany's Jews about which he could not write directly. The gaze of the Medusa had the power to turn the onlooker into stone, and alludes obliquely to the death threat to the Jews posed by the Hitler regime.
18 i.e., Istanbul.
19 The Roman Crassus was known for his infamous greed.

We live in the days of lamentation for Jerusalem.[20] It was destroyed twice in these days, once by Babylonia, then by the Romans, and we sing the same songs even today, augmented by those that are for our broken circle that was home to us, because we had grown roots inside it for centuries. But for what reason should we live in the past and let our strengths sour, as long as there is still a future for us. I must tear myself away from looking backwards and free myself from the bitterness that wants to anchor itself within me and look at you the symbol of my–our–future and now I am once again filled with hope of joy and happiness and inner salvation. The tension flows from me and a soft sleepiness overcomes me that will let me see everything more easily and fill me with hope for tomorrow after a recuperative sleep. Please be greeted, Lilongo, and love me, so much that the strength of the feeling lets us overcome everything much faster and I can be with you very soon and forever.

VERA

Journal entry, 31 July 1936, Rhyl, North Wales

I have not heard from Mope for a week. I know through Annelie that he received my last letter. Is he so lame–did something happen? I really do not worry about it, because I have been through this with him so many times before–that he did not write without having a serious reason for it. Nevertheless, I was quite disappointed to *not* hear from him at all these last few days.

MOPE TO VERA

Leipzig, 31 July 1936

After the few lines beginning with "just a few words" on the 23rd, I have heard nothing else from you. The pictures you sent that show me your lovely face and much else that is quite beautiful, heighten–if that is possible–the desire in me to have a dialogue with you. But for

---

20 Tisha B'Av (the Ninth Day of Av in the Jewish Calendar) is a solemn fast day in commemoration of the destruction of the Temple in Jerusalem by the Babylonians (586 BCE) and by the Romans (70 CE). It coincides with the time that Mope was writing this letter.

that, I need a few written words that tell me about you and remove the small disturbances in the dialogue caused by ambient noises. With the advancing radio technology, the communication between us keeps getting better and shows a fortunate harmony a lot of times, but we want to really try to remove all interruptions due to atmospheric disturbances and make our harmony complete.

Nobody knows better than I do that moods can make writing letters more difficult, but should we not participate in these moods in order to make them easier to bear, one for the other? It is an infinitely difficult task that we have posed ourselves, not only to keep up contact between us but to let it become deeper.

Please imagine: Mope comes home every evening, after the breakfast table was empty, with a fevered eagerness to see if there is a letter from you, and then he goes to bed disappointed and, instead of your eagerly awaited lines whose content should follow him into his dreams, he reads a boring newspaper article about unrest in Spain, floods in China, insolvencies in the economy and the persecution of Jews in Poland, and that fills his sleep that should have been recuperative had you just chatted with him before he went to sleep. After so much longing, we have really earned time alone together, don't you think?

My "affairs" are going their own way now. I am expecting the certificate from the emigration advisory service on Monday, and I will have to take it to the other agencies. Added to that, the liquidation of different financial assets belonging to my dear mother requires my careful considerations already overburdened by other great responsibilities. These things all move forward very slowly and I am happy about any movement in the right direction–well, slowly happy.

VERA

Journal entry, 5 August 1936, Rhyl, North Wales

I am very tired and a little exhausted and *downcast*.

Mope, how wonderful it would be if I had you here with me now! I hope that you are the right one in all practical things as well; what I mean by that is real life, the practical side of things.

MOPE TO VERA IN RHYL, NORTH WALES

Leipzig, 5 August 1936

I won't receive the certificate from the emigration services agency until tomorrow, although it was promised for Monday, and then, there will be more delays which I don't know about yet, but which everyone who has plans like I do gets to suffer. Before all of this is done, I cannot make any firm plans for the future. I have no idea as to what country and what profession comes into consideration, but Palestine is definitely not deleted off the program. I am still unable to decide, since the form has to be created before the bell is poured. In my momentary situation, it is difficult to form a picture of the future way of life. The view is too narrow and, because of that, every idea that comes from the outside and looks like it might become reality in practice is of immense importance, but it also creates a target for aimless thoughts.

VERA

Journal entry, 10 August 1936

I have Mope's picture here and I am afraid of his mouth–he looks much too unenergetic. I hope that is not true and you cannot always judge by the face alone. Mitja's face was too deceptive, and, looking at this, my future life partner seems too soft. Oh, Mope, I hope that our marriage will be a beautiful, good, and joyous one. I will do everything I can on my side to make that come true, but I am still terribly afraid that you tend to brag a little too much, are a little too dependent and a little too soft. I hope that I am wrong.

You are absolutely right for me where your human side is concerned: sensible, fine, intelligent, imaginative, and kind! Oh, I think that should be enough and everything will work out just fine (and I should not reach for the stars too much)!!!!!!!!!!!!

MOPE TO VERA IN RHYL, SOUTH WALES

Leipzig, 16 August 1936

There goes another lonely Sunday spent without you, but it brought me the happy news that your vacation begins on September 12. I have applied for a letter of credit for Czechoslovakia after I did not receive one for Belgium, but it is still questionable here if I will receive it. At this time, the only letters of credit available are to Hungary and Yugoslavia and you have to wait for those, all other requests–even if allowed–won't meet with any success for an undetermined period of time. But the main thing is that we will be together and take joy in each other, wherever that may be.

On Thursday, Fred and Hanna, arrived here and delivered your greetings. Fred and I utilized the days very well, and his help in decisions that the other gentlemen of the Gebrüder Felsenstein have to make and to which we have to bring them, was of great use to me. He accomplishes much more with these people as a "neutral" person than me, especially since he impresses them as an Englishman. By the way, it seemed to me that he was quite content with everything we accomplished and even thinks the direction taken is a good one. His affirmation concerning the matter was more than welcome to me. This afternoon, Fred traveled on to Berlin, while Hanna will stay here for fourteen more days. It is a joy for my dear mother to have her youngest daughter here.

MOPE TO VERA IN RHYL, NORTH WALES

Leipzig, 24 August 1936

After I got home quite late yesterday evening–I had attended a Hebrew class–I found your dear letter. Because I had a lot of work during the day today, I was unable to answer it, and since I cannot have any lights on tonight, due to anti-aircraft drills, I am going to hurry–it is already 7.30 p.m. and twilight–writing to you.

Yesterday, I had a visitor who requested a paper that is very important to me as a hospitality gift, and I could not refuse what he seemed to be entitled to; just a short time after that, your letter arrived–it satisfied me inwardly and I am sure that I will receive a replacement for what was lost.[21]

At this very moment, I am unable to make a decision concerning a meeting place for the two of us. We just have to bide our time to see

---

21 In his post-war *curriculum vitae*, Mope makes brief reference to the police raid of his "lodging on Ferdinand Rhode Street, where, at 5 in the morning, officers appeared to arrest me. I was able to convince them that I was innocent, but they did take my passport."

what hurdles there are to be overcome. Everything else is going on in its usual way, and we have more than enough work in the store so as to avoid thinking silly thoughts.

Hanna is staying for another week. Unfortunately, my mother does not have enough time, since she is without personnel, to enjoy her visit the way she should be able to. Added to that, she will give up her residence on September 15 and for that reason is very busy with the sale of superfluous household items and is forced to stay at home quite a lot.

I have to apologize for the cursory tone of this letter, but if I don't turn off the light now, I will be in trouble. Most affectionately, my dearest girl, Your Mope

MOPE TO VERA IN RHYL, NORTH WALES

Leipzig, 30 August 1936

I think it's wonderful that your time off had been finalized in such a way that we can meet and enjoy those free days together. Unfortunately, I cannot give you a location yet since I do not know if I will be able to get back my book in time. As inferred from your latest letter to me, you do understand me correctly!

This evening, Hanna left. My mother will find her four walls particularly lonely, especially since she is without domestic help and won't be able to find one for the few remaining weeks because none would like to take such a short time position.

There was a Zionistic conference of the mid-German group alliance all day today. Since no one knows that I am occupied with moving plans, they voted me onto the Hebrew culture commission, something I accepted rather gladly because it concerns an area that is close to my heart and gives me validation while I am still here.

Yesterday evening, I was at Annelie's who had asked several friends to her place and drank quantities of Cognac, something that was good for me and most especially my cold.

My issues are moving slowly but surely forward and trees need time until they grow up to the sky. It is probable that I will receive my Certificate of Good Standing [Unbedenklichkeits-bescheid]–a notice that declares that I am of no danger to the government–and that is another stage along the way, and I am happy about everything that brings me closer to my goal and in a completely positive mood, because a bad mood really does not help to move things along more quickly.

I am so not bent on being philosophical that my letter probably sounds rather clinical, but a writer cannot always wait for philosophical highs, because my girl would receive letters from her non-intellectual man much more rarely as is the case already. My existence here is lacking stimuli (with the exception of my Zionistic work which, due to the conditions in Palestine, requires more gritting of the teeth than it provides stimuli), so that I feel like an emptied skin waiting for the new harvest and freshly pressed juice. It is a time of intellectual slump that will hopefully be followed by a rise very soon, so that I can give you more interesting reports than I can today.

VERA

Journal entry, 2 September 1936

It is truly about Mope that I want to write!

I *want* to be perfectly clear about my current situation: I have rarely been this indecisive, thrown back and forth, and so insecure where my affection for another human being is concerned, as I am at this moment!

Should I have the courage to be completely honest with myself, see everything in *black and white*? At least where my mood today is concerned!

I am afraid that I will marry Mope *pour faute de mieux*. I am discouraged by his lack of self-reliance: a man of thirty-seven years, who lets his mother contribute fifty Reichmarks for his trip and who forgets to pay his bride who works for her living the eighty Reichmarks she spent for him. A man who says about himself that he has an extraordinary sense of direction and then cannot find the way back on a relatively straightforward location. A man whose greatest wish it is to marry a girl and make her happy, and who, despite more than enough free time, does not have the energy to cultivate the language that is necessary for his advancement. A man of thirty-seven who loves a girl completely, but would never think of calling her or sending her a bouquet of flowers, but who is kind almost to a fault. A man who loves a woman so much and still does not have enough empathy to realize that, if you send her such a scary message (like for instance this passport confiscation) and she sends him a very encouraging, brave, but still basically very worried letter, you answer this letter *immediately* so her worries will not be heightened without good reason and to show her some *resonance* for her willingness to go in for a copper, in for a gold.

Why do I want to chain myself to a German who will always be regarded as a foreigner and outsider here despite *one's own* gift of assimilation? I do not even have any kind of proof of his capabilities. His positive character traits consist only of the fact that he is sensitive and kind and that he loves me immensely? What to do????

These four days of being together, in about two weeks, are actually poisonous, because the physical longing for a sexual partner, on both sides, will sweep away everything else and those clear eyes will be darkened. We should live in the same city for a few months, like other lovers or friendly pairs, without living together, in order to get to know each other better, but when it comes right down to it, is that really all that important? Isn't it more important for someone to satisfy one's ambitious demands? Isn't it much more essential to secure someone who loves you, who will do anything for you and who will secure a home for you in the future and instill ideals in children, as far as that is possible?

Well, this is how far you have come–out of fear of being alone later and a desire for children, you are going to get married! A conjecture Mope made at the very beginning of our becoming acquainted. However, I did not want to marry Mope, he wanted to marry me, and I more than hesitated with my acceptance. What a horrible state of mind today's tiredness, disappointment and maybe even a little indignation at Mope's long-awaited lines made me put down on paper!!!

MOPE TO VERA IN RHYL, NORTH WALES

Leipzig, 5 September 1936

Between dinner and a walk with my dear mother, I want to write a few lines to you. Unfortunately, I have not received any news from you for quite a long time, so that, if there is no letter from you by tomorrow, I will send a telegram to enquire.

Nothing has changed here since my last letter and only my hope to have my book once again has grown a little.[22] Fortunately, the period of

---

22 The "book" is, of course, his passport that had been confiscated when his apartment was raided.

time between now and our reunion is untouched by any of the events and decreases so apparently if one looks at the calendar.

This evening, my cousin Julius is going to London and will stay there for at least a fortnight. I don't have to tell you how happy I would feel to be in his place, especially since he already received permission to establish his residence there. He goes over there within the scope of the company Gebrüder Felsenstein and consequently has a guarantee for the existential minimum at the same time. If one has capital, one can accomplish things much more easily than one could without. They would never have released me from this enterprise on the same basis. When I leave, it also means a surrender of all rights I have based on belonging to the family and my father's partial ownership, while the others who are wealthy through inheritances simply declare, "I am moving to Milan," "I am moving to London," and the others have no choice but to say yes.[23] But maybe, instead of money, I inherited a little more intellect and that is worth something as well, and the two of us will fight our way through, I am not worried about that. We only have to be a little more modest, until we get ahead, live more modestly than we could have ever dreamed, but even that is doable if we understand each other just as well as we both have the willpower to do.

VERA

Journal entry, 6 September 1936

I did not write to Mope, although I intended to at first. The written word is too plump and immovable for such a subtle matter as this one, I am sure of it. I will call him to account when we are together, very soon now. I am afraid of this meeting, of being disappointed. Of course, the physical, sexual will play such a great role that it will overshadow everything else, but it cannot be allowed to do that. I cannot make things that easy for us, or rather be so shortsighted. I know we harmonize in

---

23 Mope's cousin, Alfred, moved to Milan in 1933 shortly after the Nazis came to power, and from there to Uruguay. Julius had contacts in London but settled in New York, taking for himself valuable possessions of the Gebrüder Felsenstein that should have been shared but were never even offered. Both remained full partners in the business and claimed further assets after the war. The demise of the family business was escalated by the mercenary behavior of individual partners.

this one point–and that is why I think that it is not the right thing to go all the way, as I thought at first, just to see if I still yearn for him afterwards, but instead consciously and certainly not go all the way and also let him know right from the beginning, because, right now, I am afraid that it would not help me win clarity, but would take all of my senses prisoner in such a way that I would not be able to judge clearly. And right now, I need a clear and objective power of reasoning in order to make a complete and final decision concerning a yes or a no; and once you have made that decision and it happens to be positive, then you can crown the alliance by giving yourself to him.

MOPE TO VERA IN RHYL, NORTH WALES

Leipzig, 9 September 1936

Your reaction seemed incomprehensible to me until the arrival of your letter which I had to read several times in order to understand. I informed you about my being indisposed as fast as I could because I thought it only right for you to know about it. At the same time, I told you that the matter was not that important. I cannot tell you more even today.[24]

You write that you have "a lot of good will in stock for me." That is not enough for me and my answer to that is that I neither feel the notion nor the necessity to beg others for love; a store of good will is not love and I do not place any value on anything else. I have written to you several times and asked you to tell me if you have doubts and that I will always try to alleviate them if I think they are unjustifiable. But you also know that I admit to my faults, as far as I am aware of them, because human beings who want to live together have to either come to terms with that or fight against them with love through constant understanding and commitment. People separate because of doubts that eat at them if they don't talk about them. After your conduct which appears quite egocentric to me, I consider it difficult to get back on to the "old correct track," because it bears witness to self-love and unkindness

---

24 Mope is, once again, referring to the confiscation of his passport, an "indisposition" which made it impossible for him to travel. The ill temper of this letter is partly brought about by personal strain, and by a feeling that Vera's letters were more indifferent than loving. His passport was returned to him the following weekend.

towards me. It seems ridiculous for me to write essays on energy and the gift of empathy again and again; only a life together can prove that, if you did not already receive an appropriate impression from my letters. But I would suggest to you, if you still have them, to read a few of the earlier letters again in order to recall earlier conversations.

You cannot change me into someone placed to the side, as was done with your father–as I see it. You can go with me together on an equal basis or not at all. Your letter is a conscious or maybe subconscious attack on my feeling of self-worth, but fortunately, I am strong enough to withstand such attacks. It is late once again and I wish you a good sleep, something I will start as well now.

MOPE TO VERA IN RHYL, NORTH WALES

Leipzig, 13/14 September 1936

Now I am happy and sad at the same time. It is one o'clock at night and I just came back from Berlin where the meeting of the Zionist state board of directors took place. I wanted to participate in it because of the important events in Palestine. Actually, I had counted on finding mail from you on my return home, but did not believe that its content would prove to be so gratifying to me, that my assumptions were wrong and I am, under full consideration of the depressing feeling that I did you wrong. I am more than happy with the two letters you sent.

I would very much like to beg your forgiveness. I hurt you and did you wrong and I am very, very sorry because I can see that now. In return, I want to give you something to be happy about. Yesterday, before I left for Berlin, the missing book was given back to me and I am feeling incomparably freer than during the last few weeks.

Sometimes, there is an abysmal difference between what a writer wants to say and how the reader takes it in, because the mood or the electrical charge of the two participants are different and unknown to each other, and then, according to Nature's patterns, there is a thunderstorm. They are difficult to bear, but at least the atmosphere is cleared and I hope that, once we talk to each other on the telephone tomorrow night, the sky above and in us will be as blue as our stationery once again. If you are not too mad at me, I would suggest that we meet Thursday morning in Karlsbad or Marienbad. Please be so nice and contact Fred right after you get to London so he can procure the needed

Czech crowns for you. You will get them much cheaper through him than in the country.

Please let yourself be passionately embraced and kissed by me in your thoughts and write back as "Your" Lilongo to *your* Mope

VERA

Journal entry, 13 September 1936

During the day:

Yes, I would like to marry Mope and walk down my life's path with him. From now on, I will not let such tortuous doubts come over me again nor lend them my ear in the future.

I will write to him much more often, should we have to keep being separated and will see if that might not be the better and most effective method.

I really hope that he will call me this evening and I am looking forward to those days together, now so tangibly close, and I will not make any plans for them, but enjoy them to their fullest, just the way they are.

Sunday night, *same day*:

Mope did not call me. I waited for that call for over two hours.

It felt good for him to finally be tough with me, and if I have not lost everything, then this was the best possible lesson he could give me. A woman like me, or should we say a spoilt and overly pampered girl, needs a strong hand behind her, otherwise she will get sassy.

I am ashamed, not for having made Mope wait for so long, but *on the thoughts behind it all*; which I put down on paper here in a completely unbalanced hour, but now, I want to make a final decision: *Yes*, I will marry Mope and no other man shall be able to dislodge him from this place (not even in my thoughts). Pack up your teenage dreams; you really are too old for that and should be experienced enough by now to know that the only thing that counts in life is harmony between a man and a woman and that all the small outside vanities and comforts are completely inconsequential in the end.

Mope is gentle to a fault, is intelligent and you find him physically attractive, so please, let all that nagging and waffling sink into the abyss and keep sight of everything being relative: *the basic stock is good and right in Mope*!!!!!! Do not let anyone ruin your conviction; this determination is and forever shall be unshakable and holy to me!!!!!!!!

But maybe, I have already lost him! Will he be that impulsive? I think and hope not!

Vera and Mope were together in Karlsbad, Marienbad, and Leipzig from the morning of Thursday 24 September through to the evening of Monday 28 September. In 1936, Karlsbad and Marienbad (the Sudetenland) belonged to Czechoslovakia. The Sudetenland was forcibly annexed by Germany in October 1938.

Fig. 67 Postcard of Marienbad in the 1930s.

MOPE TO VERA

Leipzig, 29 September 1936

Your train is racing through the clear night and will arrive in Lehrte very soon, while I sit here alone, where you were still with me yesterday with your kisses and the gentleness of your movements. The beautiful flowers you brought me still decorate my room. They have bloomed into their full beauty, after they almost succumbed to the change in atmosphere. The moon is looking at me from outside in its fullness and, with its perfect clarity, gives the writing desk its own coloring. We saw it in its beginning at Marienbad. The tender sickle, often overshadowed by clouds, did not have enough strength to illuminate our walk in the forest. Why do the days together go by so fast that they won't even let us experience the moon's travels together?

My beloved girl, I am so happy about the beautiful days, up to and including the very last one, that we spent together in unbeatable harmony and in ever-changing entertainment, never too much and definitely not tiring. I thank you from the bottom of my soul and with a heart filled with you, that you followed my call to Karlsbad so endearingly and without contradiction and let us enjoy your vacation together, and I would like it if you considered those days among the most beautiful that life has granted us.

VERA

Journal entry, 1 October 1936

Last night, I came back from my Karlstad-Marienbad-Leipzig trip. I am completely happy in my awareness of having found that human being, the life partner who will be able to give me everything I always dreamed of: intelligence, kindness, and gentleness. Dearest Lord, I thank you!

Nineteen: Letters From a Wretched Coffee House Sitter

2 October through 11 December 1936

POLITICAL TIMELINE, SEPTEMBER 1936–JUNE 1937

- 23 September 1936: Sachsenhausen Concentration Camp opened.
- 15 October 1936: Decree that "Non Aryans" are prohibited from teaching in German public schools.
- 25 October 1936: Rome-Berlin Axis formed by Mussolini and Hitler.
- 27 November 1936: Film criticism banned in Germany.
- 10 December 1936: Abdication of Edward VIII, King of Great Britain.
- 14 March 1937: Pope Pius XI issues encyclical repudiating Nazi racism but not denouncing anti-Semitism.
- 28 May 1937: Neville Chamberlain becomes Prime Minister of Great Britain.
- 11 June 1937: Jews prohibited from giving testimony in German courts.

In Leipzig, the three-month stretch before they rendezvoused in London was a lonesome period for Mope, made bearable by Vera's dispatches. Her almost daily letters, none of which survive, had become (in his own self-consoling words) "an indispensable prerequisite on my breakfast table… [making me] almost forget the time and the necessity of going to the office." At the office, while still engaged in the daily affairs of the Gebrüder Felsenstein, he was endeavoring to extricate himself from his position as a salaried partner in a manner that would give his mother the wherewithal to emigrate to Palestine. His Felsenstein cousins, full partners in the firm, grudgingly figured out his importance to the business, and were not willing to make his departure easy.

From Mope's responses, it can be construed that Vera's lost letters from this period will have included details of her work for Marks & Spencer, where she was in charge of recruiting and training personnel at the company's new store in Kilburn (a northwest London suburb). In Germany, Mope still hoped against hope that he could persuade Vera to join him in Palestine. He alludes frequently to his protracted negotiations with Haavara, the transfer company set up with the agreement of the Nazis to facilitate the emigration of German Jews to Palestine. By the time of his next visit to London at the end of the year, those arrangements seemed at long last to be falling into place.

MOPE TO VERA

Leipzig, 2 October 1936

There is an emptiness here. When I walk through the streets, a hollow space marches along on my right side. I have to look again and again, but I convince myself constantly that my arm is missing the warmth of yours because yours isn't there to link with. I feel it most strongly in the morning when I wake up and realize that the joy of seeing you and wishing you a good morning are not accomplishable.

MOPE TO VERA

Leipzig, 8 October 1936

Finally, there is calm again inside and out. It is nighttime. No noise from traffic reaches here. I call back to mind the good advice that you gave me in that beautiful park in Karlsbad not to get upset over unfair people. Yesterday, at the Gebrüder Felsenstein, Semy, our senior partner asked me to write down my wishes regarding the assignment of my mother's legitimate share in the business and also what was due to me.[25] We reached a reasonable agreement after he expressed his amazement over the fact that I treat the whole thing not only factually, but also

---

25 A photograph of Semy Felsenstein (1883-1978), head partner of Gebrüder Felsenstein, can be found in the online resources for this book, https://doi.org/10.11647/OBP.0334#resources

emotionally. He finally understood that it is not so easy for me to forego all rights to the company as the last one of our line, a company that was raised from the ground by my blessed father–as he said himself–and in which I have worked for more than ten years of my life. He also admitted to me that I alone was responsible for the extension of the German business in the last few years–we had 90 per cent foreign business until 1933, and now we have 75-80 percent in-country business–and that it was accomplished to the advantage of the company.[26] Tomorrow, I will work out a declaration concerning a waiver of my rights under the caveat that my plans are effective in the future, because one cannot count on reimbursement for anything from these kinds of people. I don't expect much to come from that, since I know I can develop better with a certain amount of independence.

On top of all of this, the denial of every form of relief for my mother's assets that I had applied for arrived today. First, it looked like I might be successful in this and now I have to appeal, and the whole affair will take more time once again. This afternoon, I had the time to work through the files and devise the appeal. Not everything can always work out on the first try and nobody expects that anyway.

Now I have bored you enough with all this stuff. I am accompanying this note with some paper kisses, but I wish that you could feel them as if I were with you and had your beloved hands on my temples and my mouth on yours. Your Mope

MOPE TO VERA

Leipzig, 11 October 1936

This morning, there was a letter with a belly on my breakfast table. It was blue and fat, like no other letter from you before. You broke your

---

26 The significance of this becomes apparent in the context of the global boycott of German goods following the rise to power of the Nazis in 1933. Edwin Black describes the effect of the boycott on the fur trade: "On May 12 [1933]... the prestigious Leipzig annual fur auction was held. Ninety percent of the world's fur industry was in Jewish hands, and French, Dutch, British, and American furriers boycotted the event totally. Reich sources admitted that the entire auction was a failure as $3 million worth of furs were withdrawn for lack of buyers" (*The Transfer Agreement: The Untold Story of the Secret Pact between the Third Reich and Jewish Palestine*, Macmillan Publishing Company, New York and London, 1984, p. 131). Taking responsibility to extend business with German fur companies, Mope contributed greatly to the ongoing profitability of the Gebrüder Felsenstein, but as a salaried–rather than full–partner was unable to reap individual benefit from that.

own record by much with this letter and gave me an immense delight, especially with the lovingly thought-out contents. Your letters have become an indispensable prerequisite on my breakfast table. That means, that, if the mailman appears a little too early once in a while, I creep down the hall, still in an incomplete state, and covertly retrieve the blue envelope filled with your loving greetings, take it to my bedroom, sit down on the edge of my bed, happy in my knowledge of you, and read and then almost forget the time and the necessity of going to the office.

What have you done to the Mope who was once too lazy to write? Can you take responsibility in front of God and the world for the fact that he defaces so much beautiful paper with his scrawl? But I have to confess that I don't even really hate to write to you, because the pendulum between hating to write and loving to chat with you swings in favor of the latter by a significant degree. The chatting with you about things that up to now were usually handled by myself proves that writing (which is something like talking) about many things contributes to the ease of existence and with that, to elevating my mood. I have caught myself singing (or I should really say, growling!) more than once lately and have determined that such positive expressions of life have not shown themselves in many years, especially since the melodies are usually happy ones. While I am writing, I am seated at "Café Felsche's" where I am a wretched coffee house sitter. I hope that with necessary patience this bad habit can be corrected in our future shared home and a very good coffee.

Fig. 68 Kaffeehaus Felsche, Leipzig, c. 1930 (https://www.paulinerkirche.org/tmp/augusta/fel1922.jpg).

MOPE TO VERA

Leipzig, 16 October 1936

This evening, I have not felt any kind of yearning to go back to my accommodation. The letter to you from Café Felsche is now starting to become a tradition. It is supposed to go across into the red mailbox of the main post office, so that it can bring my girl her Saturday greetings on time.

Who knows if you who are so scornful of our traditions want to share what touches me today! Despite all the work that seems to fall on you, I am happy that you've become aware of the old day of rest–official holiday of the week–of the Jews. The Jewish homemaker lights two candles at the beginning of the Sabbath. They stand in silver candlesticks and even the poorest feel the difference between today and the weekdays at the sight of the decorated table, because the table appointed with the silver candlesticks is especially important to them. On this particular evening–once in seven days–they are gentlemen, kings, and this awareness lets them remain human during the entire week when they have to be servants with their heavy loads on their backs. The continuation of ethics that are deeply rooted inside of us can be traced back to this and many other customs that let the heads of our ancestors rest for one day of the week even in the days of the bitterest need and let them sit proudly on those shoulders. On this day, the spirit was taken care of and the one blessed with knowledge stood above the one rich in goods, who, on the Sabbath, bowed before the one who knew the books of Judaism and let him be superior.

Now I have slipped into my teaching mode again, after I have not sat at my mother's table in several weeks or had the candles in front of me. In the present time, they are a certainty no longer but seem much clearer to my eyes even when they are not there.

Here, they are starting to put the chairs to bed, although it is only 12.30 a.m. They are allowed to rest from the humans who devoted nothing but their backsides to them all day long. A beautiful custom that should be allowed to humans as well. I embrace you and shall carry that feeling into my sleep.

MOPE TO VERA

Leipzig, 29 October 1936

After our engagement has become more widely known, I have been receiving many letters of congratulations which include you, of course. Although I let Littauers' know about our union, they have the least right to know and no right whatsoever to complain about being told late. Back then, I told Ruth about the old story first of all and received the receipt for it. I am deeply grateful to her for it today, because the happiest circumstance led the two of us together and I shudder when I think back and try to draw parallels between you and her. But that was really not her intention anyway, and only my lucky star brought about such a happy solution.

This week, our Hebrew course was cancelled, since there was a lecture on "Jewish perception of history" by Joachim Prinz and we could not find another free evening we could share. The lecture was dialectic, as always with Prinz, extremely well presented, but he is a pseudo-scientist who wants to make an enormous impression on the majority, but he cannot impress people who have a little knowledge and therefore are better able to critique. I assume that the name Prinz is familiar to you. As a boy, at the age of twenty-three, he became the rabbi of a large congregation in Berlin and has been the cause of many a fierce discussion of late because of his Zionist influence on young people whom he enthralled, in the manner of Bernard de Clairvaux, and estranged from their parents in many cases.[27]

I will leave here tomorrow around noon and will be in Karlsbad in the evening. If it is not too expensive, I will call you from there since it will be Friday evening and you are so sweet to appoint it "our" evening.

---

27 Rabbi Joachim Prinz (1902-1988) was known for his fierce criticism of Nazism. He was expelled from Germany in 1937, and, seeking asylum in the USA, became the rabbi at Temple B'nai Abraham in Newark, NJ. He was a strong supporter of the Civil Rights Movement, and, as President of the American Jewish Congress, took a leading role with Martin Luther King, Jr., in the march on Washington in 1963. Bernard de Clairvaux (1090-1153) was a founder of the Cistercian Order of Monks.

MOPE TO VERA

Karlsbad, Czechoslovakia, 1 November 1936

The drive across the mountains was magnificent and even now still offered colorful autumn views that stood in idiosyncratic contrast to the blanket of snow already covering parts of the mountain. On the trip there, we even had a few rays of sunshine that brightly decorated our way at times and created new colors by appearing and disappearing in turn.

Now, I want to tell you about the reason for my trip here. All of a sudden, after the devaluation of the crown, my request for a letter of credit submitted on August 5 was approved for 3,000 Czech crowns at the old exchange rate. The Reichsbank did not want to lose any value in its Crown holdings and that is why everyone who had applied earlier had to withdraw the money and if they don't use the letter of credit, they have to bear the loss in the exchange rate. A critique concerning this is unnecessary. I would have had time until December 6 to withdraw the money, so it was the last possible weekend.

I was lucky that the sister-in-law of my car driver is here from England for a spa-treatment and I arranged to have some of the money paid to her. I will give her approximately 1,500 of my Crowns which she will pay back to you in London. Since we have not balanced the books yet, I don't know if there will be anything left to possibly put in this letter. [28]

MOPE TO VERA

Leipzig, 6 November 1936

A week ago today when I called you from Karlsbad, we heard our voices sing and they lost nothing of their naturalness, although they cut across earth, under the channel with its storm-tortured waves and once again moved through wires that moved in the wind, crossed borders and were led through the pulsing, loud life of metropolitan cities. We felt close to one another, not closer than usual because such strong feelings cannot

---

28 Because of currency restrictions on Jews imposed by the German authorities, crossing the border into Czechoslovakia was one of the few ways by which Mope could transfer funds to London. Until Hitler annexed the Sudetenland in October 1938, many German Jews would apply to visit Karlsbad as a temporary release from conditions under the Reich.

even be heightened by sounds that one wishes to hear all the time. But it was something special, like a gift of nature that one has heard, like the rustle of leaves that continues on through the forest. It is passed along from tree to tree and the melody rings for miles and miles. It is like a huge ringing that fills the entire forest, and we were like two trees that have suddenly plugged into this concert and our leaves were touched by others and always others making music between us until there was the contact that let us feel each other's breath. But then, the contact was dissolved again as suddenly and there was a hollow space in which we wanted to grab each other and reached into emptiness. It was as if a tendon had been cut so that the hand that reached for you sank down feebly before it could feel the softness of your skin and the breathing of your pores and warm itself in the warmth of your body. The separation was like a gush of cold, icy water on a person feeling highly aroused and one would never have felt the separation if the secret of nature, the rustle of trees that can be sustained without interruption, had been taken without also taking the continuity in the actions of nature.

Could you have felt it in the same way and not feel overcome by the gush of ice-cold water? I almost believe that such an interruption can be less surmountable in women for a longer time than in men. But maybe it is just a silly hypersensitivity in me to have felt that way but also needing to put it into words which can only describe feelings in a lackluster way.

MOPE TO VERA

Leipzig, 10 November 1936

While I am writing from here (at Zellner's),[29] I am eating the rest of my dinner. Unfortunately, it was near 11.00 p.m. when I finally found the time, since, during the day today, I had to inspect merchandise that will be sold at auction tomorrow. Semy sent me to look at the wares although I definitely will not reap the sweet or sour fruits of success. He considered my judgment on the merchandise to be completely accurate, and tomorrow, I will buy for the Gebrüder Felsenstein. It is lucky that the other partner-cousins are not here, because they would surely suffer

---

29 Jewish-owned Zellner's Restaurant was on Nikolaistrasse along from the Gebrüder Felsenstein building. Its forced closure took place in 1938. The Zellner family would be deported to Auschwitz in 1942 where they perished.

seizures in their anger over the trust shown me. Actually, I am dead tired from all the work, but I don't want to go to bed without writing to you.

My intention to drive to Berlin on Friday will likely take place. I do not know yet where I will be staying and I will let you know if you can call me Saturday evening. I am just feeling bad for the English money that you will have to spend for that, since that is a rare article that can only be acquired with much effort. Please forgive this materialistic view of the world that is necessary nevertheless.

MOPE TO VERA

Pension Gloria, Berlin, 14 November 1936

I am sitting here waiting. I wonder if you will call or even received yesterday's letter today. Since it was really late yesterday, I stayed in bed in the morning and went for a walk in the afternoon. Life on the Kurfürstendamm is tremendously crowded and cannot be any more flooded without respite in Piccadilly or Regent Street.

....

To hear your beloved voice was, just like the last time, an experience to me and it was so clear and distinct, as if you were in a telephone booth on the Kurfürstendamm. Although I was waiting for it, I did not find the right words once again, for the most important thing is not the technical stuff with its positive and negative aspects, but the fact that I love you and that I long to kiss your beautiful mouth and that I want to stride with you arm in arm, and my heart is so overfilled with it that I can only stammer, because the words that are meant to tell you that, come out in such a rush if they have to be spoken. We write to each other and we know a lot about one another and still, there is the last thing between us, that point of contact that can only be made with a kiss and for which no words would be necessary between us. Meanwhile, your voice still sounds in my ear as if we could see each other again in the morning and I could embrace you, take your hands and caress you.

By the way, I decided that once I get everything done here I will take a four-week vacation and I am counting *on you to accompany me*, because I will probably need a vacation desperately by then in order to start my new work with newfound strength. I am considering a trip to Palestine as a strong possibility. I will find out during my visit in London, and before I come over there I have to clear up a question concerning the indemnity needed with the "Haavara." The people promised me to write to Tel-Aviv, and I hope that the answer will require less time than my request in June.

Now I want to air the room a little because I smoked and will bring the letter to the mailbox in the meantime. Since, to my knowledge, there will be no airplane tomorrow, I will send it by regular mail, otherwise it will stay here until Monday.

MOPE TO VERA

Leipzig, 16 November 1936

When I arrived here today around noon, I found two letters from you. I consumed this detailed pleasure before I went to lunch and to the store. Despite the call on Saturday that let me hear your beloved voice, I really missed your reports a lot.

You will be interested in a short report about my day yesterday, since the Zionist conference was of the highest order and your director at M&S, Rebecca Sieff,[30] spoke very well and showed the same movements that Weizmann does when he speaks. That was amusing to watch. She was wearing a belt that she kept moving back and forth with her hands and while one gets to see the suspenders every now and then during the parallel activity in Weizmann, one waits for a similar "revelation" (but admittedly in vain). Her speeches were in English, of course and were then translated. In the evening, I was introduced to Mrs. Sieff with the explanation that I was the fiancé of Miss Hirsch, an employee of M&S. Immediately, she said, "I know, she is in the welfare department," and I asked, "Do you know her personally?" and she answered, "No, but I intended to meet her. She is a friend of Mrs. Braham. Do you wish that I tell her something from you?" And I said, "Thank you, no, I telephoned with her last night, but please give her my love." Then she said something about "some good looking man" and I told her, "Please tell her that!," whereupon the "audience" was ended since there was a

---

30 Rebecca Sieff (1890-1966) was the sister of Simon Marks. She married Israel Sieff in 1910, and was a prominent Zionist, and a friend and supporter of Chaim Weizmann, later first President of the State of Israel. In 1920, Sieff was one of the co-founders of the Women's International Zionist Organization (WIZO). Both her brother and her husband were directors of Marks & Spencer, the British chain store at which Vera was employed.

vast number of people who wanted to talk to her. It was a great joy to me that she knew about you, something I had not expected. Other than that, I felt a little embarrassed because so many people were standing around listening. Her picture in the *Rundschau* is extremely flattering, by the way, because she looks at least twice as old.

Sunday evening before I left Berlin, I had sat down at Dobrin on the Kurfürstendamm so I could write to you and give you my fresh impressions concerning the evening with Mrs. Sieff. However, a really unlikable guy from Leipzig had the audacity to just sit down at my table and began to talk to me, and when I finally got away from him, it was getting really late and I was too tired to continue writing.[31]

MOPE TO VERA

Leipzig, 24 November 1936

You are right when you say that clouds are now moving above us and through us and that we are influenced by their darkness just as the rays of the sun wake light and joy in us. But if we are prepared to see that and actually know it, then we are strong enough to direct the clouds and the sun if they want to influence us psychologically. And that is the reason why we meet with postal delays or zones of disturbance in the inwardly wireless contact between us that sometimes sound like dissonances–heightened by misunderstandings that can be cleared up by letter. So long as we are forced to be so far apart spatially, we want to let the joy of our knowledge of one another rule over all moods of a negative nature. Herzl said when he talked about Palestine, "If you want it, it is not a fairy tale!"[32] And we both want it!!

Unfortunately, I cannot yet determine the exact date of my trip to London because I am missing some documents that, as I have already

---

31 Café Dobrin was a famous Jewish *Bäkerei* and coffee shop. The "really unlikable guy from Leipzig" was almost certainly a Nazi official sent to spy on Mope's activities and those of other Zionists. According to Rebecca Weisner, even in 1936, it was not unusual for the Gestapo to spy on the premises and randomly arrest clientele sometimes with fatal consequences (see Eric A. Johnson and Karl-Heinz Reuband, *What We Knew: Terror, Mass Murder, and Everyday Life in Nazi Germany: An Oral History* [New York: Basic Books, 2005], 49).

32 In his preface to his utopian novel, *Altneuland* (1902), Theodor Herzl (1860-1904), the founder of political Zionism, introduced the famous motto, "If you wish it, it is no dream".

written to you, the PalTreu had promised to provide. A letter-exchange with Palestine could be accomplished in ten to fourteen days, but I am afraid that the people will take their time because they don't care that Lilongo and Mope long for each other. Nevertheless, I hope for a quick transaction since I described the matter as extremely urgent. Because I am still with the Gebrüder Felsenstein and they have now granted me unexpectedly generous liberties as long as I stay with them, I can hardly abuse this generosity in all good conscience–apart from the costs.

I already wrote to you about Mrs. Sieff, but I have no idea in what respect she is supposed to be "hard as nails." I am curious to find out if she remembers to deliver my greetings.

VERA

Journal entry, 24 November 1936

I have not written anything in here for an eternity, because, whenever I have time to write, I write to my friend and lover.

I have a lot of work, and for the most part, it is very satisfying. I carry my Mope within me and I hope that he will come home soon and that we will find work for him here.

MOPE TO VERA

Leipzig, 4 December 1936

This evening, after quite a long break, I had another Hebrew lesson which stretched out to a quarter after 1.00 a.m. so that this epistle is being written in the train station waiting room once again. Since I can sleep in tomorrow morning, I have the leisure to contemplate my peculiar surroundings during my writing.

It is the same picture as always and is interrupted in its monotony only by a very striking-looking blonde who just appeared. She looks as if she could afford to use a hotel lobby to wait for the train, but she serves a "higher purpose" with the view she offers to the ones waiting here. Her cavalier who looks more like a gigolo is virtually ignored by her.

Blondie and gigolo are fighting at this very moment. I wonder if you and I will turn out to be sulky and upbraid each other at some point. Or will we be sufficiently insightful to avoid such scenes when misunderstandings develop between us? It is certainly good to always remember that such moments are the sum of single trivialities that, seemingly insurmountable, lead to an explosion.

Now, the waiting room is filling with people in a way that I've never before observed. Most of them are not without alcohol and for that reason, things have become a little lively. The air has become thick enough to cut, despite the height of the room, because of all the smoke. At my table, two "gentlemen" sat down who are distressing themselves over street ballads in a fluent Saxon dialect, although they have not yet received their beer through which they can oil their sore throats. Blondie and gigolo left the restaurant separately–she with the suitcases. *That* marriage is broken. Then she came back one more time with inviting looks for me, but I did not feel up to serving as a baggage handler and so both of us remained lonely–but only on the outside where I am concerned.

Now I will bring the letter into the franking room at the main post office so that you will most likely receive it tomorrow. I would love to go on writing but I don't like the atmosphere here anymore.

MOPE TO VERA

Leipzig, 6 December 1936

There is nothing in the newspapers here about the affair of the King with Mrs. Simpson, except in the *Times*. Poor guy that he had to fall in love with, of all things, this young woman with a past. However, I can understand the attitude of the English who are also accusing him of not being religious while he, as the King, has to personify the head of the English church. Certainly, that thirty-eight-year-old young girl does have the strongest influence on him and takes the suggested long trip to let him come to his senses. Mistresses can be honored, but appear to me to be unsuitable as the queen and mother of an heir to the throne of a bigoted people.[33]

---

33 Great Britain was in the middle of the Abdication Crisis. King Edward VIII, intent on marrying the divorcee, Wallis Simpson, was formally to abdicate the throne on 10 December. Edward's younger brother became King George VI.

MOPE TO VERA

Leipzig, 10 December 1936

It is true that we got to know each other because of all that work you had to do for Christmas last year, but the death of a king helped us to deepen the contact just a little more; and without that event, I hardly would have come by my first kiss at that time. Today, another king abdicated. I wonder if another joy is in store for me because of that!

Yesterday evening was very successful, although we learned that some things could have been done better, as is always the case. There was a lottery at which the single very large prize was supposed to be a trip to Palestine–which had been donated. The tickets were very inexpensive at 5 for RM 1.–and people snapped them up. The trip had a value of RM 250.–and those clever people only sold 1000 tickets (that is, for 200.-) while at least 5000 could have been sold, had more been available. As you can see, the Zionists are idealists and, in all their idealism, forget the calculations.

The speech was given by a very young Rabbi Nussbaum from Berlin.[34] A vain boy who imitated Joachim Prinz's voice and used the most catastrophically unconsidered comparisons. But you could see once again how pathos–if used correctly–stirs people, because, much to my shock, they were thrilled by that uncontrolled torrent of words.

I received a rather unsatisfactory answer from the Paltreu Office in Berlin today. Those people abuse their right in the most indecent manner–at least that is my feeling. According to my calculations, we will sustain a loss of approximately 18 per cent because of them, including the fees they demand, which are added to everything else.

Now it is outrageously late once again, but I lay down for an hour before I started the letter, because I was just too tired to write. In the greatest love–Your Mope

---

34 Rabbi Max Nussbaum (1908-1974) from Suceava, Romania, served as a community rabbi in Berlin. He and his wife escaped from Germany in 1940, and settled in the United States, where he became the rabbi of Temple Israel of Hollywood. A posthumously published volume of his sermons and articles, *Max Nussbaum: From Berlin to Hollywood-A Mid-century Vision of Jewish Life*, appeared in 1994.

MOPE TO VERA

Leipzig, 11 December 1936

This evening, I lit four candles. The first half of the eight-day festival of Chanukah is over already. For years, I did not do the lighting with any regularity, but this year, loneliness tempted me into doing it since I am already counting the days, and I can celebrate every day that brings me nearer to you with a new light.

Our family business does not close over Chanukah, because this holiday did not come into being until a later time–that is, after the time of the Bible. It is a holiday of the Jews, only it does have, as all of our celebrations, a religious note as well. The Romans had desecrated the Temple in Jerusalem and, after everything disturbing (pictures of idols and so on) was removed from it, there was no more olive oil in store– olive oil that had been pressed in the prescribed manner and sealed in containers by the High Priest–other than one small bottle the contents of which would have only supplied the candelabra for one day. The miracle of it all was that the light, despite the insufficient quantity of oil, burned for eight days, until new oil was available. That is where the tradition of the eight-armed candelabra comes from and the joy does not concern the victory but the consecration of the Temple and Chanukah means consecration.[35]

Unfortunately, I haven't been able to read any books for the longest time, or I start to read them and can't go on. I cannot even finish my newspaper reading. By the way, did you read the Weizmann speech?[36] It is thought out so consummately and a historical document in its presentation of claims. You can tell from it what motivates us Zionists and what sweeps us along inwardly. We have set ourselves a high goal that is difficult to reach which we will fight for despite all resistance.

My heartfelt congratulations on the new royal family, please give them my kind regards and assure them that they are the only people that I would feel like visiting when I am there. However, in two weeks, we will spend this evening together and I cannot even describe my

---

35 Rather than the Romans, it was Seleucid forces under King Antiochus IV that desecrated the Temple, c. 165 BCE.
36 Mope is alluding to *Das Recht auf die Heimat* (*The Right to the Homeland*), a speech made in Jerusalem in November 1936 by Zionist leader and future President of Israel Chaim Weizmann (1874-1952).

delight when I look forward to that. Sleep well, my sweet wife and let yourself be kissed and embraced again and again by Your Mope

Mope was in London with Vera from Wednesday, 23 December 1936 through to 10 January 1937. Their correspondence resumes following his departure.

Twenty:
"More of a Stranger Here Now"

10 January though 3 February 1937

The agreement between the Gebrüder Felsenstein and Mope stipulated that, whilst he remained with the company, he was free to travel at will in preparation for whatever life he was planning. But he knew that he needed to be back in Leipzig to assist his mother in seeking an apartment since Nazi "Aryanization" had forced her out of her own. Additionally, he wished to further his discussions with Haavara and the PalTreu regarding emigration to Palestine. In order to satisfy British mandatory requirements, each emigrant needed to post a surety of £1,000, yet German currency restrictions prohibited the exchange or exportation of Reichmarks. In an important exchange of letters (out of which, alas, we only have his side and a short entry from her journal), Mope and Vera also engaged in discussion on questions of female chastity with hangovers that appear to be primarily of his own making.

VERA

Journal entry, 10 January 1937

This morning, my Mopelein went back, after we spent two and a half very happy weeks together.

This man is the one I have been waiting for all my life, a man with a heart, a mind, a body that is attractive to me, and equipped with so much sensitivity. I love him and I want to make him happy.

On 25 December, because of a conversation, I realized that he thought I had not been with a man before. I was very sad to have to hurt my beloved man like that, because of the thought that he might think me insincere and also because of the matter itself which cut him to the quick. All men are vain!

I know that I did the right thing back then, the thing that was necessary for me. Nevertheless, had I known that a Mope would come later, I would not have done it.

MOPE TO VERA

Leipzig, 13 January 1937

I am more of a stranger here now than I have ever been. It is absolutely not the outbreak of a depression that makes me write like this. Maybe even the opposite actually, because this feeling of loneliness only incites me to shorten the time until we are finally together again.

Yesterday evening, there was a pleasing concert of the Berlin Jewish orchestra at the local culture alliance. First a Mendelssohn overture, then Mozart's "Kleine Nachtmusik," and after the intermission, Beethoven's Third Symphony in D-major under the new conductor Professor Julius Prüwer. The former conductor, Prof. Steinberg, took a position abroad and was better than the one today by a far margin.[37] After the concert, I was at Felsche's–to digest the music–and was simply too tired to still write to you.

Today, I examined approximately 1,500 Persian lamb skins for six hours without a break, piece by piece, and then had to adjust the catalogue that had already been annotated by both Semy and a second partner. The auction tomorrow will show whose judgment was more correct.

I sent the Weizmann speech to you today and hope that you will find time to read it with as much attention as is appropriate for its very valuable content.

Once again, it is illegally late so that I have to close as quickly as possible and since I cannot do it in person, I am once again forced to do it in writing with such feeling that you will remember the real caresses

---

37 Julius Prüwer (1875-1943) was an Austrian-born conductor and a protégé of Hans Richter. He eventually fled from Germany and died in obscurity in New York. Cologne born William Steinberg (1899-1978) had been dismissed from the Frankfurt Opera in 1933, and left Germany for Palestine in 1936, becoming the first conductor of the Palestine Symphony Orchestra. After 1938, he continued his career in the United States.

and hopefully yearn for my lips that are burning to kiss you and want to whisper sweet nothings that my heart dictates to them.

MOPE TO VERA

From Erwig's Hotel Fürstenhof, Leipzig, 20 January 1937

As you can tell by the stationery, I am sitting in the hotel with my dear mother. She arrived yesterday afternoon and unfortunately, I was not able to see her until I had finished the inspection of the merchandise. Instead of me, a young man from the store met her at the train station. I found her looking a little small but not bad. Today she had to look for an appropriate room–sadly without me once again, but she has not decided on one, although I had already looked at several before. It is just not that easy to accept a little room in a city where you have run your own large household for more than forty years.

There is so much poverty and despair here among the Jews, and we hardly know anymore which way to steer.

My activities today were just as ineffectual, since the prices obtained at the auction were far above what we were able to invest so that I was able to buy almost nothing. A little dissatisfying, when one has worked so strenuously for two days and then has to go home without any results. But that is one of the quirks in this line of business, ever since the export can only take place with the appropriate authorization.

It makes me glad that you read the Weizmann speech and found it good. It is, as has often been said, really a historical document in the history of our people.

It is really cold here and it has been snowing almost without a break. A pity that one has neither the time nor the money to go on a winter sports vacation.

MOPE TO VERA

Leipzig, 24 January 1937

This morning, I went looking for a room with my dear mother, and after an hour and a half of climbing up and down stairs, we met with the desired success. We rented a room with steam heat, a room that is large, bright and friendly. The washing facilities are in a bathroom with warm and cold water. The move will probably take place on Wednesday. Until then, the dear lady is staying with Uncle Siegfried who seems to be enjoying the company.[38]

This afternoon, I was at the Kaiserhof with one of my fraternity brothers and celebrated–by myself unfortunately–the cocktail I spilled exactly one year ago in the company of Annelie and you, before we went to see the movie "Bosambo." Do you remember that? Now we are at the stage of celebrating anniversaries of our acquaintance and the love that grew from it, and still, we are so far away from each other.

MOPE TO VERA

Leipzig, 25 January 1937

If I sound downhearted and sad, I have to admit that I am indeed, in giving voice to doubts that burden me concerning your relationship with Lancelot.[39] Sometimes, I think that I love you too much to stand life without you any longer. That is where these thoughts are coming from that might appear not only unjustified to you but also silly. They might lie in a completely different area, but a woman who so completely adjusts herself to the needs of her man meets all doubts with a proof of value and lets them burst like soap bubbles. Still, I do know that you will not be angry with me for talking about what was bothering me, because you can stand above that.

I don't believe that any girl will relinquish herself to any man against her will. Nevertheless, there is no excuse for Lancelot. *If the possession of the girl had meant anything to him*, he might even be considered a nasty, frivolous bastard and criminal for whom no punishment can be hard enough. A guy who only takes a girl who has never belonged to anyone before him, in order to possess her once and satisfy his senses, can destroy that girl for life and make her unhappy, and I–maybe I am a fool and think more of women than they deserve and are worth–am surprised that you got over the deed and the following behavior of

---

38 Siegfried Felsenstein (1853-1939) was an uncle to Mope and his mother's widowed brother-in-law.

39 Mope is, of course, alluding to Vera's relationship with Mitja. He bases the name on Friedrich Markus Huebner's drama, *Lancelot and Sanderein* (1916), that both he and Vera knew. In the story, Lancelot takes advantage of Sanderein, though with the implication that the relationship is consensual.

the fellow without any psychological cracks, or even with a certain self-assurance.

Maybe I am unjust in losing all objectivity in connection with your person. In a neutral case I would most likely try to give understanding to a male subject who had acted like him and maybe even defend him. But since it concerns your person whom I love most deeply I see red and get so angry, an anger that does not find any outlet so that I don't even know myself any longer.

It is probably good for me that I am telling you about it, because in doing so I can find my way back to reason, and pose to myself the question how would I have acted. Had I been your first lover, I think that I would have acted differently or would at least have fallen deeply in love with you.

However, you do recognize that your first experience has robbed me of my objectivity. I know that this wave of rage will come over me again and again until it subsides, especially because your attitude towards the affair is psychologically incomprehensible to me and doubt overpowers me and I wonder if some small piece of this man did not stay behind that has been revived through me and keeps some small part of you from me. I ask myself whether this experience has been overcome by you completely or survived well, an experience you told me about with a certain amount of pride.

Maybe it is wrong to try to handle such a delicate question objectively when a deeply loved person is involved or to reduce the matter to its smallest psychological details. Maybe one should keep that jealousy of the past to oneself if it exists, but–maybe it is right or the right thing to talk things out with a human being that one loves as much as I love you and whom I trust implicitly, because I can count on the same honesty, *even if it hurts*, to get an honest answer. That is the only way–complete clarity even in this can be created between two lovers–and that cannot diminish my love for you.

My jealousy–you see, I am not trying to prettify anything–is based on the general claim that a girl will never forget the man whom she belonged to first, because she can never get over the love for him (and a man who loves back is worthy of that love, although real mutual love that finds fulfillment is so rare that it would have to be called perfection). Had I been a girl in the course of my soul's travels, I would surely be more understanding than it is possible for me like this. Please accept that as an apology for my behavior.

However, please understand what I am saying in relation to my longing for you, a longing that demands more, *all of you*. It is so wonderful for me that you see our future path as so straight and without difficulty in front of your eyes, and my remarks should not be obstacles on that path but should show you that we can talk to each other about inner unrest without taking offense or tripping over it, because the one who is feeling the unrest expects his best and most loved friend to be understanding.

VERA

Journal entry, 31 January 1937

A few days ago, I was too tired to go on. Today, I planned to refresh my memories of Mitja and to send a report of the events to Mope, just as soon as I have the time to write everything down.

I am so glad–no, actually it makes no sense to write such mundane sentences here. I have found in Mope my "husband"–really and truly!

MOPE TO VERA

Leipzig, 3 February 1937

We just talked–by the way, for nine minutes–to each other and I was so happy once again to hear your voice and to find out with how much interest you made my business yours. Not because you are helping me and I am really grateful to you for that help, but because the intensity of the help and the wish to help prove your love to me, and I am especially happy about that.

Tomorrow evening, I have to go to a lecture which is followed by yet another meeting, so that I don't know if I will be able to write to you afterwards. It will be quite late, I'm afraid, but it concerns the procurement of money for Palestine. During today's meeting, a report was made about the new actions that would give a guarantee that all Palestine-transfers through Haavara will function with the greatest simplification. Of course, I did not say anything to that, but just stared at the table for so long that it appeared green to me.

My beloved mother still wants to move to Jerusalem where her siblings are living as well and she also has two children in the vicinity.

In contrast, I will move to London, according to your wishes and in consideration of the circumstances.

Because the economic pre-requisites in Palestine have changed inordinately since my orientation trip last year, I have to try to get a clearer picture of the new situation. During my stay in Palestine, there was a period of prosperity following an economic depression, caused by the unrest, etc., and the plan which had been established based on importing luxury goods no longer appears to fit the current situation, or, as the case may be, no longer promises the expected livelihood. However, the alpha and omega lies in the fact that the transfer of assets to Palestine has to be arranged to the advantage of the German economy and hopefully not be too disadvantageous to me.

Today, I am writing to you from the office for a change. Unfortunately, the letter is a hopeless chaos, because I have been interrupted untold times, have served customers, have taken phoned in offers, signed bank stuff, and whatever other daily jobs and demands there are.

And now finally, an end to all that business stuff, that is necessary unfortunately and which you take on so lovingly. I considered flying there to be with you over the weekend. But that costs RM 216,–return trip and my heart is for it and my wallet so against it that the war between the two had to be decided in favor of the Mammon, much to my regret. Sometimes it is downright sad, that one is not rich enough and to have to send letters via airmail instead of oneself.

A few days ago, I wanted to write and tell you that our love does have a large dose of romanticism, because, as factually as all the economic questions have to be treated, it is an unusual path that is supposed to lead us to each other. I only regret that you have to go to so much trouble that is added to your work which takes up most of your time already. I hope that you get enough sleep anyway and that you take care of your health. I am seriously worried that people burden you with too much and would be very grateful to your dear mother if she would make sure that you don't go to bed too late and watch your food and take care of yourself. It does not matter if one or the other of the letters does not get done for a few days if it helps you relax. *Your well-being is the most important problem to me.*

I kiss you most passionately and full of great love, your Mope

On the fly, Mope opted to leave for London, arriving unannounced to an astonished Vera one evening in early February and greeting her with a bouquet

of flowers as she was leaving work for the day at Marks & Spencer. Their unplanned reunion was joyous, though during his stay Mope was obligated to take account of his fiancée's packed work schedule, patiently awaiting long hours in the frigid winter night outside the Kilburn store until Vera was free to join him. After just over two weeks, he returned to Leipzig on 21 February.

Twenty-one: "The Letter Writing Last Guest"

21 February through 22 March 1937

Worried that she lacked permission to remain a permanent resident in England, Vera was concerned that to announce that she was engaged to a Jew residing in Germany might jeopardize her position at Marks & Spencer. Contrary to this, Mope felt that her secrecy at work about their engagement was both compromising and counter-productive. To resolve lingering doubts, they decided to postpone their wedding date to the summer.

In Leipzig, Mope remained involved with the Jewish Cultural Committee, while also pursuing plans to emigrate. In the spring of 1937, though confiscation of his passport was a constant fear, he still enjoyed relatively unrestricted travel, and, coinciding with Passover, was able to visit Vera in London at the latter end of March.

Many of Mope's letters were written late at night while he sat over coffee at Zellner's or Felsche's, at which Jewish-owned café-restaurants he had become well known as the midnight penman or (as he later describes himself) "the letter-writing last guest." Inevitably, he was observed with pen in hand by Nazi informers. In his post-war curriculum vitae, Mope writes chillingly that "on one of those occasions, I was arrested by SS men who alleged that I was a spy. They beat me and wanted to transport me to jail. Fortunately, the main train station was still in the hands of the regular police, and a police officer who knew me (our company's building was located about 100 meters away from the train station) forced the SS men to go with me to the police post in the train station, where the police inspector released me." Rather than scaring Vera, he excludes reference to such encounters in his letters to her. In Nazi Germany, the brutalization of Jews was not something that could be written about in a letter that might too easily find its way into the wrong hands.

MOPE TO VERA

Amsterdam, 22 February 1937

In Amsterdam, which did not put down its rainy mantle for a short time until the afternoon, I called Wolffs'[40] and they invited me for breakfast. After, I followed the old motto "Make the best of it" and went to the Rijksmuseum in the morning where all the wonderful Rembrandts, Hals, Ruisdaels etc. can be seen. I was strongly impressed by the painting of Rembrandt's bible-reading mother. His most famous painting, "The Night Watch," also hangs in Amsterdam. That is a painting whose beauty goes beyond the possibilities of imagination. I sat in front of it for a long time and for the first time in many years felt what painting can be.

I went back to Wolffs' for lunch and Aunt Rahel showed me Amsterdam afterwards. The city with its many canals and the many picturesque corners and places is especially beautiful. We also went to the Jewish quarter where we toured the immense Sephardic synagogue (Sephardim are the Jews who were expelled from Spain around 1495, while the ones from Germany and from the East are called the Ashkenazim).

There are approximately 70,000 Jews among the 800,000 residents. Whole streets that used to be the former ghetto are now just part of the Jewish quarter. Around ten per cent of the Jews here are Sephardim. There is also an extraordinarily large number of German emigrants here who can lead relatively decent lives, although the economy is not as good due to the non-armament than in Belgium, England and also in France, of late.[41]

Though she does not know you, your Aunt Rahel sends her kindest regard.

---

40 Mope's aunt, Rahel Marx(1882-1942), had married Solomon ("Sally") Wolff in 1903. In common with many others, the Wolff family had fled Germany in the early 1930s, and were rebuilding their lives in Amsterdam. Sally died in February 1940, a few months before German forces occupied Holland. Accompanied by a son and daughter-in-law, Rahel escaped to Paris. All three fell victim to Dr. Marcel Petiot (1897-1946), a Nazi collaborator, known as "Dr. Eugène", who promised to smuggle them out of France in the trunk of his car, but, because of the dangers involved, insisted that they were anaesthetized for the journey out of Paris. He then injected them with cyanide, killing them instantly. At least sixty escapees were killed by him during the war. Petiot was found guilty of heinous war crimes and executed in 1946. See also David King, *Death in the City of Light: The Serial Killer of Nazi-Occupied Paris* (New York: Crown, 2011).

41 The Netherlands remained neutral during World War I, and maintained this policy through the 1930s. It did not prevent the Nazis from invading Holland in 1940.

MOPE TO VERA

Leipzig, 23 February 1937

Neither Semy nor the others said even one word about my prolonged absence. The staff told me that the company had been rather unusually quiet. Some customers did come in at different times and asked for me first and then for Semy, and after acknowledging our absence, they had disappeared again quietly and without saying a word. During the day today, I bought five hundred rabbit skins, and Semy remarked rather pointedly in front of the other partners that the purchase was a sound one.

Tomorrow is the Fast of Esther and Purim the day after tomorrow. If you read the book of Esther in the great Doré bible–it is not very long–you will know the reason for that.[42] At the end, it says that all Jews sent each other presents and that is still the custom on this day. Since Purim is a celebration of joy, they have a good frame of mind and–against all the present norms here–are cheerful and drink and dress up and whatever other happy customs there are. I am missing a home as much as my dear mother does in which we can celebrate with invited guests.

I just read in the "Ketty poems" of my grandmother that I actually intended to send to your dear mother. But I think that the mourning for the first child was completely different for her and do not know if it is right to show her the comparison with the loss of such a hopeful child.[43].

---

42 Incapable of reading Hebrew, many assimilated Jewish families in Germany owned the large folio bible (*Die Heilige Schrift*) in Ludwig Phillipson's translation, which was decorated with the celebrated illustrations of Gustave Doré (1832-1883).

43 After the early death from diphtheria of her oldest daughter, Ketty, in 1893, Gertrud Marx (Mope's grandmother) wrote a series of poems in her memory. These were privately printed by her surviving children in 1928 to commemorate the first anniversary of the death of Gertrud's husband, Georg Marx. It was a copy of this volume that Mope planned to send to his prospective mother-in-law, Alice Hirsch, who had lost her own first daughter in 1935, almost two years before this letter was written.

MOPE TO VERA

Leipzig, 28 February 1937

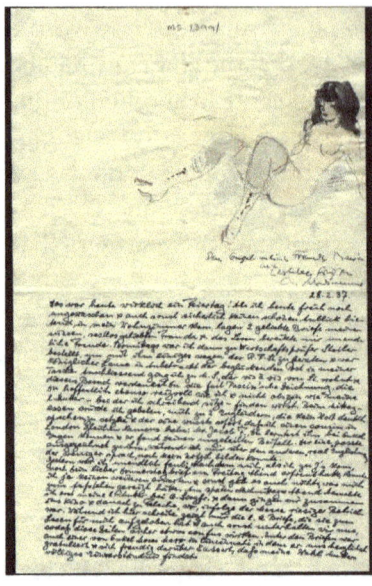

Fig. 69 Erotic watercolor by Max Schwimmer at head of letter from Mope to Vera, 28 February 1937.

As I came into my living room, unwashed and certainly not presenting a beautiful sight, two beloved letters of my sweet and completely beloved wife lay there, and reading them gave me unending pleasure. In the morning, I had an appointment with our auditor in order to consult with him on some things concerning taxes but was in such a royal mood because of that pleasurable mail in my pocket. Afterwards, I went to Max Schwimmer who lives across the street and you have to thank this visit for the drawing that I hope you will find as charming as I did and not obscene as my dear mother thinks–whom I am sitting next to while writing this. While I am writing, my mother is showing me letters that she saved for me to read and we are also talking so that these lines might appear a little confused!

I am very happy that you took pleasure in the Megillath-Esther, and even though it only repeats things you already know, the content is worth being refreshed in your memory. The Hebrew lettering is often more stylized and because of that, not as beautifully printed as in the edition I sent to you that also gave me pleasure when I saw it. Generally, I look at

Hebrew printings very critically because I love it when the beauty of the letter forms from old writings is preserved in reproduction.

MOPE TO VERA

Leipzig, 1 March 1937

The First of March. A year ago on this day, I was in the land of my constant longing and I was happy. Now I am sitting at Felsche's which is packed with people because of the Leipzig Trade Fair. As I write, an uninterrupted stream of coming and going guests sweeps alongside my arm. You will find the same picture at Zellner's from early until late. Until now, 11.45 p.m., I was at my mother's who picked me up from the store. I had to check a number of bank statements at her place (all the way back to 1934) and send part of them to the auditor with a commentary. We ate dinner at her place again.

Now to your dear letter! Are you really still thinking about spending the summer far away from London and extending our waiting period even more? I would really like it if we could get married in the registry office at Easter if you can arrange everything necessary in time. Or would you like to wait a while longer? We can move the real and most important wedding ceremony to any convenient point in time. Have you in the meantime been to the Hammersmith borough registry office? What papers will they need from me?

Although the clock is at 12.30 a.m., the traffic here has really not let up. Something like this would be impossible in solid London. But here, even the streetcars are going all night long during the trade fair. Now I have to close because work is awaiting me at home and Morpheus also has a few rights to me that I already shortened for him last night. Sleep well too, my sweet beloved. Dream only beautiful dreams and let me be with you in them at least, Your Mope

MOPE TO VERA

Leipzig, 3 March 1937

This evening, I went to a newly opened Jewish coffeehouse with my dear mother. This coffeehouse smelled strongly of new paint, was not very comfortable, but very clean and a new harbor for us, besides Zellner's. We had a very stimulating conversation–as usual, and I will miss her a lot, since she will travel to Hamburg via Berlin on Sunday. She is keeping her room here, and that gives me the hope that she will come back in the not so distant future.

Tomorrow, I will inspect another batch of rabbits, and if I like them and we can agree on a price, I will take them on. Today, I took the opportunity to complain to Semy that our telephone conversations are often monitored by one of the partners. I also told him that the monitoring of private telephone conversations proves dislikable curiosity, but that of business conversations distasteful mistrust. I am curious to find out about the result.

Everyone who finds out that I will leave the Gebrüder Felsenstein in the not-too-distant future declares that they probably will no longer deal with us and a few whom I talked to about my reasons, i.e. bad pay, are beside themselves about the pure meanness. I have already received several offers at a much higher salary because of that.

MOPE TO VERA

Leipzig, 4 March 1937

You will not believe how happy I am that you are trying to find out where you can learn Hebrew. It proves to me how hard you are trying to draw nearer to my inside feelings and interests and I thank you so very much for that. It also makes me happy that you are having Zionistic thoughts. What progress that is for Vera Hirsch from Frankfurt who was equipped with a Jewish vacuum. Such considerations just have to contribute directly to your inner equilibrium. People who are missing an arm or a leg also create a balance, but if one replaced it for them, they would realize what they had been missing.

VERA

Journal entry, 7 March 1937

Morning. A slow morning in bed. I know that I have neglected my journal in the last few weeks. Whenever I have time, I write to my man. Nevertheless, the reason why I write so little in here lately probably lies somewhere else: this book always served to help me get clarity concerning my thoughts, or should we say problems, my innermost personal problems and to deal with them. At this time, I feel so well-balanced that it might be one of the reasons for my rare entries.

I am so happy and glad in the knowledge of Mope, this man whose finely tuned instincts–his sweetness and kindness–are of the greatest. His way of dealing with the problems of this world, his sense of beauty and his joy in it is so akin to mine. His generosity and his way of loving me, just what I always wished for in my husband!–

The one thing I still am not clear about is the ability to be a daredevil in business and if he possesses the practical commercial sobriety you need to get ahead, but I guess I will have to help with that and I hope that the two of us will accomplish that together. I am happy and glad: I love Mope, not with a burning, consuming love, nor led by any kind of cold reasoning nor as an adventurer for the sake of the adventure, but deeply and steadily and growing from the inside and out of a feeling of the most beautiful and harmonious belonging.

MOPE TO VERA

Leipzig, 9 March 1937

Semy said yesterday that it was not right that I would go on another trip. He did understand that we want to get married over Easter, but that I could not be gone one half of every month. I answered that it had been agreed upon specifically that I had every freedom to travel in my own affairs and he could not expect that I would stay here over Pesach with the numerous invitations I had received from my relatives. He replied that I would have to come back right after the holidays. I pointed out to him that the registry clerks would not work just for us during the holidays, something that made sense to him.

By the way, the fur trade show is starting here on Sunday after Easter. So I have to be back here Monday at the latest and will have to leave Saturday evening. My arrival in London on Thursday before Easter has already been announced in all the newspapers–as a great event in world history. Did you not read about it? On the trip back, I will probably stay in Amsterdam for a few hours where my dear mother will be and she might travel back with me.

Now I am Felsche's last guest once again and that is why I have to say adieu to you. They are opening the windows and if I did not feel your lovely loving warmth while we are chatting I would certainly feel cold.

MOPE TO VERA

Leipzig, 10 March 1937

Because of a silly tooth that has disturbed my sleep for a few nights, I am a little tired today and was only able to follow the lecture of a Mrs. Mahler about the work of the women in Palestine through a conscious effort. Afterwards, there is another, smaller session of the board of directors of the local Zionistic group which I shirked in favor of writing, because otherwise, I won't get to it or won't get any sleep. Both of those things are more important to me today.

This afternoon, I spent an hour with Annelie and she asked me to tell you about her sorrow or the reasons for it, since it was too hard for her to write about it. After many years of fighting with her parents, she finally received their permission to go to New York to be with Fetz, and he had already procured a visa for her and had given her all the information necessary. Three days after this letter, an airmail letter arrived with the message that, in the afternoon of the day he wrote the letter he would be married in a civil ceremony to Alice Lewin (formerly of Leipzig). The reason is that the girl is expecting his child, something no one can do anything about, and after all of his relatives, friends and otherwise interested people had worked on him, he had to give in. Annelie had constantly warned him in writing about the girl who was in love with Fetz (without having been able to awaken like feelings in him). Fetz is supposed to be just as unhappy as Annelie and regards his life as messed up. In any case, that is what she took from his letter. He had already written to her on January 30 that he had committed an unforgivable stupidity and that it had taken just one hour of his life, an hour he will never forgive himself. It seems that, ever since then, everyone was kneeling on his seams and finally managed to soften him up. Annelie sent him another letter in which she asks him to go to bed with ten street prostitutes but not with the whore Alice Lewin. Now she is afraid that the newly married wife will read it.[44]

---

44 Annelie's account corroborates but differs in significant details from Mani Feniger's award-winning exposé of the life of her Leipzig-born mother, Alice Lewin (*The Woman in the Photograph: The Search for My Mother's Past* (2012). When researching the memoir, Feniger approached Annelie for information but was firmly rebutted.

Annelie is in a lot of pain, her face has changed completely and unfortunately, she can't laugh anymore–something that looked so good on her. But usually, people will get over even such sad experiences; it only takes a longer or shorter time depending on the depth of the person. She seems to have felt that I would understand her, because she would like to see me again if she stays for a few more days. It is such a shame that, at times, the most lively temperament is removed from the wine in the process of pressing, and many times has to be replaced artificially.

Early today, I had dear company in my bath once again. I went and got the blue envelope and read it in the tub and let drops fall on it that let the writing which was still fresh run all over the page. If I could cry I would be able to consider the spots tears after the fact, but there was no reason for that, or do you think so?

Today, I received my dear mother's first report from Hamburg. She had a good trip and went from a soaking wet Berlin to a snow-covered Hamburg where it is 6 ° [Celsius] cold. Unfortunately, although I talked to her about it, she did not take along her fur coat and thinks that if I sent it now the weather would turn warmer and melt the snow.

In terms of our own wedding plans, I have now made the firm decision that we need to postpone the civil marriage ceremony. Why should you let your conscience bother you if your papers have to be altered and you feel embarrassed to let the head office at Marks & Spencer know? Why should I put you into an odd situation with your friends, if the civil ceremony and the religious ceremony are far apart chronologically? Why should you be placed into the embarrassing situation of having to tell everyone something that is obviously mortifying for you? These questions are absolutely not meant to be *ironic*, but I can see that I will have to get used to your idiosyncrasies in this regard and since I love you, I am prepared to do so. I read that part of your letter to Annelie and she thought that I would have shown my respect for you with this premature wedding. However, I have great respect for you without the wedding and don't have to prove it through that. But she did not understand you and I was not able to make her understand you. By the way, today's decision, as already mentioned above, is unshakable.

The weather here is awful, rain mixed with snow, and that contributes to everyone feeling tired. Hopefully, the sun will be shining on Good Friday for a little while, just like it did last year. I kiss you with all my love and am happy in my knowledge of you. I won't feel my real bliss until I am with you completely and we can talk about everything without forty-eight hours lying between the question and the answer. My arms embrace you and I yearn for you as if we had been separated for months. Your Mope

MOPE TO VERA

Leipzig, 12-13 March 1937

1.30 a.m. in the 3rd class waiting room at the train station. Just a little while ago, I took Annelie home after I spent the evening with her at Felsche's. She has calmed down quite a bit, even if she is still quite apathetic and does not feel like doing anything. Until now, she was always on the sunny side of life and the cold shadow of her recent experience has taken away so much of her courage. Once she is a little more removed from it, she will be able to feel that the experience brought her forward. Annelie is at an age at which experiences of a mental nature grow deeply into a person and create a very vulnerable web of scars.

When we said goodbye, she promised me that she would not take a sleeping pill tonight. Her former man's birthday is on the 30th of the month and she wanted to send him a birthday present, but I advised her against it. Since she still loves him, she should write him a happy birthday letter that does not contain any kind of "regardless." That will do him good and give him pain, both of which he deserves.

The station waiting room is filling up again. Friday night is moving forward and my bed is starting to call me to sleep–like the muezzin in the minaret calling the faithful to prayer. I still wish to send off my Friday evening letter to you, my beloved, and I hope that it will await you tomorrow, after you come home from work. Your Mope

MOPE TO VERA

Leipzig, 14 March 1937

I have to return to your inquiry concerning the wedding postponement one more time. I see girls who got engaged and whose feelings which prompted the connection are so much shallower than ours, talk about their engagement happily and let friends, acquaintances and bosses know about it. With you, I keep getting the feeling as if it scares you when someone finds out about this "secret." The fact that you did not let

Annelie know for almost half a year was making me wonder back then, but I thought to trace it back to your feelings of insecurity, and so I tried to be considerate.

When one day you expect a child, will you lace yourself up so tightly that no one will be able to see it, because your private business is none of anyone's concern? If everyone knows in advance that you are getting married, they will not wonder about the child that comes from it. If you keep your marriage secret, people will gossip about you when you become pregnant. I already wrote to you once that the degree of our love is a private matter, but the marriage is not and that is why–I have so tried to overcome your inhibitions in the most reasonable way. I won't be kept a secret. I am much too self-confident for that. There are males in the animal world who get eaten by the female after mating successfully (some species of spiders, etc.), and no one needs to talk about males like that, but I belong to a completely different category. You may consider me conceited, but I expect that you be proud of me, and that is not shown if you want to keep quiet about me. It is unimaginable to me that no opportunity has come up during the last eight weeks to mention the question in principle and to fix a final date.

No, my beloved girl, I did not understand the point of view that you represented in your letter, because it touches the same area once again upon which our difference rests. You keep giving me reasons to feel that you are not only not content with me, but that I embarrass you and that is something at which everything in me bristles. Of course, I know exactly that the reason lies in completely different sentiments, but those I have to fight against, because they are capable of constantly carrying new differences into our usually harmonious togetherness.

If you want to get married to me because we belong together, then you don't have to feel embarrassed in front of anybody if you explain that the religious ceremony will only take place when we can start our life together. These are abnormal times which also pose abnormal conditions. Very often, the so-called honeymoon takes place later than the wedding, so that no one will find anything wrong with it. You would only have to let the head office at Marks & Spencer know about the registry office wedding and the trip which is projected for a later time. However, as I already told you on the telephone, I have another concern that I would like to talk out with you, and I want to do that and make the final decision dependent on it and not persist on the categorical "no" that I declared in my Wednesday letter and that I regretted later.

I don't have to assure you again–but I really love doing it–that you and *only you* are "the" woman for me with whom I will be and want to be completely happy, and that no one will ever be able to change my mind. Most likely–I don't know Fetz–I am a much more strong-willed person than he and not as easily influenced if it concerns questions of conviction. You are right, that I hurt you, because I talked about Annelie's matter and our wedding at the same time, and although it was a coincidence that both came together, I am very sorry to have burdened your thoughts like that. That is why I bow to your "scolding" and realize that you are entitled to it. Please forgive me for the fact that this letter is so ugly, but I had to talk about what I am thinking.

I love you soooooo much, my sweet girl, that I talk to you this openly and I would be unbelievably happy if I could tell you all of this in person, because it would seem much less harsh and the sounds die away in the ether, while writing remains. Tear up the letter so that it won't make you sad any longer, but please try to understand me at least. Your Mope

MOPE TO VERA

Leipzig, 15 March 1937

Now I did get a letter from you and such a sweet one, too, that I am almost ashamed of my nasty tone of yesterday. But it had to be talked about once, something that cannot be silenced inside of me, because I have the feeling that these deliberations are right. If they had been talked about in person, they would probably have sounded much milder and much more understandable, because a voice can be modulated, but on paper, they sound cold and mean when they are read. However, I do hope that you know nothing is further from my intentions than torturing you and that is why you need to give my words the desired tone.

They will throw me out at Felsche's in a minute and I want to tell you quickly that I never expect you to use excuses with me. Why should you anyway? You do know that I–despite yesterday's letter–am always trying to comprehend your intentions and deliberations and to bring about a togetherness of mutual conviction, just like you do.

I am looking forward to seeing you so very much and am exceedingly happy and content in the knowledge of you so that all ugliness along my way seems unimportant. Feel my kisses and let me put my arms around you. I will give them to you in person soon and will want them back from you so that you can start looking forward to me. Your Mope

MOPE TO VERA

Leipzig, 17 March 1937

Now, I am sitting here and my conscience is bothering me even more than before. I took all the joy from my beloved girl with that all too serious, all too dissecting letter that I thought I had to write, because that was how my heart felt, as if it had to be told.

Your loving understanding for my gruffness shames me, since it is not necessary–even if it seemed necessary to me to address these questions again–it was not necessary to do it in this form. Your letter from last Monday was written in such a way that I should have noticed that you worded the question with a certain insecurity concerning me, because you were probably afraid of my lack of restraint. Now I feel even more dim-witted and share your opinion one hundred per cent that it is high time for us to see each other again.

In the meantime, the former concert master (violinist) Schwarz from the *Gewandhaus* has sat down at my table and I showed him the new photos of you. He is always very thrilled with your pictures–how thrilled he would be if he met you in person–and begs me almost every time when we see each other to show him your picture. Schwarz is a very nice guy and a real artist who now has to try to live on an extremely small pension and the income from a few concerts that the "Mendelssohn-Trio" gives for cultural events outside of Leipzig as well. To offer such a man a real life as an artist or pedagogue would be a marvelous deed. But how and where?[45]

Tomorrow evening, I am invited to a tea of the Keren-Kajemeth Lejisrael (Eternal Funds of Israel that serves the land purchase in Palestine. The land is only passed on as an inherited lease and is the property of the Jewish people), during which the leader of the KKL will speak. Presumably, it will be an interesting evening, since one always hears about new things during such occasions. I have another date with

---

45 Leo Schwarz was the lead violinist of the famous *Gewandhaus* Orchestra in Leipzig, which, until the advent of the Nazis in 1933, had been under the direction of the legendary Bruno Walter. In common with other Jewish musicians, Schwarz was dismissed from his position, and could only perform before Jewish audiences, under the auspices of the *Reichsverband der Juedischen Kuturbende in Deutschland* on which Mope served as an elected representative. Musical compositions such as the works of Mendelssohn and Mahler were banned under the Nazis but could still be performed by Jewish groups. Although arrested after Kristallnacht, Schwarz was able to leave for the United States in 1939.

Annelie for Friday. She seems to enjoy spending time with me, and I am very glad that I can help her even a little.

Now, it is abominably late once again and I am really tired and so filled with longing for you that I do not know what nice things I should write to even express just a small part of it.

MOPE TO VERA

Leipzig, 22 March 1937

Well now, the solemn moment has arrived during which I will write the last letter before I come to you. Another and another long day has gone by slowly, and the period of time that separates us now has become shorter, although, at times, I believe that the decrease won't ever come to an end.

I am leaving on Wednesday and will, should I arrive earlier than you return home from work, wait for you and use the time to flirt with your dear mother. Of course, you cannot disturb us too early! Please, just take your time for the way home! Shockingly, I neglected to ask you if I can stay with you again, or if you sold out on me. It could also be that such a frequent guest will soon become unwelcome! Well, I will hang myself from a rope at Liverpool Street Station after my arrival and listen to what people say about that. (You could have invited me?).

I am looking forward to Thursday like an imbecile, after we have not seen each other for such a terribly long time. You see I am completely beside myself because I love you excessively and with unauthorized passion, Your Mope

Twenty-two:
"Human Beings Are Good!"

4 April through 14 May 1937

Over this short period, Mope sought authorization from the British consulate in Dresden to establish himself in England. Fearing Nazi scrutiny, his references to the consular office are couched in terms that are deliberately oblique. "H.O." and "Gebr. H.O." are shorthand for "Home Office." Simultaneously, he was chasing contacts with Paltreu/Haavara with the notion of transferring capital to Palestine to aid the emigration of his mother. In this, he had already enlisted the support of his cousin, Julius Rosenfeld, in Palestine, and his brother-in-law, Fred Rau, in London. Fred undertook a short visit to Leipzig, which Mope reports in his letters.

In anticipation of his impending resignation from the Gebrüder Felsenstein, Mope began looking for clients that he would represent once he was ready to strike out on his own. On other topics, Mope's involvement with the Kulturbund throws light on the ghettoization of Jewish culture by the Nazis. He also made regular visits to his artist friend, Max Schwimmer, whose sketches and watercolors adorn several of the letters. Primarily, his attention focused on his fiancée and their joint desire to determine a new date for their postponed wedding. Over the Whitsun weekend (15-16 May), they met and spent two days together in Brussels.

MOPE TO VERA

Leipzig, 5 April 1937

I am sitting at my desk once again, the witness to so many letters that I have written to you filled with my love for you. It is rather late. My return trip was quite comfortable and since I had decided to travel 2nd class, I was able to catch some undisturbed sleep.

During the day, there was nothing much to do today. Some of my customers who usually only work with me had been here in the past week and they found more merchandise than I had thought possible. Those people seem to be buying anything and everything that has hair on it in order to keep their businesses going.

Max Schwimmer will come to see me tomorrow and pick up the colors. He was very happy that I procured them for him.

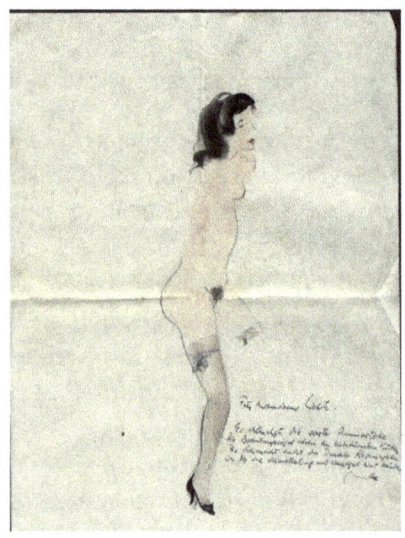

Fig. 70 Erotic watercolor by Max Schwimmer with verses included with letter from Mope to Vera, Leipzig, 5 April 1937.

For Maurice's Beloved

The gentle immortal one sobs,

The brown white birds scream along ice storm coasts,

The yearning seeks the dark wave of roses,

in which butterflies and nightingale once kissed.–Max Schwimmer

I kiss you, my sweet, beloved wife, and my arms reach out for you in vain–they yearn to embrace you.

MOPE TO VERA

Leipzig, 7 April 1937

I just got home from the very brilliant performance of *The Merry Wives of Windsor* of the culture union. Since I had not read Saturday's community leaflet, I found out about it by accident today and was happy that I went. The troupe had come from Berlin with its own orchestra.

Today, I told a few sales representatives and customers that I will leave the Gebrüder Felsenstein very soon, hopefully, something that caused genuine consternation (in the truest sense of the word). After all, no one is indispensable and I was feeling particularly replaceable at that time.

I love you unconditionally with all the intensity I am capable of, and as I have already told you, for the first time in my life without pain and therefore, not comparable to any other feeling I have had before. Additionally, I feel my love is more mature and–like a well-aged wine that has already reached its final aroma–it tastes wonderful to me, like it was pressed from the most exquisite grapes. If permission is granted, I will soon be able to drink my wine all the time and let it intoxicate me over and over without ever having the feeling that it might just be too much. I am yearning for this enjoyment and have discovered–a side of me I did not know about–that I am a gourmet who would be overjoyed if he could just have the smallest sip of the drink that will let every day become a holiday later.

MOPE TO VERA

Leipzig, 11 April 1937

Aside from a Hebrew course this morning and the reading of my mail at the store, I spent the day sleeping and reading. I have started to read books all the way to the end again, something I have not done in a long, long time, and I regard that as progress towards inner peace and balance, that I owe to you and my awareness of you, which makes me very happy.

I am expecting Fred here on Tuesday and I hope that he will also report about your well-being in his own words and according to his view. I had talked to Fred several times and at length about the matter of assets and there should be no misunderstandings in this respect.

In the meantime, I have been thrown out of Felsche's and want to finish this letter quickly, so that it can be mailed today.

MOPE TO VERA

Leipzig, 13 April 1937

I went to pick up Fred from the train station after he called and informed me about his arrival and his intentions here. Now he is at his cousin's and I did not go with him. In one hour, I will pick him up again and we will talk for a short time, because he has to leave for Freiburg at 7.00 in the morning. I will accompany him on this car trip so we can really talk in detail. We will be back around noon and he will continue on to Berlin while I have to go and inspect merchandise for an auction on Thursday. Semy seemed to attach great importance to the fact that I do the inspection that was not yet possible today.

* * *

Now I am sitting in Fred's hotel room while he is stretching his apollonian limbs in the bathtub. It is 12.30 a.m. and, since we were at his cousin's until now, we have not yet found the time to talk about business. He only told me that he received a letter from Julius Rosenfeld in Palestine on the day of his departure but could not say more than that. He will send you a copy after he returns.

MOPE TO VERA

Leipzig, 14 April 1937

I am satisfied with the discussion between Fred and me, as far as that is possible. It was really good that we had enough time while driving to Freiburg. Aside from that, the car trip was pleasant, since I had ordered quite a nice car yesterday, and the area has its charms in the first stage of Spring, charms we did not have much opportunity to admire because of concentration on the matters that occupied us.

We got back in time for the Berlin train and, after I had shown the document to Fred and took a short lunch, I went on to the inspection of merchandise which did not satisfy me qualitatively. Fred had actually not seen the document back then because of his long trip and he was completely right with his claims not to know it. You will hear about my views from Fred directly, and I am too tired today to repeat them and my opinion once again.

My dear mother is supposed to have traveled to Hamburg today where she will stay with Ketty for a few days.

On Saturday, Semy is traveling to London, and I would probably be much, much happier than he is if I could go in his place.

I kiss you and embrace you and love you, my most passionately loved wife–unfortunately only in my thoughts again and fueled by my imagination.

My sweet Lilongo, Your Mope

MOPE TO VERA

Leipzig, 18 April 1937

Early today, your very dear Friday letter made me happy, a letter that was actually written at the same time as my letter to you. In the meantime, you should be provided with more than enough mail, because I am writing every day, which is beyond comprehension to me. A year ago, I would have felt that anyone thinking me capable of that had to be damaged in the head, although I already knew you back then and we were actually engaged. Admittedly, my letters don't always get to the mailbox in the evening, often not before the morning like this one that is coming into being in my room after a long evening spent at Zellner's.

After quite an inspiring Hebrew hour, I took care of my own business correspondence at the store and taught the typewriter, after a few failed attempts, to follow my orders halfheartedly. A relatively detailed letter looked quite decent when I was finished with it. After that, I had a late dinner. Tomorrow, I will inspect more merchandise, since the auction begins on Wednesday. In the evening, I have another Hebrew instruction meeting and will go to Max Schwimmer afterwards who has invited me to come over.

MOPE TO VERA

Dresden, 22 April 1937

Yesterday morning, I received a letter from the branch office of Gebr. H.O. at the store which induced me to visit the branch office today. Unfortunately, I was not able to talk to the boss on the telephone and an employee wasted such a flood of words on me that hardly gave me any opportunity to present my offer in the way I wished for. He maintained that they received offers like that every day and had very little interest in them, aside from the fact that any order could only be made from the main office. So I could have answered the query in writing without going to any kind of trouble, but "I tried my best" and no one can do more and if you do any less to reach success, you might reproach yourself later. When all is said and done, the employee is not the one making the decision anyway.[46]

MOPE TO VERA

Leipzig, 23 April 1937

Despite all the difficult obstacles that have placed themselves between us at such great length, I am still very happy in my knowledge of you and so filled with it that my thoughts, and often my actions and reactions to events as well, are influenced by it. However, I do not want to state that there has been a change in my ego, but every human being has different possibilities to react, and now, I often follow the decisions that were precipitated by a short dialogue between us, before I react; and you are always the superior reasonable part in me during that conversation.

This morning, your dear letter from Wednesday made me happy in the bathtub, and I lay there dreaming and thinking about it in the water, until I almost forgot the time.

I got the information on the plane connections to Brussels from London today and found a connection–one that will hopefully do justice to the short time–which you will hopefully accept. In order for me to pay

---

46   The British Consulate (referred to here in coded fashion by Mope as "Gebr. H.O.") had been transferred from Leipzig to Dresden in July 1936. Its address in Dresden was 20 Mosczinskystrasse. The Consul ("the boss"), previously at Leipzig, was Henry Livingston. The "main office" was, of course, the British Embassy in Berlin. (Information supplied by Dr. Stephen Twigge, Official Historian at the Foreign and Commonwealth Office, London). Mope traveled to Dresden by train.

for the stay, Fred will have to give me a Whitsuntide present that he can send to a hotel he has to name, because I don't know of any. That is what the poor boy gets for being allowed to marry my sister!! Would you be so kind and let him know about this happy message?

MOPE TO VERA

Leipzig, 30 April 1937

Yes, it is Friday evening and I have enjoyed it all the more, because it gave me the opportunity to talk to Annelie. She looks really good, as also her parents whom we encountered as I was bringing her home, and I got the impression that she has lightened the weight on her heart a lot, even though she is not completely over it yet. Annelie said today that the veins on my left hand form a "V" and represent an "H" on my right, and it is actually really visible and I find it rather amusing. Other people have to determine the initials by throwing apple peels behind their head. For me, they are more intensely marked than if they had been tattooed, and I did nothing for it.[47]

MOPE TO VERA

Leipzig, 3 May 1937

After a walk under the stars, as far as they were observable between the houses, I have landed at Felsche's in order to give form to my daily desire to have a visible chat with my beloved. Early today, I received your loving letter from the office during the first day of the London omnibus strike, which will hopefully not be followed by others.[48]

It is really regrettable that it can come to such laying down of work by thousands of people, which, besides the usual consequences, also creates difficulties for the people on strike, because they are responsible for the maintenance of their families. The strike fund will only be of use for a short time in avoiding the distress that hunger will bring to the people. But following my letter from Thursday, I have to say that I am only really touched by the strike because my poor dear little girl has a

---

47 i.e., "V" for Vera, and "H" for Helene, Mope's mother.
48 The London bus strike lasted for four weeks, disrupting public transportation at the coronation of George VI on 12 May.

much more difficult trip to the store and through that, an even greater demand than usual is placed on her strength.

Today, I had to run the business by myself and it worked out so well that I was even able to take care of my private correspondence and still closed on time (more on time than usual). And I even took care of some business-related work that would normally not get done, because one always wants to pawn it off on the other. Additionally, I sat down in a club chair on the roof during my lunch break and gave the beautiful sun the opportunity to fry me. I have a nice tan already–at least in the face.

Did I tell you already that I had another call-back from Dresden? Of course, I answered it immediately and would be happy if I could get the final contract soon, but they are taking their time back there.

MOPE TO VERA

Leipzig, 5 May 1937

I wonder if the bus strike is over by now. I would really like it if your workday, including traveling back and forth to work, would at least be shortened by one hour. The work at Gebrüder Felsenstein during those two days of "absolute rule" was very pleasant to me and that pleasure was in no way diminished by Semy's return today. He is a good man and I can talk to him about everything, and he can give his opinion pro and con without anyone having to misunderstand it, because he is such a decent and objective man. What a difference to having to be alone with the other partners, where one feels pursued by falsehood with every step made, and add to that their obvious ineptitude that tries to hide behind an act of supposed importance.

Today, another stupid letter arrived from Dresden, and I will most likely go there next Tuesday. I can hardly help but feel that the people don't want me, but I won't lose courage, and I will work without them, if they want to give me problems.

MOPE TO VERA

Leipzig, 6 May 1937

After I was lazy all morning today–the sun did not come out until early afternoon–I went to Zellner's and into the store and then, I went for a walk with an acquaintance. While I was at the store, I wrote a letter to

Dresden–with the typewriter which is very slow–and asked if my visit would be welcome on Monday or Tuesday, and now I am waiting to see what the high and mighty gentleman will answer.

Why do you think that it is especially notable that the business at Gebrüder Felsenstein works without problems for me? It would function a lot better if I were by myself and would not constantly have to start a discussion about even the smallest matter in order to assert my opinion–in most cases anyway. It works really well with just Semy and he can oversee everything much better than I can, something that is helped by the fact that he undertakes the purchase of merchandise and its disposition. Additionally, my head has been so filled with personal matters for some time now that I am not always able to concentrate completely on the interests of Gebrüder Felsenstein, something that Semy does understand.

MOPE TO VERA

Leipzig, 7 May 1937

There are many things that can make a person mad, if that person is predisposed towards that. I have made some amusing studies concerning myself on this subject. For instance, it happens when I drop my keys and I introduce me to myself as "idiot" or "camel" or tell myself, "You are an especially stupid specimen today!" On other days, I discover that I whistle a happy tune during the same occasion so that my mouth cannot move fast enough from the pointed shape to the normal one and so I keep whistling happily. Do you whistle, too, my Veralein? Whistle for everything annoying or burdensome to you that wants to place itself in your path, because things will go much easier and better.

So, today is the last Friday on which I am writing to you before our longed-for reunion. Next Friday, I will be sitting in the train and will dream towards you, and that knowledge makes me so happy today that I would like to dance for joy. I suppose that my beloved will write to me one more time next Friday and will send her loving greetings towards me, greetings that heighten my longing for her even more (if that were possible) and will calm my agitation.

Now, your squandering husband has to tell you that he bought himself a wonderful portable typewriter for a horrible amount of money. However, he does need it and he had the choice between two models of which the better one cost about RM 40 more, and so he decided for the more comfortable one.

I will be thrown out of Felsche's any minute now. The last of the very few guests are getting ready to leave.

MOPE TO VERA

Leipzig, 8 May 1937

You will have just left the store and have started your way home which still seems to be circuitous, while I am sitting at Zellner's and make the embarrassing observation that the clock, despite my wish to make it move forward, or maybe despite of it, hardly moves. At 11 p.m., I want to call my beloved. Her letters during the last few days have sounded so downhearted that I hope to be able to lighten the mood through the telephone just a little bit. Soon you will read my letter from yesterday which–if it serves its purpose well–will also contribute to lift that little mood and make it ready for the weekend.

Early today, my typewriter which I had had furnished with £ and $ signs was delivered. I am happy like a child with it and will probably write the letters to my beloved on it, although that would be just a little impolite.

On Monday, the new Palestine film "Hatikwah" (The Hope) will be shown here, and it is supposed to be very good.[49] Everything with legs will go, because the interest in the land, in which everyone here has relatives and friends, has become exceptionally great. Unfortunately, the available location is much too small and will not be able to take, in my estimate a third of the people who would go if it was bigger.

On Tuesday, Alexander Kipnis[50] will sing arias and songs for the culture league. Unless I am wrong, I have already heard him before and was only moderately awed. It could however be a mix-up with another person.

Now I am going to the store to call you and I am really looking forward to hearing your beloved voice for a few minutes.

---

49 Released in 1937, *Hatikvah* ("The Land of Hope") was a Zionist documentary film, directed by George Engel. In 1940, for his film, *Der Ewige Jude* ("The Eternal Jew"), the Nazi director, Fritz Hippler, juxtaposed scenes from *Hatikvah* showing Orthodox Jews in Jerusalem with similar sequences from the Polish ghetto to propagandize the idea that the Jewish scourge was everywhere the same.

50 Alexander Kipnis (1891-1978) was a famous Ukrainian born operatic bass. He had become an American citizen in 1931 but continued to tour in Europe until the Anschluss (annexation of Austria) in 1938.

So, now I have talked to you and I am very happy about it, because you seemed to be in a better mood and that calms and gladdens me. I have landed in a café in the meantime where I had to talk Italian with customers from Naples, and now, it is late again and the letter is supposed to be mailed tonight.

My Lilongo, your yearning Mope

Now I am sitting here without an envelope, because I had to use the one intended for you to contact Milan about the credit worthiness of the customers!

MOPE TO VERA

Leipzig, 9 May 1937 [Envelope written with new typewriter]

It is correct that my sister Hanna was able to take care of everything in Leipzig back then. The gentleman did not move to Dresden until a short time ago. I also received my Palestine visa a year ago today. Even if it is uncomfortable to me, I cannot blame the man for the fact that he prefers the beautiful city of Dresden as his residence.[51]

In another week, two people will lie in bed around this time and be unbelievably happy together and all difficulties and hardships will be forgotten when they embrace–indescribably happy and looking forward to the future and aware that they belong together completely and without conditions.

MOPE TO VERA

Leipzig, 10 May 1937

Today, I was very lucky once again–I had two letters from a certain young lady who whistles like a cobbler's boy (please read that in French!) and manages to overcome moments of sluggishness with the

---

51 Hanna and Fred Rau had married in 1932. According to Dr. Stephen Twigge (Official Historian at the Foreign and Commonwealth Office, London), "only Consuls had authority to register lex loci marriages and marriages to be solemnized under the 1913 Foreign Marriages Act" (personal communication). Hanna was a German citizen, and Fred was British. The British Consulate at 10 Dittrichring, Leipzig, was moved to Dresden in July 1936. The Consulate was responsible for the issuance of visas for German citizens wishing to visit Palestine, which was under British Mandatory control. See also note 46 (above).

aid of that whistling. Besides the demands on different organs that are absorbed by that, whistling also supports regular breathing, and that is of exceedingly great significance for the resistance on the part of the body and the soul in cold weather as well as in bad moods. What does my beloved who has had at least eight semesters of medicine say about this brazen meddling of a chemist outsider, who might just have some small idea about the combustion processes in general biology, in the field of psychology?

But now, I have to return to being serious. Your pronouncement concerning the "ideal" marriage is, in my opinion, the main condition for such an institution. The togetherness of people has to serve the purpose of letting people grow closer together, otherwise, it is sterile and therefore a waste of time and energy. Such people find their way to each other while playing bridge; because they hope that they can at least win something from the other, and any other kind of togetherness would make them go to sleep or start to fight. Just the awareness of two people who want to get married or are already married that the pan has a lid and the lid has a pan lets those two be more than they would be by themselves. Reassurance lies within this awareness, and there is an inner balance. But once that is gone, the marriage is down the drain as well and can only be continued officially when both parties agree to tolerate adultery.

No, my beloved girl, I expect much more from our marriage and the "more" can be embodied in the most beautiful form through our fruitfulness, because we want to grow through our children and allow our mutual understanding to become keener than it is without offspring.

However, the result of your deliberations concerning the fact that you are feeling regret about not meeting me six years earlier makes me very happy, because it shows me that your love is deepening. When you wrote to me, in a different matter, that it was a sin for even one minute not spent with the one you love, it reminded me of how much you resisted any such thoughts not too long ago.

Now, I have not even told you about today's Palestine film. It was a substandard film, quite good, by an industrious photo amateur which did lose a lot of its impact however because of the small reproduction area in the relatively large room. Nevertheless, it was quite inspirational, because I was able to remember the colors and to see everything shown in a different light than someone who does not know that glorious country.

I decided not to go again to Dresden and wrote a detailed letter instead which will hopefully serve the same purpose.

MOPE TO VERA

Leipzig, 11 May 1937

Today, the Kipnis concert took place, and I could not get there until after 9.00 p.m., because I had an important meeting beforehand. The man has a wonderful baritone, and I am just a little sorry that I was forced to miss the first part. Then, a small circle of friends and acquaintances got together at Zellner's, and I am writing to you from there. I really did not want to start writing a letter, because it has been terribly late every night during the last few days and I really wanted to get to bed before 2.00 a.m. for once, especially if I want to read for a little while.

There was much to do during the day today and I was happy, as always, when I can be alone with Semy. Right now is the buying season for seals captured from Norway and since the purchase takes place via telephone and telegram and the prices can be very different, it is a really exciting affair. Additionally, our company secretary was there who took my passport along to secure the Belgian visa for me. You will also have to get one. Please don't forget.

I will think of you tomorrow and take pleasure with you in your day off. In the evening, I will be at Max Schwimmer's–I sent him a bottle of champagne, and he was as happy as a child.

They are waiting for me and the tavern is closing soon.

MOPE TO VERA

Leipzig, 12 May 1937

My lady, as the title page has already informed you, I have just come from Max who honored me with a very charming etching, beside this one. Now, I am sitting in the Park Café in order to devote myself to my beloved. I did not want to write the letter at Max's again, otherwise he will lie on his couch quite desperate, just like the last time, and says, whenever I want to leave, "but no, just stay, you are not bothering me at all." Additionally, I left one of his most intimate girlfriends with him.

Fig. 71 Erotic watercolor by Max Schwimmer accompanying letter from Mope to Vera, Leipzig, 12 May 1937.

Today was a big day for the people in London,[52] as the newspapers showed in transmitted pictures. Hopefully, my beloved did not participate in it, but used the day for rest, thankful for the day off, and recuperated a little from the strain of work. I would really be happy if you came to our rendezvous less strained and am afraid that the trip will really use up your strength.

As long as I cannot use the typewriter well enough, I will keep writing the letters to my golden girl by hand. I have been taking instructions during my lunch break every day this week and I am learning to type with ten fingers. That is, aside from the general usefulness, very good training for my left hand. The instructions demand–despite the senselessness of what is written–the most complete concentration. I write, or I type without looking at my hands or the typewriter and I am marveling at the idea that something like that is even possible and can be successful. The entire course takes about fifteen hours and I only regret that I have not had a single evening to just practice, because of other obligations. Maybe I can arrange things differently after my trip.

I am in constant contact with my dear mother through letters. She is spending a quiet but psychologically demanding time in Hamburg, since my brother-in-law has been ordered to stay in bed for the last few weeks due to a heart attack, and there has not been any kind of improvement

---

52 The coronation day of King George VI.

in his condition, unfortunately. I feel sorry for my sister, because the economic difficulties are now joined by the worry about him.

MOPE TO VERA

Leipzig, 13 May 1937

After the rather short letters of the last few days, I remained without mail today and only the thought that that can probably be traced back to the coronation hype calms me somewhat. I hope to be compensated quite well early tomorrow. Tomorrow evening at this time, I will be on my way to our rendezvous already, a reunion I look forward to so much that I have been gripped by travel nerves–a "sickness" formerly unknown to me. My things are packed already so that I won't even go back to the apartment tomorrow.

My typewriter instructor told me today that he is counting on teaching me to type with ten fingers in about twenty-five hours. For my rather modest expectations, I think I have already learned amazingly well. I would have never dared to think that my stiff fingers–every single one of them–would ever gain so much active independence. For instance, I write "aqwert" and "zuioplo" fifty times in a row, or "hassdasgas" or "als das da lag" and find less sense than satisfaction in this activity, that usually finds its end after about one and a half hours with a little back pain, because of the unusual activity and quite an appetite for the postponed lunch. After I came into my room yesterday, I practiced for another hour, although it was rather late already, something I will not repeat because I am too tired.

Yesterday's letter will hopefully give you pleasure, at least as far as the charming drawing is concerned. Max Schwimmer came looking for me at the store today, because I procured some animal skulls for him. To have gorilla, lion and leopard skulls as decorative elements in his living space seems to me to be a little eccentric, but the animal forms will probably give him inspiration for some kind of picture and in that way will fulfill a real purpose.

As you can see, I have nothing real to tell you at the moment, because what fills me cannot be recounted in words. It is all so elementary, so huge, so restlessly concentrated on the moment of the reunion inside of me, that written words will make everything else seem trivial and maybe even banal.

Mope and Vera encountered horribly cold weather during their thirty-eight hours together in Brussels, although (as he gallantly wrote to her a few days later), "it did not seem as disturbing because of your beloved presence." Their initial rendezvous proved problematic as they arrived at different train stations, and each suffered momentary panic before they succeeded in finding one other. For Mope, despite the short time, "the feeling of walking together, side by side, to hear your voice–without the influence of some bureaucrat charging fees–to watch your ever so beloved, beautiful face with its animated expressions and everything else in our togetherness has given me so much and filled me full of inner happiness." Being together, he adds "has balanced both of us inside, so that we can give each other even more with our letters when we are apart." They were not to meet again until more than two months later. In Brussels, he employed his Leica camera to take photos, of which he says "as far as can be judged by the negatives, four pictures of you and one of me came out well. All the others are out of focus or wiggly." He attributes this to Vera's "bursting with the need to move" and inability to stay still.

Figs. 72 (a) and (b) Mope and Vera in Brussels, May 1937.

VERA

Journal entry, May 1937

From 16 through 17 May–evening

Two, or rather, 1 ¾ days of perfect marriage spent with Mope in Brussels.

Twenty-three: "Every Turn of the Wheel"

18 May through 19 June 1937

Mope's final month in Leipzig was frenetic and exhausting. Working through PalTreu, and with the participation of his cousin Julius Rosenfeld in Palestine and his brother-in-law Fred Rau in London, he believed he had at last secured a legal route to transfer a significant portion of his mother's assets and much of his own out of Nazi Germany. The transportable goods that he used were furs, which he bought in astonishing quantities throughout the month. Here is how he describes the scheme in his post-war Curriculum Vitae:

I applied for a transfer to Palestine and received permission to send merchandise valued at 50,000 Reichmarks to Palestine under the condition that 25% of this amount would be paid in foreign currency. My brother-in-law Frederick Rau in London provided me with the needed amount in £ Sterling (appr. £ 1,080), because I did not have access to any money abroad. After I had already purchased a larger amount of fur merchandise, a fur business in Paris offered me a position as a fur buyer in Russia. This was in June 1937, and I did not want the merchandise, a quarter of which had been paid for by my brother-in-law to remain in Germany during my absence, but on the other hand, it could not be subjected to the heat of the summer months in Palestine, so I asked for permission to warehouse the raw furs in Antwerp until the autumn. I was given oral permission, just before I had to leave for Moscow, and I hurriedly made the necessary arrangements right before my departure, expecting that written permission would follow the oral one.

The proposal by the Compagnie Internationale de Pelleteries in Paris to represent it in Russia was one that Mope would have been unwise to turn down. The offer allowed him to resign from the Gebrüder Felsenstein effective June 15, and to set up as an independent "commission agent." The job of a commission agent required considerable knowledge of all aspects of the trade, coupled with the ability to select and purchase furs from the Soviet Union for foreign clients. According to the agreement, he was to receive salary and expenses from the Compagnie Internationale plus a small commission for each purchase, and a larger commission to be shared with his main employer for acquisitions made on behalf of all other clients that he represented. In his personal affairs his priority was to secure what would hopefully be an agreed "final" date for his wedding to Vera on Sunday, 1 August, in London.

By the time he left for the Soviet Union, he had purchased most of the furs he sought with plans for further transactions upon his envisioned return in July. In the meantime, the inefficiencies of the transfer scheme under PalTreu caused final payments to the creditors that were due no later than 10 June to be delayed. As he was in good standing because of his ten years at the Gebrüder Felsenstein, all but one of his creditors expressed a willingness to wait for the payments to arrive. Mope's discomfiture concerning the delay is evident from his letters.

Mope's frenetic final month in Leipzig was taken up too with the herculean task of planning in consultation with his absent siblings a future for his mother outside Germany. He also expedited the process of reducing his own possessions (including his extensive collection of books) and storing the remainder. In this he was helped by Erich Gödicke (known as Max), a longtime employee at the Gebrüder Felsenstein. He renegotiated his lease with his landlord, Dr. Jacobson, so that he maintained only a single room in Leipzig. His long days of purchasing furs and clearing his desk at the office would end as they often had with late nights at Felsche's or Zellner's, where he would pen his love letters to Vera. Many of the circle of Jewish friends and acquaintances that he would meet and socialize with did not escape from the grip of the Nazis and became victims during the Holocaust.

When Mope left Leipzig, he fully expected to return within the month, and so he left behind his most intimate personal possessions, the stream of letters that he had received from Vera. He took with him only two or three of her most recent, and they allow us our first direct experience of a daily two-way conversation. After 16 June, Mope was never again to set foot in the city of his birth.

MOPE TO VERA

Leipzig, 19 May 1937

After I worked on the man for three weeks, I bought fourteen thousand five hundred Reichmarks worth of merchandise for myself today. It took a long time until he was ready to sell it at a decent price. The merchandise has already arrived at Gebrüder Felsenstein. I have a sure feeling that I did not make a mistake and in this day and age, that is almost more than you can stipulate even for yourself, because the season is over and there are many other reasons that make purchasing difficult. I will most likely be able to send a precise report to Fred tomorrow as to what amount in pound sterling he has to make available to the Haavara for it.

It comes to just about exactly £ 270, and it would be best if he remitted it right now by airmail or telegram, as soon as my deposit has been confirmed, something that might possibly still happen this week. I would be very grateful to you if you would call Fred and talk to him about this matter. The transfer has to happen quickly, because I owe it to the seller who is decent enough to wait for payment up to two weeks at most to pay on time. I will probably also close on several small batches in the next few days. That's enough about business now!

They will throw me out of here any minute now (at Felsche's) and I put my arms around you tightly–very tightly and inseparably and infinitely thankful for this beloved, charming human being who loves me back. Your Mope

MOPE TO VERA

Leipzig, 21 May 1937

Today is another Friday evening. Over lunch, a lady who never wanted to know anything about being a Jew before and raised her boys accordingly told me how she now celebrates the Friday evenings and the Seder evenings and how her children who have to attend the Jewish school and have to learn about all the traditions encourage her. She has found real joy in it, just like her husband. There was actual love in her voice and a great willingness to understand, so that I was really happy about listening to her, thinking of you, because I know that you will be just as understanding when such questions relating to the upbringing of children will become acute.

I took care of some private correspondence until 9.30 p.m. and went to Zellner's for dinner. By the way, I purchased another batch of merchandise today for about four thousand five hundred Reichmarks, which was *relatively* low-priced. Hopefully, Fred agrees with everything and is ready to act.

In the meantime, I have landed in a hotel lobby, since it is after 1.00 a.m. and will finish this letter quickly, before the porter becomes ungracious.

MOPE TO VERA

Leipzig, 23 May 1937

My dear mother arrived here around midday today. I picked her up and determined the first moment I saw here that her appearance was not quite satisfactory. In the meantime, the two of us ate lunch together after we took the luggage to her room, and now she is looking a little better. Both of us are sitting in the store and are taking care of correspondence. I had to type several business letters on the typewriter, and now, I am taking care of my favorite writ to you that, contrary to all the others, is restful to my nerves.

It will be of interest to you that I have bought several thousand Reichmarks worth of merchandise since Friday. I have been bargaining for the single batches for many weeks and now, the buying is finally taking place. However, I also had to decide to invest a little more than I wanted to originally. The main point is that the market conditions are good for me at the moment. The contracts have been made in such a way that payment has to be made on 10 June. That is also an accommodation resulting from the market situation, since immediate payment is customary in our trade. How sweet of you that you passed along my two messages to Fred and that he seems to have reacted so positively.

In the meantime, it is midnight. Mother and I went for a little walk and then to Felsche's. At 7 o'clock, there was synagogue–unfortunately, early tomorrow at 7.00 as well so that I have to get up in time–and then I watched the dear lady unpack her things until 9.00 p.m. Now I am sitting at Zellner's, with my heart and soul's favorite drink–mocha– and I am with you again completely and exclusively and immersed in thoughts of you. Your Mope

MOPE TO VERA

Leipzig, 24 May 1937

Early today, at 7 a.m., we were in the Synagogue and afterwards, I took Mother to my place for breakfast, something she gladly accepted, because she does not have any of the supplies needed to make herself a decent breakfast. Then, we went to the cemetery around 12 o'clock. I was glad to be able to accompany Mother, although cemeteries are unable to make any kind of sentimental impression on me. We passed by an unending number of famous names and, aside from an interest in the history of the milieu and the art, I remained untouched on the inside, just like during earlier visits.[53]

You are wondering why the letter I was going to write to Fred has not arrived and I have to tell you that I was not able to write it yet, because the idiots at the Paltreu in Berlin have made quite a mess of things again. I am counting on being able to compose the writ by the end of this week, or to have put everything in order for it, as the case may be. So far, I have bought 30,196.74 Reichmarks worth of merchandise that, as soon as the time is ripe, can be sent off. From this, 25% minus 10% loss allowance in currency has to be made available. Expressed in pounds sterling, that means approximately £540.-.-. Please be so nice and give notice to Fred about this. This amount includes the formerly disclosed sum. I have obligated myself to pay my distributors by June 10. So everything has to be taken care of rather quickly and I intend to buy more merchandise I have already made deals on, merchandise that will add to the foreign currency exchange amount.

MOPE TO VERA

Leipzig, 25 May 1937

Your question concerning Fred's lack of clarity regarding the transfer matter made me wonder, as everything should be cleared up by now. The request for payment of the required foreign currency exchange portion will take place through me or through the carrier in Antwerp, as soon as the merchandise has been stored in the icehouse there. In the

---

[53] The visit was to commemorate the third anniversary of the death of Mope's father, Isidor Felsenstein, who was buried in the old Jewish cemetery off Berlinerstrasse.

meantime, I hope to keep buying so that the sum mentioned yesterday will keep growing.

I think it is absolutely necessary for Mother's future, which occupies my thoughts all the time, that Fred comes over here for a short meeting in front of an attorney. After all the siblings have butted in with "pros" and "cons" in the further development, I am not willing to carry the responsibility of making a final decision by myself. I want to protect myself from later accusations, because I want to have peace and quiet once I am working on the building of a new existence.

But when fourteen children and several siblings intercede, *no single person should have to take all of the responsibility by himself*.[54] If Fred flies here on a Friday around noon, he can be back on Monday, and since it concerns large amounts (at least in comparison to Mother's wealth), the expenses are worth it. I would like to ask you to let Fred know about my opinion so he can think about it carefully and hopefully follow my urgent wish.

What a terrible business letter and I have not even said one word about our personal relationship. But you will excuse that, because you do know how necessary all of that is.

MOPE TO VERA

Leipzig, 26 May 1937

It is possible that I will have to go on a very important business trip that might well decide my future, and that I will come to you from there directly so I will be there in time for the civil wedding ceremony. The matter is still very, very questionable, which is why I don't really want to tell you about it yet.[55] For this reason, it would be especially urgent for me that Fred come here for a weekend, because when I depart from here, I will also persuade Mother to go to Ketty or Grete, and the problems absolutely have to be solved before I leave.

---

54 Mope is referring to his siblings and their spouses, including himself and Vera to make fourteen.
55 This is the first oblique mention of Mope's rapidly realized plan of traveling to the Soviet Union as a buyer of furs representing a client in Paris, thus no longer depending on the Gebrüder Felsenstein.

MOPE TO VERA

Leipzig, 27 May 1937

Many thanks for your report to Fred concerning my letters. Fred called me early this morning so that I was able to talk about everything with him—as much as possible anyway. He is very willing to help and I am really very grateful to him. Shortly before talking to him, I talked to my attorney and I found out that I can count on the request for remittance for tomorrow or day after tomorrow. Since I promised my payment for 10 June, that would really be the latest deadline so I can pay on time.

But now, that is enough of those vexing business reports. As a matter of fact, the two of us have much more beautiful things to talk about—although the other stuff cannot be avoided. Your fears of having depressed me during our telephone conversation on Tuesday will have been allayed by my letters that you have received. I have such a completely confident feeling that difficulties do not depress me. We will understand how to overcome them *viribus unitis*.[56]

MOPE TO VERA

Leipzig, 28 May 1937

The Alpha and Omega is that it is not certain at all if the matter will work out and all the talking about it could be just nonsense in the end. Nevertheless, if I can obtain a visa—I will go on a business trip in eight to ten days which, if I am the right man for the job, will last until approximately 20 or 22 July.

For this trip, I will receive a salary of 750 Reichmarks per month and all expenses paid, and if I prove to be of value, I will have secure employment with a fixed allowance of £ 35 a month, but I will be traveling a lot and will get all my expenses taken care of during my travels. Since I will have to travel in the opposite direction, my beloved will have to deal with the Registry Office by herself, and ask to move the deadline for our marriage permit to the end of July.

This evening, I declared myself in agreement with the above-mentioned terms. Once the matter gets off the ground, I can build a fantastic position for myself over time (and I won't have to bow before

---

56 i.e., with combined forces.

the Dresden branch manager and his bosses any longer), and a whole new world will open to me in our trade. For these reasons, which I might have told you about a little too early, I was so intent on Fred coming here, because you will understand that I can leave here even less now when I also have to take care of everything else in the few days that I have left. My theoretical organ, I mean my heart and my soul, are divided in their feelings, but the mind tells me that I cannot let such a chance pass by, because even if I am commanded back–as the wrong man for the job–I can learn a lot of new things. But why should I not be the right man?

Poor, beloved and ever so disappointed Veralein, is what I am telling you really that bad? Will you now smile at another man instead of me? Will your patience be put to a test that is too hard? I am certain that we will spend our vacation together beginning August 1 (wedding day) and I will do everything in my power to make it up to you with my strength and love and passion.

I started writing this Friday evening letter after I put my dear mother to bed shortly after 11.00 p.m. Before that, we had been sitting on the Felsche patio in the pleasantly fresh air and were happy in our being together; something both of us had been missing for too long. When we came to her apartment, her Friday evening lights were shining through the window and made for a solemnly happy mood that I had had to go without for a long time.

I already told you about my telephone conversation with Fred, and we are, as far as I can see right now, of one mind on everything concerning the accreditation. The question of my dear mother's emigration that occupies my mind is still completely unresolved and I do not know how I can solve this with the speed necessary or even prepare for a solution, as the case may be.

The Park Café is closing in just a bit. The chairs are being put to bed on the tables for a rest and are being given valerian preparations to calm their hearts. The waiters are cleaning the ashtrays so that they will be considered new tomorrow, and are preparing themselves for a deserved rest. If everything wants to sleep, then I alone cannot stay awake and that is why I am finishing this writ which is supposed to bring you my most heartfelt wish for a relaxing and pleasing weekend and the most loving embraces and kisses and an expression of my great longing for my ever so beloved and sweet Lilongo, Your Mope

MOPE TO VERA

Leipzig, 30 May 1937

This morning, I took care of quite a bit of business correspondence. The dispatch of the merchandise will take place on Tuesday at the latest, and it will be in Antwerp within a day, stored in the icehouse. Tomorrow, I will send detailed information and would like to insure the transport as well as the storage against fire, robbery, theft and water damage in the amount of £ 2,800. The insurance is supposed to take effect on 1 June.

The time is ripe for sleeping, the sheet of paper is filled and I want to send my darling a vast number of passionate kisses that are supposed to shock and delight her. I am, despite and through all the things that occupy me, always connected to you in the most deeply felt bond of love, because in everything I do, I wonder if I can make you happy by doing it. Your Mope

MOPE TO VERA

Leipzig, 31 May 1937

An exceptionally hot day filled with humid air has made room for a wet, much cooler evening. I was at the store until after 9 o'clock and our secretary wrote a few private business letters for me. One of them, and really the most important one, was a letter to Fred. The writ that he was expecting a week ago was finally due, after everything else had been taken care of. Most likely, it will come into his possession tomorrow around noon. Tomorrow, the first shipment will be sent off.

Despite great effort, I still did not manage to buy a bigger batch of merchandise that seemed quite interesting, because the seller was asking 10% more than I could invest, even if I forced my bid up as high as possible. Buying merchandise is anything but easy.

There is a lot of great indignation over the bombing of the "Deutschland." It is really terrible how world peace is exposed to constant dangers by insane undertakings of a few wild people. Hopefully, this bad event does not result in worse.[57]

---

57 The German pocket battleship, the *Deutschland*, was attacked from the air by Republican aircraft off Ibiza on 29 May 1937 during the Spanish Civil War. Thirty-one seamen were killed. Hitler actively supported the Nationalists under General Francisco Franco.

I think that you can tell by my boring way of writing that I am exhausted. That is no wonder after the hot day and the sudden weather change. I will seek the horizontal position very soon and just add my most heartfelt greetings. I wish this constant letter writing would be over soon and I could lie down beside my darling when I am tired and cuddle and caress her, because I would never be too tired for that. Your Mope

MOPE TO VERA

Leipzig, 1 June 1937

Today, I was able to make a few smaller deals, that is buys, and hope to have made some progress concerning several larger purchases. In any case, everything will be taken care of until Fred's transfer and the request for payment of my shippers on the part of the Haavara will have been carried out. If Fred has not written to me about it yet, please ask him to confirm that he took care of the insurance for my shipment. That is of the utmost importance to me, because any kind of loss would otherwise be irreplaceable.

I turned in my passport for renewal today and was told that I would be able to pick it up on Thursday. I won't need the Dresden people *for the time being*. In the meantime, everything else can develop and be realized in its own time, and then, I could go into further talks with them.

I will take along my typewriter and Max from the store will take care of everything else. Max is rather well suited for this and he likes doing it.[58] For the time being, I gave my landlord, Dr. Jacobson, notice on one of the rooms, because two will be too much space.

This letter, like every letter I write to you, is supposed to bring you my most passionate kisses, my darling, and all my embraces and tokens of love. Your Mope

MOPE TO VERA

Leipzig, 3 June 1937

I made several purchases today. Everything is moving forward, albeit slowly. I consider today's buy especially advantageous.

---

58 "Max" whose actual name was Erich Gödicke was a trusted employee of the Gebrüder Felsenstein.

My mother made the same petition as I did–or I did it for her actually–and she can undertake the same steps as me. Her assets have gone down quite a bit over the last few years, and the Reich tax is extremely high in relation to those assets. Tomorrow or Monday, I will send off another shipment, smaller and less valuable than the first, but still something.

Today, I received my book[59] which will come in very handy until the middle of January 1938. I am very happy with it.

It is 1.45 a.m. already and I am thinking of going to bed soon. It is questionable whether the mailbox will be emptied today or not so it might not reach the airmail plane on time. Maybe I will take it to the main post office so that you won't be at a loss for mail.

I enfold you in my arms, my most passionately loved sweet wife, and kiss you again and again and again, everywhere and with all the intensity of my feeling that is filled with the knowledge of you and my great love for you. Your Mope

MOPE TO VERA

Leipzig, 4 June 1937 [Envelope contains sticker: "Opened by customs agents for foreign currency inspection"]

 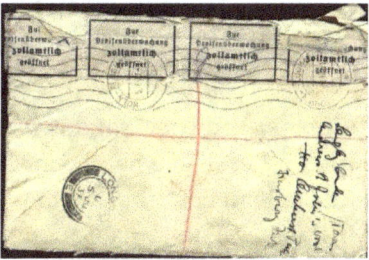

Figs. 73 (a) and (b) Front and back of envelope to letter from Mope to Vera dated 4 June 1937 with vetting stickers added by the Nazi authorities.

Today, just like yesterday, was a very exhausting day for me–I did not even have time for lunch. When one is terribly tired there are tree and rock martens running around in one's brain, besides the beloved who has a right to most of one's thinking, and there are asset calculations in number form moving around the whorls of the brain, it becomes difficult to put correct sentences and considerations down on paper.

---

59 i.e., my passport.

Tomorrow, Max is coming over, and we will talk about everything that might happen, such as how to sort my books and how my furniture should be treated. Hopefully, I will hear from Fred tomorrow whether he has taken care of the transfer or not. I need that money to be able to fulfill my obligations in a timely manner.

Years ago, I tried to learn Russian for a while, but aside from some declinations and conjugations, there is nothing left in my memory. It is still uncertain if I will be able to visit Dr. Jacobson one more time, but it is possible.[60]

At noon, I went to attorney Dr. Goldschmidt with my dear mother in order to talk to him concerning everything that needs to be done on her behalf in the immediate future, but he is going on vacation for four weeks. The bold wish that he might take care of matters the way they should be taken care of will hopefully not be disappointed, after the good man has already proven himself to be very good at failing.

Let me kiss you and hug you and whisper many loving words to you which are meant to wrap around you in a long and strengthening sleep and tell you about my great, strong love for my most beloved girl again and again.

MOPE TO VERA

Leipzig, 7 June 1937

We, mother and I, just sat down at Felsche's on the gallery—in air that is a little fresher than what the inner city usually offers. She has given me exactly half an hour to write to you.

This afternoon, I had another telephone conversation with Fred. There are constantly new difficulties to overcome that are so ridiculous at times that I can hardly believe it myself sometimes. However, I am willing to confront serious and ridiculous obstacles, and until now, I have actually succeeded quite well. I am just amazed about my mood which remains even and unchanged, and I am glad for the heat that heightens my spirit of enterprise visibly. I was able to purchase a small batch today and there will be a shipment tomorrow—nothing of great worth actually. Your Mope

---

60 Here is the first near direct reference to the fact that Mope was shortly to leave Germany for the Soviet Union. "Dr. Jacobson" (the name of his landlord) is his coded way of referring to Leipzig to which he was uncertain whether he would return en route to traveling to England to marry Vera.

MOPE TO VERA

Leipzig, 9 June 1937

Early today, your card arrived at the same time as your every so loving Monday letter. Your lovely words give me great joy every single day and such an inner peace and happiness that makes my work easier. What is going to happen when I can no longer be supplied with the ever so longed for messages as punctually and within 24 hours? Well, even this period of time will be overcome and my new boss who arrived today answered my question as to whether the wedding date fit into his plans or not by saying that it was perfectly alright with him. So: Long live August 1 and the following days which we will spend free and happy in Italy, I have been carrying my letter of credit for Lire 2650.–in my pocket since yesterday.

Around the beginning of next week, I will probably begin to travel and just hope that everything concerning my purchases will be in order by then.

MOPE TO VERA

Leipzig, 10 June 1937

It is 12.30 a.m. Until now, I was sitting at a table with my old boss and my new one, and we chatted a little and also talked about my future work, which I might already be starting at the beginning of next week. In any case, I am resigning from Gebrüder Felsenstein on 15 June. Today, I had a lot of work to do and did not have time to read your lovely letter, which arrived with the second mail delivery. I did not even get around to having lunch–this only to justify the neglect of my beloved, or her letter, as the case may be.

I was glad that I succeeded in buying another batch of merchandise this afternoon, after I had been trying for 10 days. On the other hand, there is so much turbulence, because the transfer, or better the request for remittance has not been effected as of today. I am completely in the dark, because I don't have any kind of message from Tel-Aviv in front of me, and my suppliers were promised payment for today. I am really very uncomfortable in this situation, although the delay can only be a matter of a few days and Julius Rosenfeld is hopefully expediting the matter. Other than that, my head is a fantastic labyrinth of numbers.

The things that are happening in there cannot be accommodated in any logarithm chart.

Just a few minutes ago, I explained to Semy: On the first of August, we are getting married, come what may, and the date is set. Unfortunately, I have to leave all the preparations to you. Will you please ask Fred, in case the opportunity presents itself, if he will talk to his teacher, Mr. Marmerstein about marrying us? It might also be necessary to send out a greater number of wedding announcements, which will have to be printed. You might talk to Hannalein about who should receive one in my family. Without these announcements, all the people will be bitterly offended, and we really don't want to start our life together surrounded by the anger of our friends and family, with whom we have to maintain relationships, even if the two of us are more than enough for each other. I am really sad to cause so much work for you, but can that really be helped?

I kiss you, my most passionately loved girl, with all the fervor and much greater heat than even the last few days were able to produce. Your Mope

MOPE TO VERA

Leipzig, 11 June 1937

Around 6 p.m., Fred called me to tell me about a telegram he received from Julius Rosenfeld. At 7 o'clock, I also received one. It was very good that I had been informed by Fred beforehand and, because of that, was able to bring together all the needed material and could dictate the necessary letters. Now, everything has been sent off and will arrive Monday morning in Julius's office. This new delay is very unpleasant to me, because I was reminded by several of my different suppliers today. It is incomprehensible to me that Julius did not know until today, that he did not pass on his knowledge that the invoices, etc., would have to be presented to Haavara, before the disbursement order will be given. I am afraid that Julius is not contributing to the acceleration, but to the delay of the process.

A little while ago, I went out to eat with my mother and then we sat on the terrace at Felsche's until 10.45, and the air on the terrace was a little cooler at least. Semy left again today, after we had dinner together last night. By the way, he was of great help in my matters for which I am very grateful to him, and this proved to me again that he is a dependable friend, despite all of his weakness.

Now, after hours of lightning, the thunder is finally starting to roll announcing that a loud night is on its way. This letter is meant to go to the mailbox before it gets emptied, so that it will hopefully reach you tomorrow. My Friday evening letter has turned out to be quite a silly writ again, but I feel a little exhausted and my bed is audibly calling me, so that I ask you to forgive the emptiness of this scribbling.

MOPE TO VERA

Leipzig, 13 June 1937

Yesterday morning, I went to see my new boss who asked me to inspect various merchandise for him. I did this quite quickly and with great certainty, because, after all, I do know a little bit about it. Later on, I heard him say to his companion, "He understands the merchandise. I think he is important to us!" I had not even considered that he wanted to test my professional knowledge, and that is why I did not feel any stage fright at all.

In the afternoon, I wrote a few business letters and then, around six o'clock, I met my dear mother with whom I have been sitting in cafes or gone for walks until now. In the evening, I did some calculations concerning my mother's various accounts and talked to her about her income and expenses, and then, we made a list of the people who should receive wedding announcements. Please don't be startled–we reached 120 and I am sure that we forgot a few.

If my hope comes true, my suppliers will get paid on Tuesday. I believe I wrote to you on Friday that there were new difficulties to deal with which I hope will be overcome very soon.

Just now, the violinist Schwarz sat down at our table, but I won't let him disturb me all that much. It has been hot here, without any kind of break in the weather. Just now–it is evening–a fresh breeze came up, but most people are asleep while my life impulses are gaining in strength.

I do love you indescribably, my sweetest, golden girl, Your Mope

VERA TO MOPE

London, 13 June 1937 [German sticker on back with: "opened by customs for foreign currency inspection"–also stamp on front– "inspected by customs law"]

Pepper and Mutti are sitting next to me in deck chairs and all three of us are sitting in Ravenscourt Park (entrance to the registry office is at an oblique angle across from here, if you know what I am talking about; I don't think that you saw it back then).[61]

Today, I am spending a more than lazy day; around 9 o'clock, I heard the rain hitting the windows, turned to the other side and slept until almost lunch time. Unfortunately, it turned a little cooler than I would prefer–normal temperate people think this weather is perfect–the sun is peeking down from between the clouds every once in a while and there is quite a palpable little breeze blowing.

Julius Rosenfeld does not seem to understand all that much about business matters, otherwise he could not have acted so nonchalantly and just about irresponsibly. I am sure that he will receive your letter tomorrow and will hopefully arrange everything necessary immediately.

Did the suppliers accept the reasons, or were you not able or willing to explain the details to them? And did Semy whose name they surely know very well stand by your side?

My most beloved, I know that peace and quiet is extremely hard to come by at this time or is hardly possible, but isn't it a fact that, as soon as you remember that it really is a complete waste of time to get upset and that you will only get worked up physically and psychologically without really accomplishing anything, and that there is someone on the other side of the Channel who loves you so indescribably much, then you just calm down again, not only physically, because my beloved was very calm and I admired that a lot, but also deep down on the inside, right?

How long will your trip take, by the way? I mean, until you reach your destination? Will it be cold there? Hopefully not!

I want to close and mail the letter off today, but before I do, I want to give my beloved many, many passionate kisses and snuggle up to

---

61 This was the Registry Office at which Mope and Vera were planning their official marriage. It is a happy coincidence that the first of Vera's surviving letters to Mope was addressed from outside there.

him ever so closely in my thoughts. I believe that I can feel his beloved embraces, and I caress him gently and want to be with him completely.

You–Your Lilongo

MOPE TO VERA

Leipzig, 14 June 1937

Just now, it rang midnight from all the church towers. How I missed the sound of Big Ben among all that ringing and how much better I would feel if I was near enough to you to hear it, but I long even more, much, much more, to be able to listen to your beloved voice, to lie next to my lover and forget about the world with all its worries.

My mother and I had dinner at Zellner's, after she picked me up from the store. Later on, we made a stop at my room where I wanted to show her paintings and etchings by Max Schwimmer which she had not seen yet. And because of all these "important things," it got to be quite late again.

I am still waiting for my order to depart and I am actually glad about it in some way, because I would like to have everything arranged beforehand. I hope that everything will be taken care of by Julius Rosenfeld tomorrow, so that I can go on my trip with my mind at rest, as soon as the protracted visa is here. Maybe I can make another purchase tomorrow. It is merchandise that I have been expecting for fourteen days and that arrived here this afternoon.

My suppliers have reacted very decently–quite unexpected in part– and did not present me with any difficulties. By the way, Semy made the amount needed for another purchase available to me from his private assets until the payment is made. The people know me at least as well as Semy and act quite decently towards me because of that–knock on wood.

However, I have to close now and will keep on reading your dear words in bed and go to sleep happy in the thought of how close my darling is to me. Your Mope

VERA TO MOPE

London, 14 June 1937 [postcard]

Evening

What happened? I have no message from you, neither on Saturday nor on Sunday? I am only writing a card since I am not even sure that it will still reach you in Leipzig.

If only you would call today so that I could be sure everything is fine and there is no serious reason for your silence. It is horrible to have such a great distance between us and I hope that I will hear from you tomorrow before I go to the store.

All good luck for everything and wherever you are and for all you do, Fondest love, Lilongo

MOPE TO VERA

Leipzig, 15 June 1937

Although the reason for your call early today, namely that you had not heard anything from me, seems regrettable, I was extremely happy to have been awakened by my beloved. I was still quite groggy, but you found out from my addle-headed statements that I *did* write to you.

In the afternoon, around five o'clock, after I had just received news about my departure tomorrow, I thought about announcing my telephone call by sending a telegram, but I didn't because I did not want to scare you. Contrary to the usual custom–the telephone calls are usually connected within five minutes–I had to wait for over a half hour today. As your dear father will have told you, I will call you tomorrow evening, *if possible*, from Berlin. However, I cannot give you an exact time for that. Had I talked to you today, I would not be writing this letter, because I am feeling a little exhausted and, although it is 10.30 p.m. have not met my dear mother yet, but did eat dinner just a little while ago.

I still had to take care of quite a few things at the store–correspondences, cleaning up, etc., that needed to be done–despite various earlier preparations for departure.

Unfortunately, the order of remittance still has not been carried out. Aside from this awful feeling, I am happy and filled with joy and see the new future with a large measure of hope and great expectations.

Max is sitting opposite me–the one from the store. He kept me company until now and helped me and will also help me tomorrow, I hope, with my packing. He will also move everything out of my large room, since I canceled the lease as of June 30, as I wrote to you earlier, and he will keep my things at the store for the time being. I will keep the bedroom for now.

Despite all the adversity, I am always in a good and sometimes even excellent mood. The basis for all that good mood is the awareness that my beloved–although she is so very far away–is always close to me. You have become the substance of my life in such a way that I cannot even describe and you chase away all the little quirks before they have time to find room inside of me.

I will probably come back here from my trip around the middle to the second half of July. Although I am really looking forward to it and will most likely see many, many interesting things, I would be happier if it was already behind me. It is really high time that we two lovers finally come together. How long the trip will take I cannot say and really depends on whether I go by train or plane.

VERA TO MOPE

London, 17 June 1937 [Mope in transit]

Once again, my beloved is sitting on another train and once again, every turn of the wheel takes him farther away from me, instead of bringing him closer, but despite this knowledge, I am glad and happy about his success. Mopelein, this could really not have been done any better or quicker, and I see my great friend and lover and dear, most beloved man from afar with the feeling of limitless happiness about his capabilities, his energy, his care and his stamina; and that is aside from his other much loved qualities: his goodness, his gentleness, his spiritual being and the power of expression and impression, his imagination and, yes——his love for me.

This is meant to become a birthday letter, aside from many other things! The happiness that I am experiencing now is something so complete and harmonious and ultimately beautiful and all-encompassing that I do not know anything more beautiful I could wish for my beloved for his new year of life.

How sweet it was just a little while ago to hear your dear voice so close to me, before you went to your train. How many impressions of new and sometimes strange character for you will lie between now and the point in time when this letter reaches you?

My beloved, it is very late, or better, it is very early in the morning. I will sleep myself to your side wherever you are and I love you with all my heart, all my soul, my body and everything that makes me who I am, Your Lilongo

MOPE TO VERA

In transit through Poland, 18 June 1937 [postcard]

Just now, we are going through a tunnel to Warsaw and I wanted to tell you quickly just *how* happy I am to have talked to you yesterday. Yesterday afternoon, I had to go to the necessary meetings with my boss, Mr. Ruwim Schapiro,[62] whose wife will write to you in the next few days to give you my most heartfelt regards. And he might also call you in London on occasion, which is something I asked him to do. He is a great guy and speaks Yiddish. This only so you can be prepared. I was so busy with my affairs yesterday morning that I had to say goodbye to my dear mother on the telephone, and then I just barely got to the train in time to jump on. Tonight, I have slept very well, except for the disturbance at the border and I am still a little addle-brained while I am writing. I cannot see anything of Warsaw except for a few gasometers and the train station. Maybe I will have some time to look around on my trip back. I am so exceedingly happy and relieved that some of my suppliers will finally get their money this week. With all the difficulties, everything worked out really well and I hope that Fred will transfer the amounts requested by Tel-Aviv as fast as possible, so that I can use the

---

62 Ruwin Schapiro was one of the Ost-Juden (Eastern European Jews) in the fur trade who had settled in Leipzig, though by the time Mope became his agent in Russia he had already moved the headquarters of his fur business–the Compagnie Internationale de Pelleteries–to Paris. The Leipzig Jewish database at the Leo Baeck Institute in New York records that he was born in Homel bei Mogilow in present-day Belarus on 5 January 1880, and was married to Ida Friedland (born 7 April 1901). Mope and he were to have a contentious business relationship over the next two years.

time I have in Leipzig during my trip back to make further purchases which my representative will prepare.

My most passionate, loving greetings and kisses, my beloved girl. All my best to you. Only write about personal matters to Moscow Hotel Metropol

Your Mope who is very much in love!

VERA

Journal entry, 19 June 1937

Today is my Mopelein's birthday and he is in Russia. During the last few months and weeks, my husband has proven to me that he is not lacking in drive, energy, endurance, or bravado. I am completely steeped in a feeling of joy, of security, because of the knowing that perfect, loving, strong, intelligent man.

This love is something completely new to me; it exhilarates without singeing my wings, or let them be captured by cold, as it was with Mitja two years ago. It fills me, without devouring and extinguishing me, it is within me, in every single cell of my body, like a precious metal that creates an alloy and still retains the idiosyncrasies of both source materials, and because of the mixture, it brings out new, even better characteristics. Dear God, fate, life, karma, I thank you. —and I live in trembling anticipation of the fulfillment of our mutual wishes. Dear God, I thank you for my Mopelein.

Twenty-four: "I Will Come to London Directly"

19 June through 24 July 1937

POLITICAL TIMELINE, JUNE-NOVEMBER 1937

- 16 July 1937: Buchenwald Concentration Camp opened.
- 19 July 1937: Nazi exhibition of "degenerate art" (Entartete Kunst) opens in Munich.
- 27 July 1937: Ritual murder trial of five Jews opens in Bamberg, Germany.
- 7 September 1937: Hitler declares Treaty of Versailles invalid.
- 12 October 1937: SS begins euthanasia program with crippled infants as targets.
- 8 November 1937: Opening of Der Ewige Jude (the Eternal Jew), anti-Semitic art exhibition in Munich.
- 25 November 1937: Germany signs military accord with Japan.
- 1936 through 1938: Mass arrest and execution of Trotskyites and Bolsheviks by Stalinists in the Soviet Union, known as the Great Terror or Great Purge.

Mope's left Leipzig assuming that he would return to oversee any residual credit arrangements, organize shipment or disposal of his personal effects, and tie up loose ends prior to traveling to London to marry Vera. His resignation from the Gebrüder Felsenstein was facilitated by the offer of the Compagnie Internationale de Pelleteries in Paris, to employ him as its representative in Russia. In 1937, Communist Russia was beginning to unlock its doors to international trade.

The notifications concerning the PalTreu payments that he received from Leipzig and from his brother-in-law, Fred Rau, in London appeared at last to be in order. Mope even expected to extend his purchases on his return to Leipzig in July. That expectation was thwarted. Before leaving Leipzig, he had settled in cash with the single creditor who had demanded an advance deposit. The bombshell that Mope had not anticipated was that that same creditor–a fellow Jew–denounced him to the Nazi authorities for having engaged in illegal currency transactions. It was sufficient excuse for the SS to raid his lodgings and put out a warrant for his immediate arrest. Here is how he describes this ill-fated episode in his post-war account:

While I was in Russia, I received warnings by telegram from London and Prague not to come back to Germany, because a warrant for my arrest had been issued there. One of the sellers of the raw fur materials had forced me to make an advance payment to him, because he would not have been able to sell to me otherwise. I paid him RM 4,000 under the condition that the money be paid back after he received official payment.

This man used my absence to denounce me to the local authorities, telling them that I had violated the foreign currency regulations, which was completely false, but which permitted him to keep the money I had already paid. The German authorities–aside from the arrest warrant–confiscated my bank accounts, and they succeeded in commandeering back to Germany the larger part of the merchandise stored in Antwerp, although this merchandise had been warehoused at my brother-in-law's [Fred Rau's] disposal. Additionally, all my furnishings, including a very valuable library and a number of precious paintings, were seized.

In a post-war letter to a family acquaintance in Leipzig, he reveals the identity of his betrayer, who had also found refuge in England:

Karl Herzberg has been residing in London since the end of 1938 or the beginning of 1939. In Leipzig, I bought martens from him in the amount of RM 19,500 to use in the transfer for which I had received permission from the Nazi authorities. He had me pay a deposit of RM 4,000 for the martens. Shortly after that, I traveled to Russia, and while there, I was informed that I had been denounced, and that it would not be advisable for me to return to Germany. I was told that, because of what he did, Herzberg was able to use the merchandise as well as the deposit for his own purposes. Additionally, he had curried favor with the Nazis because of it and had not been taken to a concentration camp in November 1938 [the aftermath of Kristallnacht] like everyone else. I was not the only victim of this man.

In later years, Mope never forgot the brave action taken by his cousin, Semy, through whom he was to learn that he could no longer return to Germany. The absence of a paper trail prevented him from attempting to prosecute Herzberg for his putative crime.

Mope's initial tenure in the Soviet Union saw him shuttling between Moscow and Leningrad, and his initial impressions of each are punctuated by the long hours of the fur auctions, followed by obligatory late-night vodka-filled banquets that were organized by "Sojuzpushnina," the Soviet fur trade consortium. Both he and Vera were conscious that Stalinist Russia was hardly less a totalitarian state than Nazi Germany, and, given the likelihood that their letters would be inspected, both correspondents remain careful in refraining from any overt political commentary and in deliberately painting a more than rosy picture of life there.

In England, Vera was making arrangements for their wedding in London, the date of which was now settled at Sunday, 1 August. Planning for this was made challenging as the Staff Welfare Department at Marks & Spencer sent her once again to run one of their summer camps, this year under canvas for two weeks in mid-July near Whitby in Yorkshire.

After learning of his denunciation to the Nazis, Mope was concerned that this could lead to the arrest of his mother, who had been staying with her daughter, Grete, in Freiburg. Avoiding Germany himself, Mope's journey to England was anything but direct. On his arrival at Croydon Airport, late at night on Friday, 30 July, Vera whisked him by cab to Hammersmith, where an accommodating registrar had agreed to stay until after midnight in order to issue a marriage license. The civil marriage certificate of "Ernst Moritz Felsenstein 38 Years Bachelor" to "Vera Hirsch 27 Years Spinster" is dated 31 July. Their religious wedding would take place the following day.

MOPE TO VERA

Moscow, 19 June 1937

Since our conversation on Thursday, you will have received my somewhat drowsy card from Warsaw. My trip was very pleasant and, since the clock has to be moved forward by two hours when you pass the Russian border, it was not all that long. The entire landscape from Warsaw to here alternates between beautiful forests and green meadows and fields, and only every once in a while, there is a village with its farm cottages, or a city along the way.

From Berlin all the way to the Russian border, I had two sleeper cabins to myself, because there were few fellow passengers, so that I was able to use one as a bedroom and the other as a day room; and from the border on, I had one cabin–also by myself–with a good bed and impeccable linen.

Shortly after Warsaw–in the dining car–a very nice-looking young lady sat down at my table. At first, I paid little attention to her, but then, we started to talk and I found out that she was a French teacher from Tel-Aviv, which of course meant that she had my complete attention. We talked to each other in French and stayed in my day room conversing pleasantly until Baranovica [63] where her parents live. The father is a medical doctor and since he is very ill, she flew from Palestine to Warsaw.

My first impression of Moscow–superficial naturally–is a good one. Already, I had quite a few things to take care of today and took the very attractive Metro whose stations make a much more elegant impression than those of the London underground, and I also traveled by bus–the bus was one story high, just as the cable cars and the trolleys. But everything is in very good condition and you can see very modern models. The streets are alive and you can see many satisfied people and many who seem to be quite content. They are dressed very simply, but noticeably clean. There are many hugely broad streets with beautiful, partly older and partly very modern grand buildings made of some very pretty stone material, while most houses in the countryside were made of wooden logs in the form of bungalows. There do seem to be enough forests for that.

---

63 i.e., Baranovich, a town in present-day Belarus. Before the war, the town had a vibrant Jewish community, which was annihilated by the Germans in 1942.

Since there is no airmail from here, I will send the letter by express and really hope that it will reach you on Monday, so that you won't be without any news for too long. Please don't forget to let me know when you get this letter.

I am extraordinarily relieved that my suppliers will come into possession of their money either today or Monday at the latest and really do hope that, in the meantime, Fred has taken care of further transfers, so that the later purchases can also be covered. You can let Fred know that there will be martens among the merchandise for which I paid directly, so that the cumbersome manner of payment with its allowance to the Haavara does not have to be followed this time.[64]

I was put into the Hotel National for the time being, because there was no room at the Metropole, but tomorrow, I will most likely get a room there, which will be more enjoyable for me, because my acquaintances all reside there.

I registered with the local office for furs today and was received in a very friendly manner and will inspect some merchandise tomorrow and might purchase it if it is adequate. The task here will be very interesting and educational for me, because I have never seen so much merchandise in one place.

The bad thing is that I have no knowledge of the language whatsoever, but the gentlemen with whom I will be dealing all speak German, English, or French. However, on the street, I communicate like a deaf-mute and that seems to work if I just write the goal of my travels on a piece of paper and hold it up under people's noses.

Now I am enfolding you in my arms, my beloved, sweet girl, although that has become even more difficult because of the greater distance and I kiss your beautiful mouth and many other sweet things your body has to offer and that I long for almost as much as an oral exchange of ideas with my passionately and exceedingly loved darling.

Your now very 38-year-old Mope

---

64 Mope was still trying to resolve the Haavara/PalTreu issues regarding imbursement for the furs he had purchased in Leipzig. The direct payment he had made was presumably to Karl Herzberg who responded by denouncing Mope to the Nazi authorities for engaging in financial irregularities.

VERA TO MOPE

London, 21 June 1937

Hannalein and Fred were here until just a little while ago, and we had a very harmonious evening. Fred said that he would take care of the necessary transfers, of course, and so the entire matter is taken care of and I am happy about it.

Tomorrow, I will probably receive the long-awaited letter from my beloved and I am so looking forward to it. Hanna and Fred know your new boss, they even talked to him here not too long ago and both of them acknowledged, of their own free will, your judgment, that he is a really good man. I really do like Hannalein and Fred and I think it is nice, as I have said many times before, to be given so many likeable people! Apart from the one who is my husband and whom I love and who means everything to me!

My most beloved, once again, it is after midnight! Do you feel my love all the way over there in the U.S.S.R.? Your Lilongo

MOPE TO VERA

Telegram, Moscow, 25 June 1937

= ELT = HIRSCH ADDISON COURT GARDENS BLYTHE ROAD LDN =
TRAVELING TODAY LENINGRAD 29 IN MOSCOW AGAIN SEND LETTERS TO MOSCOW HAVE WORK AM CONTENT THANK YOU SATURDAY LETTER LOVE GREETINGS KISSES = MOPE +

MOPE TO VERA

Leningrad, 25 June 1937

I arrived here this morning around 10 a.m., had a very good and very comfortable breakfast and afterwards, I went to the local office of the "Sojuspuschnina," which is the central fur trading company for all Russian furs and whose main office I had been dealing with in Moscow. Since I could not take care of any business today, I will go on a tour of the city in an open car.

When you were writing to me on Saturday at 5.45, it was 7.45 here and according to local time, I would have been done with work before too long, while you still had three difficult hours in front of you in London. Here, every sixth day is "Wychodnoi," (that is, away from work). On the 6., 12., 18., 24., 30. of each month, people have the day off and they go outside and relax. Yesterday, we saw large groups of people–from the train–who were out camping, and the surroundings are really very inviting. People use all the languages of Europe here. It is amazing how many can speak English, French and German, and if I cannot seem to get ahead with my knowledge, I will try to talk with my hands and try to use a Russian word here and there that I heard somewhere and express my wishes that way.

The handling of business here is completely different from Leipzig, naturally, because you only buy. I knew just a little bit about this kind of work and also knew some of the gentlemen through doing business with the Russian trade mission. Incidentally, I am also buying for the Gebrüder Felsenstein here.

Hopefully, everything is working out with the transfers to my Leipzig suppliers. It is very important to me and I do not have any kind of overview from here or influence over it. In any case, I am convinced that Fred won't desert me, although I cannot correspond with him from here, because I am completely uninformed concerning the status of things.

Here, the weather is warm and at this time, we have the white nights, during which it remains light both day and night. You cannot even go to bed with all the brightness and the sun, which is something I cannot afford to do while I am here.

Your photo is standing in front of me and you are smiling at me in such a way, my golden girl, that I feel all warm around my heart. Your Mope

MOPE TO VERA

Leningrad, 26 June 1937

I have been in the U.S.S.R. for a week now and have seen much and got to know many new things, but the language is still a book with 777 seals to me. Leningrad is a beautiful city with excellent streets, parks and plazas and I like it–from an architectural standpoint–better than Moscow.

As I was getting ready to send off a telegram to you earlier to let you know that I will return to Moscow today, at night, they handed me your dear telegraphed greetings, and since I found out that an "E.L.T."

telegram[65] (that is much cheaper) has to contain at least 25 words, I added to the cable that hopefully reached you on a *free* Saturday.

Yesterday, I went on a beautiful tour through the city and today, I will visit a Rembrandt exhibition that shows the complete collection of all the Rembrandt works in the U.S.S.R. and a museum with paintings by Russian artists. Actually, you were supposed to receive a reproduction of Saskia (first wife of Rembrandt) lying on her bed waiting for her husband, but I have not been able to get it yet. I know most of the paintings from books and I was very happy to see them in person. It is a good and very comprehensive collection.

Aside from the museum, I also visited the Isaac Church, which serves as a godless museum. That is a fantastically beautiful building that was furnished with extraordinary taste and riches. In order to reach the cupola, from which you have an especially nice view of the city, you have to climb 521 steps, which we did not go up because we were scared of those many steps. You need a lot of idealism for something like that.[66]

I had hoped to take on merchandise here, but that was an error and so I am going back to Moscow where I have lots to do and won't come back here until around July 3. As you can see from this description, I indulged my muses here instead of working. The high point of it all was yesterday's dinner at the Hotel Europesky. From there, one had a wonderful view of a large part of the city. I went there around 11.00 p.m. and stayed until about 1.30 a.m. People here eat at very different times than we are used to. At midnight, the dance bands began playing, and that is when the real life starts. Until around midnight, it is almost as bright as during the day, and dusk does not start until then, a dusk that is soaked in beams from a full moon so that artificial light is unnecessary.

As I already telegraphed you, I urgently hope to receive a letter tomorrow from my beloved girl and to find out if you are receiving my messages in a timely manner. I have made different experiments and put different stamps on letters: I have sent letters for 1.60 Rubles and others for 2.40 and 2.60 and I would really like to know if the more expensive letters get there faster, or if that is a certified mail fee because I always get a receipt. Beginning on July 1, a new airmail connection from London over Stockholm to Leningrad is being created, with whose help we will be able to inform each other about everything much faster. It will work

---

65 E.L.T. = European Letter Telegram.
66 St. Isaac's Cathedral was built in the first half of the nineteenth century. During the 1930s, the Soviets transformed it into a museum of atheism.

out really well, because I will be here–probably for a few weeks–since the auction here begins on 12 July, and there is a week during which the merchandise can be inspected.

Please don't forget to report my well-being to my mother, without mentioning the U.S.S.R. or any city names, so that she does not worry and please forgive me for burdening you with this. Most passionately, Your Mope

VERA TO MOPE

London, 27 June 1937

So today, my beloved arrived back in Moscow and hopefully found many letters from me. I am so curious to hear about your impressions in Leningrad and your business there.

Is it completely necessary that you visit Dr. J. one more time before we get married?[67] I am not comfortable with the thought that you want to visit this man and his entire circle once again. I know that you want to make several more purchases with him, but can your agent not take care of that for you? I think that Dr. J.'s surroundings are so unpleasant and would prefer that my husband, after he undertakes such a long and exhausting trip, were spared such extremely annoying and disagreeable things, as they seem to me anyway.

Are my misgivings exaggerated and is the man and everything that is connected to him actually not as bad as I imagine him to be? I am very willing for you to teach me better, but I would truly like to ask you urgently to really ponder it, which is something you probably have already done anyway. Although I do not know Dr. J. personally, he was described to me repeatedly and just recently by different people as "most unpleasant," and even worse. Do you understand me or are you laughing at me? It's just that to me, purchases, if you want to make more later, don't seem that terribly important, or do I not understand due to a lack of knowledge of the business situation?

It is late at night once again and now, there are only four weeks and a little left; that is not soooo terribly long, but nevertheless much too long for me. You–your Lilongo

---

67 "Dr. J." alludes to Dr. Jacobson, Mope's landlord in Leipzig, though Vera is actually referring here to Nazi Germany and her legitimate fear of the worsening situation for Jews there.

MOPE TO VERA

Moscow, 27 June 1937

Now to the answers to your question whether I have to go to Leipzig before I can come to see my darling. 1.) I have not emigrated yet and I better not stay out of Germany for longer than two months, 2.) I want to begin taking the necessary steps to officially emigrate, 3.) I might have to request my new visa for the U.S.S.R. from Leipzig or maybe from London, because I have to come back here immediately following our honeymoon. As I told you some time ago, I will have to spend a significant part of the year here and I am already racking my brain trying to figure out how you–without losing your position–will be able to manage to spend at least a few months here with me. Of course, one of the conditions is that I will be getting a permanent position here, that is, they have to be happy with me. The expenses for your stay here will be paid by the company. 4.) I will try to buy some more merchandise during my stay in Leipzig, since, as far as I can see, there is still money enough for that. Until then, the accounting from the bank should be available and I will be able to determine how highly Fred's transfers have been considered by the Haavara. I was unable to find out before my departure.

Yesterday, while in Leningrad, I received a telegram from Jerusalem to the effect that Haavara finds fault with my invoicing. I wrote immediately and in detail to Julius Rosenfeld about how the personal invoice came to be, and I really do not understand why people keep taking exception to it. I would like to ask you to let Fred know about this matter, so that he is informed. The customs clearance that is mentioned in the telegram is in Antwerp where the merchandise is stored. Only the devil knows why they are using different methods now than they did with the first three shipments. You can tell from it that all obstacles have not been removed yet.

Just now, I discovered several doves on the windowsill of my room which is on the fourth floor. How nice that they can welcome me although I don't have any crumbs I could give them.

I have not fully taken care of any of my business correspondence and so, I want to end this rather business-like letter–for the most part anyway. Your Mope

VERA TO MOPE

London, 29 June 1937

How beautiful the white nights of Leningrad have to be; and I am glad that the warmth seems to be lasting there. It turned a little cooler here today and although it still is not cold, you can definitely feel the difference after the preceding warmth.

I have heard from all sides that the climate where the camp is can be quite rough. I will prepare for a bit of cool weather when I choose my clothing, since the nights in a camp, despite the wonderful clearness and fresh air, can be a little drafty. I am looking forward to camp life, a life I really like, because it finally lets me be a little natural again, which is something I appreciate after London with all its busy people. I only hope that the camp and its inhabitants keep me just as occupied–even if it is in a different and more pleasing manner–as the store does, because otherwise, the waiting for you will become unbearable. My most deeply loved beloved, you–despite everything that I say without reservation– do not let any of it keep you from any business dealings that appear important to you, and your wife will and would like to never get in your way, but will walk with you and beside you, even if it is just in her thoughts, but with no less intensity because of it.

I am discovering your lips with mine and I am completely Your Lilongo

P.S. The precise camp address is: c/o Mr. Welford, Ravenshill Farm, Dunsley near Whitby, Yorkshire. There is only one M&S camp there.

MOPE TO VERA

Moscow, 29 June 1937

Right now, 1.30 at night, I am sitting at the dinner table, after I went to a fantastically beautiful ballet in an outdoor theater. While I am sitting here writing, a jazz band is playing in the dining room of the Hotel Metropole, and the people are constantly dancing past our table. You can see that I am enjoying my life. The food is also exceptional and I think back to Zellner's with horror. I am feeling quite strange that I can experience so much joy in life again–dancing, music, etc.–after I had not heard or seen that kind of thing in Leipzig for years.

Fig. 74 Hotel Metropole, Moscow.

As I came back from swimming today, I found a telegram announcing a telephone call. My joy knew no bounds when I found out that I would get to hear your beloved voice. Since 9 o'clock here (7 o'clock where you are), I have been sitting waiting for the call.

Just now, we talked to each other. They were only a few words and still, the awareness that I heard you one more time before you go on your trip to the camp fills me with so much joy that I am completely happy. I am so happy that our voices were so clearly audible. Usually, you can understand next to nothing, something that probably can be traced back to atmospheric influences of the summer, because communications are supposed to be much better in the winter.

I dropped my intention to go on a city tour today, which was supposed to take place during the blazing midday sun, and instead drove to the outskirts of the city with two acquaintances where we swam in the river (Moskwa). Unfortunately, the sun gave way to thunder clouds at that time and as we were driving off, it came back out freshly polished. That was the first time this year that I got around to swimming, because it was not possible in Leipzig.[68] The swim was very refreshing.

How I hope that you will adjust well to the camp and that you will rest and that you will meet pleasant colleagues and girls there.

I kiss you and embrace you, my darling, and I am happy that June is reaching its end now and that we have removed another obstacle between us. Towards the end of July, I hope and long to really put my arms around you, and the thought makes me so happy that I cannot wait for that to happen. I love you just a little bit indescribably, my sweet, beloved wife and friend. Your Mope

---

68 Under the Nazi regime in Germany, Jews were forbidden from swimming in public places.

MOPE TO VERA

Moscow, 1 July 1937

Today was an exceedingly lazy day. From 9.30 to 1.30, I sat in the office of Sojuspushnina and waited until I received permission to go to the warehouse, only to find out there that there was no appropriate merchandise for me in stock and that the warehouse manager had to leave. Admittedly, I was not the only one who had to wait, there were nine people who did arrive later than I did. My desire to be clever by arriving early (here, 9.30 is very early) did not amount to anything and the day was less than successful. By the way, that is not an exception around here, but most people who have been here for years have become used to those things that our odd trade demands and only newcomers like me think that it's peculiar, if not to say unpleasant.

It is still very hot here and the other men are glad that they don't have to work very hard, while the heat only heightens my desire to be active, as you know. Tomorrow evening, I am traveling to Leningrad, as I wrote to you already, and hope that my darling sent her mail to that address in time so that I won't be without your longed-for reports for too long. On the 5th, the viewing begins for the auction which is scheduled to take place on the 12th, and there will be lots of work, because I have to look at and describe everything closely for my customers.

The day after tomorrow you are moving to Ravenshill, and my thoughts will accompany you to the unknown region where you will hopefully have lots of sun and a happy time and most of all, I want you to take the opportunity and rest. Is Yorks. short for Yorkshire? I have no idea where that is and would be very grateful for a small position plan so that I can at least have some idea where it is. We two people roam around the world, although we wish nothing more than to be together. It is not that easy, what my beloved girl took on with the man she did not even want at first. Hopefully, my beloved does not feel any regret and remains as brave and loyal to me as she has been, because that gives me so much incentive to high achievement and most of all, it gives sense to the achievements, because I know that all the work and all the deprivation lead to a goal, a goal that seems to me the most beautiful on earth, namely to prepare a future for you and our children, children I am looking forward to so very much.

My most heartfelt and loving embracing and kissing has been waiting for you much too long now and my entire being is made of longing for you and the need to caress you, to let my lips fondle your sweet body so that you melt with me and into me, inwardly and outwardly.

Your Mope

MOPE TO VERA

Moscow, 1 July 1937

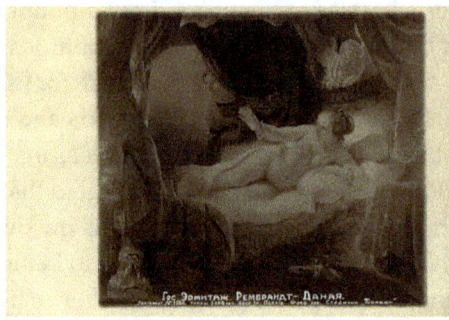

Fig. 75 Photograph of Danäe by Rembrandt, mailed with letter from Mope to Vera, Moscow, 1 July 1937.

I already wrote to you today, but since I just got a picture of "Saskia" that I had told you about from Leningrad, here are a few more words.[69]

Even if the shape of my beloved is incomparably preferable to that of Madame Rembrandt, I can imagine my girl in that same position– waiting–and I hope this reproduction that does not even come close to portray the beauty of the original will give you a little joy.

Not only the woman–so ready for the game of love–but also the old servant woman and the other small details of the painting are only foreshadowing the memory of what the reality of the painting has given to the one who is constantly occupied with his beloved.

The fine hands ready for caressing, growing from the bejeweled arm. The blanket thrown back in beautiful folds ready to receive the lover. The beautiful body waiting for the final, deepest happiness and under it, the soft sensuous pillows and on the floor, the impatiently thrown off little shoes–all of that looks so much richer in color, so much more

---

69 The painting by Rembrandt at the Hermitage that Mope endearingly describes is that of Danaë, for which the original nude model was the artist's wife, Saskia.

prepared, drunker with longing, and I feel the happiness that is waiting for me and will find complete fulfillment soon, soon.

I love my Saskia and long for the day that will have her that prepared for me, like Rembrandt's wife in the picture, to give and receive all the joys that life is ready to give at its best. How much I love my Lilongo!

VERA TO MOPE

Ravenshill Farm, near Whitby, Yorkshire, 4 July 1937

I want to use the first free minute since I arrived here to write to my beloved and to thank him for the beloved loving messages and to answer them.

One of the letters arrived here at 5 o'clock, at the same time as we did and welcomed me here, and I received the other one quite unexpectedly early today (Sunday). It probably arrived here yesterday during the late afternoon, and no one brought it up here until today. Our camp is situated on a bank that takes about five minutes to climb. At this moment, I am sitting on my camp bed, in front of me, our meadow stretches out, which is framed by a hedge. From the back fields, wonderful old trees are looking over at me and in front of us lies the sea that is wrapped in mist just now. We cannot go through the camp field directly to the ocean; we have to go down a hill, cross a street and then climb down to the beach, but it only takes eight minutes to get there; it is probably better that way, because the climate here is much rougher than in Somerset, where we were last year.

Just now, it is raining very lightly and the sound of the light click, click, on the tent roof is the only sound in the complete and wonderful silence. This morning, the sun was shining with interruptions, and now it is completely overcast, unfortunately, but the weather changes so rapidly here–before lunch rays of sunshine and warmth and a half hour after we were done, cool and rainy–that we can hope for the sun to come out again rather soon.

Our two predecessors left around 12 o'clock, after they handed over the cash box, books, supplies, medical utensils etc., etc., introduced us to suppliers, and then the ever so very important post office. I just found out that we have to pick up the mail twice a day from there, at nine in the morning and three in the afternoon, which I will do myself.

Seven girls decided to stay on for the coming week, the others left this morning, the other (new) twenty-nine will arrive during the course of the afternoon; the cook with her twelve-year old daughter and the porter who is extremely reliable also stayed here with us.

Three girls will sleep in each tent. Each one of us has a tent to herself with a table, chair and a shelf made of wooden boxes. On my table, there is a bunch of violet-colored flowers that we picked this morning from a hedge and whose name I do not know. They are deeply violet standing umbels that look especially decorative and glorious in their color surrounded by the wax-like green leaves.

Sandsend is a tiny place with a few bungalows, a few fishing huts and hotels–if you want to give them that elegant name. Whitby can be reached by a bus–every two hours–and seems to be a larger, and well frequented seaside resort. The bus takes about ten minutes to get there, so it is not far at all.

Now enough about this place and to your dearly beloved letters. As far as your projected trip to see Dr. J. is concerned, I thank you very much for your precise explanation. Should anything displeasing happen at Dr. J.'s, which is something I hope does not happen, and I don't think it will, I will travel there *immediately*, although I actually cannot do that after such a long absence, since he certainly won't remember me and, because of that, would not be too happy about my arrival, but I hope that your visit with him will be a very short one and that you will come to me right away. In your letter dated 30 June, you mention that you will probably be here towards the end of July. I will travel back on 18 July. Do you know HOW much I am looking forward to you?!

I am very glad that my beloved was able to take a refreshing swim. Unfortunately, I will not be able to go into the water for the first few days. They say that the water is ice-cold around here, but that will not bother me at all. Please don't worry–I will be very careful! Just now, the sun is trying to peek through the clouds.

My most heartfelt thanks for the telegram that reached me before I left and made my day much brighter. I still can hardly believe that we are really going to live together starting in August. You!!! It sounds so unbelievably beautiful! Completely Your Lilongo

MOPE TO VERA

Leningrad, 4 July 1937

Early during the day before yesterday still in Moscow, I was able to procure a large amount for the purchase of merchandise for Leipzig, after I had been trying for days. As I have probably already written to you, people are just not very interested, and they have every right, in selling to Germany, while the traders in Leipzig are very dependent on it in order to keep their businesses running. I was able to receive permission to take on merchandise valued at RM 42000.-, maybe a little more, that can be paid for in marks. I had to work hard during rather depressing thunderstorm weather in order to connect with Leipzig and London and consult with them as to what to buy, to inspect merchandise, to negotiate, etc. In the evening, the long-awaited storm finally came in never before seen dimensions. The rain was coming down in streams, such streams that might find an equivalent in Palestine–maybe, and the entire sky was in commotion.

Tomorrow, the inspections for the auctions start. They say, in general, that the auction work here is one of the most difficult and exhausting that is known in our trade. And there won't even be a Wychodnoi on the 6th or on the 12th. So if I should write a little less in the next few days, please blame it on the work and the business reports I have to file in the evening. At the moment, I just have my head full with work and I cannot afford to make any mistakes. On top of that, there are a lot of dinners and drinks during this time from which I cannot excuse myself completely out of politeness. I really dread that kind of company.

Now, as to why I really have to see Dr. J. again, I already wrote to you about in detail and I assume that the reasons appear plausible to you. I will not stay there longer than a day or two and then travel on to my beloved.

I kiss you there, where it lets you be happiest, with all my feeling and all my love that only belongs to you. With all my passion and all my heart, Your Mope

MOPE TO VERA

Leningrad, 5 July 1937

Today, the inspections began for the imminent auctions. We were in the warehouse until 5 o'clock and then calculated all the prices that can be spent for the merchandise whose quality we had jotted down. The banquet last night did not end all that late, since most of the participants were more or less sea-sick and left the hall around midnight. When I saw the quantity of vodka being consumed, I started filling my fourth glass with mineral water and drank to the health of "I don't know who," so that nothing happened to me, although they served white and red wine later in the evening. It is after 1.00 a.m. once again and I don't want to go to bed too late, so that I won't be yawning tomorrow. I don't think I will get to see much of Leningrad this time and I am glad that I have already been here once before despite the great and wasted expense.

VERA TO MOPE

Ravenshill Farm, near Whitby, Yorkshire, 6 July 1937

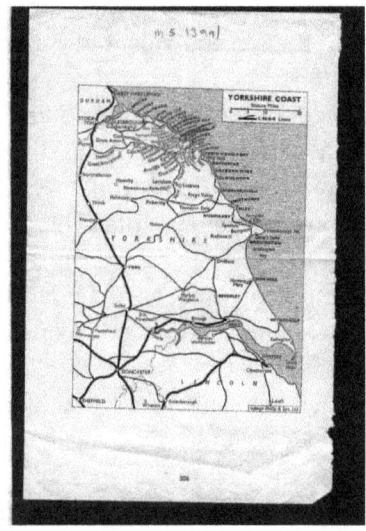

Fig. 76 Printed map of Yorkshire Coast included with letter from Vera to Mope, Ravenshill Farm, near Whitby, Yorkshire, 6 July 1937.

I am sitting in a canvas chair on our meadow, it is a little after 9.00 in the evening and although it is a little overcast and one side of the sky looks heavy with rain, but it is wonderful to be able to experience the sinking evening so entirely and completely. The sun visited us a little more often today, but I would not call it hot at all. I think that, even if it turned really warm, there will always be a wind blowing up here on our meadow. Last night, you could actually call it a storm, but that did not stop me from getting a really good night's rest.

Aside from the organization of meals, the administration of the "moneys," the so-called "first aid," putting on a dressing, etc., our main occupation consists of: buttering sandwiches, since, as you already know, bread and butter–sandwiches are prepared beforehand and forty-one stomachs devour a lot of these sandwiches during four meals a day, so this activity repeats itself every few hours, accompanied by the sounds of the gramophone and with the cook's assistance.

Fig. 77 Photograph of Vera (middle of second row) with vacationing Marks & Spencer shop girls.

The girls do not have to do *anything*, unless they volunteer and there are always at least four of them who do the dishes after the meals, something that gets done with a lot of laughter and amusement. My other work consists of enjoying the air and the sun and to be lazy. Of course, it is necessary for one of us to be present at all times, since we might be needed when one of the suppliers shows up or the girls have some kind of concern.

VERA TO MOPE

Ravenshill Farm, near Whitby, Yorkshire, 7 July 1937

I have written a letter to you every single day, and since the end of last week, I have been sending everything to Leningrad. I hope that at least the telegram I sent on Saturday after I arrived here came into your possession. It seems that they had never sent one from Sandsend to the U.S.S.R., judging by the astonished face of the postmaster.

The weather is still the same: it changes from sun to rain to wind to storms and back again to a little bit of sun about every two hours in downright regular intervals. At this very moment, the sun is coming out again and it is nicely warm (not hot), and I am lying on my blanket in the grass in front of my tent, stretched out in short white linen pants (white might be a little exaggerated, but that was the original color) and a back–and sleeveless top in order to catch all the sun's rays, after

I wore three woolen jumpers, one on top of the other, long pants and your jacket, which has served me very well once again, during my night watch and I still thought it was cold.

Yesterday morning, I went to Whitby and was lucky enough to be given a ride by a friendly soul, in a car, so that I did not have to walk down the country road for three-quarters of an hour. The female driver was a summer vacationer in Sandsend who showed great interest in the M&S summer camp, as do most people here, and the other one (male) was a Sandsend farmer who gave me the well-meaning advice to never accept an invitation for a car ride at night, and I laughed and made the promise.

Whitby is a charming old harbor with an old abbey; a pity that I did not have time to go up there; it is only preserved as a ruin and looks extremely picturesque amid old trees on a bank overlooking the red roofs of the skewed little fishermen's homes, and I hope that I will have another opportunity to visit and explore it.

Our household here is running smoothly, and the girls seem to be very happy with our meals. Most of them come from Northern England and speak a very charming dialect, and they are, with almost no exception, happy, easy going, very nice young girls, and the stay here is a real joy.

I have to stop now; the fisherman just came and told us that it would be turning very hot tomorrow; hopefully, he is right. I love you and I am very close in my thoughts, with you and beside you, passionately and gently, Your Lilongo

MOPE TO VERA

Leningrad, 7-8 July 1937

After I was without mail yesterday, I sent a telegram to your dear parents. Finally today, your letters arrived here via Moscow. Why are you not writing directly to me here? I did ask you for that in time and told you on the 27th already that I would be here from the 3rd of this month and will be staying for some time. I really don't want to reproach you, but you know just as well how longingly the two of us wait for news.

I did not write to you yesterday. I worked to exhaustion for thirteen hours yesterday without a break and I just could not do anything after that. Today, it was eleven hours, then I slept for an hour, ate dinner and have to go back to work after finishing this letter, because I still have to do some calculations for tomorrow's inspections. I am more than busy and have to work until deep into the night which is why I am wrapped in silence at the moment. Aside from that, everything is working out rather exceptionally.

Hopefully, your stay at the camp is satisfactory and favored by the most beautiful weather. It has become cooler here, something that is welcomed by everyone, except me, and so I submit to the heavens and the majority.

Most probably, I will be here until the 17th or 18th and will travel back to Moscow. Please adjust the addressing of your letters accordingly. While I am in Moscow, please address your letters to the "Metropole Hotel," because that is the location of the main post office for the local organization of the "Intourist." Starting on the 14th of this month, you can use the Moscow address again.

Unfortunately, this letter is terribly formal, but at the moment, I am lacking the leisure time to write differently, although I am always with my beloved (very, very much beloved) in my thoughts, but if I want to avoid from tearing open my mouth to yawn, I will have to go to bed soon. Your Mope

VERA TO MOPE

Ravenshill Farm, near Whitby, Yorkshire, 9 July 1937

I am a little sad today, because I still don't have any news from my beloved. To hell with all the postal, flight, train, and ship connections; in the end, they are not much good anyway. Or at least, they are not sufficient to satisfy my impatience. The only sign of my beloved husband's thoughts that I have in my hands from this week is the telegram to London, and it showed me that he was in a similar mood at the beginning of the week as I am today.

Sunday morning, most of the girls are leaving, and in the afternoon, a new shipment will arrive.

Yesterday evening–we needed a little more milk–I went to the farm that is about ten minutes away and met the owner. It was a real joy to have a conversation with this woman; she has spent her entire life up here, has never been to London, yet her perceptions on life are so broad-minded and intelligent that it proved to me once again that it is not or only in small part the outward influences that make a human being, but that you get it put into the cradle with you.—Let us hope that we will give our children many good and useful things to make their way in the world and then, let us try to take care of and cultivate it.

To come back to my farmer's wife, among other things, we got to talking about whether it would be desirable to live up here cut off from the world forever, and then she replied very simply: she could get used to any place and could be happy anywhere, as long as she had her loved ones there and a sufficient income. The farm is square and the barns are built around it, there are no electric lights and the wind blows from all sides. You have the most beautiful view down to the sea across meadows and fields that sink down gradually into the great blue water.

My beloved, unfortunately I have to close my evening–my Friday evening of chatting with you. Some of the girls are waiting with their evening walk so they can post this letter and I don't want to make them wait too long.

I love you, my most loved one, and I long for you, Your Lilongo

VERA TO MOPE

Ravenshill Farm, near Whitby, Yorkshire, 10 July 1937

Strange how irregularly plane traffic has to run. I was more than glad to finally hold another letter from my beloved husband in my hands, and it almost seems as if the heavens sympathize with my respective moods; as I was wandering down to the post office this morning shortly before 9 o'clock, the sun was shining and the sea shone deep blue; I had the feeling that, this time, there has to be a letter from my beloved.

It is 3.00 in the afternoon, the wind is blowing, the sky is completely overcast again, and it has been raining on and off. The camp participants' mood and mine as well, however, is still good. Yesterday, I was in the water for the first time despite the weather, but only for about one minute, because it was ice cold, but so much the warmer afterwards; such a cold bath, or swim as the case may be, is extraordinarily good.

For the first time here last night, I experienced a clear, starry night–the west side stayed so bright that I almost felt like I was in the land of the midnight sun. I wonder if you also had such a clear sky above you last night–Friday night–and if you looked at the same stars as I did and asked them to carry many loving words to a certain someone far in the East.

You don't have to worry: our tents are really warm and quite comfortable. They are built like sugar loaves and the radius of the base circle is about 2-2 ½ meters. The camp beds all have a well-filled straw sack lying on the beds' waterproof canvas, and there are enough blankets, and if you want, there are also hot-water bottles. I think I would live in a tent all year long if the climate allowed it–I wonder if you would move into one with me.

I kiss you again and again and am completely, Your Lilongo

VERA TO MOPE

Ravenshill Farm, near Whitby, Yorkshire, 11 July 1937

After a lovely morning, it started pouring down in buckets until the evening, and the storm was blowing so hard that we put on all the coats and woolen jumpers we could put our hands on. To compensate us, Saturday was an uninterrupted day of bright sunshine, and up here on our bank, it never becomes oppressive and it was never too hot for me. Our brown coloring deepened quite a bit today thanks to the sun.

After the rain stopped, a girl who shares my sense of adventure went on a lovely walk with me. We wandered along the country road to Whitby, and for the first time, I had the leisure to look more closely at this charming little old city. Just for that, the sun came out and we enjoyed the sunset in the church yard of the abbey–and this time, the fireball sank into the sea, which is something I really do love. A steep climb with 199 stair steps, if you want to call the bumpy stones a stair–lead up to the little church that was newly built a few meters away from the ruins of the abbey.

Since this is the last evening for the greater number of the girls, we gave them permission to bring their "boy-friends" along, served them coffee, sandwiches, sweets, etc., let the gramophone play, and the entire company sang and seemed to be in a very good mood. This lasted until about 11.30 in the evening.

I hope that my beloved is not too exhausted in Leningrad. You write that you will stay there until 18 July; are you going back to Moscow? I suppose not after you took all of your luggage; or will you go on your visit to Dr. J.?

This morning, I had a wonderful swim, that is, the waves were too high for swimming, and it was only a wonderful and refreshing sea bath. As soon as some of the photos taken here are developed, I will send them to you.

Your Lilongo

MOPE TO VERA

Leningrad, 15 July 1937

In my thoughts, I have answered all of my beloved's letters that are lying in front of me, but it has been factually impossible for me to find the time to sit down and write to you. Since about an hour ago, my work has been taking on normal proportions once again. The auction was over around noon, and, until about an hour ago, I had to complete the shipping orders of the entire bought merchandise–and that was a lot. Just now, I finished packing most of my things, and once I have written this letter and eaten dinner, the night train to Moscow will be leaving. As you already read in the last few letters, there was such an unbelievable amount of work to be done that there was not one single night when I was able to sink into my bed before 3 or 4 in the morning. I have never before seen such quantities of merchandise of such diversity in one place.

In between all that work, there were different banquets and dinners in smaller circles from which I could not excuse myself, even though I would have loved to have done so, and, instead of drinking vodka, I would have preferred writing to you. However, it just couldn't happen. Hopefully, my telegrams made up for the lack of letters just a little bit and told you that I am doing well.

I was very happy with your reports on camp life. They were refreshing for me after all the exhausting work and more important than eating and sleeping. How regrettable that your stay there did not make camping a more enjoyable activity, because the climate which is usually rough was made worse by wind and rain. Even if your tents were more comfortable than what I am familiar with, sunshine and a calm sky are requirements if you camp outdoors. I thank you for the mailing of the map. Now, I have some idea at least as to where my thoughts will meet my beloved when I send them to her–and I do that constantly.

I found out yesterday that my transfer things, which caused me quite a headache as well, are finally being taken care of. I actually felt quite weak after that tension–when I found out–and my stomach was acting like something was missing, but that was easily taken care of, and I am breathing a sigh of relief, because all of these unimaginable difficulties have been overcome.

Please excuse me for saying this, but the things you are writing about Dr. J. and that you might possibly visit him, are nonsense. You have absolutely no business there and I would be very indignant if you even approached his vicinity. There is no reason for any misgivings, but just the thought that you–for whatever reason–traveling to him is revolting.

While I am sitting here writing, many singing girls are passing by and I am happily enjoying the beautiful melodies and voices. And now, I have to stop chatting with my beloved again, because I have to get to the train on time, and since I have not eaten anything since lunch and that was in a hurry, I am feeling really hungry, and it's 10 o'clock at night.

I will send this letter, or better, this confused mess, which I ask you to forgive, to London, because it probably will not reach you in Sandsend anymore. I hope, that you, my beloved girl, will have a few more enjoyable days in camp and a pleasant trip back, after which these words will welcome you home with all the love and passion that I put into them for you. I wonder if they will get there on time. Your Mope

VERA TO MOPE

Ravenshill Farm, near Whitby, Yorkshire, 18 July 1937

In about 20 minutes, the coach will arrive and pick up our herd of campers to take all them to York, from where they will leave by train in all four directions.

Yesterday evening–after the last day was wonderfully sunny and warm again, the usual goodbye party with "boyfriends" took place; there were about 20 soldiers (there is a camp quite close to here with about 2000 residents–and I was surprised that no more showed up).

Later:

Now, there are only four girls and the cook left who will all leave around noon, and then, only my co-worker, the porter and I will stay here until tomorrow.

We two supervisors stayed awake last night, or this morning actually, until 4 a.m. (half asleep), because two girls disappeared with some soldiers and did not come back until dawn; they said nothing that sounded like "I'm sorry" but only "we did not know you would sit up for us!" Of course, it makes no sense to say something on the last day, and they know that very well and used that, and so, neither of us said a word.

It is a little later now, and once again, we climbed up and down our hill and took the cook, including her luggage, to the bus. Now, out of thirty-six little Indians, only four are still here.

Actually, I am supposed to help now with packing everything up, but the mailbox only gets emptied once on Sundays and my beloved just has to get some words from me, even if they are only gibberish caused by constant interruptions and getting little sleep.

Tomorrow at noon, we are going back to London after these two very relaxing and recuperative weeks, and maybe, I will find a few words from you at home.

My beloved, today in two weeks!!!!! Most passionately, Your Lilongo

VERA TO MOPE

London, 19 July 1937

This afternoon, or actually evening–I got home around 6.45 p.m.–I found your dear Thursday words and your telegram!! You always make sure that such beloved mail from you welcomes me, while I am afraid that I never manage to get my letters to you at just the right time.

Yesterday, we had a very busy day during which we really worked like "laborers;" among other things, 160 wool blankets had to be rolled up and tied, and after we were finished with that job, which required a lot of bending over and physical strength, our porter found us (my co-worker and me) sleeping on the mountain of blankets; on top of everything else, it was rather hot, which really does not bother me, but the previous night did not bring all that much sleep, as I told you earlier. In any case, everything was packed up by evening and all of the shipping lists were written, so that our last night in camp was a relatively early night. It was a really enjoyable stay, unburdened by all the worries of the every-day and suffused by a harmless joy, the dear letters of my beloved and the awareness that the longed day is nearing.

Tomorrow, I will go to the head office, among other things, to turn in our books and a report, and while I am there, I will ask if I can take both the long weekends that I still have and add them to my vacation–that means three extra days altogether. Of course, I will give our marriage as the reason, because there is usually no leave of absence for anyone at M&S that falls before a bank holiday, because that always is a very busy week. I hope that they will approve my plan, and I will be there to pick up my beloved on Friday at the train station–God willing, he will come home on Friday, 30 July–if only I could make time move faster!

You——I put my lips on yours and kiss you, kiss you, totally, Your Lilongo

MOPE TO VERA

Moscow, 20 July 1937

Yesterday evening, my new boss called from Karlsbad and since he needs copies of the auction catalogues, I sat there until after 2 a.m., despite my great tiredness, and wrote and wrote down all kinds of things that did not interest me at all at such a late hour. But what could I do? Today was less strenuous than yesterday and around 7 p.m., I lay down for an hour and let the catalogue scribbling be.

Afterwards, we, that is, several acquaintances and I, went to the "Eremitage." It is a kind of amusement park with a theater, cinemas, open restaurants, and very many people who relax there after work.[70] Since I have been in Russia, this was only the second evening during which I was able to do something for my private amusement before midnight.

I have given Julius Rosenfeld's accounting a cursory glance and assume that it is correct. Without the documents that are still in Leipzig, it really is not possible for me to check the accounting accurately and I won't get around to it in the foreseeable future either. Fred will have let you know that I will come to London directly and that I will postpone the visit to Dr. J. to a later date.

The fact that my dear mother's trip to London had to be postponed *really alarms me*, and I hope that there is no cogent reason that will keep her in Germany for a longer period of time???

I kiss you most passionately, my beloved, as always full of burning longing and love and will not be really happy until I can hold you in my arms. You! Your Mope

MOPE TO VERA

Moscow, 23 July 1937

I shall depart from here on Monday around 4.30 at the latest with the Northern Express and travel via Prague. I will go to Karlsbad for a day to confer with my boss and then I will fly to London on the 29th.[71] I am

---

70 The Moscow Hermitage Garden remains a popular city center recreation spot.
71 In the end, Mope had to travel by train following a highly circuitous route that avoided Germany through Austria, Switzerland and France. He arrived late on Friday, 30 July.

so very happy and glad to have this difficult time behind me and can finally travel to my most dearly beloved girl.

If only I knew what is going on with my dear mother. The postponement of her trip alarms me extraordinarily, and I have been without contact with her for about five weeks now. I don't know how she is, what her plans are, if she will be able to travel to Palestine or come to London for our wedding. This is an abominable situation, something you will understand, because you know how attached I am to that dear lady.

Now I want to close this letter, one of my last letters from here, and go to dinner. Today, there will be a grand ball in the Metropole, especially since an extraordinary number of tourists, especially from America, are here right now. The eve of Wychodnoi gives occasion to be a little happier and friskier, just as it is normal for a Saturday night elsewhere.

Please begin to consider how and where I am supposed to kiss and caress you,

Your Mope who is so very much in love

VERA TO MOPE

London, 24 July 1937

Just a few minutes ago, I heard from Muttilein that a telegram for me arrived early today and she read me its contents over the phone. I am so happy to have some kind of date for your arrival and I am so indescribably and unspeakably happy!!!

This time, I can really come to the train station in order to receive my beloved. I am on vacation until 18 August (I have to be back at work on that day) and I was happy that I saved my long weekends.

I received a charming letter from your dear mother on Tuesday. She is really hoping to be able to be here at the end of the month, and so do I! She wrote that Semy has been going out of his way for her to try and get the necessary document for her.

My beloved, I can hardly wait and would like to sleep for the four days (I am not counting Saturday, although it is only 3.30 in the afternoon) and then wake up and fall into the arms of my beloved, You—

Twenty-five: "The Alpha and Omega of My Life"

16 September through 27 October 1937

Fig. 78 (a) and (b) Photographs of Vera and Mope at their wedding, London, 1 August 1937. Vera's mother, Alice Hirsch, stands behind the couple in the second of these photos.

The marriage of Vera and Mope on Sunday, 1 August 1937 was a modest affair with family and friends adding up to a guest list of hardly more than a dozen. The only damper upon an otherwise joyous occasion was the absence of Mope's mother, who did not obtain permission from the Nazi authorities to travel to England.

On the first leg of their honeymoon, the newlyweds flew to Basle, and, to Mope's delight, his mother (along with her daughter Grete and son-in-law, Norbert, who lived in nearby Freiburg) were granted day permits to cross the border into Switzerland for a brief reunion. The honeymoon itself took place in northern Italy, the itinerary for which had been mapped by Mope before he had left Leipzig. It included a visit to Genoa, where they were the house guests of Hilde and Walter Lewy. Hilde was Vera's most intimate friend from her schooldays.

On their return to London, Vera had to go back to work at M&S, whereas the duration of Mope's stay was limited to a few short weeks. Recalling his predicament in his post-war curriculum vitae, he writes: "Since I was without any financial means, the English authorities did not permit me to stay in England or to establish my residence there. At the beginning of September, I received an order to leave within 48 hours." Fortunately for him, his replacement as representative in Russia of the Compagnie Internationale de Pelleteries had turned out to be a failure, and Mope was persuaded to take up his former position on a more permanent basis. "Since the Parisian company wanted to send me back to Russia for additional purchases and contract negotiations," Mope writes, "I had requested a new Russia[n] visa in England that arrived just in time." Concern about travel costs obliged him to travel to Moscow by sea and rail, a journey of five days.

During his earlier trip to Russia, Mope had been more than occupied during the intense days of the fur auctions, and he expected to be no less again. What neither he nor his Parisian employer had fully taken into account was the economic impact of the devaluation of the French franc. It had been devalued by about thirty per cent in October 1936, and further pressure during the ensuing year forced the French government to remove the currency from the gold standard, creating tremendous financial uncertainty. An immediate result was a flattening of demand for such luxury goods as furs. Mope arrived in Moscow to find himself made largely idle. The newlyweds were already sorely tried by their separation so soon after their marriage, and their correspondence captures well their acute depression and longing for each other.

Adding to the difficulty of being apart was the relentlessness with which Karl Herzberg pursued Mope for further payments under the PalTreu scheme.

Without full documentation, the precise details are difficult to ascertain although Herzberg's refusal to reach a settlement and the accelerated threats of legal action and confiscation leave little doubt that his actions against Mope were being directed by the Nazi authorities. "A man like Karl Herzberg would–I am quite sure–be a scourge for his contemporaries if he would have remained in Germany," writes Mope from London in 1944. "Here he tries to adapt himself to English ways and customs but this is no more than face cream."

Lacking permission to hold foreign currency, Mope had been offered by his British brother-in-law, Fred Rau, a surety to allow him to engage in the PalTreu scheme as a legal means of transferring money abroad, primarily for his mother but also for himself. The furs that he had purchased and then warehoused in Antwerp were destined for Palestine, where their sale could have released the capital that had been invested in them. The foreign currency office in Leipzig stymied all attempts to allow that to happen. The threatening letters that were sent were all addressed to Mope in London, and, in his absence, the new Mrs. Felsenstein was left to deal with these. Although she was valiant in her efforts to respond to the constant demands from Germany, Vera became increasingly skeptical about the wisdom of having engaged in the PalTreu scheme and fearful of its long-term effects upon them both.

After a month and a half of largely wasted time in Moscow, Mope's stay there was cut short by his employer's decision to recall him. He was to reach London toward the start of November. During his absence, he had missed the visit to England of his mother, before she embarked on a trip to Palestine, where her son, Adolf, and daughter, Alice, each lived. The debacle of the PalTreu plans and consequent lack of funds would have been contributory factors in her eventual decision not to settle there.

VERA TO MOPE

London, 16 September 1937

My Mopelein–When these lines reach you, you will have hopefully arrived hale and healthy in Moscow and had a pleasant and maybe even relaxing trip behind you. Let me tell you one more time and at the beginning of your stay there: I am completely and totally convinced, without any kind of reservation, that you will fill that position magnificently. I would not say that so implicitly, if I had not arrived at this definite opinion through observations, facts, and also a little knowledge about people that I inevitably have to have because of my work. A human being who has such a will to succeed, the experience and knowledge of the trade and added to that a clearly capable mind *has* to be 100% successful! It is nice, very nice to know, that the person who has all of these attributes is the man whom a very kind fate has given me as a life companion and friend and lover, and I am extremely happy about it.

My dearest, I would like to say to you one more time, as a return for those ever so rich days we spent together: They were not only filled by so many beautiful things, I also have the feeling that they brought me along a little bit as a human being, and I thank you, my beloved, for everything, for your love and kindness, your patience and your understanding and your intensity in all of your thoughts and emotions. Your Lilongo

MOPE TO VERA

On Board the M/S. England between Harwich and Esbjerg, Denmark, 17 September 1937

My most beloved, I thank you for all your love, your desire to understand, your empathy for everything that occupies me and every minute, so precious to me, that I was able to spend with you. These seven weeks have been the happiest of my life, and this happiness could not be reduced by any difficulty I encountered, other than the pain to have to leave you again.

You, my darling, I embrace across the wide sea that stretches out between us and kiss your beloved eyes and your lips and all of you, from awakening until going to sleep, with all of my love that belongs to you and only you. Your Mope

MOPE TO VERA

Helsinki, 19 September 1937

I am sitting here with an Englishman and a Greek from Egypt in a restaurant that is situated high above the city in the uppermost story of a hotel tower, and we had dinner while looking at the view of the setting sun. My two fellows are travel acquaintances with whom I spent a very pleasant day first from Åbo to here in the train and then here.

We really enjoyed the beautiful weather that finally won victory over the horrible rain. The Greek Egyptian is the most intimate friend of my good acquaintance Sistovaris in Alexandria, with whom I spent a very pleasant evening during my stay in Alexandria.[72] As my darling usually says in such cases: "How small the world really is!"

This evening, I am traveling on to Leningrad. We will pass the border, as far as I know, tomorrow morning. The departure from Stockholm yesterday was breathtakingly beautiful. We traveled for hours through the fjord with many inhabited and forested islands and the sun was going down behind them. It was a real experience. The boat is very clean, and, although it was overbooked, I had a cabin to myself which I succeeded in getting by pleading with the man that I had been urgently warned about bad smelling people. As far as I could see (or smell), this warning was actually–for yesterday anyway–not needed.

In Copenhagen, where I just barely received the last free room in the second hotel, I rushed "around the corner" to drink a cup of coffee before going to bed. The nearest tavern was a bar from where a very pretty girl waved to me after I sat down. I waved back and there she was sitting at my table with a colleague. Since everything was very reasonably priced, as in most Danish taverns–coffee, a whole pitcher of very good coffee around 16 Kronors I did not have a problem with that. We could not talk at all and I only determined that the girl who had a fine face and was built well but had rather coarse hands. After I had ordered something to drink for both girls, the one gathered all of her knowledge of the English language, pointed her finger at herself, her colleague and me and said "home." When I did not understand immediately, she took a paper napkin and wrote on it "Kronor 40." Now, that was too much for me in every way and I drank my coffee, paid and rolled into the hotel that was exactly six steps distant. I was told that was nothing unusual for Copenhagen, the Paris of the North!

The main purpose this letter is meant to fulfill is to bring you my most passionate kisses and my love and all of my emotions and feeling that exists only for you. In the meantime, I am already in the sleeper compartment of the train and want to quickly post this letter. Your Mope

---

72 The Sistovaris family were well known furriers in pre-war Egypt. Mope had docked in Alexandria en route to Palestine in 1936.

MOPE TO VERA

Moscow, 22 September 1937

I have been here since yesterday. On the 20th, I arrived in Leningrad after a comfortable trip. While I was traveling, I met three American women who want to travel across Russia for about two weeks. We visited the "Pioneers' Palace" in the afternoon and went to the theater in the evening, since I could not leave until the 12.30 train, because there was no room in the sleeper car on the 9.50 train.

The Pioneers Palace is a home for children. It is a former place of the Czar that had been reconstructed in a grand way as an entertainment home for children from about eight to sixteen years old. You cannot imagine what kinds of motivation for all different types of things the children receive. It is the most outstanding method to motivate young people and to awaken latent talents or abilities that they might have. There is, to mention only a few things among many, a chess hall, a dance hall, halls for dexterity, rooms in which someone is reading to the children or telling them stories, a café with radio music, a hall that is furnished to look like a salon on a ship, lecture halls, etc. There are about six thousand children who visit daily and, as a reward for special accomplishments in school, children are given tickets to go there. Every day, there are different children, so everyone gets his turn.[73]

In the theater, a fairy tale was performed, a tale I didn't know, but whose content was completely understandable because of its grandiose presentation. It was an opera, by the way, and the performers were really first rate. The choirs were especially good as well, so that I was happy to have taken this nice break in my mostly rainy travels.

Now I have to tell you something completely unexpected. I was greeted here by hot summer weather that is lasting through today. It is even warmer than it was for most of July; all the leaves are still green. I feel myself pushed back by two months, but unfortunately, very unfortunately, I do not have the same beautiful time ahead of me as I did then.

---

73   The Anichkov Palace, commissioned by Empress Elizabeth in 1741, was used during the Soviet era as the Zhdanov Palace of Young Pioneers, an equivalent of a Boy Scouts' Museum.

MOPE TO VERA

Moscow, 26 September 1937

Finally, finally–letters from my darling arrived today. I had really been quite desperate, without any news, and today was quite a holiday with three letters.

This evening, I am going back to the opera again. The three American women with whom I traveled from Helsingfors to Leningrad have come here for three days and ordered a ticket for me as well. When I asked them today to accept the money, they were actually offended. They are very nice and cultured and most of all, well educated, and are really enjoying their stay with sightseeing tours of art galleries and bring back very interesting reports on everything I have not seen yet while we have dinner together. Tomorrow, they are traveling on to Kiev.

If I do not close now, this letter will not reach the airmail anymore. I love you so indescribably, and I kiss you everywhere with the greatest longing and passion and embrace you again and again with so much intensity that you just have to feel it.

Your Mope

In the future, please address the envelopes with the typewriter or in block letters. Apparently, they are having problems reading your handwriting. And please address them to the Hotel National for now–maybe the letters will get here a little sooner then.

VERA TO MOPE

London, 28 September 1937

Pretty soon, you will have every right to say: *"Now she got him on the safe side, she does not write to him any more!"* Well, do you say that? Yesterday evening, I went directly to bed, because I was not feeling well at all. Nothing to get worried about and everything is back to normal now! Please don't be sad, and don't think that I have forgotten about my beloved!

My work meeting today took almost the entire afternoon at the head office, but did not result in any real new things. The essence of it was this: 1. the request to us (and the girls through us) to have as much knowledge about the merchandise as possible; 2. to not only instruct the salesgirls constantly, but also the supervisors on the floor, since they are in constant contact with the counter-girls; and 3. the request that we get involved everywhere in everything at any time. I suppose that such a meeting is quite beneficial as a reminder for self-determination and as a critique (and it was really meant as one).

I kiss you, my beloved, on your eyes and your forehead, every so quietly and tenderly.

Your Lilongo

MOPE TO VERA

Moscow, 28 September 1937

A little while ago, the three American women left. Their presence was a welcome change, although I could only share my evenings with them, of course, as far as my business correspondence left me the time to do so, and I will probably be in more need for such a change in a few weeks, since all of my colleagues are leaving here in the course of the next few days.

At the same time as the Americans were leaving, a tall, slim and really distinguished looking older gentleman was traveling to Kiev. Someone told me that he was American, but I don't believe that, since the similarity to the Archbishop of Canterbury was totally uncanny. Unfortunately, I did not find out until later that it had to have been him. His passport gave the name Prof. Johnson and was English. If I had known that, I would have returned his good wishes for a safe trip which he gave us at Easter in 1936. He looked at me rather questioningly as if he knew me, but I did not have the heart to just go and start talking to a complete stranger, and he might just have been one.[74]

The weather turned noticeably cooler here since yesterday, and I am running around in a summer coat. Nevertheless, the sun is shining all day long.

The mail has to be sent now, and that is why I have to close many pages earlier than I would like, but I am writing to you about the many, many and most loving kisses that I would love to give you personally, but this will have to do. Your Mope

---

74 Dr. Hewlett Johnson, the so called "Red Dean" [not the Archbishop!] of Canterbury had greeted Vera and Mope in the cathedral grounds shortly after their engagement. His pro-Communist leanings as a so-called Christian Marxist led to his visit at this time and to the later publication of his book, *Soviet Power* (1941).

MOPE TO VERA

Moscow, 29 September 1937

My work—especially since the correspondence that goes with it cannot be taken care of during the day—does not end until 11 in the evening. However, dinner usually takes place from 5-7 o'clock, and aside from that, I am quite lazy at this time, since I am supposed to put on the brakes concerning the purchase of merchandise. This is a consequence of the devaluation of the Franc.[75] Usually, all of us fur buyers sit in the Metropole's restaurant and you hear about business matters when people have been drinking too much, things you would otherwise hear nothing about. I usually do not participate in all the drinking, because it is important to me that I do not have a hangover the next day.

I have to tell you that my life here is meaningful only because of you. How lonely I would feel if my thoughts were not always with my sweet darling I cannot imagine at all. Your Mope

VERA TO MOPE

London, 2 October 1937

Yesterday evening, I came home dead tired after a long and aggravating day at work, and your sweet words made it so that everything looked much more bearable and made me feel happier.

I had the feeling to have wasted energy all day long for nothing, and that leaves a person with an empty and ugly feeling. The reason for all of it was that a girl's coat (if alleged or actual has not been determined yet, but I tend more towards actual), the best coat she owns, was stolen from the locker room. I spent my day to interview almost all of the girls, one by one, without any positive success. Some of them allege that the girl was wearing her old coat that morning which was actually still hanging there, but she said that she always left it here and that she had to go home dressed in just a suit a few days ago, but that she wore her good coat for a special occasion Friday morning. More details would get too

---

75   The French franc was devalued by about thirty per cent in October 1936. Further devaluation took place in June 1937 after Léon Blum's government abandoned the gold standard, and allowed the franc to float. Naturally, the fur business, a purveyor of luxury items, was to suffer considerably as a consequence.

involved here (especially since I have to go back to the store). The fact remains that the coat is gone–I left everything else yesterday and it was all for nothing; I went home tired and downhearted, so thank you once again for your letter that got me back on my feet.

I am still without an assistant today and actually should not be writing at all. However, I do have to tell you something important: There was a registered letter yesterday from Herzberg: he wants to hold the 150 pieces for you until the 9th of the month; otherwise he wants to be compensated for damages. I think that is good news and bad! The latter, because he seems to be unable to sell the merchandise at that price, good, because you won't have to pay damages and won't have to purchase the merchandise again. I passed the letter on to Fred immediately and will talk about the matter with him tomorrow. I don't believe that everything can be taken care of by the 9th, but very soon after that, and I think it would be best to write to Mr. Herzberg and tell him so. I am curious to find out about Fred's opinion and of course, I will go along with his suggestions. Actually I think it is much, much better this way than I had dared to expect, since economies do and will change again.

Many passionate kisses, Totally Your Lilongo

VERA TO MOPE

London, 3 October 1937

Today, we were able to set the clock back an hour, and because of that, I woke up at 9 a.m. instead of actually 10 a.m., which really was the actual time, I slept in and slept very well.

I talked to Hannalein and Fred on the telephone this evening. Fred advised me to make a copy of Herzberg's letter and send it to your representative in Leipzig with a cover letter referring to our last letter to him. He thought that I should not even answer Herzberg.

And your representative should try to get Herzberg to ship those 150 pieces, which could then be paid for without delay and only then. Whether Herzberg will do that remains to be seen. However, please do not worry about that–everything will be taken care of. Fred will send the correspondence back to me today, and then, I can take care of it tomorrow evening.

MOPE TO VERA

Moscow, 3 October 1937

It is Sunday night and I ordered sandwiches and tea to be brought to my room, thinking that you are probably sitting at High Tea, and I was considering if my darling's thoughts are with me as intensely as mine are with her. It was a rather odd feeling for me, almost as if I was sitting there with you, and my girl was sitting next to me, taking care of my physical well-being and thereby encouraging the psychological well-being, as she always does when I am with her.

Early today, I received the letter that you wrote after our conversation–with block letters on the envelope, and later on, the express letter from the day before arrived. How strange and still natural that you give voice to the same thoughts about our conversation as the ones I wrote down afterwards. There is a great harmony of the souls between us that causes and creates the same emotions in us despite all the distance.

I have so little to do at the moment and that is more exhausting than working hard, because I keep thinking about having to make people who are entitled and pushing to take over the merchandise understand why that is not possible at the moment.

VERA TO MOPE

London, 8 October 1937

Today, I received a letter, or better a form letter, from the head office with the following: Mrs. V. Felsenstein, wages from £3-10-0 to £3-15-0; starting this week. I am glad that I got the raise without having said anything about it, that is £1-0-0 more per month, and since I have been here for over 18 months, I will receive two weeks' pay, that is £710, as a Christmas bonus, in addition to my usual salary. This raise is not exactly great considering what those people ask me to do for it, nevertheless, it is better than no raise at all, and finally, you have to add all the benefits to the salaries: cafeteria, discounts, highly reduced dental treatments (which I am taking advantage of again now), etc.

MOPE TO VERA

Moscow, 8 October 1937

It is peculiar how far removed I feel from the entire Herzberg matter, almost as if it concerned a different Mope, but not me. Since I cannot do anything from here to take care of things, that is a good thing, because, as long as I was in the center of things, it caused me so much heartache that I am probably lucky to have moved to the periphery, before the whole affair made me sick. However, I really hate for it to affect my darling who has so selflessly taken care of all the correspondence and conferences until now, and that is why I am asking you to let matters take their course as they will or as the idiot Herzberg will. You should never push too hard in matters of business. Before my departure, we had made such fair suggestions concerning the arrangements that it is his own fault if he does not accept them. If this schlemiel still does not know that we took care of the matter in a completely correct manner and keeps going against it due to his stupid mistrust, we do not want to keep making new attempts.

Ultimately, everyone is responsible for his own salvation. I will send you a telegram concerning this matter, because I do not want my beloved to waste any more energy on this apparently fruitless business. If you get more messages, I ask you to give expression to my above opinion and then put an end to it. Your very accurate opinion that Herzberg's sudden wanting-to-get-it-done can be based on the bad economy is entirely correct. It is trending downwards in a rather bad way, and there is no recognizable point for this trend to stop. In our trade, back-treading economies often last years, and I cannot wait that long and hope that I will live to see better days. Why did the idiot not agree to my suggestion made through my Leipzig representative? I suppose that he believed he might be able to make a better deal somewhere else, and when that didn't work out, he turned back to me. However, I am too good for that and I did not find my money in a back alley either.

The textbook 1000 words still has not arrived and I have given up hope. In any case, it shows that you cannot send books.

Please send my dear mother my most heartfelt greetings. I have not written to her since the card from Esbjerg and hope that she has begun her trip to Palestine in the meantime. Mope

VERA TO MOPE

London, 11 October 1937

I just wanted to jot down a few quick words, although it is terribly late again. Early today, the mail brought me your letter from Wednesday. At the same time, there was one from Julius Rosenfeld that said, as far as customs was concerned, he was hoping to take care of matters, but that the original import permit was only good until the 31st of the month, that for further permission, either you or your mother would have to apply anew for which a 50% cash payment would be required. I sent a copy to Fred whose answer I am expecting tomorrow morning. For this reason, Herzberg's agreement has to take place immediately, or it won't be valid any longer.

I also got a letter from your Leipzig attorney that I found anything but pleasant. He raised the matter of your landlord Dr. Jacobson, rather unfavorably as a matter of fact. I read his letter again today, and he is complaining that the large room without the use of the smaller one would be absolutely impossible to rent to anyone, that August–September was the best time to find a new tenant, and since he did not have both at his disposal and if you wanted to end the lease at the end of the year, he would have the large room sitting empty for another three months, which would cause a rather large loss for him. He accounts for the expenses of five Reichmarks with telephone calls and trips on the tram to run after his rent.

It is horribly late and I am closing this hastily scribbled letter, that is supposed to bring to my beloved friend all the good things I wish for him and all my love, Your Lilongo

MOPE TO VERA

Moscow, 14 October 1937

Today, there is no mail again from my beloved. It is bad how little you can count on it, and since I am waiting with such longing for your letters, I always feel really sad when I am forced to accept a negative head shake from the lady at the Intourist mail department. She actually seems happy when she can tell me something positive, because she apparently regrets having to see my disappointed face, when a "no" from her is the cause for it.

However, quite unexpectedly, I received the little bi-lingual phrase book you sent to me on 17 September, and I am glad that it did reach its destination after all. My first Russian lesson meant a very huge demand to my tongue that earned it sore muscles. However, I think I will be able to get over that more quickly than I will learn the language for which the next lesson is scheduled for 8.30 the day after tomorrow.

I did not write to you yesterday. Snow has been falling since yesterday morning, but as soon as it hits the ground, it melts. In any case, winter has begun, and since there still is not heat–hopefully tomorrow–in the hotel, I am sitting in my room freezing and would rather stick my hands in my pockets, because they are too stiff for writing anyway. Just now, I came back to the hotel from a warming meal and for the time being, writing seems to go the way it is supposed to. Later on, I will go to the theater so that I won't have to feel like an ice block all evening long.

Unfortunately, at the moment, I am damned to complete inactivity. There are no assignments because of the miserable economy, and I am already so fed up with sitting around and doing nothing that I would love to pack my bags and leave. When the next opportunity presents itself, I will ask my boss if it makes sense to prolong my visa.

It seems that the stock exchange values in the U.S.A. are very low, because otherwise, business should start now and new assignments should come in. Has the French Franc stabilized at 147 against the British pound, or did it grow more uncertain and fall even lower?

I am so bored that I am reading detective novels by Edgar Wallace and in that, I see the sinking moral niveau. I have already read three! Your Mope

MOPE TO VERA

Moscow, 16 October 1937

Since yesterday, they have been heating and I can sit in my room again and write, something that had been impossible on the days before. Because of that, I sent a detailed report to my boss. To my question as to whether or not I should extend my visa, his unfortunate answer was, "of course!" so that the small hope that I was taking care of with utmost tenderness to see you earlier than originally expected disappeared.

Yesterday evening, we went to a concert with a wonderful program: Beethoven–Egmont Overture, 8th Symphony, and the one I love so very much: the 5th Symphony. The conductor, Oskar Fried,[76] who is supposed to have lived in Germany some time ago and already suffered two strokes, tried very hard but he still cannot touch the conductors of the Gewandhaus despite the strokes. I had never heard his name before. The orchestra was very good in their cooperation and overcame a lack in its conductor without his help, nevertheless, in the second movement of the 5th, the tempo was much too quick, because he was conducting too fast. The 3rd and 4th movements were very beautiful though and made up for the messed-up 2nd.

VERA TO MOPE

London, 18 October 1937

I found out to my surprise that the merchandise still had not been shipped from Antwerp. The shipper is now demanding money from Fred, because the extra pieces that are included had not been paid in full. Of course, Fred refused, and the shipper argued that Herzberg was holding them responsible for it. I had explained to Fred not too long ago that they had been paid in full and did not report anything else on the matter. But now, the Antwerp shipper is refusing to ship the merchandise, which of course is completely improper, because it belongs to Fred, and he sent a registered letter to Antwerp on Wednesday and threatened with a lawyer if the merchandise was not shipped immediately.

This evening, I made the firm decision that I will no longer worry about the matter, since it seems to require more strength of nerves than it is worth. Please do the same thing, because it is completely futile to keep worrying your head about it.

P.S. Late at night

I just talked to Fred one more time; he will call Antwerp tomorrow and ask them to remove the disputed forty pieces from the shipment, if the merchandise won't be sent with them included, and send the rest immediately. The Haavara in Jerusalem will be able to confirm that the amount for the back-ordered wares is still available to Herzberg. I really do not care if it will be sold at a loss or a gain, as long as everything is back in order.

---

76 Oskar Fried (1871-1941) was a German conductor and one of the foremost interpreters of Gustav Mahler. He emigrated to the Soviet Union in 1933 following the rise of Hitler. He became the conductor for the Moscow Radio Symphony Orchestra.

Fred thought it futile to call you, because no one could explain everything in three minutes and that it would just cause more expenses than what he suggested, not to mention that he would have to bother you with all of that and then that you would be unable to get a good overview in such a short time and make a decision.

Enough now, it is very late. Please don't be sad about this letter. I just had to explain everything to you. Your Lilongo

MOPE TO VERA

Moscow, 19 October 1937

At the moment, I am virtually unemployed. Other than the morning hours during which I often take Russian lessons from 8.30 to 10.15 and exercise my tongue that would look better on a snake than on me, I have nothing real to do at all. I am almost embarrassed to go to the Sojuspuschnina and report every day that I have no orders. The only other buyer who is still here besides me is at least purchasing some batch of merchandise or other almost every single day.

My life here is so uneventful that I keep reading thrillers and other novels, but to be perfectly honest, I do not find that activity particularly fulfilling or satisfying, even though I am quite curious to find out what will take place–according to the wish of the one who authored such thrillers. One pollutes one's imagination with such garbage, in which I have never had an interest.

VERA TO MOPE

London, 19 October 1937

Today, I was toying with the thought of calling you to find out if the merchandise in Antwerp was paid in full or not, because otherwise, I would almost like to suggest that the amount be paid from the account that seems to have been established with Fred, so that this terrible matter will finally be taken care of. It actually appears to me in my sleep, or at least, it is the first thing I think of in the morning when I open my eyes; and I am writing so many letters to all kinds of different people, and everything seems to be for nothing, the thing is stuck and will not move. I don't want to do anything more from here without at least talking to Fred one more time. I am sure that he is more than fed up with all of it, even if he is very pleasant whenever I talk to him.

VERA TO MOPE

London, 20 October 1937

I hope that my letter from yesterday did not depress you, maybe it would have been better not to write all of that to you, but there was no other way out and I had to say it. By the way, Fred told me this evening on the telephone that he talked to Antwerp, and I hope that everything will be shipped after the forty pieces have been taken out.

I talked to Hannalein around noon today on the telephone and she said that Ketty is supposed to arrive tomorrow; I am quite curious to meet her.[77]

How are things going with your passport extension? It will expire around the middle of January, as far as I know. As far as my residence and work permit and the extensions necessary are concerned, I would have to be present during the issuance of the recording in the alien book and in the passport, but maybe one of the senior managers can try to get it resolved around the end of December or the beginning of January, which I hope for with confidence.

You are right when you say that life is really too short to have the time to postpone being together and it already makes things difficult enough without artificially adding even more to it. Nevertheless, my beloved, I know that we have to be happy to have the opportunity to work, that we have each other, even when we are miles apart, but still in the exhilarating awareness of the other's sharing in life and emotions and thoughts.

MOPE TO VERA

Moscow, 23-24 October 1937

I have registered a telephone call to my most beloved for 3 a.m.; it should connect with you there around midnight. Since I wrote to you on various occasions that I would call you, I hope that you will be happy and not too surprised when the advance notice comes in. I did not send another telegram, because that would have caused an extra ten rubles in expenses. This time, we will be able to talk undisturbed and freely, so we

---

77 Mope and Hanna's oldest sister, Ketty Goldschmidt, still living in Hamburg, was due to make a visit to London to explore the prospect of moving her whole family to England.

should use the time to tell each other only sweet and beautiful things, since we find out about everything else in our letters soon enough.

* * *

The conversation with my sweet darling was simply wonderful. The communication was phenomenally good and we were able to really "smooch" without being disturbed, just as if we were in the same place. It was so nice to hear your beloved voice, and the feeling that you were very close and that I was completely with you and you with me gives me new strength and joy in life. To me, you really are the alpha and omega of my life.

Ever since then, I have been feeling great, and even the information you gave me concerning Herzberg and the transfer events did not upset me at all; however, the thought that this matter causes you to worry a lot gives me grief. I had no idea what new things this disgusting pig has come up with to keep burdening us. The foreign currency office has to realize once and for all, that there is good will on my side and that I am only kept from following their wishes through the intrigues of another.

Only one more remark on this: that it is irresponsible sloppiness on the part of the Antwerp shipping agent that he did not inform Fred about the delay until fourteen days after the merchandise was supposed to have been shipped. We should let him know that we plan on making him accountable for the resulting damage. Please update Fred, and even more importantly, please keep all thoughts concerning this matter from your mind. You have more than enough to deal with, so that this matter–that remained unresolved despite all your efforts–should no longer cause you any kind of depression. As you can see for yourself, the intellect of several people was not enough to break the meanness of one man.

I am enfolding you in my arms with passion and love and I return the kiss you gave me on the telephone a thousand times, covering you and enfolding you and protecting you from everything bad that you might encounter. Your Mope

VERA TO MOPE

London, 24 October 1937

My beloved, I am so happy that I was able to talk to you and hear your voice as if it were in the same room. I wonder if it was alright with you that I talked to you about so many business matters, but you told me that is what you wanted, and I can no longer carry the responsibility and burden all by myself. I was hoping, at the beginning, that I would be able to take care of everything for you without burdening you with any of it, but the matter keeps getting more complicated, and, as it seems to me now, almost more hopeless.

Hanna whom I talked to this morning on the telephone told me that Fred has not heard anything else from Antwerp since his call on Wednesday, but keeps getting the most horrible letters from the shipper. She also said that it was awful, because Fred needs to have his money back by the end of December.

I intend to be completely serious with Fred and get him to send the £ 30.–from the balance of your work account, if there is no other way to get the shipper to send the merchandise, because if the merchandise is not sent soon, the consequences, as far as I can see, will be much more far reaching. It is definitely better to pay this sum–without even considering that there will be no possibility for your dear mother to make this deal– and the fact that all of your things, books etc. will be confiscated from you, and that is the most deciding factor to me.

This letter is turning out quite different than I intended, but I think that I have just lost my courage at the moment. *I beg your pardon.* That is really very bad and I know only too well that it makes no sense to worry for months in advance and that you cannot make anything turn out better because of that worry. Don't you think that you have a really bad wife who burdens you with all kinds of things across all those miles? It's just that these things are so real to me and sometimes I just cannot get them out of my head, and then, such ugly letters are written. Add to that, of course, that I feel such awful longing for my beloved.

MOPE TO VERA

Moscow, 25 October 1937

It is really so unbelievably sweet of you that you take care of my matters with all your heart and I am ever so grateful to you for that, but you should not let it depress you like that. I have made myself as well as my beloved crazy with it for several months now, and I will not continue with it, because it eats up too many nerves. Your decision from Monday to not let those things upset you any longer was already forgotten by Tuesday.

Because I cannot have any money in a foreign country and also do not have any idea what I would use it for, it is out of the question that your credit balance with Fred is used for these matters. You should never throw good money after bad.

Most passionate, loving and totally sweet kisses, my golden one.

VERA TO MOPE

London, 25 October 1937

I am lying in bed today: I have a "silly" cold, which is really not all that bad and I don't feel quite like myself, which is completely natural; neither is it worth mentioning. It is pouring and storming outside, and I am lying here inside and really have some undisturbed time to follow my thoughts, and many of them are trying to put down on paper what has been bothering me for days now. I really do not know if I will actually mail the letter later, since I know that it will be extremely difficult and almost impossible to make someone understand something that is very difficult in itself across such a distance and in such a way that brings what is said as close to them that it really will be understood and cannot be misunderstood and also sees the reason why it was written and won't be swallowed up by it.

Mopelein, you know from all of my past letters that the Antwerp matter with everything that is connected to it really affects me a lot and constantly occupies my mind (with the exception of the time when I am involved with M&S). I have tried to understand why that is so and did not come to any kind of conclusion. It does not concern the possible financial loss. We are both young, willing to work and will hopefully get ahead without material possessions, of that I am sure; and as long as one has straight limbs and is healthy, a mere financial loss should not and cannot affect any human being, in my opinion.

What bothers me and burdens my inside is that it seems something was not planned or thought out completely to the end; or am I in error there? Mopelein, I have finally forced myself to talk about the existence of this painful unevenness on our way to overcome it, because I really do have the best will to do so, I just need my dear husband's guiding hand to accomplish it, so I can walk with him down our road together all the more sure and determined.

I wrote all of that down, although I know that it is a great risk, at such a distance, in time as well as spatially, and although I know that my beloved might not be in the best mood because of the momentary state of forced unemployment, because of our separation and the above-mentioned matter itself and the fact that I should make him feel better with my letters. But you, our friendship is too deep, isn't it, than that we should lie to each other or be able to, even if the insincerity was created with the best motives. I feel that it was right to write that down, because all of a sudden, I feel so completely relieved to have an opportunity to really put everything on paper that weighs on my soul, things that have been burdening it for days; and that was "worth much more" to me than a day at M&S!!!

I think I completely forget to tell you last night that I really liked Ketty. She is coming over for dinner on Monday and Hannalein might come as well if she does not have to accompany Fred to a lecture, and I am really looking forward to Muttilein and Ketty getting to know each other. I am sure that those two will like each other.

MOPE TO VERA

Moscow, 26 October 1937

Before you will receive this letter, I will have informed you by telegram that I will leave here in all probability on the 28th and Leningrad on the 29th to travel to London. Today, a huge telegram arrived from Schapiro, my boss in Paris, that, besides assignments, contains the following remarks: "Due to the catastrophic circumstances I think it would be better if you go back to London now. Please have a visa sent to London as quickly as possible so [giving you the] possibility to travel back to Russia."

If I were not worried that something might interfere, I would jump for joy. I am so indescribably happy to be able to take my darling into my arms again so unexpectedly soon. As you can see, I am jumping for joy in my happiness! I will leave here on the 28th and from Leningrad where I still have to inspect a few things on the 29th and travel directly to London by steamboat. I will most likely arrive there on November 3 so that we can enjoy your free Thursday afternoon together. So please do not make other arrangements for that day!!! I would like to take this opportunity to inquire if there is room for me in the Hirsch Hotel (preferably in your bed) where I can be accommodated.

Apart from the sadly awful economy, everything is working out exceptionally well, because tomorrow, I will receive the money that was transferred and the day after tomorrow my laundry is coming back from the cleaners, so that these technical questions won't pose any problems. I also hope to get my passport back tomorrow with the exit visa.

MOPE TO VERA

Moscow, 27 October 1937

It is self-evident, my girl, that you have to write to me about everything that occupies your mind and especially when it is such an ugly story as the Herzberg one, and I would probably find it more depressing if I knew that you do not tell me something–for whatever motives–even if they could be regarded as considerations towards me. I do not at all agree with the removal of the forty martens because the danger exists that they will be used for further mischief. For this reason, I sent a telegram stating "all the merchandise." Were it not for this apprehension, I would not care at all or feel even more comfortable with the idea that they stay in Antwerp.

Now quickly to bed–my last Russian lesson before I leave is scheduled for 8.15. I also have not packed yet and I am unshaven, as if my barber is a pig.

I am eternally grateful to you for the great love that rings from your dear letters, and soon, soon, I will take you in my arms and tell you everything without words, but with innumerable kisses and by caressing your ever so beautiful body, which I long for almost as much as your soul. I do have to say it that way; otherwise it will sound too sensual!! Your Mope

Twenty-six: "This Ever so Long Time of Insatiable Longing"

18 December 1937 through 27 March 1938

POLITICAL TIMELINE, DECEMBER 1937–MARCH 1938

- 21 January 1938: Romanian Jews stripped of their citizenship.
- 4 February 1938: Hitler names himself supreme commander of the Wehrmacht (German Army).
- 13 March 1938: The Anschluss (Annexation) of Austria by German troops.
- 28 March 1938: Jewish community organizations in Germany stripped of their official status.
- 31 March 1938: Polish Parliament revokes citizenship of Poles living abroad, many of them in Germany.
- March 1938: Show trial in Moscow (known as "The Trial of the Twenty-One) of so-called "Rightists and Trotskyites" with unanimous guilty verdicts.

Mope had to leave London for Russia avoiding Germany. He trod a circuitous route through France, Switzerland, Austria, and Poland. In England, Vera played host to two visitors from Leipzig. One was "Max" Goedicke, a trusted non-Jewish employee of the Gebrüder Felsenstein, whose travel was underwritten by Mope with instructions that he should bring over personal possessions that had been stored in the company warehouse. It was hoped that Max might be of help in trying to resolve the remaining PalTreu issues once he returned to Leipzig. The other visitor was Annelie Freimann, Vera's cousin. She had now qualified as a dentist and was doing everything in her power to emigrate from Germany.

For her, the visit was a brief respite from Nazi oppression, and an opportunity to explore possible openings abroad.

Both Max and Annelie were apprised of the continuing endeavors to resolve the impasse over the blocked furs under the PalTreu scheme. Shortly before they each returned to Germany, news came through to Vera in London that some of the goods would soon be released from locked storage in Antwerp. Those furs that were shipped back to Mope's denouncer, Karl Herzberg, in Leipzig were never recovered. A protracted court case to reclaim the insurance value of the lost furs was still to follow.

At Marks & Spencer, Vera (always known there as Miss Hirsch) sought promotion from the Kilburn store at which she was head of personnel. To her delight, she was offered a similar position with a raised salary at the company's larger Hammersmith store, far closer to home. Much more critical and a cause for jubilation was the decision by the Home Office that gave her permanent approval to remain in Britain almost five years after she had fled Germany. A similar request concerning Mope was denied.

During this time, Mope's mother returned from Palestine to Leipzig where she was visited by her British son-in-law, Fred Rau, though arrangements to bring her out of Germany on a permanent basis remained at a standstill. In London, Vera's parents, "Pepper" and "Muttilein" (Hermann and Alice Hirsch), each endeavored to supplement the family income, he by dabbling in the tobacco business, she by sub-letting rooms in their rented house to newly arrived Jewish refugees, giving German lessons, and offering her skills as a cook. These activities and the strains they had undergone had the effect of debilitating the usually energetic Alice Hirsch. To Vera's exasperation, when her friend, Hilde Lewy, invited her mother for a recuperative visit to Genoa, Pepper opposed, fearing to have to fend for himself during her absence.

The lull in fur trade activity that had affected Mope during his previous stay in the Soviet Union was no longer in evidence by the early months of 1938, and it was hard to persuade his clients that his need to return to his wife was his more pressing concern. He and Vera planned for themselves a "second honeymoon" in Paris with Mope traveling the route through Warsaw and Vienna that he had taken on the passage out. The Anschluss (the annexation of Austria by Germany) on 13 March thwarted those plans, while also totally panicking Vera. At the end of the month, Mope took a safer journey to England by sea via Helsinki and Stockholm. The final letter in this chapter, written from Helsinki, is his sigh of relief at being out of the Soviet Union.

MOPE TO VERA

Warsaw, 18 December 1937

Today is Sabbath and I am sitting here in Warsaw, against my plans, in the hotel and will not be able to continue my trip until tomorrow morning shortly before 9 o'clock. My train was delayed so that I was not able to make my connection. If I said that I am mad about it, I would not be lying.

Now, I will tell you about my trip from the beginning and how it went. At Paris, I was greeted in the most pleasing manner. I found out that everyone is pleased with my work so far. The merchandise I bought had sold quite well, despite the difficult business situation. If they had counted on me being able to buy so advantageously, they would have given me larger orders.

The trip through the Tyrol and Arlberg Alps would have been quite beautiful, had it not been for my inner depression. The snowy countryside and the happy faces of people who were traveling for winter sports stood in deep contrast to all of my emotions, so that I could only become sadder when I looked at the great white expanses.

Our local fur trade representative called and told me that he would come here and pick me up. We spent about six hours together. First in a cabaret with few exciting performances. However, my enjoyment might have been affected by my mood, so that I did not give enough attention to the acts. Mr. Blum–that is the name of the man–had also invited, aside from his girlfriend, her girl-friend to the cabaret as company for me, and I was quite surprised, since I had no idea of my good fortune beforehand. Unfortunately, she kept asking me if I was tired and things like that, because I did not seem to give her the necessary attention. Later, we went to a very pretty new restaurant for dinner. Mr. Blum ordered everything on the menu. He even went and picked out the hors d'oeuvres personally and found an appropriate excuse to leave the table for a while so that I was the lucky one who had to pick up the tab. Afterwards, I went to the hotel to continue writing to you, because that was more important to me than anything else.

You will have probably received the check from my commission in the sum of £87.10. Please do not forget to buy something pretty for yourself for about £20 that will give both of us joy. Please send the remaining amount to repay Fred Rau, so that it will be there before the year ends.

Now I am sitting in the hotel, waiting for a call to you.... It is 12.15 here already and the call still has not come through, so that I will go and get myself ready for bed, since I have to get up rather early. I embrace you and love you, Your Mope

VERA TO MOPE

London, 24 December 1937 [postcard]

All of a sudden Annelie is arriving here tomorrow evening. She sent a telegram yesterday. I am not free to pick her up and also not free to welcome Max, but Muttilein will take my place. Unfortunately, I still have no news from you. I hope that you are feeling very well. All my love, your L.

MOPE TO VERA

Moscow, 25 December 1937

So now you have two guests. I am surprised that Max has arrived already, since people were still working at Gebrüder Felsenstein until yesterday. I hope he uses the time in London to gain an impression that he can take home with him of the huge city. I wonder what he brought along. I hope everything has now been taken care of with that old crock Jacobson and the shack has been vacated.

I am interested in finding out what kind of impression Max made and if he is a pleasant guest–actually, I am convinced that he is. What reasons is Annelie giving for her exculpation? Is she behaving? How long is she staying? I hope that her cure is not lacking my hard and strict hand. Please don't forget to wash her head[78] and then put it back in the right place. And has she finally climbed over Fetz or is she still as depressed?

For New Year's Eve, there are a lot of things going on here. The entry ticket to the Metropole with dinner, performances, and, as I hear, ½ bottle of champagne costs 100 rubles. That is almost £4. In the Albert Hall in London, it costs £3 without dinner, so that is even more. Since I have to be without you, I am not looking forward to it at all and I would not go, if the other fur traders were not all going, so that I can hardly avoid it.

---

78   i.e., give her a piece of my mind.

The general mood in the trade is still very depressed, and in London and New York, more bankruptcies and even lower prices are expected. Here, my work program becomes more and more reduced. I am starting again with reading books. I really did not have to come here for that!

VERA TO MOPE

London, 25 December 1937 (with enclosures from Annelie Freimann and Max Gödicke)

I really survived all the Christmas bustle at M&S quite well. In the store, everything went off as planned, turkey dinner, Christmas pudding, etc., and the girls were in an excellent mood until the end. They presented two pairs of very beautiful, pure silk stockings (not M&S stockings) to my assistant and to me, which I thought was very charming. Around 10.30, we were done and at 11 p.m., I left the store; so that was not so terribly late. At home, I found Annelie and Max.

Annelie has not changed and is as charming and dear as ever. Since her passport expires on February 22, and an extension won't be approved unless she decides to leave permanently, she resolved on making the trip within a few hours. Incidentally, when should I apply for the further passport extension for you? Will you please give me the detailed information?

Max is really nice. He thinks everything here is just great; he brought along your typewriter, suits, underwear, and bathrobe and arrived here with everything without any kind of difficulty. He really is very reasonable and explained to us that he would have already taken care of matters had it not been for your attorney, but according to all appearances, everything will finally be arranged.

Unfortunately, I still have not received any letters from you, since you have been over there. Hopefully, it is not too cold and you take your medicine regularly. I think I mentioned to you that your payment check arrived. Papa cashed it for me and I will send a check in the amount of £50-0-0 to Fred; I gave Max £3-0-0, with which he was very happy. I will write to you in detail about what I buy for myself. After Christmas, everything is much more reasonably priced.

I wonder if you don't have to work either today. When is Wychodnoi? I am constantly and always with you in my thoughts! Please excuse this motley letter, but at the family table, it never works without interruptions, and Annelie is making rascally remarks in between. Totally, Your Lilongo.

ANNELIE FREIMANN TO MOPE

London, 25 December 1937

Dear Mope, I decided just a short while ago to travel to London, because it will be presumably the last opportunity for me, and I really wanted to take advantage of it. It feels to me like I have never been away from here, because I feel so at home. I am breathing much more freely, and slowly. One dares to talk again. The Hirsch couple, and not to forget Mrs. Felsenstein, are wonderful people. Yesterday evening, Veralein came home around midnight–she is such an industrious person. She looks marvelous–I am just a little in love with her, but as far as any competition is concerned, you have nothing to worry about!

I am feeling reasonably well, better than anyone should actually expect. My work in the clinic helps me get over many things, although it is still difficult at times. However, I just have to go on. Kisses, Your Annelie

ERICH GÖDICKE ("MAX") TO HERR FELSENSTEIN

London, 25 December 1937

Dear Mr. Felsenstein! After a very interesting trip, I was sorry that I was unable to meet with you. Your wife and your honored parents-in-law are very concerned about me. I brought along the items that you ordered, and I hope that you will be satisfied. I looked around in London for a little while today, but it was very foggy.

Before my departure, I talked to your attorney and found out that he still has not received the import certification from Palestine and that the foreign currency exchange does not want to continue negotiating. I will contact the attorney again immediately after my return. It is really a shame that you charged him with the matter, because the man is so anxious and awkward that he has made a mess of many things. However, there is no use to hire someone else, because that would complicate matters even further.

I also had a rather unfriendly altercation with Jacobson concerning the demand for payment, but he was unable to convince me, since I had already told him he should go ahead and rent your room together with the other as soon as he could. However, I told him not to deregister you with the police so that you won't have any difficulties. He answered that he could not wish for a better tenant who is hardly ever there and still pays his rent. After I did not relent, he told me that he would at least like to have the various expenses in the amount of 7 Reichmarks reimbursed. I consented to that and I hope that you agree. Jacobson accepted the amount as a loan, since he had been asked by the foreign currency exchange to file an application. We agreed on January 4 as the date for moving the furniture still in the room since neither one of us is able to take care of it sooner. Concerning Jacobson, I would like to let you know that we parted ways in a friendly manner. I hope that I will be able to tell you more after my return.

I bought a wardrobe trunk for you which is here in London now. Additionally, I brought along the following items: 3 suits, top hat, new hat, typewriter, warm underwear–I chose the 10 best pieces–2 sweaters, 2 scarves, bathrobe, various pajamas, dress shirts and collars; I only regret that you don't have all those things there with you.

Now I want to pass on the greetings people asked me to give to you, from Mr. Semy and from all the other employees. Gebrüder Felsenstein celebrated their one hundredth anniversary on Dec. 7, 1937. It was not announced but still, flowers and well-wishers appeared anyway in such a number that you can hardly imagine. As a jubilee present, the staff received between Reichmarks 50 and 200, depending on how many years they had been working here. I received RM 150.–and we also received a Christmas bonus this year. Business has been very quiet, after a very good start around the beginning of November. I hope that you can get a better picture of matters now. Sincerely Yours, Erich Gödicke

VERA TO MOPE

London, 26 December 1937

I would like to get back to Max's letter from yesterday one more time, after I talked to him about everything in detail. Since the price for martens has fallen by around 50% and the Haavara is now demanding a minimum of 50% in currency submission, it actually would not be worth it to make another offer to Herzberg, although I am sure he would like nothing better right now. I suggest to offer a compensation amount to Herzberg to rescind the purchase, and I am sure that he will make his own demands. With all of that, we can hope that the bank deposit will be freed up then so that the capital can be paid out, and then, you will at least have the money at your disposal so you can either give it to your dear mother or buy something for it. After the customs receipts arrive, they will hopefully remove the lock on the deposit that occurred through the PalTreu at the request of the Reichsbank since they were suspicious. Max also thinks that the locked account will be freed up as soon as the customs receipts are on hand.

Early today, we were very lazy (that is, Max went sightseeing with Pepper again, and around noon, Annelie, Mutti, and I went on an excursion to Whitechapel; unfortunately, the market was over already when we arrived, but we still did not regret our outing). Annelieschen is really a lovely person, and Max is more than nice and decent and completely enthusiastic about everything (this afternoon, he went to the movies).

I kiss you most passionately and wish you all the best and sweetest things–You, my beloved–totally your Lilongo

MOPE TO VERA

Moscow, 31 December 1937

Unfortunately, I got really upset over your letter of 26 December. All of your suppositions expressed in your letter are incorrect according to my feelings and my knowledge. I really did not ask Max to come to London to turn your heads, and I beg and beseech you to waste no more thought on this damn matter. I sent Herzberg a short-term request to send the merchandise again and directly to Palestine. He not only did not do so, but did not even answer. During a purchase, it is necessary that both buyer and seller agree to the conditions, because otherwise, the business deal cannot be made. Herzberg had the merchandise sent back without my consent. So the deal is annulled and he has no right to any kind of demand against me.

Your remark concerning the demand for the currency draft from the Haavara lacks any kind of basis, since there is neither a permit nor was one requested. So that is a supposition based on thin air. Additionally, in order to do anything further, the approval of the foreign currency department would be needed which does not exist any longer either. A pity that all of you spent so much time pondering over it! There are much more pleasant topics to warm your heads.

The amount owed to Herzberg for the forty martens is Reichmarks 180.63 exactly and I will not hesitate and pay it as soon as my money has been released. This part of my merchandise is the only one that did not get paid for in advance by Fred. You really cannot expect Max to have that much of a mind for business to have a good overview of the matter.

What comments on the last day of the 5th month of our marriage! This evening, my colleagues and I will be at the Metropole, but I really don't feel like celebrating, because I feel nothing but longing for my sweet, beloved, beautiful, golden madame. Your Mope

VERA TO MOPE

London, 1 January 1938

After another detailed conversation with Max today, I would like to write the following to you: When I made the suggestion to you to send the forty pieces back, I meant only in case that the simpler solution might be a compensation payment that Herzberg would demand, under certain conditions. However, if the customs receipts are on hand on Max's return to Leipzig, he will only need to take them to the departments concerned and show them, and then, the money will be available again. However, I really do not believe that the purchase can be so easily annulled, and I am certain that Herzberg will assert compensation claims for damages.

We sent Max to the cinema for the evening, at midday to watch ice hockey, yesterday evening to the ice ballet. So you see, he did not miss anything and is completely blissful.

My beloved, I love you and I am completely and totally convinced that we will get our way. You, I kiss you on your eyes and temples and caress you in my thoughts, Your Lilongo

MOPE TO VERA

Moscow, 1 January 1938

Was my letter from yesterday bad? I hope that you understood me and that, should I have written something wrong, my beloved will be understanding, because from so far away one's aim is never the best. The main thing is that I want to let Max know my point of view before he leaves and does not go home loaded down with inaccurate impressions.

Since your German passport is still valid, they will only keep it at the embassy for a day at most if you apply for a new one. That is why I would recommend to you to take care of that immediately, so that you won't have to wait for a long time later.

VERA TO MOPE

London, 2 January 1938

Max left early this morning, feeling quite blissful, and I am convinced that he will take the greatest pains to get everything done as well as it can be done.

Yesterday, a printed matter from Schwimmer arrived, an etching that was designed by him as a New Year's card (I will enclose it soon, because just now, I cannot put my hands on a large enough envelope). I am curious to hear if you like it. You, my beloved friend, Your Lilongo

MOPE TO VERA

Moscow, 2 January 1938

Today, the longingly awaited letter from the 25th finally arrived with its enclosures from Annelie and Max. Although I did not do anything all day long, it is almost 11 p.m. now that I am starting to write this letter.

In the afternoon, some of us were invited to a cocktail party given by Dr. Bunkley and wife. He is the doctor attached to the American Embassy and lives in a very nice apartment in the house.[79] The conversation was quite animated, since the people there had seen a lot of the world and told interesting stories. We stayed there for almost two hours. Afterwards, we had dinner in the room of a colleague who is here with his wife, and listened to the radio.

I am sure that, by the time you receive this letter, Max will have left. I am really grateful to him for all the effort he put into my affairs and I hope that the invitation to London gave him new energy to keep taking care of things for me. I really don't believe that Max would have been able to take care of everything, had he not consulted my Leipzig attorney, because, as clumsy as that man might be, I am sure that he

---

79 Lieutenant Commander William Bunkley was a Naval Surgeon assigned to the American Embassy in Moscow.

is much more experienced in those matters than Max. In any case, it cannot be changed now.

I was also very happy to receive Annelie's correspondence. It would be really horrible if Annelie did not get an extension for her German passport. That would be a bleak outlook for an unlimited number of people who would be affected as well. I would like to ask you to contact the consulate concerning my own passport extension around the middle of the month. If the extension has already been approved, please find out if it can be granted for a year–I have already given them the necessary documents. Your Mope

MOPE TO VERA

Moscow, 6 January 1938

The air here is so perfectly clear because of the cold that walking is a pleasure despite the heavy clothing. My ear warmers serve their purpose very well; I am rather pleased that I put so much effort into their purchase. Yesterday evening, I went for a little walk, because it was snowing so wonderfully. I have never seen such fine snow in my life. It looked like the finest powdered sugar, and today, everything has been swept away cleanly; they use snow shovel excavators for that, which transfer the snow to trucks with amazing speed. The heater in my room is working well–knock on wood!

It is terribly late again, but I do not want to go to bed before I send my darling at least an especially tender kiss. When I went to dinner at the Metropole a little while ago, I took stationery along, but I did not get around to writing, because all the colleagues were sitting there having dinner, and I could not have placed myself somewhere else.

Actually, it is a shame that I did not start to write to you earlier, since I did not do anything today besides write a report to Schapiro. Once you start to be lazy, you fail to do even the holiest of tasks! However, I do have to rehabilitate myself somewhat, because I had a 2 ½ hour Russian lesson, which really tires the brain quite a bit.

Yesterday evening, one of my colleagues reported that he had not smoked at all that day, whereupon I declared that, if he was able to stick to it for a second day, I would also not smoke for 24 hours. Because of that, neither of us smoked a cigarette until midnight tonight, and that first cigarette did not taste good to me at all. In the meantime, I have smoked two more anyway!

MOPE TO VERA

Moscow, 12 January 1938

Yesterday, although I really did not have anything to do, I still did not get around to writing. My colleagues and I worked in the office until 5 p.m. and then went to dinner, and since some of us, among them me, had tickets for the Jewish theater, we had to hurry so we would not arrive there late. The performance was excellent where the acting was concerned. Those people are great artists. The play did not finish until midnight and afterwards–since it was Pod-Wychodnoi–we went to the Metropole for some food and did not get home until very late. Because of that, I slept until noon today, which turned out to be really good for me, since I have a little bit of a cold. They got me some more tickets today without my knowledge, this time for the ballet "Swan Lake" that I have seen once before. They already want to pick me up for the theater and I will continue writing during the intermissions.

In the meantime, two acts have been danced. The ballet is extraordinarily good in every aspect. The orchestra, dancers, and scenery are exemplary, and every theater in the world could learn from them and use it as an example for the exactness, the feeling for the music, and the scenic composition. After the third act, which might be the most beautiful, at least the most colorful, I have remained seated so I can continue writing. My passport is serving as my writing table and naturally, my handwriting is suffering, but I hope that you will be able to read it nevertheless.

Now, I am sitting at the Metropole. We have ordered dinner, and since we will have to wait for a little while, I went to the foyer so I can continue my letter to you. You can see that every free minute is dedicated to you.

Of course, you are right that I should not have been upset over your letter in the transfer matter, but what can I do? Things just happened by themselves and I was a hapless victim, *nebbish*. As far as I can see the matter, I don't think it would make much sense to apply for further transfer permits, because, with the condition of the 50% foreign currency through the Haavara, nothing much can come from it.

The medicine for my cold is almost gone, and I will try to get more from here tomorrow. If that is not possible, I will mail you a telegram to send me three or four bottles again, because I am noticing that I feel better, and I would really hate to be without for too long especially now, while I have a cold.

I could also use some more cigarettes and I will ask Pepper to have 1.000 sent to me. Since the English customs fees are eliminated and the local fees have to be paid in London, they won't be much more expensive than the regular ones.

Now, I am sitting in my room again and the letter, interrupted so very often, is supposed to get finished. A new colleague who already has a little boy was complaining to me yesterday how bad it is for him to have been married for only four years and to be here for months on end. Such people have no idea how difficult other people have it. Today, it has been four weeks since I left and I still cannot say when I will come back.

I love you indescribably with the greatest of all loves, Your Mope

VERA TO MOPE

London, 16 January 1938

It rained without interruption today. I got a very good night's rest, which was really nice. Annelieschen has to leave on Thursday, and so, today was the last day that we could spend together–the last day of her stay here this time. After I wrote a long letter for her in English to a relative in America, who is supposed to give her an affidavit if needed, we decided to go for a little walk, despite the rainstorm.

Our walk ended in a cinema: the Broadway melody "of 1938," a very nicely arranged revue with good-looking people, some of whom had very beautiful voices and brilliantly accomplished dance techniques. Annelieschen is so sad that she has to leave again, and I would have been glad if something could have been worked out here for her. Herr Ehrmann[80] recommended America to her with urgency, and if an opportunity arises, I am sure that she will go there.

The things that Annelie discussed with me about marriages that she knows has me even more convinced–if that is even possible–that ours seems to be something completely different than those of other people,

---

80 Robert Ehrmann was a Leipzig fur trader who had relocated to London.

something much more deeply founded, all-fulfilling and delightful, independent of any outside forces.

In the matter of Herzberg, Annelie was so sweet and offered to tell Max and your Leipzig attorney in person everything you talked about in your last few letters concerning the annulment of the order from October. Of course, that is the best way.

Most passionately and close, Your Lilongo

MOPE TO VERA

Moscow, 17 January 1938

Since I cannot know when these lines will reach my darling, I will start them with my most loving and heartfelt wishes for a completely and utterly happy, healthy and successful year that will see its beginning on Sunday, fortunately a day away from work.[81] How can I put into words how happy I would be if I could spend that very important day together with my beloved, *sweet witch*? I hope that my beloved likes the new name I gave her just as well as I do, because what you did to me and what you let me become, is pure witchcraft. Until about two years ago, I was smitten at times, but never completely wrapped up in love, a man with a healthy dose of common sense and a calm demeanor, and now, although he wore out his children's shoes long ago and is approaching the years when others start the so-called contemplative way of life, he does not think about anything without considering his *little witch*. And I have to admit that I like the feeling of being bewitched *sooooo* much that I can no longer imagine any other condition or would want to.

Today, it is Pod-Wychodnoi once again, and a little while ago, I had my hair and fingernails worked on, something that should have been done ten days ago. In a little while, I will go on a pilgrimage to the Metropole in order to have dinner with my fur trade colleagues. One of my top clients will be here for the next Wychodnoi. I hope that he will be satisfied with my preparations for his visit (I am inspecting as much merchandise as possible so all he has to do is give it a quick look). There will be a lot of work, because he only wants to stay for five or six days, and I doubt that I will be able to write to you as regularly during those days.

---

81 Vera was born on January 23.

I have to keep repeating my affectionate words from darling to witch, because my vocabulary is so very inadequate compared to what I feel for you, and also my kisses which are becoming more burning because the longing for you is growing stronger, sound the same on paper and belong to that part of the letter that my girl might not read with all of her attention any longer, because she already knows it by heart. Your Mope

VERA TO MOPE

London, 20 January 1938

After work yesterday, I went directly to the German consulate. However, I forgot to take along three passport photos, but the decision was not unfavorable concerning the extension. They assured me that, as soon as I turn those in with my passport, I would receive an extension of the one that is valid until the end of April. However, they did not tell me how long that would take.

Earlier today, an invitation arrived for you and wife and grown children, if any, from K.J.V.[82] which is comprised of resettled members living here in London, and will be celebrating its first get-together on January 31 with a meeting afterwards which is supposed to be used for discussion purposes. The letter contained a list of all the local K.J.V. members here. I am sure that my beloved will be sorry to have to miss this first meeting. I will thank those people in your name and let them know that you are away on a business trip.

Nothing has shaken me in my at least somewhat developed knowledge of humanity as much as what happened in the store on Tuesday. We found out via another store and the head office that one of the most decent and most dependable girls, or so we all thought, who was already working there when I was relocated to the Kilburn store, is actually a criminal. She had worked out quite a complicated scheme to exchange club stamps that were completely worthless for merchandise. It would go too far to explain all the details here, but the most shocking thing that hit me like a sword stroke was that I should have believed that one of the girls whom I considered to be 100% beyond reproach turns

---

82 The *Kartell Jüdischer Verbindungen* (K.J.V.) was the Zionist Student Union within which Mope had been active in Germany. By 1938, a sufficient number of its members had escaped to England to form a local chapter. The London group remained active even many years after the war.

out to be a cold-blooded thief; and there is not even the excuse of no appropriate home surroundings or momentary temptation. I was deeply saddened and shaken by it and had to try to come back to myself. My beloved–how much I miss you in everything and how your intelligently thought-out judgment, your support, and your empathy and ability to analyze would have helped me to get over it much more quickly.

Completely *your* Lilongo

P.S. I wrote sideways on the paper because that was much more comfortable while lying in bed!

VERA TO MOPE

London, 23 January 1938

It was so indescribably beautiful to hear your beloved voice yesterday evening, and I have *never* before had the feeling during a telephone conversation that the conversation has to be taking place in the same room, as I did last night. It seemed unimaginable to me that so many miles are supposed to be between us, and I had to force myself to put the receiver down, driven by a guilty conscience (guilty because I allowed you to spend soooo much money on me), and afterwards, I could not believe or even fathom for quite a long time that my beloved is very far away and that he is not standing right next to me. What a pity that you seemed unable to hear or even understand me as clearly as I could hear you.

I do not think I have told you yet how beautiful the carnations are, but it is rather difficult to describe them. They are standing in a broad, high, wide vase and I haul them from one room to the other, depending on where I take up residence for the moment. Their glow is so incomparably beautiful that you just have to be happy and your heart laughs when you look at them, and every single one of them expresses so indescribably many dear things from my best loved friend, and the strength of their glow tells me of his love and their fathomless calyxes speak of the depth of his soul; their folded and frilled flower petals tell me of his quickness and flexibility and their fullness of his kindness, and the fine green of his gentleness and cautiousness. And together, they call to me: *He loves you!* And I respond very quietly: *And I love him!!!!!!!!!!!!!!!!* —

Today was a rather relaxed day, and we only went to Kensington Gardens for an hour before high tea to get some fresh air. Of course,

Muttilein spoilt me most lovingly, as always, she gave me an especially beautiful striped blouse, a very charming bed jacket, a home-baked birthday cake, and Pepper gave me Egyptian cigarettes.

Hildelein wrote me a very dear birthday letter. Here is part of it: "Since there is so little opportunity to show you my appreciation with a small token, I sent, with the same mail, the book "Reuben, Prince of the Jews," which, as far as I can remember, attracted Mope's special interest when you were with us in Genoa, and he recommended that you read it, something that did not happen due to lack of time back then.[83] I am really looking forward to reading it.

Then Hilde adds something that makes me especially happy: "What would you think if your mother decided all of a sudden to get on a train and came to visit us?" Muttilein has not had any opportunity to relax for such a long time. She looks really bad and often complains of painful joints (though she really does not complain). The Riviera sun would most likely blow all the pain away in short order, aside from the fact that Hilde would be terribly happy. *Her own* mother is not allowed to visit her and she really likes Muttilein, and her company would really be good for her.[84] What do you think of it?

Muttilein does not want any part of the idea as she says she could not leave Pepper alone. Here is just another point where I just fail to understand Pepper. Instead of helping me to convince Muttilein, he only moaned when I even mentioned the plan (not because of the possible costs as one might expect, since I will pay for all expenses, but) because he just whines like a child when he thinks that Muttilein might not be at his service just once. What can I do? Diplomacy from my side will be without success, and on top of that, it is even harder now to convince Muttilein how much she needs to relax and how good the trip would be for her and how all of us would profit from it when she comes back strong and recovered.

Hilde describes in such a dear manner what she is planning on doing to cheer Muttilein up. *One* reason I gave Muttilein seemed to change her mind just a little. I explained to her that, as soon as the matter with Cooper is taken care of, the two of us are planning on having a child and hopefully will have, and that she needed to be strong and healthy,

---

83   Max Brod's *Reubeni, Prince of the Jews* (1925; English translation 1928) was an historical novel centered on a sixteenth-century false messiah.

84   Hilde's mother was refused permission to leave Germany at this time.

because I would need her help more than ever then.[85] I did not even try to use such arguments on Pepper, because he acted like he was certifiably insane when I even tried to mention it. That surely sounds very hard, but that is exactly what happened.

In my thoughts, I nestle my body into your beloved arms, ever so close, my Mopelein, and wish that you were here with me—Your Lilongo

VERA TO MOPE

London, 26 January 1938

It was rather quiet in the store today. Since last week, I have started my staff training sessions again, and the girls are reacting quite positively after such a long break. As there is not much else to do, I held two sessions today. Outside, it is raining in sheets.

Mutti took the three photos to Carlton House[86] for me today and they told her that it would take about two months for me to get my passport renewed. That seems to be the usual thing. I also called Miss Stiebel today.[87] She said that I should let her know when you will arrive back, and then, Cooper will make contact with the people so that there will be no difficulties arising for you, even if–which I hope does *not* happen–April 15 is not too far from the date of your travel. As she told me, Otto Schiff will contact Cooper & Co. directly and she mentioned that there had been a similar case recently, and after it had been turned down repeatedly, it had finally been approved, so let us hope for the best!!!!!!! As soon as I hear anything definite and hopefully positive concerning the matter, I will let you know, of course. I just wish we were there already!

We heard from Annelie that she had a good trip and arrived hale and healthy, and that she longs to be back in London.

---

85 Vera and Mope recognized that it would be unwise to start a family before their application for permanent residence status in England was granted. Their case was being handled by Ernest Napier Cooper, a sympathetic principal in the Aliens Department of the British Home Office.

86 The German Embassy was at 8 and 9 Carlton House Terrace. Vera was seeking a renewal of her passport.

87 Joan Stiebel (1911-2007) was Otto Schiff's Private Secretary. She acted as an intermediary to Ernest Cooper in the Aliens Department at the Home Office, often (as here) funneling applications for residency status.

The book Hilde announced has also arrived in the meantime; I started reading it and I really like the way it is written (I am still at the very beginning).

So we will celebrate another honeymoon in March; that is still six weeks away! Today, it has been six weeks exactly since my beloved left and now, there is still the same amount of time left. Sleep well, my love–I kiss you and I love you *very* much, Your Lilongo

MOPE TO VERA

Moscow, 28 January 1938

Just as my sweetest beloved knows that I am always with her in my thoughts, I know that her thoughts are constantly occupied with me. That is the greatest and happiest part of our love, a love that regrettably cannot be experienced in its entirety because of the enormous distance from there to here, but despite the distance between us, it does not only not diminish in its intensity, but is cultivated and even beautified in some ways. We come to know a deep, unspeakable longing, a very, very strong feeling that people who are together constantly are unable to feel, and our being together will always be new and cannot be reduced by habit, because this longing lets us grow inwardly and teaches us how infinitely much we mean to each other. Nevertheless, *how* completely happy I would be without this ever so long time of insatiable longing, but we must and want to make the best of it, the very best, then everything will seem much easier to bear. *Your* Mope

MOPE TO VERA

Moscow, 30 January 1938

After I took my previous scribbling to the post office without reading it again, I went for a little walk with several acquaintances and then, we had coffee together. Now, I will come back to my beloved and continue the conversation we had started.

I already sent a telegram to your dear mother with my thoughts concerning her Genoa trip. It seems urgently necessary to me that she should have a change of surroundings. Such a change in atmosphere of every form will certainly be of significant benefit to her general condition, which can regrettably be read in her face, even if she does not say anything about it. Such times of relaxation contribute to extending the life expectancy of everyone, especially that of older people, and how could anyone who loves your mother as dearly as Pepper does be against it if there is a pleasant opportunity to make such a relaxing holiday possible for her. I am almost convinced that everything will be taken care of in such a way that Pepper won't lack for anything (other than his beloved wife, of course), while she is absent, and the joy of welcoming her back will more than make up for the time he was a straw widower. We men react sourly when someone tries to force something, but if my beloved–and I am sure you have never done that before–sits down on his lap and is nice to her Pepper, even he might declare himself ready to commit a burglary for you, and if you don't lose your patience, he might do even more, that is, agree to the trip.

The reason you gave your mother to talk her into making the trip makes me *unspeakably happy*. I was even happier with your news concerning Cooper & Co. It is such a pleasure to know about it, although I hope not to arrive at the last minute. For that and your ever so great effort my most heartfelt gratitude! It not only sounds unrealistic to my beloved, but to me as well, even though the facts confirm it that we have only known each other for a little over two years. I almost feel like diving into the first, still so very reserved letters and let the development of our love pass before me like a *good* film–although I do have all of it in front of my eyes.

I was told today that cigarettes sent here absolutely have to be declared there, because they cannot do it here. One of my acquaintances just paid £2-0-0 including customs fees (very cheap, as a matter of fact) for 1,000 Camel cigarettes. Unfortunately, my cigarettes are all gone and the Russian ones are not so good for my throat, because I am not used to the tobacco, which is why I have to ask the others for cigarettes, something I loathe doing.

I kiss you most passionately, my beloved, and embrace you most lovingly in my thoughts, so lovingly that I want you to dream about it, as I do, and all of my caresses and tenderness are meant to be brought to you with my words. Your Mope

VERA TO MOPE

London, 1 February 1938

Today, we have been a *married couple* for six months and unfortunately, we also cannot celebrate this half year anniversary together, and we have to console each other with the thought of "Later" when the two of us no longer have to live separated all the time! I believe that we can look back on these first six months with the knowledge that every single day brought us a little closer to each other–even if it was not in proximity– and that those days were filled with inner happiness, with harmony and the joy in the awareness of the other, and the understanding and the love the one feels for the other in such a special measure!

My dearest one, today I can finally say: next month, my beloved is coming home! Just the simple thought of that lets a hot wave wash over my body and I try to forget that, in all reality, the moment when my beloved comes home is still weeks away.

I have been able to get ahead just a little concerning the trip to Hilde since your telegram arrived on Saturday, and after I negotiated with Pepper again on Sunday; however, no final decision has been made yet and Muttilein also will not hear of it at all, but I think it is the best thing for her and really, really hope that it will happen.

At lunch today, I once again had three future staff managers with us at the store who, among other things, listened in on one of my "talks" and gave me their heartfelt approval. That is quite pleasing to me, especially since they will give a report on everything at the head-office tomorrow, since they routinely have to file a report concerning their lunchtime *store excursions*.

Joan Stiebel whom I called again assures me anew that I do not have to worry at all about your landing possibilities, and just as soon as I know the date I will let her know immediately. I just wish I already knew!!!!!! Your Lilongo

MOPE TO VERA

Moscow, 3 February 1938

Unfortunately, I did not get any news from my beloved today and I hope that I will receive mail again tomorrow. Today was a very long and exhausting day. At 9 a.m., I had a lesson with a new teacher and after that, I worked without a break until 5.30 p.m., from the office to the warehouse and rushing back, and in the end, I did not accomplish what I wished. Then, in the evening, I wrote business letters for 4 ½ hours and took care of similar matters so that I feel very tired as I begin this letter, with very good reason. While I am writing, I am sitting in the restaurant and just ordered my dinner. After that, I will go to the horizontal with the speed of an express train, because there is much work to be done tomorrow.

My colleague Mr. Aisenstadt left here yesterday for London and promised that he would give you my love over the telephone on Friday or Saturday. He also told me he would let you know that I should not write to you so often. Whenever he saw me writing a letter, his conscience started bothering him concerning his own lady. He just cannot fathom what kind of need and pleasure it can be to chat with one's darling, even though it is such a poor replacement for a face-to-face conversation, when one has to rely on letters. I wish it were that time already that we could live together and would no longer have to think of saying goodbye when we see each other again. I hope that Otto Schiff will help us achieve that. I would be so unspeakably happy about that.

In the next few days, I might have to travel to Leningrad for a day. I will not give up my room while I am gone, because I won't get one in Leningrad, since I will travel overnight on the way there and back. The matter is by no means sure yet though. Contrary to that, it is just about certain that I will travel to the auction in Leningrad around the 26th of the month and I ask you to begin sending your mail to Leningrad, Hotel Astoria, around the 21st. I am afraid that the mail sent there will take longer.

I am counting on leaving here around the 20th, March 25th at the latest. That is still a frightfully long time, but time does have to go by eventually, and then, we will begin our second honeymoon in Paris, and we will continue it with a Muttilein who will come back relaxed and well from Genoa. *Entendue, madame?* Your Mope

VERA TO MOPE

London, 4 February 1938

Just a little while ago, I received your lovely, loving, loveable words from Sunday, and I cannot describe to you *how* happy I was with them.

They tell me so many loving and tender things and they pour out such a depth of gentleness, sensitivity, and warmth that they make me feel completely and utterly happy on the inside, or to be more precise, the awareness of the writer who stands behind those words. This evening, I am very tired once again and that is why I will only send you a short greeting.

Today, after repeated negotiations, etc., I finally succeeded to order 1.000 Du Maurier for you through Pepper (yellow packaging cork-tipped), since the other ones cannot be exported, and they will be declared here. I do hope that they will arrive there towards the end of next week, and besides the fact that I am glad that you will have them for your own use, you will like being able to invite your colleagues for a smoke, especially after they seem to have supplied you with tobacco in such a kind manner.

Mr. Aisenstedt called just a short while ago, which I thought was very nice, because he did not arrive before noon today, and he gave me your greetings and told me that my beloved was extremely busy for days, and most of all, he assured me that you are in good health and doing well. I want to close and get some sleep, my love, and I long for you———Your Lilongo

VERA TO MOPE

London, 16 February 1938

This morning, when I arrived at the store, my assistant welcomed me with the question whether it was true or not that I would be relocated to Hammersmith. Around noon, head office called and disclosed the *"great news"* to me with much ado such as *"that I had done so very well at Kilburn,"* etc., and that they wanted to move me to Hammersmith, since I had recently asked for a promotion. They told me I would receive a raise in the amount of 5/–a week. Since I will also save about 4/–in traveling expenses, it will be almost 10/–a week. There has been a new manager in Hammersmith since January who is said to be very friendly, competent, and likable. I have never met him.

I have not told the girls at Kilburn anything about it yet, but things like that have a way of spreading like wildfire, and the office personnel came to me and told me how sorry they were, etc., and all of them were rather charming. I know that taking over the Hammersmith store means there is a lot of work ahead for me, and many difficulties and obstacles will have to be overcome before I get it the way the Kilburn store is now—I mean as far as the standard of the personnel–but Kilburn was not like that right from the beginning either. Hammersmith is the second largest London store, and I am curious to find out what working with the new manager will be like. The short distance from home and the raise make the farewell from Kilburn much easier, of course, although I have to admit that I feel attached to the staff after a year and a half.

At head office, I also mentioned the vacation days still owed to me, and they assured me that I could still take them in March. Tomorrow I will make some enquiries concerning train connections and weekend tickets to Paris and I will let you know what I find out. Completely and entirely, Your Lilongo

MOPE TO VERA

Moscow, 18 February 1938

Finally, I get around to writing a few lines to my beloved girl again. I hope that you will have received my telegram from yesterday in which I expressed my pleasure over the advancement that you cabled to me. I think it is great that you will be moved so close to Blythe Road, and with the fares saved, the raise will mean not a 5/-, but an 8/–raise per week. I hope that you will be able to keep your long weekend reserved for the days in Paris, because I am looking forward to that so immensely that I do not want to do without.

My Leningrad trip was pleasant. On the way there as well as on the way back, I had a sleeper compartment all to myself, which I welcomed not only for the work, but also because of sleeping alone. It was cold in Leningrad, but the sky was the most beautiful blue you can imagine, cloudless and full of sun. Contrary to that, it is snowing here constantly and the sky is covered with clouds. I have been working until now in order to calculate everything I have inspected in the last few days. Today is Wychodnoi, which I will use to catch up on everything else, because tomorrow, there is a lot of work to do again. However, I did sleep in this morning, and that was really necessary.

I had a long telephone conversation with Schapiro concerning a number of orders, among them one I just took care of, to buy merchandise for a little over £5,000, merchandise that I inspected in Leningrad and which he sold on after my telegraphed description.

Here, I had to interrupt the letter again. In the meantime, I was able to close another deal worth about £3,200. You can see that I am not sitting around doing nothing. Admittedly, it does not happen every day that you have such sales or even near that. Additionally, I had dinner, got reports on the deals others have made, and it is time to post this letter so that it will be transported today.

I love you most passionately, my sweet little girl, and in my thoughts, I am kissing you everywhere, where it gives you pleasure and joy, long and with such great passion and intensity that your beloved beautiful body arches with the sweetest excitement. Your Mope

P.S.I think the ban of the Rundschau in Germany is terrible. It was the only means through which the people there could find out the truth, even if they had to read between the lines. I hope that the ban will be lifted.[88]

VERA TO MOPE

London, 18 February 1938

It is 11.30 once again and I know that I should actually turn off the light, but since I am already lying down and therefore resting, you are not allowed to be mad at me when I write you a quick little greeting and thank you for your dear lines from last Sunday. Tomorrow is my last day in Kilburn and my successor is coming in so that I can give her some tips. All of my girls in Kilburn told me that they are very sad about me leaving.

I do not think I told you yet that I bought a very pretty dress, at least I think it is, very simple and navy blue, its decoration is white pearl embroidery and it has a very nice cut. I am very curious to find out if my beloved will like me in it, and I wish that we were in Paris already; I will

---

[88] The twice-weekly *Judische Rundschau*, published by the Zionist Organization in Germany, had remained the main conduit by which Jews living under Nazism were still able to receive more or less independent news. Because the paper strongly advocated the exit of German Jews to Palestine, its publication was initially tolerated by the Nazi authorities. However, it was temporarily banned in the early part of 1938, and finally closed down later that year, its last issue appearing on 8 November.

bring the new dress along, of course. M&S provided us with fabric for a store frock again; this time, the quality is good, it is soft, but for my taste, the color is too light, although it is supposed to be navy blue as well.

For the time being, Muttilein's trip to Genoa will not take place. I regard the trip as postponed only and I do hope that it will happen later. Muttilein has some paying guests arriving next week and several orders for baked goods, so she is to all intents and purposes very busy.

My love, today was Wychodnoi and I hope that you took the time to rest and recuperate and maybe even write a detailed letter to me. Oddly enough, I have not heard anything else from Julius Rosenfeld although I sent him the necessary forms weeks ago.

My beloved, in my thoughts I am nestling my body into your beloved embrace and dream that you are with me, and I kiss you with all my love and tenderness. *Your* Lilongo

P.S. Just now, I found out that Annelieschen was involved in a car accident and suffered a concussion. Her sister Trude is writing at her request, because she is supposed to keep absolutely still. I feel very distraught over that news.

VERA TO MOPE

London, 21 February 1938

The first day in Hammersmith is over and I am very tired today, and I just want to write a few quick lines so you can *see* that I am thinking of my beloved. I think that the work there will be very interesting. Instead of forty-nine sales assistants, there are sixty here, instead of four office girls, there are eight, etc., all in all, there are over one hundred employees there. The manager here is very young, has only been here for the last four weeks, is very interested in his work, and seems to be quite a gentleman. I hope that I will get along well with him.

I moved into a new office right away and he ordered that they install a house as well as a general telephone for me, etc. The store earns much more than Kilburn; it is significantly larger. The counter displays are much behind those at Kilburn and if I could manage that the girls do it the same way as they do in Kilburn, then the Hammersmith earnings could be improved significantly as well. It is a great pleasure to work so close to home, I was at home shortly before 7.30 already.

I received a letter from Julius Rosenfeld this evening, with a copy of a letter he wrote to Fred. In it, he writes that the matter of the customs fees refund is still not resolved, unfortunately. He had visited the department three days ago and had received notice that we can count on the final decision very shortly. Then, he will send his accounting to Fred and will also mail his check for the balance. I have not heard anything else about the furs.

MOPE TO VERA

Moscow, 23 February 1938

Usually, the mail arrives here in the course of the morning, but there was none for me. When I looked again in the afternoon to see if an expected telegram had arrived, I found the parcel with the cigarettes. They taste absolutely wonderful and seduce me to smoking, after I have spent the last fourteen days smoking Russian cigarettes exclusively, and they dry out my throat. The enjoyment I get from it is *even* greater, because my beloved went to such lengths to procure the cigarettes, and that really does mean something.

Yesterday evening, I had a lesson, and then, an acquaintance of my teacher came by, so that it was really late, before I was able to write my business report for Paris. As I was informed today, I will probably receive my exit visa around March 20. I hope that I will be able to take care of all business matters by then, so I can depart with a clear conscience.

I am very, very sorry to hear that Annelie had a car accident. That poor girl has had a lot of bad luck lately, and I hope with all my heart that she will enter a streak of good luck soon for a change. With all the bad luck, she seems to have been lucky, because a concussion–as far as I know–only needs time to get better, but usually does not leave any disadvantageous aftereffects. Maybe she will meet a nice, good Uncle Doctor who falls for her, then one would at least know why everything happened the way it did!

I am kissing you most passionately in my thoughts and enfold you in my embrace, Your Mope

VERA TO MOPE

London, 24 February 1938

Since I am extremely occupied during the day just now–I still take great pleasure in it–because the staff is *completely* untrained, at least compared to my former staff. The counters are not taken care of, and hardly anything has been organized or arranged. I was just not able to write to you when I came home last night, but simply fell into bed because I was so very tired.

The manager is very receptive to all the suggestions and improvements I have made so far–of course, I try very hard not to give him the impression Americans who come to Europe inevitably do when they say, *"Oh, we in America do this and that this way, and everything is much better, etc."* However, he is intelligent enough to see it is not meant that way and I try to be receptive to his ideas as much as I can. During our conversation, I had told him emphatically that I would be very grateful to him to tell me if he did not agree with something I do or if he wanted things done a certain way, he would please talk to me under any circumstances and not just try to ignore it, because that would make working together difficult, if not impossible; and then, after we had discussed all the pertinent points and our discussion was over, he asked me to do the same for him. Actually, that would be the polite thing to do, but for the M&S manager type I have come to know until now, that is a rather *better than average* attitude!

Hannalein who is a straw widow again, too, will have high tea with us on Sunday. Fred is on the continent and, among other things, will also go to Leipzig and see your dear mother there. Do you know that my residence permit expires on February 28? I called the head office secretary today. She told me that she had submitted all the documents weeks ago, or better, sent them to Otto Schiff, just as I had requested, and that I should not worry, because lately, it usually took as long or longer, and that it did not mean anything.

I have to close so that this letter will fly away from here with the night mail. I think it is so unbelievably beautiful to be married, although we have so very little time together to show for it, which is almost unbearable, but the awareness of your love and our harmony and our mutual consent echoes through my days like a beautiful melody. *Your* Lilongo

MOPE TO VERA

Moscow, 26 February 1938

I just got done packing my things. It is 11 o'clock and the train leaves at midnight. I was unable to get a 2nd class sleeper for the earlier train and so I preferred the later one. I am having to consider what to take to Leningrad and how to arrange the suitcases in the dumbest way possible so that the things I need cannot be added, and so on. Now, I am sitting in the restaurant and just want to send my most loving greetings to my little witch before I leave.

Today, I was without mail, but if I understood you correctly, you started sending your letters to Leningrad beginning last Sunday, and I am already looking forward tremendously to finding them there.

I did not do anything at all involving business matters today. As I was putting on some fresh socks this morning I was much enthused to find that not even a single pair was without toe air vents. So I had to sit down and darn 9 pairs. Do you admire that feat as much as I do? However, I did not cut the old darning patches out, as I have often watched my dear mother do, but let my own work use the old frame. I hope they won't pinch!

I am so very happy that the month of February is almost over now, and then, we only have March, and we two happy lovers will celebrate our second honeymoon. Your Mope

VERA TO MOPE

London, 28 February 1938

Today, I have *very good news*! Mrs. Stiebel called today to let me know that I now have a *permanent permit to stay in England* and that I should please send my passport to her so that it could be entered in it. I called her today during lunch and she assured me that *all conditions are cancelled*, and that means that I am not only allowed to stay here but also take any kind of work. Added to that, she told me that Otto Schiff would go there again this week and try to do what he can concerning your application to reside here. I just wrote to him and put the matter close to his heart once again. I did not expect this result and I am afraid that our two applications might collide at some point in the end. My beloved, if we get lucky with Cooper and Co. now, I would be *completely* happy!

I arrived home at 7.15 this evening, although I had lunch there because I want to try the store cooking first. It seems to me that it is not too bad. However, my assistant's management abilities–my predecessor seems to have given her free hand–are questionable. The cafeteria shows a loss, although double the number of personnel stays here for lunch than did in Kilburn and so should definitely be profitable, and that even though the portions are smaller than in Kilburn and the quality most certainly not better. I have already found different things she does unnecessarily, and I told her how they can be done differently, and she was very responsive, at least up to now. I now know every staff member by name and I know in which department they work, and of course, that makes things much easier.

Unfortunately, I have not heard anything from Annelieschen, although I sent her a bouquet of spring flowers last week. I do hope that she is feeling better and that your loving wishes for her will come true; she really deserves to have a little bit of good luck for a change.

My Mopelein. I am counting the days with the greatest impatience, and despite my work and the new sphere, I am constantly with you in my thoughts, ever so close and so filled with passion. Your Lilongo

MOPE TO VERA

Leningrad, 1 March 1938

So today really is the first of March! And it brought me *such* a dear letter from my sweet little witch that I feel completely happy with everything. But, I find it less satisfying than you that you have to do such exceptionally exhausting work in Hammersmith, and hope that it will only be a temporary matter and that the girls will soon be trained well enough to relieve the burden on you. There is one thing I want to suggest to you in connection with the new work. They will not estimate your work all that highly if you introduce all of your improvements at once than if you keep introducing one thing after another and reorganize things over a period of time. Then, your success will be all the more obvious to them, because the brats will be able to understand things so much better if you advance one step at a time, than if the "new broom" (how awful to call my beloved something like that) starts sweeping away everything dirty right from the beginning and wears out its brush right away so that it can no longer reach into all the corners. And it is really the higher art to rebuild slowly–with everyone's comprehension —because that takes the talent of finding just the right sequence.

It is like being married–you should never go for broke and always keep something in reserve to keep the partner's interest, and so it is while working if the work is meant to be creative. If you follow the work method suggested, your new manager will never have the feeling that you think everything is bad and only see that things could be done better, and psychologically speaking, that is most definitely the best way where he is concerned–to show him that you are especially able, since he seems to be open-minded and intelligent.

My stay here was extended to the 20th and as soon as I return to Moscow, I will apply for my exit visa, so I believe that I will be leave Russia right on time, and I should be able to leave here around the 20th.

I am really happy that Fred went to visit my dear mother. She has to feel horribly lonely over there. I wonder what will happen to her in the future. I keep thinking about it all the time but I can see that the longer she waits the worse the prospect becomes to get her out of that damnable country in reasonable shape. Unfortunately, all of my suggestions have been ignored and it has been proven that the path I originally chose for myself was not the most fortunate one either.

VERA TO MOPE

London, 3 March 1938

Just now, I received your dear lines from Sunday, the ones from before your departure. Monsieur, I am impressed, nine pairs of socks–that is really quite an achievement, and if you can actually walk in them, then that is all the more wonderful!

I just heard from Hannalein and Fred that your dear mother looks very well, was feeling well, and has a pretty room, something that made me feel very happy. Fred visited her last Wednesday. He really congratulated me for the permit and said that that would also make things easier concerning your matter in this area. I hope he is right!!!! I just wish that the furs would finally be sold and the debt to Fred paid back. I find this debt so unpleasant and I hope that we will be able to settle it soon. Yesterday, I received the Jewish Rundschau once again.

So my beloved will have started his main work from today. I hope that it is not too strenuous for you. The difference for my beloved between the auction last August and this one is the fact that, back then, aside from the exhausting work, you had so many stressing worries resting on your shoulders, while these kinds of worries have almost completely dropped away this time. And so I hope that my love is feeling less drawn before, during, and after the auction than in the summer. I can hardly believe it: today in a fortnight, my beloved will hopefully begin his trip back!!!!

You hit the nail square on the head in what you write concerning my work, my beloved: it will definitely prove to be much more successful and effective to proceed gradually and with a plan in reorganization and improvement; in the meantime, I have come to that realization myself–it happened when I bumped my nose–admittedly, just a tiny bit–your prediction came true. There was *one* moment at the end of the first week during which it seemed to me that the manager felt rather uncomfortably touched–to have to see so much all at once as needing to be changed, when he had not noticed those things at all before. It was–as I said–just for a moment, and he immediately gave in and changed his mind; and *so did I*!! And I mean drastically, and I came to the conclusion that my beloved, even from afar and without practical groundwork, formulates things so clearly and intelligently.

Thank you, my Mopelein, for your interest, your overview, your ability to place yourself in situations, and your intelligent advice that I will take to heart completely and entirely with a renewed appreciation for its accuracy. It is something immensely necessary in my field of work, but also something that is very difficult for me and goes against my nature–it wants to act quickly and precipitously–and that is only possible for me if I engage all of the brain cells available to me or better, the activation of their functioning.

I want to close, because I would still like to go to the post office and take care of a few errands. *Your* Lilongo

MOPE TO VERA

Leningrad, 5 March 1938

After working for thirteen hours today without a break and dinner with customers following immediately after work and then more work after that, I am dead tired, but I just cannot go to bed, before I write a few lines to you. Tomorrow afternoon, the auction will start, after a banquet during which there will probably be a lot of drinking once again in order to put the customers in the mood.

I already sent a telegram yesterday congratulating you on your permanent permit, and I would like to repeat that here with all my love. I am so tremendously happy about it, and your independence, as far as work is concerned, as Miss Stiebel told you, has been achieved.

In a bit, it will be 2 a.m. again, and tomorrow will start at eight in the morning. So, off to bed, after I have given my beloved my kisses and all my tenderness through this paper. I am expecting you in my dreams, full of longing and love and my entire being, so I can embrace you and pull you close to me, and you know about everything else, and I am sure that you are waiting with the same feelings as your Mope who loves you with all his strength and his soul.

VERA TO MOPE

8 March 1938

I talked to Mrs. Stiebel on the telephone. Otto was there on Friday, and for the time being, they did not give their permission for you. They would *not* object to a visit every six months or so, but they would not permit a permanent *stay*. It is supposed to be a *matter of principle* and *not* to be taken personally, on the contrary, Mr. Cooper was looking at our matter with all possible goodwill. Otto wrote me a letter today that I will bring to Paris for you, in which something is mentioned about that month long stay. He said, when you are here, both of us should see him; then, he will try again; despite everything, he thinks that it is just a matter of time. I think it best that you do *not* mention this matter to your colleagues. For all they know, the case is still with Mr. Cooper and still moving forward, and no decision has been made yet. I will not let that ruin my good mood–and not for you either, my love, I hope and beg. We are strong and young and one day, with perseverance, patience, and a good disposition, things will hopefully come to pass. *Completely* and *Entirely* Your Lilongo

MOPE TO VERA

Leningrad, 10 March 1938

Now, all that auction work is finished, and I am really glad and relieved to have that behind me. As I let my darling know yesterday in the telegram, it was completely impossible for me to write to you during the last six days. At night, once I was finished with making calculations, writing catalogues, composing telegrams, etc., I just keeled over totally exhausted. Actually, the exchange of letters with you is supposed to be relaxing and joyous and a much-needed change and diversion from the daily vulgarities, but a condition for that is that I have a clear mind and do not see everything doubled because I am so tired, as has been the case in the last few days.

I am exceedingly happy that my sweetheart now has a permanent residence and knows where her home is. Hopefully, I will get there as well in the near future.

I can walk very well in those stockings I darned myself, but unfortunately, to the side of the darning, new holes are forming. I wonder if that is always the case or if it lies in a mistake made by the darner, but that escapes my judgment, since I have never before paid much attention to such things. In the greatest love, Your Mope

VERA TO MOPE

London, 10 March 1938

I wrote a detailed letter to your dear mother, and I assume that she was especially happy with the letter this time, because it was filled with good news. I told her about the permit, the new store, that my beloved is doing well, and that he is working successfully.

I sent £50-0-0 to Fred, and I feel glad and relieved this debt is shrinking so visibly. By return, I received the receipt from Fred, and I have the feeling that he was very pleased. I think I already told you I am glad that another piece has been paid back, and I am sure that my beloved feels the same as I do.

I wonder when you will know for certain on what day you will be able to leave. I hope that your boss will not try to keep you there. It almost seemed to me as if he intended to do so, when he announced that there would be much more work after the auction than *during and before it*. Is that true?

By the way–I think I did not tell you Wednesday night–I received another copy of Cooper's letter to Otto Schiff–a letter that really does not sound all that unfavorable and says that it is going to be that way *for the time being*. I hope that, once we have talked to Otto together, the matter will be resolved somehow. He seems to be rather optimistic himself. *Your* Lilongo

MOPE TO VERA

Moscow, 12 March 1938

The decision Otto Schiff let you know about is a little progress, at least when compared with the last time, and I am really very satisfied with it. Please give Otto and Mrs. Stiebel my most heartfelt thanks. Somehow, the matter will and has to be cleared; we just need a lot of patience. At the moment, all the signs make me believe that my path so far has been the correct one, and we cannot know the future in advance. Anyway, I am happy to have turned my back on that deadly land of my birth.

It is really very sweet of you that you wrote to my dear mother again, and I am very happy that Fred found her well and apparently quite content. I hope that she did not pretend to be in good spirits just for him, because she is too proud to complain.

VERA TO MOPE

London, 14 March 1938 [written immediately after news of the Anschluss]

Mopeleinchen, I just called Fred to ask for his advice, because I am really worried! I would like you to alter your traveling plans, by all means necessary, that is, that you take a different route back, either Warsaw, Yugoslavia, Trieste, Paris, or through Sweden and Denmark, like you did when you traveled there. Mopeleinchen, please let me know immediately! *I am worried*, my love. If only you were with me already. This last week of our current separation, I hope it is the last one anyway, is virtually unbearable to me. I do not know *how* I could bear it if I was not so occupied at work.

My beloved, hopefully, Schapiro does not put obstacles in your way and postpones your departure, that would really be horrible. It really has been long enough now——that is, if you think that you have to stay longer, then please do so, but I do hope very much that that will not be necessary. *I am worried to-night and cannot think about anything except that I want my beloved husband back !!!*

Mopeleinchen, I just cannot write a letter this evening–please send me a telegram immediately! So I can meet you at the right time, that is, should you come directly to London, so I can pick you up. *I think life is sometimes very, very difficult!!!!* If it is not absolutely necessary, please do not stay there past the 20th.

My love, what a horrible letter! But I am sure that my beloved will understand me. Maybe, by this time next week, you will already be on the way to Paris, over Warsaw and Trieste!!! I kiss you, my beloved, and I love you indescribably, *Your* Lilongo

MOPE TO VERA

Moscow, 14 March 1938

Just now, I talked to the most wonderful of all bosses. He gave me quite a few orders and supposed that I would have to extend my visa. But if I do not want to, it will not happen, and I do not want to! I will try to get everything done by the 20th, if possible, and I hope that things will work out. It is still a puzzle to me as to how I will travel back, because, if I travel by boat via Stockholm, I have to go to London first and then to Paris, because–so I hear–none of the boats make a stop in Amsterdam or some other harbor. Another possibility would be to travel to Prague and fly from there via Amsterdam or Rotterdam to Paris, but my beloved writes much to my surprise that I should not fly under any circumstances! Although I do not understand the reason, I will try to act in accordance with your wishes. Now I will try to get information concerning the possibility to get to Amsterdam via Riga, without setting foot on accursed territory.

I kiss you, you beloved, and embrace you full of the most heartfelt tenderness and love, and I am so happy that the 15th has started now. It will probably not even be 14 days now–I hope, only 10–until we can finally snuggle close together and find compensation for all the deprivation. I love you sooooooooooooooooooo much, my girl, you! Your Mope

VERA TO MOPE

London, 15 March 1938 [Telegram]

Fig. 79 Telegram from Vera in London to Mope in Moscow, sent via Berlin, 15 March 1938.

ELT FELSENSTEIN NATIONALHOTEL MOSCOU
RADIO BERLIN
KLITSHUGINA
B LONDON 41
2524 2250
TRAVEL ROUTE WARSAW YUGOSLAVIA TRIESTE OR SWEDENPLEASE CABLE REPLYWAITING IMPATIENTLYHOPE SUNDAY DAY OF DEPARTUREMOST LOVING KISSESALL MY LOVE YOUR VERALEIN

MOPE TO VERA

Moscow, 15 March 1938

Today, I was without mail from my beloved. Actually, that is not true at all, because I received a very worried telegram this morning. So today, I went to get exact information concerning the connections. It looks like I will leave next Monday or Tuesday evening to travel to Leningrad. The next evening to Helsingfors. Again, in the evening over Åbø to Stockholm. The night after that to Copenhagen and from there to Esbjerg, from where a ship leaves for Dunkirk on Saturday, but just once a week. Since I can only travel overnight the entire trip, as there are no daytime connections, the trip will be very long, but what can I do? I have to make the best of the fact that I will be separated from my darling for a few days longer than I would have imagined.

In any case, I am counting on arriving in Paris on Monday in eight days. I am asking you to get information as to when the boat traveling from Esbjerg (Denmark) at 5 p.m. on Saturday to Antwerp-Dunkirk will arrive in Dunkirk. Should you have a good connection that makes it possible to meet me in Dunkirk without having to wait too long for each other. Please write to me about this to Stockholm, because your answer would not reach me here in time. Should my exit visa from here be issued for precisely the 20th, I would leave on the evening of the 19th, but I think that they will give me a few days leeway. In that case (I mean if I do leave on the 19th) I would have to alter my plans in such a way that I would come to London first and pick up my sweet beloved, since I would have to wait around for days to take that boat otherwise. As soon as I know, I will send you a telegram. By the way, I would like to ask you to add the remark "via Northern" to your telegrams in the future, so that they will not be sent through Radio Berlin of all things, like the one today.

MOPE TO VERA

Moscow, 17 March 1938

Today was the feast of Purim. I am sure that you know that famous story. I only wish that the current enemies of the Jews suffered a similar fate to that of Haman. Unfortunately, it seems that my wish will not come true, and, if it did, that would really be much more important to me.

I talked over the telephone to Schapiro in Paris three times. Twice, we were interrupted. I explained to him that I will probably leave here on Monday the 21st. Actually, I was told today that my passport will not be ready until the 22nd, so that I would not leave until Wednesday the 23rd at the earliest, if that is the case. I asked if it might be possible to have the exit visa issued earlier–I should get the answer to that on the 20th and will send you a telegram then.

Tomorrow is Wychodnoi, so this evening I will go to the Metropole, although I feel very tired, to spend some time with my colleagues. *How happy I would be if it were a week later and there really were only a few days left between now and our reunion. I cannot describe it or say anything, but only talk about the fact that it occupies my senses and thoughts completely, and there is no room in my brain for anything else besides envisioning the reunion and smearing all the beautiful and more beautiful colors on the palette to mix them into the most beautiful* color of all. We have now been separated for over three months and that is a longer period of time than I have ever lived through, because my innermost being was always with my sweet, most beloved little witch, to protect her, to take care of her and to read all of her wishes in her eyes and on her lips and make them come true, despite the distance. And that is how I experienced that time.

It is difficult for me already to imagine your beautiful body in my head, that is how long I have not been able to see it. I still have to wait!! How difficult that is!! I kiss you, my beloved, and my hunger for you is so great that the kissing will be more like biting and never letting go, until we go to sleep drunk with love. I wish it were that time already!!! I am beginning to hate the paper I have to trust all these dreams to, because I cannot experience them yet. *How* much I do love you!!!!! Your Mope

MOPE TO VERA

Moscow, 18 March 1938

Because of the quick mail transportation, I had the great pleasure not to be without mail today, as your loving and worried sounding letter from the 14th of the month reached me. I am very, very sorry that you were so unnecessarily worried. As you were able to see from my various letters, I made up my mind to travel via Stockholm or a similar route, as soon as the unheard-of measure that gives reason for the alteration of my travel plans happened. Just now, I finished writing the weekend telegram to my sweet darling to give Tuesday the 22nd as the anticipated date of departure and hope that that will work out.

I still have a big program for the last few days, and Schapiro will call me again later and most likely make it even bigger or at least try to make it bigger. How far I can get things done, I cannot say in advance, since the prices and other wishes of the clientele can only be brought under the same roof as other demands here with the greatest difficulties.

It has become cold here again since yesterday evening, and an icy wind contributes to making it even more uncomfortable outside– whereas over there, things are beginning to bloom. Now, I will close this writ, which will probably be the last I will write from here before I leave. By the time these words reach you, you will be able to pack your suitcases in order to meet me.

With limitless love, Your Mope

MOPE TO VERA

Helsingfors, Finland, 27 March 1938

"Who never ate his bread with tears"[89]–can never understand how good my breakfast tasted today. I cried tears of joy on the inside, and they added spice to the wonderful warm toast and did not ruin the taste of the excellent coffee. And at the same time, even the sweetness of the honey that flowed so golden yellow on my bread could not lessen the bitterness to still be without you–my everything, my dream and my desire, my most beloved and longed for girl. All my organs, my pores, my entire being is filled with longing for you as if with electricity! An electric light bulb placed against me would flare and die, because the wire would burn and melt–it will still be days before I can take you in my arms to be led back to balance and to normal thoughts and emotions through your love and tenderness.

I sent my weekend cable to my sweetest little witch from the first station outside of "the" country, and I hope that it gave joy, even though it was late. Today is Sunday and I have a Sunday feeling, after I went into the bathroom here at the hotel that was gleaming with cleanliness–without resembling a terrarium. I kept looking here and there at a bold head to see if it was a cockroach or some other kind of zoological monster, but alas, there was just nothing to beat to death.

My trip until now has been very pleasant and undisturbed. Two female guides from Intourist took me to the train in Leningrad, both of whom were named Vera, and one of them said that they each represent one half of what my beloved means to me. They told me that–if I came back with you–there would be three Veras. They want to take care of you lovingly while I work, show you the city and take care of your entertainment so that you won't feel lonely. Everyone is expecting my darling to come with me the next time. All of Moscow already knows that I am not human without you, because the longing is eating me up inside and I just could not bear it a second time to be separated from you for such a horribly long time. All the colleagues, every porter, and every hotel manager already knows that my sweet one will accompany me the next time, and only I–I still have not received your confirmation! Why

---

89 Mope echoes the opening verse of "The Song of the Harper," a short poem by Goethe.

do you leave me without an answer to this question and often repeated request???

From Stockholm–tomorrow–tomorrow–I will call you and then, I will come to you, and *everything* will be good!! So you love me as unspeakably as I love you? Were you as loyal to me as I to you? Are your thoughts as filled with me as mine, mine with you? Soon, you can give me your answer and make me happy and glad, my most beloved!

Once again, I trust my kisses and caresses to the paper that is meant to bring them to you. You, finally–Your Mope

P.S. Please tell me nothing, nothing, nothing related to business for the first two days!

Twenty-seven: "10,108 White Foxes"

30 May through 31 July 1938

POLITICAL TIMELINE, APRIL–SEPTEMBER 1938

- 26 April 1938: Decree requiring all Jews living within the Reich to register all of their assets with severe restrictions on moving assets abroad.
- May 1938: Following the Anschluss, Austrian Jews forced to scrub the streets to the delight of onlookers.
- 19 May 1938: German military manoeuvers along border with Czechoslovakia gave rise to widespread fears of an imminent invasion. The "May Crisis" was averted by warnings from Britain and France that they would respond in the event of an attack.
- 28 May 1938: Intensified boycott of Jewish businesses in Frankfurt.
- 31 May 1938: Germany outlaws so-called "decadent art".
- 9 June 1938: Main Synagogue in Munich set on fire and burned to the ground.
- 15 June 1938: Any Jew in Germany "previously convicted" of a crime (even a traffic offense) is to be arrested.
- 25 June 1938: Law passed under which German-Jewish doctors only allowed to treat Jewish patients.

- 6 TO 15 July 1938: International conference at Evian-Les-Bains to discuss "Jewish problem" fails to open doors abroad for persecuted refugees.
- 23 July 1938: Jews in Germany ordered to carry identity cards to be shown to police and other officials on demand.
- 25 July 1938: Licenses of German Jewish doctors canceled.
- 8 August 1938: First Austrian concentration camp established at Mauthausen.
- 10 August 1938: Great Synagogue in Nuremberg destroyed.
- 17 August 1938: Law passed by which male and female Jews must adopt the respective names Israel and Sarah by the following new year.
- 26 September 1938: Hitler promises that Sudetenland will be his final territorial demand in Europe.
- 29-30 September 1938: British Prime Minister Neville Chamberlain and French premier Edouard Daladier sign the "Munich accord" with Hitler, permitting the annexation of the Sudetenland by Nazi Germany.

The two months that Mope enjoyed with Vera in England before being obliged to return to the Soviet Union at the end of May 1938 culminated with the "sympathetic" allocation of provisional residency papers, stipulating that he could now spend four weeks in Britain no more than twice a year. With his German passport no longer valid and loss of his natal citizenship imminent, the British authorities granted him a "stateless document" that allowed him to travel back to Russia, where his work visa would be subject to renewal every few months.

The validity of the Certificate of Identity issued by the British to take the place of a passport was to prove problematic causing snags for Mope whenever he entered or exited another country. The original Certificate had an expiration date. Its later replacement is illustrated here.

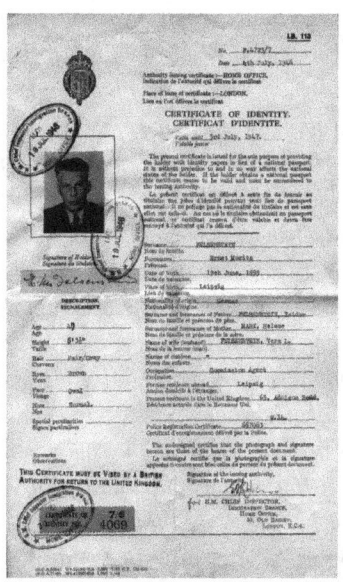

Fig. 80 Later Certificate of Identity issued to Mope by the British Home Office in 1946. The earlier certificate has not survived.

In Russia, the prolongation of his permit to stay depended on the good will of Sojuzpushnina (the state-run fur trade organization) and his continuing success in the purchase of furs—white foxes setting the trend during 1938—for his western European and American clients. Although well treated for the most part, he lived in constant fear that the visa would be rescinded with the likelihood that he would be deported, or that he might be randomly arrested and taken away as did happen to at least one of his fur trade colleagues.

Before his departure from England, he was able to share with Vera a short vacation, which they spent in Downderry, Cornwall, though during most of his stay she was occupied with her work at Marks & Spencer. As his earlier route through Austria was now shut off to him, Mope planned his return to Russia via Paris (a required stopover in order to consult with Schapiro), and Strasbourg, flying over Germany to Prague (where he still retained several business clients), and then on to Moscow via Warsaw. In both Czechoslovakia and Poland, his newly issued stateless papers only granted him short duration transit permits. But for his sheer determination, good luck, and quick thinking, he was almost forced to abandon much of his belongings during his stopover in Warsaw. During the succeeding four-and-a-half months, he quartered in Moscow, making several trips to Leningrad, the most significant of these being for the main fur auction in the first two weeks of July.

In England, Vera was promoted with a small salary increase to the new position of "staff manager-staff supervisor," with responsibility for overseeing four stores, including her "home" store of Hammersmith. The soon-to-be-opened store at Ealing would occupy much of her time during the next months. As in previous years, she was also assigned camp duties for two weeks, this time from the end of June at the Marks & Spencer staff summer camp at St. Anne's, outside Blackpool, in the north-west of England.

Just before her departure for Blackpool, Vera responded to a demand to visit the German Embassy in London, where she was told that she must surrender her passport as her citizenship was revoked. In Germany itself, a new law (14 June) called for the compulsory registration of all Jewish-owned businesses. Very shortly thereafter, the Gebrüder Felsenstein, now a shadow of its former self with Mope's hapless cousin Semy as the sole partner still in Leipzig, was Aryanized and sold at a fraction of its value to Nazi accessories. To Mope's relief, his mother (Oma Lenchen) was finally allowed to leave Germany and dwell in England, arriving in mid-July. In faraway Moscow, he was able to rejoice at "the fact that my beloved mother got out of that hell healthy and happy" (18 July 1938).

MOPE TO VERA

Prague, 1 June 1938

When my beloved receives these words, she will have certainly overcome the amazement that overcame her when I called her from Prague. I will explain with a chronological report about everything that has happened. The trip was very comfortable, although the sea rocked the boat quite a bit, as I noticed when I was awake for a short time. Schapiro picked me up at the railway station in Paris. The man does not speak one word of French, but he sticks his nose into everything, and that is why they would not give me the checked suitcase because it contained tobacco. After I showed them my ticket to Moscow and many expenses, "Air de France" brought my suitcase to the airport accompanied by a customs official, which took more than two hours of coaxing.

By the way, the flight was wonderful. After we left Strassburg behind us, we flew, in the most beautiful summer weather, over Baden, Herrenalb, Karlsruhe, Stuttgart, Nürnberg, Marienbad and landed here. I had never before had such a clear view while flying. It was rather pleasing that they gave me a map with which I could get my bearings.

When I wanted to depart from the airport, people explained to me that I only had a transit visa and would have to commence my air travel immediately. They were very determined and would not listen to any explanations, until I said that I had a headache, that I would not get back on an airplane today and would just have to take the train. After waiting and negotiating for an hour and a half they agreed, and I was told that only the police directorate would be able to make any changes, as far as issuing a permit to stay here until Friday was concerned. (The Warsaw plane only leaves on Mondays, Wednesdays, and Fridays). When I arrived at the police station, the top person had already left for the day and so, I will have to go again tomorrow. In the meantime, I went to see a doctor who gave me a written report stating that I need a few days' rest before traveling on.

Until now, I have only visited Mrs. Adler here who is a very charming woman who runs her husband's entire and quite significant business all by herself as an authorized partner.[90] Around here, the furriers close at 4 p.m. during the summer months, so that further visits were not possible, and then, the visit to the doctor including the waiting had taken a full hour and a half.

Now I will go and have dinner, since I have not eaten anything since Strassburg, besides a piece of cake.

I love you all the way into my innermost heart–unutterably–you! Your Mope

MOPE TO VERA

Prague, 2 June 1938

While I am beginning to write this, I am standing in the post office to get instructions concerning my trip. *How* happy I was yesterday to talk to you and I am still really sad that you were worried! *How* awful that we could not say good-bye yesterday. Since the call costs more than ten shillings for three minutes, I had demanded that they would let me know as soon as three minutes were up, and those idiots just cut us off without saying a word about ending the conversation.

I already wrote that I had to go to the police director's office *immediately* after arriving here in order to avoid unpleasantness. Then,

---

90 Perhaps foreseeing the deteriorating political situation, Mr. Adler, in conjunction with his son, had recently opened a branch of their business in London.

it was necessary to get some of the local currency, and following that, I determined that the consultation hours of the doctor who had been recommended to me only lasted until 4 o'clock, and I arrived at his office one minute before four. The whole story there took about an hour and a half, and I arrived at the hotel around a quarter to six. First thing tomorrow, I will have to get more Polish money, before I can confirm my time of arrival in Warsaw.

I made a number of purchases today, shirts, lipsticks, skin lotion, a smaller briefcase for me, since it is uncomfortable to have to carry the heavy "suitcase" around in Moscow, a bathing suit, lady's stockings,[91] and on top of that–after I received permission to stay here until tomorrow–I visited customers. Several promised to give me smaller orders as soon as the political situation gets better.

Life here plays out exactly the same as always: people are sitting in the coffee houses and take walks around Wenzelsplatz, the main traffic center, as if war had not almost entered this country ten days ago.[92] Human beings really are the strangest creatures living on this Earth. Contrary to others–at least that is what they claim–they can reason and have the ability to think; and after such a very short time, they have already overcome the greatest nervous crisis they can possibly meet, as if nothing had happened at all.

It is a quarter after midnight, and I have a lot of work ahead of me tomorrow, which is why, despite my need to keep chatting with you for hours on end, I have to close so I can climb into bed. The music has stopped already, music which is produced here in the hotel lobby during the evening at a pleasant volume, and they are drawing the shades. Only a few customers are still sitting around, much to the chagrin of the tired

---

91 Fashionable ladies' stockings from the West were a particularly prized commodity in the Soviet Union. These and boxes of western cigarettes could be used both for currency and tipping purposes.

92 On 21 May, the Czechoslovak government had ordered the partial mobilization of its armed forces following reports that Hitler was about to attack the country in furtherance of his claim that the Sudetenland, which had a large ethnic German population, belonged to Germany. The ensuing "May Crisis" had the world believing that war was imminent. Hitler finally annexed the Sudetenland in early October 1938 as his prize, following the fateful Munich conference. The area included Karlsbad and Marienbad where Mope and Vera had vacationed together in September 1936, and where many German Jews had found a temporary respite from Nazism.

waiters, and I do not want to be the last one to leave. I hope that I will receive mail from my darling tomorrow.

Your Mope, who is the last guest to leave, after all.

MOPE TO VERA

Warsaw, 4 June 1938

Early yesterday, I made quite a few visits in Prague and schmoozed with the customers. Then, Mrs. Adler drove me to the airport. My plane took off after a forty-minute delay. It rained today as if all the water gates in heaven had been opened, and we were flying between the clouds and only saw a small ray of sunshine in the cabin here and there for the last half hour of our flight. You could see lightning strikes shoot down towards the ground left and right, but our pilot was extremely capable and avoided the thunderstorm. By the way, he told me later that a thunderstorm is not dangerous to an airplane. Interestingly enough, we were much faster than the bad weather, which did not arrive here until two to three hours later. I have now been roving about Middle Europe in this way for all of a week. I shall be departing for Moscow early tomorrow morning, where I will arrive in the morning on the 6th. The reason for this is that here they do not want to extend my transit visa under any circumstances, so that I do not have any other choice.[93]

Today, I was extremely busy, since I spent most of the morning at the mayor's office because of my passport. However, that was nothing compared to the afternoon. Yesterday, at the airport I had requested that my luggage, which was supposed to go all the way to Negoreloje (Russian border), be sent to the customs office at the railway station, but they explained that that would not be possible until today. When I got there, they reported that the suitcase was there, but that the customs office had closed immediately after it had arrived and would not be open again until Tuesday. I had a man from the hotel with me as a translator, but he was not aggressive enough for the impending difficulties, so I took another man from *Air France*. After we found out who was the

---

93 The Polish authorities treated German-Jewish citizens particularly harshly as many so-called "Ost-Juden" (Polish Jews) had been expelled *en masse* from Germany to Poland by the Nazis, thus intensifying an already endemic anti-Semitism. Traveling with "stateless" documents, as Mope discovered, greatly compounded the problem of obtaining visas.

director of the customs office and could not find his telephone number in the directory, we took a taxi and learned that he had moved to a new residence. We worked on finding the new address, and when we arrived, he was sleeping. They were afraid of his divine wrath if they awakened him, but I insisted and then heard that he did not have the keys at all. He gave us the name of a clerk whose address we found after waiting at the train station for half an hour. Despite the wonderful weather, that man was at home as well and promised to come to the train station within a quarter of an hour. After he got there, he leafed through all of his files–and there were quite a few–again and again, and could not find any documents concerning the suitcase. Finally, he determined that the suitcase was still stored in one of the customs rooms within the customs enclosure, for which another clerk had the only key. However, this man lives far outside of Warsaw. So back into the taxi and filled with fear that he might have gone out for the day, I went to find him. Had we got there ten minutes later, we would not have caught him at all. So we took this man and drove to the first man–or better, the second one–and after four hours of fear, agitation, anger, and finally joy that the no longer hoped for success was achieved, we landed back at the train station where I could hand in the suitcase to be sent to the border station, after paying the overtime hours for both clerks. And that even though those people readily admitted the unbelievable mistake had been made by the airport customs people, and said it was very unjustified that I should experience such expenses and lost time because of it.

    This detective story was a small piece of bravura because of my complete ignorance concerning the language, and I am convinced that, halfway there, most people would have let the matter go. Add to that the fact that the translators certainly spoke Polish very well, but other than that, spoke very little French. What a long story and how little does it tell you about the feelings it excited.

    It is now terribly late, and tomorrow, I have to get up at 7 o'clock. Tomorrow, I will go to the station at approximately the same time as it is with you, because there is no time difference here during the summer. However, in Russia, there will be a difference of two hours. *Your* Mope

VERA TO MOPE

London, 5 June 1938

Today, beginning at 1 o'clock, I was in Ealing where I would like to hire five or six old girls (that is, girls who have left the company of their *own* free will for some reason or other–mostly *married women*–who are already trained). Especially during this time of year, no one is fully capable of working continuously in the warm air in the store between seven and nine in the evening. I expect that the arrival of fresh girls at that time would make a significant difference. I have a lot of extra work because of the Ealing store, as I have had to interview girls for the new store here in Hammersmith and also do not want to neglect my own store, if at all possible. Next Wednesday, I will go back to Ealing and hire more personnel, for the opening of the new store that will take place during early autumn.

Yesterday afternoon, I was at the *head office* for a *camp supervisor meeting* where I heard more ranting than anything else, but still–it was a restful change from the store. I am leaving here on Saturday, 25 June, around noon and will be in Blackpool around 4.30 in the afternoon. My address there is: M&S Holiday Camp, Blackpool Road, St. Annes, Lancashire.

I heard yesterday that, according to a new German law, no more than RM 5,000 will be allowed to be taken out and then only as *Sperrmark*! Professor Immelmann is back from Germany where they let him know today that they will not pay him *another* penny in pension, because he has a home here! He is supposed to be quite beside himself, Muttilein said, and is also quite thunderstruck psychologically, because oddly enough, he still feels quite attached to all of that—[94]

My love, it is very late again–I love you unspeakably and completely, and I am *totally your* Lilongo

---

94   Immelmann and his wife were family friends of the Hirsches who had left Germany in 1933 after he had been dismissed from his position as a university professor. He appears to have revisited Germany in 1938, and learned there that his pension was permanently rescinded. The *Sperrmark* system limited the amount of cash that could be taken out of Germany, and particularly affected Jewish refugees.

MOPE TO VERA

Moscow, 6 June 1938

I was unable to get a room in the National, because nothing was available, and so I booked in at the Metropole. Tonight, my colleagues and I drank a lot of alcohol while having our dinner. Unfortunately, I could not get away from it, because we had been invited by the gentlemen from the Sojuspushnina. Until now, we have not been able to do anything, but I really hope that we can soon get down to business. I will do what I can for my part.

The weather here is extraordinarily pleasant once again. The sky is clear and the sun is shining, but it is not too hot. It seems to me like I have been here for several weeks now, although it has only been fewer than two days. People greeted me everywhere in the friendliest and most pleasant manner, so that I would be able to feel quite at home, if I did not miss you so terribly. Most people asked me why you did not come with me. No one can understand why my darling leaves her husband so alone, though if you had to travel here at my expense there would really be nothing left of my salary, because the trip would gobble up too much money, but *life would be beautiful*!

This tired letter did not turn out all that nice, but nevertheless, it brings my gentlest kisses to my beloved little witch. Your Mope

MOPE TO VERA

Moscow, 9 June 1938

If my beloved only knew how happy I was today to receive mail again, writing would surely give her even more pleasure–I am assuming that she does take pleasure in it! At the same time as your letters, I received one from Hugo Fränkel in Stockholm, in which he lets me know that the office of the Russian embassy there wrote that they would issue a transit visa for me if necessary. Without that, granting it would otherwise take more than fourteen days, and I cannot wait that long, if I want to leave some day.[95]

---

95 Hugo Fränkel (d. 1940), a longtime Leipzig fur trader, had moved his fur business to Stockholm. He generously undertook to act on Mope's behalf if it became necessary at this politically charged time to obtain a transit visa at short notice.

I did not expect anything other than that they would take Professor Immelmann's pension away some day. He should have thought about that earlier if he cannot do without it and made different decisions. There is an infinite number of people who suffer just like him, but they are forced to suffer that kind of treatment only because they are Jews, and they did not volunteer for it. I do not feel any pity for him.

Now I will lay me down in my chaste bed and dream of my darling and be ever so close to you, caress you and kiss you, put my arms around you and be ever so happy with you, just as I am in my knowledge of you. Your Mope

VERA TO MOPE

London, 12 June 1938

A few days ago, the manager of the Hammersmith store and I had a longer conversation during which he asked me what kinds of plans I had made for the future, whether they lay in the company or in my *"married life."* I told him that my immediate future was in the company, of course, and he asked me if I was hoping for a larger store, or what else I was thinking about as a future. I explained to him that I was not thinking of anything specific, aside from wanting to advance, and since they were drawing on me so much for the new store opening, the future might lie in the position of a supervisor. Why he asked me, I am not quite clear about. However, I would have considered it completely wrong to say anything about my *actual* plans.

But maybe, you, Sir, might be interested what kinds of plans they are: *no matter what kind of position M&S offers me in the near future*, I am hoping to have a baby around May or June next year, and that I wish for with all the fibers of my being!! So that means that I will quit my job around Christmas time, or sometime around then, have my child, hopefully, and as long as it is still small, I hope not to have to go back to my job. What will happen then, whether I will go back to work, when the child is past its infancy is very difficult to know, and a position a little higher up than the one I have now would naturally appeal to me very much, but first of

---

His son, Jury Fränkel (1899-1971), was a friend and contemporary of Mope. Jury's posthumously published memoir, *Einbahnstrasse: Bericht Eines Lebens* (2 vols., Murrhardt: Rifra-Verlag, 1971, 1972), includes many insightful descriptions of the pre-war Leipzig fur trade.

all, I want my, *our* baby!!!! Do you agree with that, my beloved, or do you not completely agree with the *proposition* presented to you?????

You–totally and completely, *Your* Lilongo

MOPE TO VERA

Moscow, 18 June 1938

After I inspected approximately 8.000 white foxes piece by piece from nine in the morning into the evening around six o'clock, I was so tired after dinner at 8.00 p.m. that I lay down on the bed–despite the need to get work done–and slept for a few hours. After that, I worked until five in the morning and examined approximately 4,000 more white fox pelts today. I bought 10,108 white foxes yesterday and today, after I had already bought 6,094 before. That is almost twenty-five per cent of the entire Russian white fox harvest and a very significant transaction. On top of that, I also bought other things, and I think that Schapiro will not be dissatisfied. Despite all the work, I am uncommonly fresh and feel excellent, as long as I disregard the impact of the longing for my sweet little witch.

I came here for the first time a year ago tomorrow, and when I consider how lost I felt without any knowledge of the language whatsoever and how different that was compared to now, I become aware of the fact that 365 days have gone by, a long time that has just flown by. My knowledge of the language is still laughable, but at least they seem to understand my stuttering when I want something.

The new law would mean a complete catastrophe for the poor Jews who are still living in that country of pigs! It is really inconceivable what kinds of dirty tricks that rabble comes up with and on the other hand, it is proof of how bad they are doing economically, that they have to keep devising new shabby tricks despite the opinions of foreign countries.[96]

Now I want to get something to eat before I go to sleep. I wish you a wonderful trip to Blackpool and much satisfaction for your stay there! Your Mope

---

96   A new German law that came into effect on 14 June made it compulsory for all Jewish businesses to be identified and registered. As Mope may have foreseen, this was simply a prelude to their confiscation.

MOPE TO VERA

Moscow, 19 June 1938

The last birthday before the end of the fourth decade of my existence is almost over, and I will begin the new year just like I ended the old one with a letter to my darling. Early today around 9 o'clock–usually, the mail does not come in until the afternoon–I received your ever so beloved letter from last Sunday and your loving congratulatory telegram, and I would like to thank you so much for all your love and friendship, which make life so beautiful to me and make me happy. It really was the *best* decision of my life. Since I did not work all that much today and the weather unfortunately did not entice me to go outside, I spent most of the day alone and enjoyed the peace and quiet.

Your conversation, or better, your answers to your store manager's questions were very intelligent and appropriate. It is no one else's business that we are already looking forward to producing a baby of our own. So you want to place it on my next birthday table and I cannot begin to tell you how happy that will make me some day, to carry a photograph of my own child instead of pictures of other children, or maybe even two of our own (if that is not too much for my beloved).

How long I will have to stay here I cannot say at this time, but I will only stay here past the beginning of September if my beloved will join me here; if not there is no way! In any case, I recommend that you file an application for a visa soon so that you would have it in time, if that should come to pass. It would not cause any problems if you did not use it. It is valid for three months after receipt and for two weeks after it is recorded in the passport until the entry takes place. Now I will go to sleep, I am very tired and hope that the letter does not prove that.

Mope who only belongs to my Veralein!

VERA TO MOPE

London, 21 June 1938

After my beloved wrote to me once again how important the question of citizenship is to him, I went to see Mr. Treger, Carlton House Terrace, with Muttilein during lunch yesterday. He asked for my passport, which was supposed to belong to me until the end of September, and explained to me that the two of us would *never* receive one again. They kept mine and demanded that I also bring yours. Mr. Treger is a decent man, at least I think so, and he had told me the other day that I would not have to see him until you were back. I hardly think that the matter could have been handled differently by me, since they only sent the letter of invitation for *both* of us last Thursday.[97]

VERA TO MOPE

London, 23 June 1938

At the moment, it is hot and oppressive, and everyone is tired and exhausted and probably more touchy than normal. Yesterday, Muttilein went to the Home Office first where she had to wait in the heat, and then, in the afternoon, she went to Carlton House Terrace where she was forced to wait for several hours. As they told her, they will send me a receipt for both of us in the next few days. Over the telephone, Joan Stiebel assured me that, even without a receipt, if she described the circumstances of the case to Mr. Cooper for me, we would get everything we wished and would have nothing to worry about!!! I am happy with that.[98]

MOPE TO VERA

Moscow, 24 June 1938

Just a few minutes ago, I arranged for a six-minute telephone call to my darling–I would like to talk to you one more time before you set off for camp tomorrow, because I feel such immense and intense longing for you and would really like to hear your beloved voice again.

And now, the call has taken place. I want to take the opportunity to express my joy over the excellent connection for our conversation. You cannot communicate all the love you carry within yourself on the telephone, but you feel so close all of a sudden, and contrary to what I have said before, I have to say that, despite the separation that came

---

97 Mr. Treger was the official in the German Embassy in London who was in charge of the renewal of passports and identification papers. Despite his apparent "decency," he had no compunction about confiscating Vera's passport to indicate her de-naturalization.

98 Mr. Cooper was the Home Office official acting on the couple's behalf, and Joan Stiebel the secretary to Otto Schiff.

much too soon, a feeling of deep happiness has remained on the inside that cannot be described, because words are too poor to express it.

The news you gave me is really astonishing. So they denaturalized my darling and me without cause–just because we are Jews. That should also mean that we will not be able to get my things out of that filthy country, unless my dear mother can take some part with her. I really do hope that she will soon get out of this realm of dehumanization. That vile country has stolen so enormously much from me without any justification. What the newspapers are reporting concerning spitefulness and brutality is almost incomprehensible, but fortunately, everything on Earth does find its revenge eventually. I guess that the extension of my British residence papers will now be more effortless, as you told me, and that is very satisfying to me.

By the way, I heard that the business has been sold.[99]

It has become downright cold and windy here, although the sky glows deeply blue and is filled with stars tonight–one of the shortest nights of the year, it seems. I actually enjoyed my walk to the post office, because the color of the sky was–already being brightened by the returning sun in the East like a wonderfully gleaming Burma sapphire– of a rare beauty tonight.

Do you know that I have earned more in commissions this month than what my salary amounts to? I was not prepared for that and feel quite satisfied with it. Just imagine that I bought 21,100 white foxes single-handedly and inspected them piece by piece. Besides that, I bought some Persian lamb, ermine, Kohlinski deer[100] lining, etc., and took over several contracts. I am telling you about this with the expectation that you are a little interested in finding out a little about my work, in which my beloved can also participate, should she come here.

I have to go back to the warehouse, and that is why I have to close this letter definitively, and with most passionate kisses and tender caresses, just like the ones my dream showed me last night. I was with my beloved completely, and we were tightly entwined, until the telephone pulled me back to reality with its loud ringing, and I realized how alone I am, and my longing for you is still growing stronger, if that is even possible.

---

99 The Gebrüder Felsenstein in Leipzig was forcibly Aryanized at this time with minimal or no compensation.
100 Deer from the Kola Peninsula in the western part of the Soviet Union.

MOPE TO VERA

Moscow, 26 June 1938

Finally I have time for my beloved! Yesterday evening, I could not write to you, because I had too much work to do and then could not stay away from the furrier table because of my colleagues, a table that had been set up in the hotel restaurant to celebrate Pod-Wychodnoi. Actually, I did not have the expected Wychodnoi today, because I had to work, and now, it is way past 11 p.m., and I was not able to send my telegrams until now or take up my most favorite occupation with leisure. Following your good example, I lay down for two hours earlier and slept rather well, so that I feel quite fresh now.

As I heard, it is best to make a statement concerning one's assets remaining in Germany, because otherwise everything will be seized irrevocably once and for all. I will ask at the local embassy that the appropriate paperwork be sent so I can fill it out and note down the numbers, as far as I can remember them. The matter has to be taken care of by the 30th, so that I have no time to lose. That gang of pigs!!

I embrace you and kiss you in your tent bed, which probably only has room for me in the imagination but would actually be much too small for both of us! You! Your Mope

VERA TO MOPE

St. Anne's, near Blackpool, 26 June 1938

It is almost 4 o'clock and the first opportunity to write. Sundays are always very busy in camp, because the change of occupants takes place. The ones leaving have to clear the area by 11 a.m., but some of them leave very early in the morning, and the breakfast and everything else has to be ready for them (sandwiches for the trip, etc.). Then, beginning at 11 o'clock, the new ones arrive at all hours, because they come from different parts of England, some by bus and some by train; a few arrived as early as 8 a.m. today after they had driven through the night.

The location of the field here is a closed part of a former racecourse, and there are still some half decayed grandstands in the background. The ocean is not visible; it takes about fifteen to twenty minutes to get to the water, and before dinner, I went for a short swim with some of the girls; it was not warm enough to stay in the water any longer. Those who accompanied me were the girls who will stay here for the two weeks and so already had a week of their stay behind them. As I already told you, the enthusiasm for swimming is not all that strong in the English girls, and only three of those who went into the water had a bathing suit with them, and only *one* actually went in with me and seemed to be an excellent swimmer.

The surroundings of the big field seem to consist of homes, a gas works, and Blackpool's entertainment/look-out tower in the background. It was the wish of many of the girls to come to Blackpool, but there seems to be very little in the surroundings that is attractive. Blackpool is an entertainment center for the masses par excellence. We are three pence per bus–far distant from the center, and I am very happy about that. The air is very pure and beautiful; until now, it has been very windy, and just a little while ago, it started to rain. Despite the weather, and although I have not even been here for 24 hours, I already have "camp color" in my face. The ocean wind causes that, and it will certainly get rid of all the London air in my lungs.

My co-supervisor whom I know only fleetingly does *not* have my complete approval. In my opinion, they made a mistake at the head office. She is a *"bl[oody] foreigner"* as well, and just for political reasons, they should not have sent two supervisors who suffer from the same condition, but of course, that is not her fault. She is probably a very well-educated girl, but she is lacking all the typical English attributes: *the absolute politeness, discretion, and lack of personality*, and it is these attributes that are so especially likable in camp. Although I am not all that enthused with my co-worker, I will get along with her and learn how *not* to do things.

My tent is very large and warm; I have more than enough wool blankets and hot water bottles at my disposal whenever I want them, and I slept through the first night like a sack, without waking up even once.

Thursday evening, there was a card for me from Walter Levy to let me know that a healthy baby girl had arrived in Genoa and that Hilde was doing well. I was really happy about that, and immediately sent our congratulation in the name of Hirsch and Felsenstein and also wrote to her parents in Frankfurt. I would be very pleased if you could find the time to write a few words as well, but only if time allows.[101]

---

101 Having escaped from Germany, Vera's closest friend from schooldays, Hilde, and her husband Walter Lewy, were still living in Genoa at the time of the birth of their daughter Renata.

MOPE TO VERA

Moscow, 27 June 1938

You are really sooooo very sweet. Despite all of your work, you take the time to go to Mr. Treger during lunch in order to be of help to me, knowing that it is very important to me to find out about the final decision in this matter. It is really unbelievable how that band of vermin demands the passport papers back–seemingly without any kind of reason. I hope that they gave you or Muttilein the receipt for both of us. As long as that dirty mob has the right to make the rules there, I do not want to have anything else to do with them. Who knows what kinds of elephants they made of mosquitoes! Right now, I really do regret to have incurred all those expenses in order to send the merchandise to Palestine. I am not in the position to spend much more on it, but our chances at achieving British naturalization should have increased significantly because of this new turn of events, and I suggest to you that you should have Otto submit your application as soon as possible.

The British consulate here should be contacted as soon as possible concerning the extension of my papers. That has to happen from there– as far as I know–and I hope that I am not creating too much trouble for you again. In any case, I will also take steps here.

How is that for a love letter? No, that is not a love letter at all! But it was *meant* to be one! Instead, I talk about all kinds of business matters, but at least, I have the good fortune that my sweet little witch will see it as a love letter anyway, because she knows how filled with love for her I am, that there is an especially tender kiss in every single letter, even if the combinations sound completely different. Your Mope

MOPE TO VERA

Moscow, 3 July 1938

My departure for Leningrad has been delayed until tomorrow, presumably, since I have been unable to get my papers, which will hopefully happen tomorrow, because the inspections will start on the 5th and with that, such an enormous amount of work, which will probably keep me from writing to my darling for several days.

This afternoon, Sojuspushnina arranged a picnic excursion in our honor. We left the hotel around 4 o'clock and drove to Chimki. Because of the bright sun and the most beautiful weather, the colors of the landscape were quite striking, and we were not in a hurry to move on. On the terrace in the lower level with a view of the canal–as far as I know, it is 85 meters wide–a table had been set, and it could not have been set more decoratively and beautifully. They put a very grand dinner in front of us. There were exquisite hors d'oeuvres, caviar, of course, crabs–a local delicatessen suckling pig–halved Russian cucumbers, hollowed out like little ships and filled, tomatoes filled with something that tasted excellent, but I cannot define it, mushroom pastries, etc. They served fish Solianka[102] as the soup, then poultry, and for the finale, frozen whipped cream with fresh strawberries. I have never before eaten such good ice cream and I am thirty-nine years and fourteen days old! And of course, everyone drank a lot. There was Vodka, and then, they served a very good white wine. When dinner was finished, we were taken to a boat, and went for a ride along the canal, and then along the Moskwa (river) to Moscow, which we reached around 11 o'clock. Between Chimki and Moscow, the canal has a gradient of 42 meters, which has to be counterbalanced by sluices. As far as they told us, such big sluices do not exist anywhere else. The usual gradient is between 6 and 8 meters. It is admirable from a technical point of view, with what precision these giant sluices function, and usually, they contain three or four ships at the same time.[103]

The surroundings of the canal are partly wooded and flat land that makes a beautiful impression with its summer green and grazing animals. Then, we came closer to the city and moved past great factories and many new houses still being built, and also interesting older buildings, for example, a giant former cloister with its picturesque towers and walls. At the end of our outing, we walked through the park filled with people to the underground which took us home. All of us are highly satisfied with the undertaking which had been organized most excellently. My beloved will think that a dinner without mocha afterwards can hardly have satisfied her Mope. So I forgot to mention one very important point. The coffee was served–once again with a lot

---

102 A traditional Russian beef soup.
103 The Moscow Canal connects the Moskva and Volga Rivers. It was constructed between 1932 and 1937 by two hundred thousand Gulag prisoners, and was heralded as a showcase for the achievements of Soviet Communism.

of alcohol–on the boat, and I drank innumerable cups, because it was excellent and also neutralized the alcohol at the same time.

Today, I dressed in my beautiful white silk suit for the first time, with a blue shirt and the wonderfully matching tie that you bought for me in Venice, and I felt extraordinarily comfortable in it, despite its sensitivity to spots. Did I already tell you that there was a downright tropical heat wave in Moscow in the last few days? Today, it was 28 º [Celsius] in my room at 7.30 in the morning. Because of that, my white suit was a real comfort.

There is nothing going on here concerning purchases at the moment. Aside from an insignificant batch of merchandise, I have not bought anything in July yet, and I am curious to get to the auction. Since a few days ago, the market is supposed to be much firmer, so that everyone is counting on good prices during the auction. The higher they are, the better that I bought before. In any case, I have been right so far in my economic prognosis, which stood in exact opposite to a client of mine who was expecting a Persian lamb downturn. However, that could still take place by the time October gets here. Then, the season is over.

The weather and the location outside Blackpool seem to have brought nothing but disappointment for my beloved little witch, and I feel really sad about it. Nevertheless, I do hope that you will have a good rest and can return to London much strengthened.

I enclose you in my heart. Lost is the little key. You will have to stay inside forever.

Totally and Utterly, Your Mope

VERA TO MOPE

St. Anne's, near Blackpool, 6 July 1938

It is 7.45 in the evening, I am lying comfortably in a lawn chair on our meadow in front of my tent; the sun is shining on my nose (I am wearing the nice blue glasses from Venice, which serve their purpose excellently and which I could not be without now that we have such beautiful sunshine). The air is absolutely calm, and I had not known until now that such a thing as a lull was even possible in St. Anne's. I am feeling great and well-rested.

This morning I received an answer from Joan Stiebel. She wants to write a letter to Mr. Cooper immediately, although the receipts from

Mr. Treger have not arrived yet. Muttilein called him again and he said that he would send them very soon, that he had forgotten about it completely with all that had happened lately. I think he is quite proper! I answered Joan right away today and told her you had been informed that everything would have to be taken care of from here and immediately at that. She told me that she would let me know as soon as she had an answer, and I believe her and hope that the matter is in good hands. You write that you think that my chances at becoming naturalized are greater now. My love, don't you know that I am not counted at all where this is concerned, but only the husband, and that I as the wife am automatically the same nationality as you, at least that is how it is according to English law.

As soon as I get back, I will order the cigarettes for you–maybe Pepper can order them for me in the meantime.

I long for you, a great, great, great longing!!!! Your Lilongo

VERA TO MOPE

St. Anne's, near Blackpool, 9 July 1938

I have to quickly tell you about a small, but very good thing: I heard from Muttilein today that Mr. Treger sent her a receipt for both of us, which she passed along to Mrs. Stiebel immediately. Since I had informed her in detail yesterday–according to your instructions from Mr. Cooper's colleagues–as to where everything should be sent, I hope that the entire matter will be taken care of soon now. I was really relieved!

Today, one of my co-workers who is very nice, but a common girl who worked her way up from the counter to staff floorwalker asked me if I had been born here or *abroad*, and when I told her *abroad* (I did not say where), she asked me if I preferred to live in England or abroad. My most energetic answer was England, but that is not really true. It is any place where I can have my most beloved human beings with me and can make a living, and aside from that, I have actually only lived in two countries, so I cannot really judge if here or *abroad* is better, because the *abroad* we left is truly not a desirable place to stay.

Afterwards, I asked myself if it is not cowardly to tell people what they want to hear, but as I told you at the beginning, she grew up without having been taught to think, and I do not know if it would be right in such cases to say what one is actually thinking concerning such "delicate issues." She told me immediately that she had never been abroad, but no matter what kind of well-paid position she were offered in a foreign country, there was only England for her! *And why should I hurt her feelings!!!*Would you think differently?

My love, despite the miserable weather–it stormed throughout the night and the rain poured down and it also rained during the day–I enjoyed being here for a second week and was really able to relax.

As an approximate limit, we can spend on the girls one shilling and nine pence a head per day here, and of course, it really does not matter if we spend a little more. Our average spending is, bread and jam and marmalade, an apple between breakfast and lunch. Meat and vegetables and a dessert for lunch, a high tea around 6 p.m., and between 9 and 11 p.m. sandwiches, soup, cocoa, and crackers, etc. The girls have all gained a few pounds in weight, and I am sure that I have as well.

Yesterday evening, there was dancing, playing ping-pong, and singing, and everyone seemed to be highly entertained. The rain was coming down in rivers against the tent, but inside, it was so loud that the noise of the weather could be ignored. Although it was very loud, such amusements never overstep the boundaries of a nice and polite tone, despite the fact that the majority of the participants are shopgirls at M&S, contrary to similar entertainments which I participated in with so-called educated people of the university in Germany. While I am writing this, it is storming again, so much so that one could think that someone is shaking out the tarpaulins. I have to close. This will be my last letter from St. Anne's.

I am looking forward to your first report from Leningrad, which I will hopefully receive on Monday. You calculated the mail transportation excellently, since there will be no mail delivery anyway tomorrow. Your little witch

MOPE TO VERA

Leningrad, 10 July 1938

It is 2 o'clock at night, and there is still a lot of work I have to get done before morning, but after I only sent my darling a telegram on the day before yesterday and nothing at all yesterday, I cannot let another day pass by without telling you in writing something I repeat in my thoughts every single minute–and wish that it would get through all the way to you–that I love you unspeakably, without limits, and with everything that I am. Yesterday, your dear letter from the 3rd reached me, and today the one from the 4th, and I am so happy, even when I just see one of those familiar envelopes in my key box, that all the exhaustion caused by the stressful work of the days seems to be gone in a second. We have to get through all the merchandise by tomorrow afternoon, because the banquet that opens the auction will start at 5 o'clock, and following that, a batch of ermine will be auctioned off.

On the day before yesterday, we were invited to a private dinner with the gentlemen of Sojuspushnina during which there was a lot of drinking, which is why I was not feeling well at all yesterday. It lasted from 7.30 p.m. until after 2.00 a.m. and I lost a lot of good work time. Yesterday, I worked until 4 o'clock, and it will probably be even later today. The catalogues for the customers just have to be prepared perfectly, and aside from that, there is a lot of work and a lot of time lost because of certain customers who order me to attend to them for the most trivial things. And during all of that, I have to constantly show a friendly face and ask if the gentlemen had a relaxing afternoon nap, a good night's rest, and something different to eat for dinner.

By the way, we went for a one hour walk today, beginning around 7.30 p.m. We drove to the local cultural park, a wonderful facility that is situated on one of the three islands near Leningrad. I was very glad that I let my colleagues talk me into it, because smelling merchandise all day long and having to breathe inside air becomes unbearable over time with this kind of exhausting work. Nevertheless, people keep complimenting me on looking well, and I do feel in excellent health–knock on wood!

Tomorrow, one of my London-based clients has offered to compose a letter to the Home Office asking for an extension of my papers. According to the papers, they are assuming that I am supposed to stay here until October. It would probably be best to ask Joan Stiebel about what should be written. The number on the paper is "F 4723"–it was issued on May 14 and is valid until August 13. If the extension does not reach the British Consulate in Moscow by June 25, I will have problems, because I would have to apply for my exit visa by then, if the extension does not come through, in order to leave the country on time. *Your* Mope

VERA TO MOPE

London, 10 July 1938

I had a very good trip from Blackpool and arrived here tanned and healthy, and I have been talking to Muttilein until just now–it is past midnight. Now, I am lying in a wonderful, fresh bed–that is a true pleasure after the camp cot. I feel very relaxed and well rested, and I am sure that I have gained a few pounds.

I received a very sweet letter from your dear mother who writes that Grete and Ketty will come to see her in Leipzig and will be there to spend the last few days with her, because she will leave from there permanently around the 15th of the month. I am extremely happy about receiving this news. She and Grete write some especially nice greetings and wishes for you. Ketty had not arrived in Leipzig yet, otherwise, she would also have written something. *Your* Lilongo

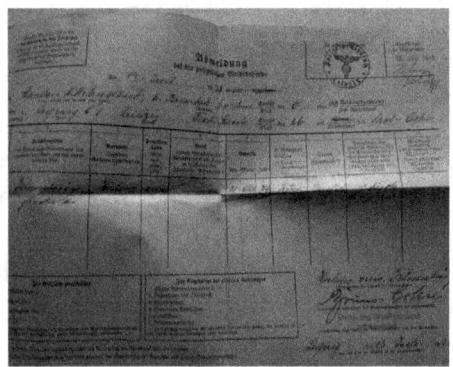

Fig. 81 Helene Felsenstein's "Abmeldung" (Exit Accreditation), Leipzig, 15 July 1938.

MOPE TO VERA

Leningrad, 15 July 1938

While we are waiting here in the Leningrad harbor–in the Sojuspushnina warehouse–I will start to write these lines to my darling –and one of the people traveling home to England is supposed to take them. I did not write to you either yesterday or the day before yesterday. There was such an enormous amount of work that I did not even go to bed during the night from the day before yesterday to yesterday, but had to work through. Yesterday, it was 2 a.m. before I went to bed, but now the main thing is over and I intend to sleep a little more during the next few nights. Tomorrow evening, we will travel back to Moscow and I think that my main customers will stay on for two more days before I can relax just a little.

I love you and long for you unbearably–you!!! Your Mope

VERA TO MOPE

London, 15 July 1938

Just a little while ago, I talked to your dear mother on the telephone. She arrived here safely and seemed to be in quite a good mood. She is staying with Ruth–as I already told you–and will leave in the car with Ruth and her husband for Sheringham[104] early Sunday to visit Hannalein who is on vacation there. Unfortunately, I will not be able to see her before she leaves. I had really hoped that I would be able to go and see her Sunday morning, but that is the time when she is leaving. Your dear mother told me that she had been issued an exit visa for a year, that she is doing very well. In Leipzig, they told her that your things were all free and *not* confiscated.[105] She sends you many loving greetings and wishes and is glad that she is finally here.

She told me that she was already becoming accustomed to being here and that she is very glad to be here and that *everything* had gone very smoothly. Now, she is hoping that all of her things will also arrive soon without any problems, just like it had been planned. Her main wish is to get Grete's and Ketty's families out as well.

I had written to her when she was still in Leipzig to ask if she would not like to stay with us–whilst Hannalein is away. That was Muttilein's wonderful idea and also that we could procure some plates, pots, etc., so that Oma Lenchen can supervise the kosher kitchen herself. I made the suggestion that I would like her to teach me how to cook like she does–as far as my free time allows, because I know that my beloved would be very happy about that. I had hoped in vain that she would perhaps come here!

My love, how indescribably difficult the inspection week with the writing of catalogues must have been, and the necessity of making polite conversation and playing host for the customers. I want to mail this letter

---

104 A seaside resort in Norfolk on the east coast of England.
105 Unfortunately, this turned out to be incorrect, though Oma Lenchen succeeded in retrieving some of Mope's personal items that had been stored in the warehouse at the Gebrüder Felsenstein prior to the confiscation of the business by the Nazis.

today and hope to hear my beloved on the telephone yet today, as soon as I have sent off this letter. Totally and completely, *Your* little witch

MOPE TO VERA

Leningrad, 18 July 1938

I thank you for all your efforts concerning my papers and I am so relieved that everything is coming together and I can do without that gang of pigs who refuses to extend my earlier papers. I think that you can fill out the questionnaires the tax department sent in my name with the remark that the declarations were made from memory. I do not want that gang to be able to accuse me of failing to do something. By the way, I gave a copy of my long letter to a Leipzig "Aryan" who is quite influential there and was here for the auction. He will take the matter on and I am curious to see if that will lead to a more positive result. He has already helped several Jews, which has to be considered very decent coming from an "Aryan" in this day and age.

Now I have to talk about something that makes me a thousand times happier than the order brought to my paperwork and many other things–please forgive me–and that is the fact that my beloved mother got out of that hell healthy and happy. I cannot express in words what that means to me and I ask you to tell her in my name that I feel so much lighter now that that ton of weight, which bore me down, has been taken from me. Had she acted according to my wishes, her emigration would have taken place many years before under much more advantageous circumstances, but it is silly to repeat old news and thereby reduce my happiness which is great indeed.

I kiss you on all your sweet places, those with little nipples, little hairs, little clefts, with my lips and my tongue, until both of us swim in our juices and we fall asleep embracing in exhaustion. How I long *for that*, you sweet, beautiful beloved! Your Mope

MOPE TO VERA

Moscow, 20 July 1938

The trains to and from Leningrad always leave at night so that no one loses any work hours. The trip took between twelve and thirteen hours. Most likely, I will have to go again in a few days to take on more merchandise, but I will probably stay no longer than a day or two. The sad thing is that I will be unable to write to you while I am traveling, because usually I am not alone in the compartment. During the journey back to Moscow, there were *four* of us, and one of those was a farmer's wife who was surely eighty years old. When you travel, you absolutely *have* to travel first class on the trains, because then, there will be two per sleeping compartment instead of four.

I still have a lot of work to do. I took on another three and a half thousand white foxes yesterday. Rather unexpectedly, this article has become quite an important part of our business and I only hope that the customers will do well with it. Their handling takes an inordinate amount of time. Since I have been here, I have bought over £150,000 worth of merchandise, including the auction purchases. That means commission earnings of around £100–apart from my salary. I hope that my darling is satisfied with that.

MOPE TO VERA

Moscow, 23 July 1938

Today, I inserted into my schedule a very lazy day, and tomorrow is Wychodnoi so that I will be able to really rest for once. A year ago, on July 26, I left here to travel to my beloved sweet girl, to you–my wife. We were *very* good friends then and loved each other a lot, but neither one of us had any idea that this year of our marriage would bring us so much closer to each other and ignite our love into such a blaze. Our ability to feel has grown to such dimensions–formerly unknown to us– and because of the two of us, we, or at least, I have become a completely happy and satisfied human being because of my most beloved, sweetest, intelligent Veralein, and the only thing I long for now is to put an end to these unbearable periods of separation so I can feel all the happiness a human being can give to another.

These words will most likely reach you before August 1, maybe even on July 29, the anniversary of my arrival there a year ago, and I feel like thanking the pleasant gentleman at the registrar's office one more time for his help in letting me win my happiness. Do you remember when I was jokingly complaining that I was put in a taxi and "dragged" to the registrar's office? Your dear mother was quite offended at that remark.

What I would not give if I could be with you–at least during these days–and tell you about my love, my joy in you, and my happiness because of you in person, to take you in my arms and kiss you and forget about the difficult times of separation for just a little while.

My most heartfelt thanks for the greetings from my dear mother and I would like to ask you to return them with my love. She will probably arrive back in London around the same time as these words will reach you. So she has decided to move to Ruth's for the time being. Unfortunately, because of the distance, you will most likely not get to see her all that often. A short time ago, I wrote to Fred concerning a potential possibility for Grete and Ketty, but I have not received an answer yet. I would be very happy if we no longer had to deal with that gang of criminals.

Now, I want to go to bed and fall asleep thinking of my sweet darling so that my dreams will carry me to you and let me embrace you and kiss you most tenderly. How bitterly I miss you and all the sweet caresses that our togetherness always brings. I hunger and thirst for you like a desert wanderer. But *no* mirage can pretend to show me my oasis where I can and will slake my thirst. I love you unspeakably and more than anything, you, most beloved!!! *Your* Mope

VERA TO MOPE

London, 25 July 1938

I have quite an exhausting day behind me today. Earlier today I was in Hammersmith–I did not leave there until around 11 o'clock although I was supposed to be in Kilburn at that time. The main discussion centered on the new store in Ealing. They instructed me to hire another forty sales assistants by the end of August! Between now and September 2, I am supposed to go to Ealing as often as possible to interview staff there, to follow up on the establishment of the store, etc.

I was in Kilburn until around 7 o'clock where the entire staff greeted me and said hello in the most touching manner. I never thought it possible that a well-organized and smooth-running machine could become so completely off kilter. My successor, who was fired, left last week. Her successor might be intelligent and very eager and probably even suitable, but her education and training are inadequate, but they have *no one* else, and I tried to give her as much training as possible today, but what is an afternoon for an uncountable number of things!

None of my well-ordered files is there any longer; forms and paperwork are lying in heaps all over the desk, some from as far back as June and some from the beginning of this month, paperwork that has not been taken care of yet. Never has the personnel turn-over been as great as it has been in the last five months. Despite all of that, the store's proceeds have increased while they have gone down just a little in Hammersmith compared to last year's income, because the British Home Stores have become better known.[106]

Just now, I wrote a letter to your dear mother and sent her a word for word copy of the passage in which you express your joy at her emigration. Warburg sent you a bank statement today. It is the itemization of your foreign assets and contains the remark that they have been blocked. Do you want me to send it to you?

I want to get these words to the post office tonight.

Completely and utterly and full of the gentlest love, Your Lilongo

MOPE TO VERA

Moscow, 27 July 1938

I am dead tired and cannot even think right any longer, but I do want to write a few words to you anyway. After I came back from the warehouse, I worked until about 1 a.m. The continuing heat here makes you feel a little exhausted, especially if you sleep little and very restlessly; otherwise, I would not be so tired at this hour of the night.

Tomorrow, I have to pack all my stuff again, because I am traveling to Leningrad. Before I leave, I will receive my extension which arrived at the embassy but will not reach the British consulate until tomorrow, because they have different buildings in different parts of town. I will probably stay in Leningrad for just a few days, so you should keep sending your mail here, because otherwise, I will not have mail in either place.

That is how far I got last night and then, I was unable to continue because my bed was actually screaming for me. Tonight, on the train, I will not be able to write to my darling, unfortunately, because I am sure that I will not be alone in the compartment, since a lot of people are traveling during the tourist season. Now I will close because there are still a few things to be taken care of today. I will try to send the letter by airmail and

---

106 British Home Stores, founded in 1928, became a rival to Marks & Spencer, though aiming at a less affluent clientele. It remained in business until 2016.

I am curious to find out if it will reach you sooner this way. I long for you terribly, because I love you unspeakably and for all eternity, Your Mope

MOPE TO VERA

Leningrad, 29 July 1938

Another long day has gone by and I finally get around to my darling to whom I was unable to write yesterday–before the departure to here. After I had the visa in my hands around 4 p.m. yesterday, I went to see the consul who received me in a friendly manner and extended my papers until the end of the year. A large burden was lifted off my shoulders and I thank you, my beloved girl, from the bottom of my heart for all your efforts.

My trip here appears to be for nothing, unfortunately, because I cannot see how I will be able to come to a business deal. We, a few colleagues and I, arrived here around 10.00 this morning. The trip took place on one of those especially organized first class trains–for a *"cruise"* of Americans–on a German ship, no less–and it was quite comfortable. I shared the compartment with one of the colleagues and next door, there were two American women–we talked to them for a few hours before turning in for the night. In the end, I gave one of them your telephone number and address–she is going to London in a few days–so that she can pass along my most loving greetings to you.

Today, a young father from New York told me during dinner everything a woman should do during pregnancy and after the birth of the child, and I so wish to put my new knowledge to practical use with my beloved in the near future. Actually, I do not agree with his statement that a young mother should not breastfeed her baby. He claimed that– one of your prettiest decorations–the breast would be irreversibly enlarged. I think that that is not correct, and even if it is, we do know that it would be necessary for a very important reason, and I would not like you even *one iota less*. Additionally, he said that a woman should not gain any weight during pregnancy which is something I cannot judge at all. The child would not have to be heavier than six pounds and would have more room to move in the mother's womb, room that would not be available for very heavy children. Here I am divulging all my wisdom much too early–wisdom I lack any kind of proof for–because I think that you are interested as well, since you are the one who will experience all of that in person.

In my thoughts, I embrace you and kiss you with all my love and filled with boundless longing for my sweetest, most beloved being, my beautiful Lilongo. Your Mope

VERA TO MOPE

London, 29 July 1938

I had the afternoon off today and since I was dead-tired I lay down and rested for a little while. This morning, I trained five new girls and talked to them for about two and a half to three hours with the utmost concentration and drilled them, and beforehand and afterwards, I took care of a lot of things I deemed necessary. I only found *one* girl for Ealing and I am not all that sure of her yet. I am hoping to find two additional floor walkers who have already held that position for some time and would like a relocation and a raise. Enough shop!!!!!

Today, after dinner, I called Fred at the office. He was getting ready to depart for Sheringham again for the bank holiday. He said that the court case concerning the Antwerp merchandise will begin after September 15, after the court recess is over.

Most heartfelt, passionate kisses, my friend and the only man I love, my husband. I am completely and utterly, body and soul, *your* Lilongo

MOPE TO VERA

Leningrad, 31 July 1938

I have already put all my words of love into my letters in the last few weeks and now, they are just repetitions but the feelings are so great and new every day and, if that was even possible, heightened daily in infinite love for you who are the substance of my life. I hope that all my love letters have reached you in time and give my beloved a little joyful feeling on this special day by what they would like to and are meant to express.

It is going to be 11 p.m. soon where you are and my golden girl will lie down in her lonely bed and think the way I do, that two people who love each other so boundlessly and completely should be able to lie together on this day and give each other all the tenderness and love they feel. How my fingertips yearn for the voluptuous feeling of caressing your skin and come closer and closer to your sweetest Muschi and feel it become excited and swell, and how your entire body begins to yearn for the union with mine. How all the muscles loosen and everything prepares itself just for one thing, to receive the seed, just like the blooms in the field and on the meadow are waiting devotedly to be inseminated by the dust that will be brought to them. How my entire body and my entire soul is enlivened by the wish to be united with you in the highest delight, with you, feeling you with all my pores, to call out to you, "Come to me quickly, my beloved, and let us enjoy *this* day and the many that separated us, because they are now part of the past–and we can make up for lost time."[107]

When these lines reach my beloved, there will still be a month between us, such a terribly long time when so much homesickness and such burning, smoldering longing has to be bridged. We have been married a year today and it seems to me as if we have been together for a lifetime and it seems like the day of our wedding was yesterday. What an infinite abundance of experiences lies between those two great days!! Do you really know *how* much I love you? You! Mine, MINE!!! Completely and utterly Your Mope

VERA TO MOPE

London, 31 July 1938

My beloved! One year ago today, we were together and celebrated our wedding. I was Mrs. Felsenstein already and the wedding celebration was still in front of us. Yesterday evening, when I arrived home around 9.45 p.m., I found a card telling me that flowers had been left there for me. I found a box with sixty carnations and each one prettier than the next. They glow and fill the small writing room in which I am putting these words on paper with their peculiar fragrance. They are dark red, pale pink, white, and violet and beautify my free days and liven up my loneliness.

---

[107] Mope is very loosely echoing the lines from the biblical Song of Solomon, 2:10-14.

Twenty-eight:
Visas, Visas, Visas

1 August through 21 September 1938

To conserve the limited time allocated to his visits to England, Mope was encouraging Vera to join him in the Soviet Union for the duration of her upcoming vacation. Since she too would now be traveling using stateless documents, the process of obtaining permits was less than simple, particularly so as it involved two-ways transit visas for Denmark, Sweden, and Finland, in addition to a visitor's visa to Russia. The correspondence provides fascinating details of a convoluted process, and of their shared frustration when the denial of a transit visa through Finland prevented Vera from traveling to Russia. In hindsight, given the political crises of late summer 1938 that led to the Munich accord, it was for the best that she did not venture east. As a fall-back, Mope advised applying for French visas with the notion that they could meet on the Riviera.

For Vera, Friday, 2 September, the due date for the opening of the new M&S store in the west London suburb of Ealing, was already a red letter, both because of the necessity to hire and train nearly seventy shop girls for the store, and because she knew that she could not travel to join Mope until after the "big day" was done. Her letters give some indication of the level of her success.

With the change of season and the limits imposed on Mope's residency in England, the south of France was a preferable place for them to unwind and rediscover their intimacy. "I will always keep preserved in my memory," voices Mope, "those most beautiful nights filled with the most tender and wildest love making with my most adorable darling." For each of them the ultimate expression of their love was the desire to start a family. The first entry for more than a year in Vera's private journal records her thoughts on this. After their return to London in October, Mope had to count down to December, when his visa restrictions would force him to depart once again.

From both sides, the correspondence is peppered with mainly pessimistic news and observations about the situation of Jews in Germany. Mope's brother-in-law, Dr. Norbert Moschytz, in common with other Jewish physicians, was on the point of being dismissed from his position in Freiburg and looked with despair for employment elsewhere. Mope's sister, Ketty Goldschmidt, and her family, were still in Hamburg, waiting to emigrate once the necessary permits were granted. Cousins from Karlsruhe, Carl and Lies Rosenfeld, were on a brief visit to England in hope of finding work there for their two young sons as a means of getting them out of Germany. To her relief, Annelie Freimann, who announced her engagement to marry, had now obtained most of the requisite papers to settle in the United States. After getting her parents out of Germany, Vera's best friend and her husband, Hilde and Walter Lewy, still living in Genoa, were also looking toward the United States, having finally awoken to the precariousness of their lives in fascist Italy. The expanding list provides a microcosm of the frenetic circumstances and limited options still available to Germany's Jews in their search for political refuge in countries that might yet offer them the security of a new home. The violence against those Jews that was to take place on Kristallnacht (9-10 November), often seen as the pogrom that ushered in the Holocaust, underlined the absolute urgency of this search.

MOPE TO VERA

Leningrad, 1 August 1938

It will be 11 o'clock soon and the day of our wedding anniversary is approaching its end. My colleagues and I came back from the harbor around 5.00 p.m. and decided to have our dinner in the roof garden of the Hotel Europejsky for a change. That was more than welcome to me, because I wanted to have the opportunity to drink to my darling's well-being. Our mood improved gradually and I ordered a bottle of champagne—everyone was quite happy with that—and we emptied our glasses to your happiness, your well-being, and *our* hoped for offspring. When I wanted to pay, they refused and divided the expenses. They told me that the idea was the most important thing, not paying the bill. I thought that was marvelously decent.

It will be midnight soon, and a completely different anniversary begins, the one of the declaration of war twenty-four years ago.[108] Since that time, small fires are burning again everywhere, and the

---

[108] Germany declared war against Russia on 1 August 1914 in the chain of events that began the First World War.

irresponsibility of some countries' "leaders" has brought a new danger of war closer than the grim experiences should permit. Four years ago, for the twentieth anniversary of the declaration of war, they issued anti-war stamps here, stamps that I am using on my letter today. All the peoples should be shown such horrifying pictures of terror in order to bring them back to reason and make them refuse sacrificing their loved ones again for such nonsensical cruelty, as they are already doing in Spain and China.[109]

I kiss and embrace you filled with the gentlest love and with my happiness in the knowledge of you. Most passionately, you! Your Mope

VERA TO MOPE

London, 5 August 1938

I was very interested in what you told me in your letter of July 29 concerning your conversation about pregnancy. Of course, I intend to breastfeed our child, once we have one, because that is most certainly the best thing for it. It is utter nonsense that a woman should not gain any weight and you can tell your friend so (please don't!), because most of the organs change temporarily during pregnancy, as any beginning medical student learns during the first week.

Thank you for having had a drink to my health on August 1! Did you feel how close to you I was???!!! And am?!!! When will you know how long you will be able to stay and when you will be able to come back?!!! Or if we will be together there, you!!!!

Please let me know once again about the ticket to Russia–single or return,–the travel agent seemed to think a return ticket would be better. I applied for a French, Danish, Swedish, and Finnish visa. And I received the identification paper valid for one year![110] *Your* Lilongo

MOPE TO VERA

Moscow, 6 August 1938

Although today was Wychodnoi, I worked the entire day until late into the night. Around 12.30, there was a telephone call from Schapiro. He

---

109 Mope is referring to the Civil War in Spain and to the Second Sino-Japanese War.
110 As her passport and papers had been confiscated by the German authorities and her citizenship revoked, Vera would have had to travel using a "stateless" identification paper issued by the British authorities.

told me that I should have my visa extended, and I responded that I would be applying for my exit visa. "Well, whatever you want," was the answer and then, "Didn't your wife write to you that she is coming?" I told him that that would not happen at my expense, that I could not afford that. He: "Well, we shall see about that later." I acted as if I did not know anything and then he asked if I had not written to you to tell you that you should apply for a visa which I answered in the affirmative, of course. In the letter to him I wrote, "Concerning my wife's travel to Moscow, I have to consider if that is the right thing to do. If I have to work until late into the night, she won't get anything out of her vacation!! After all, she is supposed to relax when she is on vacation." If we cannot have at least fourteen days we can spend together in peace and quiet, the trip will be nothing but a strain for you.

I am exhausted and my brain is filled with nothing but business. And when you are here, my heart would be so engrossed with you that there would have to be conflict between heart and mind. I will make everything dependent on your extra vacation time. Please let me know about your decision as soon as possible and don't be annoyed at me for blackmailing you like this. Please show me how much you love me by getting some extra vacation time approved.

Tomorrow evening, I will travel to Leningrad again for a few days. The last visit did show some success as I ploughed through a deal for a little under £ 5000. It was anything but easy, but I do feel more satisfied now.

I hope that Hilde Lewy is doing well and that the child (boy or girl?) is growing. I have to affirm that it would be right to let her parents come to Genoa as well, because, if the older generation can no longer enjoy their children, their lives lose all meaning under the current conditions. Unfortunately, danger reigns all over Europe and in any event, the youth is more threatened than the older generation to whom the anti-Semitic methods in Germany seemed to be more bearable. I would like to ask you to definitely talk to Fred about my things and find out about any possibility that might exist to get them out of Germany. The longer we wait, the more difficult it will become. Your Mope

VERA TO MOPE

London, 7 August 1938

My love, I am wondering what you were doing today. You had Wychodnoi yesterday, didn't you? I would really like to know if you are still in Leningrad or on your way back already, maybe you are back in Moscow by now? Yesterday, our travel agent sent me the identification paper. It is valid for one year until August 1939. He also sent me the paperwork for a Finnish, French, and Swedish visa, and I sent all of it back with photographs today. He is going to send the Danish one soon.

When it comes down to it, the only thing I want is to be with you, you!!!!!–And I am feeling quite sad when my love doubts my wishes and my longing to be with him!!!! You do know that I have a job by the way that does not allow me to be completely free and make decisions on my authority alone, and that my most important fulfilling job is to be your wife. That I hope you know and feel as well!!!! Please believe me when I say that I will never forget my beloved because of M&S!!! You seem to think that I try to numb myself with M&S, because how else would I be able to stand it otherwise??????? For me, it is the only salvation–to have an occupation that takes up all of my time, in which I can immerse myself completely–otherwise, I would simply *not* be able to bear these times of separation. I am sure that my beloved will accept that and agree with it.

Your dear mother and Hannalein and children will be coming back next Wednesday and as soon as I have had a chance to talk to your mother and received more information about the matter of your furniture I will talk to Fred immediately to see what can be done. Your boss, with whom I talked about the matter, considered it impossible to get your things out and also senseless to contact a shipping agent in Leipzig from over here. As I said, I will do what Fred advises me to do! Completely and utterly, Your Lilongo

MOPE TO VERA

Leningrad, 8 August 1938

After I worked in the Moscow office of Sojuspushnina until 7.45 in the evening, I left around 8.25. Since I was by myself in the train compartment, I intended to write another typed letter to my beloved, but all of a sudden, such a tiredness announced itself that I decided to lie down for a little while and when I woke up, the train had arrived at the Kalinin[111] station shortly before midnight, according to the people talking at the station platform. At that late hour, I did not want to risk

---

111 Present-day Tver, a city situated at the confluence of the Volga and Tvertsa rivers.

disturbing my neighbors with my typing and really went to bed, that is, undressed. I hope that my sweet girl will not be too sad to have been without news for a day.

My day today was quite busy. I went to the harbor where I inspected merchandise until 2.30. After that, I made some visits to the various rooms of my colleagues to find out what kind of merchandise they had seen, where I have to watch out for the competition, how they rate the merchandise, etc.

That's enough about work! This afternoon, I went on a wonderful outing to Zaoskojc Selo–now it is called Puschkin–to the former castles of the Czar. One of the castles, immense and beautifully furnished, was built by the daughter of Peter the Great. They told us that, after construction was finished, the architect went to her and said that something was missing, that the castle was such a jewel it needed a treasure chest to which she answered that the castle was the treasure chest and she was the jewel that was placed in it. The lady seems to have been quite taken with herself. The second smaller castle was built by his grandmother for Alexander I. While the first one was constructed mainly in the baroque style, the second one is of pure classical construction but it was spoilt by paintings that were hung in such a way that they disturb the classical lines. The newer wing that was inhabited by the last Czars was built in the hideous Art Nouveau style. However, it is very interesting because everything was left exactly as it was when the family left on 31 July 1917. Enormous numbers of family portraits, icons of saints, and small, rather worthless household items can be seen everywhere. Actually, it is the residence of a wealthy bourgeois family that was not exactly blessed with good taste. The most beautiful things are the library rooms that Nicholas II supposedly had little interest in and had been established by his ancestors. There are also quite a few mementos of the criminal, arrogant, but nevertheless historically important priest Rasputin. His pitiful handwriting shows that he must have been little more than an illiterate. The Czarina, a princess from Darmstadt, appears to have been the stronger one in the marriage but she was so horribly superstitious that one becomes convinced that these people earned their fate. It is terrible to think that such human beings were responsible for the fate of a great and powerful people. Some women who were with us were extremely interested in all the photographs and personal items and seemed quite excited in looking at all the things once considered taboo for "ordinary mortals." It was also quite interesting to me to watch that reaction.[112]

With all these stories, I completely forgot to tell my beloved that the cigarettes arrived yesterday and tasted so good to me, after several weeks of smoking Russian and various other mooched cigarettes. My most heartfelt thanks for taking care of that for me! You did a great service of love for me by doing that. The expense also seems to have been less than for the Du Maurier you sent to me the last time, because the price of the cigarettes was only 23/–to which you have to add shipping and customs, of course, but I do not know how much that was.

I am sure that you were able to talk to my dear mother in detail in the meantime and were informed about how her emigration took place. I really hope that she did not suffer too much upset because of it. I would be interested in finding out whether or not Max (Erich Gödicke) is still a decent person or if he can now be counted among the pigs because of the times we live in. I would also like to hear about Semy's plans. I really do feel sorry for him, even if he did not always go along with our wishes. *Your* Mope

VERA TO MOPE

London, 9 August 1938

I suppose that my beloved is still in Leningrad just now. I was so very happy that your earlier trip showed such success and I hope and wish that this one will also show such positive results, because I know how success in your work heightens the mood, even if a lout like Schapiro does not acknowledge it. Please, my love, do not let that one depress you; he is too ill-mannered and loutish for you to even react to him in any way or show that you do. I am sure that you agree with me on that?!!!

Today, I called the travel agent once again: he will apply for a Finnish, Danish, and Swedish transit visa for my trip there and back and also

---

112 The town of Pushkin (Tsarskoye Selo) outside present-day St. Petersburg, is the site of the Catherine Palace, built by Czarina Catherine II (known as Catherine the Great), and of the Aleksandrovsky Palace, which was the home of Nicholas II, the last Czar. The Catherine Palace was destroyed during the Second World War but has been reconstructed. Mope is mistaken in believing that this palace was built by the daughter of Peter the Great.

for a stay in France. I told him that we also wanted to spend some time in Sweden and he thought that it would be difficult to get a visa for a stay there. Would it not be better if you were to apply for a Russian exit visa so that you have the alternative of coming to me right away if I do not receive my visa? Or maybe I can meet you in Sweden but that is not possible because the visa will be issued for transit only. What should I do???

Please send me your answer immediately and also instruct me concerning the various visas! You have a much better overview on just how many business deals you might miss out on if you do not stay there. You are still a better judge than I can be from over here. Do others stay as long as you??? It seems to me that you are *the only one* among your colleagues who has to stay there for that long!!! Should you depart from there around the beginning of September, I would suggest that I arrange to meet you in Sweden or Holland or somewhere else, or maybe *France*.

From noon on, I was in Ealing today and everything was going topsy-turvy. The replacement staff floorwalker who comes from Richmond is absolutely not equal to the task. She is working under unusually difficult circumstances because she is facing a staff that is completely untrained, and works in a store in which a smooth course has not been established yet. I was there until around 7.30 this evening and I will go back tomorrow afternoon. The store has more personnel than Hammersmith and needs a *capable* staff manager, but there is *none* at the moment! If those people paid better salaries, they would not have any problems to find able staff managers. Altogether, I have been very, very busy in the store: I now have forty-four *sales assistants* for Ealing and altogether, I will need between sixty and sixty-five.

I love you completely and utterly and passionately, *Your* little Lilongo-witch

MOPE TO VERA

Leningrad, 10 August 1938

Your last, ever so beloved letter that reached me was dated July 31 and I almost feel forgotten, without news. I am expecting a telegram from you with such huge yearning, almost as if it were a small piece of my beloved herself. I have no idea yet how many days I will have to stay here. It could be that I will travel back to Moscow tomorrow or in five days. For this reason, I cannot have your mail forwarded to me, because that usually takes at least two days *if* it is sent off right away which is something I cannot count on.

I waited for a telegram from you until late into the evening, and instead Schapiro's cable arrived announcing that he would call that night. That means that I will have to wait up until late into the night, and more likely than not, for nothing. Why doesn't that idiot telegraph like every other normal human being? It is much better for me when I have things in front of me in black on white and can show, if need be, what is wanted, while such a conversation, difficult to understand at best, only informs me of half of it. That man is incorrigible with all that telephoning.

Outside, a full moon is beaming brightly. It is looking down on both of us at the same time. Right here, it is looking down into my window. If I could just be–for just a minute even–the man in the moon and look down on my sweetest little girl and then return to my desk, calmed and content. However, the moon does know that I would not be happy with that one minute, because, if I were in it, I would want to look and look until I was satisfied and there would be no end to it. That is why the man in the moon does not switch places with me and is taken aback when I look at him so filled with wishful thinking, because he knows that wishes, filled with such enormous longing, can be stronger than he, and he would like to just hide behind a cloud. But there is no cloud to be seen near or far. So everyone has his own worries and it is almost satisfying to us poor residents of earth to know that even the man in the moon is not free either. I am sure that my darling is laughing at me now because I give way to my imagination which is why I am telling you that the gentleman himself just told me that–how else could I come up with such a story (a story you might believe or not!)???—

There has been no trace of Schapiro's call and it will be 1.30 a.m. soon. I will wait for another half hour and then let the telephone department know that I will no longer accept the telephone call if it does come through. I will no longer consider letting myself be made crazy. Why does that man use such enervating methods to make business more difficult for me and for himself?

I will now wish my darling a good night; it is high time that you go to sleep! I kiss you everywhere and caress and bite and open your sweet little legs so I can give you all the love and your Muschi will react to this love in the sweetest way and your entire beautiful body can concentrate on sharing all the feelings and share all the desire I am able to make you feel. When will it finally, finally be that time when all of it will come true, everything I dream of and long for with such pain? When will I be allowed to take you in my arms and bring every pore of your body close to mine, to feel you and relish in the enjoyment of having you close to me?

My little girl, you!!!! Your Mope

The announcement of the telephone call from Schapiro came in at 2 a.m. and we finally talked at 2.30!

VERA TO MOPE

London, 12 August 1938

Yesterday, after dinner, I talked to Hannalein on the telephone. She asked me to inform you that starting this fall, Norbert and all his colleagues of the same race may *no* longer practice medicine, which is terrible, of course.[113] After that, I talked to your dear mother who is at Ruth's at the moment. She said that her things have not come in yet from Germany and she is quite annoyed about the delay and hopes that that is all it is. Ruth whom I talked to on the phone for a short time as well told me how disastrous the business situation is at the moment and how happy she would be if Heinz had a steady income she could rely on. And that she often did not know how and with what to take care of everything.

I have to close now! This morning, I will go to Hammersmith first and then to Ealing.

I have to go, it is late! I was *not* able to read through this scribble!

Most passionate, most loving, sweetest kisses, you—

MOPE TO VERA

Leningrad, 12 August 1938

Apart from a leisurely drive along the Newa and an evening walk, I spent this Wychodnoi in my room reading. It is still very hot here but

---

[113] A decree of 25 June 1938 barred German-Jewish doctors from treating non-Jewish patients with effect from the autumn. Mope's brother-in-law, Dr. Norbert Moschytz, was still in practice in Freiburg im Breislau, and his wife (Grete) and their four children remained with him.

there is a breeze which is refreshing. It has not rained even once in Leningrad since July 8 while there have been a few thunderstorm rains in Moscow now and again but they do not bring any cool-down either. If I get done with my work in the harbor on time tomorrow, I want to go to Peterhof, a castle with many fountains in front of it–it is supposed to be very beautiful. The work here actually takes up much less time than the work in Moscow, but you have to wait for an eternity until it is your turn for the drive to the harbor for the merchandise inspection because only two people can work there at the same time. Sometimes, we get around to discussing what we inspected, usually in the evening around 9 p.m. or even later so that it is difficult to do anything else. The scheduling is better in Moscow and I would really like to go back soon because I am sure that there are many letters from my darling waiting for me.

Tomorrow in three weeks is September 3 and I assume that my sweet girl will leave by boat from Hull to Helsingfors that same day or will fly to Riga via Stockholm on the 5th. If you took the boat, you would arrive here on Friday, September 9, so that you would be in Moscow on Saturday, September 10. If you fly, which I consider the better choice, you would arrive in Moscow on the 6th–aside from the Sunday in between which you can use to pack your things. The plane leaves Croydon in the morning at 9.50, via Amsterdam, then Copenhagen-Malmö to Stockholm where it will arrive at 16.20. The next morning, you will leave Stockholm at 9 a.m. via Riga to Moscow where I will take you in my arms at 18.05 (Russian time) and be *indescribably happy* to *finally* see you again. Completely and utterly, *Your* Mope

VERA TO MOPE

London, 12 August 1938

Today, I made up my mind definitively to leave here on September 4 by air. We will just have to pay the difference between air and boat from our own pocket. Should I fly to Moscow or to Leningrad????? Schapiro sent me £40.–today and enclosed a letter to me with the following content, which, for him, was extremely *friendly*:

> "I believe that your husband will have to remain in Moscow for business reasons. I have already written to him concerning the matter. I do not know for how long, since that does not depend on me, but is dictated by business. In order for Mr. Felsenstein to stay as long as possible, I

suggested that you join him there. Unfortunately, we cannot promise that he will travel back with you. I do not oppose you staying over there for a longer period of time and wait until he can depart, but I do not know if that is possible for you. It is possible that he will have to stay for another month after you leave to travel home, but maybe that will not be necessary. However, it is impossible at this time for me to make any firm commitment, as I mentioned above. No one can say if he will leave at the beginning or the end of October."

My love, today, I filled out a fourth French visa and enclosed four passport photos and I sent my identity paper and book to our travel agent, since he needs both of them for the consulates. I will leave here in three weeks from Sunday–hurrah, hurrah, hurrah!!!!!

MOPE TO VERA

Leningrad, 17 August 1938

Tomorrow, I will find out if and what kinds of merchandise can be expected to arrive here in the next few days. Once I am back in Moscow, I will try to reach you by telephone because this surrogate–writing–is not as good as talking on the telephone–and I want to hear your voice at least! As soon as you receive your visa for here, send me a telegram and also let Schapiro know immediately. It should be much easier to get the other visas.

My work here seems to be mostly done. I am thinking of inspecting a few more things on the 19th and then go back to Moscow in the evening where I will hopefully be able to stay at the National this time. You cannot imagine how much I am looking forward to, and long for, finding your beloved letters there. The time I spent here was very difficult to bear and I am ever so grateful to you for having beautified that time twice with your telegrams which also let me feel much calmed where your well-being is concerned. Your Mope

VERA TO MOPE

London, 17 August 1938

This morning, your telegram arrived and I found out that you are still in Leningrad. I keep sending my letters to Moscow. I hope that someone brought them to you from there. I filled out all of the paperwork for the

Swedish consulate today and I hope that everything will be taken care of soon. The travel agent received the Danish one today, the one for the return trip as well, as he told me, and he will let the Swedish and Finnish consulates know about it because he hopes that that will help. I got in contact with the Swedish consulate by telephone because the agent wrote this morning that I would have to go there myself. However, that was not necessary–I only had to give them the dates of my travel. My love, tomorrow, it will be three weeks ago that the Russian visa was applied for at Intourist, or actually the day after tomorrow, and this evening, our agent said on the telephone that it usually takes around three to four weeks. I just wish that it would finally, finally come through!!!!!

It is really a good thing that I am so very busy right now and have so many things to do. They left the entire personnel question to me. If I were not so occupied, at least in my thoughts, during the day, I do *not* know how I would get through these last two and a half weeks of our current time of separation. Tomorrow, I will go to Ealing to interview more staff there during the afternoon. I went to the labor department around noon today and hired seven of the fourteen girls I saw there. I still have to hire around thirteen more and have a lot of work ahead of me since I am supposed to find floor walkers for the other stores.

I received a letter from Hildelein in Genoa yesterday evening in which she tells me that that they are strongly considering the possibility of a second emigration. I was quite shaken; her brother-in-law's children are no longer allowed to attend school there. I wrote to her that she and Walter should visit us for an investigative trip just as soon as possible. Actually, she asked me if they would have a chance over here. She had been told that it was completely out of the question to ever be allowed to come to this country. However, since we have seen that such things are considered on a very individual basis, I do not consider it impossible. In the meantime, they have added their names to an immigration list for the U.S.A., although they have not made any definite plans yet. The furniture from Hilde's parents in Frankfurt has arrived and they hope for calmer times now.[114] Things really are not all that nice right now and one has to be grateful all over again every single day to be at some distance from all of that; for how long it will remain in the distance remains to be seen, of course.

---

114 Hilde's parents had by now succeeded in emigrating from Frankfurt.

I hope that I will be able to find something out for Grete and Norbert concerning Costa Rica.[115] Fred and Hannalein came by for a little while yesterday evening, and we compiled a series of questions concerning emigration prospects with further help from your dear mother, who looks very well indeed. She really is a very special woman, who possesses intelligence and kindness in the same measure. She and I got along famously. She did not take *anything* out with her when she left Leipzig, and they promised to send her personal things but nothing has arrived here to this day. Max (Erich Gödicke) seems to have been quite decent. However, he did say that he did not have any of your personal things anymore when your dear mother questioned him.

My love, it seems completely improbable, but when you looked at the moon so closely Wednesday evening and charged it with all those wishes, I went for a short evening walk down Northend Road with Muttilein and the full moon shone down on us and I said (there is an eye witness for this) how much I wished to be the moon who can look down on my beloved!—

Completely and utterly Your Lilongo

MOPE TO VERA

Leningrad, 18 August 1938

Our outing today was definitely worth the time. The drive to Peterhof, a wonderful park with various castles which were begun by Peter the Great[116] and then continued and expanded by several other czars and czarinas leads along a well-built road that nears the ocean at the halfway mark. The first castle in the park that should actually be called a pretty bungalow was built by Peter the Great himself directly on the water of the Finnish Bay and ever since then has been preserved as a museum or a memorial of this unique great one of the house of Romanov. His wife Katherine I had a different castle which was built of wood but that

---

115 In 1937, land had been purchased in Costa Rica for the purpose of settling Jews from Central Europe, but, in the face of government anti-Semitism, it was decreed that this was illegal. Very few Jewish refugees were able to settle in the country, and Mope's brother-in-law, Norbert Moschytz, opposed attempting such a move.

116 Peter I (called "the Great"), 1672-1725, became Czar on his father's death in 1682. It was he who founded the city of Saint Petersburg (Leningrad). Peterhof and its palaces became a sumptuous summer retreat for the Czars of Russia.

was replaced by her daughter with one constructed of stone. Peter's bedroom is a tiny room with a very small bed in it, a bed that makes an extremely chaste impression. I would have furnished it differently after I met my sweetest girl but earlier, I would have been very sympathetic of this method of sleeping in separate rooms.

Peter the Great seems to have been quite taken with fountains which he created in such a way in part that he could satisfy his desire to play tricks on people. Directly in the vicinity of his house, for instance, there is a bench he used to sit down on when he received guests who would stand in front of him filled with reverence. In the ground in front of that bench, nearly invisible water pipes were installed which could be activated from a distance at a wave of his hand. The water would spring from the ground up to three meters high from both sides and the two streams would then unite in the middle and cool the guest down to the skin. At a little distance from there is a mushroom-like construction with benches arranged in a circle around the stem. If someone sat down there, he would have water bubble from the outer edge of the mushroom roof, and it was impossible to leave the area which was so nicely protected from the sun without getting thoroughly drenched. Well, this is not the main side of this very progressive monarch who is still much beloved by his people, but it is interesting to see how people "amused" themselves back then.

In the 1760s, in his last years or shortly after his death, they built a wonderful arrangement of fountains with the help of a French expert that made Peterhof into a second Versailles. The water needed was brought in from about 25 kilometers away by laying down the appropriate water pipes. In my opinion, Peterhof is more beautifully situated than Versailles because of the adjacent ocean (of course, they could not use the ocean water for the fountains because, despite its relatively low salt content, it would have clogged and corroded the pipes very quickly). The immense and especially beautiful park has been open and available to the public since 1926. There are bands there every afternoon–they play concert and dance music and in some places, people can be seen dancing in the park. On display in one of the walkways, there are extraordinarily humorous caricatures–painted on canvas–which show the generals of the world war and also the current enemies of Russia. These caricatures show the visitors whom they got away from and what they might have to face if they are not careful. A very interesting method of education for the masses that look at these paintings with great interest!

My little girl, the day is over and the new one has begun already and I want to go to bed and continue chatting with you–not as visible to you though–until, instead of my darling, Morpheus takes me into his arms. I hope that that will make you jealous and gives you even more reason to come as quickly as you can. Your Mope

VERA TO MOPE

London, 18 August 1938

Today, I did not have the afternoon off and hired an additional four girls in Ealing so that I have sixty-one girls now. The new store will open tomorrow in two weeks and all in all, I need sixty-five girls, that is salesgirls, on top of that, I need a presser and another three weekend girls, added to the two I have already hired. About forty of them are training in other stores, like Chiswick, Fulham, and Hammersmith, and the other twenty-five will come to Ealing on the 29th where a staff trainer and I will train them until opening day. This morning, I found a few more serviceable girls in Chiswick and so, everything seems to develop satisfactorily, at least where the staff is concerned.

What was very interesting is that quite a few girls from *British Home Stores* and other similar stores in the vicinity of Ealing applied for positions with us, although they would not receive higher salaries from us for the most part. They told me, "*We have heard that M&S is such a good firm to work for! And that one has a chance to get on there and to get promotions!*"

One of the directors, Simon Marks' brother-in-law, came to Ealing last Tuesday for a tour and I suppose that the entire company will appear for the opening or at some time during the first two days.[117]

My love, this morning at the station in Chiswick, before I left for Ealing, I called the Intourist bureau and they told me that my visa was expected to arrive with the next mail from there and will probably be here next week. I will be in Leningrad on Monday and on Tuesday, my beloved will claim me at the train station in Moscow.

---

117 Simon Marks's brothers-in-law, Israel Sieff (much later Lord Sieff of Brimpton), and Harry Sacher were both directors of M&S. It is uncertain which of the two was the visitor that day.

I wonder what my beloved is doing right now. It is 10.45 here now and I am writing from the chaise longue in the dining room and Muttilein and Pepper are playing cards. I will close now and go to bed and dream myself to you. Your little witch

VERA

Journal entry, 21 August 1938

It seems to have been a long time since I wrote anything here the last time. The reason for that is not a lack of experiences, but simply the fact that my beloved man spent most of the year separated from me–and even now, he is still gone–and I already wrote down everything that worried me when I wrote to him every day. Today, I also sent him a very detailed report, but still, I reach for this little book.

The reason: there is something bothering me, something I want to come to terms with for myself, for the time being anyway: Both of us would like to have a child. Mopelein received his residence permit around the end of May. I am 28 ½ years old, so what is keeping us from fulfilling our wish? I will probably have to give up my career after about four months, at least temporarily! So I will no longer be able to help out my beloved Muttilein on my own, and what shall she and Pepper do then? I know that my Mopelein will do everything he can for them here; but will he be able to do that? It is entirely possible that he will lose his current position during my pregnancy, and that means he will get *no* visa!!! What to do? And on top of that: you want to bring a human being into this world that is full of hatred, strife, and spitefulness?

No, I am allowed to do it anyway! Even while I am writing all of this down, my thoughts are clearing and I realize: I can bring *one* child into this world for us–we need it!

1. We want to give living expression to our love!
2. We want to learn with and from our child and stay young and agile because of it.
3. It will provide us–maybe and I hope so–with the answer to why and what for. It's not that I wish to get an answer from our child and not from each other, but I hope that our child will be such that it will *also* mean an answer to us.

4. Since I am not all that young any longer, we cannot wait much longer.
5. I have more than enough (jewelry and other things) to help my Muttilein until I can work again!
6. I hope that I will become more mature and understanding because of the experience of pregnancy and childbirth.
7. I am looking forward to *our child*!

MOPE TO VERA

Moscow, 21 August 1938

If you only knew what a relief it was for me to receive a large number of most beloved letters from you waiting for me in Moscow. Back in Leningrad, I had been so unsettled waiting to get newer messages from my beloved. Since I do not belong to those people who want to enjoy things a little at a time, but to those who want to enjoy everything to the fullest, I called you in the evening and was overjoyed when I heard your beloved voice and to assure myself of your well-being–as far as that can be done by telephone. Since it was difficult to understand anything at first, I complained immediately after the call, and so, I had the great joy of having a really nice chat with you. They were decent enough to only charge me six minutes for the entire call, that is, they did not charge for the unintelligible part at all.

I was unable to do anything when in Leningrad concerning your visa, and yesterday and today I tried to hurry things up. Since you will receive an Intourist and not a consulate visa, there seems little that Sojuspushnina can do for it. Please keep the choice whether your first stop will be Moscow or Leningrad open for the time being. The first stay overnight has to be in the city the visa is made out for. The matter is a little complicated.

Your plan to fly to Helsingfors and then take the train to Leningrad sounds great to me. However, I do not think that you will be able to reach the evening train to Leningrad. The airplane arrives at the Helsingfors airport at 9.40 in the evening and train leaves Leningrad at approximately the same time, as far as I know. Maybe, the train can be reached on time after the airplane lands? If not, you might have to stay in Helsingfors for a day. In that case, I recommend either the Hotel

"Torni" where you can take your meals in the restaurant on the top floor with a wonderful view of the entire city, or the Grand Hotel. Do not go to the Hotel "Kämp" *under any circumstances*, because they are Nazis. And most importantly, please do not forget to let me know of your good arrival *immediately* by telegram, if you decide to stay in Helsingfors for the night. In any case, please do so at the first opportunity that presents itself, at the border station for example where you will probably have more than enough time for that. Should I happen to be in Leningrad at the time of your arrival, I will have to know when I should be at the train station to pick you up. If I receive the telegram too late, I might be in the harbor when it arrives.

Did I already tell you that you will need at least three passport photos here? Please don't forget to take care of that in advance and order them with time to spare. I would also like to mention that, when you cross the border here, or better, during customs inspection, you have to declare all jewelry you have with you, and they will add a statement in your passport or give you paperwork so that you can take it back with you. Otherwise, you will encounter unpleasantness when you try to leave the country.

If I get my own passport[118] returned to me tomorrow, I will go to the French consulate and apply for a visa which will require a little time.

I think it is horrible that Hilde's family has to consider emigration. Why don't you tell Hilde about Costa Rica? The main business there is exporting fruit and I am sure that Walter would be able to become acquainted with that business rather easily. I am sure that it is much better to show your back to Europe. The new decision concerning Jewish doctors in that country of filth is such a cultural disgrace that I just have no words for it. How glad I would be if my suggestions concerning Costa Rica are of some kind of help to Grete.

It really astounds me to hear that the economic situation is supposed to be so catastrophic in London. At this time, there is very little merchandise here and a lot of demand, and in Leningrad, people are sitting on top of each other while they wait for further shipments.

I already wrote to you concerning my return trip–that I cannot stay here for much longer because of my clothing which is not suitable for winter–and I am still hoping that I will be able to travel back with my beloved. Your Mope

---

118 Mope's "passport" was the stateless document issued by the British.

VERA TO MOPE

London, 22 August 1938

The day in Kilburn was quite interesting for me today, as usual, and it was pleasant to be among all those familiar people. This evening, shortly after 7 o'clock when I was getting ready to go home from the Kilburn store, I was told, "*A lady is waiting for you downstairs who has asked for you.*" The store was already closed and when I arrived downstairs, can you guess who was waiting there for me?? Your dear mother! During our conversation Saturday afternoon, she had heard that I would be in Kilburn today and so she had decided from one minute to the next, after she had spent the afternoon sewing as she told me, to get on the bus at Mill-Hill and meet me since I was so close for once!! (How close that really is, you know all too well, my love!!).[119] I was so touched and so pleased and so happy all the way to the innermost heart over such a dear thought.

After I showed her the personnel rooms, we went out into the fresh air for about a quarter of an hour and then, sadly, she had to make her way back. I put her on the bus so she would not get back to Mill-Hill too late. We had a heart-to-heart talk and she was so completely understanding and loving and attentive! I told her how, just how terribly difficult it was for me to make you understand that I simply cannot get away for more than a total of four weeks and that the only alternative would be for me to quit my job completely which is something we really cannot afford at this moment and I do not really want to do anyway.

Your dear mother agreed with me completely and even suggested that she would write to you about it which I refused however since I explained to her that the two of us would come to some kind of agreement on our own. The more I get to know your dear mother, the more I feel drawn to her and the more admiration I feel for her; she is a really extraordinary woman: intelligent, kind, broad minded, and understanding.

VERA TO MOPE

London, 24 August 1938

I am really sad and *downhearted*; I called the United Travel Bureau and Intourist today and both of them told me that the visa still had not arrived yet. The Russian consul can only be reached until 1.00 p.m. and

---

119 The distance from Mill Hill to Kilburn is a little over five miles.

I will try to talk to him during my lunch break. This state of waiting and uncertainty and insecurity is downright horrible. I contacted the Travel Bureau once again today: they told me that there is usually a layover between the arrival of the airplane in Helsingfors and the departure of the train, but I do not even have my visa yet! And I am wondering if I will get it and if I do, will I get it in time? I think that the airplane is supposed to arrive around 9.00 p.m. and the train departs around 11 p.m. Maybe the travel bureau here is making the mistake of taking the two-hour time difference into account or does it not exist in Helsingfors?!

Much later in the evening

In the meantime, your dear mother and Hannalein came by for a visit. And both of them were charming and sweet as always. Your mother told me that she had had it reported to her that Max (Erich Gödicke) could not and was not allowed to send any of your things. Well, nothing can be done about that! Your dear mother's things have not arrived yet either.

I have assembled the complete Ealing personnel now and I am curious to see how many will abandon me on Monday–I am sure that a few will and I think that is quite normal in most cases. After several of the girls I had already hired canceled, I hired more staff for Ealing. And now, I have all I need except for one ironing girl and maybe one more weekend girl. I really do hope that everything will work out well now. The entire staff is supposed to appear there next Monday and we have until Thursday to introduce the twenty-five to thirty girls who are completely new and have not had any training in one of our other stores.

VERA TO MOPE

London, 25 August 1938

My most heartfelt thanks for your dear telephone call! I felt quite desperate today! I left the store early because the Russian consulate is only open until 1 p.m. and when I arrived there, the sign said *NO office hours on Thursdays*! I rang the doorbell anyway and with much coaxing, I got all the way to the consul who could not do anything as he told me. I just wanted to cry! Then I called Intourist and went there myself in the afternoon; they cannot do anything for me either and I was downright desperate! I am soooo glad to have talked to you and to hear that you are sure everything will work itself out. I was told today that the train leaves Helsingfors about two hours after the plane arrives, so there is normally enough time to get there. So now, the only thing I need is the visa!!!!!!

MOPE TO VERA

Moscow, 26 August 1938

It is terribly hot here and they say that they have not had such a consistently high temperature in forty years. Today, I turned in my application for the extension of my visa and would be very thrilled if I received it in time, together with my passport, so I could welcome you in Leningrad. I have to go there anyway at the beginning of September to handle a Persian lamb contract and would save my darling from having to travel through two nights in a row. I think you should wait with the stamping of your Russian visa until the very last minute because you have to give them the name of the city of your first stay and that depends on whether I am here or there and that again depends on when I will receive my passport. Have them give you your "tourist book," that is the one with the coupons for room and board, in tourist class, that is III. class, but demand that they give you first class for train travel within the U.S.S.R. I will hopefully receive the report concerning your visa which was promised for yesterday evening sometime early tomorrow and if it gives any specific information, I will send you a telegram.

I have to make a few more suggestions to you that seem important to me. Bring an ample supply of stockings–they do not have to be the best–because you will tear many of them up here. Additionally, equip your handbags with powder boxes and take along powder, skin lotion and small perfume bottles. Also bring a good choice of clothing, because we cannot buy anything here with our money. Please do not forget to bring toilet paper.

And now, I will climb into my chaste bed. And my dreams will once again carry me to my beloved and let her rest in my arms and I will kiss her most passionately and caress her gently. Please think of me and my plea to take care of yourself which comes from the heart.

Your Mope

VERA TO MOPE

London, 28 August 1938

Last night, it got to be very late again. I did not get home until around 10 o'clock since our typist is going on vacation this Monday and she had taken some letters in shorthand for me but she had not typed them yet–unfortunately, it got to be too late to get them all done. Since her replacement who is starting on Monday cannot read her shorthand I will have to go back to Hammersmith in the evening and dictate those letters again, whether I like it or not, after I have spent the day in Ealing. There is no typist in Ealing, unfortunately. The personnel rooms there which are finished now give the impression of a *hotel lounge* which means that they are excellent. They were photographed yesterday and will be published in the local paper sometime soon!!!!!! I am curious to see how many of the sixty-five girls I hired will *not* appear tomorrow morning. There were several who dropped out last week and I was able to replace them with others.

Just now, I received a card from Annelieschen with which she tells me in a roundabout way that she has become engaged, to a Dr. So and So, she did not give me his name, a journalist in Berlin–she had told us about him several times last January, but she only talked about him as a friend and never as a potential marriage partner. She wrote a very funny card and everything I told you about her *husband-to-be*, I was able to get from what was hinted at between the lines. She wrote that she feels *very* cheery once again and I am very pleased about that. I just wrote to her and told her how genuinely happy I am for her.[120]

Yesterday, during lunch time, Carlchen Rosenfeld called and told us that he is here with his wife for a few days to take care of the accommodations of his children. We were expecting both of them after dinner yesterday evening, but unfortunately, they called around 9 o'clock to tell us that they were too tired to come over. I hope to be able to see Rosenfelds before they leave again and would really like for Muttilein to meet Lies Rosenfeld.[121]

My love, in one week from tomorrow–God willing–I will be with you instead of all alone and lonely here, you—

Completely and utterly and without reservation, Your Lilongo

MOPE TO VERA

Moscow, 31 August 1938

I am writing this date with a heavy heart, because I had counted on being able to send my sweet darling a telegram concerning her visa

---

[120] Annelie had become engaged to Arno Herzberg.
[121] Carl and Lies Rosenfeld, Mope's cousins from Karlsruhe, were in England to try to place their two boys in work there. The elder one, Georg, found a position, whereas his brother, Benjamin, was able to settle in Palestine. Their parents were obliged to return to Germany after their exploratory visit.

by this date. After I had been told in the morning that they were counting on receiving positive news in the evening, I got the same bitter disappointment once again a little while ago, just like every single day before. My girl tells me that she feels *down-hearted*–you cannot even imagine how depressed I am over the fact that I still do not know when the sorely awaited answer will finally arrive. I am so scorched with longing for you that I can no longer think of anything that does not concern you. During the last few days, I have asked about the visa so many times and everyone at the Sojuspushnina already knows about my great worry and everyone asks me on a daily basis about how things are going with my beloved's coming.

Why is everything combined with such indescribable difficulties? And there is no possibility to have some kind of influence on it because everything has to work out in its own way. I have not been able to write to my darling in as detailed a manner as usual during the last few days because with all the inner tension, I do not know what to tell you and until now, I also wanted to avoid pouring my heart out to you and make you feel even sadder.

When will I finally see my beloved again? Alas, I cannot even imagine that our beautiful plan can no longer be realized. I am soooo sad and so crestfallen–and I kiss you–still only in my thoughts–most passionately and filled with indescribably great and deepest love for you, my sunny girl, Your Mope

VERA TO MOPE

London, 31 August 1938

My Mopelein–Today is the last August day of 1938 and I still do not have my visa. I called the travel agent again today and he told me that the Finnish visa was not there yet either, only the Danish one, so I seem to have misunderstood him because I was totally convinced that the Finnish visa had been received!!!! I will only receive the Swedish one with the condition that the Finnish one is approved and all three cannot be stamped into my papers until the Russian one is on hand because I can only get them then–if at all. All of the consulates close at 1.00 p.m. on Saturday. The agent thought if the Russian visa is received by Friday noon at the latest that everything could still be taken care of on time. I no longer believe now that I will be able to travel on Sunday, maybe Monday or Tuesday!!

My love, no one makes things all that easy for us! But on the other hand, the two of us should *not* complain at all because we do have each other and our mutual deep love that shines above everything and that is the greatest and highest and quintessential thing most human beings can ever reach or own.

A little while ago, I called your dear mother who was very sweet, as usual. She sends you her heartfelt love and greatest sympathies for our experiences. She told me that she had received a very unhappy letter from your sister Alice in Palestine. Her husband has nothing to do and they would like it best if they could go to America. I hope that that is a passing crisis period there.[122]

I have a very bad conscience: I have not called Carlchen Rosenfeld yet. He and his wife went to see your dear mother last Sunday afternoon and he was rather *down-hearted*, unfortunately. I will try to call him tomorrow.

I spent the entire day in Ealing today and in the afternoon, five girls from Reading (about twenty miles from London) visited me–they had their free afternoon today and had met me in summer camp. They went to Hammersmith first where they were told that I was in Ealing and they appeared there around 5.30 p.m. I served them tea and showed them the new store and then I found out that one of the girls is a virtual expert at displaying canned items, and both the manager and supervisor in Ealing were so enthused with her ideas that they prompted her to come to Ealing tomorrow morning instead of going to Reading. I wrote a letter to her manager and the supervisor signed it in order to explain her absence tomorrow. The girl was beaming! And the other four also asked if they could not be used in Ealing as well. It was an odd coincidence that the five of them came to see me on this particular Wednesday!

MOPE TO VERA

Moscow, 2 September 1938

A really red half-moon makes its way across the sky and I have to think of the moon letters I exchanged with my beloved three weeks ago. Back then, I believed that I would have her here with me by the new full moon and to draw her near to me filled with happiness that the terrible

---

[122] Mope's sister, Alice Homburger, a trained nurse, and her husband, Julius, a medical doctor, had landed in Haifa in November 1935. He had great difficulty in making a living there.

separation is finally over, and to make up for many of the things we missed out on–even if we cannot make up for everything. Today is a half-moon and in another week, it will have rounded itself and where will my darling be then? I can no longer tell you because it is not given to me to be able to address my feelings in all their fullness and depth of experience in words.

They promised me a decision for the late afternoon this morning as well and my hope which still survives to some small degree received another blow and I am not sure that it can recuperate from that. Today, I was "put off" again for two or three days and explained that I will apply for my exit visa if no decision has been made by Monday.

I registered a telephone call to my girl for later today. I have to talk to you and will try to make you feel better and ask you to postpone your leave by a few days so that *our* time–should you be able to come after all–does not suffer any reduction. I only know one thing, that I need you, that I long for you, that I will break if it takes much longer until I have my sweet one with me again.

All day long, I was thinking about the exciting and stressful work my darling will have today and I hope with all my heart that everything works out well so that you will find some satisfaction in that at least. My entire thinking and being is so completely dominated by you, waking and sleeping that I cannot comprehend that my will to have you with me is not strong enough to move all obstacles out of the way. I kiss you with the most painful longing, and I embrace you again and again, you, you! Wholeheartedly, Your Mope

VERA TO MOPE

London, 2 September 1938

I just put myself into the horizontal position and this writing tablet is the only one within reach, so please forgive me! I was soooo happy to hear your beloved voice just a little while ago. Hopefully, I will arrive in the U.S.S.R. before this letter does–how I wish for that!!! It was so nice to be able to understand you so well–the connection was exceptionally good today!!!

I am *very* tired–today was a big day![123] Hundreds of customers were standing in front of the glass doors with their noses pressed flat and

---

123 Vera is referring to the grand opening of the Marks & Spencer store in West Ealing, for which she had recruited most of the staff.

at 10 o'clock when the doors were opened they came streaming in like a migration of nations. The *takings* were much higher than expected! Around 10.30 about twelve city representatives came by for a tour and a snack. We had prepared sandwiches, tea, coffee, etc., and my deputy and I served as "hostesses." One of the directors (who knows me, Simon's brother-in-law) was there,[124] the manager, supervisor and various other people from the head office. The councilor and one of the directors each made a short speech and the entire company left after a detailed inspection, apparently highly satisfied. In the afternoon, I had the two managers from the Labor Department here for tea, and everything with legs at the head office came by. Apart from Simon Marx and Israel Sieff who will come by tomorrow, I believe.

When will the visa finally get here???????!!! Most passionately and see you soon???

Your Lilongo

MOPE TO VERA

Moscow, 3 September 1938

Although there will be no plane tomorrow because it is Sunday and this letter will lie around until Monday, I still want to tell my beloved how happy I am to have talked to her yesterday and that I could listen to your beloved voice so very well. I had feared that you would be even more depressed than me because of the postponed trip. Then, I was so very pleased to find out that my darling has come to terms with the unalterable facts.

A week ago, I would not have thought it possible that I am still writing to you and I still do not know when you can finally begin the flight to me. I was so convinced that my girl would be with me on Tuesday at the latest that I cannot tell you just *how* bitter every minute I am forced to spend without my little witch is to me. I am abysmally fed up with work and I think of nothing but your arrival which will make my life worth living and happy again. However, your later arrival might make it possible for us to travel back together. Whether or not I can come to Leningrad depends on when I get the extension of my visa which I applied for on 26 August. I do so wish to be able to meet you there so I can save you the second night trip.

---

[124] Harry Sacher (1881-1971), who was married to Simon Marks's sister, Miriam.

They told me today that your visa had *not* been refused but that you were the only one who could find out about its issuance; that could not be done by "Sojuspushnina" because it is not a consulate visa. I now live in the hope that the visa will be sent with the next courier which means that it will arrive there either Tuesday or Wednesday, and I beg you to send me a telegram the minute you find out anything. As far as I can see, it will be difficult for me to get to Leningrad before the 13th because my papers will not be ready until then.

And now, I have to finish a letter to Schapiro so that it will reach the 11 o'clock mail. I do hope so very much that the stress of the Ealing opening gives way now to a calmer work day, until you can finally, finally come to me. Your Mope

VERA TO MOPE

London, 4 September 1938

I did not write to you yesterday although I had the afternoon off. I came home and slept for several hours. I was just so completely done in after the opening. Yesterday, I talked to one of my superiors at Head Office on the telephone and she told me that she wanted to congratulate me "*on the opening.*" She asked the manager, the supervisor, etc., in Ealing and all of them said that they had thought I must have managed a dozen openings before this one. I thought it was very nice of her to tell me. The takings during the first few days exceeded *all* expectations.

This morning, I slept well into the morning. Yesterday evening, Carlchen and Lies Rosenfeld were here and both of them were as charming as ever. He is feeling very depressed; they hope to get their older boy hired on in a factory here soon.

Hopefully, hopefully, this note will get into your possession *after* me!!! How I wish for that!!!!! You, I feel such indescribably longing for you, my love! Well and truly, *Your* Lilongo

MOPE TO VERA

Moscow, 6 September 1938

Today was Wychodnoi but I worked for most of the day and did not give myself one free minute aside from business meetings and shining my shoes, a pleasure I had not indulged in since I got here. It is still very hot here but there was a bit of a cooling wind today which I felt made it much more comfortable.

I wait for my beloved's telegram hourly although I know that a few more days might pass until the visa arrives. This waiting is too horrible and unbearable to me and I could feel how hard it was for my little girl, and I know that you are waiting just as longingly for the reunion as I am. As I already told you, the cardinal mistake lies in the fact that you are expecting an Intourist and not a consular visa. It seems that Sojuspushnina lacks any kind of influence at the former agencies to hasten the process. However, I am glad to know that it has not been denied and I keep hoping from hour to hour to receive your message that will free me from a ton of weight. You did not write to me yet about the French visa but I hope that you have received it.

So Annelieschen has become engaged once again and I do wish with all my heart that she will be happy and married. The fact that she chose a journalist of all people makes me a little skeptical but she has to know best. The main thing is that she is happy again and stays that way.

It is really bad that Alice's husband lacks any initiative. I never liked him all that well and I thought it was really silly that she was more or less forced into marrying that boy. But my blessed father's view of the matter was that a girl has to be married off and the husband had to be Orthodox, and so, it was done under pressure on her good conscience. And I even believe that she loves him but you cannot put any bread on the table with that. If she were not such a brave soul and got the money out of that accursed country, the two of them would be starving with their three children. By the way, in my opinion, the crisis does not bear any blame because one of my mother's cousins, who reached Palestine at the same time as the Homburgers supposedly has an excellent medical practice.

I wonder if you talked to Carlchen and Lies before their departure. I really feel sorry for that one. He has such a penchant for depression anyway which is probably heightened quite a bit by the immovable prosthesis,[125] and there should hardly be any way for him to get out of that damnable country as long as his sons do not earn any money.

I feel such a weight on me today because I still do not know when I will see my beloved once again. Every single day, I decide to apply for my exit visa, but then, I pat myself on the back and tell myself in the

---

125 Carl Rosenfeld had lost one leg beneath the knee when fighting for Germany in World War I.

most convincing tone–just wait one more day. Maybe the visa will come in after all and it is your duty after all to wait just a little while longer. It is a horrible test of nerves that has been placed on both of us and actually–we are like the two royal children who could not find their way to each other because the water was too deep and probably loved each other just as deeply and burningly as we two entirely non-royal ones. [126]

I kiss you full of the greatest and deepest tenderness and love, you, my everything, Your Mope

VERA TO MOPE

London, 7 September 1938

I talked to your dear mother on the telephone yesterday evening–she sympathizes deeply with our plight. Norbert arrived in London yesterday to have a look around and he and Hannalein and your dear mother spent time together. I am afraid that Norbert will be very disappointed in connection with his medical prospects, but I hope that another chance for somewhere overseas with a good climate will offer itself.

Monday evening, I talked to Rosenfelds on the telephone and I told Carl that I was actually quite sad because I thought that the call was from you. Lies told me that Georg, their eldest son, will begin working here around the beginning of October, and I am glad that at least one member of the family will have turned his back on that "beautiful" country.

This morning, I called our travel agent again and he told me that there was nothing that could be done and that I just had to wait!!!!!! My love, if it arrives tomorrow, I can still fly Sunday morning. Would it not be better if you applied for the exit visa so that you have the alternative of coming to me right away if I do not receive my visa? Or maybe I can meet you in Sweden but that is not possible because that visa will be issued for transit only.

---

126 Mope is invoking from memory a traditional German folk ballad, "*Es waren zwei Koenigskinder*" that can be traced back to the fifteenth century. In the nineteenth century, Heinrich Heine cites his recollection of the ballad, "an old old story that no one now believes" which opens with the lines "There were two kingly children / Who loved each other truly; / They could not come together, / The water was too deep —" (*Italian Travel Sketches*, trans. Elizabeth A. Sharp [London: Walter Scott Ltd.], n.d., p. 36). [http://library.umac.mo/ebooks/b32309181.pdf].

I do not think that I can wait much longer, because I will put myself into a blue envelope and fly to you as a letter–maybe the decision will come tomorrow after all!

Most passionately and tenderly, *Your* little witch

MOPE TO VERA

Moscow, 10 September 1938

Right now, the outside is bathed in moon light and because of that, the beauty of the great Red Square is lit most strikingly. The clock on the wall of the Kremlin just struck 10 and I jumped out of my bed from which I enjoyed the grand vista to write to my beloved. However, I just remembered that there is no point in hurrying because no plane is leaving tomorrow.

On September 12, as things stand now, I will probably travel to Leningrad in the evening, if my passport gets here in time. Should my little girl not come during those days, I will apply for my exit visa immediately after my return here. I also telegraphed Schapiro the same by giving him the 15th as the date so that I will most likely be able to depart from here around the 20th and arrive in London that evening. Should my exit visa not be ready by the 20th, I would not be able to leave here until the 24th because I do not want to travel on the Sabbath, and there is no plane traffic on Sundays. I do not see any sense in sitting around here any longer, since there is hardly any merchandise available aside from Persian lamb which I will buy in Leningrad, and the new harvest does not begin until December, and I will have to be back here by then anyway, as *horrible* as that thought is to me.

I kiss you, filled with the most burning longing, and I embrace you with a love that is so unspeakably great and deep. *Your* Mope

VERA TO MOPE

London, 13-14 September 1938

My love, this evening, I feel more than depressed! I found a letter from our travel agent this evening letting me know that the Finnish visa had been denied without giving a reason for the denial.

I had a terrible day today! Someone called early this morning and told me that the telegram I had sent to you on Sunday to Leningrad had been forwarded to Moscow since my beloved was not staying at the Astoria in Leningrad. I spent the entire day worried as to why you did not travel to Leningrad after all. My love, this state is really becoming unbearable and I implore you with all the intensity at my disposal to come to me as soon as it is possible. I worry terribly and constantly and dream the most horrifying dreams and even at the store, I can hardly manage to master my expression any longer, and I do not even try when I am at home. As I said: *Life is* not *too good just now!*

I kiss you in my thoughts filled with the most painful longing! Completely and utterly and without reservation, *Your* little witch

MOPE TO VERA

Leningrad, 13 September 1938

My trip here was quite comfortable and I was terribly tired after I had to work all day before leaving Moscow to get my Swedish and Finnish visas, which I finally succeeded at around 7 in the evening. I feel that the knowledge of having this running around and waiting behind me is quite a relief. After my arrival this morning, I had a quick breakfast and then inspected merchandise until around 4 o'clock. It is much colder here than in Moscow and right now, there is a storm raging outside which lets everyone hear that autumn is here.

Later today, I went to see the film "Professor Mamlock," which, based on a novel by Friedrich Wolf–until now, this author was unknown to me–was filmed here during the time of the auction in July. It shows the beginning of Nazi rule in Berlin and the horrifying excesses against Jews.[127] It was almost too harmless compared to what those swine actually perpetrated. Nevertheless, a very real psychosis took hold of me and when I left the cinema; I thought at first that I was surrounded by SA or SS-people. That is proof of the success of the play and the terrible time that one had to experience under the rule of that rabble so that one still has not completely freed oneself from the inner pressure that was put on us. And that in the fifteenth month of freedom!

---

127 Friedrich Wolf's play, *Professor Mamlock* (1933) tells the story of a Jewish professor of surgery who remains blind to the threat of Nazism. The play was intended as a wake-up call. In the Soviet Union, it was made into the film by Adolf Minkin and Herbert Rappaport, and it was this version that Mope went to see. In 1961, Friedrich Wolf's son, Konrad, directed a new version of the film in East Germany.

I really do not expect much from Norbert's visit in London. Aside from the fact that the climate would not agree with him and he would have to make up with a number of exams, there will hardly be a chance for him. I hope that he will find something reasonable as soon as possible. What is to become of the Goldschmidts? The fate of the siblings occupies me very much and I would be more than happy to hear something positive very soon. Carl and Lies Rosenfeld's future also weighs heavily on my heart and I feel deep sympathy for them. I wonder which one of the two will bring Georg to London and where and how should he be housed? I am sure that the boy will adjust to the new milieu quickly and one should try to help him to get over the initial feeling of homesickness.

It is rather late already and my sweetest one's husband is very tired and wants to place himself into the horizontal. I no longer believe in my beloved's traveling here and when I hear the storm whistling outside, I would be ever so worried about letting you fly. And it will be much more beautiful if both of us are free and unburdened by work and enjoy our vacation together than if I were occupied by work from early until late and my little witch would have to wait for me and I would be exhausted. Most passionately and most, most lovingly, Your Mope

VERA TO MOPE

London, 16 September 1938

Yesterday, I did not write to you after I received your longed-for telegram which let me know that you had applied for your exit visa. There was another telegram today that gave me your address as Hotel Metropole in Moscow and was supposed to tell me, I guess, that my beloved seems to think that mail from me will still reach him there, and I do hope ever sooooooo much that the time period still between us is too short now to let letters from me come into your possession. My Mopelein, this waiting is becoming downright horrific and the restlessness and worry pursues me day and night and makes me feel more than *downhearted*! I talked to your dear mother in detail on the telephone yesterday and as always, her loving compassion and care made me feel better.

My love, it seems that there is something like telepathy after all, because around 8 p.m. (10 p.m. where you are), I went outside with Muttilein to get some fresh air and made some more observations concerning the moon and said to Mutti that I was wondering if my

Mopelein was having another conversation with the full moon; and it seems that he was and at about the same time as I did.

Actually, I no longer have the words to tell you how much I need you and how much I worry about you being so far away from me at this particular point in time.

Completely and utterly, *Your* little witch

MOPE TO VERA

Train Leningrad-Moscow, 15-16 September 1938

Right now, I am sitting in the train again and despite fierce protests from Schapiro, I will apply for my exit visa tomorrow, something I telegraphed to my darling just before I left the hotel. Schapiro had the audacity–or should one consider it stupidity?–to telegraph me that some other business clients of his want to come here around the 20th or 25th of the month if the situation has cleared itself up by then. I do not believe that the customers will make the trip, and that the desire is the father of the thought where Schapiro is concerned. Of course, he uses all his influence on those clients in order to talk them into making the trip.

And me, am I dirt? Should it actually come to war, those people would want to be at home and with their families.[128] Whatever happens to me and what my sweet one is going to do plays no role at all. The main thing to him is that the capitalists who help to fill his pockets feel safe and secure and are satisfied. I received another telegram from him in the afternoon in which he suggests to wait with the application for the visa (he means the exit visa). Should I leave, he might lose part of his earnings after all and because of that, he does not care about whatever happens to the two of us. In any case, the fur season has reached its end and there is no more decent merchandise to be had, or very little. So it would really be best to come home, even if circumstances were normal.

I also believe that, after Chamberlain has visited that criminal, a way will be found to satisfy everyone. Unfortunately, it will happen at

---

128 Hitler threatened to go to war in order to annex the Sudetenland of western Czechoslovakia, and, as a consequence, the political situation in Europe had become extremely edgy. As part of his policy of appeasement and wishing to preempt a war, British Prime Minister, Neville Chamberlain, met with Hitler at Berchtesgaden on 15 September. This was a prelude to his ill-conceived Munich Accord that was signed by the two leaders on 29 September.

the expense of the Czechs and on top of that, the "Great Albion" will embarrass itself with that step for all times to come. It is a shame that an English prime minister lends himself to being a poor matchmaker between a painter gone crazy[129] and a state that is being led under the same auspices of democracy as England itself, and abandons the principles which control his own government and probably appear incontrovertible to him where his own country is concerned for the smaller and weaker partner.

I did not write to you yesterday. Although I really did not have all that much to do, I was so agitated until I heard about the trip of the Prime Minister that I was unable to have one calm thought and also could not sit still enough to begin something rational. All of us colleagues were together the entire time and were trying to decide what action might be most prudent. Of course, all of us came to the same result that the ones living in Europe should try to get home as fast as possible. The Americans whose continent will hardly be dragged into any kind of affair for the time being can wait with greater calm to see how things develop.

Now, I will finally get into the horizontal because I am rather tired and I suppose that my neighbors will soon begin complaining about the clatter of the typewriter which is something I do not want to happen. I hope to finally and truly embrace you soon and give you all the tenderness which has been waiting for our reunion in vain for so very long.

Completely and utterly your Mope

MOPE TO VERA

Moscow, 20 September 1938

It is a horrible feeling to be without news for days on end. I go to the National every single day and ask for mail in vain. I will continue writing to you on a daily basis, because I want to spare you this worry, although I really do hope that I will leave here on the 24th. I do not think that it is possible before then because of the exit visa which was promised for the 23rd. If I do not leave on the Sabbath, I will have to stay here for a few more days. There is no plane on the 25th (Sunday) and the Jewish New Year begins on the 26th and 27th. I would not work on those days anyway,

---

129 Hitler was a one-time house painter.

and aside from that, the exit visa would probably expire by then. So there is no other possibility and apart from that, the unending longing for my sweetest darling urges me to get home as quickly as I can.

If everything remains quiet and we receive the necessary visa to France in time, the two of us will spend our vacation on the Riviera. That way, we will not be lacking sun and warmth and we will not have been cheated entirely out of our summer, as my sweetest one seems to fear. To me, the main thing is that I will have you with me again and can take joy in you, which is something I have been slavering for these last four months.

So you do not like Norbert *at all*? I think that you do not know him well enough yet since he does not deserve such a derogatory verdict. Because of his religiousness, he is always feeling tense, which shows in his entire demeanor, but he is a quintessentially good man and his religiousness which is not founded in knowledge, not like in Fred's case, contradicts inwardly with his intelligence, which is something he will not admit to himself. In his desire to respect himself, he becomes loudmouthed and I am sure that it is that which you like least. And his fixed opinion on the so-called homeland in Germany can be explained that way.

I am so excited in anticipation of our conversation and I feel such immense longing to hear your beloved voice, but I can understand so very well that you might not bring yourself to write to me following our call. I usually feel like that as well, because "writing" is such a poor substitute for "talking" as a means of expression and is so very slow and takes even more time to get to you that you cannot really call it communicating. Your Mope

VERA TO MOPE

London, 21 September 1938

These lines are accompanied by just *one* wish–that they will no longer reach you there and that I can tell you about all of my wishes for you and all my love for you, my most loved one, in person and nestled in your arms. Why do I reach for a sheet of paper once again? Because I just have to talk to you, my love, and tell you how indescribably and infinite my longing for you is, you, my most beloved! Completely and utterly and without reservation, *Your* Lilongo

Twenty-nine: "Today, for the First Time in My Life, I Wished I Were a Man!"

1 December 1938–23 January 1939

POLITICAL TIMELINE, OCTOBER 1938–JANUARY 1939

- 1-10 October 1938: German army occupies Czech Sudetenland.
- 1 November 1938: Polish Jews living abroad have their citizenship renounced.
- 7 November 1938: Herschel Grynszpan, a seventeen-year-old Jew, shoots dead German diplomat Ernst vom Rath in Paris.
- 9-10 November 1938: As reprisal for Vom Rath's assassination, Nazi leaders instigate a nationwide pogrom against Jews, known as Kristallnacht (Night of Broken Glass). Multiple synagogues destroyed, properties looted, and scores of Jews killed. Thousands rounded up and sent to concentration camps.
- 12 November 1938: Jewish community fined one billion Reichmarks to pay for damage done during Kristallnacht.
- 15 November 1938: All Jewish pupils are expelled from German schools.
- 25 November 1938: In the Soviet Union, Lavrentiy Beria appointed People's Commissar for Internal Affairs (Chief of Police).

- November 1938: British Government allows 10,000 unaccompanied Jewish children to be admitted into Great Britain (the so-called Kindertransport).
- 3 December 1938: German decree that all remaining Jewish businesses are to be "Aryanized."
- 6 December 1938: Germany and France sign a nonaggression pact.
- 1 January 1939: Jewish men in Germany must adopt the middle name of Israel, Jewish women the middle name of Sara.
- 11-14 January 1939: Neville Chamberlain visits Mussolini in Rome for appeasement talks designed to draw Italy away from supporting Hitler, but nothing is achieved.
- 30 January 1939: On the sixth anniversary of his accession as Chancellor, Hitler announces that, in the event of war, the Jews of Europe will be exterminated.
- January 1939: Defying blockage, "illegal immigration" from Germany to Palestine begins.

Shortly after Mope reached England in late September, the couple set off on their postponed vacation. During their stay in the south of France, Vera was to become pregnant. After their return to England toward the end of October, they counted the days before Mope's unavoidable departure in compliance with his restricted residence permit. His route to Moscow took him by plane through Paris, Stockholm, and Helsingfors (Helsinki), and then by train via Leningrad. Once there, a poor global market, which brought little business for Mope, only compounded his unease.

Much of the correspondence from this time period concerns Mope's mounting fear that the demands of Vera's work at Marks & Spencer risk endangering her pregnancy. Her exhilaration about her personal career when she received word that she was to be put in charge of the company's new flagship store, the Pantheon on Oxford Street, brought only "deep depression" to Mope, who worried that, with a baby due in the summer, she was taking on far more than she should. He was relieved when the head of the welfare department at M&S ruled that the promotion was indeed too demanding for an expectant mother. Vera's disappointment was palpable.

Meanwhile, the situation of the Jews in Germany (and slightly less so in Italy where Vera's best friend Hilde still lived) was more and more dire, Vera receiving almost daily letters to try to help family, friends, and even complete strangers, to escape. For all that, there were spots of light. Through the newly initiated Kindertransport scheme, Ketty Goldschmidt, Mope's eldest sister, was able to send the first two of her four children–Lassar and Gertrud–to England, to be cared for by their grandmother and other relatives until the anticipated arrival of their parents. Grete Moschytz, his other sister still in Germany, took her four children to join her husband, Norbert, in Davos, Switzerland, though permission to settle there was denied. Released from Buchenwald, where he had been incarcerated following Kristallnacht, Mope's hapless cousin, Semy, the former head partner at the Gebrüder Felsenstein, also received papers that permitted him to leave for England, though on the non-negotiable condition that he relinquish the company's remaining foreign assets to the Nazis.

This section takes us through to Vera's twenty-ninth birthday on 23 January 1939.

MOPE TO VERA

Stockholm, 2 December 1938

I was so pleased and happy to have talked to my most beloved girl yesterday evening and I hope that you will be able to fulfill my most intense and passionate wish–to remember to take care of yourself.

I need to report to you that my extensive conversation with Schapiro in Paris followed a very harmonious course. He is counting on me participating at a commission rate of 7%. He expressly told me that his business partners are very satisfied and have great trust in my work and knowledge. That is how one bluffs oneself through life!

Please go and see the doctor, send him whatever he wants, take the medicine regularly, and take care of your health for the future citizen more so than for M&S, because that is something even the highest salary could not buy. Your Mope

VERA TO MOPE

London, 2 December 1938

Thank you, my Mopelein, for your telegram from Stockholm, the content of which Muttilein read to me over the phone shortly after 6 p.m. while I was at the store, and I was happy and relieved and now, I am waiting, full of impatience, for the one from Helsingfors which will arrive here, God willing, tomorrow evening.

I hope that my most beloved friend will have a good night's rest in a comfortable hotel bed tonight. I talked to Fred on the telephone a little earlier–he had called me this morning. He heard from you that I know Mr. Cooper and wanted to know how well I know him and if I could do something for his cousins who come from the same town as Uncle Joseph, or ask Mr. Cooper for help on their behalf. I told him that I only knew Mr. Cooper from his office and not, as he seemed to believe, privately, and that it would be much better to ask Otto Schiff who knows Mr. Cooper much better than I do and through whom I was introduced in the first place. He understood that and suggested that he get in contact with Joan Stiebel once again and I offered to contact Joan or Otto in the matter if he could not make any headway. I hope that you agree with the above–it seemed the right thing to do.[130] Your Little Witch

MOPE TO VERA

Leningrad, 4 December 1938

Yesterday in Helsingfors, I bought a few things–a number of books, rubber shoes, and some other things–before I went out to eat. The only thing I could not get was a pocket calendar with all the Jewish and Catholic holidays, weights, measurements, etc. Maybe you could send me one when the opportunity presents itself.[131] Since dinner at the Hotel Torni, I asked for a day room there, lay down on the bed, and went to sleep immediately. I was dead tired. Then, last night, I went back to sleep on the train and hope that I can do the same today on my trip to Moscow. The preceding days were quite exhausting and the body demands its rights.

---

130 Joseph Felsenstein, Mope's uncle, was a younger brother of Isidor, and lived in Fürth, where Fred Rau also had relatives. Following Kristallnacht, Fred made frequent trips to Germany, rescuing family members by smuggling them into Holland, often in the trunk of his car. From there, he provided papers to allow them to travel on to England. In late December 1938, using identification papers that he had acquired, Fred escorted four children of his cousins from Fürth, the Rosenbaums, across the border into Holland. Ernest Napier Cooper was the British Home Office functionary who had helped Vera following her arrival in Britain in 1933. It is unclear whether he was able to issue Fred Rau with the necessary documents to aid the escape of the Rosenbaum children and their subsequent settlement in England.

131 The complications of the Soviet dating system in the 1930s made it essential for Mope to have ready access to a western calendar.

Just now, I hear that I have to leave for the train station in half an hour. I think the letter will reach you sooner if I post it in Moscow, so I will mail it tomorrow morning. By then, it will be around 11 o'clock here (now, it is 1 o'clock here, that is 10 o'clock your time). Completely and utterly, Your Mope

VERA TO MOPE

London, 8 December 1938

My love, this afternoon, I went to see Mr. Nixon on Harley Street.[132] He is about thirty years old, quite likable and very pleasant. He did not even examine me, only took my blood pressure and wrote down what I should be eating, more or less what I eat anyway. He asked me if I can drink milk and suggested taking in about one and a half pints per day, since I would get one gram of calcium without medication which he considered best, considering that it would also be advantageous where milk production is concerned. I asked him about sports and he said that swimming and playing tennis were both *extremely favorable* if one did not overdo it. Additionally, he thought that I would certainly be able to work until April which satisfied me quite a bit. So, now you know approximately everything!

A little while ago, I was on the telephone with your dear mother who is doing very well and who sends you all her love. She told me, and remarked that you would probably be very interested–Hugo Hoffman from Frankfurt was able to get out of the camp.[133]

The mail brought me a letter from the Home Office this evening in which they ask me to mail your expired German passport to them. I found one in the desk which expired in January 1938 and if I do not find

---

132 William Nixon was already a leading figure in his field; see Geoffrey Chamberlain, *Special Delivery: The Life of the Celebrated British Obstetrician* William *Nixon* (London, 2004).

133 Approximately 30,000 Jewish men were incarcerated at Buchenwald, Dachau and Sachsenhausen concentration camps following Kristallnacht, and only freed after they agreed to relinquish their assets and leave Germany. Hugo Hoffman (1893-1941), the husband of Mope's cousin Frieda (née Weil), was arrested and sent to Buchenwald, from which he was released on account of his service in the German Army during World War I. He escaped to England, where (with funds provided by a brother-in-law who had settled in London many years before) he opened a boarding house in Buxton, Derbyshire. Unfortunately, he was run over by a bus during a blackout in 1941 and died from the injuries he sustained.

a different one, I will send that one. I am wondering when your first letter from the U.S.S.R. will get here.

I have to close now and go to bed early for once. *Your* little witch

MOPE TO VERA

Moscow, 9 December 1938

During the last two days, I was unable to write to my sweet little girl. Yesterday evening, I participated in a banquet where people drank a lot, as usual, and I was glad that I had a few "Alka-Seltzer" tablets which helped to clear up my head!

Until now, it has not been cold at all here, and I put the fur coat in the closet. However, the cold will come soon enough. Nothing is free! Generally, people are unhappy over the fact that my beloved did not accompany me, despite all the efforts they put into procuring the visa for you. Unfortunately, I had to explain to those people that the time right before Christmas is your busiest time at work and that your coming here right now was completely out of the question, but that I had every reason to hope and was counting on you coming here in February. You will most likely have to interrupt your work anyway at that time and the only thing I fear is that the traveling might be too strenuous for you. Otherwise, that would be a wonderful diversion for you because, when one is suddenly out of work and has to sit at home without anything to do–seemingly without a reason–it is anything but pleasant. Please discuss the question with Dr. Rothschild and the other doctor in detail. You would be able to stay here until the end of March and travel back with me then, as long as the two of them consider such a trip to be *completely* without danger to your condition.

I am *very* interested in finding out what will become of Grete and Ketty. I do hope so very much that they will be able to get out of that damned Germany soon. I wonder if Lassar will receive his permit before his sixteenth birthday. After that, it will be much more difficult to bring him in or out because he will be considered a child only until then.[134] I would also like to know what will become of Carlchen Rosenfeld, Semy, etc.

---

[134] Mope's nephew, Lassar (Leslie) Goldschmidt, the oldest son of Ketty and David Goldschmidt, was born on 17 December 1922. Under terms agreed by the House of Commons in response to Kristallnacht, Jewish refugee children below the age of seventeen could be admitted into Britain through the so-called "Kindertransport"

I kiss you and embrace you most tenderly and lovingly and would be so very happy if you could come here in February. Completely, Your Mope

VERA TO MOPE

London, 11 December 1938

Today, I made a date with Hannalein to meet her for a walk. She is a straw-widow for two days, because Fred drove to the city where your former representative Michel lives to find out about an acquaintance of his.[135] Hanna told me that on either Tuesday or Thursday of this week, Lassar and Gertrud will come here; the former will stay with her and the latter with your dear mother. When Grete's children come over, Gertrud will be moved to live with your mother–she has already been registered at a tailoring school, and although it was *full-up*, they made a concession for her after Hanna explained the circumstances: namely that the child would not receive a permit to enter the country if she had not been accepted at a school. I will write a few lines to Ketty today to tell her how happy I am that her children are coming.

My love, I completely agree with you: that it is *the* main duty or one of the main duties of any woman to do everything within her power and her abilities to ensure that the future child will be strong and healthy, as far as that is possible. You can depend on the fact that I will do everything possible and assure you that I will do the right thing.

I still want to write a card to Annelie to find out how she is doing. My love, I wish you the best of luck for all your work, and all the most heartfelt and loving thoughts! *Your* Little Witch

MOPE TO VERA

Moscow, 15 December 1938

I am very happy to hear from you that Hugo Hoffman was released and hope that Eugen Weil, his brother-in-law, is also free.[136] It will not

---

scheme. Approximately 10,000 children escaped from Nazi Germany in this way before the start of the war. Most of the children would never see their parents again.
135 Vera is writing in coded fashion to indicate that Fred was visiting Fürth to secure the escape from Germany of family members. "Michel" was a former functionary of the Gebrüder Felsenstein.
136 Mope's cousin, Eugene Weil (1881-1947) was among the many Jewish men who were arrested and incarcerated by the SS after Kristallnacht. Following his release,

be any consolation that so many others are feeling just as bitter about the fact that they cannot help their friends in that damned country. I am exceedingly worried about my sisters with their families and I find the helplessness against that gang of criminals and their criminal laws deeply depressing.

This evening–it is 12.30 now–I still have to go to the post office, write a letter to Schapiro, and copy my calculations, among many other things. For this reason, I now have to interrupt the conversation–I kiss you, embrace you most passionately, ever so lovingly and gently and filled with the most ardent longing, you, most beloved, you!

VERA TO MOPE

London, 17 December 1938

Lassar and Gertrud arrived here yesterday and I already talked to him on the telephone. He will get a welcoming tie from me and Gertrud an overall. As Lassar told me, the Raus are trying to get visas for Ketty and her husband to come here, and the two younger children have been invited by your dear mother's sister to come to Amsterdam–she offered to take care of them.[137]

Fred called a short time ago and told me–in a very dear manner–I had asked Hanna about it last Sunday–about a method that could be used to bring people out illegally.

Completely and utterly, *Your* Little Witch

MOPE TO VERA

Moscow, 18 December 1938

As far as business is concerning, things are not working out the way I would like them to, since they do not want to give me the contracts I had negotiated–I would really like to finalize them–for the time being, and I

---

he and his family emigrated to the United States in May 1939.

137 Oma Lenchen's sister, Rachel Wolff (née Marx) lived in Amsterdam. After the Nazis occupied Holland, she fled to Paris with her son and daughter-in-law, where, in the fall of 1942, they were among the murder victims of Dr. Marcel Petiot, a collaborator who posed as a member of the resistance. The horrific circumstances are described by David King, *Death in the City of Light* (New York: Crown Publishers, 2011); see pp. 168-171, and passim.

am afraid that the prices–by the time I will be able to finalize them–will be too high to complete them. However, I can do no more than make the best effort possible, and I have been doing just that day after day.

Today is the first day of Chanukah and I really hope that you will go to Fred's. That might be a little much for my little girl, but nevertheless, I am curious to read your report, and it would really please me if you were to see a little bit of the anniversary of the Maccabees and the celebrations. The story is probably not unknown to you, but if so, it is interesting enough to become familiar with it. It even made quite an impression on Peter the Great, or so I read quite by accident today.

I love you most passionately, my little girl, and I kiss you, filled to the brim with the greatest longing, and all those little places of your face and body, where it gives you the most pleasure. I embrace you tenderly and wish that I could do so for real, and then, I could go to sleep feeling your beloved body close to mine, and the happiest thoughts would accompany me into sleep, as has happened many times before and still so *very* rarely. *Your* Mope

VERA

Journal entry, 18 December 1938

A few dates concerning my pregnancy:

last menstruation 27. 9. 38

I assume (I would rather say I am convinced) date of impregnation after October 15 (Nizza).[138]

16. Oct.: swelling of the outer genitalia for about 2-3 days and complications

17. Oct.: heaviness in the limbs, temperature, headache

18. and 19. Oct.: completely unable to take any nourishment, slight apathy, weakness, repeated vomiting

20. Oct.: slow return to feeling normal

21. Oct.: got up and walked to the flower market

26. Oct.: arrival in London

27. Oct.: store, continuing constipation that can only be resolved by laxatives

---

138 i.e., Nice, the city on the French Riviera.

Constipation lasts for about 11–14 days after arriving in London, then goes away completely. After that, during the first two weeks of November, during the morning at the store, slight feeling of sleepiness and queasy lightheadedness until about 10.30, time of regular bowel movement, after that complete feeling of being unwell.

19. Nov.: slight flickering and headache (very light) in the morning

20. Nov. (Sunday): around 6 p.m., slight flickering again and onetime vomiting–very light

Other than that, *completely* normal; very tired in the evenings, which is to be expected considering the Xmas rush.

2nd half of Dec.: after prolonged period of standing, a very slight pain in the abdomen, similar to the preliminary phase of menstruation–after sitting down for short period, pain subsides.

All of the above-mentioned things very light and hardly worth complaining about.

I am very glad, content, and happy; I have an intelligent, kind, and fine husband whom I love most passionately and who loves me just as much. I have a career that lets me accomplish things, and I am grateful to a very kind fate every single day.

I will not and cannot make a statement about the "coming one" until later and I hope that it will be healthy and intelligent.

MOPE TO VERA

Moscow, 19 December 1938

Those last long and content-less days of the year go by at lightning speed. It is rather strange to realize how many, many hours each day has, and to have the feeling that they are flying by anyway. My thirty-ninth birthday was an eternity ago and that is just half a year ago, and just a few hours ago, I talked to my most beloved from Victoria Station, and that took place nearly three weeks ago. Because of all that traveling, I have lost all feeling for time, but *everything* I did together with my most beloved is so infinitely close as if it just happened, and everything else that takes place away from you is in an almost forgotten past; even yesterday and how much more that which took place half a year ago?

This evening, after dinner, I slept for a little while, because the cold outside and the heated rooms produce much need for sleep, a need I give in to, since I now have the time. Today, I was able to buy another larger batch of merchandise, but there is not much merchandise to be had right now, because the season is over and I have relatively little to do. Since it is the custom here, my colleagues and I played some games, a stupid card game the name of which I do not know. I am too untalented for the ones that require more brain power, and that is why they played a stupid one out of consideration for me–and out of decency, I cannot exclude myself. Tomorrow, I will wear the fur for the first time, because I am beginning to feel cold in the other coat. I am very glad that I have it here. There will be another big ball for New Year's Eve and we *Pushniki* [139] reserved a table.

It is very late at night again and I do not want to climb from my chaste bed too late tomorrow, and that is why I will close. However, before I do, as always, I want to send you my gentlest kisses and my most passionate embraces and gently caress you and your beautiful body in my thoughts. I do so long for that reality and I love you infinitely, my most beloved, you!!!

Completely, Your Mope

VERA TO MOPE

London, 20 December 1938 [postcard]

I did not write yesterday as this week is more or less like your weeks during the big sales! I promise you and it is really true that I am taking very good care of myself and as you see, I am even neglecting my sweet husband by going straight away to bed. I shall try and write to you probably to-morrow during the day. Please do *not* be sad that I have not written a letter. I am *continually* with you with my thoughts! Completely, *Your* Lilongo

---

[139] The pet name given to themselves by the foreign contingent of fur buyers working with Sojuzpushnina, the Soviet agency in charge of the sale of animal skins.

MOPE TO VERA

Moscow, 20 December 1938

There are children one has to constantly keep under control with a stick and my darling is one of those! If I were not constantly endeavoring to temper your fervor for M&S with letters and telegrams, I am convinced that, with all your zeal for your work, you would do a lot of things that would be especially bad for your health at this particular time. I hope that I have been able to limit your wild impulse to overwork, and that means that at least *something* has been achieved. I do know you share my views that everything has to be done to let our offspring become strong and healthy, but, there is too intense an urge to work in you and someone has to keep putting on the brakes and try to reduce the respect and lessen the urge. And is there anyone besides me who has more of a claim on you and is more entitled to do so?

I embrace you with the most passionate love and the greatest longing and I kiss your eyes, your beloved mouth and many other beautiful things. *Completely*, Your Mope

VERA TO MOPE

London, 22 December 1938

Today, I have such wonderful *"news"*!! And now I hardly know how to tell you!! They tell me that they will relocate me to the Pantheon "Store"[140] beginning January 9!!!!! I could hardly breathe!

My love, I would have sent you a telegram but I know that you (probably quite beside yourself) would send one back saying, "Do not accept under any circumstances!" I called Dr. Rothschild and he said I could work until May without any problems (actually, as far as I am concerned, even longer, but since it will become obvious by then that I am expecting, it will most likely not work well for the store). My love, *please, please,* do not write in anger that I should not accept it under any circumstances. I am so very happy about it and find it so very incomprehensible that I as a foreigner will get the Pantheon Store! I would have never dreamt of it! I just talked to your dear mother on the

---

140 This flagship Marks & Spencer store was built in 1938 on the site in Oxford Street where the Pantheon, an eighteenth-century structure, had stood.

telephone and gave her the news and she was also very happy. What do you have to say, my love!?

Please, please, please, do *not* say that you will not give your permission! I am sure that it will not be any more strenuous than Hammersmith and a lot healthier because the rooms in Hammersmith are cold and damp! Should they even keep the offer open after the revelation of my pregnancy, which I highly doubt unfortunately, I would have a *staff manageress* for an assistant and below her, two more assistants. On top of that, I would have *every* Saturday afternoon off and an entire Saturday off once a month. I am also curious to find out what kind of raise I will get. And now, I am afraid that I counted my chickens before they are hatched.

Today, for the very first time in my life, I wished I were a man! But nonetheless, I am anyway looking forward to our little child very, very much, and you just have to understand and forgive such a passing wish which lasts for a moment only, and it is not meant seriously anyway! Nevertheless, I was terribly pleased about the matter as such.

I love you–very, very, very much and I am very pleased and happy and content with my lot in life. Most passionately and completely, Your Little Witch

MOPE TO VERA

Moscow, 22 December 1938

After I finished working, I went down to the restaurant to have a glass of tea and write, but it was my bad luck that there were still a few acquaintances sitting around despite the late hour and so I had to, more unwilling than willing, sit down with them. There was a married couple sitting at the table, at the end of a one-year long trip around the world. These people opened a mink farm in Wisconsin in the U.S.A. four years ago and are now working so successfully that they can afford such a long trip. The man told me that he has two thousand minks and that one thousand and five hundred of them will now be slaughtered and brought to the fur market. However, he has no idea about the prices that will be paid for his pelts at this time. As it happened, I had heard a report on the New York auction and because of that, I knew quite a bit about it. Each one of the mink females bears at least four young in the course of a year so that he can count on another large harvest next year.

The average price he will get for his merchandise lies around $15 per piece so that he will take in approximately $30,000 with relatively small expenses for feeding and upkeep. It is a very lucrative business that, just a few years ago, had many a farmer lose everything because they were not sufficiently informed about the question of how to feed the critters.

Today, I inspected a lot of merchandise but I was not able to make quite as much as I would have liked and I think that it will be even more difficult to make any deals during the next few days due to the *Christmas holiday*, because the Western Europeans laze around and I will be forced to wait for answers in vain.

Just now, I am reading *The Oppermanns* by Lion Feuchtwanger and it is depressing to have that disgusting time of the beginning of the Nazi era before your eyes and to relive it.[141] The descriptions of the individual siblings and their reactions remind me strongly of the individual responses from the diverse people at Gebrüder Felsenstein who just did not want to believe that they would be excluded from everything despite all the traditions and the recognition of their fellow citizens as highly respectable contemporaries.

While I am writing, my sweet beloved is watching me from six different photographs and I feel such an indomitable longing for the original that I can no longer describe it. On one of them, I am looking down your bathing suit, down to two of the sweetest half spheres ever and I could not imagine them to be more beautiful than the real thing, and my thoughts let me dream of other beloved places of your body, and that makes me so excited that I have to keep looking so I can imagine them as well in all their hills and valleys, even if reality keeps them hidden from me, unfortunately. I kiss all of those sweet places, which I can only imagine in my mind, sadly, and I will now take myself to my beloved in my dreams and caress her tenderly and pull all of your seductive limbs close to me and breathe in their warmth, as if I were really with you.

Completely and utterly, Your Mope

---

141 Feuchtwanger's novel, published in 1933, is a particularly prescient account of the effect of Nazism on the Jews of Germany, and of the inability of assimilated Jews to comprehend the full extent of the terrors that were about to be unleashed against them.

VERA TO MOPE

London, 23 December 1938

My most heartfelt thanks for your dear telephone call! I was soooo happy to hear your dear, beloved voice. And I was sooo very happy that you seem to be rather *pleased* about the Pantheon Store, to all appearances. Today, I will only write this very short note to my beloved, because I want to go to bed since tomorrow is another "big" day at the store! I am feeling *very well*!

I received a letter from Hilde Lewy in Genoa on Monday. Her mother-in-law received a visa to Palestine, and she is going to the U.S.A. to stay there with her sister until her departure. Hilde had to let go her girl who had been with her for three years because of the latest law passage and now has to take care of the baby, the move, and the household by herself.[142] They have to leave over half of their possessions behind and hope to be able to depart towards the end of January or the beginning of February. She seems very charmed by her baby.

Once again, thank you and all my love and many most loving kisses, you, my *sweetheart*!!! Most passionately and completely, Your Little Witch

MOPE TO VERA

Moscow, 23 December 1938

I am so very happy to have talked to my darling just a little while ago, and your beloved voice sounded so happy that my mood turned happy and light as well. When the call came in a while ago, I had gone downstairs, because of Pod Wychodnoi,–resigned to the fact that I would have to do without the sound of your most beloved voice today–to get something to eat and was just going to begin with very little appetite when they called me to the telephone. If you could have seen how much better everything tasted after that!!!

And now, I have not even congratulated you yet on your excellent success and advancement and I do so with *the greatest joy*, because I know and can measure what this acknowledgment–which was so very unexpected–means to you. It is really a great thing that they have chosen

---

142 Mussolini introduced a raft of anti-Jewish laws in 1938, with the intention of bringing fascist Italy into line with Germany.

my loved one for such an important position and it proves how capable you are, especially after they did not take you, as a *foreigner*, as seriously as they would the *natives*. I assume that they will ask my beloved one to come to the head office for the announcement of the great event. Now, I would advise you to write a letter to your head of personnel beforehand and put it in your handbag, a letter in which you tell her about your expectant condition and give her the time at which you will most likely have to take a break from your work. You can back-date the letter just a bit if you like!

Then, when she tells you about your advancement as well as your raise, you pull out the letter and say that you had intended to let her know about the matter some time ago, but that you had hesitated because you can never be too sure during the first few months. Now, however, you felt duty-bound to call her attention to the facts, etc. This way, you will find out first of all what they were thinking concerning the raise and it proves your *fairness* with the already proven plan to call attention to your condition. I hope that these lines will reach my darling in time.

After dinner, I went for an hour long walk through the wonderful, cold, snowy night and drank hot tea afterwards. It is quite cold here but I consider the cold rather comfortable. My bronchial tubes are clear and I can breathe so very well and unimpeded. Last year, the minus temperatures were much less welcome to me. Unfortunately, the snow is removed immediately here–even while it is still falling–that is great where traffic is concerned, but I would absolutely like to experience a real winter picture of Moscow, with sleigh rides, snowball throwing children, and whatever else there is on the street where winter enjoyment is concerned.

Now I want to hurry and get to bed and try to remember the conversation with my beloved and the sweet long kiss you gave me which I did not hear, unfortunately! I embrace you with the greatest longing and filled with the *greatest* love and *great* pride for my little girl who is so capable and so successful. Completely, *Your* Mope

VERA TO MOPE

London, 28 December 1938

So–I called the *head office* this morning and was able to get an appointment for 4 o'clock with the head of personnel. I shared *that I shall have a baby in July*! And that they would have enough time to find a replacement for the time during which I will not be there. They explained to me right away that they did not have anyone else whom they could send there and that they would be glad if I could work there until May with the condition that it is *alright for me*. And I said, "*All I wanted to know was whether it's alright with you! And I only wanted to be fair and tell you!*" And that was the end of the conversation. And I was so elated!!! I am all too curious to hear about the *increase* (my estimate is 10/-). Hopefully, the offer letter will come through soon.

I talked to your dear mother on the telephone a little while ago (since we closed very early today I did not go back to the store). I will go to visit her on Sunday afternoon. Alice arrived on her doorstep all of a sudden Monday evening and I am looking forward to getting to know her.[143]

My most heartfelt thanks for your two dear letters from the 19th and 20th which I received earlier today and made waking up all the more pleasant! My love, although I do not put immense distances behind me in a short period of time, as you do, but stay in one place most of the time, I also lose all feeling for time quite often. It seems completely incomprehensible to me that I am supposed to have known my beloved for just three years at the end of next month, or better, met him back then for the very first time, and I cannot imagine, no matter how hard I try, what my life was like before that.

I just talked to Hannalein on the telephone–the poor child will also be a straw-widow over the holidays. Fred helped a few more strangers to get out of that damned country,[144] which is something I think is very decent of him, and next Wednesday, he has to go on another big business trip for two months. Hannalein explained to me on the telephone that she is really *fond of me* and she congratulated me on the biggest store. I thought that was very charming of her!

My love, I do not think that anything will come of my plans to join you there in February, but I also doubt that Dr. Rothschild would have agreed to that anyway.

---

143 Mope's sister, Alice, had unexpectedly traveled to London from Palestine with the intention of exploring the possibility of her family resettling in England. A surviving letter from her sister Hanna to their brother Mope enunciates her plight: "Alice runs around every day in order to find a chance to build an existence for her husband, herself, and her children. Sadly, they cannot seem to get ahead in Palestine. But even here, things are difficult, as she has found out" (23 January 1939).

144 The Rosenbaum children (see note 130).

Are you happy with the Pantheon? Even if I only stayed for a very short time, two or three months, I am glad that I got M&S's biggest store and one in the West End of London, because that will be important for any kind of future work, whether for M&S or somewhere else.

My Mopeleinchen, I will close now and go to bed. I kiss you in my thoughts, with the greatest tenderness, you, my love!!! *Your* Little Witch

MOPE TO VERA

Moscow, 28 December 1938

It is not early anymore and on top of that, I had two glasses of tea with three cognacs each as medication against my cold, but I had a little rest earlier and I do not want to get up from sitting at the desk before I have sent *at least one* loving kiss by letter to my sweet one before I go to bed. Unfortunately, I was without my darling's mail again today and that means that the last of your beloved letters I received was from nine days ago today. Had I not talked to you last Friday, I would be completely beside myself, but knowing how you were feeling on the last day of the most exhausting period before *Christmas* and the following free days, I feel much calmer. I would really love to know if those three days of rest brought real rest and relaxation for my little girl and that the first day back at work today was not too exhausting.

It seems to me that the first *actual* good deed of Mr. Chamberlain was that he gave Tuesday to the London residents as a day off,[145] because the things he did before prove to be misdeeds over time, and I am afraid that he will add to those. Sadly, I can see more and more that my judgment concerning his politics back then was quite correct and that my rejection of the Munich surrender of the Czech Sudetenland was clearly seen, even if my darling did not want to admit it because you were under the influence of popular opinion.

Hopefully, Ketty and David can soon make it to London. It will be difficult for them to know that their children are living so dispersed, but it is a good thing that there are relatives among whom they can be distributed. What is going on with Grete and her children? I would really like to know more and hopefully nothing but good things! Also if

---

145 Christmas was on a Sunday in 1938, and, as a consequence, Parliament declared Tuesday, 27 December (the day after Boxing Day), a public holiday.

Semy will come to London now! You do not seem to have heard anything else about Carlchen Rosenfeld and his Lies and children, because if you had, you would have reported it. Their eldest boy is of that dangerous age and I hope that those swine do not do anything to him.

Today, I bought another batch of merchandise and I hope that my customers will be happy with the purchase. During this month, I have now made deals for around £28,000, which means that I earned £20. That is not really all that much, but the timing is not the best right now, since the fresh merchandise did not start to arrive until now. In any case, I hope to be able to take care of a few smaller things before the end of the year.

This morning, I went to my Russian lesson and even though, to the trained ear, I probably made some awful grammatical errors, I was able to make myself understood. That is not all that great, but nevertheless, it is something, and at the moment, I tend to be less critical, because otherwise, I would be and should be ashamed to open my mouth in Russian. Unfortunately, there is little opportunity to speak and hear the language, since our circle only speaks English or German and I hardly ever get together with real Russians who do not also speak English or German as well. And those Russians are from the Sojuspushnina and it would be careless of me to speak to them in their own language and risk misunderstandings that could be very expensive for the customers.

Tomorrow, I have to inspect an enormous amount of merchandise and because of that, I will close now, so I will be well-rested. There is a lot more work here now than just a few days ago, because–as I said–the new harvest has begun to come in.

I kiss you with the greatest tenderness and the most passionate love, and I am so very pleased and happy to know that you are really feeling well and that the new citizen to-be causes you little discomfort. I wonder what the decision concerning the Pantheon Store will be. Please do not be upset if you do not get it because of the expected baby. I hope with all my heart that the child will give you much more joy than all the *chain stores* on earth could give you, even if they belonged to you. Completely, *Your* Mope

VERA TO MOPE

London, 29 December 1938

It is very late again! I am very tired and that is why I will only write a short greeting today, although I lay down in bed for a while around lunch time today. My love, if I do not get a decent increase for the Pantheon store, I will leave M&S, and if Dr. Rothschild and Co. do not have any objections, I will join my most beloved. Your belief that it might take until April before you can come home makes me feel very sad and maybe I can come to you after all–how much I wish for that!!! Most passionately and completely, *Your* Little Witch

MOPE TO VERA

Moscow, 30 December 1938

I had a lot of merchandise to inspect today and I am also expecting a lot of work for tomorrow. Tomorrow evening, there will be a big New Year's Eve party in the hotel restaurant, but if I am as tired tomorrow night as I am tonight, I might go to bed. We do not work on 1st or 2nd January and then, I will be able to rest. I can see from the letter in which you tell me about the Pantheon store just *how* happy you are with this advancement and I have to admit today that the sheer joy you took in the suggestion is worth it all, even though it is not actual coin. Sadly, your all too egotistical husband just cannot come to terms quite as quickly with the fact that he will have to forego your coming here, and I do not want you to be sad about that. After all, these long periods of separation are much more difficult for me than for my most beloved one who continues to live in the circle of the people she has chosen and only has to forego my company. That is not meant to sound bitter at all and should not be understood any differently than just a statement of fact.

I wish that the new position will bring you the satisfaction you expect from it. When I come home in April and, should you keep working until May, I would rather not come to London, because I will have to come back here in May or June. And then, I better look for one who also has time for me and leave you to M&S. Most passionately, Your Mope

VERA TO MOPE

London, 1 January 1939

I did not wake up until a half hour ago; I slept well into the New Year and that was a nice thing, too, because waking up called up the end of the old year clearly into my consciousness, and I am sad and *downhearted*: either you, my love, are not well and the cold I can feel despite the vast distance is more than just a sniffle and my beloved even has a fever and does not feel well? That is the first thing I am thinking and worrying about. Hopefully, hopefully, this thought is wrong and unjustified, but the fact that you did *not* go to the New Year's Eve party which had been announced some time ago makes my fear stronger and my heart heavy. Did you consult a doctor? Are the colleagues taking care of you? Did you stay in bed for a few days in order to let the warmth and even temperatures have an effect on you?

At 9 o'clock on the dot, when I left the store yesterday evening (we closed at 8.30), I imagined that my beloved was probably receiving the telegram (around midnight your time) I had posted in person around 7 p.m. and that he would drink to my health and to the health of our future little offspring who will hopefully turn out to be *just* like I imagine, for the two of us.

Mopeleinchen, this is the *first* day of 1939 and *I am downhearted* and I hope that the next few years will bring us nothing but good things. I wish for us: good health, peace, sufficient professional success so we will not have any financial worries, a little child that turns out just the way it is in our dreams, and that our mutual love in all its depth and perfection will stand the test of time and stay just the way it is today. Your Veralein who is feeling just a little sad!

MOPE TO VERA

Moscow, 2 January 1939

When man was first created–so says the first book of Moses–God declared that he created him in his own image. Later, when he gave him the laws, he said, you may not have a God besides me, I am the Lord, your God, an "agitated" God. I am sure that that is not supposed to mean agitated, but jealous. Against my better judgment, I am both agitated and jealous of M&S if it begins to take over more room in my girl's heart than I am forced to give it, and for making my beloved have such blasphemous thoughts as regretting not being a man. It seems to me that this rather innocuous remark, if made at a normal time, but at this time when my sweetest one moves toward the highest and most beautiful goal of her womanhood, added much to the bleakness I felt during the last few days of 1938. I read that and then it wormed its way into my innermost being and caused the most insensible considerations, doubts, and sadness in me. Even now, when I consider the matter in a much calmer light, I can understand that all too well, because, if your enthusiasm for your work–which can only be done by a woman in a rational manner–brings you so far that I and our togetherness appear burdensome to you, then everything has been moved from its normal channels.

Following that, you wrote that you, as a man, would have to do without me and my love and that you would rather not do that but that could only be compensation in a childless marriage. In this time of bearing fruit, I think that a woman–*my wife*–would not even be able to entertain such treasonous thoughts. After all, the remark was aimed mainly at the child you are expecting, because, without its development, you would be given the same opportunities as any man–namely the undisturbed continuation of your work. So your words mean this to me: if only I were rid of the child I would be uninhibited in my professional development. I am writing this in such a longwinded and detailed manner to make you understand my deep depression, now that it has been overcome and made way for happier thoughts. Maybe I am a little too sensitive and it is a little crazy to give so much importance to a rather hasty remark!

However, my beloved's impregnation was not just a happy experience of a few minutes to me, but with the experience I took on the responsibility of its consequences and part of those is the upshot that you will have to interrupt your work. If that places such a heavy burden on my girl, then the goal of my wishes to make you into the mother of my child is an unforgivable act of egotism on my part, an act that forces you to make sacrifices contrary to your wishes. Maybe, the real feelings of motherhood are not awakened until later in you girls, when the little creature lies in front of you visibly and its existence begins to fill your heart with joy. For me, the feeling began the moment I saw you lying there so helplessly and sick in Nice. You seemed like a small animal struck down by my lust, a small animal I had robbed of its strength and the agility of its movements. Back then, it was only a foreshadowing of the fact that I was the guilty one, but that has been confirmed in the meantime, and the picture of those days stands in front of my eyes today, as if the knowledge had been in me even back then.

I kiss you, you poor, sweet, most beloved little girl who has been robbed of your free will by me–filled with the most immense longing for you and I wish for both of us that you will be limitlessly happy with this robbery some day and that you will feel full of joy.

Completely and totally, Your Mope

VERA TO MOPE

London, 3 January 1939

After I was ever so filled with joy and contentment last week and also wrote to you about it from the store, there was an immense "damper" on all that high-spiritedness today! But after all, I guess that is the way it is supposed to be, because otherwise, life would not be just. I was informed by the M&S management that as I was expecting a baby, it would be better and the *only* right thing to stay in Hammersmith. As I already knew myself, it would take several months to learn the inner workings of a new store, and if I were in their place, would I give "Miss Hirsch" the Pantheon under the current conditions? The only answer I could give them was that I was *unfortunately of their opinion*.

I did not tell anyone else in the Hammersmith store about all of this, and although quite a number of girls had heard about my relocation, English people are much too polite to ask for a reason if one does not volunteer it. I am sure that *no one* can tell yet that I am expecting by looking at me, because, until now, the only sign is that I have become *much* smaller in the face and most people ask me if I have lost weight.

I took the little bottle with the urine sample to Dr. Rothschild this evening. Mutti went with me. He was very nice today and said that I could not work any longer than the end of April. I asked him in quite some detail about a trip for me to pick up my beloved, but unfortunately, he was very much against the idea; he said that, if it was a "must," then maybe one could do something like that, but otherwise *most decidedly* not. He said that if one traveled by sea, one could not only do damage to the baby, but also to oneself. You can see that I had a *very sad* day today!

Dr. Rothschild also took my blood pressure again and told me that he would not be able to feel anything for another month and that any examination before that would not make any sense, and he is completely right, of course. He advised me to also take the calcium medication you recommended from now on.

I am very, very tired this evening–that is the reason for this less than beautiful letter. I want to close now and go to sleep. Sadly, the mailman did not bring me anything from my beloved today. *Completely Your* Little Witch

MOPE TO VERA

Moscow, 3 January 1939

Towards the evening I received your telegram with the news that nothing will come of the Pantheon store–I am sure that made you bitterly sad. My most beloved took such great pleasure in the advancement and I am sure that my complaining is the reason that nothing will come of it now. I feel such a profound aversion towards the relocation that it seems to have flowed out of me in waves, all the way to your bosses at M&S. I wonder if my sweet one is upset with me now for those emotional waves. You see, I was discouraged by the longer commute, the greater difficulties getting home, the stress that is connected with getting to know all those many new girls, and the entire getting used to the new store. I had not realized, before reading your last few letters, just how immensely close the matter was to your heart, and I finally became a little more comfortable with the idea, and now, even I feel a certain sense of woefulness that the position already given to you was taken away again. The reason is probably the short time you would be able to devote to the matter, and I can understand only too well that those people want to avoid making this important store into a test case. Well, maybe there will be another opportunity for you later, to receive that or a similar position. After all, the main thing is that they picked you as the best qualified staff manager, and that is where the main acknowledgment lies.

So my sister Alice did finally arrive in London! That young girl seems to have been gone from home for nearly two months already and apparently told herself à la Chamberlain: *try, try, try again*, until she received her visa. I wonder if you have met her in the meantime. I am very curious to read your report.

Now, it has almost been three years since we met for the first time. Everything in me and on me, every pore, every hair, and every little piece of skin longs for your sweet nearness and I have no idea how I can stand that for another three and a half months until I can finally pull you close to me again. Completely, Your Mope

VERA TO MOPE

London, 5 January 1939

Yesterday, the evening with your dear mother and Alice, was very harmonious. I liked Alice (and I was just a little prepared for that *not* to be the case), and I think that all of you wrong her just a little where her appearance is concerned, because I think that I would call her rather *good-looking* than not. Your dear mother told us that Grete has gone to join Norbert at his urging (he had a passport for both of them, after all), but that Grete really did not appreciate having to leave everything behind, while she had been hoping that she could sell the house before leaving and to take along at least part of her belongings. She had gone and taken the two smaller ones to Freiburg and they would come over in the same way as the older siblings.[146] I also found out from your dear mother that Semy is here now and that his wife will arrive in the next few days.[147]

Around lunch today, we were in the city, which is why I went to lie down as soon as we returned home shortly after 7, and I took care of all of my correspondence from there. We stopped by Radio-Rentals in Regent Street and ordered a radio–it will be delivered tomorrow, or rather, several will be shown so we can choose one because the different

---

146 Mope's sister Grete (twin sister to Alice) followed her husband, Norbert, to Davos, Switzerland, where he was sheltering. Grete and their four children (aged between two and nine) were refused asylum in Switzerland but could not return to Germany, their house in Freiburg having been confiscated by the Nazis. Their fate remained uncertain at this time.

147 Mope's cousin, Semy Felsenstein, had been arrested and sent to Buchenwald concentration camp following Kristallnacht. He was forced to barter the remaining assets of the Gebrüder Felsenstein, including funds that were outside Germany, in order to obtain his release and the reactivation of a dormant visa to travel to England.

ones work differently, depending on the district. I agreed to rent and not buy the apparatus, and the rent, depending on the radio, is between 2/–and 3/–per week, and all repairs are taken care of by the company. I am really looking forward to having the radio, and since I so rarely get to the cinema or go to the theater now–it is usually too late for that–I am looking forward to the diversion all the more.

I want to close now and go to bed soon, but before I do, I want to send you innumerably many of the most passionate kisses–Your Lilongo

MOPE TO VERA

Moscow, 5 January 1939

Unfortunately, I remained without your longed-for mail today, especially now when they are filled with sorrow over the Pantheon after all that joy you felt. I would so like to help you overcome all this, which would probably be much easier if I had knowledge of the particulars. I have to show more patience than I have and just keep waiting for my darling's mail. I am always speculating that that gang of criminals in Germany polices the transit mail and that is why the delivery takes place so irregularly. Nothing can be put past that rabble.

By the way, they announced on the radio yesterday that it had snowed again in London. I am sure it is very cold there and I hope that you are dressing accordingly, that is, very warmly, especially since the Hammersmith store does not really offer the ideal kind of protection from the rigors of the weather. It also snowed here today, but only very little snow has fallen so far this winter. The snowflakes are itty-bitty, but for all that, the snow is much more compact than we are familiar with in Western Europe. I still do not feel the cold as uncomfortable yet, something that has not been the case with me for the last few years. I am much less frozen and so very well equipped with my woolen underwear. The new socks your dear mother procured for me really prove to be invaluable.

A little while ago, we had a long conversation concerning the faithfulness of traveling businessmen to their wives. I seem to be the only one of the colleagues who does not dally with the local girls and in the course of the conversation, I realized that this daily writing to my little witch is a strong tool to curb my desire for sexual activity (because of the deep concentration on my dearest one) as far as it does not

Twenty-nine: "Today, for the First Time in My Life, I Wished I Were a Man!"

concern you, and sadly, there is no chance for that anyway. One of the boys mentioned that quite a few of the Russian "virgins" wonder who I am, but they advise them not to approach me to save their graceful womanhood from being turned down. I know about a few people who are attached to their wives with deep love but they do not feel equal to being away from them for such a long time.

Today is Pod-Wychodnoi and I look back at the work period with shame, but it lasted only three days, and I did not earn even one penny. I tell you that because shared pain is half the pain and I wish nothing more than reducing your pain the same way. Other than that, my "failure" does not bother me all that much, because no one else here has been able to enter any contracts. The Russians are now asking for such high prices that I seriously doubt that there will be any contracts made. The politics driven by that is in consolidating the prices despite the bad world market, and that is actually very necessary. If the people accommodated the economic situation of the capitalized nations at the very beginning of the season, today's prices would be well under the existing contracts and a lot of merchandise would be left lying around. This way, they can be retained until the auction in March and maybe, by then, the entire situation will hopefully be much better. The main thing needed is that those fascist criminals become weakened in the meantime and I fear that Mr. Chamberlain's visit in Rome will have the opposite result. That one will sell anything that does not belong to him at give-away prices and I am curious to see what will happen when they start kneeling on his seams. I consider his politics ruinous and undermining all of Europe and it seems to me that the U.S.A. has taken the more intelligent and farsighted path with its strengthened pro-Russian stance. England will realize that soon enough. Hopefully before it is too late![148]

My only regret is that I cannot be with you during this time and do everything possible to make things easier for you. Everything else, like yes Pantheon or no Pantheon, and yes contract or no contract, will soon sink into the past, and is so unimportant next to the prospect of a

---

148 Mope refers here to the impending visit of Neville Chamberlain to Rome, where, in line with his policy of appeasement, he was to meet with Benito Mussolini whom he hoped would persuade Hitler against going to war. No promises were made by Mussolini. In his State of the Union address on 4 January, Franklin Roosevelt had warned that "A war which threatened to envelop the world in flames has been averted; but it has become increasingly clear that world peace is not assured."

positive future, and I wish my sweet one would come to the same way of thinking and quickly get over the lost Pantheon. Your Mope

VERA TO MOPE

London, 8 January 1939

Dr. Rothschild, who requested that I bring him another two little bottles, one from the morning before the store and another one after, called yesterday evening to tell me that everything was in order and he wanted another two bottles next Friday, just to make sure. I am feeling excellent and I am sure that the tiredness is caused by the weather.

When I came home on Friday, the radio was there and it works really well and we can hear all the foreign stations very clearly. The installation cost 10/6 and the rent is 9/6 per month, and after six months, the rent becomes cheaper. The official fee from the post office is 10/–per year, so it is a pleasure one can afford and I am terribly happy to have it. This evening, I listened to an act from the opera *Faust* with great enjoyment and also heard the *Rhapsody* by Liszt. You can hear foreign and inland broadcasts equally well, and *the entire family* takes great pleasure in the radio.

MOPE TO VERA

Moscow, 8 January 1939

I had thought that I could see a logical sequence in my thinking and became so obsessed with those depressing ideas that I forgot to consider, for the most part, what kind of upset I would cause for my darling. I now see my guilt more clearly than I did a few days ago and I beg you to regard the unforgivable which found its expression in unjustified jealousy of what occupied your mind so strongly, namely your work. I know how little of life my beloved can enjoy because of my being away for so long, and instead of supporting the pleasure you take in your work, I am constantly making the mistake of arguing against it. I will try very hard to do better and not allow any more of those impulsive reactions. Many things can be contained and controlled and I am making an effort, but I beg you that when I wrong you, and unfortunately, that possibility exists because of these long periods of separation and the ever so imperfect method of communicating through letters, to not get upset.

As you have already read in my earlier letters, it cost me the same amount of strength to get used to the thought of the Pantheon, especially since I was rather prejudiced against it in general. But when I heard the sound of those bitter words "Pantheon canceled" in your telegram, I started to regret having been against the entire matter and that I had to accept part of the blame for its failure. However, when it comes right down to it, it is probably better that it happened this way and we should regard the matter as postponed and not put aside, and my beloved can look forward to working at a Pantheon in the future. After all, the sheer amount of acknowledgment you have received for your work gives you a certain amount of satisfaction–more for the soul than material gain–and the knowledge that you will be able to get work at *any* time should add more than enough to make up for the material side of it. It is really not an easy life that the two of us have to lead, so terribly far apart from each other, and still belonging together. But when it comes down to it, we should be glad that we have such a decent way of feeding ourselves–and multiplying–after we both got out of that pig sty with our health, but without any means.

I am very happy to hear that you liked Alice. People who meet her without any preconceptions usually like her, and she has many friends. But around us when we were children in Leipzig, because of her more beautiful sisters who were in part more intelligent and who were preferred as company by the brothers as well, she felt pushed against the wall so that she answered to everything in the defensive instead of reacting normally. That certainly created a skewed impression of her character. I know very well that she is much more good-hearted and eager to help than many other human beings, probably even more so than some of her siblings, who were always trying to subdue her. Added to that was her love for food which would not allow her to let a bowl of potatoes leave the table without being emptied first, despite all her wishes to retain a slim figure. I am sure that that is a little exaggerated, but the slimmer sisters ate fewer potatoes while two souls–the slim soul and the potato soul–did battle in her breast and also created disagreement in other things in her innermost being which is something she could not hide completely. I hope that you spend a pleasant Wednesday evening with her.

Your Mope who loves you indescribably!!!

VERA TO MOPE

London, 13 January 1939

From the Office

I called your dear mother a little while ago and I will see her and Alice either tomorrow or Saturday around noon. Gertrud started attending school here on Monday, and Lassar is supposed to be registered at one in the next few days. He was complaining to me that he was not allowed to take his stamp collection out of the country with him, and I will give him a few from you, my love.

Yesterday morning—we are now selling small cakes and tarts in the store—I took the three girls who work at the new counter as well as the floorwalker responsible for that area on a tour of the "model bakery" where all these sweet things are produced mechanically in very hygienic conditions. I was very interested in seeing the operation: the bakery is in Hayes in Middlesex and it took over an hour for us to finally get there; and since we had had no idea of the distance, we had started much too late and did not get back to the store until about 2 o'clock. Beginning next week, M&S will introduce a forty-five-hour work week. On Mondays, Tuesdays and Wednesdays, one third of the personnel is allowed to go home at 6 o'clock, and the morning break has been extended from ten to fifteen minutes. The girls responded to this innovation with great enthusiasm, and I think that it is a step in the *right* direction!

I have not heard *anything* from Hilde in Genoa since December and she still has not answered my *long* New Year's letter: maybe they have traveled on already, because otherwise, her silence is baffling to me. Most passionately and completely and utterly, *Your* Little Witch

MOPE TO VERA

Moscow, 13 January 1939

Unfortunately, I was without your mail again today. It has now been three days I have been waiting without success, and only the knowledge that I talked to you for a short time yesterday and having received your telegram calm me just a bit. Of course—I am sure that it is a mistake—I am starting to think too much again, worrying about what the reason for the lack of mail could be. I am wondering if I might have written something during those days when I was feeling so depressed that might have made you cross with me. Your voice also sounded rather matter of fact, almost cold, out of which there is a mean ghost whispering in my ear right now telling me that it could be proof of your being cross. And all that, although I am completely convinced of your love for me–it is just a constant pondering that takes hold of my brain because I have nothing better to do, because I miss you so very much and because of the infernal waiting for your ever so longed for news. Should I even write down such thoughts?

In order to show you just how difficult my job is in making a business contract, around 11.00 this morning I went to the branch office of Sojuzpushnina. I was finally received at 2.30 p.m. During the whole time, three and a half hours of waiting, I had to tell myself that this attempt would fail with a ninety per cent certainty. Although my proposal was not completely declined, and the chances for success might have risen from ten to fifteen per cent, I remained quite skeptical, and understandably so. After my visit to the branch office, I went to the warehouse. There, I waited another two hours exactly before I was admitted, and there the result was entirely negative. I did not see any merchandise at all today. Now you can imagine how the brain occupies itself during such long waiting periods and you will hardly wonder about all that brooding.

By the way, I had a conversation with a man from Hanover today–he is an employee of an animal shop and arrived here yesterday with an African elephant which comes from the Hanover Zoo. He will trade that elephant for snow leopards, reindeer, and Russian deer and take them back to Hanover. After a while, he became a little more relaxed and told me how exceedingly bad the living conditions in Germany are. For himself with a wife and child, he receives half a pound of butter per week, and the bread is moldy. You can no longer find decent fabric for suits and clothing. The discontent of the population is supposedly very great and growing at a constant rate. People in all decent circles are beside themselves over the slaughter of Jews which took place in late fall–that is when the government people showed their true faces once again.[149] They had tried to prepare himself for how bad living conditions were here. Now, he is completely amazed to see what excellent bread and any desired quantity of good food can be had here. They showed him the underground train and he is completely thrilled with it. There

---

149 The reference is to Kristallnacht.

are, after all, no grander and more beautiful stations in the whole world and everyone shares in the admiration for what was accomplished here. I wonder how he will find his way again once he returns to that country of barbarians.

After this report, I see even more confirmation in my opinion that this regime worthy of condemnation cannot hold its grip on power much longer. I just wish that my opinion had already been confirmed in fact. I am happy and overjoyed to have nothing more to do with that country and I am completely satisfied with my fate, to be a Jew, which is why I am no longer part of it. We had to get out of there, not because we are vermin, but because they knew without a question that Jewish people would have rebelled against the reigning dishonorable methods. You cannot use such methods on an old cultured people, as we Jews are, and they had to do it without us, or after we had lost all human rights.

I am looking forward immensely to the gift of a healthy, strong, intelligent child that my beloved will give me in the course of the coming year. Completely, Your Mope

VERA TO MOPE

London, 15 January 1939

After I spent the entire Sunday morning in bed sleeping and reading, I went to Hannalein's for lunch. She and I had a very pleasant chat after lunch until about 5 o'clock, sitting by the fire in her drawing room, completely undisturbed for once. I really do get along ever so well with her and I do like her a lot. Later, your dear mother and Alice joined us. As you state so correctly, Alice is a *very* dear little animal and I often feel just a little sorry for her, because she obviously means well and often does not get to the intended goal, but is completely off the mark. She is very nice and friendly to me and talks about you ever so sweetly and keeps expressing her regret over the fact that you are not here (and I?!!!!!!!!!!).

Hanna is very worried about Ketty and David and her two younger ones (I think I already wrote to you that Holland no longer admits any refugee children, so they cannot go to the sister of your dear mother). I promised her, if she sends me copies of the papers that have already been submitted, that I will write to Mrs. Stiebel concerning Ketty. Hanna said that they have a good and more than sufficient guarantee for Ketty, and that David has good business connections here so he can build a new business. You will be happy to hear that Grete's two little ones have joined her in Switzerland now.

Dr. Rothschild who had requested that I send him another two little bottles,[150] one from Friday morning and one from the evening, called a little while ago to inform me that everything seems to be going well and that Mr. Nixon has found a *nursing home* in Courtfield Gardens (that is in the vicinity of Gloucester Road Station). As soon as I have the time, I will have a look at it with Muttilein and find out about the cost, and I will make a decision then. If you do not book a room here months in advance, you might not get one at all.

It is 1.00 a.m. now where you are and you are probably asleep by now, or maybe you are writing to me. My love, I have to close now so I can still mail this letter! *Your* little Lilongo

MOPE TO VERA

Moscow, 15 January 1939

Before I started writing this letter, I had a little rest, because this letter is of special importance. This letter is meant to bring my most beloved my most loving, most heartfelt and gentlest good congratulations on her birthday. How I wish that I could fill this letter with all the beautiful things in the world! I wanted to make the paper like a wishing rod which makes all my beloved's wishes come true when she touches it. It is supposed to unite all the good powers of heaven and protect my sweet little girl from everything evil and sorrowful. It brings you my most longing wishes for the best health, a little one who will bring you nothing but great joy, whose character comprises everything to be a constant fountain of happiness to you; a *husband* who will always love you as hotly and passionately as he does now and will never again make the beginning of a New Year sad for you with his depressed prattle and will always be able to give you everything beautiful the world has to offer and that your heart desires.

My most beloved one is twenty-nine years old now and will be a grown little mother by the time her next birthday comes around, with all the personal knowledge of what nature demands in order to enable

---

150 i.e., urine samples.

a woman the fulfillment of her intrinsic purpose. How much I wish for both of us that this introduction will be easy for you and accompanied by as little pain as possible, a pain which will seem like nothing compared to the new little transaction you will give to us. I would so like to take away some of the burden that the little product is causing you in the true sense of the word, but nothing can be changed in the arrangement that the better part of creation–the *ladies*–have to deal with that by themselves.

My beloved girl, I embrace you with the gentlest, most longing, burning love. My soul and my body are filled with desire for you and I want to kiss you while you snuggle close to me, everywhere, on those little hills and in the valleys of your ever so beautiful body which seems even more delightful to me than usual now with its ripening to bear fruit, although that is difficult to imagine. Just thinking of it brings my blood to a boil and my body longs to give your body more seed to add to the one already ripening. Now, I will come to you in my dreams and become one with you so that our desire is sated and the wish for new desire awakens.

Completely and utterly, Your Mope

VERA TO MOPE

London, 19 January 1939

It is almost 11 o'clock and our visitors, a really extremely likable couple, just left. I think I already told you about them–the daughter with husband and child of a friend of Mutti's are staying here until their number to the U.S.A. is called. He is in his early forties I suppose, and she is about thirty-six, and they have a sixteen-year old son who goes to school in Switzerland and a fifteen year old daughter who started going to school here yesterday.[151] I regretted ever soooo much that these two ever so very likable people did not get to meet my *husbandlein* this evening, and I told them *a lot* about you–since they have no idea yet when they will be able to leave for the U.S.A., and, when you come home, you will probably get to see them as well. It is such a rare thing, although it should be something that is self-evident, to meet people

---

151 Vera does not identify them further. A good few German-Jewish refugees used England as a staging-post toward emigration to the United States.

from *especially* good and even luxurious surroundings who come here and immediately develop the right attitude towards everything new: their status as refugees, the strange country with its utterly strange and odd customs, their hosts (they are living with friends who invited them to stay), in short, everything their new existence brings with it. I am certain it is a question of *intelligence* and *tact*–it is really refreshing to meet people who seem to possess those characteristics and do not bring along bad manners from their former home country. My Mopeleinchen, you already know how happy I am that you belong to those noteworthy exceptions so completely, and your dear mother belongs to them as well, but other than that, they are far and few between.

This evening, I received your beloved lines from January 13. I wish you were right with your prophesy that the Nazi reign has lasted long enough already and is facing its end, but unfortunately, I do not believe that to be the case yet, but to the contrary, I am afraid, *very* afraid that it will take root more deeply and extend its reach. As much as I like being here, the conviction that a country so close to Germany cannot be all that safe becomes more firmly rooted within me. I hope that I am wrong.

My love, often, there are doubts welling up inside me which I should not even put down on paper, with such a *great* distance between us–these are doubts I try to suppress immediately with very weighty reasons that speak against them: should we bring a child into such a world?!!!! I no longer think that and as I said, it is very wrong to write something like that to my beloved who is so many miles away from me and by the time he receives these lines, I can no longer understand why I ever thought that way, because I know that our child will hopefully allay all and any doubts within me and will probably add a new and so far unknown answer to the question "what for" to both of our lives. And just like my beloved has told me repeatedly: one cannot know and could not have known at any one point in time what the future will bring, and that is a good thing, too, and I am a bad person for putting such temporary thoughts on paper at all. However, on the other hand, if I did not do so, I would tell myself that I am keeping something from my beloved, even if it is something that is *not* good.

This evening, I also received a letter from a Hilde Lindheim, born Abraham, Leipz. N. 22, Goethner Str. 54 III. It was an express letter to you, in which she requests most urgently to talk to someone in person at the Woburn House[152] or somewhere else on her behalf and that of her husband, and her one year old son, because they have to be out of that filthy country by the end of the month and they do not yet have permission to go to the U.S.A. despite the necessary affidavits, etc. Since she also mentions your dear mother in the letter and also her possible intervention, I forwarded the letter to her, because I do not know these people at all, and I hope that that was done with your approval! She will be a better judge than I to see if there is anything that can and should be done in this matter.[153]

Yesterday evening, I received a letter from Hilde Lewy in Genoa, and in the meantime, she, Walter and the baby had visited the American consulate in Naples and they hope, since all their papers, etc., appeared to be in order, that they will be able to leave on February 22. She asked me to do something for a Mr. Fuchs. It seems—I suppose it is a matter of his physical condition—he cannot go to the U.S.A. However, he cannot stay there either and would like to go to Australia and use England as a *transit station*. She enclosed his vita and excellent recommendations, among other things one from a Berlitz School in Genoa where he worked as a teacher until last November, and also a list of his assets—he has £475 in free foreign currency at his disposal and is prepared to give a potential guarantor I might find for him here a security deposit of £200. Hilde writes that he would never be a burden to any guarantor but where can one find someone who would be willing to do that for a man without a wife or children? I think that anyone who is willing to take on a guarantee for someone should have £1000 in his bank account as security, and as sorry as I feel for Mr. Fuchs, I do not see where I might find someone here who is able to take him on, or whom I might even interest in the matter.

I can understand Hilde and the worry for a friend of "her house", and also that, with her current worries concerning the many physical and psychological demands life is placing on her just now, she cannot

---

152 Anglo-Jewish communal headquarters in London.
153 Hilde Lindheim was born on 19 June 1911, thus sharing a birthday with Mope, who was twelve years her senior. Her husband was Werner Lindheim, and they had a son, Ralf, born on 14 January 1938. They left Germany for France, where Hilde was killed by a bomb on 17 June 1940 during the German invasion. Werner escaped to America via Marseilles and Casablanca. Their son, Ralf, was hidden from the Nazis in France for most of the war, and was later reunited with his father in the United States.

make herself sit down and write to me or even find the time to do so. Nevertheless, it pains me for just a short moment that she only turns to me lately when she wants something, but I am sure that I am unable to put myself in her shoes right now and I would probably not act differently either, and if I am able to do anything for Mr. Fuchs or Hilde respectively in this matter, I will try to do so, although I doubt that it will be possible.

I believe I told you last Saturday that I want to put in a good word for Ketty with Mrs. Stiebel–just as soon as Hanna sends me all the necessary paperwork with all the details, or better, the copies. I have not received anything yet and it is impossible for me to expect Mrs. Stiebel to get all the details for the Goldschmidts, which Hanna seemed to understand. She told me that Fred's secretary has all the files and that she would get in contact with her.

Although all of my clothes still fit me as before (and most of them are not loosely hanging dresses, but were made to fit rather tightly), I believe that I am gradually gaining a little belly, even though it is not really visible, or better, noticeable at all; and since Dr. Rothschild said that he would be able to feel for the expected child during the next examination around the beginning of February, that is actually rather appropriate. Completely and utterly, Your little Lilongo

VERA TO MOPE

London, 21 January 1939

This afternoon, I am going to the *nursing home* in Courtfield Gardens to meet with the *matron* there, and Muttilein will accompany me.

I forgot to tell you in my detailed Thursday letter that an extremely tall policeman appeared the other evening and asked for Mr. and Mrs. Felsenstein. He was very charming and polite, as *all* officials here tend to be, showed me a letter from Bow Street which requested that we go there *at our earliest convenience*. I asked him to come in and showed him my papers and he was more than nice and grumbled about Hitler– after I told him that we were *Jews born in Germany*. I called Bow Street the following morning and it concerned your extension, just as I had suspected, and my name was on the paperwork quite by accident. I explained that and also why you had only received an extension from the *local office* and did not go to Bow Street after you had received your extension. They replied that everything was in order and once you were back in the country, you should come in to have them check your papers again.

Yesterday evening, I received a letter from Annelie's mother in which she asked me to undertake steps for her and her husband in order to make it possible for them to come here until their resettlement in the U.S.A. They did not make a request until December 1938. Since she cannot give me any kind of information concerning the assets at their disposal, their case will probably be a very difficult one and I will see what can be done and will write to the Woburn House. Among other things, Mrs. Freimann writes, "Annelie sent us a telegram today to let us know that she is getting married today."[154]

Just a little while ago, there arrived a very dear birthday letter from Hilde Lewy in Genoa! They are now moving from their home and everything is being packed. They will ship out on either 2 or 22 February. She writes, the one thing that gives her consolation and joy despite all the difficulties is her sweet one who compensates her for everything. I wrote back a detailed letter, and I let her know that I am also expecting a baby. I am very curious to see what and when she will answer. By the way, she also told me that her brother-in-law had been offered a position at a college in the state of Georgia, U.S.A., and they are very pleased and happy to be done with the worry for him and his family.

As far as Mr. Fuchs is concerned, I learned that the chances to go to Australia for someone who has as much money as Mr. Fuchs does are quite favorable. On top of that, if an Englishman could be found as a guarantor, he would not actually run any risk, since Mr. Fuchs had more than enough assets at his disposal to pay for his stay here, so there is no need for £1000 in the bank. I do not know if that is correct, but in any case it seems reasonable to me, that if the application has already been made to the Australian government, it would be much easier to get a visa for a transit stay here. I will send all the application papers to Genoa today, since Hilde wrote to me that Mr. Fuchs has to leave Italy by January 31.

I have not heard anything from your dear mother or Hannalein since last Wednesday–I do not know if they are or will be able to do anything in the matter of Mrs. Hilde Lindheim.

You, my most beloved!! Completely, *Your* Little Witch

---

154 Annelie married Arno Herzberg, a journalist who had escaped Germany for the United States.

MOPE TO VERA

Moscow, 22 January 1939

Today was a beautiful day full of sunshine, so I tried to exploit it as much as possible. A few colleagues and I went on a 2-4 hour sightseeing tour by car. Then, I had a bite to eat and worked until 10 p.m. At 10 o'clock, I went to the theater where I saw the film *Lenin in October 1917* which was shown to celebrate the anniversary of the death of that great man and leader of the Russian people. The film is excellent and even I was able to understand it. It shows Lenin's return to Russia and the preparations and execution of the revolution up to the dismissal of the provisional Kerenski-government.[155]

Today, your dear letter from January 15 reached me. My most heartfelt thanks for that! Just a little while ago, I was able to express my best wishes to my beloved over the telephone and I was able to hear your ever so beloved voice perfectly clearly, almost as if we were in the same room and not all those innumerable miles apart. It was so wonderful to talk to you and to feel your closeness at least with the ears, a closeness all five of my senses hunger for so unspeakably. Someday people will be able to see each other as well, but no matter how far technology advances, the ability to taste and feel, which belong to the most beautiful things, will never be achieved at those distances. If only time would go by faster, so I could come back to you sooner!!! However, that cannot be done either and we have to acquiesce because, through these times of separation, we will actually gain the opportunity to found an existence for ourselves which will permit us to establish our lives in a meaningful way by procreating and hoping for a sweet baby that fulfills all of our wishes.

Your letters from Sunday and Monday are lying in front of me waiting for an answer, since I only touched on the Saturday letter earlier today. As far as I remember, the Lewys had planned on turning their back on Europe around the beginning of January. You should not be surprised if they did not find the time to write, with all the jostling of the last few days, and we should expect that they will write in more detail once they are onboard the ship.

---

155 As letters were randomly opened by Russian censors, it was tactical of Mope to include praise of the Soviet Union and its first leader.

My sweet one already seems to be looking beyond the surface where Alice is concerned. She is an unlucky girl, because, as you say, she always means well, but she does everything just a little off so that it constantly creates the wrong impression and sometimes even misses. I am very pleased that the entire Moschytz family no longer belongs to those one worries about acutely. If only Ketty and her people were out already as well! I also think that David will be able to rebuild an existence in no time at all, once he is in London.

But now, I have to seek the horizontal. My fruit-bearing little fruit tree has been asleep for quite some time already. I embrace you most tenderly, my most beloved one, and I am thinking of you always, filled with the greatest and strongest love.

You little apricot tree–fertilized by orange seed–full of yearning and love—

Completely and utterly, Your Mope

VERA

Journal entry, 22 January 1939

I wonder if other "expectant mothers" have strong motherly feelings for their child before it is born and if I might just be egotistical and not normal. I *wanted* a child and I *would like* a child, but still, it was unbelievably difficult for me to forswear the Pantheon store and the professional advancement connected to it. And still, it is not easy for me to see my rather good figure disappear–even if it is only temporary. Although up to now, those people who do not know cannot tell, I am sure. And despite all the rational arguments that keep telling me again and again how important it is *not* to be childless, I am often afraid to have to go through childbirth in a time that looks so forbidding, and to be no longer master of my own body. The reasons, as mentioned above, are simply rational arguments; even that might be abnormal and egotistical, because other women long for a child emotionally, I believe.

However, with my marriage, when I entered into it, did not pure rational arguments play a large role? And today, today, our marriage is flooded with the purest feeling of love, friendship, regard for the other, and friendliness? Most likely, because of this so completely harmonious and fulfilling marriage and on top of that, my work that satisfies me and offers me— field to use all—I actually do not know yet, not until I have a child–so let us say, many of my feminine abilities and fulfills me in such a way that it also represents a reason as to why other women apparently have a very pronounced longing for a child that will fill their lives with purpose, while mine is anything but strong. I hope that my child will find and conquer its own place in my life with its appearance–how I hope for that; and that the child will take away any feelings of mourning that the loss of professional advancement might bring, and that it will give an even deeper sense to our already so deep and harmonious love and marriage partnership–and children, especially those born out of love, are supposed to do that.

Until now–I am sure it is a shame to even write something like this down–aside from the reasonable arguments (which I already listed here earlier), I only wish that I will experience everything I do not know yet–and that is another reason. My interest in living and experiencing life and exploring it in all its strangeness. I do not know if this has anything to do with being egotistical nor if other women, at least in part, feel unfulfilled and would rather exchange their reasonable arguments with that much more gentle and feminine word "emotion," be it consciously or more often than not subconsciously. I would really like to know. I am sure that the moment I *see* the product of our love, strong and intelligent, I hope, I will feel completely overwhelmed by love.

Thirty: "The Little Fruit That Fell From the Tree"

25 January through 19 March 1939

POLITICAL TIMELINE, FEBRUARY–MAY 1939

- 3 February 1939: Bomb destroys a synagogue in Budapest, Hungary.
- 9 February 1939: Anti-Jewish legislation passed in Italy.
- 20 February 1939: Massive pro-Nazi rally in New York orchestrated by the German-American Bund.
- 21 February 1939: Decree in Germany that Jews must surrender all gold and silver to the government.
- 2 March 1939: Election of Cardinal Eugenio Pacelli as Pope Pius XII.
- 15 March 1939: German troops occupy independent Czechoslovakia, soon after stripping Czech Jews of their livelihoods.
- 20 March 1939: Public incineration of so-called "degenerate art" in Germany.
- 25 March 1939: Huge "Stop Hitler" march in New York City.
- 31 March 1939: British Government affirms its commitment to defend Poland in the event of war.
- 1 April 1939: End of Spanish Civil War with victory by Francisco Franco's Fascists.
- 30 April 1939: Tenancy protection for Jews in Germany revoked.

- 3 May 1939: Stalin appoints Viacheslav Molotov as his Commissar for Foreign Affairs.
- 15 May 1939: Women's concentration camp officially opened at Ravensbrück.
- 17 May 1939: British Government issues a White Paper restricting Jewish immigration to Palestine.
- 22 May 1939: Germany and Italy co-sign a "Pact of Steel," a military and political alliance.

Vera was to visit a number of London maternity hospitals, eventually opting for the London Clinic, and Mope used his letters to express his ongoing belief that a woman in her condition should slow down her grueling schedule at Marks & Spencer. Vera was still trying to conceal her pregnancy from the shop girls that she trained, while (despite Mope's admonitions) keeping up her demanding agenda.

In Germany, Mope's sister and brother-in-law, Ketty and David Goldschmidt, were still trying to escape from Nazi rule. Through the Kindertransport scheme, they gained permission to send their two younger children, Gabriel and Alfred, to join their two siblings already in England, but they themselves were still trapped in Hamburg. In panicked response to a letter from Ketty pleading urgently for help, her youngest sister, Hanna Rau, demanded of Vera that she write to Otto Schiff, the head of the Jewish Refugees Committee, to ask him to intercede on behalf of the Goldschmidts' application for refugee status in England. Vera counseled that approaching Schiff without supporting documentation was unlikely to get anywhere, but Hanna insisted that an approach must be made. Vera reluctantly agreed to write to Schiff though warning Hanna that the absence of important particulars would likely derail the effort. Inevitably, despite best efforts, the application failed, and crucial time was lost. It remains uncertain whether a more considered intervention on Ketty's behalf would have made any difference. The Nazi authorities continued to demand full payment by the Goldschmidts of back taxes and putative liabilities before they would permit them to emigrate.

There were similar expectations and fears concerning Mope's cousins from Karlsruhe, Carl and Lies Rosenfeld. In early February, Vera learned that their older son, Georg, had been offered employment in England, and their younger son, Benjamin, had joined a Zionist youth group that would soon settle in Palestine. The hope remained that Carl and Lies would receive permission to depart for a new life in Jerusalem. Elsewhere, Vera's friend, Hilde Lewy and her family, traveled from Genoa with papers permitting them to board a ship at Naples that set sail for New York.

In Moscow, Mope's work was still sorely affected by the economic slowdown. At the end of January, approximately two months after he had left England, he became ill with a high fever and influenza, which confined him to bed for more than a week. During the time of his confinement, he was too debilitated to be able to write to Vera, deciding also that he would rather not add further worry to his pregnant wife by revealing his sickness to her.

The long hours and strenuousness of the auction itself, in which Mope more than made up for the lean months before, left him with a "deeply depressing awareness of having neglected my darling so terribly all that time." Vera's daily letters had greatly helped to sustain him through a difficult time. The details of her own condition, as unraveled through their correspondence, provide a fateful counterpoint to his own struggles. Apprised of the situation and the Leningrad auction behind him, Mope traveled back at once to be with his wife.

VERA TO MOPE

London, 25 January 1939

Today is January 25 and three years ago today, I was introduced to my beloved, or better, he was introduced to me, or it might be better to say that he met me, because that was hardly the case on the 24th. I remember the long side of the ballroom very well and the place where we sat and drank coffee and your astonishment that the "ravishingly beautiful Englishwoman"–you surely had to be *terribly* disappointed–works for a living and of the fact that we were actually dancing towards the end of the evening, although you had told me earlier that you never dance. All of that seems years ago to me, and the following years during which my love slowly and constantly and visibly appeared to be taking on a more important, then the *most* important role in my life, fill me with happiness and joy and harmony and inner peace, despite all the difficulties of the outside happenings in the world and the bitterly long separations the two of us are forced to endure.

Today at lunch time, I received a letter from the Leipzig tax department. In it, they demand that you pay a total amount of RM 2600 as Jewish asset taxes, in payments of RM 60, with the first payment due Dec. 15, 1938, and if the payments are not made on time, a late charge in the amount of 2% of the amount will be imposed. Nice people, aren't they? I will not send an answer and I hope that you agree with that.[156]

My love, I am feeling very well: I take a calcium supplement every day and also milk and cheese, just as Dr. Rothschild recommended. Although no one at the store or anywhere else for that matter has noticed anything yet, I can tell by looking at myself that *I am gradually starting to lose my slim figure*, although I can still wear my dresses. Aside from being very tired in the evening, the baby gives me hardly *any* hints of its development, with the very small exception that, if I do not eat something immediately after getting up, I start to feel a little sick around 9 o'clock without, however, feeling the slightest bit nauseous after that. So you can see that I am really doing very, very well and I am absolutely able to work. I have to close now and get this letter to the post office. Completely, Your Little Witch

MOPE TO VERA

Moscow, 25 January 1939

As has been the case all month long, I still cannot make any deals and I find the sitting around here and having to wait downright unpleasant. As far as I can judge things, the situation in Western Europe is extremely tense once again and I am sure that that contributes to the fact that no deals can be made.

Do you have any idea about the further plans of Grete and Norbert? They can hardly sit in Switzerland forever with four kids and no money and depend on the mercy of others. If they intend to wait for visas to the U.S.A., that can only be regarded as a partial solution to the problem in the far distance. It is only a partial solution because it can only satisfy the question of location, but not the material one. As far as I know, Norbert would have to pass several exams there before he can even think of engaging in any kind of financially beneficial work. I am wondering if he has even started preparing for that. The biggest worry concerning all of these questions is the worry about Ketty and David. We have no idea of the psychological burden that is bearing down on all those poor people, but we have to try to help them before they are crushed. It is a

---

156 German demands for Jewish assets extended even to those it had now denied citizenship.

difficult knowledge to me that I cannot do *anything* at all from here that could contribute to helping them.

The tiredness produced by all this idleness has really taken such a hold of me that I am forced to wish my most beloved a good night and I am giving her a long and ever so tender kiss before I go to sleep. You sweet little fruit tree with an even smaller fruit, Your Mope

MOPE TO VERA

Moscow, 26 January 1939

Despite the fears of my beloved that my optimistic supposition concerning the coming end of the Nazi criminals in Germany lacks any justification, I will continue to believe in it. However, one should not hope that everything can be brought back into even and cultured tracks immediately, tracks in which the country found itself in the past, but even a change in government in which somewhat more moderate views prevailed could dam the spread of the Nazi plague. But that does not eliminate the danger of a European war, although despite all the critical moments speaking for a war, I believe that we will escape unscathed for this year. Whatever the future will bring for us Jews is only contingently tied to the general development.

History shows in the strangest way that every time the assimilation of the Jews in any country became too prevalent a catastrophe happened to them. That can be proven again and again through thousands of years, and since the degree of assimilation does not depend on any one person but shows itself in the entirety of the Jews, I can understand my darling's thoughts and doubts concerning the right to procreate. The path of your education led to the ground being pulled out from under you, just like it was for many others, when they began to officially declare us as inferior.

Our experiences show that you have to prove to a child from the very beginning that it should be valued just as positively for what it is, namely a Jew, as any other human being, and in order to give it secure footing that will withstand all possible attacks no matter how strong they are, he has to be given Jewish knowledge and with that Jewish self-confidence. Every creature is at its natural enemies' mercy if it is not prepared, be it physically or with a strong inner footing, to meet them. Flight is only a partial escape if the spiritual equilibrium is disturbed by it, because the achieved outer security does not help to restore this equilibrium. For this reason, one has to work at prevention and try to construct the spiritual balance as massively and firmly as possible.

When they began to race through the countryside with cars, many field and forest animals and even pets were killed and injured. The chickens, hares, and deer did not give up procreating because of it, or because people hunted and slaughtered them. The pet animal which has been robbed of its instinct to be free can only minimally protect itself against its enemy by screaming and thereby awakening the pity and emotions of its owner. The free animal teaches its young to avoid the country road, to escape the hunter, and to use its mimicry in the most appropriate way in order to protect itself. We have to learn from that in order to guarantee *those* freedoms to our children that life has to give, and that is only possible if they are familiar with all the factors that can help them understand life and arm them against all enemies, just like the animal living in freedom. As a consequence of your upbringing, you regard being a Jew as a weakness. How many people who tower above the average have made their weaknesses into factors of strength and perseverance because they acknowledged them, and those very weaknesses helped them to get above the prevailing niveau. Let your children recognize their "weakness" as strength and that is how you give yourself the right to have children.

All the other reasons to have children that my darling lists are of a much too egocentric nature to be sufficient reason on their own to give justification to the desire. Hilde Lewy's joy in her little daughter, just like the childlessness of Mr. Fuchs and the lack of the world's interest in him which results from it, is not sufficient proof that procreation is justified, but the free creature's will to procreate and the awakening of the instinct to be free and its cultivation in the newly created creature include nature's right, because freedom is natural.

It is not only not wrong that my little witch writes to me about such understandable doubts in these times, but I am deeply grateful to you for giving me the opportunity to comment on these doubts! You write yourself that our little fruit will give us another answer unknown to us to the question "what for" and without it, the answer would remain unknown, and so you say exactly the same thing I said, just using different words, when I was talking about freedom. Freedom is the will and the strength to procreate and the "what for" is the product that results, which we will come to know–with any luck.

"This lady Hilde Lindheim née Abraham" is a lady I told my beloved about some time ago. She was in love with me once and was a virgin, and when she offered herself to me, I could not bring myself to physically put an end to that condition. So she decided to go skiing and took the cold opportunity to be deflowered just to tell me that every obstacle had been removed and now, would I please?! Regrettably, I was even less able to make a decision, despite the removal of the obstacle, because I had been *ethically* unable to comply with her wishes. Poor girl, she has to be in the worst situation to turn to me for help and I would really like to help her if I knew of a way, because she is a dear and good person, and after all, one should be grateful for unrequited love that was ready to make sacrifices–even if the sacrifices themselves were wrong psychologically. The girl comes from a good middle-class family. The father was the owner of a small department store in Gohlis (a suburb of Leipzig). When she got married, I recommended to her to go abroad as soon as possible, especially since the husband was already working abroad, as far as I remember, or had some connections to foreign countries which he neglected rather stupidly because of his marriage.

I heard that people who have an affidavit for the U.S.A. and can count on being included in the quota in the near future, will be able to stay in Sweden for up to six months. The consul general for Sweden in Leipzig, Dr. Paul Hollender, told me that today.[157] He will probably travel back to Leipzig soon and maybe Hilde Lindheim can turn to him. Maybe other people can be helped to escape from grave danger with this knowledge. If you have a German passport, you do not even need a visa, as far as I know.

Shouldn't it be possible for Mr. Fuchs who lived in Davos often and for a long time because of his ailment, to have himself sent to Switzerland by his doctors? If he can prove that he would not be a burden to anyone, I cannot imagine that he would meet with any difficulties. Aside from the technical difficulties, the English climate might be dangerous for him. I can understand completely that Hilde wants to help her friend, and since she is not asking for herself, but, in order to help, asks for help for someone else, I find her plea understandable —just like the quickly and bravely overcome pain my beloved felt over only receiving letters with pleas from her friend. If you cannot turn to your best friends in

---

[157] Paul Hollender, a gentile, was the President of the Leipzig Fur Merchants Association and joint partner in the fur business of Thorer and Hollender.

times of need, who can you turn to and when the hand reaches for the ink pen in cataclysmic times–how can the brain dictate anything other than that which forms itself into a plea for help in what the brain is constantly worrying about?

It is unbelievably late and I am a bad example for my girl who also writes to me much too late at night. I kiss you on your belly which is rounding just a little and on many of those other sweet places of your beloved body and I am longing so indescribably for you and your love and the fulfillment of my love for you. Your wistful Mope

VERA TO MOPE

London, 27 January 1939

Just as I was leaving home, Hanna called and although Muttilein told her that I was already late and in quite a hurry, she insisted on talking to me since it concerned something of *great urgency*! When you read the following, please try to be *completely* objective towards me, and if you think that I am wrong, or overly sensitive or hard hearted, *please* tell me so! Women often judge things in a narrow-minded way and I know that my most beloved only wants the best for me when he tells me that I am wrong. If he explains to me where my fault lies, I will be more than happy to have him lead me!

So–Hanna told me she had received a letter from Ketty and her brother-in-law. David writes that Ketty and his family *have* to get out of Germany immediately. Hanna told me that she is *terribly alarmed*, which is only natural, and since the matter did not seem to be progressing at all, she had hired an attorney yesterday, who had written a letter on their behalf to Woburn House. Since I had promised to intercede and contact Otto Schiff, she maintained that I should please do so forthwith. So, the first thing Hanna says to me is that I will have to go to Mr. Schiff in person. I told her that she would need to inform me of all the details first, and most of all supply me with the copies and reference numbers of the files. I asked for further details: Hanna said she assumed that David was not doing well at all where his health is concerned (at most: *a breakdown*). Then: He has excellent business connections to an English firm and they would take him on as a *half commission man*. When I asked for the name of the firm, she said that Fred thought it would be better not to mention it because it was not certain yet and the firm would not like it!

It would have been much easier if Hanna had sat down and written down all the reference numbers, the date of the application, the name of a relative who was willing to back them financially and what plans David has once he is here, so that I would have been able to give Mr. Schiff all the necessary information. Since she did not do so, I had only half the information I actually needed and I really hate to go to Mr. Schiff and then expect him to find out the rest!

When I came home I immediately, composed the enclosed letter to Otto Schiff by racking my brain as to how I could avoid mentioning the missing documents, for fear that the letter would fail to accomplish its purpose. I think the last page may change the angered look on his face back into a smile, and it was 10 o'clock by the time I was done with the letter, and I was so tired that I just fell asleep. Here is a copy of the letter that I wrote:

Dear Mr. Schiff,

I understand that my sister-in-law, my husband's eldest sister, Mrs. David Goldschmidt and her husband who are residents at Hamburg have to leave Germany. Mr. Oscar Philipp[158] has filled in a declaration to the effect that he is prepared to guarantee for them and their two children aged 11 and 8, should they be allowed to come over to this country. Their two elder children are already in England.

On 25 November 1938, an application for them was made to the Home Office stating all the details. Mr. Goldschmidt has been an insurance broker in Hamburg and was also an agent for an English firm there. I understand that his business connections in this country are very good. Should he get the permit, he would be able to establish himself here.

I was informed that Mr. Goldschmidt has suffered a complete breakdown and that he and his wife do not know what to do, so that I just had to try and help them to get their case through.

My husband is away in Moscow, and like everybody else, I continually get letters from Germany, mostly from people whom I hardly know, imploring me to help them. I have tried to do what I could, but in the

---

158 Oscar Philipp (1882-1965) was a successful metal trader and a cousin by marriage of the Felsenstein family. His wife, Clarisse, née Weil (1888-1971) was a niece of Oma Lenchen.

above case, I feel that everything that can be done has been done and I know you are the only person who can proceed to get their case through successfully. Mr. Schiff, I cannot tell you how terrible I feel to have to approach you and ask you for a favor and your help in a time like this where I know you receive no end of applications every day.

To give you some lighter news: I was asked to take over the staff management of the Pantheon Store, the newest and largest store of Marks and Spencer's in Oxford Street, but I could not go there as I shall have to interrupt my work in a few months' time because I hope to have a baby in summer, and alas, one cannot have everything in life! I was surprised and very pleased that I was asked to go to the new Oxford Street Store, as I never thought they would choose me to undertake this job.

Many, many thanks for your great kindness! Yours ever, Vera Felsenstein

Mopelein, I know and can understand that Hanna is really terribly worried and probably acted the way she did because of it. Or is it wrong of me to judge her like that? Please let me know exactly what you think! I keep asking myself full of fear: am I just like so many other ladies in the family way, playing "the overwrought and overly sensitive one"? I do *not* think so but I want your opinion and your calm, clear view.

My love, it is very late! What a letter!!! But my love will probably understand it correctly and help me. Most passionate kisses, you, my love——Completely, *Your* little witch

MOPE TO VERA

Moscow, 28 January 1939

This morning, when I was told that a letter had arrived for me, I thought that it would be from you. Instead, it was a letter from Hannalein–I was happy to receive it, but in no way could it trigger the kind of joy that each one of your beloved reports gives me. I already wrote to you about Ketty these last few days and how much I care about getting her the necessary help, and now, I see that Hannalein turned to you again in the matter.

Hannalein wrote that all of the Felsensteins, including Semy as well as Uncle Joseph and his son Erich,[159] have come to London with their wives and children, though she has not heard from Semy himself. She still cannot see what *else* she can do for Ketty and has already tried everything possible, and none of it has shown any kind of success. I wonder if she has turned to you once again in the meantime?

By the way, Hanna writes that Alice is putting a lot of effort into building a new existence for her husband and herself, but that she had to realize how "indescribably difficult a task" that proved to be. It should actually be her husband's job to take care of the relocation, but it is always the same where that one is concerned. The wife has to prepare everything and if he is dissatisfied, he gets upset because she did everything wrong. Other doctors have been able to create a new field of work for themselves in Palestine, although the relocation of people in that particular profession took on such an extraordinary configuration after they lost their health insurance in Germany. Had he gone to the countryside, he would probably have been more successful, but he did not want to do that because initially, his wife had brought out enough money to allow him to lead a life of indolence.

The old Freimanns really deserve to be beaten. How long have they known that their children are going to the U.S.A. and that he will have to give up his practice, and they did not start taking care of their own emigration until December 1938!?[160] I congratulate you as "close relatives" on Annelie's wedding! I hope that she was lucky in her choice and will not have to feed him as well. It is really horrible what kind of cruel disaster this rabble of criminals has brought to so many human beings, and no one can oversee when that will come to an end, because those poor refugees have no hope at all for a new existence, which is not so easily established nowadays, despite their emigration.

I did not get out into the air at all today, but that is no pleasure at the moment anyway. It has been snowing for four days now without pause, and the very fine snowflakes hit your face like little whips. My room is

---

159 Joseph Felsenstein's family had been responsible for the branch of the Gebrüder Felsenstein in Fürth, near Nuremberg, that specialized in the preparation of animal bristles for the manufacture of brushes. It too had been confiscated by the Nazis. The escape from Germany of the Fürth Felsensteins was aided and made possible by Fred Rau, Hanna's husband.

160 Annelie's stepfather, Dr. Freimann, was a doctor in general practice in Leipzig until the Nazis dismissed all Jewish physicians.

heated wonderfully and I feel no desire to leave it. These lines will reach my darling more quickly than usual, because a colleague who is leaving tomorrow has agreed to take them to you. Aside from the letter, he will probably also take a broken horn comb along. Your awful *husband* broke his best one when he was cleaning it and if the same thing happens to the second one, Mope will have to wander through the streets uncombed. It would be very sweet of you if you could find a similar replacement and send it to me with one of the colleagues who is traveling here.

My little fruit-bearing tree, your male bee who fertilized you. He would so love to "fertilize" again!!!

VERA TO MOPE

London, 29 January 1939

I talked to your dear mother for a long time yesterday evening and we talked about many things. I also told her about my telephone conversation with Hannalein and my letter to Otto Schiff and everything that is connected to that. Although she did know that Hanna had asked me to contact Mr. Schiff, she thought that it concerned the two younger children of Ketty's. Among other things, she told me that Ketty was writing about that with such deeply felt desperation, because they have large debts there, mainly tax debts, which is why they are not permitted to leave at all. Hanna did not mention that with so much as *one word*! So how much good would a potential intervention by Otto Schiff do?! I do *not* think that was right of Hanna!

Just a short while ago, I talked to your dear mother on the telephone again, and to Alice as well. Both of them send you their heartfelt love and Alice told me how moved and overjoyed she had been that you had mentioned her in your telegram, and that she had insisted that they give her the telegram so she could take it home and show it to Julius. Then she said that she feels so much closer to Mopeleinchen because of me and that she is so very happy that "we have you!" is what she said to me! What that is based on or why, I do not know, but I found it downright heart-warming of her, although I did have to smile just a little–but no one saw that.

How sweetly and *thoughtfully* and reasonably my love judged my friend Hilde! I have tried to base the long break between her letters on outside circumstances, but it is so good to have that affirmed by you.

This letter is supposed to go to the post office today, but before that, I want to give my beloved many, many, long, sweet good night kisses in my thoughts! I love you, my Mopelein, *very, very* much! Completely and utterly, Your Little Witch

P.S. In the store, *no one* has any idea yet that I am expecting a baby!!!

MOPE TO VERA

Moscow, 31 January 1939

Although I am dead tired and exhausted, I am still reaching for paper so I will not leave my beloved without news. After I worked all day, I was informed that the first contract for Persians had been finalized. It is of great importance to receive the first offer after closing a contract, because the prices increase from contract to contract, and I was very proud of having achieved that! Since shortly after 6 p.m., I have been trying to contact Schapiro by telegraph and telephone. Just now, a little after 1 a.m., I was finally able to reach him just to find out that a decision will not be made by him until the day after tomorrow, although the Russians insist on a decision by tomorrow morning. Since they have been kept informed through me of the activities there, that is an inexcusable sluggishness on his part and–if you lose a contract–will cost a lot of money because the prices will have risen already in the meantime. Anyway, the difficulties encountered in finding the old boy have enervated me completely.

Please do not be sad about this silly writ, but I am just too tired to try writing a "prettier" one, but at the same time, I do not want to leave my darling without any news! I kiss you most passionately and most lovingly, my little orange tree including the little orange and I long for the two of you so indescribably and tremendously. *Completely* and *utterly, Your* Mope

VERA TO MOPE

London, 31 January 1939

I had a bad day today, but I suppose those kinds of days do happen here and there, and I really should not complain about it at all at such a mile-wide distance, because, by the time these lines reach you, the "bad" day will have been forgotten already, most likely. I received the following letter from Otto Schiff earlier today:

"Dear Vera,

Many thanks for your letter of the 26th, and first of all, let me congratulate you on your wonderful news. It is indeed sad that you cannot take over the staff-management of the Pantheon Store, but I do not doubt that your baby will be ample compensation for this! Anyhow I think it is simply splendid that you were chosen for the post!

As regards your sister-in-law and her husband, I am not absolutely clear from your letter as to whether the necessary application has been lodged. If the application has been put through already I personally can do nothing as all applications have to go through Woburn House now, and the Home Office accepts them only from there. I do not quite understand what you mean. As soon as I hear from you I will do my best to be of assistance.

Yours ever, Otto Schiff

I immediately wrote to Hanna to tell her that the details she had given me over the phone were absolutely insufficient nor clear and definite. It is very *disconcerting* to me to be forced to bother Mr. Schiff twice, since he is already *overburdened* with similar requests. I asked her to send me the details that Mr. Schiff needs as soon as possible, because, since I wrote in my letter to him how extremely urgent the entire matter is, I can hardly make him wait for an answer now. Although Hanna did not offer me any other choice, I was convinced that I was not doing the right thing!

I wrote to Hanna this morning before going to the store. I have not heard a single word responding to it yet–actually, I have not heard anything else from Hanna since last Thursday, although the matter is ever so urgent. I called your dear mother a little while ago and she was kind and understanding as always. I told her about the letter from Otto Schiff and also about my letter to Hanna and asked her to use all of her influence and make Hanna realize the importance and consequences of a clearly written and most of all quickly assembled report on the facts of the matter. On the one hand, Hanna seems to be a little too casual to me and on the other hand, she cannot of course help being completely uneducated where business matters are concerned and is unaware of the importance of a clearly written report, because I am sure that she is completely willing to help Ketty. I hope that you do not think I am judging her too harshly. I cannot change my opinion that she is not behaving correctly in this matter.

Enough now with this letter of complaint, especially since all the complaints seem more than *inane* compared to the horribly depressing newspaper reports of the last few days.[161]

I long for your understanding and intelligent advice, and everything else! Completely, *Your* Little Witch

VERA TO MOPE

London, 2 February 1939

I am beginning my lines to you now, although I know that I will probably not be able to finish them before this evening. Mutti and I went to Kensington High Street to buy a pair of shoe insoles, but we were unable to find them. I am not rounded enough yet for *maternity frocks* and it would be a complete waste right now to buy anything else, so I postponed this purchase. After we got home, I lay down for a while and now, I am writing to my beloved from the horizontal. I am feeling very well and I do *not* feel even the slightest discomfort.

I called through to Hanna after she sent me the following letter with the requested information yesterday:

Dear Vera,

Many thanks for your letter which I received yesterday evening. I am very sorry that Mr. Schiff has to be bothered twice because of us. The application was sent from Woburn House to the Home Office on 25 November 1938, where it received the Reference No. S.11378. From there, it was sent back to Woburn House for further details and approval. I had hoped that Mr. Schiff would be able to expedite the matter through his connections at the Home Office.

This should answer all of Mr. Schiff's questions and I hope that everything is clear now.

Once again, my thanks for your efforts! Greetings, Your Hanna

---

[161] Vera is referencing Hitler's widely reported speech to the Reichstag on 30 January 1939, the sixth anniversary of his appointment as German Chancellor, in which he threatened the extermination of Europe's Jews should there be a breakout of war.

Since I did not want to let any tension rise between the two of us–Hanna and me–*I* called her and told her rather candidly what I thought of the matter. *She* said that I had to have misunderstood her on the telephone. I told her that such things should never be discussed on the telephone in a hurry, but that she should have either come to me in person or documented everything in writing. I gave her my views on all of those things, since I consider honesty between two people who are friends the best and most intelligent policy, because otherwise, some kind of thorn will be left behind. After all of that was said, the conversation ended on a friendly note.

I kiss you–only in my thoughts, sadly–and put all my tenderness in it, you –

Completely and utterly, *Your* little Lilongo

VERA TO MOPE

London, 3 February 1939

Today, I am starting my letter to you at the office for once. Sadly, I have *not* received any more news from you. I am wondering if my love has forgotten about me!!!!!?!!! I come back to your beloved lines from 26 January. You explained the right to procreate in such a loving way and in such an intelligent manner and I thank you for that.

I received a very sweet letter from Hilde Lewy in Genoa this evening. They are departing from Naples on 12 February. She wrote in the most charming way about our expected little child and that the joy such a little one will bring cannot even be imagined beforehand. *Your* Little Witch

MOPE TO VERA

Moscow, 6 February 1939

What kind of a guy was my poor, golden girl bamboozled into marrying? Since the night of 31 January, he only let his most beloved have one telegram and no other news besides that–and of course, now, my darling is thinking that I have been working very hard? No–the *husband* was lazy, like he has never been before and his bones are so stiff from all that lying around that he can hardly write. Today, I am feeling well again. I am completely free of fever, but still feel rather weak, which the doctor projected, but I think that I will be back to being the old Mope in just a few days.

After I had finished the letter to my little witch Tuesday night, I felt a sudden chill and the thermometer showed 38.2.[162] So I decided to stay in bed on Wednesday, but I did not count on the nonsense lasting as long as it did. When there was no improvement Wednesday night, I asked for a doctor to come and see me on Thursday. He examined me thoroughly and determined that there was nothing wrong with me organically, and that I did not even have a bad cold. Apparently, the reason the matter dragged out for as long as it did was that I had taken quite a few aspirin and other such garbage during the days before to get over the thing I was feeling. Tomorrow, I will start working again, after I have not worked for a whole week. That is, I did do *some* work, since I was able to close the contract for the Persian pelts despite my temperature. But enough of that now!

I still have to answer many things in your dear letters in detail and I promise that I will do so, but these lines are supposed to get to the post office right away in order to put an end to the long break in my messages. Unfortunately, this writ is less than beautiful. I wish with all my heart to find just the right words to make you aware of my tremendous love for you, a love I have only been able to tell you about it in my thoughts, not in letters, for many days now. Completely and utterly, Your Mope

VERA TO MOPE

London, 7 February 1939

Muttilein went with me to the *nursing-home* in Courtfield Gardens that had been recommended by Mr. Nixon. Unfortunately, we were unable to look at any rooms, because we were there at *feeding time* (there is no elevator or running H2O there either).[163] The matron is a woman of approximately thirty-eight to forty years, intelligent, reasonable, and likable, and since the matron of such a home is usually, or actually always, the main midwife and because of that, will be present during the procedure, it is of great advantage, of course, if she is likable. I made

---

162 100.8 degrees Fahrenheit.
163 i.e., no wash basins with running water in individual rooms.

arrangements with her to come by again on a free afternoon or a Sunday afternoon in order to inspect a room. The price is 10 guineas and up from there, and she said that there would be an extra 2 guineas per week. However, she also suggested that she would gladly give me a list of all the medical things that would be needed and would be much cheaper if one were to purchase them oneself (I get a fifteen per cent rebate at Boots[164] anyway). On top of that, she said that she would be happy to put together a list for me with all the necessary things for the baby, which it would need during its stay at the *nursing-home.*

Just as soon as I have gained a little more girth, I will buy a really *smart maternity frock.* Since I will probably not like myself at all with a rounded figure, I will have a much easier time accepting it if I can wear a well-cut dress that does justice to my temporarily altered appearance!!! By the way, I know that you are interested in it: I took my measurements on Sunday after I got up, just out of curiosity: Before, they were: bust 36 inches, hips 38 inches, waist 26 inches. Now, they are: bust 36-37 inches, hips 38 inches, waist 29 inches. I determined that I now look the same as those so frequently criticized madams who do not have very good figures but insist on wearing very tight-fitting dresses that emphasize all of the imperfections of their bodies in the most disadvantageous manner.

Yesterday evening, the mail man brought me a small package from Italy with a beautiful little baby jacket, hat, and little socks, everything in white decorated with pink and light blue from Hilde. I thought that was a very touching gesture–it arrived without an accompanying letter as a sample shipment–and since they are leaving next Sunday, she probably wanted to send me this dear thoughtful gift from European soil, after she had sent me a very charming letter, in which she expresses her great joy over the expected little baby.

Otto Schiff wrote the following earlier today:

"My dear Vera,

Many thanks for your letter of the 2nd of the month. I will certainly drop a note to the Home Office and ask them if they can speed up the application for Mr. and Mrs. David Goldschmidt and hope this will not take too long.

Yours ever, Otto

---

164 The British pharmacy chain.

I called Hanna *immediately* after the store and read the letter to her. I hope that the matter will now be expedited. That could have already happened last week, had one used a little more diligence, a *whole* week sooner, so to speak. I hope that I will soon be able to report to you about the desired success.

Alicechen called me yesterday evening because an inordinate number of relatives had announced their visit at your dear mother's to say good-bye to her. I had sent her a few lines yesterday, enclosed a few Russian postage stamps–she had asked for them–and also a small powder box in brown calf leather. I thought that it would give Alicechen a little pleasure. This evening, a letter from Carlchen Rosenfeld arrived in which he tells us that his eldest son has been here for the last eight weeks and has started to work; the younger one will go to Palestine on February 22 with a youth group, and in April, they hope to resettle in the same city[165] as his brother Julius. I will write to him as well and also invite the boy.

MOPE TO VERA

Moscow, 8 February 1939

You know, I have a guilty conscience towards my little girl because of my illness, as I was forced to leave you without news for so many days. If I get to talk to you today, I will have to tell you that I was ill, because I cannot make you understand that long break in writing any other way. *Hopefully*, this news after the fact will not upset you! I am feeling *completely* well again and went back to work today. The temperature is back to normal again and by eating milk porridge and similar children's food, I was able to regain my strength.

So Hannalein has provided you with the necessary information in the meantime and I would be very glad just to know that your intervention with Otto Schiff will lead to a positive result. It is really dismal to think what endless worries one is constantly burdened with in these times, and then, we know that, with the creation of an opportunity to get out of that damned country, the main worry of rebuilding an existence will begin, and I hope that David, with all of his connections, will not be too bitter once he escapes. I am wondering if I will see those two once I

---

165 i.e., Jerusalem.

get back to London. I think it is very right that you expressed yourself very succinctly to Hanna. Now, I hope that the matter is cleared up and your friendship is back to the way it was. You have to explain to her *most resolutely* that, should she feel the desire to see you, she will have to come to you now, and you can tell her that I forbade you to undertake that difficult trip twice under the given circumstances, that is, to spend nine and a half hours on the bus. I already think that my darling takes on way too much and I would be ever so grateful to you if you took better care of yourself.

I am sad over the fact that you were so frightened by my having been ill. I asked the doctor from the American consulate to take over my treatment–he is very thorough–and he came over immediately, had people give him a report in the evening and asked if he should come over again and then, he came over every single day and listened to my breathing on a daily basis, brought medicine and was really great. On top of that, he demanded that I come to him sometime this week during his regular hours so he can convince himself of my complete recovery. So you can see that you have *every* reason to be pacified.

Now, I have to jump into my bed as soon as possible, because I am terribly tired. Good night, my most passionately beloved golden girl. Sleep well and sweetly and in good health and dream yourself to me, as I dream myself to you so I can take my little fruit tree into my arms in my dreams and give you a *very*, very long, *very*, very sweet good night kiss.

Completely and utterly, Your Mope

VERA TO MOPE

London, 9 February 1939

I had *no* idea, my love, that you were ill, and apparently spent an entire week in bed. I can still hear the sound of your beloved voice in my ear and I did not like it at all, because it sounded tired and exhausted. My love, after coming down with the flu, people always feel terribly weak for another week or so, and it is *terribly* important that you take very good care of yourself during the week after, otherwise–and please, please have yourself examined for that–damage to the kidneys or the heart might be left behind. Please, please, have a urinalysis done, go to bed early and stay in if it is harsh outside until you are *completely* well again. I know just *how* exhausted one feels after the flu and how necessary it is to watch out for oneself *afterwards*.

I am supposed to go and see Dr. Rothschild Sunday morning–he wants to see me once a month; actually, that is really not necessary at all since I am feeling excellent.

I completely forgot to write that I received a postcard from Annelie from New York at the beginning of the week, and she tells me that she has been married for five days and is very happy and that her husband is busy working.

Alicechen left for Palestine early today–she called me again last night and was unable to reach me, sadly.

Most passionate kisses and all my love, you, my beloved! *Your* little witch!

MOPE TO VERA

Moscow, 10 February 1939

I will have to travel to Leningrad in the next few days. During the upcoming auction, there will be a terrible amount of work–because the quantity of merchandise is simply enormous–and this time, I have to try even harder to satisfy the customers, since I am increasing my demands. When I talked to Schapiro about my contract with him, he was surprisingly pleasant. However, I am sure that my demands are anything but pleasing to him, but he will not be able to do without me without some difficulties, because slowly but surely, the customers have come to believe that I know a little bit about the merchandise. Life is making me modest!!! Schapiro is just a parasite, after all, and he probably does not suffer any illusions as to his role. With me, he has taken a snake to his breast, while he thought that he had caught himself a dumb one.

It is very late again and I still want to climb into the tub, after I was unfaithful to my custom of bathing in the morning for all those days. I take you in my arms most passionately, you, my beloved little orange-peach tree and hope with all my heart that you will not worry unnecessarily about your ill-bred *husband*. *Your* Mope

VERA TO MOPE

London, 12 February 1939

I went to see Dr. Rothschild who found everything in the best order–he took my blood pressure and touched my belly and determined–I already knew anyway–that I have very strong stomach muscles (that is because of all the gymnastics I used to be involved in) which he considered to be a very positive condition for a birth (which I also knew already). He asked me to send him another little bottle and told me that, as a former medical student, he would have expected me to bring a new one without being told. He said that I would be able to work for another two months (I think longer than that, but we shall see!!!!!).

It is 10.30 in the evening and Carlchen Rosenfeld's son, Georg, whom we had invited to join us for high tea, just left. He seems to be a very nice and humble boy and has been here since the end of January, works in a factory, and lives in Ealing with his cousin.[166]

Fig. 82 Georg Rosenfeld, later George Rosney, in 1937 (courtesy of Audrey Rosney, his widow).

Yesterday evening, I took care of all of my letter debts; I wrote to Annelie and congratulated her in both our names. Today, I gave Muttilein a check for £26-3-8, and hope that that is alright with you. It is to pay for her rent for January and February. Since Mutti had very high gas, electricity and telephone bills and also had some additional expenses like the purchase of additional bed linens, I knew that it would be very difficult for her to pay the bill, and I hope that my actions are alright with you.

---

166 Born in 1921, Georg Rosenfeld (later George Rosney), although still a teenager, was beyond the age to be admitted under the Kindertransport scheme but found refuge in England.

In the meantime, it is 12.30 and I have made my way to the horizontal and the ink in my pen is all gone. My love, I am happy in the knowledge of you, your love, and your intelligent and kind understanding. I am looking forward to our little baby and hope that it will represent everything I wish for in it. Completely and utterly, *Your* Little Witch

MOPE TO VERA

Moscow, 16 February 1939

After a rather busy day–I had to work out all of my Leningrad auction specifications and send them to Schapiro and also inform him that I had acquired some other merchandise today–I had my porridge and read a little of the newspaper.

You know, I am constantly worried about whether you are really well or not. Sometimes, I am downright afraid, because the mail takes so horribly long, and what kinds of vexation and sorrows or physical discomfort can make an appearance during those everlasting days until the mail gets here? For the last few days, ever since I talked to you, I have been so worried about my beloved little witch's well-being, and I hope with all my heart that those worries are completely baseless.

How are things coming along with the *nursing home*? How blundering of the matron in Courtfield Gardens that she has no running water in the house, because it seems that she would have otherwise met with your approval! It is unimaginable in such a huge city as London that people there are so far behind the rest of the world where such simple matters of hygiene are concerned. I already wrote to you that you should pay no attention to the price, please, because it is completely wrong to try to save money in things like that.

I am very happy to hear that the tension between you and Hannalein has been dispelled. It would have been very sad if this friendship had been loosened. My opinion of the good little chick Alice seems to have also carried over to my little witch. She really appreciates it when people show themselves to have friendly feelings towards her. In any case, I am glad that you got to meet another one seventh of us and I hope that you were not too loathe to take her into your circle as well. Even as a child, she was our "funny old one" and I am sure that she will be just that as she gets older.

Apparently, we will be moving our future field of activities to Leningrad. Merchandise will now be shown in the beautiful new Palais of the Soyuzpushnina and not, as previously, in the area of the harbor. I was told that our operations will have to move there for good in the future, since most of the merchandise will be sent there for sale or auction. The climate there is not as favorable as it is in Moscow, since the air is very moist because of the many canals and the River Neva, especially in the transition period. That is exactly the time, in the spring and the fall, that I am usually with my darling, so I will hardly have to suffer under it. The warehouses around the harbor are terribly cold at this time of year, while the heating emanates the most wonderful heat in "our" new location.

Now, however, I have to get into the horizontal as quickly as possible. It is unbelievably late and I have to work tomorrow. I take my most beloved girl into my arms and I kiss you with the most beautiful and sweetest kisses which are meant to make you happy innumerable times. You, sweetest little mother-to-be, you! Most tenderly, Your Mope

VERA TO MOPE

London, 16 February 1939

It is past 10.30 and I just jumped into the horizontal. I had the afternoon off today. After lunch, Muttilein went with me to Kensington High Street, and, at Barker's, I looked at a skirt model which I will be able to wear until the end of July, because it is a *wrap-over* skirt which can be adjusted according to the increasing girth by re-sewing a snap which I consider very practical. I intend to invest in a well-made *maternity frock* just as soon as I more noticeably gain in fullness.

Yesterday at the store, one of our *floorwalkers*, who let me know not too long ago that she will get married in March, appeared in my office crying and saying that she had to tell me something that no one, not even her mother, knew about yet, namely that she is expecting a baby towards the end of June and asked if I could help her. Since the *young man* who is part of it knows about it and is pleased with the news and since they will get married at the end of March instead of during the summer, as originally planned, I calmed her down by telling her that I did not see why she was crying and what else was making her heart heavy, and she assured me several times that since I was taking the matter that way, she was feeling completely relieved. I arranged an appointment for her at the hospital immediately so she could be examined and a bed reserved for her for June. Although I could *not* tell anything by looking at the girl, she sobbed and told me that the girls in the store had made ugly remarks concerning the changes in her appearance and that they were talking about it. I fancy that no one knows about me yet. I wonder if that is just wishful thinking. Actually, I do not care one way or the other, but I would really like to know out of pure curiosity.

When I arrived at the Kilburn store, the typist there welcomed me–she is a Jewish girl of around twenty, an excellent stenographer and typist who probably attended a better middle school. I knew her from my time in Kilburn; she is quite intelligent and most likely grew up in a proletarian or middle-class milieu. She held out her left hand to me and showed off the *wedding-ring* on it with pride and said, *"You can wish me: all good luck, I got married on 26ᵗʰ December"* which I did, of course, with the greatest pleasure and I assured her that a life shared between two people is so much more beautiful! Then, she asked if she could talk to me and if I were willing to advise and help her, because there was *no one* else she could talk to: despite her two-month long marriage, she had not been with her husband yet, although she loves him; she is afraid and he respects that, and what should she do? I advised her to go to a doctor–I thought, from my point of view and since I was no more than halfway informed–that was the best advice. She agreed to go after another period of two weeks that she gave herself. Additionally, I tried to calm her down on the one hand, because she seemed to be *worried*, and on the other hand, I explained to her how important a visit to a doctor was after another fourteen days, *important* for the future of her marriage. The husband (also a Jew), if he is healthy, seems to be good-natured and unintelligent. Or is that diagnosis wrong?

These are a few sketches from the day of a *staff manageress*!!!

I am waiting for your next letter with much impatience, because that letter will probably tell me about the result of your visit to the doctor last week. I hope that he found *everything* in the best order! I am feeling *very* well, apart from an *immense* longing! Completely and utterly, *Your* Little Witch

VERA TO MOPE

London, 19 February 1939

I called your dear mother a little while ago. She asked me if Schapiro had paid you and I told her yes, a few weeks ago, and then, she said that Hanna had come to her and told her that the expenses for Grete's flat and everything else in Davos had been *much* higher than expected and since Fred was not here, she would really like it if you could contribute £25-0-0 of the promised £75-0-0 now. (Fred will be back from South Africa in a week from Friday!). Of course, I told your mother that I will send her the £25-0-0 and I just put the check and letter for her in an envelope. I know that the agreement said payment during her stay *here*, but I could not tell your dear mother that, and I hope that it is alright with you. What I find completely *wrong* in the matter is that Norbert virtually forced Grete to go *there* with the children although she does have a permit for here. I do not know about the costs there, but I cannot imagine that Davos is a very inexpensive place. I can understand only too well that he prefers having his wife with him, but other people want that as well and have to make the greatest sacrifices in this regard! Do you agree with me? The application to Switzerland for permanent residence was denied and the permit for her to stay there is only valid until March, so Grete and the children would have to come here in May. It is up to you whether you want to comment from there on the check that is to be sent to Davos! It will be difficult from such a great distance and most likely altogether futile to respond. It probably will not make much sense.[167]

Hanna called a few minutes ago!!! She asked when we would be able to see each other again and I told her you had requested that she come to me, because I have to work standing up so much, but although you had said that, it would not be absolutely required to abide by that request since I am feeling *very well*. Among other things, Hanna told me that she had been informed today that a notice from the Home Office had been received yesterday and that Ketty's visit had been turned down. When the application was submitted, a petition for a work permit was

---

[167] Mope had agreed with Fred to underwrite affidavits that would allow Grete and children to immigrate to England. Their mutual brother-in-law, Norbert Moschytz, Grete's husband, appears to have leaned for support on the generosity of the larger family without full consideration of their circumstances.

made at the same time and I am sure that all of these cases are weighing heavily right now. I felt very sorry and I would like to know if Otto Schiff's intervention had arrived there in good time. In any case, since Hanna will make another petition, I hope that his letter, had it not been received yet, will prove to be successful.

When will you finally know the date of your return, my love? But of course, I do not want you to come back earlier than is feasible to you and before you get everything done the way you think is right in order to satisfy your customers.

I kiss you innumerable times full of the gentlest love, and I am happy to know that we are together, you——Completely and utterly, *Your* Little Lilongo

MOPE TO VERA

Moscow, 20 February 1939

Belatedly, Sojuspushnina arranged a banquet to celebrate the conclusion of the Persian lamb contracts. They called us around 6.30 to ask us to make an appearance at the Savoy Hotel at 7 o'clock. Having postponed several writing tasks, I still had a lot of work to do, so I decided work first and then "pleasure" and did not go over there until 9.20 while three of my colleagues had appeared on time. As punishment for my being late, I had to drink a wine glass full of vodka and after that, another half glass. I am not quite drunk, but feeling a little addled and the letter to my most beloved, sweetest girl will turn out accordingly and I might be reluctant to send it on its way tomorrow morning.

It would have been a serious affront, had I not shown up at all after the invitation and I had hoped, in my carelessness, that the late arrival would save me from a significant part of the alcohol consumption. As you can see, this was a complete misjudgment on my part! Nevertheless, the others also seemed to have been drinking a lot and one of the colleagues, whose wife is supposed to arrive tomorrow, drank quantities I had never thought possible, and that after I got there. Had I taken in even near that amount of alcohol, I would probably be lying under the table where the banquet took place until the July auction.

There is only *one* thing, the most *important* one, that I would like to raise here, as I have done all the days before. Please decide on the London Clinic immediately–if you have not done so already! I can hardly see a difference in the cost compared to the earlier offers and soooo much desired comfort that there can be *no* doubt that this is the right place for my darling.

Because of that report on all the boozing, I completely forgot that we drank a toast to you as well as to our expected baby's health. I had to explain to the president of Sojuspushnina back then why it became impossible for you to come here and so, he used the occasion to drink to our son's well-being. However, I told him that I did not care if we had a boy or a girl and was only interested in your health as well as the child's.

Now, I want to close this funny, drunken letter and prepare myself for going to bed immediately after the telephone call. I am sending the most passionate and sweetest kisses that might be a little fragrant with alcohol to my most beloved little fruit tree. Most passionately and completely, *Your* Mope

VERA TO MOPE

London, 21 February 1939

At home, I found your loving telegram concerning the London Clinic. I just called the people there but I still feel like I am a terribly wasteful person and I am not completely clear whether I have the right to have a clear conscience in this matter! Most of all, my love, I would like to thank you for your love and caring and kindness and tell you that I am very *glad and happy*, once I get over my guilty conscience, to be able to go to such a hygienic and modern *nursing-home*. That is the disadvantage of my medical half-education, that I know too much to be completely untroubled and because of that, face a matter like this without critique, but still not knowing enough about medicine to actually use it for some practical purpose, or even be able call that little bit of unimportant knowledge as medical knowledge at all.

My love, it is very *good* and *sensible* of you to alter your diet to porridge and milk rice after that flu because meat, and with it protein, place too much of a demand on the kidneys. Vegetables and fruit are good as well and I hope that my beloved takes in as much fresh fruit as humanly possible, even if you do not do it gladly–*do it for* my *sake!!!*

My love, I have been reading the newspapers during the last few days with such extremely fearful emotions. There is so much in them about *how* ready to attack that dirty gang in Germany is and that people were expecting bad things to happen at the *beginning* of March. Even the thought makes me feel cold and I would really like to know your view and your opinion concerning the matter, and if you see things as darkly as the newspapers.[168]

Most passionate, longing kisses—*I love you with all my heart and soul and everything that makes me the person I am. Your* little Lilongo Witch

P.S. I am feeling extremely well!!!

MOPE TO VERA

Moscow, 22 February 1939

You will probably have received yesterday's telegram with the request to make immediate arrangements with the London Clinic and I hope that you contacted the people there right away. I like their prospectus and from it, I can see that this place is the only appropriate one for my girl to bring the expected little child into the world. Hopefully it will work out to where they have to give you a sixteen guineas room for fourteen guineas—then you will at least have the feeling to have got something for your money. I am sure that the price will seem *reasonable* to you then! I am so exceedingly happy that the pregnancy does not seem to place too heavy of a burden on you—according to your reports at least.

You might like to find out that I procured my Finnish visa yesterday—it is valid for three months—so that I will not have to come back here again before my departure from Leningrad. I asked to have the Swedish one sent to Helsingfors. Quite a burden fell off my soul when they issued the visa immediately which was probably done because I already had the one from London in my passport!

And now, it is high time to come to the end of this letter. It is a chronometer that results from the size of the paper, because otherwise, I would continue writing ad infinitum. I kiss you, my sweetest little peach tree, full of the most passionate love and most tremendous longing, *Your* Mope

VERA TO MOPE

London, 23 February 1939

Today, I had an especially *good* day! The mail brought me three most beloved letters as well as a telegram which requested the address change

---

168 Hitler continued to threaten to annex the rest of Czechoslovakia, and occupied the country in the middle of March, only a few days later than Vera had predicted.

for the cigarette shipment. Just yesterday evening, I received a letter from Abdulla in which they inform me that the February shipment will be sent next week and ask me to let them know if another shipment is supposed to be made next month. I called them today and informed them that the February shipment should be sent to Leningrad and that I would call them again, as soon as my beloved lets me know if he wants another shipment in March; I do so hope that that will not be necessary and that my beloved will be *here*, in my company, when the next shipment is ready to be sent.

My tummy is now beginning to grow little by little–but my waist and bust measurements have increased about five centimeters as of late; by the time you come back, my love, you will find a *wife* whose measurements have undergone quite a transformation. My love, I am really feeling very well and ever since the night from 21 to 22 February I feel how the little one makes the tiniest movements within me. They say that that usually begins at the halfway point–that is, after about four and a half months into the pregnancy–and that is approximately right. I feel it during the day as well now–it is definitely not uncomfortable at all or even painful–it feels more like something moves ever so slightly and gently in the intestines.

This morning, I received a letter from our insurance agent in which he informed me that the *war-risk* has been included in our finalized insurance policy and because of that, there is an additional payment due in the amount of £1-11-0. When I called him not too long ago concerning this matter, he also said that he regarded the inclusion of *war-risk* absolutely necessary.

Mutti's good friend Emma Oppenheimer came by this afternoon– you met her once and she is a very intelligent and likable woman. The reason for her visit was that she wanted to bid us farewell since all of her paperwork for South Africa is done and she intends to leave around the beginning of April; but before she leaves, she wants to visit her grandchildren in Switzerland–they are half-Aryan and their father is still in Berlin, while their mother, Mrs. Oppenheimer's youngest daughter, is already in the U.S.A. It is difficult to say what will become of such a marriage and more than dreadful.[169]

Completely and utterly and most passionately, *Your* Little Witch

---

169 Many mixed marriages foundered because of the fierceness of Nazi racial laws. The children of such marriages were deemed *"Mischlingen"* ("crossbreeds") and

MOPE TO VERA

Leningrad, 26 February 1939

I am really doing *very* well! I arrived here at the Hotel Astoria at 9.30 a.m. after I had a very pleasant trip–I shared a compartment with one of my colleagues. At 12.30, I received two most beloved letters from my sweet one and I am really happy about *how* lovingly you provide me with your longed-for reports. By 4 o'clock, I got caught up with all the work that had been left undone yesterday, then I went to dinner and ordered a theater ticket for this evening because I will probably not have any time for things like that in the next fourteen days or will be forced to go with customers and think of all the work waiting for me the entire time.

By the way, your friend Krämer the dentist is a big bungler. The provisional filling he claimed would last quite a while has splintered and now, I am living with a huge hole in my mouth and the hope that I will not be tortured by a toothache during the auction work. As usual, something like that happens at the most inconvenient time! I now eat compote more often in order to fulfill your wish that I eat more fruit in some form. There are enough apples and oranges available here to eat raw fruit as well, but I have a difficult time bringing myself to do that.

It seems *very* right to me that my dear mother approached you for the money for Grete, and not Hannalein. As a matter of fact, as the mother, she is *the* person to take care of things like that, since she is in London now, fortunately. Of course, it was perfectly correct of you to agree immediately and not delay the matter further by asking me first. My most beloved, you know just as well as I do how difficult it is to have to live separately and it might even be more expensive if Norbert has to pay hotel expenses in Davos and Grete keeps a household with the children in London. So, what was done is not entirely wrong, or so it seems to me anyway. There is another reason that can be mentioned, namely that resettling the children into the moist London climate might be more conducive in May than it would be right now. However, what do those people want to do after May? They can hardly be a burden on the family for the rest of their lives and I would like to know if Norbert is

---

were therefore deemed to be Jewish and subject to a precarious existence if they remained in Germany.

doing anything to create a new existence for himself or if he is just sitting in Davos doing "scientific" work–at least that is what he calls it–and wants to continue living the life of a parasite.

The rejection of Ketty's petition weighs heavily on me. The poor girl has had such a difficult time, but neither she nor David can be blamed. David has done some stupid things, but that happened more or less because he was deceived. In any case, both of them–and Ketty completely blameless–have had to suffer heavily, and I wish with all my heart that their luck will finally change.

I am really happy that my little girl has now made an agreement with the London Clinic and I do not have to worry about that any longer–that is a lot worse than the minor additional charge compared to the shack at Courtfield Gardens. So you see that you provided me with a lesser burden and not an increased one! You would only have a reason to feel guilty if you had left me up in the air during the auction. It might be a good idea to make a down payment of around five guineas to make sure that you will be accommodated. That would also have the advantage that the later *bill* would seem lower to you.

I do not believe that war will start before the summer, under any circumstances, and even then, there is not much chance for that. I am sure and hopeful that all of your worries are unjustified. It would be against all statesmanlike intelligence and foresight–although that cannot necessarily be expected from the rabble in those fascist countries–to begin a war before the harvest has been brought in. You will find that confirmed in world history.

Now, however, I have to gallop off to bed, otherwise, tomorrow's first inspection will turn out badly. I send the most passionate, most loving, sweetest kisses to you, my golden girl. Most passionately, *Your* Mope

VERA

Journal entry, 28 February through 2 March 1939

On Tuesday, 28 February, in the afternoon between 3 and 4 o'clock, I lost our baby. On Tuesday, 21st, when I went to bed (I was at the store during the day), there were slight traces of blood. I stayed in bed on Wednesday and the doctor gave me injections. It stopped *completely* on Friday and Saturday. On Sunday, it started again, very lightly, and it came with diarrhea this time. Sunday evening, Dr. Rothschild examined me on the inside and found my cervix closed. During the night from Sunday to Monday morning, the blood loss became heavier.

Mr. Nixon and Dr. Rothschild came over early Monday morning and Mr. Nixon also examined me and he found the cervix closed as well. He doubled the dose of Vitamin E from 3 to 6 capsules a day. No injection on Monday, because a Zonderk-Aschheim[170] was supposed to be performed Tuesday morning. My temperature had been around 37 degrees during the last few days (under the arm).

Was prescribed a sedative on Monday–no appetite.

Around noon, pain in the abdomen about every 10 minutes, way down, for about ½ to 1 minute, then pain spread to the entire abdomen.

Dr. Rothschild came back again around 11 o'clock to bring the bottle for the Zonderk-Aschheim. I talked to him by myself for just a moment and told him that it would probably not be necessary any longer, because I expected that the child would come during the night. By the time, we had settled down (Muttilein and I), it was around 12 o'clock and at 3 o'clock, I woke up and the pains were coming in 5-minute intervals. Towards morning, I went back to sleep for a little while, for how long or how short I do not know.

Dr. Rothschild came back early that morning and because I was bleeding, he thought that it would be better to wait with the ZA; he gave me another injection and told Muttilein that the room should be darkened and that sleep was the best thing now. After about ½ hour, the pains that were still localized in the abdomen subsided a little for about ½ hour, but then, they resumed tenfold, in intervals of about 2 minutes across the entire abdomen.

Between 12 and 1 o'clock, I took morphine twice, but the pain did not relent at all and came in intervals of 2 minutes and kept getting stronger. Then, around 3 o'clock, the doctor came back. I drew up my legs (before that, I had vomited twice, but since I had only had a little tea, nothing much came out) and I was lying on my back and as long as I did not move, the pain was a little more bearable.

Then, the doctor got on the telephone and asked for a nurse and I vomited again, with very strong tremors. Muttilein was there and afterwards, I said to her that I thought the child had come out with that. The doctor checked and there it lay together with the placenta. I felt very lightheaded, that is, physically, because the pain had stopped. The

---

170 A now obsolete pregnancy test drawn from urine samples.

doctor gave me an injection to make sure that my uterus regained its original shape as quickly as possible. Then, the nurse arrived, wrapped a terry cloth towel around my belly, washed me with warm water, and then put a pad on me rather tightly. Yesterday, she poured a disinfectant on me (she came over for about 1 ½ hours, in the morning, and I was feeling much better. In the afternoon, there was a little blood.

Yesterday morning around 7 o'clock, I wrote to my darling (as the Tuesday letter and yesterday towards evening as the Wednesday letter).

I took pills to avoid infection and more capsules to ensure that my uterus kept drawing back together. Aside from the fact that I felt a little tired, I felt quite well, but I had a great need for rest.

In the evening, I took the sleep medication again and slept through the night, until now.

This is the description of the purely physical events. I felt really well during the entire pregnancy. I did not lift anything heavy nor did I do anything that could have caused this miscarriage, in my opinion. However, was I really prepared, I mean psychologically prepared, as one should be?

1. I wanted to hide the changes in my figure.
2. I was very disappointed that I could not go to the Pantheon.
3. I was sad, or rather, I had not reconciled myself with the thought that I would have to interrupt my career.
4. I was–although, from a purely intellectual point of view, and that is probably where my biggest mistake lay–that the want I felt for a child was based in intellect and reason, not in emotion, in the heart. I would really like to know to what this miscarriage can be attributed. I ask myself if I rested enough and if I should not have been working, but I hardly think that is the reason, or maybe I am lacking some hormones or there is something wrong with my abdomen. If only I knew the reason!

There is something there and I have been feeling that for a while now: that something had to happen in my life that would show me that things will not always go smoothly and that things had been going way too well for me.

Besides my beloved Mopelein, I have an angel Muttilein and what worry and trouble I caused her and how indescribable she was to me and what pain I must have caused her. That and the horrible pain and the disappointment that I am causing my Mopelein is the worst thing of all to me! And I really, really hope that I will soon bring a healthy child into the world.

VERA TO MOPE

London, 28 February 1939

I did not write to you yesterday.[171] It got to be very late, and as soon as I put myself into the horizontal position, I fell asleep. I am *so* happy to hear that you have already received your Finnish visa and I hope most longingly that you will be successful in procuring your visa for Sweden as quickly as possible.

So, my Mopelein was a little, pardon me, a large drunkard last Monday. Your beloved kisses did not smell of that all the way to here and I almost said–unfortunately not! My love, I determined with regret that it seems to be very late there lately when you write and that is *not* good–you have a lot of work to do, you suffered from a bad flu not too long ago, so you *must* get enough sleep, otherwise, your kidneys will suffer!!!!!

I am feeling very well and I only wish that my beloved could be with me. Nevertheless, I do know just how grateful we have to be that you have this job, and as I have told you many times before, I am *very, very* proud of my beloved who was able to become familiar with and so very good at this completely new and difficult work.

I love you, my darling, with all my heart and with all the intensity at my disposal.

God bless you and I am looking forward to seeing you so indescribably, and I kiss you again and again in my thoughts and full of the gentlest passion—

Completely and utterly, *Your* Little Witch

How long will you have to stay there *after* the auction is over?

---

171 This letter was penned on the day that Vera suffered her miscarriage. Wishing to conceal the very sad news from Mope until the end of the Leningrad auction, she continues to write to him on a daily basis affirming her own good health, though (reading between the lines) the letters she writes at this time are understandably distraught and less focused than usual.

VERA TO MOPE

London, 1 March 1939

Today is the first day of March!!! I can hardly tell you how happy that makes me, because I am hoping with so much longing that my most beloved will be here with me by the end of this month and that I will be able to finally feel his beloved embrace again. *How* I look forward to that and to everything that makes him the man he is!!!!

My Mopeleinchen, hurrah that it is March!!!!!! I cannot describe to you just how happy that makes me! And now, I can think that my beloved is coming to me *this* month, can't I???? I love you very, very, very much, more than I can write to you about!!! Mopeleinchen, do you know that you make me very, very, very, completely and utterly and totally happy? *Your* little Lilongo Witch

MOPE TO VERA

Leningrad, 1 March 1939

Just now, it is 2.30 a.m., I am interrupting my work, because I cannot leave my beloved without mail for a third day in a row. Yesterday and the day before, I worked until 3 o'clock, and 3.30 respectively and since I have to get out of bed again at 8 o'clock, there is not much time left for sleeping. The catalogue of the first section, that is, foxes, martens, European polecats, etc., is twice as strong as usual, and there is an immeasurable amount of work. We are busy inspecting the merchandise from 9 to 5.30 with an hour break for lunch. In the evening, it is time for taking care of calculating the prices which is very difficult this time as well, since numbers have been printed in the catalogue, and they have to be checked in order to do a self-check concerning the particular descriptions. This only to explain to you that I only have to neglect my sweet one where letters are concerned, but never in my thoughts! All of my customers want filled-out catalogues and the auction begins Sunday afternoon and should last until Friday.

As I already told you, I will remain in Leningrad now and not go back to Moscow at all, so that the mail will also be awaited here with great longing. I intend to leave on the 30th and arrive in London in the morning of 3 April. That is a Monday and the day before Pesach.

I am deeply touched and delighted that our expected one has begun to move in a noticeable manner and I hope with all my heart that it will not give my beloved one any discomfort, because I would have to be mad at it, although I do not really know it all that well yet, and I am sure that it does not want that. I hope that the matter with the London Clinic has now been firmly finalized—please let me know!

I went to a dental clinic here because of my emptied tooth and had it filled again temporarily. It was very quick and painless and I am happy that I will not have to worry unnecessarily about getting a toothache.

Now, I have to hurry and get to bed and I will come running to you soon in my dreams–beneath your picture–and open the door ever so quietly to convince myself that my sweetest one is sleeping well and then kiss you most tenderly and take you gently into my arms so that I will not disturb your sleep, you sweetest little orange tree, and I am looking forward to the little fruit ever so much and I kiss you and it most lovingly and gently. Completely, *Your* Mope

VERA TO MOPE

London, 2 March 1939

Today, I have the afternoon off and I sandwiched in another very lazy *half-day*, but before that, I went out into the fresh air right after lunch. Now, I am writing to you from the horizontal and I am enjoying the peace and quiet. Today, my beloved is celebrating Wychodnoi and I hope that he was able to get some rest, despite the many inspections and all the work. And that he did not have to write catalogues without pause!!!

Early today, I received a rather convoluted letter from Annelie in which she asks me to do something for her parents and make it possible for them to use England as a transit station. I had not heard anything from her parents since I sent them the application form. I will send Annelie a copy of my letter to her parents and then wait to see what she thinks of it and also bring Sweden to her attention, as you advised me to do earlier. Among other things, she writes that she had just received the news that her sixty-six-year-old father-in-law who had been sent to a concentration camp in perfect health died in the hospital. Aside from the fact that this news shocked her, she is even more worried now where her parents are concerned. She also writes that her only consolation is her husband and she would write to us about her life and her activities another time. She had not received my letter yet when she sent her letter off to me.

I just talked to your dear mother and she sends you all her love; she was very sweet and charming, as always. She had a half fast day today and I think it is wonderful how closely she observes everything.[172] Among other things, she told me that your brother Adolf had spent some very restful vacation days in the Lebanon and she is very happy about that because he works very hard. Your sister Alice had written from Cyprus, the return ship was not as comfortable as the one on the way there, but that is really not all that bad after all.

My Mopeleinchen, most of all, it is meant to tell you that I love you, that I am well, and that I feel such great, great, and even greater longing for you.

Completely and utterly and totally, *Your* Little Witch

VERA TO MOPE

London, 3 March 1939

Today, I received two most beloved letters from Moscow and the detailed one from the 26th from Leningrad. I was happy to hear that my mail arrived in Leningrad at just the right time and welcomed my beloved there! By the time these lines reach you, you will have passed the zenith of the auctions already. I was so very happy to hear that you were able to finalize a few more deals before your departure from Moscow.

I do hope that the tooth Krämer put a temporary filling in which fell out again will not give you any pain. Oddly enough, your judgment concerning Mr. Krämer coincides with Muttilein's whom I had sent to him a few weeks ago and she was not pleased with him at all. I have always been quite satisfied with him until now–although I do not have any expertise in this matter. In any case, I really do hope that that particular tooth will *not* give you any problems during your current stay there.

My love, I was very sad to hear that you believe you will not be able to come home before April!!!!?? It has never been that long before–but if it has to be, it just has to be!!! Nevertheless, I do *not* find that wonderful

---

172 The Jewish Fast of Esther, preceding Purim, occurred on the roman calendar date of 2 March in 1939.

at all, and why is that necessary? Schapiro thought that your trip would make no sense at all unless you stayed there for the entire month of April. Do you happen to share that view????? I most decidedly do not!!! After all, we only live once and the beginning of April is bad enough, but as has been said before, if it is necessary, I do not want to stand in your way!—

I am feeling very good and I feel such a limitless yearning for my beloved!!! It is nice to know that the mail from Leningrad and back appears to take less time! Do you really know that I love you very, very, very much and *even more*, you?! —Your Little Lilongo Witch

VERA TO MOPE

London, 5 March 1939

Today–Sunday–was a beautiful day filled with sunshine and aside from the fact that the wind was blowing rather strongly, one could really believe that spring has arrived. As usual, I spent the morning being very lazy and did not go out until the afternoon to catch a little fresh air, and I took the little bottle to Dr. Rothschild so he can examine it. I am feeling very well and the only thing missing is *you*, my love. Dr. Rothschild is very pleased with my progress and I hope that you are as well.

Yesterday evening, I received a huge bouquet of dark red tulips: I remembered that I had mentioned to the assistant cashier some time ago, when she was in my office, that tulips are my favorite flowers and that red is my favorite color. A while ago, towards the end of December, I pushed a raise through for her, but getting it through created some trouble for me. She had been working for us for ten years, left to give birth to a baby (she was married) and came back after two years. They rehired her at a ridiculously low salary and even after she had been retrained and became re-familiarized with the work, they hardly gave her an appreciable raise. I talked to the chief branch accountant, and she finally got her raise and she knew that I had procured it for her. And it appears that the bush of red tulips which was delivered without a note is meant as a sign of her gratitude. In any case, I was very happy to receive them. Generally speaking, I think and have observed that human beings on the same social background as our girls (the *assistant cashier* used to be a *salesgirl*) have a much better developed and unadulterated sense of gratitude and express it much more freely than so-called educated people.[173]

Maybe you will come home at the end of the month? That is my quiet hope anyway! As soon as you have some kind of idea concerning your arrival date, please let me know about it *immediately*!!!!!!!!! So that I can look forward to that date and I can do that a lot more once I know the date or at least the approximate date.

Most passionate, loving kisses, you, filled with longing, my Mopeleinchen –

Your Little Lilongo Witch

As a matter of fact, do you know that I love you very, very much and that all of my emotions are concentrated on doing something loving for and to you, you?—

VERA TO MOPE

London, 6 March 1939

Your dear mother spent the evening with us–she left just a little while ago–and she was sweet and charming, as always. She read a very detailed letter from Grete (Davos) to us–Grete seems to be quite comfortable there. They are still in negotiations with the U.S.A. and they still hope that things will work out for them after all, which would be a very desirable conclusion. The children seem to be very charming; she does not mention anything about her *husband*, as far as I remember. As I understand from her letter, Alice traveled over Switzerland on her way back and they met for a short time. In the meantime, your dear mother received the news from Palestine that Alice had arrived there hale and healthy and that everything went smoothly during her entry, aside from a few customs difficulties.

Yesterday, your beloved lines from 1 March arrived, so it seems that the mail is *significantly* faster from there. I was very happy to read that you now have an exact date for your arrival here, my love; so, unless Schapiro places something in our way, which I really hope will not happen, my love will be with me in four weeks. *How* I am looking forward to that day!!!

---

173 Likely, the anonymously sent bouquet of tulips came from the management at Marks & Spencer, who had been informed of Vera's miscarriage, and not (as she takes pains to explain to Mope) from the assistant cashier.

I hope that the first day of the auction yesterday went by pleasantly: I was with you in my thoughts all day long, my love!!!!!! Enough, enough–it is very late!!!

Completely and utterly, *Your* little witch

I am doing very well!!!

VERA

Journal entry, 7 March 1939

I am still lying in bed and today, I have to think about a few things: I would really like to talk to my husband, when he is back, into *giving up his job*. The reasons for that are as follows:

1) A marriage is not a real marriage if you are together for 2 months and then separated again for four months. After all, you only live once; you can suffer through such hardships if you *have* to, if there is no other way, which was the case for us 1 ½ years ago.

2) If my beloved does not spend more time here, he will never get British citizenship.

3) There will come a point when they will no longer give him the Russian visa, so it would be better to put an end to it yourself and of your own accord than to wait until you are no longer *able* to do it.

4) It could be rather bad for our marriage if this constant separation continues. If I had given birth to a baby now, in July, the matter would be quite different, but the way things worked: We are in a position to take some risks, because we are only responsible for adults, not for a child.

On top of that, I want to have a child as soon as possible, but the doctor says that I am not allowed to until I have had at least two normal periods, and by then–if my beloved continues with this job–he would be gone again, so we would have to postpone the arrival of our baby by another four months, so that would be six months altogether. Should we do that? I am twenty-nine years old, not so young anymore. I want to talk to my beloved about the matter when he comes back and see what he thinks about my perspective.

I would really like to have my husband here with me–this is not a natural marriage and maybe, we can find some kind of solution, some kind of satisfactory solution, to this problem.

I really hope so!!!!!!!!!

MOPE TO VERA

Leningrad, 11 March 1939 [postcard]

As I already told my most beloved in my telegram last night, the auction is over now. I had an indescribable mountain of work to take care of the entire time and on average, I had about three hours per day for sleeping. Nevertheless, I feel excellent, apart from the deeply depressing awareness of having neglected my darling so terribly all that time. Unfortunately, I am just simply not able to do anything besides constantly preparing the catalogues for the auction, check the billing, etc., because otherwise, I would not have been able to finish it all.

These words are meant to be a most heartfelt little greeting to you and tell you how indescribably I love you and how unbearable my longing for you is!!!

Completely and utterly, Your Mope

VERA TO MOPE

London, 11 March 1939

My beloved,

In the enclosed letter, I have to tell you about something that will *not* please you at all! *Please*, before you read it, go to your room or somewhere else where you can be completely undisturbed; and do not read it, should you be in a mood that is not the best.

And promise me that you will not let your head droop and that you will *not* be too unhappy!!!

Most affectionately, *Your* little witch

Thursday, 2. III. 39

I will work on this particular letter a little every day until it is sent off, so that it will make it possible to hurt my most beloved as little as possible–and I want *nothing* more than that! My Mopeleinchen, please help and advise me as you have done so often and always in such a loving and gentle way and still do.

What would you have done in my place, if you knew that your beloved husband (it might be difficult for you to imagine that, so wherever I set a masculine sign, please choose a feminine one) is very busy with merchandise inspections and that he needs all of his strength, his physical strength as well as his power of concentration, one hundred per cent to be up to the demands his profession places on him; that customers expect increased achievements, the highest performance from him since he is making increased demands on his employer, and that customers come to Leningrad from all four corners of the world to have him advise them advantageously, intelligently, and carefully?

Then add to that the fact that you love your husband without limits and know that this love is mutual and that everything your wife experiences affects you deeply, and the same for the other way around.

Mopeleinchen, I am afraid to continue writing–can you understand that?–and I have thought long and hard about whether I should wait until your return to continue this report. Then, you would be able to look at me. Then, I could caress you gently, kiss your eyelids, and continue quietly, ever so quietly with this narration which weighs so very heavily on my soul; so here goes:

There once was a young woman who had so much happiness in her life that it made her feel afraid at times.

Friday, 3. III. 39

She had a husband she loved completely and he had the same feelings for her; the two of them harmonized intellectually, spiritually, and physically. They assisted each other, helped each other, loved each other, supported each other, and a wondrous harmony suffused their union.

6. III. 39

Even outwardly, life was good to them; they started with nothing and were able to get ahead through diligence, energy, competence, and both of them found a lot of joy in their work.

The only thing missing from making their happiness complete was a product of their love, a visible one: a child!

Mopelein, my beloved, we will have *another one*, I hope. *This one was a boy.* I am feeling completely well, my darling! Had it made sense to call you back such a short time before the auction??? You could not have helped me anyway, my beloved. It happened on: Tuesday, 28. February, in the afternoon between 3 and 4 o'clock. At home. And Dr. Rothschild was there, and, my darling–I know, and that is another deep sorrow to me, from now on, it will be difficult for me, very difficult, to get you to believe me, and that is a terrifying thought!

Tuesday, 7. III. 39

And now, I am doing very well again, but I do not think that you will believe me until you have convinced yourself of it in person, and God willing, you will be able to do so relatively soon *after* you receive these lines....[174]

Wednesday, 8. III. 39

The moment the child came out all further pain subsided immediately, and since the afterbirth and everything else had come with it, complete, I had no fever and there was no need for any interference by the doctor, and no further discomfort arose.

The first thing I said was: "Poor Mope!" and I have repeated the same thing every day and *uncounted* times now and I keep thinking it endlessly, and I wish nothing more than to be right next to you while you are reading these lines. The next thing I said right after that was: "When can I have a child again?"

When Mr. Nixon was here, he remarked that statistics show that 20% of all pregnancies end in *miscarriages*. The only reason I can see for me being part of this 20%, as I already mentioned earlier, is the fact that the two of us were doing *too* well, and life wanted to remind us that not everything can always proceed smoothly and unobstructed and according to our wishes.

Dr. Rothschild determined that it must have been dead for at least two weeks and it was completely impossible to establish a cause. (What I had taken as probably movements by the child, must have been movements of some inner organ!). My love, I did not lift anything heavy nor did I stretch or do anything I did not do every single day prior to this. As I said, I lay in bed, absolutely sedately, for an entire week before it happened.

Today, I left the bed for the first time so I could take a bath. I feel completely well, but since the doctor insists, I will stay in bed until the end of the week. My love, please be assured that I am doing *everything* the doctor tells me to do because I do want to have a strong and viable child very soon and I do understand that that makes it very necessary for me to follow the doctor's orders implicitly. I am trying to be very sensible!!! My Mopeleinchen, I know that it is almost impossible to

---

174 There follows here "a chronological report," omitted here since most of the details are already contained in Vera's journal entry describing the miscarriage.

understand anything on the telephone from Leningrad, but you might feel relieved if you talked to me and convinced yourself that I am really feeling completely well again today.

By the time these lines reach you, I will have been out of bed for a while and you will realize when you hear the sound of my voice that I am fine.

My beloved, I plan on sending these lines either Friday or Saturday of this week and will be downright relieved that I will not have to send you any more letters with store reports, etc.

My letters must have shown you that I was doing well the entire time despite the events of February 28, otherwise, I would not have been able to write them at all.

Friday, 10. III. 39...

Please do not come back earlier because of the above report, under any circumstances, than you had planned initially. I am really feeling completely well and what sense would there be in you neglecting your duties towards the end of your current stay and offend Schapiro. Then, all of the effort I put into keeping the events secret until after the auction would have been for nothing, my love, and it cost me more, so much more energy than everything else....

My Mopelein, what I would give could I spare you this fright. My love, what would you have done in my place?? Had you come back, you would not have been able to help me anyway, and had you stayed there knowing what had happened right before the auction, your thoughts of me would most likely have paralyzed you.

Saturday, 11. III. 39

In the course of this day, I will send this report off; my love, I am feeling as good as ever!!!

Would you have preferred it if I had waited until your return and not written to you about it at all? I just could not have done that!!! And you can see why I did not write to you about it before, can't you, my love?!

I am looking forward to *you* and I am already looking forward to the next child even now, and I hope that I will carry it within me very soon and I hope *so* very much and with *so* much longing that my beloved–even after he reads these lines–is looking forward to all of that with me!!!

MOPE TO VERA

Leningrad, 12 March 1939

With this letter I will begin to provide my sweetest with regular mail once again, and in just a few weeks' time, I myself will follow them. Outside, the sun is shining and it is beginning to awaken the happiest feelings inside me at the thought that it is becoming so easy now to count the days that still separate me from my little witch. I am actually quite amazed how good the enormous amount of work was for me. I was in a constant hurry in order to get everything done which was more or less successful. During the entire auction, I had an average of three and a half hours of sleep a day, but nevertheless, I was in my best form during the merchandise inspections.

Today is Sunday and Wychodnoi at the same time and I am so glad to have the same day to rest as you do. I stayed in bed until 2 o'clock although I woke up repeatedly. In my brain, there still is no real chronological order of the events during the auction and I am reporting a jumbled mess to you, but I am sure that you can understand that and excuse it as a result. By the way, my beloved really helped me in everything with her regularly arriving reports, and the greater half of the merit of having done decent work is *due to you* and I thank you for that, my little girl.

My most passionately beloved little witch, I feel such an unbearable longing for you and your love and everything that has to do with you, and I am happy to know that I will be with you in three weeks tomorrow, if everything goes according to plan. The time together will help us get over all the difficult times of separation. I am looking forward to you as never before, because this time, you will show me more loveliness than ever before.

Filled with the greatest love and longing, you, my little peach tree–
Your Mope

VERA TO MOPE

London, 14 March 1939

This morning, with the 11 o'clock mail, I received your beloved lines from Sunday quite unexpectedly–my most heartfelt thanks! Once again, I am certain that it was right to keep the sad news from my beloved during the auction! I hope that you agree with me! I just wish that the day was already over–I assume that you will receive my Saturday letter tomorrow, since the mail is being transported much faster now–and I would finally know that my beloved has that behind him already. My thoughts are with you constantly and without pause and I am really worried about *how* you will take the news.

Muttilein called your dear mother this morning to let her know that I am doing well, and your dear mother said that, as soon as she could manage, she would come over again to visit me. I am always very happy to see her. She reported that Ketty's two younger children have received the permit to come over and will be here soon.

My love, if I only know what kind of mood you are in right now– if only I could kiss away all the sorrow from your forehead–but soon, soon, God willing!!!!!! My love, please do *not* be sad!!!

I kiss you innumerable times, sadly, via paper only, my beloved–*Your Little Witch*

MOPE TO VERA

Leningrad, 16 March 1939

I got married because I loved a girl with all the truth of my soul, with all the faith of my heart. That girl knew that our happiness depends on absolute honesty towards each other and is based on that. Even before our wedding, she realized that keeping a fact that could not be kept from me shook me to my innermost core and weighed heavily on our togetherness for a long time. It was only overcome because I was convinced that this experience had given my girl a lesson for life.[175]

Now, we have been married one and a half years. My love for my girl has grown to immeasurable limits. Every moment, every second of my being is dedicated to her, in loving thoughts, whether I live near her or far, far away. Our love was supposed to reach its zenith through the creation of a child. My worries for my girl, my worry that she might not take care of herself, that she remains aware of her task that the carrying of a baby in the womb demands, originated in that great love I feel for her.

In February, around the 10th of February to be more exact, an almost inexplicable fear took hold of me rather suddenly, a fear that something

---

175 Mope is alluding to Vera's relationship with Mitja.

had happened to my girl or the child inside her, and I also expressed that in my letters and begged, pleaded, for *truthful* reports on her well-being. I asked for telegraphed messages and I was deeply worried and concerned. Despite all the telegrams and letters that were supposed to calm me, my fear continued well into March. How many nights I lay awake and tried to imagine how my girl was doing! But that does not matter now!!!

Last night, I received a long letter which tells me that my girl has lost the child. Since February 22, she has lain in bed and she knew that there was danger, and on the day that the child left her, she sent me a telegram with the words "Very well aside from longing." I am an enemy of all heroics, because there are more lies than bravery in heroics. Instead of letting me know on February 22, that danger was approaching and letting me share in her pain as much as in her joy, my girl gave me falsified reports on experiences that were not experienced. Not only did she treat me like a wimp and feared that I would not be able to handle the facts, but she lied to me the entire time. How can I believe her now when she tells me that everything is fine??? How should I read your letters in the future? Veralein, *what* did you do?

Our love is built on truthfulness, and that is the only way it can be good and beautiful and great! And love also gives strength, more strength than necessary to overcome difficult blows of fate if they are not disfigured by lies into a horrible vision, because they will be increased a hundred-fold through falsehood. You cheated me out of sharing your pain, Veralein. You did not give me the trust I deserve–and trust is the basis of our union! I know that you wanted to make up for it, I know that with all the pain you already feel this piece of paper will give you more of the same, but should I now answer untruth with untruth? There are no diplomatic tricks between us, as far as I am concerned, and I have to tell you what I think and feel, if our love is not to be crippled by this.

Veralein, my Veralein, you knew of the joy I felt in the expected little child, but *your* well-being is much, much, much, indescribably much more important to me. If only I knew now, truthfully, that you are well again, it could help me begin to forget the sadness for the little fruit that fell from the tree before its time. But after what has happened, I can only convince myself of your well-being *in person*. You told me, via telegram and telephone, not to come home.—You send me a telegram in Dr. Rothschild's name "coming home absolutely nonsensical."—

And I love you with all my heart and share all your pain so completely and I am sitting here because Schapiro wants to earn a few more pounds and that is why my coming home would be "nonsensical!!!" I no longer understand anything, anyone! Your Mope

MOPE TO VERA

Leningrad, 16 March 1939

I have been sitting here in my room all day today, waiting for the telephone to my beloved which was supposed to come through at 10.30 this morning. After I wrote to you a little while ago, I feel a little less overwhelmed by bleak thoughts, although I have to believe that the letter will not give you any great satisfaction. Earlier today, I did not believe that it would be possible for me to write to you at all with the awareness of having been deceived like that. However, little by little, the feeling that you wanted to do something good for me is alleviating the pain just a little. My darling cannot know me well enough to anticipate all of my reactions, because I am so very far away from you so much of the time and so often, and most of all, I know what psychological and physical pain you poor sweet girl had to suffer and how difficult it must have been for you to tell me about it after it was all over. In the beginning, you did not count on having to give up the child without carrying it to term and then, yes, then, everything was over already and you wanted to spare me. Deep within me, I am happy that there were no complications at least, no fever added to it, or that is what you tell me anyway!

You know, I have been afraid all this time that you overdo things. Once, I saw you jumping on a moving bus and I am certain that the child probably fell victim to something like that, because what else could be the reason? On top of that, I have often thought that you did not care all that much about having a child. Your vanity rebelled against it and all of my attempts to make you feel love for the developing little creature, a love that was supposed to be stronger than all the sorrow over the lost Pantheon store were not enough after all. You wanted to have the child out of love for me (and I thank you for that), but not because of your own motherly desires.

It is not right to say that fate envied our happiness and that it wanted to show us that not everything will go smoothly. There are no goddesses of vengeance one has to make sacrifices to in order to satisfy them. We make a great part of our own fate ourselves and if the will to reach a goal is influenced by doubt, the goal will be impacted as well. Of course, many who want to rid themselves of a developing being within do not succeed despite everything they try to do, and others who wish for nothing else and wait for it with the most deeply felt motherly yearning, because they regard being a mother as the highest and most beautiful task of their womanhood, will never find that hope fulfilled. Concerning my beloved, there seems to have been a mix of both. You wished for a child because of me, but the sacrifices that ambition and vanity would be forced to make often seemed too great to you, because your yearning for a child was not as strong within you as those two characteristics controlling you.

You finally resigned yourself to losing the Pantheon store after my desperate reaction to your deeply felt sorrow, but deep inside you, you were neither able to accept the loss nor could you accept that this little creature wanted to affect your beautiful forms. But since that apparently could not be prevented, you wanted to be athletic, at least, and show everyone what a Vera can achieve despite a pregnancy. And how many things happened that I know nothing about???

But why am I writing all of this? Do I want to make stupid accusations now, after the fact, which cannot bring back what is irretrievably lost? I only want my darling to see everything clearly! My perspective might be wrong, but my thoughts are meant to stimulate yours to get as objective a picture concerning what happened as possible. You write to me that you want to have another child, but I do not want it to bring you nothing but sorrow and no joy, or causing the same worries for you as the first one. You should and have to consider if the required sacrifices seem equivalent to what you will gain by making them. You should not have a child because I long for it–like it was with the first one.

It is 7 o'clock in the evening and I have not left my room at all today, still hoping that I will be able to talk to you and also hear you. Tonight, after I had just cancelled my request so I would not disturb you after midnight, your call came through. Sadly, I had to guess what you were saying as, with a poor line, I did not really understand a single word. I take you into my arms with the gentlest love, and I cannot say what I would give if I could be with you right now!

Your Mope

VERA TO MOPE

London, 17 March 1939

How I look forward to the day when I no longer have to put things down on paper. My Mopelein, *how* would *you* have handled the matter in my place? I can only tell you again that I did not have the slightest idea, until Monday, February 27, that I would lose our child. And on Tuesday, the only day when I really did not feel well at all, it happened, and what sense would it have made then to let you know? You would have come back, you would have lost your position, you would *not* have been able to change *any* of the facts, so what would you have done in my place??????

When I received your beloved Sunday letter, in which you tell me so lovingly how my regular letters had helped you get over the difficult auction work, I felt so relieved and happy and I had the feeling that I did something good and right. And now, I no longer know what is right–although I still feel, when I think about it, that I did not have any other choice. However, I did not count on one great factor: I did not think it would ever be possible to lose my *beloved's* trust because of it. I was too sure and too convinced that the two of us trust each other so completely that my love, after the initial shock, would be able to understand the situation in such a way that the thought of my being unable to send him truthful reports would disappear in the background completely. My beloved, it is terribly difficult to be forced to be so far apart for such a long time!!!! —

I can only say and repeat: please, please, come as *soon* as you can, that is, as soon as you are finished with your work there. I wish I could have some idea of what my most beloved has to take care of now, after the auction is over, and could judge how important it is. My love, please take care of *everything* related to business the way you usually do, so you can leave there with a clear conscience, and then, as soon as everything is done, come to me, but *not* by air!!!

Oh, so, after our telephone conversation, you do not want me to read the next two letters?!!?!!? What would you do in my place? Of course, I will read them and *I love you*, even if you wrote angry letters to me. In my thoughts, I snuggle into your beloved and yearned for embrace and I kiss you quietly and tenderly and gently, here and there and everywhere, you, my beloved. I am completely and utterly, *Your* little Lilongo-witch

VERA TO MOPE

London, 19 March 1939 (mailed to Mope in transit through Stockholm)

Yesterday evening, as your cable was read to me on the telephone, I was more than happy, and I hope that you will have received my telegraphed answer very shortly after. As far as I know, it only takes about an hour for a telegram to arrive, at least that is what the Via Northern clerk told me. I am *so happy* I can hardly tell you just how happy. When and where will you arrive, my love? Apart from everything else, I do not like the political developments of the last few days at all, and so, I am relieved to know that you will begin your trip home tomorrow.[176]

Yesterday morning, I received a very dear and detailed letter from Hilde Lewy from New York. I had written her a letter at the beginning of this week but had not sent it off yet–because I had lost her address, or rather, the address of her brother with whom they are staying temporarily. She seems to have been so pleased with the telegram from "Vera Mope" and she said that it had been the last greeting from Europe before they left and the first good wishes on their way to the U.S.A. They want to go to the south of the country, maybe even to Atlanta, because Hilde's brother-in-law found work in the south and they do not want to be too far away from him. For the time being, they have no firm plans as to what they want to do, but they do not want to stay in New York under any circumstances. Hilde's entire letter made me very happy. I finished mine to her this morning and sent it off.[177]

My love, I really can hardly wait now until you are finally, finally here. And in the meantime you have come to understand, haven't you, just why I had to send reports that were not quite in line with the truth for those two and a half weeks? First of all, everything happened so suddenly, secondly, you would not have been able to help me, my love, and right afterwards, I was feeling completely well again, thirdly, you would have lost your position, most likely, and fourth, I love you so indescribably, my Mopeleinchen, and I know that now, after you have had the time to think about everything again, you understand me, don't you, you??!!!

---

176 German forces invaded Czechoslovakia on 15 March. The inaction of the western nations greatly emboldened Hitler's territorial ambitions.

177 The descendants of Hilde and Walter Lewy still live in Atlanta, GA.

I am looking forward to you and I hope that we will have a child very soon, very, very soon!!! In my thoughts, I kiss you full of tenderness and love and I wish you a good and comfortable trip and I accompany you with my thoughts, you–

Completely and utterly, *Your* little Lilongo-witch

Thirty-one: "No Life Without You"

17 May though 27 August 1939

POLITICAL TIMELINE, JUNE–SEPTEMBER 1939

- June 1939: German refugee ship, the St. Louis, turned away from Cuba and the United States.
- 12-21 August 1939: Anglo-French Mission meets with Soviets in Moscow but they fail to reach an accord over the defence of Poland.
- 22 August 1939: Hitler calls for the liquidation of Polish people to make room for Germans (Lebensraum).
- 23 August 1939: German-Soviet non-aggression pact signed in Moscow by Foreign Ministers Joachim von Ribbentrop and Vlacheslav Molotov.
- 25 August 1939: Anglo-Polish Alliance whereby Britain undertakes to come to assistance of Poland in the event of war.
- 1 September 1939: German troops march into Poland.
- 3 September 1939: Britain and France declare war on Germany, marking the beginning of the Second World War.
- 17 September 1939: Russian troops occupy Eastern Poland.

When Mope left for the Soviet Union in the third week of May 1939, he had exceeded almost by a month the terms of his permit to remain in England. His five-day return journey to Leningrad took him by sea from Harwich to Helsingfors, followed by a long train journey into Russia. As a stateless person, he again had had to obtain valid transit visas through Sweden and Finland as well as an authorized work permit for the Soviet Union.

Once back in the USSR and with Europe in a state of turmoil as a consequence of ongoing German militancy, Mope was conscious more than ever of his vulnerability and loneliness. The operator-dependent telephone connections between Leningrad and London were sporadic and unreliable, and he and Vera were to resort to cable telegrams to supplement their daily correspondence. The wireless that Mope brought over with him provided an additional lifeline to the West, giving him contact with Great Britain through the BBC. On 19 June, he was to "celebrate" his fortieth birthday, on that particular day no less than any other, ruing the physical absence of his wife.

Communication from his boss, Ruwin Schapiro, was also intermittent, and the resultant slackness in Mope's work schedule made him question again the value of his being so far from home. For all his misgivings, he was to conclude that it was prescient to hold on to his present position as Schapiro's man in Leningrad at least until the expiration of his contract in April 1940. Given his "stateless" circumstances, there was really no other choice.

Mope was able to use free time to visit grand palaces and stately homes in the vicinity of Leningrad, and his reports give us vivid pictures. Many of Vera's letters to him express her care for his health–he was troubled with a tenacious bronchial cough–and campaign to reduce his consumption of cigarettes. At home, both she and her parents grappled with health issues. After her miscarriage in the spring, she was fulfilling a promise to disclose to Mope rather than "whitewash" any unanticipated disorders or ailments that might arise.

Just before Mope's departure from England, his sister, Grete Moschytz, arrived from Switzerland, with her four children, bringing them to Buxton in Derbyshire. To the consternation of the whole family, her husband Norbert concluded that it was not in his best interest to join them. He was to remain in Davos, Switzerland, for the duration of the war in company with his widowed mother who escaped from Germany days before the start of hostilities. Grete and her three younger children were to rejoin him there in 1948. In 1954, despite the unspeakable tragedy wrought by the Hitler years, Norbert was to return to his "native" Germany, setting up a medical practice in Stuttgart. There was no love lost between Mope and Norbert.

News from Germany left the family on tenterhooks. The welcome news from Mope's sister and brother-in-law in Hamburg, Ketty and David Goldschmidt, was that permission was being granted for her to come to England. And once he had sorted various tax demands, David would be allowed to follow. She was *left with the dilemma of whether to join her children in England immediately or to stay the course with her husband until his papers were in order. Suffering from ill health, he was encouraging her to remain with him. The efforts of Georg Rosenfeld to aid his parents (Mope's cousins), Carl and Lies, to emigrate to Palestine were encumbered by a British White Paper, curbing the number of Jews authorized to settle there. Among those who did receive permission to leave Germany for England were Oma Lenchen's two elderly aunts from Berlin, Helene Simon and Klara Reichmann. Mope's heroic brother-in-law, Fred Rau, was instrumental in bringing this about.*

By August, Mope sensed correctly that war was imminent, and began to apply for the necessary visas to return to England via Finland and Sweden, the same "safe" route he had used on the journey out the previous May. Unfortunately, the Finnish and Swedish Consulates in Moscow showed little readiness to re-issue transit visas to a person carrying "stateless" papers. In addition, far from coming to his help, his heartless boss, Schapiro, tried every trick in the book to persuade him to remain in Leningrad. On 25 August, Mope was granted permission to leave Leningrad for Moscow. Two days before that, the widely publicized Soviet-German non-aggression pact had been signed by Molotov and Ribbentrop in Moscow, removing the last hurdle to a Nazi assault on Poland. On the very day of his departure from Leningrad, the Anglo-Polish Alliance, by which Britain undertook to come to Poland's aid should Hitler invade that country, was ratified. In Moscow, despite personal pleas, the Finnish and Swedish Consulates continued to refuse Mope the required transit visas to travel home. Vera's rising fears for her husband are evident in her letters.

MOPE TO VERA

At sea, on board SS Suecia, 17 May 1939

It is shortly after 9 o'clock and two hours have passed already since I was able to wave to my most beloved, sweetest girl for the last time.–My little girl cried some little tears and they burned on my skin, because our good-bye was more difficult than ever before; and we have had to part from each other so many times before! Unfortunately and happily, one just cannot get used to bidding each other farewell; unfortunately because I would so like to alleviate my cute little witch's pain, and happily because the pain is an expression of your great love for me for which I am *unspeakably* grateful to you, and I return it with the fullest heart and *with all my being* in such a way that the knowledge of it should lessen your pain. We are connected by such a wonderful friendship and harmony that spatial distance permits just as close a togetherness as if we were actually together. However, we do miss and long for the mutual caresses that represent the sugar crust on the torte on which both of us are snacking.

I know there is much more than that missing during the long and difficult periods of separation. Just the awareness that one is able to see the other in just a few hours and exchange the experiences of the day makes for such a happy feeling that helps overcome all the obstacles standing in the way. For this, the two of us have created a real replacement by writing daily letters to each other, because, by writing down our thoughts, we experience an exchange of ideas which aids us in finding a way out of labyrinths. The complete concentration of one on the other lets us observe everything much more clearly and deeply than we would be able to do without the joyous awareness of each other. It is something so great that we have each other; and we feel how empty our existence would be without this community. I think that the mutually bitter and deeply felt longing is not only painful, but also beautifies life, because we feel how fulfilled it is through our love.

Now, I am comfortable in my cabin. There is a porthole with a view of the ocean, which also allows me to get some fresh air, as long as the ocean is quiet. I will go to sleep now in order to be able to go on deck early, if the sun is shining, and so get something positive out of the trip.

I am completely with you, awake and asleep, because I love you *deeply* and most passionately. Good night, my sweetest one! Your Mope

VERA TO MOPE

London, 17 May 1939

It is 10.15 p.m. and I just got home. I really hope that they gave you a nice and comfortable cabin, that you had a good dinner, and that you will sleep deeply and well. My lovielein, I still cannot get used to the fact that you will be away from me again for months on end and that the two of us will have to make do with letter lines. Of course, I know and keep telling myself again and again that we have to be grateful that we, as emigrants, are making a good step forward, or better, an extraordinarily good step, on the way to building a new existence. I hope with all my strength that we will be able to eliminate these miserable periods of separation in the foreseeable future; and until then, we just have to take it and try to make the best of it. And I think that the two of us do a very good job of that!

My Mopeleinchen, do you know that the separation is becoming more difficult for me every time and the pain is greater, but I really did not want to tell you that at all! At most, I wanted to tell you just to show you how much I love you!!! I am completely happy because you married me!!! *Your* Little Witch

P.S. *Please don't forget: sweets are very often much better than cigarettes!!!!!!*

MOPE TO VERA

At sea, on board SS Suecia, 18 May 1939

Right now, almost thirty hours have gone by since I saw your handkerchief waving brightly in the wind even when I could no longer see anything of my most beloved. Today was a long and lazy day that I spent reading and sleeping, and hardly exchanged so much as one word with anyone. I read the little book *"The ordinary man's answer to Hitler"* by Evan John, which your dear mother gave me yesterday to read during the trip.[178] Besides a comparison of Hitler with Frederick the Great (no women, outrage against poverty, an inclination towards art, a feminine inclination that was forcefully suppressed, a guarantee to Silesia against attacks and the immediately following occupation by him) whose military abilities he seems to be lacking, fortunately, it did not give me anything new. However, it is to be welcomed that such books–cheap enough that everyone can buy them–are being published, because the average Englishman has absolutely no idea what danger threatens his country and himself from these criminals if they are given a free hand much longer.

The sea has been agitated all day and the dining room that was not fully occupied during lunch showed great empty gaps this evening. The food tasted very good with just my own company and I did not feel the slightest desire to seek others. Early tomorrow around 7 o'clock, we will arrive in Göthenborg. While I am writing, I am sitting in the very pretty lounge, which is furnished in early 19th century style, all by

---

178 Evan John, *Answer to Hitler; Reflections on Hitler's "Mein Kampf" and on Some Recent Events upon the Continent of Europe* (London: Nicholson & Watson, 1939).

myself, because the few passengers who are not yet in the horizontal are sitting in the smoking salon. I lay on my bed for two hours this afternoon and slept deeply (sitting in the deckchairs was too cold, despite warm blankets), so I am not all that tired right now, not like I felt yesterday when I was writing.

I will probably post this letter as well as yesterday's in Stockholm, since there is a plane connection from there, which I doubt exists in Göthenborg. Now, I will go to sleep and go to my sweetest one in my dreams in order to snuggle very close to you and satisfy you with my caresses. Your Mope

VERA TO MOPE

London, 21 May 1939

I did not write to you yesterday evening. *I was terribly worried* because I still had not received any communication from Leningrad. There was nothing this morning either and just now, at 8.00 a.m., your cable was read over the telephone and I feel more than relieved!!! I cannot understand the delay at all, because in the past the air transport used to work quite regularly during the summer months.

I am happy to know that you arrived there in good health and I hope that you are well and that you are not coughing so much!? I wonder if you could ever decide to do something–which is actually quite contrary to your nature–like writing down at the end of the day how many cigarettes you smoked. I can imagine that that would give you a greater self-control and you would then be able to work on decreasing the number slowly, almost like a sport. Something like that would present a kind of self-satisfaction to me, but I know that my beloved is a little different where things like that are concerned; and looking at the matter from your point of view, I can only say that you would do something really great for me if you tried.

I had called Georg Rosenfeld and invited him to join us for lunch. I promised to meet him at Chiswick Park Station around 11.45 so that we could go on a walk through the beautiful park around Chiswick House. He turned out to be extremely nice and pleasant. I wrote a few lines to his parents in Karlsruhe in your name as well as mine and told them how dear their offspring is.

Now to reporting some very *good* news: Ketty and her husband have received their visa to come here!! And now, your dear mother is trying to find someone who will help them to pay the back taxes there, and then, hopefully, they will come and most likely–which I consider a *very* good idea–stay with your dear mother, and I am sure that she will have quite a bit of help in her household that way. Gertrud spends so much of her time lying in bed and I am sure creates a lot of extra work for Oma Lenchen. She and Gertrud have been invited to Buxton where they intend to spend a week with Grete.[179] Most affectionate and sweetest kisses, *Your* Little Witch

MOPE TO VERA

Leningrad, 22 May 1939

The train trip from Helsingfors to here was very pleasant, because a new train car which is very comfortable has been put into service now. The horrible rainy weather in Helsingfors gave way to the most beautiful sunshine; nevertheless it is still quite cool in the shade and I am happy that I am not wearing my summer underwear yet. Since it was almost 3.30 by the time I moved into my room, I did not work yesterday, but joined my colleagues instead–they wanted to drive to a culture park that is situated rather beautifully on the Bay of Finland. We spent about an hour on a river steamboat going down the Neva, and after we arrived, we went for a walk in the park. By the time we got back to the hotel, it was after 11 o'clock and we were hungry again, so that I did not get back to my room until 1 p.m. and then started to unpack. Before that, a colleague had helped me unpack the radio and we made the pleasant discovery that it works very well and it is playing music the whole time while I am writing. If I understood correctly, the music is coming from Buenos-Aires, however, that seems a little improbable to me because of the distance. A sad piece of news to me was the fact that I can no longer do anything with the money I brought with me–they no longer

---

179 Fourteen-year-old Gertrud Goldschmidt, who had arrived in England under the *Kindertransport* scheme, was living with her grandmother. Traumatized by being away from her parents and fearing for their safety, her behavior was wild and unruly. In the spring, her aunt, Grete Moschytz with her four children, had left Davos, Switzerland, for England, where they were temporarily housed in Buxton, Derbyshire.

exchange Reichmarks at all. I can get by for the time being, but I do not know what will happen then.[180] It is a good thing that I left some money here so I can use that until more is sent to me. Where business is concerned, I was unable to come to any result today. Schapiro will be beside himself when he does not find a telegram telling him about great business deals, but what can I do about that? Yesterday, I felt quite depressed because of that.

But now, I have to go and climb into my chaste bed. It is terribly late and I am quite tired. I will come to you in my dream in just a little while, my Lilongolein! By the way, you lose all feeling for time here, because it is still very light at 11 o'clock so that you could read the newspaper on the street. Most affectionately and completely, Your Mope

VERA TO MOPE

London, 29 May 1939

I finally wrote a detailed letter to Annelieschen and I will also enclose the one that was sent back as undeliverable in the middle of February and just now, I am sending my congratulations to Grete on her settlement in England in a longer letter. As I heard today, your dear mother will stay there with Gertrud for another week, which I think will be very good for her. I am sure that the peace and quiet and the good air will do her a lot of good. I am not sure if I told you yesterday that Grete gave a letter to you to Hanna to pass along to me and she misplaced it. I mentioned that in my letter to Grete and asked her how pleased you would be about receiving mail, especially from her.

I am waiting most longingly for news from you and I am very curious to hear how business is going and if you really have so many orders in front of you that the early departure is justified. I hope that you are now receiving my mail regularly–I have written to you *every* day!

I talked to Hanna on the telephone yesterday. She with Fred will travel to the countryside to inspect a youth training country home in

---

180 It seems that Mope still held a quantity of Reichsmarks. Until May 1939, the Soviet Union had been pursuing an anti-fascist policy, and the refusal to exchange German Reichsmarks may have been part of this.

which boys are trained for Palestine.[181] And on Tuesday, she will visit the two little Goldschmidt boys.[182]

I want to close because I need to go to sleep now–I am already in the horizontal.

Most passionately, *Your* Little Witch

Mopeleinchen, I am worried about your chest cough–do you have enough throat lozenges there? I wonder if you are still thinking about cigarettes.

MOPE TO VERA

Leningrad, 29 May 1939

Today, I was without a message from my sweet darling once again and I cannot tell you often enough just how difficult the walk to my room is without your letters after they have told me in the lobby that no greeting from you arrived. Just now–it is almost midnight–I asked them again in vain and now, I have to give up hope for today. Tomorrow is Wychodnoi once again and the colleagues are downstairs and want me to come down to the restaurant as well. Last time, I did not go, but this time, I will have to go, although I really do not feel like it. In preparation for that, I slept for an hour earlier today. My little witch will have to work again tomorrow and I am so curious to hear how you spent the days off–hopefully very, very nicely.[183] I did not do anything today either–besides waiting, and outside, it rained all day long.

Here, it is almost daylight, because the nights are extremely short during this season. At the same time, there is music being broadcast from the BBC and I am surprised that they are still working at such a late hour, while I am usually able to get broadcasts from the fascist or Nazi criminal gang early in the morning, but I am not willing to

---

181 In 1939, Bnai Akiva, the Orthodox Zionist youth group, began running training centers in England for young Jews who were planning to settle in Palestine.
182 Since reaching England the previous month, Gabriel (aged 11) and Alfred (aged 8) Goldschmidt had been enrolled as boarders, along with several other *Kindertransport* children, at Macaulay House School in Cuckfield, Sussex. It was one of several schools that helped to accommodate the influx of German-Jewish children during 1939.
183 Vera had recently left Marks & Spencer after accepting an offer to head the personnel department at the Odeon organization, an expanding British cinema chain. For reasons of space, I have omitted from this book details of her experience at her new job.

listen to that at all. It really is high time that the democratic countries acquire stronger transmitters as well and broadcast more of their own propaganda.

I am more than happy about the issue of the permits for Ketty and David and I hope that they, as the last ones from our family, will be able to leave that wicked, damned country as quickly as possible and will adjust to life in London. I think it is very reasonable for them to move in with my dear mother, because I hope that it will mean a relief for her. It will also be good for Miss Gertrud, because, contrary to the all too loving grandmother, Ketty will not let her get away with anything. Someone should make Gertrud understand how unbelievable this matter is, since she does not seem to have grasped it on her own, unfortunately.

What can I tell my beloved about my former and already forgotten cough? If I tell the truth, that it is gone, you do not believe me, and if I say that I am still coughing, I am lying, so what should I report??? My breathing is quiet and my nostrils are unbothered, a fact I have just ascertained in the mirror! I smoke less and, following your orders, have some candy instead, although a cigarette would taste good with it, but I try to control myself. Today, I only smoked fifteen cigarettes and will only have one more.

Now, I want to go to bed. My most beloved, I take you into my arms most longingly and kiss you long and most passionately everywhere to give you joy and to make you recall the real caresses through these written ones. Completely and utterly, *Your* Mope

VERA TO MOPE

London, 1 June 1939

I would like to tell you again how happy I am if your cough was really measured by my standard (that is, especially in the morning and also at night) and is really better??!!!!!! I am so very happy about it if this is actually the case. You have, as I believe, a very bad wife who torments and badgers you and doubts your dear reports, but I actually believe seven-eighth of it!!! Especially since my beloved writes–something rather unexpected and therefore all the more pleasing–that he controls his daily consumption of cigarettes!

I learned of some very sad news from Annelie in New York: her sister, Gerda's youngest–he was three years old–died very suddenly of an infected appendix that was recognized too late; and on the day of the funeral, her elder child, Helga, became ill with appendicitis and had to undergo surgery immediately. It is a terrible beginning in a new country. On top of that, in Leipzig, Dr. Freimann has been in the hospital for the last few weeks. Annelie wrote and asked for Ray Braham's address; she wants to use her as a guarantor (as a nominal one since the brother-in-law who is an American put up the bond) and the guarantor has to be British. In my letter last Monday, I asked Annelie if I could do anything in the matter and I will write to her again now. I really do feel sorry for her. I know how attached she was to the little one. I do not know if the senior Freimanns in Leipzig have been informed of the terrible event and because of that, I will not send them my condolences.[184]

It is late and I will close. *I love you, my sweetheart* and I miss you terribly, more than ever!!! Completely and utterly, *Your* Little Witch

So, in your last letter, you write to me about 16 cigarettes. How many is it now? Maybe fourteen and a quarter???! But you do *not* have to write to me about that!!!

MOPE TO VERA

Leningrad, 3 June 1939

I had a lazy day today, because I could not go to the warehouse before 2 o'clock, for which, since a few days ago, we are required to obtain special permission. Tomorrow, I have an appointment at 10 o'clock and with a different department at 2 o'clock, so that I will be rather busy. This new method seems better to me, because until now, we had to sit around and wait until our turn came up without being able to do anything profitable. Most of my colleagues played billiards and I also tried this art several times, but I am glad that I do not have to kill time with that any longer, because I prefer reading a book, but I could not do so in the warehouse without being disturbed.

---

184 Gerda was Annelie's half-sister. Dr. Joseph Freimann and his wife, Rosalie (d. 1951) did eventually succeed in escaping from Germany, but only after the start of the war. They were among the approximately one thousand Jewish refugees crammed aboard the S.S. Navemar, a barely seaworthy Spanish freighter equipped to carry twenty-eight passengers, which reached New York from Seville in September 1941. Sadly, Dr. Freimann died not long after their arrival.

I think I have finally become used to the fact that this profession provides a lot of work at times so that I do not know where to steal another half hour in order to get it all done, and at other times, there is no work at all. I do believe that my average daily work hours are around eight, because there is a lot of written work that needs to be taken care when I get back to the hotel around 5 or 6 o'clock. Until now, I made the mistake of not going out into the fresh air at all, with the exception of the first day here, but I have decided to change that, because a daily walk would certainly be very good for me. I was replacing that walk with a plate of plum compote which I usually devoured before breakfast. But enough now about my conduct which is so far removed from the rest of the world, because the constant babbling of my colleagues is beginning to bore me and I feel most comfortable in my own company so that I am taking my meals in my room as well.

It has become much cooler here and I am content that I did not let the warmer days seduce me into changing my underwear–I mean from winter to summer underwear. It is also raining quite a lot, but my non-coughing condition seems to persist–knock on wood. If I had my golden girl here with me, I would feel completely happy, but this is no life without you. This year, Rosh Hashanah is on September 14 and I would be *very* saddened to not be with you at that time, as I have been every year up to now.

I would like to give you the most passionate, gentlest kisses, but also rousing ones, and I want to do all those things that give you joy and desire, and with that, give them to me as well. Completely, *Your* Mope

VERA TO MOPE

London, 6 June 1939

Yesterday evening, I went to Oma Lenchen's for dinner. She told me about Grete. Apparently, Norbert will come to Buxton in just a few short weeks. Oma Lenchen claimed that she had had a very relaxing time there. I found her looking well. She was as charming and dear as ever and I like her more every time I see her. I was *very, very* happy to have Oma Lenchen all to myself. She told me again that she had been so very pleased with my lines and Grete had commented very positively on the manner in which they were composed. Actually, I simply wrote what I was and am feeling for her.

MOPE TO VERA

Leningrad, 6 June 1939

When I woke up around 10 o'clock this morning, the sky was so gray that I thought the planned excursion to Pavlovsk (that is the summer palace of Paul I., the father of Alexander I. who fought against Napoleon) would be softened by rain, before we could even get on our way. Instead, it brightened up and we left around noon. The drive leads through Pushkin, the former Zarkoje Selo where the last czar lived and where I was last in March of this year. Back then, we waded through deep snow and this time, spring showed itself with the prettiest tones of fresh green in the trees and the bushes and a blue sky, decorated with heavy gray and white clouds. Right now, it is a short time before the blooming of the lilacs here whose deep blue buds are shining from many bushes. First of all, we drove through the area that houses the Sojuzpushnina house that connects to the newly projected center of Leningrad which lies even further outside of the city proper. It is just unimaginable what huge housing complexes are being built there–there was no trace of them back in March, but the new city promises to be very beautiful and will group around the huge Soviet House that has progressed tremendously since March and seems to be very monumental. The palace in Pavlovsk is built very generously and contains a few wonderful tapestries from the late eighteenth century. The park that belongs to the palace is absolutely wonderful, and if you consider that this parcel of land which would have been so beneficial to the health of the people was closed to humanity for the last one hundred years and was not opened until after the revolution, one can only be glad that the monstrous former methods were thrown by the wayside.

In the park, there is a building called the "Pavilion of Roses", and connected to that is a great hall. The others went rowing, but I preferred to pay a visit to the children's theater taking place in that hall. There were hundreds of children, some of whom were sitting, some standing, because there were not as many seats as there were visitors. The ages of the children was anywhere between two and around fifteen and one could see ten-year-olds watching while holding their younger siblings. One could have heard a needle fall–without the voices of the actors–that is how quiet the guests of the performance were and such suspense suffused the little faces that it was a pleasure to watch them. And what was shown??? Children performed the fairy tale "Little Muck" by Hauff–as far as I know.[185] The stage was completely primitive and aside from a bench and a carpet in front of it, there was no background. The costumes were rather pretty and were complemented by grotesque masks. It was difficult for me to separate myself from the view of the audience and actors, after the car had been driven up to pick us up– that's how charming the whole thing was. I am writing this to you in such detail, since I was shown, quite unprepared, the confirmation of the impact of fairy tales on children. One can see that children can be captivated by the most primitive means and actors from their own ranks at the age of around twelve. How much more can one offer in a film???

What made me very sad was what you wrote to me about Annelie's little nephew. That really is a bad beginning in a new country and I hope they will be spared any further worries which affect their lives and well-being so deeply. I hardly think that I will write to Annelie from here, but I suppose that my girl will write in my name as well. Actually, the fact that her father is in the hospital does not say that he has to be ill. I have heard repeatedly that people, I mean Jews who felt they were in danger, went to hospitals which until then had protected people from unnecessary direct interventions. The two Bambergers are like that and they are waiting longingly for permission to be allowed to immigrate to a foreign country.[186]

Now, I want to climb into my chaste bed, but not before I tell my darling about my unspeakably great love which has made me a happier person because of and through you. Despite the horrible separation which goes so *entre coeur*, I constantly feel so very close to you and I am always connected to you ever so intimately in my thoughts that nothing but space could come between us. Most passionately, completely and utterly–*Your* Mope

---

185 The children's play of "Little Muck" was based on a fairy tale by the German writer, Wilhelm Hauff (1802-1827), in which a dwarf obtains magical powers that lead to many adventures.

186 Gustav Bamberger (born Worms, 1880) was one of Mope's Leipzig friends. He and his brother, Ludwig (born 1882), had been co-owners of Bamberger und Hertz, the leading department store in Leipzig specializing in men's clothing. The store was destroyed by fire during Kristallnacht, and the Bamberger brothers were arrested and falsely charged with committing arson in order to collect insurance on the building. Neither brother succeeded in escaping from the clutches of the Nazis. Gustav is believed to have perished in the Stutthof Concentration Camp in Poland in 1942. He was unmarried. His sibling, Ludwig, died in Theresienstadt in 1942.

VERA TO MOPE

London, 7 June 1939

The summer weather is blistering here, just the way the two of us love it, and I wish for nothing more than if you could enjoy it with me–I never feel better, just like you, than I do in temperatures like this. Yesterday evening, when I came home from my writing place in the park, I had a great fright and much excitement: Muttilein was lying on the chaise longue–something that she *never* does normally; ever since Monday, she had been telling me that her calves were hurting a little and yesterday afternoon, they started swelling up all of a sudden and she was hardly able to walk. Whenever something like that happens, Pepper is indescribably impossible and egotistical and moans and blusters and acts like a small child and that makes *everything* much worse; and it actually forces Muttilein to say not a word no matter how bad she happens to feel. After she had lain down for a while and I had rubbed her legs with *pond extract,* it was almost over this morning, fortunately, but nevertheless, I had Dr. Rothschild come over, because swollen legs are often a sign of something serious. I feel more than relieved after I heard that he said it was based on overexertion coupled with the great heat–which Muttilein always has a hard time dealing with, and he prescribed two special elastic leg wraps with which she is supposed to bind her legs.

This evening, I called Oma Lenchen who told me that she has been wearing elastic wraps just about every day for the last 20 years now, because otherwise, both of her legs would swell! I feel a lot calmer now, but yesterday evening, I was completely beside myself and terribly worried. Completely and utterly and most passionately, *Your* Little Witch

MOPE TO VERA

Leningrad, 8 June 1939

Because of yesterday's strong storm, which still has not calmed down today, it became rather cool again here, although it was not all that warm before. Unfortunately, nothing was done for my psychological warming either, that is, I remained without news from my sweet darling so that I am behind by almost a week once again. Where is the postal logic in that?

What do you hear about Ketty and the date of her emigration? Hopefully, this will not drag out for too long, because you never know what the Hitler gangster rabble are up to next. As far as foreign policy is concerned, they seem unable to achieve anything–apart from those few ridiculous non-aggression pacts which are meant to pull the wool over the people's eyes! But it also increases the fear that they will have to do something inside the country in order to divert the people's attention, and who makes a better victim that is completely at their mercy than the Jews, again and again? This is why I am really worried, if the departure is delayed much longer!

I wonder if you have already talked to our Helenchen since her return from Buxton. I would so like to know if Grete has settled in well. It seems that her husband intends to keep nursing his health in Davos. Ladies and Gentlemen, will that man ever be healthy!!!!!

VERA TO MOPE

London, 10 June 1939

I feel that being without you daily is becoming more unbearable all the time; after all, we only live once and it often seems to me that the two of us are cheating ourselves out of the most beautiful years of our togetherness!!! My beloved writes to me that Rosh Hashanah will be on September 14 and he does not have any idea if he will be back here by that date??!!

I am sure you know just how happy I would be if I could come to you. How do you feel about that? I think my "passport" expires on August 1, so I have to have it renewed in time. My love, please write to me and tell me about your thoughts concerning your return home, a vacation, my coming there, etc. *I am waiting for* your *comments, Sir*!!!

I called Mr. Cooper at the Home Office this morning and asked about my naturalization. He replied that that is *completely* out of the question at present, but he was very *nice* and told me that they had not *cancelled the conditions* for you yet, and he would make sure to take care of that with the next application–at the end of the year. I was quite astonished at so much kindness and he said that I should call him again soon and not wait until the end of the year when your papers have to be renewed. I was completely *happy* with this! On top of that, Mr. Cooper told me something else; but it was expressly unofficial: he said that if you apply for naturalization five years from August 1937, under the condition that you spent the last year in England, something might have been done by then, but as I said, this was completely non-committal and no "official notification." For me, he said the only thing that could be done right now would be *"if you want to divorce your husband,"* and I told him that was *completely* out of the question, and he invited me to tell you about my decision concerning the choice between being married to you and British nationality, and he thought that you would probably be pleased with it!!

Hopefully, your cough is behaving and you are feeling well–please write to me about that! *Do you still think of the cigarettes, my lovielein?* I really do hope so!!! Your Little Witch

MOPE TO VERA

Leningrad, 11 June 1939

When I set off for the post office around 11 o'clock [p.m.] today, I discovered, to my complete elation, your letter in my box at the front desk. On the way to the post office and back, which would be between 11 and 11.45, I read my mail on the street which should give you some idea of the daylight during the night here. Of course, no streetlights are turned on which might seem downright odd. Today is Pod Wychodnoi once again and around 1 o'clock, after I listen to the news, I will go to the restaurant. Today, we finally had a warm day again and tomorrow, if the weather holds, I will go on another outing.

In the meantime, I went downstairs and now, I am enjoying the somewhat fresh air by the open window while I continue these lines to my darling. Just so I do not forget, I have to ask my most beloved for a couple of things:

1. My supply of candy, which served me very well, has dwindled. I assume that one can have such things sent here by Lyons through customs, just like the cigarettes. Please only do so if it can be done without too much trouble.

2. Please call Abdulla, or even better, confirm the conversation in writing that they should, like before, send me 1,000 cigarettes as quickly as possible, and keep sending the same number on a monthly basis until the order is revoked. I found out that the transport takes about two weeks which is why the matter needs to be expedited, although I am

adequately supplied at the moment. I know only too well that my little girl will not like fulfilling my request for cigarettes, but I do smoke less than before and give away *a lot* which should be of some comfort to you.

So it seems after all that Norbert is finding his way to Buxton and therefore, he must have received his permit. I wonder what he is going to do to keep busy all that time. I suppose that his own family will not provide him with any means and I am sure that Fred will not give him any money so he can sit around in Davos some more.

Most affectionately and passionately, my golden girl–*Your* Mope

VERA

Journal entry, 11 June 1939

I am fed up with having to spend my life separated from my husband and I do not want to do it anymore!!! This is going to be his last longer stay in the USSR, unless I go with him on his next trip. I am becoming rather single-minded–I spend all my time writing letters (I am sooo tired and will continue writing this another day).

MOPE TO VERA

Leningrad, 13 June 1939

Today, I received my darling's letter from the 7th. I really regret hearing about your mother's being unwell due to swollen legs and I hope that she is back to complete health now. I am sure that the cool down will be pleasant to her and so, all disadvantages always have certain advantages. I know that Helenchen has had bandaged legs for many years, because she and some of the sisters have a tendency to develop varicose veins. My little witch, why are you surprised that Pepper is beside himself when there is something wrong with Muttilein? You find it egotistical, but *just like him*, I am completely beside myself, too, when there is something wrong with you, and I hope that you find that completely understandable when it concerns me! Why so little understanding for the good old man? A husband who shows himself indifferent when his wife is suffering should be judged much more harshly than one who demonstrates a little too wildly that he is not indifferent to it.

But now, I have to close once again! The sun seems to almost stop in its tracks here, just as it did back in the Bible, because some king–no, actually, it was Joshua, I think–wanted to bring a battle to a successful end, but the mean clock keeps on going and that is the decisive factor for the division between day and night.[187]

Sleep sweetly, my love, and feel the constant nearness of your Mope who loves you sooo completely!!!

VERA TO MOPE

London, 13 June 1939

I hope that these lines will come into your possession on the 19th;[188] they are meant to bring you all the love and good things in the world I can think of. I will try to describe to you just exactly *what* they are supposed to wish for you. First of all, *health*, probably the most important condition for *everything* positive in life; next, *inner peace and happiness*, the preconditions for being able to get real enjoyment out of life; furthermore, the preservation of your fortunate ability to "land on your feet" in order to meet the outside *"ups and downs"* of fate head on and well prepared. And *last not least, happiness*, my love, and in such an abundant measure as I can imagine. Those are my wishes for you.

How indescribably happy I would be if I could be with you on your birthday, my *sweetheart*, and most especially on this one which will lead you into a new decade of your life. I think that the forties are the most perfect years for a man: he is in full possession of his bodily strength, he has the experience of a grown-up of decades and the strength that comes with it, the inner equilibrium, and has found *the* outward attitude towards life that makes it possible for him to enjoy it to its very depths. And if he then also has the advantage of looking like a man in his thirties, which most certainly is the case with you, there cannot be any doubt whatsoever that the forties has to be a more than positive decade.

As far as the coughing and the smoking are concerned, there are actually no demands for you to report to me, as I already told you repeatedly, and your conscience–if there was a reason–would be what makes you feel concerned. It is no secret that I wish nothing more than

---

187 See Joshua, 10.12-14.
188 Vera writes in anticipation of Mope's fortieth birthday on 19 June 1939.

for my love to reduce the number of cigarettes—*but I leave—it entirely to you—and I trust you.*

A little while ago, I had a long telephone conversation with your dear mother. Among other things, Oma Lenchen told me that Fred went to see Ketty during his last business trip and also the old aunts in Berlin who also have their permit for here now.[189] He found Ketty in good condition, and as soon as everything is settled–which could take from a few days to a few weeks or months–Ketty and husband will come here, as Oma Lenchen told me.

Norbert is supposed to come here too, or rather to Buxton, shortly. Mutti called Oma Lenchen yesterday and asked if Grete needed bed things, like pillows for instance and feather beds and your dear mother seemed to be very happy about that and will ask Grete right away, and as soon as we hear from her, we will send her everything she would like to have. Apparently, she feels cold a lot and the feather beds will be more than welcome, and I am glad if we can do something for her. I will enclose a toy monkey for each one of her kids. On top of that, I found a black, rather worn looking dog that used to sit in the sun on the window sill by my desk and was supposed to keep me company while I was preparing for my prelims–it was given to me by Heising and is too worn to send it to Grete and the kids, while I am sure that the different monkeys will give them a lot of pleasure. Just *a few* years ago, I would have *never* given them away under any circumstances!

My love, I am so unbelievably happy and it really gives me energy when you write to me that my little bit of work is helpful in our building of a new existence and that you regard that as competent. I consider myself so absolutely *average* and sometimes even less, and when you write to me in such an appreciative manner, I feel a renewed energy to work and a greater trust in myself, although "competent" seems to spring from a non-objective and skewed attitude towards me. I was lucky enough to have had good training, and under those conditions, everyone else could probably achieve the same or even more. That is my opinion in the matter!

My little birthday child, I kiss you with all the intensity at my disposal and for such a long time and so filled with tenderness that you

---

[189] Oma Lenchen's aunts, Dr. Helene Simon (1862-1947), the well-known sociologist, and her sister, Klara Simon Reichmann (1867-1952), were still living in Berlin.

will feel it all the way over there, in Leningrad, you, my beloved. *Your Little Witch*

P.S. Muttilein's legs which she now bandages regularly have fortunately been much better since then.

MOPE TO VERA

Leningrad, 17 June 1939

I am feeling *terribly* good today! As a matter of fact, I received my little witch's letter from 10 June which I had been waiting for with much longing, like all of your beloved letters. Apart from that, they also brought me Mr. Cooper's birthday present and I am completely enthused by his message. It is the one thing I had been hoping for in my wildest dreams, but I did not believe that it would ever come true. You cannot imagine how happy you made me with that, because I belong to those people who feel infinitely better when they know that they have a home. And his prediction concerning further facilitations for the year 1942 also rings beautifully in my ears.

Do I have to be jealous of Mr. Cooper, since he was so nice to you and asked you to call him again soon? Fortunately, you said no to his question if you would get a divorce so you could become naturalized, which I think is *very* sweet of you, because you have to give up something very pleasing to you. However, I would not have let you run away anyway, because I love you way, way, way too much, and I am a great egotist who is only too happy to be able to add to the many hours we want to spend united in the most passionate love!

Completely, and utterly only your Mope

VERA TO MOPE

London, 19 June 1939

Today is my beloved's birthday and my thoughts are *constantly* with you; I called Oma Lenchen a little while ago and congratulated her on the birth of her son. Oma Lenchen told me how well she remembers the day forty years ago and how the doctor had asked her in surprise how she came by such a *light blonde baby*!!!?!!! By the way, I have always thought that my lovielein is a cuckoo's egg anyway and has nothing in common with the Felsensteins (at least those I know).

Many especially extra-sweet birthday kisses, my *sweetheart*!!! I feel such an *indescribable* longing for you–more, *much* more than I could possibly describe.

Your Little Witch
Don't forget that cigarettes are very bad for you and your throat, you!!!

MOPE TO VERA

Leningrad, 19 June 1939

My sweet little witch was very artful and managed to send off her so beloved letter with the many good wishes for the beginning of my fourth decade in such a way that it reached me at the right time and really put me in an elevated mood, the kind of mood children are usually in on their birthdays. As far as I can judge up to now–it's been an hour–forty is a very agreeable age! I do feel much too young to take this number any more seriously than the one that informed me ten years ago of turning thirty, at least according to my papers. Today, I had begun by imagining that I am not really even thirty yet, but only twenty, because the development that the body goes through until the age of twenty is comparable to the intellectual-spiritual development from the twentieth to the fortieth year. You write something very similar about two decades of being an adult which made me especially happy in connection with that, just like your declaration that I look like a man in his thirties, which I hope was not only made to make me feel good. Two years ago today, I came to this country for the first time and I look back, with a certain satisfaction, on this time that let me become used to a completely different milieu and it has not been without success. In this, my little girl helped me in a way that can never be sufficiently appreciated with her love which makes me happy and her trust which makes me proud.

Your philosophy concerning my right to the great satisfaction and joy in your great and energetic collaboration in our build up lacks any basis. You personally participate in our work in a manner far above average and with your love and friendship and even just your being, you give me such initiative that I will be forever grateful to you for everything. You say that you were lucky, but good luck wants to be earned, unless it just happens to be in the lottery, and with you, it is effort and your effort gives me an incentive just so I do not fall behind.

* * *

And now, I have to tell you that your lazy *husband* took a lazy Monday today. My various offers were insufficient or remained unanswered. In the warehouse I would just have had to sit around there for nothing. I agreed to join a few colleagues to visit Peterhof. The weather is as beautiful today as it was yesterday and we left to make the beautiful drive around 1 o'clock in an open car, and–as usual–I had the pleasure of sitting in the seat next to the chauffeur–because of my long legs. At Peterhof, we–that is, only two of us, me among them–went swimming. The castle is situated near the Gulf of Finland and the water was wonderfully warm and I really enjoyed the *swim* as well as the extended sunbathing afterwards. We did not get back to the hotel until around 6 p.m. and brought a tremendous hunger back with us.

When I returned to my room, I found out, much to my disappointment, that the radio which was performing perfectly this morning did not work anymore. The only determination I and a knowledgeable colleague have been able to make so far is that the so-called *"miracle eye,"* a lamp (*valve*) that usually lights green when the radio is working, refuses to function properly. It is unknown if there is another reason and could only be determined by testing the *valves* of which there are ten. I do not know if they can do the testing here. In any case, it would be very, very sweet of you if you could give one of the people traveling here two replacement *"miracle eyes,"* but please wait a day or two because I need to get some more information first.

Later on, at the hotel, I stretched out lazily after I had prepared hot chocolate for myself and dreamed of you so intensely, until I had to go to join colleagues at the Europeysky. There, we sat over three hours under a pale sky that was lit up by fireworks which looked rather strange against the light-colored background (the fireworks took place in the culture park). On top of that, the setting sun spread the most beautiful, constantly varying colors across the entire horizon–what we could see of it–and the splendid buildings of Leningrad gradually changed to silhouettes that looked magnificent against the evening sky. It was an incomparable natural spectacle and I only wished–as always–to sit beside my darling instead of these others who mean so very little to me. Most of us did not drink any alcohol, and I certainly did not. When I just came back to the Astoria, I received my sweet little girl's telegram with all your loving wishes.

My most heartfelt thanks–my birthday began and ended with mail from my little witch! How happy that makes me!!! Your Mope

VERA TO MOPE

London, 20 June 1939

My *lovielein*, I do realize that the two of us have to be patient a little while longer, and *I am sorry* if I was a little unrestrained the week before last. Mr. Cooper's dictum might turn out to be very helpful to us, or rather, the taking effect of what he said. I do understand that we have to be patient, but I really do not like it at all! I hope with all my heart that it will not have to be for several more "years."

Yesterday evening, I received a long letter from Annelie; she writes very sweetly and asks me to get in contact with her parents' lawyer here so that the matter of their emigration will go forward a little more quickly. Coincidentally, I had talked to the lawyer in the evening, before I received her letter, and asked him to contact Lady Rochdale[190]–without referring to anyone specific–since I found out from the lawyer that the children in the U.S.A. will guarantee for their parents, but that some nominal person has to post a guarantee here–maybe the lawyer can get a little ahead with Lady Rochdale's help (among other things, he contacted Ray at Annelie's request, but she herself was not able to do anything in the matter). Annelie has opened a polyphoto shop; she reported that she had learned to handle the cameras before they left Germany, and I find that very capable, especially since she writes that it was doing rather well. She remains silent concerning her husband's occupation, but aside from that, she writes nothing but positive things about him. The loss of the baby and the illness of the older child must have been a terrible blow for the whole family which is more than understandable. Annelie is a really brave person.

---

190 Lady Beatrice Rochdale (1871-1966), the wife of the Liberal politician, George Kemp, first Baron Rochdale, seems to have been recommended as a guarantor by Ray Braham, of whom she appears to have been a friend. Earlier in life, she had been active as a suffragette, marching nearly three hundred miles from her home in Keswick to London in 1913 in support of women's right to the vote.

Yesterday evening, Abdullah's confirmed the cigarette order and right now, I have to make a bit of a confession to you: instead of every *four* weeks, I asked them to send another shipment every *five* weeks. Is that right with you or should I, or better, do I have to change it to every *four* weeks??? I am so very happy to hear that your cough has "retired;" I really hope that the retirement will last without limitation!!!! And maybe a partial retirement for the smoking as well?!!

What do you think of the momentary situation in Europe? I am afraid but that is not very helpful and I am trying not to think about it.[191]

The sweetest, most loving kisses here and there and everywhere, you–*Your* Little Witch

MOPE TO VERA

Leningrad, 21 June 1939

I just got back to the hotel from a walk along the Neva and I am–although this path is the same one I always use–completely thrilled with its beauty. I can stand there on the bank for a long time and look across the river with the Peter and Paul fortress–Peter the Great had it built as the first beginning of Petersburg and it also houses–besides the burial chapel of the czars–the terrible prison of the time of the czars, and even the bare mention of its name instilled fear in all who heard it. It was mainly a political prison and many idealists had to leave their lives there. Even the famous Duke Kropotkin whose work "Mutual Aid in the Animal World" you might have read once starved there.[192] Before that, you pass the Winter Palace of the czars which was built in a mix of baroque and renaissance styles and many other palaces, always along the water, and the evening sun plunges everything into pink and sky blue.

Today, a colleague tried out my "miracle eye" with his radio and behold–it glowed. So the fault must be somewhere else. I would

---

191 Vera is probably alluding to the situation in general but may have had in mind an incident three days earlier, on 17 June, when a small bomb had been detonated inside a Jewish café, the Riva Restaurant, in Prague, injuring thirty-nine people. The news also contained disturbing reports of German troop movements on the border between Nazi-occupied Slovakia and Poland.

192 Peter Kropotkin (1842-1921), the so-called "anarchist prince," was the author of *Mutual Aid: A Factor of Evolution* (1902), which proposed alternatives to Social Darwinism. Because of his revolutionary activities, he was imprisoned in the Peter and Paul fortress in 1874, but escaped from there to Switzerland in 1876.

like you to write a letter to Selfridge's radio department concerning warrantee #3902399 and tell them that my radio "Ferguson 503 receiver" functioned perfectly for a full month until the 19th and that I was able to receive London and all other stations very well and that people admired the apparatus in general, but all of a sudden, it refused to work when I attempted to turn it on, that is, there was no sound whatsoever coming from its throat. Should it not be possible to repair it here, I want to at least be able to make use of the warrantee when I come back. Please excuse my causing effort for you once again. I really do hate doing that!!!

How awful that we still do not have any idea how long it will take with Ketty's emigration, because, apart from everything else, every single day that postpones the re-establishment of a new existence represents a great loss of strength.

This letter is supposed to get into the mail today so that my girl will not have to wait in vain for news from me. You, most beloved, most longed for one, Your Mope

MOPE TO VERA

Leningrad, 23 June 1939

I am sitting at my desk and beginning to write to you and while I am doing that, I am listening to an interlude from the opera "Tiefland" by Eugen D'Albert—on the radio.[193] Yes, ever since this evening, the damage is repaired, after Intourist sent a radio mechanic at my request, and he looked around for a little while and then determined that something had come loose between the speaker and other parts –at least from what I was able to understand. Something like that should not happen, of course, but the main thing is that I can listen again and no longer have just a mute witness of earlier and ear pleasing noises standing in front of me. The fun actually cost forty Rubels–that is approximately thirty-two shillings–and so, even Mr. Schapiro had to contribute something in the matter, after he refused to compensate me for the purchase earlier.

---

193 Eugen d'Albert (1864-1932) was a German composer, born in Scotland. He studied under Franz Lizst in Weimar. *Das Tiefland* (*"The Lowlands"*), first performed in 1903, is his most popular opera. During the Second World War, it was adapted for film by Leni Riefensthal, using slave labor (mainly gypsies) for extras. Post-production, many of these extras were deported to Auschwitz. The film was only released in 1954.

Today, it is Pod Wychodnoi once again and we went to the restaurant after the technician left around noon today. So this time, it was not work that made me write so late, but the repair to the radio.

Today, I was able to take something on contract again, but things are very slow, although I am really trying very hard. On top of that, I received my passport today with a visa extension until Sept. 20, but if my little sweetheart cannot make up her mind to come here, I do not feel like staying here that long. If you apply for a visa for here, you have to tell them that there is one here, but that it has probably expired in the meantime. It is possible that it will only have to be extended. On top of that–but that is really self-evident–you will have to inform me immediately on *what day* you turned in your application. You will remember from the last time that the visa is valid for three months, as long as it has not been entered in the passport. From the day it is entered, you have fourteen days to arrive here at the latest. Please apply for a one-month visa, because you might encounter problems with leaving if the visa was too short, that is, you might need an exit visa. You need a so-called consulate visa and will have to make the application in person at the consulate, where you will have to fill out three forms, and they will need three passport photos.

And now, it is terribly late once again, but I can sleep in in the morning so it's not all that bad. I kiss you most tenderly and longingly on all of your sweet half orbs and on everything that lies between them and above and below them and I caress you in my thoughts until our blood begins to boil and we can go to sleep sweetly and most satisfied. *Completely, Your* Mope

VERA TO MOPE

London, 26 June 1939

It is very late and I am writing to you from the horizontal position. This morning, the mail brought me *two* most beloved letters. The moon is clearly visible in the sky in its ¾ full glory and the air that is streaming in through the window is so clean and refreshing that one would like to actually drink it in with the deepest breaths. I am wondering if you are also looking at the moon right now and tell it something for me, just as I am doing for you.

I especially liked the description of your walk along the Neva, because I think that I could picture everything quite vividly thanks to your good description. I wonder if it will come to the two of us enjoying that moment together in the foreseeable future.

Yesterday, Oma Lenchen came by with Gertrud and she was ever so charming. I have to repeat again and again what an especially intelligent, *progressive*, and charming human being Oma Lenchen is!!! She spoiled us–something she should not have done because it cannot be easy for her–and brought along a very good cake and a box of Lindt chocolates. Gertrud behaved as usual; when Ketty can finally come is not sure yet since they still have to pay the taxes.

I received a very nice letter from Grete and her children this morning in which they express their joy in the feather beds and the monkeys. This week, Grete received the first part of her boxes of furniture. Completely and utterly and totally, *Your* Little Witch

How is your cough??? And the cigarettes! Think of me with each one!

MOPE TO VERA

Leningrad, 29 June 1939

As of yesterday, it has been six weeks, forty-two days, since I bid farewell to my sweetest darling. The time seems infinitely long and short at the same time because I am always with you in my thoughts and not gone from you at all. Even the minutes of our goodbye are so present to me as if they just happened a few days ago, because I let them pass before my mind's eye so many times and try to reconstruct the beloved face of my little witch in all its minute details and tones, just as the camera of the eye recorded it.

This morning, my *wireless* lost its voice again all of a sudden, after it was working just fine last night. I had the man come over and this time, he brought along a voltmeter which he did not have with him last week. He determined that a condenser was causing a short circuit. He took it out completely and now, the good thing is working again and just let me listen to the very interesting report on the speech of Lord Halifax from London this evening.[194] Finally, those boys are starting to show a

---

194 In his speech of 29 June, Lord Halifax, the Foreign Secretary, had iterated that Great Britain stood by a policy of resisting aggression while also endeavoring to

little more decisiveness and no longer take all those criminal ventures of the aggressors in complete silence. I hope that they will be successful in cowing that rabble, if that will even serve a purpose now that these criminals have gone so far that putting the brakes on might lead to their carts being overturned. I am sure that nothing will happen before the auction. That we know from previous experience. First, one pays high prices and then, there is something that shatters the value of the world market in such a way that the customers no longer know how they will receive some of their money back in a sale.

You know, I think a lot about us and about a man living with a woman in general. It really is an astonishing, but probably also good aspect that most women, when they love a man, nestle close to him with their souls as much as they do with their bodies. They also adjust to him intellectually and are irrevocably convinced of his abilities–at least for as long as the love lasts. At the same time, most men experience the desire and the need to make her into his creature. My girl now exhibits a more independent attitude in which the most important thing is to make her own decisions. I am happiest about the fact that you love me so much that you nestle close to me and are completely devoted to me. And because of that, I am trying very hard to foster your individual attributes and to cultivate them and to free you from anything that might inhibit something inside you. I try to advise you, to make your path free of most obstacles, if possible move problems out of the way, but still, I want you to take your own path in complete independence and I can do that because I trust you implicitly. All of these considerations result from the fact that I have seen women stand there all alone and helpless, because all of a sudden, they lost the love of the men who ruled them completely. Just because I hope to be your life partner for an infinite time and I am sure that I do not even have to think about a cooling of our love for each other, I only wish that I will let your own being come to its ultimate realization and uninhibited development, which will let you grow into a strong human being by my side and will let us be two strong human beings who work and build together in the greatest of trusts.

I do not know why I am writing all this to you–it is probably because it has been occupying my mind lately, born of the wish to make your

---

settle differences by negotiation. However, he also spelled out that his country would not stand idly by if the independence of Poland became seriously threatened by German aggression.

life happy and to prevent anything that might affect this happiness. I am certain that two people who harmonize as much in all the most important facets of life as we do are much more capable to develop and much more encouraging towards each other and bring ourselves close to a certain perfection than two people who become "one with a shadow," because the second person is forced to follow the first one due to some inner imperfection, and if the sun is not shining for once, that other person seems to disappear. All of those considerations seem to me–though quite underdeveloped at this time–to show the right way and I would love to know what my darling thinks about all of this and if you agree with me.

Sleep well and sweetly and restfully and feel how intensely and filled with the most tremendous love and longing I am! Completely and *utterly*, Your Mope

VERA TO MOPE

London, 2 July 1939

Today was more April than July; the sun came through quite often, but in between, it rained and it was not warm at all–except when the sun came out. It is shortly before 6 p.m. and, before Hanna and Fred arrive, it is now my love's turn. First of all, I have to tell you that I have a very guilty conscience, my love, and that I almost penned another letter to you last night, but unfortunately, it got to be very, very late, since I also had to take care of some correspondence for Pepper. My guilty conscience comes from the fact that I am accusing myself of having let myself go much too often lately in my letters to you and that I was very unrestrained. My love, if I think about it reasonably, I do realize that the two of us just *have to* accept the long periods of separation for the moment, and I am afraid that I only made things more difficult for you with my letters in which I complained about the separation and talked about putting an end to them, and they are difficult for both of us. I know very well that my love will not impose these separations on us any longer than absolutely necessary, and if I really think about it, I realize, again and again, that the two of us have it so *very, very* good despite the fact that we long for each other's company: we are glad and happy in the awareness of each other; we do not have any material worries at this time; we are healthy; so we have to be very, very ashamed if any complaint is made and if we dare to utter even one word besides that we are happy and overjoyed, especially when we consider that many people lack one of the things mentioned above or even several. And I would like to tell you once again: I am very cheerful and happy because of you, my love; I have a professional job that will allow me to achieve something, I hope, and I am looking forward to the day when you will return, so: *please forget* all *about what I said in my previous letters*! And again: I am ashamed of that!

I have to close now–the Raus have just arrived. If possible, I will write more later.

* * *

My *sweetheart*, it is midnight now and I am writing to you from the horizontal after I had to interrupt my partial letter to you so abruptly. The evening with Hanna and Fred was extremely pleasant. Fred told me–and assured me that you knew all about it–that the lawsuit had been won, that is, with the condition that a notarized statement, or better, a confirmation could be presented that the merchandise belonged to him. He said that he had been unable to devote himself to the matter due to lack of time, but that he thought that, with the help of Julius Rosenfeld's attorney, the necessary letter could be secured. The whole thing sounds rather hopeful.

Among other things, Fred told me the following: Norbert wrote that, for the time being, he preferred not to come to Buxton, because applying for an immigration visa to the U.S.A. would probably be a complete waste of time, since it could take up to ten years, before a new existence as a medical doctor could be established, and since he would be going back to his home country anyway within the next two years, he thought it best to stay in Middle Europe for now. Grete is supposed to be terribly depressed over the news and Fred said that he had written a letter to him which would most likely make him change his mind, that is, decide to join his family in England. What do you say to something like that? That man is either not normal or completely and incomprehensibly bad, but I consider that almost impossible, that someone can be so irresponsible and unconscionable, and I really think that all of the events have taken hold somewhere in his head and that the man cannot be taken seriously– both things are equally terrible!

My lovielein, I can understand that you smoked more during those exciting days of buying and I hope that your breathing is really free.

How often do you cough in the morning when you brush your teeth? And do you cough a lot in the evening? If it is possible, my *sweetheart*, please try to reduce the cigarettes again, because every one you smoke pains me.

I kiss you full of the most passionate love–Completely and utterly, *Your* little Lilongo-witch

MOPE TO VERA

Leningrad, 2 July 1939

This afternoon, ten of us went to Peterhof, but only two of us, I and another guy, went swimming. It was a wonderfully relaxing experience and my skin has turned red-brown. Should they see me, my clients will think that I am here for relaxation, because I tan so quickly! If I can arrange it, barring lack of time, I will repeat the outing, which took four hours including the swimming, before the auction begins. While there, we laid ourselves down in the sun and we chatted. During that conversation, I found out from a colleague that he thinks of me as an ice-cold human being who can probably also be quite brutal. I was quite charmed by that, because I do not think that people need to be able to read me all that easily and determine right away what kind of a person I am. This only as an aside!

When I got back to the hotel, I found a *sweeeet* letter from Schapiro. I will answer him right away in which I will tell him pretty much the same thing I told you. He will burst at the seams, and he is supposed to, although he claims to have deposited £284.19 at the bank in New York. Sometimes, I wonder if the man expresses himself so badly in the German language that his letters cause such displeasure, or if he is really that stupid to think that he can make me feel small with such methods.[195]

It was only right of Grete to write a nice letter since you spoiled her so sweetly. It is good that she seems to be getting her things from that land of criminals now. I do not need to hope for mine, although there are quite a few things I would *really* love to have. It would be soooo good

---

195 Mope was all too often kept waiting by Schapiro who was perpetually tardy in settling his salary, expenses, and commissions, a proportion of which were to be paid into a New York bank account.

if Ketty could come soon and take her children back into stricter hands and alleviate some of the work Helenchen has now.

Just now, I am hearing that Chamberlain held a speech, which supported Halifax's, as the volunteers were marching past the King in Hyde Park. How much I hope that that will intimidate those criminals who completely disregard human rights, just like the appeal of the general assembly of the English workers which seems quite reasonable and impressive to me.[196]

I wonder if this will be the last letter to my sweet one for the next few days. In the morning, all the hoopla will begin. It will be a bustle beyond comparison. The quantities of merchandise for pre-auction inspection have never been this big and I am by myself, while others–as I have told you already–are working in threes and even fours. Unfortunately, during the next few days, the mail man will start to think that I have become unfaithful to you and will have *no idea* how much more wonderful it would be for me if I could write to my darling instead of doing without chatting with you.

But for now, I want to get these lines to the post office and then go to bed. I am with you *all the time* and wish for nothing more intensely and longingly than to really be with you and no longer have to enjoy our union through letters alone. Completely and most passionately, *Your* Mope

VERA TO MOPE

London, 5 July 1939

It is 9.30 in the evening and I have so much to tell you that I do *not* know where to begin. I spent a large part of my evening on the telephone, until just a little while ago, and talked to Georg Rosenfeld; he wrote to me at the office and asked me if I could please call him soon. He told me that his parents are hoping to be allowed to go to Palestine in the next six months, but that nothing had been decided black on white yet concerning the matter, and Mr. Weißmann,[197] Carlchen's friend, will

---

196 Neville Chamberlain's radio speech of 2 July (which Mope was able to hear in Leningrad) warned that Britain would stand up to any further aggression by Germany. The speech was given shortly after 20,000 National Service volunteers had marched past King George VI and Queen Elizabeth in Hyde Park. Their march was intended to demonstrate Britain's solidarity in the event of war.

197 Unidentified.

not give an unlimited guarantee, but only one for six months, in other words, for both of them: £100-0-0, but Woburn House or rather, the Home Office, will not accept something like that and will only issue a visa if an unlimited guarantee is presented. Georg asked me if I knew of any English guarantors and I gave him Lady Rochdale's name, but I still have the feeling that I did not do enough to help.

Georg is hoping to receive the final confirmation from the Palestine office within the next two weeks, allowing his parents to immigrate in the course of the next six months; once that is on hand, I also think that the six-month long guarantee of Mr. Weißmann will be enough or at least, I hope it is. In this one, good advice is hard to come by–what can be done? Should I–just in case the Palestine office does not want to get involved or rather, is not willing to confirm anything in writing and Lady Rochdale cannot do anything–contact one of the directors at M&S in writing? Or what else can I do? A guy like Norbert has the permit which means he has a guarantor and makes no use of it–and such delightful people as Carlchen and his wife, who have every right to it, do not have one and have to suffer because of it. I invited Georg for Saturday evening and he will come over by bicycle. He really is a *very* nice young man and among other things, he told me that his parents would be able to survive here for six months very easily on £100, or maybe even longer, and that he was putting back a little every week which was meant for them and would also help out a little. He earns thirty shillings a week and, as far as I know, he does not qualify for a weekly bonus from his employer yet. The difference between Georg and the Goldschmidt children is obvious to the naked eye. And it is incomprehensible to me that those children are so completely untouched by the momentousness of the events and they think that they have to have everything there is to be had.

I just called Oma Lenchen who asked about you ever so lovingly. Among other things, I told her about the Rosenfelds, and she said that Fred was very involved in matters of that sort. Supporting the family Moschytz costs him *much* more than he had estimated, since Switzerland is very expensive and they (I assume *Norbert*) had to buy so many new things there. I have to admit that I do not understand Fred in this regard and I think the only right thing to do would be to not give this conceited parasite–and I do *not* find that expression too harsh for him–another penny. I feel very sorry for Grete and I hope that she does not suffer too much because of all of this. Completely and utterly, *Your* little Lilongo-witch

VERA TO MOPE

London, 10 July 1939

My love, I will finally respond to your thoughts that you talk to me about in your letter from the 29th of last month concerning the relationship between men and women and the danger that a woman who loves her man might adjust blindly to him under certain circumstances and sometimes even submit to him intellectually and spiritually and the connected possibility that the man turns the woman into a complete slave and she becomes his creature in such a way that she loses every initiative and self-reliance.

I believe that it is in a woman's nature to surrender herself and to want to nestle close–physically as well as in intellectual and spiritual matters, in a greater or lesser manner, and if she cannot do so, she is not a real woman.

How far she surrenders herself to becoming dependent by doing the latter and in what measure she succeeds in finding the right balance depends on three points: 1) the intelligence of the woman, 2) the intelligence and niveau of the man, and 3) and maybe most importantly, how far and to what degree both partners harmonize and are able to lead a satisfactory life together. And if that is the case, they will become dependent on each other, or better, will be so tuned in to each other that they will feel free at the same time and be and remain uninhibited in their personality.

To come back to point 1): if the degree of intelligence of the woman is not all that high, she will never have thought or acted all that independently–even before she falls in love with a man–and of course, as soon as she surrenders to a man completely, she becomes his creature and will follow him blindly and adore him without judgment, without the ability to judge him.

If the condition of number 2 fits the situation and the degree of intelligence in the man is below average or is lower than that of the woman, a woman, out of the disappointment and realization that she cannot nestle and will not find the necessary resonance, will fall into the extreme that goes contrary to her very nature and become the enslaver and through that, will lose a lot of her natural charm and her natural equilibrium.

I am so inexpressibly grateful to you for being able to nestle close to you, completely and totally and in every sense of the word and that you make it possible for me to retain my independence. I believe that I told you and wrote at the very beginning of our love that the most pleasing part of our relationship, and completely new to me, was the wonderful harmony and balance that rang through it and that there was nothing inhibited, unnatural, or even untrue about this relationship.

I did not go into your lines from the 29th in more detail before today–they have occupied my mind quite deeply–because I wanted to spend some time thinking about them, to feel them and carry them around with me until my thoughts had ripened enough for me to put them down on paper or even into words.

I shall be writing to Hilde Lewy who sent me her long-awaited news today from Atlanta. Walter still has not found anything and for the time being, they have rented a two-room furnished apartment, until they can have the part of the furniture they did not sell. She writes about her little child in such a delighted manner and says that now that she is a year old she has become such a charming little person that she already outshines most people, or so she writes with great delight.

Oma Lenchen told me that the aunts arrived from Berlin yesterday. She will visit them tomorrow and I hope that I will get to meet them soon. Ketty might come over in the next two weeks. Oma Lenchen was able to transfer a little money to her account there, which will help her to get away. It will be very good to have Ketty here, because Gertrud really needs a strong hand, and Oma Lenchen with her kindness and leniency is *no* match for her. Completely and utterly, *Your* little Lilongo-witch

MOPE TO VERA

Leningrad, 11 July 1939

Yesterday evening, for the first time since the beginning of the inspections, I went to bed before 1 a.m., while it was usually between 4.00 and 5.00 in the morning every day or better, every night. Actually, I had intended to write to you last night, but that just did not work. I was so completely exhausted and tired. Most of all, I want to send you my most heartfelt gratitude for all your beloved and loving letters that reach me here daily.

Although Schapiro is downright bombarding me with telegrams concerning this or that article, I am now sitting around without a single order and the only reason I am grateful to him is the fact that I can take the time to draw on this piece of paper. With all the work that needs to be done right now, I feel that the most difficult thing is that I have to interrupt those letter chats with my darling for days on end, though my heart is full of love and longing. In the meantime, it is 2.15 a.m. and I was interrupted and did not find the time to continue until now. I am so tired that I keep thinking I will fall asleep on the spot. Tomorrow morning, at 9.15, it will be time to go back to work, and I have come to the point now where I can stop working with a clear conscience. I hope that I will get up on time in the morning so I can continue this letter, because right now, I would not be doing you much of a loving service if I continued writing and do without that little bit of sleep.

Good night, my golden, most beloved little Lilongo-witch, sleep well and in your dreams, feel those innumerable kisses and gentlest caresses that I would like to give to you in unimaginable numbers.

VERA TO MOPE

London, 11 July 1939

I just had a long conversation with Oma Lenchen–it took place as a replacement for a visit; she is so very sweet and it is a pleasure to have her within the reach of the telephone, at least. Ketty now has permission to start packing and might get here next week.

I received a confirmation from Selfridges concerning your *wireless set* and they want to *overhaul* it after you get back. They want to know if the *faulty valve* can be sent back to them since they only guarantee the *valves* for three months. Maybe you can have someone bring it to me.

I am sorry but the ink ran out on me and I have landed in the horizontal in the meantime. I will close now, because my eye lids are closing on me.

I love you and I kiss you with the most passionate and tender love,
Your Little Witch

MOPE TO VERA

Leningrad, 13 July 1939

I did not get around to continuing these lines until now, although I carried this sheet of paper around with me in my pocket, so I would be able to use any opportunity to finish this letter. However, I also need some inner calm in order to be able to have a conversation with my darling and I only have that when I know that I am not neglecting any of my duties while I concentrate on you. Tomorrow evening, the auction will be over. Up to now, everything has worked out somewhat well–knock on wood–although I am extremely annoyed with Schapiro, as you know.

Under the given conditions, I no longer feel able to continue working with Schapiro. I told him that constantly feeling out of tune was anything but beneficial for my work. My reasons have nothing to do with financial concerns, although I do not like to have to beg for every single penny owed to me, but rather that I feel constantly attacked by him in my self-confidence as he uses every opportunity to say things to me that are supposed to be statements made by clients in order to subdue me. In any case, I do have to really think about all of this before I come to the end with or without a decision. This parasite Schapiro who always has his wife with him and also takes her with him on his travels, most of the time, does not show even the slightest understanding, but does everything in his power to make it even more difficult because he does not seem to feel all that secure up there on his throne.—

Wait, wait–what kind of garbage am I writing to my adorable, sweetest Lilongolein? You are not supposed to get a letter of complaint from me after such a long break in my letters!!! Since I began writing this, I have been interrupted and called away uncountable times and I also have not responded to your beloved letters in any way. What you write about Carl and Lies Rosenfeld is really depressing to me and I almost feel like terrible ingratitude to a much more favorable fate to grumble the way I have in this letter. I do not know if the refusal you should really expect to get from the people at M&S is worth risking. It might be better to go via Fred and talk to him about the matter.

I really have no idea what to think of Norbert's behavior, but it would make no sense to force that idiot to join his wife whom he would just torment if that was done. I really do hope that Fred does not support him financially. There is absolutely no reason for him to do so and he also does not have that justification when so many other people who are much closer to him are forced to call on him. I find it completely insane to speculate on a possible return to Germany in two years instead of dealing with reality and establishing a new existence, even if it takes a long time. I really hope that Fred puts his foot down most energetically and decisively refuses to provide for his upkeep in any way if he does not want to listen.

It will be 2 a.m. soon and I still have to go to the post office to send a few telegrams and I also want to send this letter on its way to my most beloved little witch.

Completely and utterly, *Your* Mope

VERA TO MOPE

London, 15 July 1939

My *sweetheart*, it makes no sense to always be so annoyed with Mr. Schapiro. I hope that I am not giving you bad advice, but I have come to the conclusion, more and more, that these difficult separations, and added to that the sweetness of a Mr. Schapiro, are only acceptable for as long as you are *forced* to put up with them. There is no advantage in making personal attacks on such people–who are not fine characters, after all. I have to remind you of your own "wise" method of sleeping on such things for *one* night. Sleep makes it possible to see things more coolly and to be more impersonal in one's decision making the following morning. I am only telling you this, because I know that you–as every sensible person would–might tend to take his remonstrances just a little too personally, but it does demand prudence when one is dealing with someone like a Mr. Schapiro.

My *sweetheart*, you are still in the middle of the auction now and I hope that you are *not* too overworked and that going to bed at 3.20 in the morning was just a *one-time* occurrence. Completely and utterly, *Your* Little Witch

MOPE TO VERA

Leningrad, 15 July 1939

The auction has been over since yesterday evening, but there was still a lot of work that needed to be done and my sweet one is the one who has to suffer because I was forced to neglect you so badly all that time, at least where writing letters was concerned. In my thoughts–but I do not really think that I need to make special mention of it because my girl already knows–I was constantly with you, as always, and it is just as difficult for me not to write to you as it is for you not to receive any letters.

I had really thought about the entire matter during the last few days and that I have come to the decision to allow the contractual arrangements with Schapiro to proceed as before. I am hoping that his letters with the stupidest accusations which upset me so much will come to an end. I would really prefer not to stay here that long and that I would consider it more advantageous for business if I came back here towards the end of September. However, it will not be possible to make any decision about that right now. We shall have to watch the business developments in the next few weeks. The auction was quite weak for most people working on commission. Many orders from smaller customers were canceled at the last minute due to the unstable political situation in Europe. America also reacted similarly. Contrary to that, the larger dealers were the largest buyers so that, against all expectations, the prices remained relatively stable. It seems to me that Sojuspushnina can be well satisfied once again with the results that were achieved. My purchases will not get much above £10,000. If I did that on my own expenses, independent of my salary from Schapiro, I would have had around £75 in expenses and £150 in commissions, so that would not be sufficient to let the issue be profitable.

I am extremely interested in hearing about the final result of the court case and I also hope that Fred will not put the matter off for much longer now. I find it less than pleasing that we still have not found out about the effect of the court case and what really annoys me is the fact that time goes on and the expenses just keep growing, and we are not even sure if we will ever get any of that money back.

Sleep is now overwhelming me quite strongly so I *must* close these lines, although I would just love continuing to chat with you. I have ordered a wake-up call for 9 o'clock in the morning while I was rung out of my chaste bed at 7.00 a.m. for the last week.

Most passionately and *completely* without reservation, *Your* Mope

VERA TO MOPE

London, 16 July 1939

I talked to Oma Lenchen on the telephone last night as well as this morning. She is very sad because Ketty and her husband are not able to come over this week, as anticipated. The entire matter was delayed again! I do not know if you have read about the new law that forbids all immigration to Palestine for the next six months (that has nothing to do with Ketty), since the number of illegal ones has been so high in the last few months.[198] That poor Carlchen Rosenfeld and his wife! If they do not find anyone who gives them an unlimited guarantee here things will become very difficult for them as well. I think I already wrote to you that their acquaintance is prepared to post a £200-0-0 guarantee, but that does not seem to be enough. Completely and utterly, *Your* Little Witch

MOPE TO VERA

Leningrad, 17 July 1939

The day before yesterday, I wrote just a few lines to my beloved girl with the hope that they would reach you early Monday morning through a man who is flying directly to London, but to me he is most inappropriate as a *postillon d'amour*. The man is Mitja Simonoff and you do not need any further explanation![199] That man turned a few waitresses' heads and they were fighting over his photograph today. It seems to me that his method of making an impression on women is so cheap that I just cannot understand that they even react to it in the first place. His way of strutting around like a rooster and wiggling his hips seems almost whore-like, but maybe, my most beloved one thinks that I am prejudiced against him. I was indifferently friendly towards him since I do not estimate him highly enough to have any kind of feelings of hate for him, and after all, seen with clear eyes, all of that was only a mistake, albeit a grave one, and it is almost silly of me to come back to that, and I do not think that I would do it if it did not present such a psychological problem and riddle that I have not been able to solve to this very day.

I wonder if my sweet one has applied for the visa by now. With the tension that exists between Schapiro and me, it is questionable whether he will be willing to carry the traveling expenses, but if I have to stay

---

198 As the Mandatory power over Palestine, the British government published a White Paper in May 1939, effectually limiting Jewish immigration to 75,000 over the following five-year period (10,000 per year plus 25,000 refugees). Its subsequent enforcement was tantamount to a death sentence for countless European Jews.

199 This is the same Mitja with whom Vera had lost her innocence, and Mope has not forgiven him.

until September, I do not want to wait that long for my little witch and as a matter of fact, if I stay another month, I will earn so much more because of being here for that month than the traveling expenses could possibly amount to, so the matter is not quite as extravagant as it seems to you.

I am very happy to hear that the aunts are there now, too, and I really hope that you will get to meet them soon. Both of them are half deaf and you have to speak very loudly and clearly. You will find a very understanding soul in Aunt Helene Simon, because she was one of the best known social workers and publicists in Germany and was given an honorary doctorate from the University of Heidelberg. Sadly, she is very old now and very hard of hearing and I do not know how her sensitive soul dealt with the recent difficult events. However, you should try to get to know her. As far as I am aware, both of the Aunts are very fond of me, and I am sure they would be very pleased to meet my sweet one whom they only know from a photograph. I would also be very happy if you visited them soon.[200]

Georg Rosenfeld seems to have felt quite comfortable there with you– please give him my thanks for his note and give him my best regards. I really like the idea that he visits you quite often because he is a nice and pleasant young man and on top of that, his parents are very close friends of mine. I really hope that they will have the opportunity now to emigrate as quickly as possible.

It is Pod Wychodnoi today and now, I have to go to the restaurant and join my colleagues for a little while before I go to bed. I kiss you filled with the most passionate love and most affectionate tenderness on all of your x–that means innumerable–sweet spots (do you know which ones I mean?) and I caress you in my thoughts with all my ability to make you content and happy–if only I could really do that again finally, then I, your Mope, would be completely happy, too.

VERA TO MOPE

London, 17 July 1939

---

[200] Helene Simon (1862-1947) was a pioneer in the theory and practice of social welfare in Germany, and was deeply influenced by the work of Beatrice and Sidney Webb, the leaders of the Fabian Society in England. After fleeing Germany, she and her sister Klara found basic accommodation in a boarding house in London's East End.

Today, I am beginning my letter with very sad news: Pepper is *not* feeling well at all. Last Wednesday evening, after he had spent the day in the city, he started shivering and went to bed around 8 o'clock and then, felt better again afterwards, that is, he has been very tired and exhausted every day ever since then, and Mutti is not at all happy with the way he looks. Yesterday around lunch time, he told us how much more well he was feeling, and this morning, as usual, he wanted to go into the city, but while he was shaving, he started shivering again all of a sudden, and we called Dr. Rothschild. A little while ago, Mutti told me on the telephone that Dr. Rothschild had been there for about an hour and that he diagnosed pneumonia which really frightened me. On top of that, Pepper complained or rather did not complain but just mentioned it as an aside that he was feeling a burning sensation in his urinary tract, and Dr. Rothschild said that that was probably due to prostate hardening which is rather common in older men–it can be treated, but it has nothing to do with the other matter.

Now, I am home again and Pepper is doing *much* better. Dr. Rothschild gave him some medicine that brought the fever which was above 39° this morning down to 38.8° centigrade, which is relatively good for the evening. Mutti told me that Pepper slept for just about the entire afternoon. She is feeling very depressed and worried. Dr. Rothschild will come over again very early tomorrow morning. There is a new medication for pneumonia that he prescribed to Pepper and it is supposed to be especially good and effective.

My love, I wish I could give you much nicer news and I only hope that, by the time this letter reaches you, Pepper will be much, much better and allowed to get up again. By the way, his breathing is not heavy and Dr. Rothschild said that it was a very mild form of pneumonia. Nevertheless, at his age, that is not a good thing. He is such a touching patient who does *not* complain and all the while, he kept saying that it was nothing and he was just a little tired and yesterday, around midday, after he had slept, he said that he was feeling very well again. He maintained that he did not have a fever and did not want to have his temperature taken.

I have to close now so that this letter will get into the mail this evening. I hope that I can give you better news tomorrow. Completely and utterly, *Your* Little Witch

MOPE TO VERA

Leningrad, 18 July 1939

I feel more longing than ever before to come to my most beloved girl and it is completely unimaginable to me that I might have to be without you until September. If Schapiro is not willing to pay for your traveling expenses, I am sure that I will come back earlier and I regard *that* as the solution to the problem. You might write to him that you have applied for the visa or that you intend to and ask him if he will now pay for the trip he still owes you from last year. You can do that in my name and at my request. From what I have heard, it is almost out of the question to get a Swedish or Finnish visa on a passport that is only valid for another six months. For this reason, I do not have any other choice but to fly back, and I will have to go to Moscow for that. Nevertheless, I am going to try to get the Finnish visa and for that reason, I will travel to Moscow in the next few days. The visa will be valid for three months.

I love you so tremendously, my sweet Lilongolein–*Completely,* Your Mope

VERA TO MOPE

London, 18 July 1939

Please excuse the pencil, but I am writing from the horizontal, because it is very late already. Fortunately, Pepper is doing much better today; that is, he was feeling very weak, which is a result of the medication or rather the pills, but his temperature was 37º this morning and 38º rectally this evening. Dr. Rothschild came by this morning around 8 a.m. and was very satisfied with him. In the last ten months, the formerly so very dangerous disease, pneumonia, has become an illness that is now being treated extremely successfully, thanks to an invention of pills that make the pathogen that causes pneumonia innocuous–and it really works wonders! The difficult thing is–and Dr. Rothschild is great in that regard–to recognize a case of pneumonia immediately. The pills make the patient feel very weak, but Dr. Rothschild says that that usually disappears within three days and that Pepper will be back to his old self in no time at all. He will come back again tomorrow at 8 a.m. The poor Pepper is really unfortunate and as I already said yesterday, he is an extremely brave and good patient. Dr. Rothschild explained to me that these pills are also useful for the prostate enlargement since they disinfect all inner organs. It is really fantastic how well these pills work, because yesterday, Pepper really looked wretched, but today, he looks quite well. Dr. Rothschild told us that he should be completely well again within a week, thanks to this new invention![201]

I am so late today because I wrote a detailed letter to Annelie this evening. I wrote to her because I received a downright frantic letter from her this morning. Her parents still have not been able to make any progress and I went to see their local attorney. It seems to me that the various sons-in-law mismanaged the matter somewhat, and Annelieschen's husband does not seem to be the brightest light, at least not according to the letter he wrote to the local attorney, even if he seems to mean well. The newest project is that Dr. Friedman and the grandmother might possibly immigrate to Chile, but that is not possible before April of 1940. And if there are no flawless documents on hand for that, the desired stop over here will not be granted. According to all appearances, it was strongly suggested to them to leave Leipzig as soon as humanly possible, but there has not been a chance up to now. In my letter, I tried to explain all the different possibilities mentioned by the attorney and maybe, the matter can be taken care of after all.[202] Sweetest, most loving kisses and filled with the greatest longing, *Your* Little Witch

MOPE TO VERA

Leningrad, 19 July 1939

I hope to be able to transport these lines quickly as well so that they will reach you on Saturday. I have not received an answer yet from Schapiro, but I will probably not have to wait for too long. Should it come to a break with him, I will just have to see how I will get ahead without him. According to my calculations, we have a little over $2,400 in the New York bank and the London account is not much smaller. I hope that another £100 will be left over from the court case and

---

201 The first antibiotic medication, a sulfa drug, was made available in 1936, preceding the use of penicillin on patients by about six years. It was prescribed as a cure for bacterial pneumonia. The same drug was successfully used to treat Winston Churchill's pneumonia in 1943. During Vera's student days at medical school, antibiotics had not yet become available.
202 In fact, several of Annelie's relatives did find refuge in Chile.

Schapiro owes me more than £200 in commissions. I am supposed to receive another £130 for July and August and I am quite sure that more commission will be added to that. On this trip, I have earned around £76 in commissions so far, maybe a little more, and I really hope that this calculation, representing the result of two years of work, will please my darling just a little and will make the suffering caused by the seemingly intolerable separation a little easier to bear. In any case, the time was not completely wasted which fills me with a certain satisfaction, even if it is not a significant amount.

But now, I want to climb into my chaste bed and in my thoughts, I want to kiss my most beloved girl all over and especially on those delightful thighs and between them most passionately and longingly and caress you ever so gently. You just simply cannot fathom what a burning longing I feel for you, my golden little angel, and how unspeakably happy I would be to have you with me and to take joy in your beloved sight and all the other things. Most passionately, Your Mope

VERA TO MOPE

London, 19 July 1939

When I came home, Pepper was feeling better. He does not have an elevated temperature today, which is completely great with pneumonia, and not until the invention of the pills I mentioned to you yesterday has that become possible. As a candidate in medicine, I saw cases of pneumonia at the hospital and I know only too well what a terrible and disconsolate picture they presented. Of course, Pepper still feels terribly weak and miserable, but Dr. Rothschild assured us that now that the fever has gone down so abruptly he will get better every day. Poor Muttilein was *terribly* worried all those days! It is really bad: I think that she looks much worse than Pepper! I will take Saturday off and insist on her resting. Dr. Rothschild will come back tomorrow morning at 8 am.

Just like you, I am very sad about Lies and Carl Rosenfeld, especially after the new law was passed which prohibits any further immigration to Palestine until next March. Fred is out of town, and he is already doing sooooo unbelievably much for all the siblings that there is no way anyone should bother him while he is away on a family vacation in Cornwall.

I have to close now and get to sleep. *I love you, my sweetheart, with all my soul and heart* and completely and utterly, *Your* Little Witch

MOPE TO VERA

Leningrad, 22 July 1939

Tomorrow, it will be two years from the day I left here to come to our wedding, and my longing for you overwhelms me in such a way that I am completely *fed up* and only want to go home. I feel like a small boy who is away from home for the first time and does not know what to do in all his homesickness. Sometimes, it is not nice at all to have to be an adult who is not allowed to let himself go, because he has to make allowances for "being an adult." And I have to say that I never suffered from homesickness as a boy, at least I do not remember ever feeling the kinds of emotions that consume me now.

It is really a fact that our most beautiful years of youth go by and we only get to see each other on rare occasions and can only enjoy our mutual caresses so rarely that this state has to be ended as soon as possible. Unless it comes to a break before that, I will have to fulfill my duties until the end of the contract and I assume that I will have to travel a lot, but absences as long as this one will not happen again. I am firmly convinced that I will be able to make a living for us with a commission business in Russian merchandise and trips here during the auction and a few weeks before and after, and I really do not want more than that. I am sure that there are not too many people with as much merchandise experience as I have gained here, and I am sure that I would easily find another position.

I am deeply saddened by the further delay in Ketty's emigration and I would be much happier to have her safely in London, because otherwise, you can never be sure that she will really come. I am aware of the six-month immigration ban for Palestine and I have already thought of Carlchen and Lies, but I hope that they will be the first to leave just as soon as the six months are over. However, I feel that this law only encourages illegal immigration and then, there is the worry that the six months will be extended by a further time period. The strongest immigration there–as you might already know–is the inner *immigration*, and every woman who can manage has taken on the obligation, for that very reason, to have another child.

All the people with an eye for reality are leaving old corrupt Europe so that their children, at least, will no longer be affected physically by the powder keg the old world has turned into. A number of my colleagues are in process of leaving and moving with their families to New York, where they seem to be able to settle in quite well. Of course, that is speculation with a view into the distant future which could be completely off the mark, because the U.S.A. can experience changes as well and rapidly developing technology could draw the now still far away continent into the focal point of events here. The only country in which one can pursue one's occupation calmly and undisturbed is the U.S.S.R. where no one has to feel disquiet because of incidents in other parts of the world, since the people feel such an enormous trust in the great homeland and they can make themselves independent of the outside world without suffering the least deprivation.[203] But if the most beloved people–as is the case for me–live so far away, that same calm cannot be felt and the worst thing of all is the terrible longing that consumes me above all possible measure. *Completely, Your* Mope

VERA

Journal entry, 22 July 1939

My lovielein is still so very far away from me and I have had enough of this constant separation. I miss my husband's impact, and I think I have *much* too little initiative. Pepper has been sick since the 17th of this month, Muttilein is heart-warming and good as an angel and I do not help her enough and complain too much about being separated from my husband. I will have to try to get my husband to stay with me for good.

MOPE TO VERA

Leningrad, 24-25 July 1939

Outside, it is pouring in buckets and ever since yesterday, the sun gave up insisting on being seen by the people of Leningrad, although yesterday was Wychodnoi after all and we thought that we had a right to its rays.

---

[203] Mope's opinion here appears to have been written more to appease any possible Soviet censor reading the letter than necessarily reflecting his own views.

Around noon yesterday, we drove out to Pavlovsk again, but, because of the weather, we could not stay out in the park, so we visited the castle instead, which I did not mind doing again, because there are quite a number of very beautiful pieces of art. Among other things, there are several wonderful Brussels tapestries and their colors just about outdo the French ones. I did not get to my room until 8 o'clock where I had to take care of quite a bit of business correspondence.

Around 10 p.m., my darling's letter from the 19th arrived and I am deeply pleased to read that Pepper is doing better and that Rothschild's treatment seems to show some success. Then, I felt so tired all of a sudden that I preferred going to bed and to write these lines this morning. For this reason, I got up a little earlier this morning and I hope that, by the time I have to go to the warehouse, this awful weather will have improved. I was very interested in your description of the effect of the pills that change pneumonia into a much less harmful illness, since that was not possible until just recently. I had not known that pneumonia is so difficult to diagnose and actually, I am wondering about that, since listening to the lungs and back is easier than the examination of most internal organs and their illnesses can be determined as well. In any case, Pepper is a *clever boy* for waiting with his pneumonia until after this new invention and not only spared us a lot of worry, but also saved himself from a long illness. My sweet one has every reason to acknowledge his competence more than ever and I am very happy to hear that he is a pleasant patient and does not absorb too much of the strength of his fellow men, which is also worth a certain acknowledgment.

I am really very sorry to hear about Annelie's parents, but those people simply refused to listen and always thought that that gang of criminals would invent an extra special treatment just for them and then, their decision of leaving the grandmother there all alone did not show much heart. How many discussions have I had with Dr. Friemann to make it clear to him that there is only one decision and that would be to emigrate as quickly as possible, but he did not even want to consider that for himself.

I am wondering what has been going on with Ketty in the meantime. What a relief it would be to know that she finally got out! I am also concerned about the fate of Carlchen and Lies and I really wish to get better news about them soon. It is a depressing awareness that we cannot help or even advise them and I find it a crying shame that Carl's friend does not stick up for those two more than he does. I wonder if it would help for my darling to talk to this man. Maybe you should ask Georg what he thinks. Maybe the intervention of a woman might work better in such matters, especially when it comes from such a sweet girl like you, and I would be very, very grateful to you and I do not believe that paying a visit to this old guy would be a greater sacrifice than the awareness of having done everything possible justifies.

But now, I have to hurry up and get to work! Most passionately, you most beloved one, you! *Completely* and *altogether, Your* Mope

VERA TO MOPE

London, 25 July 1939

I am lying in the most beautiful sunshine and there is *absolutely* nothing wrong with me at all; this morning, my temperature was 36.9º centigrade rectally and I am really ashamed of lying around the house being lazy and to have caused such an upset in the first place. The entire thing was more than silly: on Sunday afternoon, I felt completely well and then, around 9.30, I felt a little bad all of a sudden, went to bed, and got the shivers and a temperature and gave poor Muttilein a bad scare. She called Dr. Rothschild late that night and he arrived after 1 a.m., and stayed for about an hour and thoroughly examined me, and my temperature was above 40º, and since I felt pain on the right side of my body, I was afraid that it might be appendicitis, but he said he was certain that was not the case and gave me the same pills Pepper had.

I wanted to send you a telegram that same night–since I had made a promise to you–and explained to Dr. Rothschild that, if I did not do so, I would break my promise. He said I should wait until morning and I asked him if he would be responsible for maybe ruining our marriage, and he answered: "Yes!" In the morning, the temperature was at 37.8º and in the afternoon 38.5º and Dr. Rothschild came back and said that he had examined my urine and he was *sure* that it was *not* appendicitis and prescribed several most intensive enemas, and today, I feel as well as anyone can and I am ashamed of having been such a burden on the poor doctor and such a worry to Muttilein.

I was convinced that it was my appendix and I started being afraid, because my love was so far away and it would have been terrible to me to have to worry you like that. Now, I remember that, after my first tennis game this year last Saturday, I drank a vast amount of tea, since

I apparently felt the need and it was teatime just then. Last time, it was around lunch and so, I will have to accept Dr. Rothschild's explanation that my silly temperature can be traced back to dehydration and constipation that led to a quasi-poisoning. Silly, silly to be that stupid!!!

Strangely enough, Dr. Rothschild told us that he had an identical case in his office yesterday and also following a game of tennis, or rather physical activity, that causes an excessive loss of H2O. I would have gone to the office today, because I feel completely well and an elevated temperature does not say much in my case, since I always run a very high fever that goes as quickly as it comes, but because I am not completely at my best today, though without any pain or other complaints, I am using the day to be lazy and lie in the sun and I am enjoying it.

My love, I would not have told you this really rather boring story in so much detail, but actually, I am pretty *sure*, that you will believe me 100% after this detailed report which even included the exact temperature. Dr. Rothschild called this morning and he agreed that I can go back to the office tomorrow. I hope that you will not worry at all, and that you are not upset with me!!!!!!!!!! Can you tell how afraid I am of my *husband*!!!!

Pepper got up for the first time today and is sitting in our room on a comfortable chair. Really, I feel sorry for poor Muttilein, with such "patients," that is, Pepper was really not well, but with me, it was just a stupid and unnecessary thing–then again, being ill is always unnecessary, but with me, it was actually self-induced–however unintentional it may have been. As a "reward," we have the most beautiful sunshine for the first time in days and I feel like I am in a health resort. *Your* little Lilongo-witch

P.S. *Do you ever think of the cigarettes??????*

VERA TO MOPE

London, 26 July 1939 [Postcard]

Dr. Rothschild was here just a little while ago and now, I am on my way to the office, since I have neither a temperature nor anything else–and Dr. Rothschild agrees. He has encountered three very similar cases in his practice since Sunday and because that has never been reported medically, he will publish it in a medical journal. In one of those cases, he was not consulted until later, after they had already removed the appendix and had to determine that that had not been the cause of the illness. I am convinced that 99% of all medical doctors would have had them remove my appendix as well and I am more than grateful to Dr. Rothschild. Had I been the doctor, I would have also made the diagnosis of appendicitis. I am feeling as well as ever. Dr. Rothschild really is an excellent doctor! Most affectionately, *Your* Little Witch

MOPE TO VERA

Leningrad, 30 July 1939

Tomorrow is the anniversary of our civil marriage ceremony. Last night, two colleagues kept me company while I was waiting for a telephone call with you which, as usual, did not connect, and we opened several cans of sardines, salmon, Prague smoked ham, and compote that I had collected over time–I do not like opening them when I am by myself, because food is not all that important to me–and drank wonderful Cadbury chocolate with it. The radio took care of the dinner music. At 2 o'clock, we went for a walk that was extended quite pleasantly when a bridge across the Neva that we had just crossed was raised to let a bigger barge through, and we had to march to the next bridge to get back to the hotel side of the river. Then, we drank tea and by the time I turned off the lights, it was 4 o'clock. By the way, we were very lucky where the weather was concerned, because right now, it is pouring down from a lead grey sky. Just now, I realized that the streetlights in Leningrad have been turned on for the first time. The white nights are over and it will not take much longer for it to start turning autumnal.

The floor servant woke me up at 8 o'clock with my darling's longed-for telegram. After receiving that, I spent the entire Sunday morning in bed and rested very well and then wasted the afternoon reading, writing, and talking, and after that, I went on a drive to Lyssi-Nos ("Fish-Nose"), a town on the Finnish Bay, across from Peterhof. The air was great and the two-hour drive with a twenty-minute stay there was a real pleasure. After returning to the hotel, I had dinner and drank an excellent coffee a colleague had donated to me yesterday. That stuff is called Nescafé and is a product of Nestle, and you put one heaping coffee spoon in a cup or glass and pour hot water over it and then, you have an excellent, aromatic coffee with no grounds. Until now, I had only known one product like that from the U.S.A. that does not taste as good.

I wonder if my dear Helenlein visited you today and convinced herself of your and Pepper's recuperation. I did not hear anything on the radio about the weather there today. Fortunately, the other news did not bring anything out of the ordinary and will spare humanity from those things that spring from such insane criminal minds as those of the fascist rabble.

It has become terribly late and now, I have to climb into that chaste bed again. But before I do and afterwards as well, I want to send you my most loving, gentlest, and sweetest kisses, my most adorable, most beloved little angel, and tell you that I love you most extraordinarily and tremendously and feel the most horrible longing for you. *Your* Mope

VERA TO MOPE

London, 31 July 1939

These lines are meant to tell you that I am completely happy because of you as we enter the third year of our marriage. My *sweetheart*, sometimes, I can still hardly believe that it has only been three and a half years since a very kind fate led you to cross my path. I wonder if you feel how intensely and completely my thoughts are with you and surround you and envelop you in my love. I think that it is a wonderful feeling to look back on these first years of our marriage with the knowledge that our friendship and love and our mutual understanding has deepened with *every* single day. I am soooo completely happy that you married me, so completely happy from the inside out in my awareness of you.

Before I started writing to my beloved again, I made a telephone call to Georg Rosenfeld who told me that his parents received a notice from Woburn House informing them that their case is nearing the *final decision*. He is hoping for a positive answer and I would really be very happy if everything worked out well. Should the matter not move forward from there, he thinks the only remaining way possible would be through his father's friend here and he welcomed your suggestion that I would then try to talk to him most enthusiastically. Georg will keep me informed on how things stand and just as soon as he or his parents hear anything further from Woburn House, he will let me know.

I hope that in the meantime your Swedish visa will have been entered in your passport. Please let me know about that *right away* when you get it. When will you go to Moscow for the Finnish one? I hope that you will receive both of them, that way you can prove that you have your *home* here.

Pepper is doing much better. He still feels weak, but that is understandable. Of course, his wish to go into the city for an entire day twice a week makes no sense, but I am sure you do not think that Pepper would let one of us stop him? For the time being, he can't go, but as soon as he can, he will not be able to help himself! He is being extremely difficult, impatient, and pedantic and is giving Mutti a very hard time–she is much too self-sacrificing and lets herself be ordered around without pause, and I am worried about her.

It is *terribly* late; I have not answered your beloved letters yet and will probably do so tomorrow. Many most passionate kisses everywhere, *Your* Little Witch

MOPE TO VERA

Leningrad, 2 August 1939

Today, I had a very happy day, because of your sweet and most beloved letters, which reached me after I came back to the hotel from the warehouse. Before that, I had felt tired and exhausted, but then, the sky became my private sky–blue again although it was raining outside and my sun was shining for me. Both of us found ourselves in the grip of the most heartfelt desire yesterday to at least spend this ever so important anniversary together, since our most dearly held wish to spend our lives together cannot be fulfilled at this time, alas. But even that remained impossible, at least not physically! But on the inside, both of us were so intensely close that both of us could feel it, and no distance, no matter how great, had the power to separate us. If you had seen me when I was reading your dear lines and perceived how my face brightened up and could have watched the joy I felt when I read your words telling me that you are happy to have married me, you would have been happy with me.

Of course, I believe my little witch when she tells me that you are completely well again. Just as soon as I see that you inform me about everything, subject to change, of course, there can be *no* doubts, and as you could see in my last few letters, I was not worried at all, which should prove to you that I put complete trust in your reports. It is such a calming feeling for me to be able to believe and not to become distrusting due to false considerations. I feel easier when I know for certain that you are not trying to whitewash anything and I can rely on your reports and get a good picture of what had been wrong with you.

In the next few days, my passport will be taken to Moscow for the Finnish visa and I really hope that I will not have to make that trip myself. I will know by the middle of next week at the latest and should that not work itself out, I will have to take the train after all. I am sure that you have read my letter, or rather, the copy to Schapiro concerning my travel objectives, and at this time, I am not able to say anything else about any specifics. In any case, I will not let him intimidate me any more than he did before when it came to traveling home.

Completely and utterly, Your Mope

MOPE TO VERA

Leningrad, 3 August 1939

Today, I had a rather idle day. There is hardly any merchandise that might be of interest for me. I have not heard anything further from Schapiro and I am completely convinced of his anger over our wish to have a life together. Parasites always lack any kind of understanding for the fact that others will not work for them continually like machines and wish to run away when it gets to be too much. I have come to the *firm* decision not to sign a new contract with that guy, or rather, not to renew it. I am sure it will not be easy for him to find a new "Man in Leningrad" but that is his problem and I cannot recommend becoming my successor to anyone.

However, it is *much* more interesting for us to find out what else I can start doing and I really hope that something can be prepared during my next stay there so that not too much time will pass when I am not earning any money while I am trying to establish myself. At the moment, that is a little difficult for me to prepare for, especially since I hardly know the London market which is overfilled with refugees, and my trust in other people is a much reduced one, because all of them, especially with such an oversupply of people who are not earning any money, try to fleece the others.

I am following the news from around the world with great eagerness and I hope with all my heart that reason will prevail and that peace will be preserved. It has been twenty-five years since the insanity began in

1914 and we should hope with all our strength that those people who had to be part of it back then have enough influence on the young (and their lust for adventure) who think that war is an enjoyable departure from the constraints of the mundane.

My passport traveled to Moscow last night and I hope to be in possession of the Finnish visa on the day after tomorrow. This visa represents the first step towards returning home which is something I long for so very much in order to be able to take my Lilongolein into my arms and press your ever so ravishingly beautiful breasts against mine. I feel downright hot when I think about that and I am more than happy that I am finally allowed to think about that again, little by little.

Today, the cigarettes arrived and I gave part of them to some colleagues–since I still had two hundred–because they were starving for them and kept mooching. All of them are waiting, but Abdulla seems to deliver most promptly, much to my satisfaction.

Now, I have to climb into the horizontal, because the clock demands it, and I will dream myself to my most beloved, sweetest, and so indescribably beloved little witch.

Completely and utterly, Your Mope

VERA TO MOPE

London, 5 August 1939

It is late afternoon, and after it had been raining without pause since last night, the sun came out for just a little. Today, in the morning, it was pouring so hard that it even woke *me*–and that will tell you a lot!!! The rain was slapping down as if someone was continually pouring out buckets of water and I closed the windows right away in order to protect our drapes.

Dr. Rothschild came over yesterday morning. Pepper does not have a temperature any longer, but he is not supposed to get up yet, because the ear is now showing a pussy flow, which is a *good* sign, because everything that is supposed to come out will come out with it. Pepper says he is feeling better. He shows a good appetite, but is still feeling very weak, is in a *bad* mood, and every little noise irritates him.

Just a little while ago, Georg Rosenfeld called me and gave me some very pleasing news. His aunt went to the Woburn House today and found out that it had turned over his parents' case to the Home Office and that it would take approximately 4-6 weeks until the decision would come in. I was recently told that, if Woburn House turns a case over, the Home Office hardly *ever* makes things difficult. I am really very happy about that and I am sure that you are too. I thought it was very nice of Georg to let me know right away. I intend to invite him here for tomorrow–his factory closes next week (bank holiday week), and he is staying at home, because he wants to save all of his money for his parents, as he told me. He really is a nice young man.

You ask how high the household expenses are. Until now, I have given Mutti £5–every week. Of course, because of Pepper, who needed various medicines, ear syringe, disinfecting material, etc., her expenses were much higher in the last few weeks. On top of that, she bought quite a few canned goods and other groceries, because all the newspapers say that people should do that, but I hope that it will be an unnecessary precautionary measure. How strange–you mentioned Nescafé and I had never heard of it and when I asked Mutti about it, she said that she had bought some that very afternoon because they had really recommended that drink to her, and we tried it and found it to be excellent.

My lovielein, I was *very* happy that you gave away to your colleagues so much of the last cigarette shipment! And I am downright *grateful* to you for that, as I am grateful for every single cigarette you do not smoke! And I hope *so very much* that your cough is better????

Completely and utterly, *Your* Little Witch

MOPE TO VERA

Leningrad, 5 August 1939

On my radio just a little while ago, they played a German lullaby "Good Evening, good night, presented with roses, slip under the blanket," and then, the chimes of Big Ben followed and told me that it is midnight.[204] Today is Pod Wychodnoi and I had just arrived back to my room after a short walk after all of us colleagues had dinner in the restaurant when that ever so familiar melody was played. I had already been on another walk earlier and listened to the sounds of the quietly moving water on

---

204 *Guten Abend, Gute Nacht, / Mit Rosen gedacht, /... Schlüpf unter die Deck* is a traditional German lullaby for children. On his radio, Mope will have heard a German transmission while tuning for "the chimes of Big Ben" and the BBC.

the banks of the Neva and enjoyed the view of the river lying in the light of dusk. The moon was still sitting very low and glowed like a split orange, reddish yellow, in the sky.[205] I gave it my most, most loving wishes for my little witch and now, it has reached the middle of the horizon. Its color has now changed to white blond and that heightens the strength of its light which is supposed to call your attention to it and my greetings of love before you fell asleep. It and I now guard your dreams so that they are happy and joyful and are not disturbed by any demons while they move through your sleep, which is supposed to stretch late into the morning until the sun–I hope, after those first few rainy August days–and the singing of the birds wake you.

Yesterday, they let me know by telephone from Moscow that the Finns are causing problems with the visa approval and because of that, I will either fly back or maybe take the Russian ship from Leningrad to London, that will take five days, which will unfortunately cut into our time together. As I heard today, the next auction will definitely take place towards the end of October. I doubt that much business can be done before then, because they will start collecting merchandise for the auction and will withdraw it from open sale.

I made some inquiries today as to when the next boat leaves for London from Leningrad and to my horror, I was told that there will not be another one between tomorrow and the 29th. And the day of departure is never completely reliable and can even be delayed for a few days. Should I encounter the same problems with the Swedish visa that I had with the Finnish one, I will not have any other choice but to fly to London, while I would only fly to Stockholm otherwise. It is completely incomprehensible to me why they are making things difficult as there is no reason.

I have not heard anything from Schapiro concerning my projected return trip. He seems to watch himself quite closely now in his letters, because apparently, he really does not want to lose me. I will have to wait and see if he can make up his mind.

I kiss you most tenderly with the sweetest kisses on all your sweetest places who long for my kisses just as much as I long for you, you most adorable little angel, you–

Completely and utterly, Your Mope

---

[205] During the "white nights" of summer, the moon had not been visible in Leningrad.

VERA TO MOPE

London, 8 August 1939

Today, such an agitation gripped me all of a sudden.[206] I have been feeling like that ever since yesterday evening–worrying about you. I do not like the newspaper reports at all, and every morning after I have read the newspaper on the bus, I feel quite depressed and *downhearted*, because the reports sound so grim and dark. If only humanity could learn how futile all that strife is and everyone would try a little harder to regard a fellow man as a companion and not as a rival. Last night or rather yesterday at night, I dreamt that you had come to me and I was completely happy about it and then felt very sad when I woke up and realized that it was only a dream. *When* will you finally be able to give me the exact date of your arrival, my beloved?!

I talked to Oma Lenchen on the telephone and she promised to come visit us next Sunday afternoon. Your dear mother still does not have any more positive news from Ketty. They *hope* to be able to get out soon and that is all there is at the moment. Georg Rosenfeld came over around noon today and after lunch, he and I went for a long walk from three to shortly after six o'clock. Georg hopes–as he said–that his parents will be able to come here in about four weeks.

This evening, I received a letter from Mr. Fuchs (Hilde Lewy's friend) who has been here for the last few days and he asks if he can get room and board with us. I called him, and told him that I will invite him for a visit just as soon as Pepper is completely well again, but that we could not take him as a boarder. I also told him that it might be possible for him to rent a room from your dear mother. I called her right away and she will get in contact with Mr. Fuchs by telephone. The extra income would be more than welcome to her.

I really do hope that you have received the Swedish visa in the meantime and even more that I will find out the date of your arrival very soon. Georg will take this letter to the mailbox for quicker posting.

---

206 Vera's agitation was brought about by news reports of a massive German troop mobilization that was being countered by parallel military measures by the western European powers and by smaller states in the region. The so-called "white war" (the flurry of diplomatic activity and flaunting of military power) in August 1939 came to be seen as a dress rehearsal for an inevitable global confrontation.

I really enjoyed the three days off [207] and I feel extremely well-rested and recuperated. Pepper too is doing remarkably better. He took care of some business letters a little while ago and smoked a cigar that tasted *very* good to him.

Sleep well, my *lovielein*, and I am looking forward to you more than I can say. Most passionately and completely and *utterly*, Your Little Witch

MOPE TO VERA

Leningrad, 10 August 1939

I have not heard anything further from Schapiro and I am beginning to speculate that he is looking for a new man who is more easily intimidated than me and that he does not want me to irritate him any longer. As long as he has not found that man, he will let me wait for an answer and he thinks that he can then present me with a *fait accompli*. Of course, that is only speculation that lacks any kind of confirmation and then, there will be problems with getting my money from him, of course, and apparently, he has not even paid my July salary yet. That swine has never given me anything in writing concerning our agreement, but always left it to me to confirm everything we agreed.

I am wondering if Ketty was able to leave that damned country in the last few days or is still facing difficulties. Those poor people must be losing their nerve completely and are being made more unable to rebuild with all that waiting and uncertainty. I assume too that Carlchen and Lies have not moved ahead any further and I often have to think of all these people who are so dearly beloved to me, and I am depressed because I cannot help them. I still do not have an answer to my question if my most beloved can make up her mind and go to Mr. Weißmann, or whatever his name is, who calls himself "Carlchen's friend." I think you should do it, because nothing should be left untried. I am very happy that you asked Georg to come over once again.

I assume that Fred has returned from his vacation by now and I would be *very* grateful to you if you asked him about the situation concerning the lawsuit. It is horrible how long that affair is dragging

---

[207] The August Bank Holiday in England.

out, and, without seeing a practical result, messages telling me that the affair was decided positively cannot satisfy me.[208]

So Pepper smoked a cigar already and even enjoyed it. That is the best proof that he is feeling better, because otherwise, smoking does not taste good at all. I find it less necessary that he has taken up his business correspondence again, but it probably gives him a certain satisfaction and there is nothing that can be done about it.[209] I am happy to hear that your dear mother looks a little better once again, after Pepper has smoked his first cigar, and I really hope that her worries have been calmed and her well-being has been restored completely.

Today, the English-French military mission arrived here and continued on to Moscow this evening. I regard that as a great step forward and admire the intelligence of the Russian government people who made this wonderful suggestion. I did not get to see much of those people, because I was busy and I am not a friend of rubbernecking anyway.[210]

Since I have not received an answer from Schapiro, I intend to apply for my exit visa on the 15th and travel to Moscow around the 20th, where I will try to get my Swedish visa so I can take the boat from Stockholm. We will talk in detail about your plan to accompany me on the next trip when I am home. I cannot tell you often enough just *how* happy I will be to have you with me, but there are so many "buts." First of all, my adorable girl wants to have a baby. Do you think it would be right to spend those difficult months here in the horrible cold of winter, if we succeed in laying the foundation for that? And then, you might have to make the trip back in your fifth or sixth month by sea which is very stormy at that time of the year!!! The second thing is that I would have loved to have you here in the summer, while it is especially beautiful and one can enjoy the fresh air by the sea or take a boat down the Neva while the famous white nights glow all around you. You can even play

---

208 War was to prevent any settlement from being fulfilled.
209 Mope is being ironic since Pepper's business ventures were invariably unsuccessful.
210 The much-publicized negotiations of the Anglo-French military delegation with the Soviet authorities turned out to be futile. Many historians now believe that Stalin and Molotov (the newly appointed People's Commissar for Foreign Affairs) deliberately intended to wrong-foot the delegation as a prelude to the non-aggression pact with Hitler, that was signed on 23 August. Before that date, Chamberlain and his cabinet as well as the public at large were unaware of the secret mediations between the Soviets and the Nazis.

tennis and I watched today and decided that there are some rather good players among the Pushniki. So there would be some diversion for you, while the winter does not offer anything besides the theater which you cannot visit every day either–and the language is completely unfamiliar anyway–and there would be nothing but the warehouse or the hotel room. But the "buts" seem stronger to me, and I did not even talk about the fact that your own earnings are of great importance to us, for as long as you can continue working and could help bridge any period of time during which I might be unemployed.

Now, I want to crawl into my chaste bed and dream of my most beloved, sweetest little witch and kiss you many, many times in your sleep, but unfortunately only in theory. Your Mope who longs for you most irreconcilably.

VERA TO MOPE

London, 10 August 1939

Tonight, all the lights have to be turned off in London from midnight to 4 a.m., because of the aerial defense maneuvers, so I have to hurry. The peace and quiet that we enjoy at home stand in stark contrast to all those disquieting newspaper reports.[211] My love, I am filled with worry and I only hope that I see things too bleakly.

Today, I received a very dear and detailed letter from Hilde Lewy from the U.S.A. It does not appear to be all that easy for newcomers to make a somewhat adequate living. Among other things, she also congratulates us on our *wedding anniversary* and wishes that all of us can live in one place at some point in the future.

My *lovielein*, I also believe that, if you can come to an amicable agreement with Schapiro, you should not break off the contract a year early, and since I now firmly intend to apply for the visa together with you, it will not mean another separation for us, I hope.

Most passionately and completely and utterly, *Your* Little Witch
Please think of the cigarettes!! I love you!!! I love you!!

---

211 Hitler had just threatened to wipe Poland from the map if it did not concede the disputed city of Danzig to the German Reich. The threat of war became more imminent by the day during August 1939.

MOPE TO VERA

Leningrad, 14 August 1939

You know, the tension inside me has grown to such immense proportions that I feel like someone who has ignored his hunger for such a long time that he can no longer imagine what eating food is like. My nerves are so hyper-stimulated because of it and this terrible waiting for news from my adorable little witch contributes to that in a rather acute manner– of course, my sweetest one is not to blame for that, but the damnable transportation.

I cannot do anything on the business side either and my work is mainly limited to begging for contract merchandise on a daily basis, since I would like to move ahead as much as possible, naturally, before I leave, so I will not have to tell myself that I neglected my duties because I left too early. But all my questions and pleas fail, because there is no merchandise and all of us who do not get any purchase orders are terribly dissatisfied and lose a lot of time that could be ever so precious if it were spent in a different way.

I still cannot give you an exact date for my return, since my traveling route depends on whether I will get a Swedish visa and how long I have to wait for it to be issued. Also, it takes about four to five days until I get my exit visa. I hope that I will be able to at least purchase some of the merchandise that has to be taken on right away during that time. I am quite sure that I will be able to stick to the 20th as the date of my departure from here and then, I have to spend two days in Moscow, so that I will fly from there to Stockholm on the morning of August 23. Should I get the Swedish visa, and I am quite sure that I will, I will travel by boat from Göteborg to London in order to avoid having to fly over that land of criminals. I wish the sea was already rocking me back and forth!

I see that Georg Rosenfeld felt quite at home again with you and I would welcome it if he could repeat his visit soon. So, I can already look forward to seeing his parents in London and I really wish that his optimism concerning four weeks will not meet with disappointment.

576 *No Life Without You*

Fig. 83 KADDISH (IN MEMORIAM): Photograph of Lies and Carl Rosenfeld typing letters to aid their escape, Karlsruhe, July 1939 (courtesy of their daughter-in-law Audrey Rosney).

Alas, Mope's wish was never fulfilled as Carl and Lies Rosenfeld were unable to get out of Germany. In August 1942, they were sent under arrest on a transport to Theresienstadt Concentration Camp, where they survived for a further two years. In October 1944, they were placed on separate transports to Auschwitz, where they were each liquidated upon their arrival. Their son, Georg (who anglicized his name to George Rosney), served in the British armed forces, and, at the cessation of hostilities in 1945, was given permission to search for them, only to discover the terrible truth.[212]

MOPE TO VERA

Leningrad, 15 August 1939

This morning, I received your most beloved message from 10th of the month and when I opened it, I ripped a small hole in the envelope from

---

212 For information on this, see Helen Fry in *The King's Most Loyal Enemy Aliens: Germans Who Fought for Britain in the Second World War* (Sutton Publications, 2007), 208-209. During my own post-war childhood, George was the closest thing to an elder brother to me.

which the words *I love you* shone into my eyes—you had written them on a corner of the sheet. That gave me such a joyful and warm feeling and made me happy that my sweetest one had created a little window for herself in order to speak those lovely sounding words to me.

Today, I applied for my exit visa and I have to say that this simple formal act improved my disposition many degrees, because I had been afraid for the last few days that there would be objections from Mr. Schapiro. The fact that there was no objection from him lets me believe more and more that the end of our relationship is near. That idiot is unable, like other people, unfortunately, to use information concerning the current business situation, but keeps looking for mistakes on my part. One cannot even really be mad at him because he cannot help it. He received my telegrams and on top of that, the copies of those telegrams are forwarded to him, but nevertheless, he forgets what is in them. If he could call by telephone, the situation would be simpler for him and the letters less abusive and stupid, because his memory would function better. If no interesting merchandise comes in, I will probably leave for Moscow on 20th August, and I have already let you know about the rest of my schedule—at least as far as it could be made, anyway.

The political tension is quite high at the moment, but I do not believe that it will come to an explosion before September and that should bring the end of the most disgusting criminal of all times, Hitler the damned. I wish we were past that already. I can hardly imagine that it will come to war and I am not looking towards the future all that pessimistically, since the strong democratic countries U.S.S.R., England, and France are banding together now.[213]

So my little angel really wants to travel with me—in the event I have to leave for here again? I wonder what you will have made of my conveyed misgivings. The auction inspections begin on October 22 and the auction itself on October 25 which means that I will have to be back here again on the 15th at the latest. And how will that be compatible with our plans of having a baby?

Please excuse my scribbled handwriting, but I am terribly tired and still have some work to do. *Your* Mope

---

213 By this time, Mope was increasingly aware of the imminence of war, and his remarks appear to be intended to assuage Vera's justifiable worries and fears.

VERA TO MOPE

London, 16 August 1939

Earlier today, I received your beloved lines from the 10th of the month. I am really hoping that these lines will not reach you in Leningrad, because you will already be on your way home when they arrive there. My *lovielein*, actually, I do not get the feeling that Schapiro is looking around for someone else; though if that is the case, it's just as well, or even, so much the better!!!!! So my *sweetheart* does not want to take me along in the winter!!!! Well, we shall see and hear what Dr. Rothschild has to say to that, just in case we need his advice, which I hope we do.

I do not know if I have told you that I asked Hanna, when I called her, where things are standing with the court case and she said that Fred still had not heard anything. It seems to me that he really is not attending to the matter and he probably has way too much to do anyway which is something I completely understand, and I think that we have to take the matter into our hands as soon as you are back.

I hope that my beloved has been receiving mail regularly. I do not think that I will write to you again on this trip but my greatest and best wishes accompany you constantly and without pause. *Completely your Little Witch*

MOPE TO VERA

Leningrad, 17 August 1939

I heard just a little while ago that my exit visa has already been approved and I will receive the passport on the 19th. Right after that, a telegram from Schapiro arrived asking me not to leave Leningrad before having fulfilled a new order for best quality Persian lamb skins. I replied that my exit visa had already been issued, and that I have to leave in the next few days because of it. I firmly intend not to extend my stay here and I am curious to see what I will hear in answer to my cable. About four days before I applied for the exit visa, I had telegraphed him one more time, just to be sure, that I would file the application on August 15 and did not receive an answer at all. And now, he wants to tell me anyway that I did not fulfill my duty because I left! I fail to see why I should stay here any longer since I am quite sure that it will come to a break between Schapiro and me anyway, and it is not my responsibility to retrieve the hot potatoes from the fire for him under these conditions. In any case, I will probably travel to Moscow on the 20th and, should I receive the Finnish visa, I will come back here for another day or two and try to get something done before I depart. If I do not get the visa, I will leave Moscow and fly to Stockholm, as I already told you, and I hope to reach the boat from Götenborg on the 23rd, which will arrive at Tilbury on the 25th around 10.30 in the morning. Despite all of it, it is more than unpleasant to me to leave with a request unfulfilled, because it is very important to me to try to maintain a good relationship with my clients.

In the meantime, I went on a long walk with a colleague, and that walk really felt good. As usual, we walked along the Newa, in which the streetlights were mirrored brightly, under the black sky with just a few stars, that has a calming effect on me. Tomorrow is Wychodnoi and all of us will go, or rather almost all of us, will watch an air show that is being held tomorrow around 3 p.m. I hope that the weather will be nice so that we can enjoy the sun. In the afternoon, I intend to start packing, because, as usual, there will be more work in the last two days than in the preceding two weeks.

Good night, my most beloved, sweetest girl. You have been asleep for quite a while already now and I wish you a good, peaceful, and recuperative sleep filled with beautiful dreams.

I am *most lovingly, completely,* and *utterly my* little Lilongo's Mope

VERA TO MOPE

London, 18 August 1939

I am afraid that I have treated you badly during the last few days, that is, the day before yesterday, I sent a letter to you airmail express to Leningrad and afterwards, after I received your telegram, I sent a postcard to Moscow, and since I hope that you will leave on the 20th, I only sent another card. Just a little while ago, my *sweetheart*, because I fear that you are pretty much without news from me there, I also sent you a telegram so you will not feel completely forgotten and alone. I can simply hardly wait until you are finally here with me safe and sound. Your Little Witch

MOPE TO VERA

Leningrad, 18 August 1939

When I got back to the hotel around 6 o'clock, much later than anticipated, from the air show, which took place in the most beautiful sunshine, I received a telegram from Schapiro, ordering me not to leave Leningrad before acceptance of the Persian lamb deal. I do not have any other choice but to extend my stay a few days and be terribly sad about that, because I was looking forward to our reunion ever so indescribably, a reunion that has now been postponed several days, and just how many is still not evident. I sent a telegram to my darling today to let her know and my heart ached and still aches, because I had to disappoint you. I do not dare to believe that I will receive the merchandise in the next few days and even if I do, it has to be good merchandise, which will have to be seen first. In any case, I intend to go to Moscow for the visa on the 20th so that I could travel via Finland, if necessary! Oh, it is just awful!

The flight performances at the air show were quite remarkable and I was greatly impressed when six big airplanes arrived all of a sudden and people actually rained down from them. At least 150 people jumped out of those airplanes within one minute, and their parachutes opened above them immediately. That was a unique and awesome spectacle. I hope that humanity will be spared and not be forced to get to know this same practice in war. As a sport however, it is beautiful to watch. I do not fancy trying it out myself, though!

My sweet one writes that she hopes her letter will not reach me here, but the transportation was so exceptionally speedy that it still would have reached me here even under altered circumstances. And now, you will have no idea where to send your beloved messages to me, and I am sure that I have confused you completely, but even I do not really know what will happen so that I cannot tell you anything more concrete. It seems to be nothing more than a dirty trick by Schapiro in order to keep me here longer. He is surely to blame for his stubborn refusal to accept any of my earlier offers. In all of his stupidity, that man wants to believe that he is smarter than anyone else. *Most lovingly* and *totally*, *Your* lover and Mope

VERA

Journal entry, 19 August 1939

This morning, I received a telegram from my beloved telling me that he will not be able to come back now, as planned, but he hopes that he will be back around the end of the month. I am disappointed and sad and I have had enough of this miserable separation! The next time, I will either travel with him or Mopelein will have to try to find something else. First of all, I will go to the *Home Office* with him in order to get *all visiting conditions cancelled*. And then, even if it means a smaller income, we will look around here for something. This is *no* life! I want to experience my life together with my husband and this time, an end has to be put to these endlessly long times of separation!!!

MOPE TO VERA

Leningrad, 19 August 1939

Today was another day without results and I fear that it will not be any better tomorrow. Nevertheless, I sent a telegram to Schapiro today to let him know that I will go to Moscow on the 20th and then, probably on the 23rd, I will come back here for two days in order to fulfill his wish, if at all possible. If everything goes according to my wishes–which have to undergo some alteration now–I will leave here via Helsingfors–no flying–on the 24th and if I am very lucky, I will catch the *Suecia* [214] in Göteborg on the 26th–I will arrive at Harwich at 10.30 on the 29th and at 1.04 p.m. at Liverpool Station. I hope that that is the last possible target date and of course, I will keep you informed as to when I will arrive. My desire to work has been reduced to a minimum, and understandably so, and all my thinking and being is concentrated 100% on my return home and the reunion with my little witch. After all, it is not all that important to me now what Schapiro thinks.

On 28th July, I had written to Schapiro that "I will travel home on August 10 at the latest, because I have only been at home for six weeks this year and under no circumstances can I let my wife wait any longer. I will also see if she can accompany me on the next trip, because this cannot be called living." On 11th August, I telegraphed that I would

---

[214] This was the same ship that Mope had taken on his outward journey.

be applying on the 15th for my exit visa. And neither the letter nor the telegram were answered, which I can only interpret as consent. As you can see, I was *very* fair and have already postponed my departure date a full two weeks, but more is out of the question!!! On top of that, those people in Paris do not recognize good will in any way and it is really out of place here anyway after the disgusting treatment on the part of Schapiro. There was a telegram from him today, "Stay requested otherwise great unpleasantness." My answer: "Greatest unpleasantness begging in vain for hard-earned money expenses," but after I calmed down a bit, I did not send it, because I am too good for that. However, he really deserves that answer and if he makes another sound, he will get it anyway.

My little witch will have a few days without letters and I hope will not be sad, because they are the days before my homecoming. Tomorrow is Sunday there and I hope with all my heart that it will offer you calmness and recuperation from the work week. I wish I had already left here, with a clear conscience knowing that I had fulfilled my duty. If it comes to the altercation with Schapiro, and I expect that to happen, I would rather not be forced to listen to unjustified accusations as far as that is possible. I am sure that you can understand that.

I cannot even write about my longing and my feeling of homesickness any longer, because these feelings overwhelm me and you keep me prisoner completely and with everything I am, my sweet little angel. *Completely* and *utterly*, *Your* Mope

MOPE TO VERA

Leningrad, 20 August 1939

And now, I did not leave here after all and the only good thing is that I am able to write to my most adorable darling this evening and thank you for your beloved telegram that was read to me on the telephone this morning. The reason for my not traveling is that my papers are not in order yet and it looks like that might take a few days. I am deeply depressed over this delay and I would like nothing more than to follow your telegraphed wish for a swift departure. Had I left for Moscow today, I would have tried to reach you tomorrow and I was already looking forward to that. Now, that has also been delayed for several days because of the Persian pelts, and I can only hope that I will not have to wait too long before I get everything done here so I can finally leave and come home to you, my most beloved.

A little while ago, I saw a red crescent moon of enormous size ascend the sky, so another new moon whose beginning we cannot experience together, but at least, we are counting on being able to spend its middle and descent together, and I cannot tell you *how* infinitely I long for that time!!! While I am writing this, I am hearing an opera unknown to me from somewhere, since the noise of the music takes away a little of the feeling of being alone, but while I am writing to my little witch, I really do not feel it at all because of our conversation, but other than that, I feel it quite strongly. I do not have a single human being here I can confide in and the letters take so infinitely much time before they are answered and the answer gets to me.

I kiss you, my sweetest, most beloved, most adorable Veralilongolein, overfilled with burning, loving longing that is ever so *painful* and *bitter* and I embrace you with infinite tenderness again and again. *Completely* and *totally* and *utterly*, *Your* Mope

MOPE TO VERA

Leningrad, 21 August 1939

Unfortunately, I expected things to work out differently where my departure is concerned, differently than it turned out to be due to the Persian lamb purchase, and asked you to send your mail to Moscow; and now, I am hoping to get there very soon, because your beloved letters will be waiting there for me. As I told you in my telegram earlier, I do not consider the situation quite as dangerous as it appears to you. Humanity will not be that insane and let itself be driven into a war in which not only the states will lose their wealth, but people will have to sacrifice their health and their lives. Everyone is aware of the fact that a new war would far surpass the previous imperialistic one in cruelty and would also put women's and children's lives in extreme danger.[215] Nevertheless, I am making every effort to leave here as soon as possible and come to my little witch after this interminable time of separation. Do I have to assure you of that?

---

215 Again here, Mope's remarks are intended to assuage Vera's worst fears, while he was doing everything in his limited power to quit the Soviet Union.

It seems that most of the colleagues are harboring thoughts of leaving, because there is not enough merchandise to make a stay worthwhile. After all, the expenses have to be met. After much effort, I was able to finalize a deal today that will give us about £1 after all is said and done, while another deal I had been counting on failed, because they want to reserve the merchandise for the auction. This auction is making business extremely difficult, because they are collecting all the merchandise instead of offering it on the open market.

In planning my departure, I will probably fly from Moscow to Stockholm, so I won't lose any more time on my way home, and then continue my travel by boat so that it should not take more than three days, while it would take at least five days from Moscow via Helsingfors. However, I cannot give you anything definite.

I am wondering if Ketty and David have finally arrived in London. You do not write anything about that in the last few letters, although you told me earlier that they were definitely expected last week.

Fig. 84 KADDISH (IN MEMORIAM): Card sized photograph of Ketty and David Goldschmidt.

Mope's urgent appeal was left unanswered. Ketty and David Goldschmidt did not get to England. In the weeks before the war, their brother-in-law, Fred Rau, had twice traveled to Hamburg with the express purpose of persuading them to leave Germany at once, but was apprised by David that first he needed to "take care of something of great importance" and only then would he be ready to leave. Though Ketty had received the requisite travel documents for herself, David was jailed just before her intended departure on charges of currency irregularities and attempting to conceal the family silver. In deciding how she should act, Ketty will have been torn between love for her four children in England and loyalty to her husband in Hamburg. Buckled by ill health and psychological stress, David is believed to have threatened to end his own life should she leave him, and so she opted to stay on. By the time he was released, hostilities had already commenced, and, when a transit visa through Norway was refused, the door out was permanently shut. The couple remained in Hamburg until June 1943 when they were deported to the Theresienstadt Concentration Camp. The following year, in September 1944, they were transported to Auschwitz and murdered in the gas chambers on 1 October. For all his herculean efforts, when recounting their tragic story, Fred commented with deep sorrow that "you see how essential it is to get one's priorities right!"[216] In his own desperation to return to England, Mope will have understood that only too well.

MOPE TO VERA

Leningrad, 25 August 1939 [Postcard]

I am leaving today!!! Today, I will begin drawing nearer to my sweetest, most adorable darling and turn into reality that which is continually on my mind: I am coming to you!!!! My heart is feeling lighter, my heart that longs for you ever so eagerly. I am beginning to feel happy again, because I will be with you soon.

How was it possible to bear this longing? I can see how much it depressed me by the way that feeling now gives way to the joy of looking forward to our reunion. I feel so much lighter every single minute that I am drawing nearer to you in time. I have started to feel happiness again. You, most beloved!! I am coming to you!! Your Mope

---

216 Fred Rau's lamentations are recorded by his children in a privately printed *Family Story: Fred and Hanna Rau and Their Forebears* (Jerusalem, 2019), 76. Through the most terrible tribulations both before and during the war, it is known that Ketty and David retained their profound religious faith until the end. For their children, that was their sole consolation.

MOPE TO VERA

Moscow, 26 August 1939

Just a little while ago, I talked to my most beloved, ever so beloved, sweetest girl. If you could feel *how* happy I am to have listened to your beloved voice!! Actually, I think I am farther away from you spatially here in Moscow than I was in Leningrad, but because of the opportunity to make that phone call, I am one thousand miles closer to you.

In just a few days, I will be with my most adorable little witch and I am happy. Oh, how I am looking forward to you!

Most passionately, most lovingly, *Completely* and *totally* and *utterly*, *Your* Mope

MOPE TO VERA

Moscow, 27 August 1939

I am leaving tomorrow morning!

There are no words for my joy in being able to take my adorable, sweetest, little witch into my arms again in just a few days and to find compensation for the difficult, unbearable time of separation in our caresses.

There are very few things I know for sure, but I am *absolutely* certain of one thing: I love you with all my ability to love, with all my heart, with my entire soul, with every drop of blood I have in me and I am my Lilongolein's Mope.

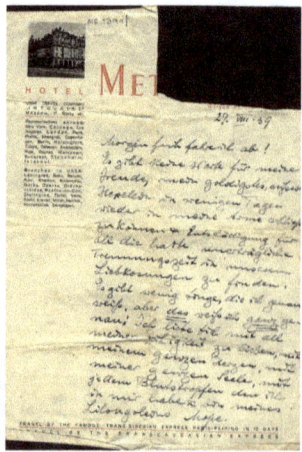

Fig. 85 Mope's final letter from Moscow, 27 August 1939. Pepper, an enthusiastic stamp collector, tore away a corner from the sheet while removing the stamp from the envelope.

The single egress for Mope that now remained open was by air and, providentially, an exit visa to leave the Soviet Union was issued to him. That in itself was insufficient. A seat still had to be found on an airplane traveling west when every flight was overbooked with frightened passengers endeavoring to escape Russia in advance of the now inevitable war. After waiting for at least a further day and failing to secure a direct connection, the flight that Mope boarded was from Moscow to Brussels, crossing over Germany. His itinerary would allow him to change planes in Brussels and then fly on to Croydon. Vera's reiterated fears about flying over Germany turned out to be far from illusory. Shortly after entering German air space, the pilot received a radio warning that, due to thunderstorms and poor visibility, he might not be able to bring the plane into land at Brussels. He announced to his passengers that he would be forced to take temporary shelter by landing in Berlin, which was directly below their flight path. Had they stopped in Berlin, it is certain that Mope, against whom there was a longstanding arrest warrant, would have been taken off the plane and never seen again. Fortunately, the pilot received a further radio signal that it was safe to continue with the flight, and he was able to touch down in Brussels according to schedule.

However, despite his relief of getting out of the Soviet Union and successfully flying over Nazi Germany, Mope was not fully in the clear. He learned at Brussels Airport that, because of the international situation, flights were cancelled, including his connection to Croydon. At least from Brussels, he could now be in telephone contact with Vera, though it remained indeterminate when and how he would be able to return to England. Following another day of uncertainty, he found himself free to travel to the coast and take the sea voyage across the English Channel to Dover, arriving close to midnight on Thursday, 31 August. After his documents were scrutinized by a single on-duty immigration officer, provisional entry was granted, and he was able to fall into the arms of his very relieved wife, who had traveled to the port in order to welcome him home. Both of them surmised that his arrival late at night had worked in his favor as his papers were subject to less scrutiny than would have been the case during the working day. The following morning, the Germans marched into Poland, and the Second World War began shortly after. Within days, cross-Channel ferry services were suspended indefinitely.

An entry in Vera's personal journal, written a few months after, revisits the events of August 1939 and lends a summation to those final days of extreme fear and uncertainty before Mope returned to her. It ends with some self-reflection and doubts about her own ability.

VERA

Journal entry, 28 December 1939

Strange that I take this book in hand on Dec. 28!!! After not having touched it for such a long time. For the last four months, the country has been at war. It brought my husband back to me, and now, while most families have been torn apart through the war, we can finally live our lives together.

The last days of August, until he returned, were very difficult, filled with fear and uncertainty. Many a times, I intended to take up this book during those days to put down exactly what I felt: to know that war would come, must come, and the man so far away, without even knowing if the authorities of this country would allow him to re-enter this country. The war did break out; what it meant, one was not quite able to realize at the time nor is one or am I really able to now.

Like all selfish people, I can only or I am in the first place concerned with what this war has brought for us (quite apart from thinking what horrors and what hardships, suffering hardships and pains, it is daily bringing to an unknown but surely large number of human beings, with whom one naturally and deeply empathizes).

What the war has brought us:

1) Mope back home and for the first time the possibility of living some continuous time together;

2) The chance for me to be at home and to get some practical experience in running a home, cooking, catering, etc.

3) The necessity of putting all our energy and strength into something new again, to adapt ourselves to new circumstances.

4) Mope has lost his position and a lot of trouble is connected with the way he was more or less pushed out of his employment.[217]

5) Difficulties at the Tribunal for Mope which have not yet been overcome.[218]

---

[217] Schapiro showed no sympathy with Mope for leaving the Soviet Union.

[218] Mope faced major problems with the British immigration authorities during the first two years of the war. These are summed up in his curriculum vitae where he writes: "Fortunately, I succeeded in getting an exit visa from the Russians three days before the German invasion into Poland, something I had applied for many weeks before, and I arrived in England during the night of the invasion. When the war broke out, I was ordered to appear before the police and was taken before a tribunal. My long stay in Russia and my return to England so immediately

The sad and weak part of *my* character is that, although I can see my flaws and realize I have them, I do not do anything to make things better, to solve the problem!!!!!!!–

I think it is pathetic that I, at almost thirty years old, with a rather normal brain and a good variety of training (university studies, business, welfare work, etc.) and a rather decent face still have not amounted to anything!!! It is high time to do something about that!!!!!!!!!!!!!!!!!!!!!!!

---

before the outbreak of the war really spoke against me, and for a long time, I was threatened with being sent overseas before I was interned."

Thirty-two: Afterword

Mope's precipitous flight from the Soviet Union had undoubtedly saved his life. In the early years of the war, before Hitler attacked Russia in June 1941, many Jewish refugees who had found asylum from the Nazis in the Soviet Union and some (like him) who had been there for business reasons were dispatched to certain death in Germany following the Molotov-Ribbentrop pact.

But, even in England, Mope's fate still hung in the balance. There was much that was suspicious for the British authorities when they considered that he had been allowed to leave Moscow on a stateless passport so soon before hostilities began. Within days of his arrival, he was arrested and hauled before a tribunal set up to ascertain whether he had been assigned to London as a Soviet undercover agent. It was within the latitude of the tribunal to ship him abroad or to incarcerate him as a suspected spy. Fortunately, he was able to give a convincing account of himself and he was released.

The war brought Vera and Mope together at last but it did not release them from the everyday responsibility of making sufficient income to sustain themselves and their immediate family. During most of the war, the couple's primary source of income was through Mope who established himself in the London fur trade. As well as also providing for Alice and Pepper, who had almost no assets, they needed to contribute on a regular basis to aid Mope's sister, Grete Moschytz, with her four young children. Additionally, along with Fred Rau who carried the lion's share, they helped with financial support for the four children of Ketty and David Goldschmidt, escapees from Germany under the Kindertransport scheme.

Widespread fear in Great Britain during 1940 that German refugees might harbor a "fifth column" led to mass detentions. On Wednesday, 17 July 1940, Mope was arrested for the second time since his return to England and held as Internee No. 80321 at Kempton Park Internment Camp (Sunbury, Middlesex) for more than a month, moved to Sutton Coldfield (outside Birmingham) during August 1940, and transferred once again to a camp at York Race Course from the end of August through September.

Surviving letters between husband and wife from this time (written exclusively in English rather than German and often labeled with a sticker, "OPENED BY CENSOR") indicate that conditions in these camps were bearable, Vera being permitted to visit her husband on several occasions. Because he spoke English rather better than many others, Internee No. 80321 was elevated to the position of "Clerk" with the task of acting as a liaison between the British officers and their prisoners. At York, he was entrusted among other things with the possession of a key, which (as he later expressed it) "I was charged to guard with my life until I would be ordered to relinquish it." A wooden tag on the chain shows that the key fitted the lock to "H.M. QUEEN'S W.C.," the royal family having been avid racing fans and regular visitors to the track during peacetime. Mope was never bidden to return the key, and to this day it remains under the close and rigorous guard of his descendants! The anecdote confirms his remark in one of his letters to Vera from Kempton Park that his time of internment seemed to him like "an unwanted but rather pleasant summer-holiday" (30 July 1940), reminding him not a little of her camping experiences for Marks & Spencer.

Fig. 86 Key to Her Majesty the Queen's W.C., York Race Course, entrusted to internee 80321 E. M. Felsenstein, appointed Clerk, September 1940.

In discussions with them many years later, they would express admiration both for the humanity shown for the most part by the soldiers that guarded the internees, and for what seemed to them the scrupulous fairness with which the British authorities in a time of war were disposed to study each individual case before deciding upon the possibility of release. For them as refugees, it was a significant marker of the difference between a vibrant democracy and a totalitarian state. During the period of his internment, Vera assembled numerous personal affidavits attesting to Mope's good character, his visceral hatred of Nazism, and loyalty to Great Britain. Among these, Otto Schiff, the influential Chairman of the Jewish Refugees Committee and early patron to Vera, emphasized that Ernst Moritz Felsenstein's "one wish is to remain in this country as a permanent resident and to help this country in its present struggle" (5 August 1940). Their friend, Frank Braham remarked of the couple that "as Jews their sense of appreciation of the freedom accorded them here is probably greater than that of refugees of other denominations" (5 August 1940). Several commented on Mope's capacity as a fur buyer to augment trade.

Upon his release, and no longer suspected of being an enemy alien, Mope was recruited into the Home Guard (an equivalent to the US National Guard) in which command he served until shortly after the end of the war, receiving a British Defense Medal for his service. Although awarded in different wars, he must have been among a small minority of soldiers to have been decorated both by the Germans and the British. As his unit was based in London, he was also able to combine his military duties with the pursuit of his fur-trade activities, having secured a position as a part-time buyer of pelts for a clothing company.

Fig. 87 Mope (middle row, third from left) with his Home Guard unit, in which he served from November 1941 through to November 1944.

Uncertainty over the course of the war and fear of a possible German invasion had led Mope and Vera to postpone their plans to start a family until they could be more confident of an allied victory. Entries in Vera's journal capture their decision-making. Significantly for one who had once shunned her ethnicity, her aspiration was that their child should be raised to be consciously Jewish.

VERA

Journal entry, 8 June 1943

Mope and I decided that we should try again to have a baby. We did not discuss it beforehand, but we both agreed and felt it was the right thing.

I am happy that we at last consider it right to produce a child. There are no signs of one yet, but I hope there will be soon. I feel though that I am hardly fit to bring up a child in the right way. I do not have the necessary self-discipline nor do I know anything of the meaning of life. But I just have the great desire to have a child. I want to try my best to care for it as well as possible; not to make it dependent on me; to bring it up to be a conscious Jew(ess) and not ashamed of its origin as I am.

Journal entry, 4 December 1943

It was a week yesterday since I have had some reason to believe that I am expecting a baby. I dared not write in here during the past week. Since 30 November I have been in a state of doubtful nervousness and apprehension and then of grateful joy. I was afraid it might not be true. In October I waited three days and then was terribly disappointed. Since June I have cried every month with disappointment and grief. I am happy now, pleased, grateful, hopeful! I don't mind at all whether it will be a boy or a girl nor does Mope. I would like twins best, as I think we should as a minimum have two children. I will try my very best to become a good mother and at the same time to continue to be a devoted wife. I have already told Mope that I do not know whether I am primarily a wife or a mother but that I hope to be both. I think of the coming child and the fact of its development with great happiness continuously. It is lovely to be expecting a child.

Journal entry, Westminster Hospital, 26 July 1944

Our first baby is to come! We expected the date of arrival to be August 8th. Actually, I was sure it would be two or three weeks later than that, and now I am in here two weeks earlier than I had expected.

I was born two days later on Friday, 28 July 1944 to the echoing of German flying bombs dropping on London. Vera's journal records my birth weight (6 lbs. 4 ounces), and daily feeding schedule –

"On first day, Friday 28th inst., had him 3 times: he only nibbled";
  "On second day, Saturday, feeding most painful, also on Sunday. Used zinc breast shields (tin hats) to heal soreness.";
  "On 2nd August as milk did not flow properly (ducts were blocked) breasts massaged and milk forced away with pumps, most painful";
  "On 7th August, weight went down to 6 lbs. 1 ounce";

"On 8th day, i.e. 4th August regained birth weight";

"Circumcision at 11 a.m. on 10th August, gave him a 4 minute feed on each side directly afterwards; went to sleep with some stroking and patting; all other feeds perfectly normal; good night", etc.

—and, "On 3rd September, first smile."

Vera describes these as "Just a few facts", though I doubt that many people of my generation will have so much recorded detail of their first days out of the womb. Perhaps we should see these entries as a late echo of her medical training that had been so cruelly cut short, though I am vain enough to interpret them as markers of a long-held aspiration finally fulfilled.

There was another significant episode that my parents recounted to me with some regularity. Mope's reserve duties in the Home Guard, and limited visiting hours at the hospital where I was born, obliged him to wait until the afternoon of my day of birth before he could gain access to the maternity ward. During the morning, he booked himself in for an early afternoon celebratory lunch at the Wooden Horse Restaurant on Kensington High Street, not far from their home. He also used the morning to telephone friends with the news that he had become a father.

Ray and Frank Braham, who had first succored Vera on her arrival in England some eleven years before, were ecstatic with the good news. Ray immediately invited Mope to join them for lunch at their home. With a confirmed reservation elsewhere, Mope refused. In addition, with the Brahams living on the eighth floor of a block of flats in Maida Vale, and flying bombs dropping indiscriminately on London, Mope considered it a far greater risk to be in their building. Ray was nothing but persistent, calling Mope numerous times, and insisting that he lunch with them. With reluctance, Mope agreed to join them.

As they sat down to eat at 1.30 in the afternoon, air raid sirens were sounded warning of another flying bomb attack. Mope was in trepidation that the Braham's tall building would be hit. Instead, they heard explosions coming from a distance before the "All Clear." Shortly after, he set off for the Westminster Hospital where he was able to visit Vera and meet their long awaited newborn for the first time.

On the journey home, he caught the Number 9 bus that connected through to Kensington. Looking out from the window, he was dismayed when he noticed that it was traveling a different route. When he enquired, the bus conductor told him that they had been diverted, and showed surprise that he hadn't heard that a flying bomb had fallen on Kensington High Street outside the Wooden Horse Restaurant and that everyone inside had been killed. I owe my father's life to

Frank and Ray Braham. In recognition, I was named after Frank and my sister after Ray.

It was on his initiative that, parents at last, Mope and Vera created their first child's birthday journal that they maintained each July 28 for the first four years of my life with the intention that "maybe, it will give you some pleasure later on; maybe some knowledge of your parents, and their thoughts; maybe some knowledge about yourself." Here are several extracts that capture their thought processes as they grappled with the realities of parenthood.

VERA

28 July 1945

This last year has been full of great events in the world. At last, peace in Europe came; will it be a lasting one this time? Will it? It is not possible to express how anxiously we wish and hope for it. If only you will be spared the experience of this most inhuman of all human doings.

Many thoughts have crossed our minds prior to your and since your arrival, centering about you, and also our relationship to you.

The problem wife/mother seemed to have worried me before you were born. It has solved itself quite easily during the past year. Let me try and explain how:

My husband is my trusted friend, partner of my life, lover. You have been given to us both on trust. We have to look after you to the best of our ability, to aim on making you independent of us, and be ready to let you fly off one day. You are an individual of your own, and of another generation with perhaps different ideas to our own. May we be able to help you develop your personality to its fullest capacity. Let us hope that your fundamental outlook on life will not be entirely different from our own.

28 July 1946

On your 2nd birthday my sweetheart, I want to put on record the part you play in our life: that of a common source of love, and of interest, and pleasure, and an object of deep, mutual responsibility.

As to the outside world, it has probably become even more politically unstable, and economically insecure than before. The position of the Jews in the world in general is most difficult, and their lot most deplorable. How deeply, we wish you to become a happy, considerate, imaginative, and active citizen of the world, and a well-balanced Jew.

Thirty-two: Afterword

Mope's gestation into fatherhood as witnessed in this first and only shared journal measures his first offspring's intelligence vis-à-vis his own. It is impossible to read these extracts without recognizing that his prognoses for his son are no less a reflection of his own struggles to confront and overcome the adversities with which he had had to contend.

MOPE

28 July 1945

You have got a very ambitious father, Franklin! More ambitious still for those next to him than for himself. His main concern since you have been on this world was–next to your health–the thought that you might or might not be intelligent. Feeling the back of your head was a good reassurance of the former! Really of much greater importance would have been to wish you to have the happiness to own a good character. Your parents hope to be sensible enough to help you retain such a disposition for all your long and happy life which I wish you on your first birthday.

28 July 1946

It is always a great event for me to see you when I wake up in the morning and when I come home at night. It is an event because you seem to enjoy seeing me just as much as I, seeing your laughing welcome. Very often I wonder whether, besides your charm, your intelligence will help you be on top of life when you are a grown-up man. I wish it for you, as intelligence in the right boundaries makes life so much more enjoyable. Intelligence will help you to understand and be grown up to the difficulties life is bound to throw on to your path. They will look like landslides, unsurmountable rocks blocking your way. But well administered brains will make obstacles shrink to nothing and let you overcome them stronger and with more self-confidence, and you will be proud of what you are and, even more so, of what you have made of yourself.

With the allied victory marking the end of the war, the physical and psychological strain that Mope had for so long endured caught up with him, taking its toll through excruciating pains caused by stomach ulcers, which forced him to interrupt work. That was to culminate at the end of 1946 with a total physical collapse and hospitalization. As had happened at the end of the Great War in 1918 when he was still a teenager, Mope found himself poised between invalidity and recuperation. Convalescence was slow. Approaching his late forties, it would take him at least six months to recover sufficiently to be able to contemplate a return to work. Even then, given his still precarious health and his stateless circumstances, the options before him remained uncertain.

It was only after the war that Vera and Mope became eligible for naturalization, first applying for British citizenship in 1945. These processes were slow, and they both had to wait approximately two years before that was granted. New citizenship seems to have given Mope a new lease of life and new hope. He simultaneously anglicized his first names from "Ernst Moritz" to "Ernest Maurice," while retaining the family surname which he felt his offspring should carry with pride. Starting again almost from scratch, he rebuilt his career as an independent fur trader, attracting back several pre-war clients of the long defunct Gebrüder Felsenstein and many new ones. With his increasing success, Vera eventually left personnel management and joined him as his office manager, and (as she put it) chauffeur, cook, wife, and sweetheart.

In the spring of 1948, looking to expand his business, Mope traveled to France, Switzerland, and Italy, visiting potential clients and returning with contracts to represent them at Sojuzpushnina's newly reconstituted fur auction in Leningrad that July. For a dozen years or more after that, Leningrad in late July became an annual event, Mope's mimeographed end-of-auction reports circulating widely and valued greatly by members of the international fur trade community. With his newly acquired British passport, travel to the Soviet Union was at once far easier. While a visa was still required, Sojuzpushnina made that a formality, though perhaps also harboring a secret agenda. During one of his first post-war visits to the USSR, the KGB attempted to bribe Mope into becoming a spy for Russia, and, upon learning of this after he returned to London, the British secret service urged him to enlist as a counterspy. Respectfully but firmly, he declined both invitations.

Shortly before this, Mope and Vera had purchased their own family home in an outer London suburb. My sister, my only sibling, was born there in September 1947. As parents, their paramount aim was to bring up their children in a happy and normal environment. In that, they succeeded brilliantly. Amid the joyful hullabaloo of everyday family life, the traumatic experiences that Ernst Moritz and Vera Hirsch Felsenstein had undergone and shared together as refugees were but rarely mentioned. To be able to look forward with confidence and hope rather than to dwell on the upsets and dislocations of the past was how they envisioned our lives.

In a new millennium, as I assembled and edited my parents' letters, I came at last to understand that their story and experience was–and is–a large portion of my birthright and who I am today. The realization is humbling, yet also a source of fulfilment in that I find myself uniquely positioned to convey their incomparable love story and refugee experience to the next generation. Vera and Mope, my dear parents, I thank you and wish you to know (if you don't already!) that I think of you every single day. At the very heart of my own being I have come to appreciate that, in far more than one sense, there would be no life without you.

Fig. 88 Photograph of Mope and Vera, undated but early 1950s.

Fig. 89 Post-war photograph of Mope and Vera at a family celebration in 1960.

Glossary of Names

Aliyah
"Making Aliyah" is the shorthand allusion to the immigration of Jews from the diaspora to the geographical land of Israel or Palestine as it was in the 1920s and 1930s. It is considered as one of the most basic tenets of Zionism.

Alice (also known as Alicechen) > See Homberger

Annelie > See Freimann

Braham, Ray and Frank
Ray Braham befriended Vera shortly after her arrival in England in 1933 and, learning of her predicament as a refugee, offered her accommodation in her Chelsea home. Born Ray Rockman in San Francisco, she had trained as an actress under Sarah Bernhardt, who described her as her most gifted pupil. After marrying Frank Braham, a former colonial administrator, she became well known in the upper echelons of London society as a highly accomplished organizer of charity events. The couple, who were childless, remained very close friends of Vera and Mope, who named their own offspring after them. Frank died in the mid-1950s, and "Granny Ray" (as she was called) lived for another twenty years, passing away at the grand old age of one hundred and two.

Cooper, Ernest Napier
Principal of the Aliens Department at the British Home Office, Ernest Napier Cooper, OBE (1883-1948) was deeply committed to alleviating the plight of Jewish refugees from Nazism. Vera was introduced to him by Otto Schiff (q.v.) in 1933, and he remained her chief contact with the British authorities during the following decade. In the correspondence, his name ("Cooper & Co."; "Mr. Cooper's colleagues") is often used as a shorthand and partially covert reference to dealings by Mope and Vera with British government officialdom.

Felsenstein, Adolf and Gretl
Born two years before him, Adolf Felsenstein (1897-1977) was Mope's only brother. He was an officer in the German army during World War 1, and then joined the Gebrüder Felsenstein in his native Leipzig. A committed Zionist, he relinquished his partnership in 1935 so as to move to Palestine, for which he trained as a plumber. He was married in 1928 to Gretl Felsenstein, née Stiebel (1904-1991), a physician's daughter from Frankfurt.

Felsenstein, Ernst Moritz (Mope)
The co-correspondent of this volume, Ernst Moritz Felsenstein (born 19 June 1899; died 27 June 1973) anglicized his given names to Ernest Maurice after the Second World War. His nickname was Mope (rhyming with "coper" or "hoper").

Felsenstein, Helene
Born in Cologne, Helene Felsenstein (1874-1963), Mope's mother, was the second daughter of Georg and Gertrud Marx of Königsberg. She married Isidor Felsenstein on 1 January 1895, and they had seven children. In the family, she was known as Oma Lenchen (i.e. Granny Helen). She left Leipzig in 1938, settling in London. Her relationship with Mope, her second son and third child, was particularly close.

Felsenstein, Isidor
Born in Fürth, Isidor Felsenstein (1866-1934), Mope's father, was the tenth child of Noah Abraham and Hanna Felsenstein. In 1889, he was sent to Leipzig to establish what became under his guidance the new headquarters of the Gebrüder Felsenstein, the family-owned fur trade business. In 1895, he married Helene Marx. They became bastions of the Leipzig Orthodox Jewish community. When he died in 1934, he had been for many years head partner of the Gebrüder Felsenstein. His relationship with Mope, his second son, was often tempestuous, though they began to understand and appreciate one another better during his final years.

Felsenstein, Semy
After the death of Isidor in 1934, his nephew, Semy Felsenstein (1883-1978) became the senior partner in the Gebrüder Felsenstein. A placid individual, who rarely showed his emotions, Semy often had to play the part of mediator in company disputes. In 1937, it was he who warned Mope not to return to Germany from the Soviet Union after the SS had

put out an arrest warrant against him. Following Kristallnacht, Semy was arrested and sent to Buchenwald. He was forced to sell the company's remaining foreign assets to buy his way out of Germany. In England, where he settled, he continued in the fur trade for many years. Mope always spoke of his "decency," though his undemonstrative character did not always endear him to Vera.

Frank > See Braham

Fred > See Rau

Freimann, Annelie
During the 1930s, Annelie Baruch (1914-2008) took the surname of her stepfather, Dr. Freimann, a Leipzig internist. She was a distant cousin of Vera. It was when visiting Annelie in Leipzig in January 1936 that Vera was introduced to Mope. Despite the Nazi regime, Annelie qualified as a dentist and practised in Berlin for a short time. In late 1938, she received permission to settle in the United States, where she married Arno Herzberg, another refugee.

Goedicke, Erich
Known as "Max," Goedicke was an employee of the Gebrüder Felsenstein in Leipzig.

Goldschmidt, Ketty and David
Mope's oldest sister Ketty (1896-1944) married David Goldschmidt (1890-1944), an insurance agent in 1922. They lived in Hamburg. They were unable to escape Nazi Germany and perished at Auschwitz. Their four children, Lassar (1922-1992), later known as Leslie, Gertrud (1924-2010), Gabriel (1927-2020), and Alfred (1930-2018), were all rescued and came to England under the *Kindertransport* scheme in 1938 and 1939. Ketty and Mope were particularly close to each other.

Grete > See Moschytz

Haavara
"A company for the transfer of Jewish property from Nazi Germany to Palestine. The Trust and Transfer Office Haavara Ltd., was established in Tel Aviv, following an agreement with the German government in August 1933, to facilitate the emigration of Jews to Palestine by allowing the transfer of their capital in the form of German export goods. The

Haavara Agreement is an instance where the question of Jewish rights, Zionist needs and individual rescue were in deep tension.... The amounts to be transferred were paid by prospective emigrants into the account of a Jewish trust company (PALTREU – Palestina Treuhandstelle zur Beratung deutscher Juden) in Germany and used for the purchase of goods, which the Haavara then sold in Palestine.... The Haavara continued to function until World War II, in spite of vigorous attempts by the Nazi Party to stop or curtail its activities." – see https://www.jewishvirtuallibrary.org/haavara.

Hanna; Hannalein > See Rau

Heinz > See Littauer

Heising
A fellow student with Vera in the medical school at the University of Frankfurt. She treated him with some disdain, which was more than justified when he joined the Nazi party and spurned future contact. Although his later identity remains insecure at present, he may be Dr. Helmut Heising who won the Iron Cross and other awards for his wartime service and affiliation with the Third Reich – see the website of *Traces of War* at https://www.tracesofwar.com/persons/14604/Heising-Dr-Helmut.htm.

Helenchen > See Felsenstein, Helene

Herzberg, Karl
Leipzig-based furrier who denounced Mope to the Nazis.

Hirsch, Alice
Vera's mother, Alice Hirsch (née Ettlinger) was born in Frankfurt-am-Main on 9 November 1875. She married Hermann Hirsch in 1900, and emigrated from Germany in 1934. She was naturalized as a British subject in 1947, and died in Epsom, Surrey, on 31 March 1956 at the age of 80. In the correspondence, she is referred to by her daughter as "Mutti" or "Muttlilein."

Hirsch, Gretel 1901-1935
Vera's mentally incapacitated elder sister.

Hirsch, Hermann

Known as "Pepper," Hermann Hirsch was Vera's father. He was born in Hanau, Germany, on 23 September 1870 and died in London on 7 July 1944 at the age of 73.

Hirsch, Vera (Vera Felsenstein after 1 August 1937)

The co-correspondent of this volume, Vera Hirsch was born in Frankfurt-am-Main on 23 January 1910 and died in London on 18 September 1992. She and Mope married on 1 August 1937. Among terms of endearment used by Mope when addressing her in the correspondence are "Lilongo" and "Hexelein" (translated here as "Little Witch").

Homburger, Alice

Mope's sister and twin of Grete Moschytz, Alice was born in 1901 and, when she died in 1993, was the last surviving child of Isidor and Helene Felsenstein. She married Julius Homburger, a physician, in 1926, and left Germany for Palestine in 1935.

Intourist

"A Russian tour operator, headquartered in Moscow. It was founded on April 12, 1929, and served as the primary travel agency for foreign tourists in the Soviet Union. It was privatized in 1992." (Definition from Wikipedia, https://en.wikipedia.org/wiki/Intourist).

Jacobson

A retired state notary, Hermann Jacobson was born in Dresden in 1875. He became Mope's landlord in Leipzig. In several letters "Jacobson" is used as a coded reference to Germany or Leipzig. Although his fate is unknown, it is thought that Jacobson did not survive the Holocaust.

Ketty > See Goldschmidt

Lewy, Hilde

Hilde Lewy, née Mayer, born in 1909, was Vera's closest friend and confidante from schooldays. In Genoa in 1934, she married Walter Lewy, an attorney whose family had emigrated from Germany to Italy. Vera and Mope visited them on their honeymoon in 1937. With their baby daughter Renate, the Lewys left Italy for the United States in 1939, settling in Atlanta, GA. Vera was heartbroken by the early death of Hilde in 1956.

Lilongo > See Hirsch, Vera

Littauer, Ruth and Heinz
Ruth Littauer (1902-1971) was Mope's fourth sister. She married Heinz Littauer (1893-1973), a fur merchant. They emigrated to England in 1935. Their daughter, Eve (1932-2016) was born in Leipzig, and their son, Ernest, in London in 1936.

Max > See Goedicke and also Schwimmer

Mitja > See Simonoff

Mope; Mopelein; Mopeleinchen > See Felsenstein, Ernst Moritz

Moschytz, Grete and Norbert
Grete Moschytz (1901-1975) was Mope's sister, the twin of Alice Homburger (q.v.). She was married to Dr. Norbert Moschytz (1895-1974). Before the war, they lived in Freiburg, Germany. With her brother-in-law, Fred Rau (q.v.), as her main financial guarantor but also with help from Mope, Grete brought their four children to England in May 1939. Norbert had left Freiburg for Davos, Switzerland, prior to Kristallnacht in 1938, and remained there through the war. Later, Norbert with Grete settled in Stuttgart, Germany.

Mutti, Muttilein > See Hirsch, Alice

Norbert > See Moschytz

Oma Lenchen > See Felsenstein, Helene

Pal Treu > See Haavara

Pepper > See Hirsch, Hermann

Pushniki
The informal name, derived from Sojuzpushnina (q.v.), applied to themselves by the small group of western fur traders permitted to work in the Soviet Union in the years leading to the Second World War.

Rau, Hanna and Fred
Mope's youngest sister, Hannah (1910-1957) had married Fred Rau (1906-1956) in 1932. Fred came from a prominent Orthodox Anglo-Jewish family with roots in Germany, and was a partner in a successful

metal commodities business. At considerable personal risk and financial outlay, he traveled to Germany on numerous occasions before the war to help secure the emigration of family members and others. They had three children, John (b. 1933), Stephen (b. 1936), and Doris (b. 1938).

Ray > See Braham

Rosenfeld, Lies and Carl (Karl)
Karl Rosenfeld (1883-1944) of Karlsruhe, Germany, was a second cousin to Mope. Karl fought for Germany in World War 1, and was severely wounded in battle. Elisabeth "Lies" Rosenfeld (1997-1944), née Willstater, was Karl's second wife, and the mother of their two sons, Georg and Benjamin. Mope befriended the Rosenfelds when he was a student at the Technische Hochschule at Karslruhe in 1923 and 1924. Despite strenuous and nearly successful efforts, Karl and Lies were unable to leave Germany. They were deported to Theresienstadt in 1942 and died at Auschwitz in 1944.

Rosenfeld, Georg
The elder son of Karl and Lies Rosenfeld, he emigrated to England without his parents in 1939. He anglicized his name to George Rosney (1921-1991) and fought in the British Army during World War II.

Rosenfeld, Dr. Julius
Younger brother of Karl Rosenfeld, Julius (1887-1948) emigrated to Palestine, and tried without much success to help Mope navigate the complex rules of the Pal Treu scheme (q.v.).

Rothschild, Claire and Paul
Born in Mannheim, Dr. Paul Rothschild (1901-1965) worked with Dr. Franz Volhard (q.v.) in Frankfurt. Shortly after the Nazis came to power, he emigrated to England, and, by chance, met Vera in Hyde Park. He became of Mope and Vera's physician. His wife, Claire, née Wohlgemuth (1898-1985) was a close family friend.

Schapiro, Ruwim
Mope's absent boss during his two years in the Soviet Union. He was the head of the Compagnie Internationale de Pelleteries, based in Paris. Their relationship, which began well, became increasingly antagonistic. It is not known to me whether Schapiro survived the war.

Schiff, Otto
Nephew of the banker Jacob Schiff, Frankfurt born Otto Schiff (1875-1952) settled in Britain in 1896 and became a partner in his family's merchant banking firm. He founded the Jewish Refugees Committee that provided a vital support network to aid refugees from Nazi Germany seeking escape in Great Britain. He was President of the Jews' Temporary Shelter set up in London. In Frankfurt, he had been a friend and admirer of Alice Ettlinger, his exact contemporary and later, as Alice Hirsch, Vera's mother.

Simonoff, Mitja
Russian born short-term suitor of Vera prior to her meeting with Mope.

Sojuzpushnina
The name of the Russian company which from the 1930s ran major fur auction sales in Moscow and Leningrad (present-day St. Petersburg).

Stiebel, Joan
Christian born Joan Siebel (1911-2007) was secretary to Otto Schiff (q.v.) from 1933. Later, she was awarded the M.B.E. for her work in bringing Jewish concentration camp orphans to the United Kingdom

Volhard, Dr. Franz
Vera's principal teacher at the medical school of Frankfurt University, Franz Volhard (1872-1950) advised her on her course of action following the coming to power of the Nazis in 1933. Despite his status as the university's leading clinician, his refusal to comply with the new regime led to his dismissal. He was reinstated in 1945 but died prematurely in 1950 following an automobile accident.

Wychodnoi; Pod-Wychodnoi
In the Soviet calendar of the 1930s, every sixth day was known as "Wychodnoi", i.e. a day off work. Pod-Wychodnoi was the eve of Wychodnoi.

Select Bibliography

Black, Edwin, *The Transfer Agreement: The Untold Story of the Secret Pact between the Third Reich and Jewish Palestine* (New York and London: Macmillan Publishing Company, 1984).

Bouverie, Tim, *Appeasement: Chamberlain, Hitler, Churchill, and the Road to War* (London: Tim Duggan Books, 2019).

Ed. Cassel, Chava, *The Felsenstein Family Chronicle* (Jerusalem: Privately Printed, August 2000). [The text to this book was based on a personal account of the Felsenstein family written by Dr. Ernst Felsenstein of White Plains, New York, a first cousin of my father. The Chronicle version has been heavily bowdlerized. Dr. Felsenstein's daughter, the late Anne Warner, supplied me with a copy of her father's original typescript to which I am indebted for several significant details. She gave me full permission to utilize the full text where it supplied additional information.]

Chamberlain, Geoffrey, *Special Delivery: The Life of the Celebrated British Obstetrician William Nixon* (London: Royal College of Obstetricians and Gynaecologists, 2004).

Drucker, Peter F., *Adventures of a Bystander* (New York: John Wiley & Sons, Inc., 1994).

Dubrovsky, Gertrude, *Six From Leipzig* (London: Vallentine Mitchell, 2004).

Felsenstein, Ernst Moritz, "Das Palästina-Amt Leipzig", *Leipziger Jüdische Zeitung*, 24 March 1922, pp. 2-3, https://sachsen.digital/werkansicht/268758/1?tx_dlf_navigation%5Bcontroller%5D=Navigation&cHash=87bb86b787064412e683b4455dc8a3dd

Felsenstein, Frank (curator), *Max Schwimmer 1895-1960: Works in British Collections* (Exhibition Catalogue, University Gallery Leeds, March 1984).

Feniger, Mani, *The Woman in the Photograph: The Search for My Mother's Past* (El Cerrito, CA: Keystone Books, 2012).

Feuchtwanger, Lion, *The Oppermanns*, translated from the German by James Cleugh (New York: The Viking Press, Inc., 1934).

Fränkel, Jury, *Einbahnstrasse: Bericht Eines Lebens* (2 vols., Murrhardt: Rifra-Verlag, 1971, 1972).

Friedländer, Saul, *Nazi Germany and the Jews, Volume 1: The Years of Persecution, 1933-1939* (New York: Harper Perennial, 1997).

Fry, Helen, *The King's Most Loyal Enemy Aliens: Germans Who Fought for Britain in the Second World War* (Stroud, Gloucestershire: Sutton Publications, 2007).

George, Magdalena, *Max Schwimmer: Leben und Werk* (Dresden: VEB Verlag der Kunst, 1981).

Grenville, Anthony, *Jewish Refugees from Germany and Austria in Britain 1933-1970* (London: Vallentine Mitchell, 2010).

Harmelin, Wilhelm, "Jews in the Leipzig Fur Industry", *Leo Baeck Year Book IX* (London, Jerusalem, and New York: East and West Library, 1964), pp. 239-266 [Information for this article was provided by EMF].

Johnson, Eric A. and Reuband, Karl-Heinz, *What We Knew: Terror, Mass Murder, and Everyday Life in Nazi Germany: An Oral History* (New York: Basic Books, 2005).

Kaplan, Marion A., *Between Dignity and Despair: Jewish Life in Nazi Germany* (New York: Oxford University Press, 1998).

King, David, *Death in the City of Light: The Serial Killer of Nazi-Occupied Paris* (New York: Crown, 2011).

London, Louise, *Whitehall and the Jews, 1933-1948: British Immigration Policy, Jewish Refugees and the Holocaust* (Cambridge, UK: Cambridge University Press, 2000).

Max Schwimmer: Liebling der Musen (Exhibition Catalogue, Galerie Himmel, Dresden, 2017).

Rau, John, Stephen, and Doris, *Family Story: Fred and Hanna Rau and their Forebears*, translated from the Hebrew by Esther Toledano Boreda (Jerusalem: Privately Printed, 2019).

Scholem, Gershon, *From Berlin to Jerusalem: Memories of My Youth* (New York: Schocken Books, 1987).

Shatkes, Pamela, *Holocaust and Rescue: Impotent or Indifferent? Anglo-Jewry 1938-1945* (London: Palgrave, 2002).

Stuhr, Inge, *Max Schwimmer: Eine Biographie* (Leipzig: Lehmstedt Verlag, 2010).

Weber, Louis, publisher, *The Holocaust Chronicle: A History in Words and Pictures* (Lincolnwood, IL: Publications International Ltd., 2000).

Ed. Winston, Richard and Clara, *Letters of Thomas Mann* (2 vols., London: Secker & Warburg, 1970).

Index

Amsterdam 206, 211, 342, 391, 424
Anschluss 8, 228, 307–308, 341, 349
anti-Semitism 2–3, 5, 8, 31, 43–45, 48, 52, 62–71, 65, 67, 73, 82–83, 89, 98, 100, 119–121, 168, 181, 205, 257, 268, 355, 360, 363, 382, 384, 393–394, 417–418, 424, 447–448, 459, 463–464, 469, 486
Antwerp 102, 235, 239, 243, 258, 266, 287, 299–304, 306, 308, 344, 379
Aryan 6–7, 45, 48, 64, 70, 74, 82–83, 120, 181, 374, 488
Aryanization 51, 82, 159, 197, 352, 363, 418
Auschwitz 48, 188, 538, 576, 585, 603, 607
Austria 2, 8–10, 228, 283, 307–308, 351

Balfour Declaration 1917 8, 99
Bar Mitzvah 25, 28, 73–74, 95–96, 98
Bavaria 41, 119
Belgium 3, 7, 170, 206
Berlin 60, 62, 99, 102, 119–120, 154, 161, 163, 170, 176, 181, 186, 189, 191, 194, 198, 210, 213, 221–222, 224, 239, 252, 260, 343–344, 403, 412, 488, 515, 532, 548, 587, 603
Blackpool 352, 357, 360, 364–365, 368–369, 372
Braham, Frank 92
Braham, Ray Rockman 90–92, 110, 190, 523, 536, 593, 595, 595–596, 596, 601, 603, 607
Britain 2–3, 7–9, 34, 83, 88, 110, 119, 181, 193, 308, 349–350, 418, 420, 422, 513–515, 540, 545, 576, 591–592, 608
Buchenwald 9, 257, 419, 421, 441, 603

Canterbury 139, 142–144, 292
Central British Fund for German Jewry (CBF) 8–9
Chamberlain, Neville 181, 350, 414–415, 418, 421, 434, 440, 443, 545, 573
Christmas 21, 45, 194, 295, 311, 313, 359, 422, 430, 434
citizenship 83, 121, 307, 350, 352, 361, 383, 417, 462, 499, 598

Cold War 55
Communism 9–10, 56–57, 367
Communists 4, 6, 50, 61–62, 257, 292
Compagnie Internationale de Pelleteries 235, 254, 257, 286, 608
concentration camp 62, 259, 350, 441, 460, 495, 608. *See also* Auschwitz, Buchenwald, Theresienstadt
Cooper, Ernest Napier 88, 323–324, 326, 335, 339, 341, 362, 368–369, 420, 528, 533, 536, 601
Czechoslovakia 7, 9, 159, 170, 177–178, 186–187, 349, 351, 414, 417, 434, 459, 487, 510
  Sudetenland 178, 187, 350, 354, 414, 417, 434

Dachau 9, 62, 421
Dominican Republic 2
Dover 146, 149, 155–156, 587
Dresden 219, 223–224, 226, 229, 231, 242, 244, 605

England 7, 9, 14, 56–57, 67, 69–70, 81, 83, 86, 88, 91, 93, 103–104, 120, 123–124, 139, 145, 152–153, 187, 205–206, 219, 246, 258–259, 276, 286–288, 301, 307–308, 321, 324, 335, 350–352, 364, 369–370, 372–373, 381–382, 403, 415, 418–421, 433, 441, 443, 450, 452, 460–461, 467, 480, 484, 495, 513–515, 519–521, 529, 543, 554, 572, 577, 584–585, 587–588, 591, 595, 601, 603, 606–607
English 14–15, 17, 20–21, 36, 57, 86, 94, 99–100, 103, 110, 112, 125, 149, 151, 189–190, 193, 261, 263, 286–287, 289, 292, 319, 323, 365, 369, 415, 435, 439, 465–467, 545–546, 573, 587, 592
escape 7, 9–10, 14, 42, 52, 57, 74, 78, 82–83, 86, 194, 198, 206, 236, 308, 321, 365, 419–421, 423–424, 452, 454, 460, 463–465, 469, 514, 537, 576, 587, 603, 608

Fascism 9

Fascist 10, 50
Felsche's cafe 184, 198, 205, 209, 211, 214, 216, 222, 225, 228, 236–238, 246, 248
Felsenstein, Adolf 24, 26, 28–29, 31–32, 73, 75, 75–77, 77, 82, 100, 131, 287
Felsenstein, Alice 24, 77–78, 100, 131, 155, 287, 405, 409, 440–441, 445–446, 448, 456, 470, 477, 479, 481
Felsenstein, Ernst Moritz. *See* Felsenstein, Mope
Felsenstein, Grete 24, 80–81, 155, 160, 240, 259, 286, 372–373, 376, 390, 394, 399, 419, 422–423, 434, 441, 449, 462, 484, 489, 498, 514, 519–520, 524, 528, 532, 540, 543–544, 546, 591, 603, 605–606
Felsenstein, Hanna 24, 78, 81, 128, 139–140, 170–171, 229, 248, 262, 294, 301, 303, 305, 334, 337, 373, 385, 390, 394, 401, 410, 423–424, 433, 448, 453–454, 460, 466–470, 472–474, 477–478, 481, 484–485, 489, 520, 542–543, 578, 585, 602, 604, 606
Felsenstein, Helene 24–25, 39–40, 42, 53, 75, 81–82, 96, 98, 100–101, 113, 140–142, 144, 146, 151–152, 154, 159–160, 162, 168, 170, 173, 183, 185, 197, 199, 202–203, 207–209, 211, 213, 218, 223, 225, 232, 236, 238–240, 242, 245–246, 249, 252, 254, 259, 265, 283–284, 286–287, 296, 303, 308, 314, 325, 334–335, 337, 340–341, 352, 363, 372–377, 385, 387, 390, 394, 400–401, 405, 410, 413, 421, 423–424, 428, 433, 441–442, 446, 448, 451–452, 454, 467, 470, 472, 477, 484, 489, 496, 498, 505, 515, 519–520, 522, 524, 527, 532–533, 540, 546, 548–549, 552, 554, 571, 573, 602, 604–606
 emigration to England 352, 372–373, 394
 marriage to Isidor Felsenstein 40
Felsenstein, Isidor 24–25, 27–29, 41–42, 49, 73–75, 79–82, 96, 142, 155, 160, 183, 239, 409, 420, 602, 605
 death 75, 81–82
 escape to Prague 73
 marriage to Helene Felsenstein 40
 return to Leipzig 74

Felsenstein, Ketty 9, 24, 80, 160, 207, 223, 240, 301, 305, 372–373, 376, 382, 419, 422–424, 434, 448, 453, 456, 460, 462, 466, 468–470, 472, 484, 490, 505, 514, 519, 522, 528, 532, 538, 540, 545, 548–549, 552–553, 559, 561, 571–572, 584–585, 591, 603, 605
Felsenstein, Mope
 and Palestine 76, 95–102, 131–147, 151, 182
 army service 24, 29–32
  wounds 31, 40
 arrest in Britain 591–592
 arrest in Germany 205
 close relationship with mother 39, 40–41, 42, 81
 denounced to Nazis 258–259. *See also* Herzberg, Karl
 difficult relationship with father 28–29, 39–41, 42, 49
 early romance 80
 education 40–41, 42
 escape from bomb 595–596
 experience of fatherhood 596–597
 family business 42, 49, 82, 183–184, 195, 363. *See also* Gebrüder Felsenstein
 flight from Russia 578–588
 future ambitions 26, 49
 independent businessman 598
 jealousy of Mitja Siminoff 198, 200–202
 library and art collection 50–51
 marriage proposal to Vera 139–153
 meeting Vera 124–126
 religion 26, 30–31, 40–41, 95
 service in the Home Guard 593, 595
 smoking 31, 150, 317–319, 323, 326, 333, 354, 369, 387, 488, 514, 517–518, 521–523, 529–532, 534, 537, 540, 544, 563, 568–569, 573–574
 temper 30
 wedding to Vera 259, 285–286
 work in Russia 257–284, 286–306, 310–345, 358–381, 382–416, 420–457, 461–511, 515–588

Felsenstein, Ruth 24, 78–81, 140, 144, 186, 373, 376, 390, 606

Felsenstein, Semy 82, 154–155, 182, 188, 198, 207, 210–211, 222–223, 226–227, 231, 248, 250–251, 259, 284, 313, 352, 387, 419, 422, 435, 441, 469, 602–603

Finland 346, 381, 514–515, 519, 535, 580

First World War 3, 5, 7–8, 28, 31, 41, 70, 95, 98, 119, 206, 382, 382–383, 409, 421, 598

France 2–3, 7, 17–18, 20, 29, 31, 33, 37, 57, 79, 183, 206, 229, 260–261, 263, 283, 286, 293, 298, 307, 349–350, 352, 356, 381, 383, 385, 388, 392, 395, 399, 409, 416, 418, 425, 452, 513, 561, 573, 577, 598

Franco, Francisco 18, 119, 243, 459

Franco-Prussian War 18

Frankfurt 3, 13–14, 16–21, 33, 35, 48, 63, 65–67, 70–71, 73, 84–85, 87–89, 103–104, 107, 141, 198, 210, 349, 365, 393, 421, 602, 604–605, 607–608
  Oberlindau
    Hirsch family home 19–21, 103

Freiburg 80, 160, 222, 259, 286, 382, 390, 441, 606

Freimann, Annelie 120–121, 123, 125–127, 149, 155, 162, 167, 171, 200, 212–216, 218, 225, 307–308, 310–312, 314, 316–317, 319–320, 324, 332–333, 336, 382, 403, 409, 423, 454, 469, 479–480, 495, 520, 522–523, 526, 536, 557, 561, 601, 603

Gebrüder Felsenstein 27–29, 40, 49, 73–76, 81–82, 154, 170, 174, 181–183, 188, 192, 197, 210, 219, 221, 226–227, 235–237, 244, 247, 257, 263, 307, 310, 313, 352, 363, 373, 419, 423, 430, 441, 469, 598, 602–603

Genoa 286, 308, 323, 325, 328, 332, 365, 382, 384, 393, 431, 446, 452, 454, 461, 474, 605

Goldschmidt, David 63, 80, 206, 246, 301, 382, 419, 422, 424, 434, 448–449, 456, 460, 462, 466–467, 476–477, 490, 514, 519, 521–522, 546, 584–585, 591, 603, 605

Great Depression 4–5

Haavara 101–102, 159, 161, 163, 165, 182, 189, 197, 202, 219, 237, 244, 248, 261, 266, 299, 313–314, 318, 603–604, 606

Haifa 75–78, 132–133, 136–137, 405

Hamburg 9, 64, 80, 160, 210, 213, 223, 232, 301, 382, 460, 467, 514, 584–585, 603

Helsinki 288, 308, 418

Herzberg, Karl 120, 258–259, 261, 286–287, 294, 296–297, 299, 302, 306, 308, 313–315, 320, 403, 454, 603–604

Hindenburg, Paul von 3–5, 62, 73

Hirsch, Alice 15–19, 21, 24, 48, 57, 70–71, 83–84, 86, 103, 105, 107, 112–113, 121–123, 129, 140, 142–146, 161–163, 207, 212, 250, 284–285, 305, 308, 310, 314, 323–324, 327–328, 332, 357, 361–362, 366, 369, 372–373, 394, 397–398, 403, 405, 413, 419, 433, 439, 449–450, 453, 466, 469, 473, 475, 480, 482, 488, 491–492, 496, 498, 505, 517, 527, 530, 532–533, 555, 558, 560, 562–563, 566, 569, 591, 601, 604–606, 608
  emigration to England 57, 84, 103, 103–104, 105
  marriage to Hermann 18–19

Hirsch, Gretel 15–17, 19, 86, 103, 103–108, 104–107, 605
  death 106–107
  disability 15–16
  hospitalisation 104–106
  institutionalized 16

Hirsch, Hermann 15, 18–19, 43, 67, 86, 103, 121, 144, 160–161, 176, 250, 308, 314, 319, 323–324, 326–327, 329, 369, 397, 527, 530, 542, 555–558, 560–563, 565–566, 568–569, 571–573, 591, 604–606
  emigration to England 57, 84, 103–104, 105
  financial ineptitude 19, 43
  marriage to Alice 18–19

Hirsch, Vera
  birth of Franklin 594–595
  birth of Mimi-Ray 598
  brief relationship with Mitja Simonoff 109, 111–115, 156, 169, 200, 202, 255, 505, 553, 606, 608

career at Marks & Spencer 14, 110–111, 115, 120, 139, 144–145, 159, 182, 190, 204–205, 213, 215, 259, 267, 275–276, 282, 286, 291–292, 295, 304–305, 308, 311, 321–322, 329–330, 332, 334, 338, 351–352, 357, 359, 370, 376–377, 379, 381, 385, 388, 396, 401, 403, 405–407, 406, 418–419, 428, 428–434, 431, 434–440, 442–446, 456, 460, 468, 472, 483, 492, 497–498, 498, 507–508, 521, 546, 550, 592, 598
close relationship with mother 17, 71, 129
difficult relationship with father 18–20, 43, 103–104, 308, 323
doubts about marriage to Mope 161–178
early romances 43–48, 65, 532, 604
emigration to England 68, 70–71, 83, 83–84
experience of motherhood 596–597
friendship with Heising 43, 45–48, 65, 532, 604
marriage proposal from Mope 139–153
medical training 35–37, 44, 44–47, 63, 84, 84–87, 88–89, 94, 103, 110, 230, 311, 319, 390, 419, 478, 486, 555, 558
  withdrawal from 63–71
meeting Mope 123–126
planning for pregnancy 359, 397–398, 499, 573, 577, 593–594
pregnancy 418, 421, 425–426, 428, 432–433, 435, 438–440, 444, 450–451, 453, 456–457, 460, 462–464, 473, 476, 480, 487–488, 495, 497, 594
pregnancy loss 490–492, 499–503, 504–511, 514
saleswoman at Eve Valère 88, 93–94, 103, 109, 110–111
school education 33–35
sports 45
wedding to Mope 259, 285–286
Hitler, Adolf 3–6, 10, 32–33, 43–44, 48, 51, 58–64, 73, 119–121, 166, 181, 187, 243, 257, 299, 307, 350, 354, 414–415, 418, 443, 453, 459, 473, 487, 510, 513–515, 517, 528, 573–574, 577, 591
Mein Kampf 5, 62, 517
Holocaust 10, 14, 60, 63, 74, 236, 382, 605
Homburger, Julius 77–78, 102, 174, 198, 219, 222, 235, 247–248, 250–251, 266, 283, 297, 332–333, 405, 470, 477, 543, 605–607
hyperinflation 3, 19, 28, 42–44, 57
Idstein 104–107
  Kalmenhof 104–106
inflation 20, 43
Intergovernmental Committee on Refugees (ICR) 2
International Refugee Organisation (IRO) 2
Iron Cross 3, 31, 604
Italy 10, 17, 57–58, 79, 131, 229, 247, 286, 382, 410, 418, 431, 454, 459–460, 476, 598, 605–606

Jerusalem 26, 133, 167, 195, 202, 228, 266, 299, 460, 477, 585
Jew 30, 40–41, 63, 65, 67, 70, 83, 100, 151, 205, 228, 237, 257–258, 349, 417, 448, 463–464, 483, 594, 596
Jewish 3, 6, 8–9, 21, 23, 25–26, 32–34, 40, 44–45, 48, 50, 57, 60, 62–70, 73–74, 78–79, 82–83, 87–89, 94–98, 100–101, 104, 106, 119–121, 123, 132–133, 139–140, 151, 160, 167, 183, 185–186, 188, 191, 194, 198, 205–207, 209–210, 217, 219, 228, 236–237, 239, 254, 260, 307–308, 318, 337, 349–350, 352, 355, 357, 360, 382, 390, 394, 399, 412, 415, 417–418, 420–423, 431, 448, 450, 452, 459–463, 469, 483, 489, 496, 521, 523, 537, 553, 591, 593, 601–604, 607–608
Jewish Refugees Committee 70, 83, 460, 593, 608
Judaism 41, 70, 95, 145, 185
  Orthodox Judaism 3, 23, 26, 30, 40–41, 78, 95, 137, 228, 409, 521, 602, 607

Karlsbad 159, 176, 178–179, 182, 186–187, 283, 354
Karlsruhe 41–42, 101, 352, 382, 403, 460, 518, 576, 607

Kent 9
Kilburn 182, 204, 308, 321, 329–332, 336, 376, 400, 483
Kindertransport 9, 418–419, 422, 460, 480, 519, 521, 591, 603
Kitchener Refugee Camp 9
Königsberg 29, 602
Kristallnacht 6, 8–9, 74, 217, 259, 382, 417, 419–423, 441, 447, 526, 603, 606

Latin 14
Lawson-Johnston, Betty 84–85, 90
Lebensraum 5, 513
Leipzig 3, 14, 23–28, 30–31, 39–42, 49–51, 53–56, 73–76, 78, 80–82, 96, 98–100, 120–121, 123–128, 132, 139, 142, 149–150, 152–155, 159–163, 165, 167, 169–171, 173, 175–176, 178–179, 181–188, 190–195, 197–200, 202, 204–205, 207–212, 214, 216–229, 231–233, 235–241, 243–249, 251–252, 254, 257–258, 261, 263, 265–268, 272–273, 283, 286–287, 294, 296–297, 307–308, 315–316, 319–320, 334, 352, 358–359, 363, 372–374, 385, 394, 445, 461, 465, 469, 523, 526, 557, 602–606
Leibnizstrasse
  Mope family home 25
Leningrad 259, 262–267, 269–270, 272–276, 279–280, 289–291, 305, 328, 330–331, 335–336, 338, 340, 343, 346, 351, 366, 370–372, 374, 377–379, 382, 384–385, 387–388, 390–392, 394, 396, 398–399, 402, 407–408, 411–412, 414, 418, 420, 461, 479, 481–482, 487–489, 493–494, 496–497, 500–501, 503–505, 507, 513–515, 518–519, 521, 523, 525, 527, 529–530, 533–535, 537–538, 540, 544–545, 548–549, 551, 553, 556–557, 559–560, 564, 566–567, 569–570, 572, 575–576, 578–583, 585–586, 598, 608
Lewy, Hilde 34, 36, 286, 308, 323, 325, 327, 365, 382, 384, 393, 399, 418, 431, 446, 452–454, 460, 464–465, 470, 474, 476, 510, 548, 571, 574, 605–606
Lewy, Walter 217, 286, 365, 382, 393, 399, 410, 452, 510, 548, 605
Littauer, Heinz 78–80, 191, 390, 604, 606
  emigration to England 78

London 13–14, 21, 23, 43, 55, 70–71, 74, 78, 83–85, 87–89, 91–92, 101, 103–106, 110, 120–121, 123–129, 131–132, 135, 137, 139–140, 143, 147, 151, 174, 176, 181–183, 187, 189, 191, 196, 203, 205, 209, 211, 219, 223–225, 229, 232, 235–236, 250, 252–254, 257–260, 262–267, 273, 277, 281–287, 291, 293–295, 297, 299–302, 304–305, 307–308, 310–316, 319, 321–322, 324, 327–332, 334–335, 337, 340–344, 352–353, 357, 359, 361–362, 365, 368, 371–373, 376, 378–381, 383–384, 387, 390–392, 396, 399–402, 404–406, 408, 410–411, 413, 416, 419, 421, 423–428, 431–437, 439–442, 444, 446, 448, 450, 452–453, 456, 460–461, 466, 469–471, 473–475, 478–479, 481–482, 484–487, 489–490, 493–498, 500, 504, 509–510, 514, 516–518, 520, 522, 524, 527–528, 531, 533, 536, 538–540, 542, 545, 547, 549, 551–554, 556–559, 562–563, 565, 567–568, 570–571, 574–575, 578–579, 584, 591, 593–595, 598, 601–602, 605–606, 608

Mann, Thomas 57–60
Marks & Spencer 14, 110–111, 115, 139, 159, 182, 190, 204–205, 213, 215, 259, 275, 308, 351–352, 377, 406, 418, 428, 460, 468, 498, 521, 592
  Ealing 352, 357, 376, 379, 381, 388, 390, 393, 396, 401, 403, 405–406, 408
  Hammersmith 308, 329–330, 332, 336, 352, 357, 359, 376–377, 388, 390, 396, 403, 405, 429, 439, 442
  Kilburn 182, 204, 308, 321, 329–332, 336, 376, 400, 483
  Oxford Street 111, 418, 428, 468
  Pantheon store 418, 428, 431, 434–436, 439–440, 442–445, 456, 468, 472, 492, 507–508
Mengele, Josef 48
Molotov-Ribbentrop Pact 1939 10, 460, 513, 515, 573, 591
Moschytz, Norbert 80–81, 286, 382, 390, 394, 410, 413, 416, 419, 441, 456, 462, 484, 489, 514, 519, 524, 530, 532, 543, 546, 550, 591, 603, 605–606

Moscow 124, 126, 143, 235, 255, 259–260, 262–270, 272, 276–277, 279–280, 283, 286–287, 290–293, 295–301, 303, 305–307, 310, 314–318, 320, 325, 327, 330, 333, 335, 337, 341–346, 351–352, 354–355, 358, 360–362, 364, 366–368, 371, 373–375, 377, 383–385, 388, 391–392, 396, 398, 402–403, 405, 407–408, 411–415, 418, 420–424, 426, 428–429, 431–432, 434, 436–437, 440, 442, 444, 446, 449, 455, 461–463, 467–468, 471, 474, 477, 479, 481–482, 485, 487, 494, 496, 513, 515, 556, 565, 567–568, 570, 573, 575, 577, 579–584, 586–587, 591, 605, 608

Munich 5, 58–59, 132, 257, 349–350, 354, 381, 414, 434

Mussolini, Benito 5, 58, 120, 181, 418, 431, 443

naturalization 362, 366, 369, 528–529, 533, 598, 604

Nazification 7, 48

Nazi Party 2–10, 14, 21, 32, 34, 43, 45, 48, 50–52, 60–67, 69–70, 73–74, 76, 82, 89, 91, 96, 100–101, 104, 106, 119–121, 123, 126, 132, 154–155, 159, 174, 181–183, 191, 197, 205–206, 217, 219, 228, 235–236, 245, 257–259, 261, 265, 268, 286–287, 308, 331, 350, 352, 355, 373, 399, 412, 417, 419, 423–424, 430, 441, 451–452, 459–460, 463, 469, 488, 515, 521, 526, 537, 573, 587, 591, 603–604, 607–608

Nazism 5, 34, 57, 186, 331, 354, 412, 430, 592, 601

Netherlands, the 7, 206

Nuremburg Race Laws 1935 6–7, 82–83, 121

Palestine 8, 34, 40, 67–68, 75–78, 95–96, 98–102, 119, 123, 125, 131–133, 135–137, 139–140, 143–146, 151–152, 156–157, 159, 165, 169, 172, 176, 182–183, 189, 191–192, 194, 197–198, 202–203, 212, 217, 219, 222, 228–230, 235, 260, 273, 284, 287, 289, 296, 308, 312, 314, 331, 366, 403, 405, 409, 418, 431, 433, 460, 469, 477, 479, 498, 515, 521, 545–546, 553, 558–559, 601–605, 607

Mandate of, 1923 8

Paltreu ("Palästina Treuhandgesellschaft", the Palestine Trust Company) 101, 191, 194, 197, 219, 235–236, 239, 258, 261, 286–287, 307–308, 314

Paris 6, 137, 206, 235, 240, 254, 257, 289, 305, 308–309, 328, 330–331, 333, 339, 341–342, 344, 351–352, 417–419, 424, 582, 608

Passover 21, 139, 205

passport 159, 170, 172–173, 175, 205, 231, 244–245, 292, 301, 306, 311, 316–318, 321, 324, 335, 344, 350, 352, 355, 361–362, 366, 383, 392, 399, 402, 411, 421, 441, 465, 487, 528, 539, 556, 565, 567–568, 578, 591, 598

Pod Wychodnoi 431, 529, 539, 554, 569

Poland 99, 119, 168, 228, 254, 307, 351, 354–356, 417, 459, 513, 515, 526, 537, 541, 574, 587–588

Prinz, Joachim 186, 194

Purim 135, 207, 344, 496

Rau, Fred 78, 101, 139–141, 146, 155, 170, 176, 219, 221–224, 229, 235, 237–244, 246, 248, 254, 258, 261–263, 266, 283, 287, 294, 297, 299–305, 308–309, 311, 315, 333–334, 337, 340–341, 376, 379, 384–385, 394, 416, 420, 423–425, 433, 453, 460, 466, 469, 484, 515, 520, 530, 532, 542–543, 546, 550, 552, 558, 572, 578, 584–585, 591, 603–604, 606–607

emigration to England 78

refuge 7–8, 34, 96, 258, 382, 480, 557

refugee 1–3, 6–10, 21, 34, 57, 78, 83, 87–88, 91, 93, 103, 110, 121, 308, 350, 357, 394, 422, 448, 450–451, 460, 469, 513, 523, 553, 567, 591–593, 598–599, 601, 603, 608

Reichstag 5–6, 61–62, 473

fire 6, 61–62

residence permit 71, 334, 397, 418

Rhyl 159, 163, 167–168

Rosenfeld, Georg 41, 207, 403, 410, 413, 460, 480, 515, 518, 545–546, 554, 562, 565, 568–569, 571–572, 575–576, 602, 607

Rosenfeld, Julius 101–102, 219, 222, 235, 247–248, 250–251, 266, 283, 297, 332–333, 543

Rosenfeld, Karl 41–42, 101, 191, 382, 403, 405, 408–410, 413, 422, 435, 460, 477, 480, 515, 545–546, 550, 553, 558–559, 561, 572, 576, 604, 607
Rosenfeld, Lies 41–42, 382, 403, 408–410, 413, 435, 460, 515, 550, 558–559, 561, 572, 576, 607
Rothschild, Paul 20, 89, 422, 428, 433, 436, 439–440, 444, 449, 453, 462, 479, 490–491, 497, 501–502, 506, 527, 555–558, 561–564, 568, 578, 607
Russia 10, 14, 99, 111, 124, 235–236, 240, 246, 254–255, 257–260, 262–266, 275, 283, 286, 290, 298–300, 305–308, 317, 326, 333, 337, 350–351, 354–356, 358, 360, 363, 367, 381–383, 387–388, 391, 393–395, 400–402, 404, 406, 412, 417, 422, 435, 443, 447, 455, 477, 499, 513–514, 520, 559–560, 570, 573, 577, 583, 587–588, 591, 598, 603, 605–606, 608

Sabbath 78, 137, 185, 309, 411, 415
Sachsenhausen 9, 65–66, 120, 181, 421
Sandsend 272, 275, 276, 281
Schapiro, Ruwin 254, 305, 317, 330, 342, 344–345, 351–352, 360, 383, 387, 389–392, 408, 411, 414, 419, 424, 471, 479, 481, 484, 497–498, 503, 507, 514–515, 520, 538, 544, 548, 550–553, 556–558, 567, 570, 572–574, 577–578, 580–582, 588, 608
Schiff, Otto 8, 70–71, 83, 87–88, 90, 92–94, 103, 105, 110, 324, 328, 334–335, 339, 341, 362, 366, 420, 460, 466–468, 470, 472–473, 476–477, 485, 592, 601, 608
Schwab, Anna 70–71
Schwimmer, Max 4, 49–56, 194, 208, 219–220, 223, 231–233, 236, 244, 246, 251, 253, 307–308, 310–311, 313–317, 320, 323, 387, 394, 401, 603, 606
Second World War 21, 31, 55, 387, 513, 538, 576, 587, 597, 602, 606
Spain 10, 168, 206, 383
Stiebel, Joan 324, 327, 335, 339, 341, 362, 368–369, 371, 420, 448, 453, 602, 608
Stockholm 264, 289, 308, 342–345, 347, 358, 391, 418–419, 510, 518, 570, 573, 575, 579, 584

Sunderland 14
Switzerland 59, 283, 286, 307, 419, 441, 449–450, 462, 465, 484, 488, 498, 514, 519, 537, 546, 598, 606

Tel-Aviv 101–102, 161, 163, 165, 190, 247, 254, 260, 604
Theresienstadt 526, 576, 585, 607

United Nations Refugee Convention 2
United States of America 7, 31, 34, 40, 61, 74, 145, 194, 198, 217, 284, 298, 319, 334, 382, 393, 405, 424, 429, 431, 443, 450, 452, 454, 462, 465, 469, 488, 498, 510, 513, 536, 543, 552, 560, 564, 574, 603, 606

Vienna 308
visa 8–9, 99–100, 125, 212, 229, 231, 241, 251, 266, 286, 298, 305–306, 333, 337, 342, 344, 350–351, 353, 355, 358, 361, 371, 373, 378, 381, 383–385, 387–388, 392–393, 396–404, 406–416, 422, 424, 431, 441, 454, 462, 465, 487, 493, 499, 514–515, 519, 539, 543, 546, 553, 556, 565, 567–568, 570–571, 573–575, 577–580, 582, 585, 587–588, 598
Volhard, Franz 69, 71, 84, 89, 94, 607–608

Wall Street Crash 5
war 9, 14, 21, 25, 28–32, 34, 41, 51, 55, 57, 69, 78, 164, 170, 174, 203, 205–206, 235, 258, 260, 286, 289, 321, 354, 359, 382–383, 395, 414, 418, 423, 443, 452, 459, 463, 473, 488, 490, 513–515, 523, 545, 568, 571, 574, 576–577, 580, 583–585, 587–589, 591–593, 597–599, 606–608
Warsaw 254, 260, 308–309, 341–342, 351, 353–356
Weimar Republic 3–5, 44, 57
Whitby 259, 267, 271–272, 274–279, 281

Zellner's cafe 188, 205, 209, 223, 226, 228, 231, 236, 238, 251, 267
Zionism 8, 95, 97–99, 102, 151, 171–172, 191, 194–195, 210, 212, 601
  Blau-Weiss 98
Zionist 8, 40–41, 77, 95–96, 98–99, 101, 159, 176, 186, 190, 195, 228, 321, 331, 460, 521, 602, 604

About the Team

Alessandra Tosi was the managing editor for this book.

Lucy Barnes copy-edited and created the index for this book.

Anja Pritchard proof read this book and created the Alt-text.

Jeevanjot Kaur Nagpal designed the cover. The cover was produced in InDesign using the Fontin font.

Cameron Craig typeset the book in InDesign and produced the paperback and hardback editions. The text font is Tex Gyre Pagella and the heading font is Californian FB. The candle icons are from Flaticon.com.

Cameron also produced the PDF, XML and HTML editions. The conversion was performed with open-source software and other tools freely available on our GitHub page at https://github.com/OpenBookPublishers.

Jeremy Bowman produced the EPUB edition.

This book has been anonymously peer-reviewed by experts in their field. We thank them for their invaluable help.

This book need not end here...

Share

All our books — including the one you have just read — are free to access online so that students, researchers and members of the public who can't afford a printed edition will have access to the same ideas. This title will be accessed online by hundreds of readers each month across the globe: why not share the link so that someone you know is one of them?

This book and additional content is available at:
https://doi.org/10.11647/OBP.0334

Donate

Open Book Publishers is an award-winning, scholar-led, not-for-profit press making knowledge freely available one book at a time. We don't charge authors to publish with us: instead, our work is supported by our library members and by donations from people who believe that research shouldn't be locked behind paywalls.

Why not join them in freeing knowledge by supporting us:
https://www.openbookpublishers.com/support-us

Follow @OpenBookPublish

Read more at the Open Book Publishers **BLOG**

You may also be interested in:

The End and the Beginning
The Book of My Life
Lionel Gossman (editor), Hermynia Zur Mühlen (author)

https://doi.org/10.11647/obp.0010

Breaking Conventions
Five Couples in Search of Marriage-Career Balance at the Turn of the Nineteenth Century
Patricia Auspos

https://doi.org/10.11647/obp.0318

Mendl Mann's 'The Fall of Berlin'
Maurice Wolfthal (translator)

https://doi.org/10.11647/obp.0233

www.ingramcontent.com/pod-product-compliance
Lightning Source LLC
Chambersburg PA
CBHW050300010526
44108CB00040B/1900